Reminiscences
of a Stock Operator

*With New Commentary and Insights
on the Life and Times of Jesse Livermore*

EDWIN LEFÈVRE

ANNOTATED EDITION
BY JON D. MARKMAN

WILEY

John Wiley & Sons, Inc.

Published by John Wiley & Sons, Inc., Hoboken, New Jersey.

Published simultaneously in Canada.

For general information on our other products and services or for technical support, please contact our Customer Care Department within the United States at (800) 762-2974, outside the United States at (317) 572-3993 or fax (317) 572-4002.

Wiley also publishes its books in a variety of electronic formats. Some content that appears in print may not be available in electronic books. For more information about Wiley products, visit our web site at www.wiley.com

Library of Congress Cataloging-in-Publication Data:

Lefèvre, Edwin, 1871–1943.
  Reminiscences of a stock operator : with new commentary and insights on the life and times of Jesse Livermore / Edwin Lefèvre. —Annotated ed. / by Jon D. Markman.
     p. cm.
  Includes bibliographical references.
  ISBN 978-0-470-48159-2 (cloth)
  1. New York Stock Exchange. 2. Speculation. 3. Livermore, Jesse L. (Jesse Lauriston), 1877–1940.
  4. Stockbrokers—United States. I. Markman, Jon D., 1958- II. Title.
  HG4572.L4 2010
  332.6'2—dc22
  [B]
                                                            2009042600

Printed in the United States of America

10 9 8 7 6 5 4 3 2

CONTENTS

FOREWORD

I first read *Reminiscences* in 1976. It was given to me by my first boss as the most important book I could read. It resonated with me on a variety of levels. First, Livermore started with but a few coins in his pocket, and as a relatively penniless 21-year-old when I first read it, it was both reassuring and hopeful. His stories of making millions, hobnobbing with other great financiers and stock market operators, trading from a yacht, and deftly maneuvering through the great commodity and stock corners of the day was the financial equivalent of "sex, drugs and rock 'n roll" to a young man at the advent of his financial career. Secondly, his facility with numbers was very similar to mine. It was as if he spoke straight to my soul in this regard. Finally, probably the greatest message I took away from my first read had to do with understanding price action. There are times when every market has a story to tell. And you have to train yourself to be both a great observer and listener, or you will be too late to enjoy the full story that will be told.

I have read the book countless times in my career, and I cannot remember a single time when I haven't discovered something new. As I was reading it again for umpteenth time, I noticed on page three it reads that Livingston used to journal both "the determination of (probable price) movements" as well as "assorted record of my hits and misses." I have been doing this semi-religiously for most of the past three decades, and I always thought it was my own invention. Over the years, I guess I deluded myself into taking credit for a brilliant practice integral to my success by conveniently forgetting the inventor. And this points to why this book is so important to me and why anyone looking to take up trading as a profession should read and study it. It is a textbook for speculation. Indeed, I hand a copy to every new trader we have, regardless of his or her considerable experience. I am always looking for the next Jesse Livermore.

—Paul Tudor Jones
Chairman and Chief Executive
Tudor Investment Corporation

For more of Paul Tudor Jones' thoughts on the book, please see page 399.

PREFACE

Imagine it is 1923. The horrors of World War I, in which 37 million men and women were killed or wounded, are still fresh in your mind. So are the horrors of the great flu pandemic of 1918–1919, which killed more than 50 million people worldwide. So are the great economic and psychological setbacks of two terrible postwar recessions in 1919 and 1921.

The cumulative gloom produced by the ravages of man and nature is hard to shake. Business in most industries is perking up a bit finally, but the stock market is reflecting a sour mood. Despite some dramatic ups and downs, prices are still pretty much where they were eight years ago.

Yet in this fallow ground of despair and fear, seeds of hope are being planted—and the dreams of ambitious, hardworking Americans are beginning to stir.

Families are starting to pour into cities from the countryside in the largest urban migration that the country has ever witnessed, and they all need new homes, water systems, transportation, offices, factories, and entertainment. Banks are beginning to feel more confident, and are doling out loans to industrialists with good ideas for cars, railroads, consumer goods, and resorts. Mass-market advertising is emerging for the first time to hawk goods over the radio, which has just begun to broadcast jazz music and baseball games after low-cost vacuum tubes have made home receivers affordable. The first talking motion pictures are emerging, a dazzling innovation that has begun to transmit American values worldwide for the first time.

Amid this growing sense of comfort and confidence, the stock market has finally begun to arch higher, and popular weekly publications are soon filled with stories of average people leveraging their wages to make a killing in stocks. Newspapers are covering Wall Street with élan, offering detailed reports on commodities and equities and the people and forces behind their mysterious movements.

Little did anyone know at the time, though in hindsight hints were abundant, that the market was about to surge 400 percent in the greatest single six-year span in its history. And so the time was ripe for the emergence of heroes to enthrall investors' imaginations and spark latent animal spirits.

Witnessing this swelling sentiment for speculation was a veteran magazine writer and novelist named Edwin Lefevre. Born in Panama to American parents, and already well traveled in Asia and South America by his twenties, Lefevre was attracted to the New York financial markets as an observer, and after finding regular work as a journalist he parlayed his keen analytical skills and buoyant personality to become one of the era's savviest chroniclers—writing and editing dozens of articles on Wall Street personalities and strategies. He stood apart from the boosterism of colleagues by primarily focusing on the gray underside of the change in stock prices, preferring to uncover tales of scammers, swindlers, and tricksters who preyed on the public's gullibility to fatten their own ledgers. He was no moralizing prude, however, and counted giants of speculation like James Keene among his friends.

By the early 1920s, at about 50 years old, Lefevre recognized that even the smartest journalism failed to get at the very essence of the truths he had uncovered about Wall Street, so he decided to shift gears and try his hand at transcending the bounds of quotes and facts by writing a new type of fiction. Casting about for a central character on which to hang his story, he had a great number of candidates to choose from, as he was well regarded by many of the era's top players. Most were relentless self-promoters well known to the public, so it was a little odd that he ultimately chose the notoriously reticent Jesse Lauriston Livermore as his foil. Perhaps it was the challenge.

Livermore had been raised on a rocky farm in Massachusetts and had risen through hard work, ambition, necessity, persistence, guts, and a sharp mind for numbers to become one of the greatest traders of stocks and commodities of the first two decades of the twentieth century. He had made and lost more fortunes by the age of 25 than most people will see in a lifetime, and though he rarely spoke to the press about his exploits and eschewed the companionship of partners—preferring to play what he called a "lone hand"—he possessed an unusual level of self-knowledge and could express his tradecraft and mental state in colorful, perceptive ways that eluded most professionals.

The two met for an initial series of interviews to size each other up. Lefevre was impressed by Livermore's cool intelligence, while Livermore appreciated Lefevre's willingness to tell uncomfortable truths. Both were frustrated at how the public blamed their misfortunes on the market and the big operators of the day when, in fact, they had only their ignorance and overconfidence to blame.

The author apparently viewed the trader's little-known rags-to-riches story as an ideal vessel into which he could mix his own views about all that was deceitful, wretched, and corrupt, yet also energizing and transcendent, about Wall Street. Although Livermore was reclusive and shy, he proved more than willing to share his life's story with someone of such rich creative talent. The tale that emerged—*Reminiscences of a Stock Operator*—was without doubt far greater than either could have told alone. In fact, Livermore later wrote his own book about trading, and Lefevre wrote another book centered on a single trader, and neither of those efforts came close to the glory that they had found when teaming together.

First published as a series of illustrated articles appearing in the *Saturday Evening Post* throughout 1922, the work in your hands became a classic for its pitch-perfect dialogue, insightful epigrams, daring raids, and heartbreaking failures. Told in the first person, as if it were the memoirs of protagonist Larry Livingston, it is a historical novel centered on the life of Livermore, yet it defies many of the conventions of the genre, as it lacks much of a story arc, the emotional development of other characters, a climax, a denouement, or, for that matter, much of a conclusion.

What the book lacks in typical plot points it makes up in psychological depth as Lefevre uses the Livingston character to probe the collective mind-set of all the traders he has witnessed and interviewed over the years.

Although most readers assume all of the thoughts articulated are those of Livermore as channeled by the author, the truth is that many of the locutions and beliefs can be found in other journalism and conventional novels penned by Lefevre. Indeed, most of the last five chapters owe much to a separate series of articles that Lefevre wrote on his favorite subject, stock manipulation, though of course they are cleverly altered to appear as if they were an integral part of the Livermore saga.

Moreover, the book may start with the protagonist's innocent attempts to make money as a gambler in bucket shops and as an increasingly cagey trader in equity and commodity markets, but the last half centers on his efforts as a stock "operator"—a term of art for a market pro hired by investment pools to manipulate a moribund stock for the benefit of insiders. It is not quite right to call this fraud, because it was mostly legal at the time, but Lefevre lets us know that the fine art of ripping off the public was not exactly admirable.

Most readers of *Reminiscences of a Stock Operator* today do not realize that while the Livingston name is fiction, about 90 percent of the other proper names of people and places in the book are real. The fact that the book can be appreciated without knowing anything about its historical context and its cast of characters is a testament to the strength of the central narrative.

After several rereadings of the book of my own, I began to be more curious about both the real historical backdrop as well as the people whose identities are essentially name-dropped. People like J. P. Morgan, Jay Gould, William Jennings Bryan, and Bernard Baruch were at least superficially known to me, but James Keene, John "Bet-a-Million" Gates, Dickson Watts, Jacob Little, Daniel Drew, and William Travers might as well have been made up. Likewise, events like the "cross of gold" speech by Bryan at the 1896 Democratic convention, which figures prominently in the early chapters, was a distant memory from a college U.S. history class, but its meaning to investors in the early part of the twentieth century completely escaped me.

The more I dug into the fascinating stories of the men and events that serve as props for Lefevre's narrative, the more I realized how much of the book's deeper meaning was lost on modern readers. I began to feel like an art restorer who, in delicately cleaning a master's painting, discovered much more vibrant colors than modern viewers had ever seen, along with hidden characters covered by decades of dust. Gates, Drew, Gould, Little, Travers, and other minor characters mentioned in *Reminiscences* led amazing lives that were well known to Lefevre's contemporary readers in the 1920s but have largely been lost to the sands of time.

The author also regularly but obliquely refers to events that evoked an emotional response to readers in the 1920s but have zero resonance for modern readers. Prime examples are descriptions of trading during milestones on the road toward U.S. involvement in World War I, including early submarine warfare battles; the economic impact of bruising fights between Bryan and William McKinley over the gold standard; the explosive onset of the Spanish-American War; and the near depression that followed the end of World War I.

In this new edition of *Reminiscences*, I have tried to breathe new life into these people and events through annotations that will help current readers understand the book in an entirely new way. Whether you hopscotch through the annotations to learn about historical figures one by one or reread the book from start to finish, using the annotations as a guide to strengthen your understanding of the original text, you will discover that Lefevre was a truly masterful interpreter of a most remarkable period in U.S. financial history.

This is not to diminish the profound insights that are lying right on the surface of the book, like gold nuggets lying in plain sight on a riverbed.

Through the voice of the Livingston character, Lefevre reaches out through time to remind us, with the panache of an artful storyteller rather than with the scolding finger of a professor, that there never is anything new on Wall Street, because speculation is as old as the hills; that in a bull market you must trade with the bulls, while in a bear market you must trade with the bears; that anticipation and fast reaction are the trader's key assets; that you should never argue with the tape; that you do not know until you bet; that the game teaches you the game; and much more. But the bottom line is that there is much more to *Reminiscences* than a list of do's and don'ts for traders, and updating the book's breathtaking sweep is what I hoped to accomplish with these annotations.

The book is often mentioned by famed traders today as their bible, or the work that inspired them to go into the investment business, so it is worth noting that the sentiment would most likely dismay Lefevre, or at least amuse him. This is because it certainly appears that he meant *Reminiscences* to be a cautionary tale more than an instruction manual. The character Livingston laments numerous times that no man can consistently beat the stock market and that human nature condemns virtually everyone to being a sucker. And yet he recognizes that they must keep trying.

Livermore himself ultimately fell victim to the game, as he was never able to adapt his methods to restrictions put in place by the Securities and Exchange Commission in the 1930s. The trader made a fortune by being short stocks in the panic of 1907 and in the 1929 crash—at his peak owning mansions, a fleet of limousines, and a massive yacht—but he was plagued with depression and repeatedly discovered ways to blunt his brilliance with bad plays. After a long series of setbacks that sapped his pride and confidence, he took his own life in November 1940 with a .32-caliber handgun at age 63 in the cloakroom of the Sherry-Netherland Hotel in New York, leaving a rambling suicide note that read, in part, "Things have been bad with me. I am tired of fighting. Can't carry on any longer. This is the only way out."

Knowing that Livermore's life slipped into darkness 20 years after the publication of *Reminiscences* should nevertheless not detract from the value Lefevre gleaned from his genius in its prime. The book has lasted because its wisdom is timeless.

Before moving on, I would like to acknowledge the work done by my researcher, Anthony Mirhaydari. He spent many hours prowling university libraries to uncover biographies and histories of the era that had not been checked out for decades. He also discovered that Google had digitized many out-of-circulation books dating from the 1850s to the 1930s, and harnessed them for our benefit. This edition would have been a lot less rich, and taken a lot longer to come to fruition, without his steadfast passion for uncovering and unraveling clues about the people, places, and events of the era. His notes and observations were invaluable to me in compiling these annotations.

Anthony and I were both amazed at the quality and depth of financial news reporting in newspapers and magazines of the late 1800s and early 1900s, particularly in the *New York Times* and *Time,* as well as the elegant prose found in several autobiographies. One of our favorites was *Fifty Years in Wall Street,* by Henry Clews, a titan of nineteenth-century finance who loved to dish on the men and women with whom he dealt in public and private service starting in 1857.

I would also like to thank several traders who helped me understand the era better. You will find my interview with Paul Tudor Jones about *Reminiscences* in the back of the book. Others who provided hours of guidance were Larry Williams, Tom Demark, John Burbank, Edward Dunne, and Terry Bedford. Thanks to my patient editors Meg Freeborn, Kevin Holm, and Chris Oster. And of course I could not have completed this effort without the tremendous support of my wife and children, Ellen, Joe, and Janie.

And finally, for busy readers who would like to view a stripped-down version of the book without the frame of the narrative, I have compiled a "Selected Quotes" section that could serve by itself as one of the pamphlets of epigrams that were popular among boys like young Jesse Livermore in the late 1800s. Plus for reference, in the Appendix is a chart of the Dow Jones Industrial Average from 1896 to 1930.

So follow me now into a time of limitless prosperity, the Roaring '20s. A time when the Dow Jones Industrial Average was about to soar from 90 in 1923 to a high of 381 in 1929. A time when a great journalist combined forces with a great trader to explain to the masses how to make a fortune in the great game and, above all, not be a sucker.

—Jon D. Markman

I went to work when I was just out of grammar school. **⟨1.1⟩** I got a job as quotation-board boy in a stock-brokerage office. I was quick at figures. At school I did three years of arithmetic in one. I was particularly good at mental arithmetic. As quotation-board boy I posted the numbers on the big board **⟨1.2⟩** in the customers' room. One of the customers usually sat by the ticker **⟨1.3⟩** and called out the prices. They couldn't come too fast for me. I have always remembered figures. No trouble at all.

There were plenty of other employees in that office. Of course I made friends with the other fellows, but the work I did, if the market was active, kept me too busy from ten A.M. to three P.M. to let me do much talking. I don't care for it, anyhow, during business hours.

1.1 *Reminiscences* is a historical novel told in the first person by the fictional Larry Livingston. The character and all of his dialogue were based on the trader Jesse Lauriston Livermore, who was born on July 26, 1877, in Shrewsbury, Massachusetts, to a family of subsistence farmers. The cold climate and poor soil in their area demanded backbreaking labor and provided a meager yield. Livermore's first job was to move the dense rocks turned up by his father's plow. Hard physical work was difficult for him because of his slender build, and he was often sick. Although he excelled in school, especially math, his father wanted him to stop his education and work all day on behalf of his family. Livermore, who was way too curious about the world to stay home, conspired with his doting mother to escape. She provided an extra-large suit so that he would not have to buy another one for a while, and $5. With that, Livermore set out for Boston in 1891 at age 14.[1]

1.2 In the days before electronic tickers, prices were manually updated on a large wooden board as they clattered in from exchanges via telegraph wires. Boys working the board would write the latest prices with chalk. They wore alpaca coats to keep from smudging the board. The use of blackboards coincided with the rise of the bucket shop, since it was necessary to display price fluctuations to many customers at once. As late as 1902, traditional brokers resisted the installation of quote boards because their absence distinguished their conservative establishments from the more liberal practices of bucket houses. The use of the term "Big Board" for New York Stock Exchange is a throwback to this era.[2]

1

1.3 ▶ The ticker was a printing
telegraph adopted widely soon
after the Civil War, and it
revolutionized the function
of capital markets. Invented
by Edward Calahan in
1867, its popularity was
boosted by Thomas
Edison's invention of
the quadruplex in the
1870s—a system that
allowed a single wire
to carry four messages
simultaneously. West-
ern Union and its rivals
leveraged this increase
in capacity to lease
telegraph connections to
financiers and speculators
outside the exchanges. The
volume growth allowed the
New York Stock Exchange to
expand in 1871 from twice-daily
auctions to continuous trading in
listed securities.[3]

Until 1872, ticker service was available only
through 700 machines in New York City. After Western
Union purchased the Gold & Stock Telegraph Co., service
was widened to its national network; by 1886, there were
2,200 tickers coast to coast. In 1903, financial writer
Sereno Pratt quipped that ubiquity of the ticker offered "no
better proof...of the universality of speculation."[4]

Popular participation in the stock market soon rose sharply: The number of American stock owners tripled between
1900 and 1922 to 14.4 million. Observers described the
device's magical attractiveness. Horace Hotchkiss, founder
of the Gold & Stock Telegraph, said that when the ticker
entered commercial service it "created a sensation as the
quotations made their appearance on the tape. The crowd
around it was at least six deep."[5] Financial writer George
Gibson noted that "dealers...intently watch the 'ticker' as it
rapidly unwinds the tangled web of financial fate."[6]

Before the advent of the ticker, middlemen called "pad
shovers" would get the latest quotations from brokers,
scribble them in notebooks, and then go from office to
office. A character in Edwin Lefevre's 1925 book, *Making
of a Stockbroker,* tells of how they "came up to you and
shoved the pad with the quotations on it right under your
nose, hence the appellative. They were the walking tickers.
Rushing the pad, they used to call the process."

But a busy market did not keep me from thinking about the work. Those quotations did not represent prices of stocks to me, so many dollars per share. They were numbers. Of course, they meant something. They were always changing. It was all I had to be interested in—the changes. Why did they change? I didn't know. I didn't care. I didn't think about that. I simply saw that they changed. That was all I had to think about five hours every day and two on Saturdays: that they were always changing.

That is how I first came to be interested in the behaviour of prices. I had a very good memory for figures. I could remember in detail how the prices had acted on the previous day, just before they went up or down. My fondness for mental arithmetic came in very handy.

I noticed that in advances as well as declines, stock prices were apt to show certain habits, so to speak. There was no end of parallel cases and these made precedents to guide me. I was only fourteen, but after I had taken hundreds of observations in my mind I found myself testing their accuracy, comparing the behaviour of stocks today with other days. **1.4**

It was not long before I was anticipating movements in prices. My only guide, as I say, was their past performances. I carried the "dope sheets" in my mind. I looked for stock prices to run on form. I had "clocked" them. You know what I mean. **1.5**

You can spot, for instance, where the buying is only a trifle better than the selling. A battle goes on in the stock market and the tape is your telescope. You can depend upon it seven out of ten cases.

Another lesson I learned early is that there is nothing new in Wall Street. There can't be because speculation is as old as the hills. **1.6** Whatever happens in the stock market to-day has happened before and will happen again. I've never forgotten that. I suppose I really manage to remember when and how it happened. The fact that I remember that way is my way of capitalizing experience.

I got so interested in my game and so anxious to anticipate advances and declines in all the active stocks that I got a little book. I put down my observations in it. It was not a record of imaginary transactions such as so many people keep merely to make or lose millions of dollars without getting the swelled head or going to the poorhouse. It was rather a sort of record of my hits and misses, and next to the determination of probable movements I was most interested in verifying whether I had observed accurately; in other words, whether I was right.

Say that after studying every fluctuation of the day in an active stock I would conclude that it was behaving as it always did before it broke eight or ten points. Well, I would jot down the stock and the price on Monday, and remembering past performances I would write down what it ought to do on Tuesday and Wednesday. Later I would check up with actual transcriptions from the tape.

That is how I first came to take an interest in the message of the tape. The fluctuations were from the first associated in my mind with upward or downward movements. Of course there is always a reason for fluctuations, but the tape does not concern itself with the why and wherefore. It doesn't go into explanations. I didn't ask the tape why when I was fourteen, and I don't ask it to-day, at forty. The reason for what a certain stock does to-day may not be known for two or three days, or weeks, or months. But what the dickens does that matter? Your business with the tape is now—not to-morrow. The reason can wait. But you must act instantly or be left. Time and again I see this happen. You'll remember that Hollow Tube went down three points the other day while the rest of the market rallied sharply. That

1.4 ▶ Livermore describes his method of recording hundreds of price changes in his head and sifting through them on the fly to determine which "parallel cases" and "precedents" were accurate enough to help him anticipate future changes. This is a crude but effective version of what we would now call a quantitative approach to technical analysis, in which practitioners use computers and mathematical models to forecast future price changes based on past patterns.

1.5 ▶ Horse racing was the second most popular public sport in the early 1900s, after baseball. *Reminiscences* is full of racing references, including "dope sheets" (reports on horses' conditions); "clocked" prices (timing price-change intervals as one would use a stopwatch on a horse); and "the tape is your telescope" (watching prices changes via the ticker tape as you would use a telescope to watch a race at the track).

1.6 ▶ This is the central message of *Reminiscences* and has made the book a timeless classic. Throughout the book, we see manipulations, speculations, booms, busts, and panics that could be ripped from the pages of financial news reports in any era decades later, with only the names changed. No matter how much each new set of investors, executives, and policy makers believes their times are unique, Lefevre observes correctly, "Whatever happens in the stock market to-day has happened before and will happen again."

1.7 "Bucket shops" were storefront operations where speculators who could not afford a regular brokerage account could bet on the price movements of stocks and commodities using small sums of their own money, plus margin borrowing. No actual transactions in the stock or commodity took place since these were not investments but simple wagers on price changes.

The term originated in England in the early 1800s, when poor youths would visit pubs with a bucket, drain beer kegs that had been thrown out, then congregate in abandoned shops to drink, smoke, bet, and carry on. The expression was later applied to shops where grain and stock transactions were counterfeited.[7] The proliferation of bucket shops was spurred by low-cost access to stock tickers. Shops would lease wires from brokers and telegraph companies, in many cases maintaining redundant connections to ensure reliability. To the untrained eye, their fancy offices, newspaper ads, tip-sheet mailers, and near-real-time stock quotes made bucket shops look very similar to Wall Street brokerages. The big difference was that while a broker acted on behalf of its clients, earning a commission on each transaction, the bucket shop maintained an adversarial relationship with its customers since it profited at their expense.

Bucket shop operators were a nefarious bunch, with one observer at the time calling them "pool-room sharks or 'sure-thing' card men with no standing in the business or social world."[8] Although U.S. bucket shops got their start in New York around 1877, they rapidly spread to small

was the fact. On the following Monday you saw that the directors passed the dividend. That was the reason. They knew what they were going to do, and even if they didn't sell the stock themselves they at least didn't buy it. There was no inside buying; no reason why it should not break.

Well, I kept up my little memorandum book perhaps six months. Instead of leaving for home the moment I was through with my work, I'd jot down the figures I wanted and would study the changes, always looking for the repetitions and parallelisms of behaviour—learning to read the tape, although I was not aware of it at the time.

One day one of the office boys—he was older than I—came to me where I was eating my lunch and asked me on the quiet if I had any money.

"Why do you want to know?" I said.

"Well," he said, "I've got a dandy tip on Burlington. I'm going to play it if I can get somebody to go in with me."

"How do you mean, play it?" I asked. To me the only people who played or could play tips were the customers—old jiggers with oodles of dough. Why, it cost hundreds, even thousands of dollars, to get into the game. It was like owning your private carriage and having a coachman who wore a silk hat.

"That's what I mean; play it!" he said. "How much you got?"

"How much you need?"

"Well, I can trade in five shares by putting up $5."

"How are you going to play it?"

"I'm going to buy all the Burlington the bucket shop will let me carry with the money I give him for margin," he said. ◁1.7 "It's going up sure. It's like picking up money. We'll double ours in a jiffy."

"Hold on!" I said to him, and pulled out my little dope book.

I wasn't interested in doubling my money, but in his saying that Burlington was going up. If it was, my note-book ought to show it. I looked. Sure enough, Burlington, according to my figuring, was acting as it usually did before it went up. I had never bought or sold anything in my life, and I never gambled with the other boys. But all I could see was that this was a grand chance to test the accuracy of my work, of my hobby. It struck me at once that if my dope didn't work in practice there was nothing in the theory of it to interest anybody. So I gave him all I had, and with our pooled resources he went to one of the near-by bucket shops and bought some Burlington. Two days later we cashed in. I made a profit of $3.12.

After that first trade, I got to speculating on my own hook in the bucket shops. I'd go during my lunch hour and buy or sell—it never made any difference to me. I was playing a system and not a favorite stock or backing opinions. All I knew was the arithmetic of it. As a matter of fact, mine was the ideal way to operate in a bucket shop, where all that a trader does is to bet on fluctuations as they are printed by the ticker on the tape.

It was not long before I was taking much more money out of the bucket shops than I was pulling

towns across the Midwest as ticker service expanded. By wrapping themselves in an air of respectability, achieved mainly through appearances, bucket shops were not seen as dangerous by the public. Men were not embarrassed by being seen in a bucket shop, as they would be if caught in a poker room.

Bucket shops found the most success in small agricultural communities where the fast action delivered via the ticker brought excitement to dull, tradition-bound lives. Chicago Board of Trade historian Charles H. Taylor noted in 1917 that they were initially viewed as a sort of democratized exchange "where the common people could speculate."[9]

Eventually brokerages and exchanges launched a campaign to stamp out bucket shops because they feared the competition and believed they undermined public support for legitimate investing. In 1889, the *New York Times* estimated that bucket shop patrons were wagering the equivalent of 1 million shares per day at a time when the average daily volume on the New York Stock Exchange was 140,000 shares.[10]

Rising public anger toward bucket shops' unsavory practices also escalated. Some owners would boast about "cleaning up a town"—draining the locals of their savings—before closing up to repeat the game in a neighboring town.[11] Lefevre's colorful narrative brings this bygone era to life.

down from my job in the brokerage office. So I gave up my position. My folks objected, but they couldn't say much when they saw what I was making. I was only a kid and office-boy wages were not very high. I did mighty well on my own hook.

I was fifteen when I had my first thousand and laid the cash in front of my mother—all made in the bucket shops in a few months, besides what I had taken home. My mother carried on something awful. She wanted me to put it away in the savings bank out of reach of temptation. She said it was more money than she ever heard any boy of fifteen had made, starting with nothing. She didn't quite believe it was real money. She used to worry and fret about it. But I didn't think of anything except that I could keep on proving my figuring was right. That's all the fun there is—being right by using your head. If I was right when I tested my convictions with ten shares I would be ten times more right if I traded in a hundred shares. That is all that having more margin meant to me—I was right more emphatically. More courage? No! No difference! If all I have is ten dollars and I risk it, I am much braver than when I risk a million, if I have another million salted away.

Anyhow, at fifteen I was making a good living out of the stock market. I began in the smaller bucket shops, where the man who traded in twenty shares at a clip was suspected of being John W. Gates in disguise or J. P. Morgan traveling incognito.◁**1.8**▷ Bucket shops in those days seldom lay down on their customers. They didn't have to. There were other ways of parting customers from their money, even when they guessed right. The business was tremendously profitable. When it was conducted legitimately—I mean straight, as far as the bucket shop went—the fluctuations took care of the shoestrings. It doesn't take much of a reaction to wipe out a margin of only three quarters of a point. Also, no welsher could ever get back in the game. Wouldn't have any trade.

1.8 **John Warne Gates** made his fortune selling barbed wire in the late nineteenth century and parlayed the proceeds of a deal with J. P. Morgan into a brokerage and a company that would become Texaco. His nickname, "Bet-a-Million," was earned by a lifetime of heavy betting at the racetrack and card tables.

Born on a farm in Illinois in 1855, Gates showed promise as a capitalist at 16 when he contracted to husk a neighbor's cornfields and used the proceeds to buy a one-third interest in a threshing machine—a venture that proved profitable when the next harvest was abundant. By age 18, Gates had accumulated $1,000 (worth $17,000 today), with which he purchased a hardware store in his hometown.

Gates's career took off when Isaac Ellwood, who had purchased the manufacturing rights to newly invented barbed wire, offered him a job as a salesman. Gates set off for Texas but met little initial success from skeptical cattlemen who disparaged use of "such a flimsy material."[12] In response, Gates rented Military Plaza in San Antonio, built a barbed-wire corral, and invited ranchers to "bring in your worst fence-busters." His pitch: "This is the finest fencing in the world, light as air, stronger than whiskey, cheaper than dirt, all steel and a yard wide." After crashing into the barbs, steers eventually gave up. Sales poured in, exceeding Ellwood's factory capacity.[13]

Gates applied for a partnership stake from Ellwood but was denied. Convinced of his abilities and the promise of the new invention, Gates built his own barbed-wire mill and became a competitor. A patent infringement lawsuit followed, but Elwood eventually joined with Gates in what would become a lifelong partnership and friendship.[14]

Gates consolidated power within the industry, buying competitors large and small until, by 1892, he became the king of the wire industry. Gates then began moving up the supply chain and became active in raw steel, ultimately becoming head of one of the largest players at that time, Illinois Steel Co. His effort culminated with a deal with J. P. Morgan in 1901 to help form U.S. Steel.[15]

Gates thus acquired great wealth and became a large operator in Wall Street after forming a global brokerage, C. G. Gates & Co., which at its peak invested as much as $100 million ($2.3 billion today) at a time. Due to the prominence and speculative fervor of its partners, Gates found itself at the center of many of the era's most inglorious stock manipulations.[16]

As part of his stock operations, Gates gained control in the open market of the Louisville & Nashville Railway from financier and horse-racing pioneer August Belmont. He then sold his stake for a $10 million profit in a sale arranged by J. P. Morgan in the Waldorf-Astoria hotel in April 1902. Gates also became active in the oil business via a stake in the Texas Co., the predecessor to Texaco.

C. G. Gates suffered a huge blow in the Panic of 1907 and was liquidated after suffering a loss estimated by the *New York Times* at $6 million (roughly $137 million today).[17] Gates then announced that he was "through with the Wall Street game" and exited the scene after leasing a shooting estate of several thousand acres in the Savoie region of France.[18]

I didn't have a following. I kept my business to myself. It was a one-man business, anyhow. It was my head, wasn't it? Prices either were going the way I doped them out, without any help from friends or partners, or they were going the other way, and nobody could stop them out of kindness to me. I couldn't see where I needed to tell my business to anybody else. I've got friends, of course, but my business has always been the same—a one-man affair. That is why I have always played a lone hand.

As it was, it didn't take long for the bucket shops to get sore on me for beating them. I'd walk in and plank down my margin, but they'd look at it without

1.9 Livermore's nickname Boy Plunger stemmed from the word *plunger*, commonly used at the time to describe a speculator, or a person who risked big losses for the potential to capture big gains. In some usages, the term implied recklessness. Livermore also always had a very youthful appearance. In a 1908 interview in the *Evening World* newspaper, reporter Rose Tillotson describes him at 31 years old: "The first impression was of extreme youthfulness. His flaxen hair and his blue eyes seem to subtract ten years from the age he frankly acknowledges. But the determined lines of his mouth and chin belie this effect after a moment's scrutiny."

1.10 The ubiquity of the bucket shop was driven by the rapid adoption and low cost of the stock ticker. Within just a few years of the ticker's introduction into commercial service in 1867, America's speculative fever resulted in its appearance in banks, hotels, restaurants, and even saloons and cigar stores.[19] It was only natural that bucket shops should appear where crowds gathered to watch the action of faraway trading floors on the tape. Bucket shop operators sometimes appeared in hotel lobbies in places like Boston, preying on out-of-town guests caught up in the excitement of fast money and the big city.[20]

making a move to grab it. They'd tell me there was nothing doing. That was the time they got to calling me the Boy Plunger. **1.9** I had to be changing brokers all the time, going from one bucket shop to another. It got so that I had to give a fictitious name. I'd begin light, only fifteen or twenty shares. At times, when they got suspicious, I'd lose on purpose at first and then sting them proper. Of course after a little while they'd find me too expensive and they'd tell me to take myself and my business elsewhere and not interfere with the owners' dividends.

Once, when the big concern I'd been trading with for months shut down on me I made up my mind to take a little more of their money away from them. That bucket shop had branches all over the city, in hotel lobbies, and in near-by towns. **1.10** I went to one of the hotel branches and asked the manager a few questions and finally got to trading. But as soon as I played an active stock my especial way he began to get messages from the head office asking who it was that was operating. The manager told me what they asked him and I told him my name was Edward Robinson, of Cambridge. He telephoned the glad news to the big chief. But the other end wanted to know what I looked like. When the manager told me that I said to him, "Tell him I am a short fat man with dark hair and a bushy beard!" But he described me instead, and then he listened and his face got red and he hung up and told me to beat it.

"What did they say to you?" I asked him politely.

"They said, 'You blankety-blank fool, didn't we tell you to take no business from Larry Livingston? And you deliberately let him trim us out of $700!'" He didn't say what else they told him.

I tried the other branches one after another, but they all got to know me, and my money wasn't any good in any of their offices. I couldn't even go in to look at the quotations without some of the clerks making cracks at me. I tried to get them to let me trade at long intervals by dividing my visits among them all. But that didn't work.

Finally there was only one left to me and that was the biggest and richest of all—the Cosmopolitan Stock Brokerage Company. ◁**1.11**▷

The Cosmopolitan was rated as A-1 and did an enormous business. It had branches in every manufacturing town in New England. They took my trading all right, and I bought and sold stocks and made and lost money for months, but in the end it happened with them as usual. They didn't refuse my business point-blank, as the small concerns had. Oh, not because it wasn't sportsmanship, but because they knew it would give them a black eye to publish the news that they wouldn't take a fellow's business just because that fellow happened to make a little money. But they did the next worse thing—that is, they made me put up a three-point margin and compelled me to pay a premium at first of a half point, then a point, and finally, a point and a half. Some handicap, that! How? Easy! Suppose Steel ◁**1.12**▷ was selling at 90 and you bought it. Your ticket read, normally: "Bot ten Steel at 90$\frac{1}{8}$." If you put up a point margin it meant that if it broke 89$\frac{1}{4}$ you were wiped out automatically. In a bucket shop the customer is not importuned for more margin or put to the painful necessity of telling his broker to sell for anything he can get.

But when the Cosmopolitan tacked on that premium they were hitting below the belt. It meant that if the price was 90 when I bought, instead of making my ticket: "Bot Steel at 90$\frac{1}{8}$," it read: "Bot Steel at 91$\frac{1}{8}$." Why, that stock could advance a point and a quarter after I bought it and I'd still be losing money if I closed the trade. And by also insisting that I put up a three-point margin at the very start they reduced my trading capacity by two thirds. Still, that was the only bucket shop that would take my business at all, and I had to accept their terms or quit trading.

1.11 ▷ Cosmopolitan is likely a pseudonym for Haight & Freese Co., which was characterized as "the largest bucket shop swindling concern in the country" with extensive operations in New York, Philadelphia, Boston, and other cities.[21]

In 1902, Haight & Freese had more than 70 offices through the United States and Canada, and was headquartered in Boston. It was founded as a partnership in 1890 as a member of the Consolidated Stock Exchange in New York. Following its expulsion (legitimate exchanges forbid members from conducting bucketing operations), the firm found it difficult to prove that it was able to execute orders without exchange connections. So in 1903, the firm's principals became associated with the Consolidated Stock Exchange of Philadelphia. Although chartered by that city with good intentions, the firm was soon overrun by bucket-shop operators looking for cover.

1.12 ▷ Livermore appears to be referring to U.S. Steel, which wasn't created until 1901. The time period he is describing is the late 1890s. So when describing his early trading in this book, Livermore allowed a little color from the 1920s to slip through. U.S. Steel was one of the most widely held stocks of the early century after it was cobbled together in an extensive set of mergers by J.P. Morgan. Traders referred to their favorite stocks with pet names, such as Steel for U.S. Steel; Sugar for the giant American Sugar Refining Co. controlled by the Havemeyer family; or Omaha for the Chicago, St. Paul, Minneapolis & Omaha Railway.

Of course I had my ups and downs, but was a winner on balance. However, the Cosmopolitan people were not satisfied with the awful handicap they had tacked on me, which should have been enough to beat anybody. They tried to double-cross me. They didn't get me. I escaped because of one of my hunches.

The Cosmopolitan, as I said, was my last resort. It was the richest bucket shop in New England, and as a rule they put no limit on a trade. I think I was the heaviest individual trader they had—that is, of the steady, every-day customers. They had a fine office and the largest and completest quotation board I have ever seen anywhere. It ran along the whole length of the big room and every imaginable thing was quoted. I mean stocks dealt in on the New York and Boston Stock Exchanges, cotton, wheat, provisions, metals—everything that was bought and sold in New York, Chicago, Boston and Liverpool.

You know how they traded in bucket shops. You gave your money to a clerk and told him what you wished to buy or sell. He looked at the tape or the quotation board and took the price from there—the last one, of course. He also put down the time on the ticket so that it almost read like a regular broker's report—that is, that they had bought or sold for you so many shares of such a stock at such a price at such a time on such a day and how much money they received from you. When you wished to close your trade you went to the clerk—the same or another, it depended on the shop—and you told him. He took the last price or if the stock had not been active he waited for the next quotation that came out on the tape. He wrote that price and the time on your ticket, O.K.'d it and gave it back to you, and then you went to the cashier and got whatever cash it called for. Of course, when the market went against you and the price went beyond the limit set by your margin, your trade automatically closed itself and your ticket became one more scrap of paper.

In the humbler bucket shops, where people were allowed to trade in as little as five shares, the tickets were little slips—different colors for buying and selling—and at times, as for instance in boiling bull markets, the shops would be hard hit because all the customers were bulls and happened to be right. Then the bucket shop would deduct both buying and selling commissions and if you bought a stock at 20 the ticket would read 20¼. You thus had only ¾ of a point's run for your money.

But the Cosmopolitan was the finest in New England. It had thousands of patrons and I really think I was the only man they were afraid of. Neither the killing premium nor the three-point margin they made me put up reduced my trading much. I kept on buying and selling as much as they'd let me. I sometimes had a line of 5000 shares.

Well, on the day the thing happened that I am going to tell you, I was short thirty-five hundred shares of Sugar. I had seven big pink tickets for five hundred shares each. The Cosmopolitan used big slips with a blank space on them where they could write down additional margin. Of course, the bucket shops never ask for more margin. The thinner the shoestring the better for them, for their profit lies in your being wiped. In the smaller shops if you wanted to margin your trade still further they'd make out a new ticket, so they could charge you the buying commission and only give you a run of ¾ of a point on each point's decline, for they figured the selling commission also exactly as if it were a new trade.

Well, this day I remember I had up over $10,000 in margins.

I was only twenty when I first accumulated ten thousand dollars in cash. And you ought to have heard my mother. You'd have thought that ten thousand dollars in cash was more than anybody carried around except old John D.,  and she used to tell

1.14 Short selling at a bucket shop was quite different than short selling at a legitimate brokerage. Legitimate shorting involves the borrowing of shares you don't own, normally from another of your broker's clients, and then selling them with the expectation of buying them back at a lower price and pocketing the difference. But since the bucket shops did not buy or sell actual securities, the transaction was not much different from going long. A "buy" or "sell" order ticket was issued with a price that, in reality, was a one-way bet against the house. If a stock went down as expected, then you just redeemed your ticket with the clerk. Bucket shop owners were usually in cahoots with corrupt floor brokers, who would run prices up to knock out stops—triggering losses for short sellers—if customers were making too much money on their wagers.

me to be satisfied and go into some regular business. I had a hard time convincing her that I was not gambling, but making money by figuring. But all she could see was that ten thousand dollars was a lot of money and all I could see was more margin.

I had put out my 3500 shares of Sugar at 105¼. There was another fellow in the room, Henry Williams, who was short 2500 shares. I used to sit by the ticker and call out the quotations for the board boy. The price behaved as I thought it would. It promptly went down a couple of points and paused a little to get its breath before taking another dip. The general market was pretty soft and everything looked promising. Then all of a sudden I didn't like the way Sugar was doing its hesitating. I began to feel uncomfortable. I thought I ought to get out of the market. Then it sold at 103—that was low for the day—but instead of feeling more confident I felt more uncertain. I knew something was wrong somewhere, but I couldn't spot it exactly. But if something was coming and I didn't know where from, I couldn't be on my guard against it. That being the case I'd better be out of the market.

You know, I don't do things blindly. I don't like to. I never did. Even as a kid I had to know why I should do certain things. But this time I had no definite reason to give to myself, and yet I was so uncomfortable that I couldn't stand it. I called to a fellow I knew, Dave Wyman, and said to him: "Dave, you take my place here. I want you to do something for me. Wait a little before you call out the next price of Sugar, will you?" **1.14**

He said he would, and I got up and gave him my place by the ticker so he could call out the prices for the boy. I took my seven Sugar tickets out of my pocket and walked over to the counter, to where the clerk was who marked the tickets when you closed your trades. But I didn't really know why I should get out of the market, so I just stood there, leaning against the counter, my tickets in my hand so that the clerk couldn't see them. Pretty soon I heard the clicking of a telegraph instrument and I saw Tom Burnham, the clerk, turn his head quickly and listen. Then I felt that something crooked was hatching, and I decided not to wait any longer. Just then Dave Wyman by the ticker, began: "Su—" and quick as a flash I slapped my tickets on the counter in front of the clerk and yelled, "Close Sugar!" before Dave had finished calling the price. So, of course, the house had to close my Sugar at the last quotation. What Dave called turned out to be 103 again.

According to my dope Sugar should have broken 103 by now. The engine wasn't hitting right. I had the feeling that there was a trap in the neighbourhood. At all events, the telegraph instrument was now going like mad and I noticed that Tom Burnham, the clerk, had left my tickets unmarked where I laid them, and was listening to the clicking as if he were waiting for something. So I yelled at him: "Hey, Tom, what in hell are you waiting for? Mark the price on these tickets—103! Get a gait on!"

Everybody in the room heard me and began to look toward us and ask what was the trouble, for, you see, while the Cosmopolitan had never laid down, there was no telling, and a run on a bucket shop can start like a run on a bank. If one customer gets suspicious the others follow suit. So Tom looked sulky, but came over and marked my tickets "Closed at 103" and shoved the seven of them over toward me. He sure had a sour face.

Say, the distance from Tom's place to the cashier's cage wasn't over eight feet. But I hadn't got to the ca-

1.15 ▶ Lefevre uses many words for "swindle" that are no longer in wide use. The thimblerig was a shell game, typically using three shells or thimbles, and a foam ball the size of a pea. Portrayed on the street as a gambling game, it was instead a con game. The operator would shuffle the pea under the fast-moving shells, then invite a passerby to bet on its location. Co-conspirators would amp up the betting until the mark, or victim, was invited to make the final bet. Then the operator would use sleight of hand to move the pea and cheat the mark. Livermore describes many market operations in which insiders con both buyers and short sellers into elaborate forms of shell-game swindles.

1.16 ▶ One of the most searing experiences for market participants at the turn of the twentieth century was the 1896 presidential election between Democratic candidate William Jennings Bryan and Republican candidate William McKinley. Contemporary readers of *Reminiscences* were well versed in the history of this event and its impact on monetary policy. The debate is echoed today among investors persistently concerned about the debasement of U.S. and European currencies.

Renowned as one of America's greatest political orators, Jennings was a populist, suspicious of the banks and the railroads, and an enthusiastic supporter of the restoration of "bimetallism"—a pre-Civil War monetary system that viewed a currency redeemable in both gold and silver as a way to expand the money supply, stoke inflation, and ease the debt burdens of America's poor farmers.[22]

Bryan is most famous for his speech at the 1896 Democratic National Convention in St. Louis in which he attacked wealthy East Coast interests for supporting the gold standard at the expense of impoverished workers and farmers in the South and West. To rowdy applause, he declared: "Having behind us the commercial interests and the laboring interests and all the toiling masses, we shall answer their demands for a gold standard by saying to them, you shall not press down upon the brow of labor this crown of thorns. You shall not crucify mankind upon a cross of gold." Besides clinching him the presidential nomination, the speech secured Bryan's status as an opinion leader and the nickname "the Boy Orator." At 36, he was the youngest nominee of a major party in American history.

The origins of the fight for "free silver" date back to the Coinage Act of 1873, which moved the United States to the gold standard and demonetized silver. Before then, anyone who possessed uncoined silver could deposit it at a U.S. Mint, where it would be made into coin. The law was spurred by the discovery of huge silver deposits in the Comstock Lode of Nevada, which effectively diminished the value of silver as money. Twenty years of economic distress

shier to get my money when Dave Wyman by the ticker yelled excitedly: "Gosh! Sugar, 108!" But it was too late; so I just laughed and called over to Tom, "It didn't work that time, did it, old boy?"

Of course, it was a put-up job. Henry Williams and I together were short six thousand shares of Sugar. That bucket shop had my margin and Henry's, and there may have been a lot of other Sugar shorts in the office; possibly eight or ten thousand shares in all. Suppose they had $20,000 in Sugar margins. That was enough to pay the shop to thimblerig the market on the New York Stock Exchange and wipe us out.◁**1.15** In the old days whenever a bucket shop found itself loaded with too many bulls on a certain stock it was a common practice to get some broker to wash down the price of that particular stock far enough to wipe out all the customers that were long of it. This seldom cost the bucket shop more than a couple of points on a few hundred shares, and they made thousands of dollars.

That was what the Cosmopolitan did to get me and Henry Williams and the other Sugar shorts. Their brokers in New York ran up the price to 108. Of course it fell right back, but Henry and a lot of others were wiped out. Whenever there was an unexplained sharp drop which was followed by instant recovery, the newspapers in those days used to call it a bucket-shop drive.

And the funniest thing was that not later than ten days after the Cosmopolitan people tried to double-cross me a New York operator did them out of over seventy thousand dollars. This man, who was quite a market factor in his day and a member of the New York Stock Exchange, made a great name for himself as a bear during the Bryan panic of '96.◁**1.16** He was forever running up against Stock Exchange rules that kept him from carrying out some of his plans at the expense of his fellow members. One day he figured that there would be no complaints from either the Exchange or the police authorities if he took from the bucket shops of the land some of their ill-gotten gains. In the instance I speak of he sent thirty-five men to act as customers. They went to the main office and to the bigger branches. On a certain day at a fixed hour the agents all bought as much of a certain stock as the managers would let them. They had instructions to sneak out at a certain profit. Of course what he did was to distribute bull tips on that stock among his cronies and then he went in to the floor of the Stock Exchange and bid up the price, helped by the room traders, who thought he was a good sport. Being careful to pick out the right stock for that work, there was no trouble in putting up the price three or four points. His agents at the bucket shops cashed in as prearranged.

A fellow told me the originator cleaned up seventy thousand dollars net, and his agents made their expenses and their pay besides. He played that game several times all over the country, punishing the bigger bucket shops of New York, Boston, Philadelphia, Chicago, Cincinnati and St. Louis. One of his favorite stocks was Western Union, because it was so easy to move a semiactive stock like that a few points up or down. His agents bought it at a certain figure, sold at two points profit, went short and took three points more. By the way, I read the other day that that man died, poor and obscure. If he had died in 1896 he would have got at least a column on the first page of every New York paper. As it was he got two lines on the fifth.

followed the passage of the act, as tightened monetary conditions led to deflationary pressures and the panics of 1873 and 1893.

The Bryan Panic, which roughly ran from the time Bryan was nominated in July 1896, until McKinley was elected in November that year, was a consequence of swelling concerns that a Bryan presidency would undermine contracts, disrupt market prices, and erode the wealth of the business class. For many, Bryan's nomination was an unpleasant surprise: On the eve of the convention, the *Commercial & Financial Chronicle* noted that the "thought of rallying around, as a battle cry, a plan for paying one's debts with a fifty-cent dollar, and presenting that as a subject of discussing for three or four months to the people of the United States, is a folly not affording a shadow of a promise."[23]

Soon after Bryan's nomination, stocks sold off, commodity prices plummeted, bank lending seized up, and industrial activity slowed amid plunging demand, as merchants feared the Democrat's monetary policies would result in a severe recession. By the middle of August, the stock market reached the lowest point in 17 years as commercial bankruptcies rose.[24] Toward the end of October, fears escalated in the money markets and currency was redeemed for gold at an alarming rate. Interest rates, previously at 15%, rose to 127% as gold reserves in New York were depleted. Conrad Jordan of the New York subtreasury, predecessor to the New York Federal Reserve Bank, wrote Assistant Treasury Secretary William Curtis, "The banks are hard up for currency and may need more to-morrow and Monday, but I think aid will come from Morgan."[25] He was referring to J. P. Morgan, who helped organize a banking syndicate that made $10 million available to the subtreasury to prevent financial collapse.

After the votes were counted in November and McKinley was declared the winner, *Dun's Review* wrote on November 7 that "a crushing weight has been lifted and rolled away."[26] It must be said that the election of 1896 was one of the most questionable in U.S. history, with widespread voter coercion reported amid a massive propaganda campaign against Bryan and the free silver movement. The themes would resonate for decades.

ENDNOTES

1 Richard Smitten, *World's Greatest Stock Trader* (New York: John Wiley & Sons, 2001), 20.

2 Ibid.

3 David Hochfelder, "'Where the Common People Could Speculate': The Ticker, Bucket Shops, and the Origins of Popular Participation in Financial Markets, 1880–1920," *Journal of American History* (September 2006), 339.

4 Sereno Stansbury Pratt, *The Work of Wall Street* (New York: D. Appleton and Company, 1903), 189.

5 Horace L. Hotchkiss, "The Stock Ticker," in *The New York Stock Exchange: Its History, Its Contributions to National Prosperity, and Its Relation to American Finance at the Outset of the Twentieth Century,* ed. Edmund Clarence Stedman (New York: The Stock Exchange Historical Company, 1905), 434.

6 Thomas Gibson, *The Pitfalls of Speculation* (New York: Moody's Corporation, 1906), 47.

7 John Hill, *Gold Bricks of Speculation* (Chicago: London Book Concern, 1904), 39.

8 Ibid.

9 Charles H. Taylor, *History of the Board of Trade of the City of Chicago* (Chicago: Robert O. Law Company, 1917), 585.

10 "All Tickers Ordered Out," *New York Times,* June 1, 1889, 1.

11 Hill, *Gold Bricks of Speculation,* 22.

12 *The Cyclopædia of American Biography*, vol. 8 (1915), 61.

13 "Bulls and Bears," May 15, 2009, www.oldandsold.com/articles11/port-arthur-7.shtml.

14 E. M. Kingsbury, "John W. Gates: The Forgetful Man," *Everybody's Magazine* 10 (1904): 82.

15 *Cyclopædia of American Biography.*

16 Henry Clews, *Fifty Years in Wall Street* (New York: Irving Publishing Company, 1908), 802.

17 "Gates & Co. to Quit; Big Losers, It's Said," *New York Times*, May 1, 1907, 1.

18 "Last of C.G. Gates & Co.," *New York Times*, June 22, 1907, 11.

19 Hochfelder"Where the Common People Could Speculate," 340.

20 "Inquiry Disastrous for Bucket Shops," *New York Times*, February 22, 1922, 30.

21 "Winds up Haight & Freese," *New York Times*, October 23, 1909, 15.

22 James Anderson Barnes, "Myths of the Bryan Campaign," *Mississippi Valley Historical Review* 34 (1947): 367–404.

23 "Financial Situation," *Commercial & Financial Chronicle,* July 4, 1896, 2.

24 "The Week," *Dun's Review* 4, no. 159, August 15, 1896.

25 Barnes, "Myths of the Bryan Campaign."

26 "The Week," *Dun's Review* 4, no. 171, November 7, 1896.

Between the discovery that the Cosmopolitan Stock Brokerage Company was ready to beat me by foul means if the killing handicap of a three-point margin and a point-and-a-half premium didn't do it, and hints that they didn't want my business anyhow, I soon made up my mind to go to New York, where I could trade in the office of some member of the New York Stock Exchange. **2.1** I didn't want any Boston branch, where the quotations had to be telegraphed. I wanted to be close to the original source. I came to New York at the age of 21, bringing with me all I had, twenty-five hundred dollars.

I told you I had ten thousand dollars when I was twenty, and my margin on that Sugar deal was over ten thousand. But I didn't always win. My plan of trading was sound enough and won oftener than it lost. If I had stuck to it I'd have been right perhaps as often as seven out of ten times. In fact, I always made money when I was sure I was right

(continued)

trading volume. On the far side of the room was a rail that kept the public at bay; clerks and messengers passed messages across it to the floor traders.

Up above, three ornate chandeliers carried 198 electric lamps. An advanced ventilation system provided not only heating and cooling as needed but also perfumed air. Upon arrival in the morning, brokers would ask the superintendent what the day's bouquet was. At 9:50 A.M., the floor traders were allowed to enter the Board Room. At 10 A.M., the gavel would fall and immediately "a dozen blending thunderstorms break loose," according to one account. Traders would fill the air with explosive cries, yells, and gesturing hands in a scene that would be familiar to NYSE floor traders today.[1]

2.2 This is one of the pillars of wisdom that Lefevre conveys repeatedly through his depiction of the evolution of Livermore's development as a trader. Because the market is open six and a half hours a day, five days a week except for holidays, and some stocks are always rising and falling with the news to great fanfare, most new traders think they should have positions open at all times. But Livermore learns to avoid being dragged into the fray by all the commotion and to trade only when he has "sufficient knowledge to make his play an intelligent play."

2.3 Another of Livermore's important messages is that traders should never trade to get even or in an effort to buy something in particular, such as a car, because the market tends to punish anger, desperation, and naked greed. Throughout the book, we witness Livermore learning that mastery of the market demands mastery of his own emotions and biases.

before I began. What beat me was not having brains enough to stick to my own game—that is, to play the market only when I was satisfied that precedents favored my play. There is a time for all things, but I didn't know it. And that is precisely what beats so many men in Wall Street who are very far from being in the main sucker class. There is the plain fool, who does the wrong thing at all times everywhere, but there is the Wall Street fool, who thinks he must trade all the time. No man can always have adequate reasons for buying or selling stocks daily—or sufficient knowledge to make his play an intelligent play.

I proved it. Whenever I read the tape by the light of experience I made money, but when I made a plain fool play I had to lose. I was no exception, was I? There was the huge quotation board staring me in the face, and the ticker going on, and people trading and watching their tickets turn into cash or into waste paper. Of course I let the craving for excitement get the better of my judgment. **2.2** In a bucket shop

where your margin is a shoestring you don't play for long pulls. You are wiped too easily and quickly. The desire for constant action irrespective of underlying conditions is responsible for many losses in Wall Street even among the professionals, who feel that they must take home some money every day, as though they were working for regular wages. I was only a kid, remember. I did not know then what I learned later, what made me fifteen years later, wait two long weeks and see a stock on which I was very bullish go up thirty points before I felt that it was safe to buy it. I was broke and was trying to get back, and I couldn't afford to play recklessly. I had to be right, and so I waited. That was in 1915. It's a long story. I'll tell it later in its proper place. Now let's go on from where after years of practice at beating them I let the bucket shops take away most of my winnings.

And with my eyes wide open, to boot! And it wasn't the only period of my life when I did it, either. A stock operator has to fight a lot of expensive enemies within himself.◄**2.3** Anyhow, I came to New York with twenty-five hundred dollars. There were no bucket shops here that a fellow could trust. The Stock Exchange and the police between them had succeeded in closing them up pretty tight.◄**2.4** Besides, I wanted to find a place where the only limit to my trading would be the size of my stake. I didn't have much of one, but I didn't expect it to stay little forever. The main thing at the start was to find a place where I wouldn't have to worry about getting a square deal. So I went to a New York Stock Exchange house that had a branch at home where I knew some of the clerks. They have long since gone out of business. I wasn't there long, didn't like one of the partners, and then I went to A. R. Fullerton & Co. Somebody must have told them about my early experiences, because it was not long before they all got to calling me the Boy Trader. I've always looked young. It was a handicap in some ways but it compelled me to fight for my own because so many tried to take advantage of my

2.4 Stock exchanges viewed bucket shops as competitors and, during the 1880s and 1890s, tried to run them out of business by blocking their access to price quotes. In the summer of 1887, for instance, Abner Wright, president of the Chicago Board of Trade, threw the equipment of the Postal Telegraph and the Baltimore & Ohio Telegraph companies out of his building for supplying quotes to bucket shops. A few months later, Wright took an ax to some mysterious wires in the basement of the exchange building—inadvertently severing cables to the police and fire departments.

In response, bucket shops secured legal injunctions to prevent Western Union and the exchanges from removing their ticker equipment. Judges were sympathetic: They saw little difference between brokerages and bucket shops, and wanted to preserve the competition. Many federal and state court rulings between 1883 and 1903 upheld bucket shops' rights.

To mount a more effective legal fight, exchanges decided to try to draw a distinction between stock speculation and stock gambling. Their argument: Trades through brokerages, routed to exchanges and resulting in delivery of equity shares or commodities, produced value by contributing to an orderly market. Whether the trade was made for long-term investment or short-term speculation, the result was a constant stream of quotations on the ticker tape that enhanced liquidity. In comparison, they argued that bucket shop operators were parasites that fed off the trading volume of legitimate brokers while contributing nothing of value.

In 1905, the U.S. Supreme Court finally ruled in favor of the Chicago Board of Trade in a case that determined that exchanges had property rights to data they generated. Exchanges finally were able to cut off the information flow that was bucket shops' lifeblood. Justice Oliver Wendell Holmes supported the exchanges' separation of speculation and gambling, stating that the former amounted to "serious business contracts for a legitimate and useful purpose" while the latter were "mere wagers."

Besides the legal challenges, bucket shops were increasingly vilified in the media. A four-part exposé by Merrill Teague in *Everybody's Magazine* in 1906 was enough of a threat that infamous bucket shop king C. C. Christie (who was once a legitimate broker and said in 1887 that "the bucket shop is a thief") defended his operations in the same magazine.[2] Noting that 99% of all trades on the Chicago Board of Trade were settled for cash based on price differences—and not in delivery of grain—Christie charged that the CBOT was the "biggest bucket shop on earth."[3]

(continued)

Teague replied that the primary difference was that "bucket-shoppers always bet against their clients, whereas regular brokers actually buy or sell; that they strive to turn the market against clients so that those who are not losing may be MADE to lose."[4] All of these accusations are vividly brought to life as we see Livermore evolve as a trader and find the skills necessary to operate effectively on the legitimate exchanges just as the bucket shops fade into history.

EVERYBODY'S MAGAZINE

VOL. XIV.   JUNE, 1906.   No. 6.

Bucket-Shop Sharks

By MERRILL A. TEAGUE

EDITOR'S NOTE.—The Bucket-Shop thief is the jackal that sneaks along on the trail of the big beasts of prey—the Frenzied Financiers—picking up their leavings. He drags down the maimed, the weak, and the small who are disdained by the larger and more daring plunderers. The Bucket-Shop thief invades fields into which the Frenzied Financier does not think it worth while to go—the small town and city—and lures the storekeeper and the business man to their ruin by the glitter of his false "Banker & Broker" sign. Mr. Teague led a famous fight last year on a notorious pack of these unclean creatures in Philadelphia. He has been engaged by EVERYBODY'S to explain what a bucket-shop is, who the thieves are that run bucket-shops, and where they are.

IN the summer of 1903 Ridgway Bowker, then more than sixty years old, had saved $5,000 from his wages as a typesetter in a daily newspaper office. There was no dishonest penny among those dollars. Nor was there taint of dishonesty in the man who had saved them. For his wife and for his nine children Bowker had worthy aspirations. He wanted to do better by them than his scant earnings had made possible; he wanted to leave them secure from want.

On a Sunday morning in July, 1903, while reading a Philadelphia newspaper famed for moral tone and intelligence, Mr. Bowker, whose home is in Camden, N. J., came across an advertisement.

Into the fathomless depths of speculation Bowker had never thrown a financial sounding-line. Wherefore, as he read, he reasoned in this fashion: Why may not I, as others have done, use my means in the purchase of stocks, hold my purchases until prices advance, and then, by selling, realize profits to the increase of my small savings? Now this was the advertisement:

We Positively Provide
For Fractional Lots
The Best Service
in Philadelphia

Haight & Freese Co.
Stocks — Bonds — Grain — Cotton
Manhattan Life Building,
S. E. Cor. 4th and Walnut Sts.
and Suite 710
Betz Building, Philadelphia, Pa.

youth. The chaps at the bucket shops seeing what a kid I was, always thought I was a fool for luck and that that was the only reason why I beat them so often.

Well, it wasn't six months before I was broke. I was a pretty active trader and had a sort of reputation as a winner. I guess my commissions amounted to something. I ran up my account quite a little, but, of course, in the end I lost. I played carefully; but I had to lose. I'll tell you the reason: it was my remarkable success in the bucket shops!

I could beat the game my way only in a bucket shop; where I was betting on fluctuations. My tape reading had to do with that exclusively. When I bought the price was there on the quotation board, right in front of me. Even before I bought I knew exactly the price I'd have to pay for my stock. And I always could sell on the instant. I could scalp successfully, because I could move like lightning. I could follow up my luck or cut my loss in a second. Sometimes, for instance, I was certain a stock would move at least a point. Well, I didn't have to hog it, I could put up a point margin and double my money in a jiffy; or I'd take half a point. On one or two hundred shares a day, that wouldn't be bad at the end of the month, what?

The practical trouble with that arrangement, of course, was that even if the bucket shop had the resources to stand a big steady loss, they wouldn't do it. They wouldn't have a customer around the place who had the bad taste to win all the time.

At all events, what was a perfect system for trading in bucket shops didn't work in Fullerton's office. There I was actually buying and selling stocks. The price of Sugar on the tape might be 105 and I could see a three-point drop coming. As a matter of fact, at the very moment the ticker was printing 105 on the tape the real price on the floor of the Exchange might be 104 or 103. By the time my order to sell a thousand shares got to Fullerton's floor man to execute, the price might be still lower. I couldn't tell at what price

I had put out my thousand shares until I got a report from the clerk. When I surely would have made three thousand on the same transaction in a bucket shop I might not make a cent in a Stock Exchange house. Of course, I have taken an extreme case, but the fact remains that in A. R. Fullerton's office the tape always talked ancient history to me, as far as my system of trading went, and I didn't realise it.

And then, too, if my order was fairly big my own sale would tend further to depress the price. In the bucket shop I didn't have to figure on the effect of my own trading. I lost in New York because the game was altogether different. It was not that I now was playing it legitimately that made me lose, but that I was playing it ignorantly. I have been told that I am a good reader of the tape. But reading the tape like an expert did not save me. I might have made out a great deal better if I had been on the floor myself, a room trader. In a particular crowd perhaps I might have adapted my system to the conditions immediately before me. But, of course, if I had got to operating on such a scale as I do now, for instance, the system would have equally failed me, on account of the effect of my own trading on prices.

In short, I did not know the game of stock speculation. I knew a part of it, a rather important part, which has been very valuable to me at all times. But if with all I had I still lost, what chance does the green outsider have of winning, or, rather, of cashing in?

It didn't take me long to realise that there was something wrong with my play, but I couldn't spot the exact trouble. There were times when my system worked beautifully, and then, all of a sudden, nothing but one swat after another. I was only twenty-two, remember; not that I was so stuck on myself that I didn't want to know just where I was at fault, but that at that age nobody knows much of anything. ◁**2.5**▷

The people in the office were very nice to me. I couldn't plunge as I wanted to because of their

2.5 This type of self-examination and inward scolding followed by an epiphany is what has endeared *Reminiscences* to traders over the decades. In his early years, Livermore regularly finds himself losing money in new ways. Instead of complaining about his bad luck, he studies his personal habits, thought processes, and procedures and determines how he can improve to adjust to new circumstances. His constant effort to mold his methods to fit fresh observations of the economic or structural environment sets him apart from more ordinary traders who rationalize their losses as stemming from changes beyond their control. Lefevre wants the reader to learn that in order to succeed on Wall Street, it is more valuable to be adaptable than to be merely smart or rich.

2.6 ▶ The brokerage house of A. R. Fullerton, where Livermore bases his operations early in his career on Wall Street, was in reality the offices of E. F. Hutton & Co. and its predecessor, Harris, Hutton & Company. And "old man" Fullerton, who lent Livermore $500 to take on the bucket shops in St. Louis, was actually Edward Francis Hutton himself. *See more about him in Chapter 4.*

margin requirements, but old A. R. Fullerton and the rest of the firm were so kind to me that after six months of active trading I not only lost all I had brought and all that I had made there but I even owed the firm a few hundreds.

There I was, a mere kid, who had never before been away from home, flat broke; but I knew there wasn't anything wrong with me; only with my play. I don't know whether I make myself plain, but I never lose my temper over the stock market. I never argue with the tape. Getting sore at the market doesn't get you anywhere.

I was so anxious to resume trading that I didn't lose a minute, but went to old man Fullerton and said to him, "Say, A. R., lend me five hundred dollars." **2.6**

"What for?" says he.

"I've got to have some money."

"What for?" he says again.

"For margin, of course," I said.

"Five hundred dollars?" he said, and frowned. "You know they'd expect you to keep up a 10 per cent margin, and that means one thousand dollars on one hundred shares. Much better to give you a credit——"

"No," I said, "I don't want a credit here. I already owe the firm something. What I want is for you to lend me five hundred dollars so I can go out and get a roll and come back."

"How are you going to do it?" asked old A. R.

"I'll go and trade in a bucket shop," I told him.

"Trade here," he said.

"No," I said. "I'm not sure yet I can beat the game in this office, but I am sure I can take money out of the bucket shops. I know that game. I have a notion that I know just where I went wrong here."

He let me have it, and I went out of that office where the Boy Terror of the Bucket Shops, as they called him, had lost his pile. I couldn't go back home because the shops there would not take my business. New York was out of the question; there weren't any doing business at that time. They tell me that in the 90's Broad Street and New Street were full of them. But there weren't any when I needed them in my business. So after some thinking I decided to go to St. Louis. ◁2.7▷ I had heard of two concerns there that did an enormous business all through the Middle West. Their profits must have been huge. They had branch offices in dozens of towns. In fact I had been told that there were no concerns in the East to compare with them for volume of business. They ran openly and the best people traded there without any qualms. A fellow even told me that the owner of one of the concerns was a vice-president of the Chamber of Commerce but that couldn't have been in St. Louis. At any rate, that is where I went with my five hundred dollars to bring back a stake to use as margin in the office of A. R. Fullerton & Co., members of the New York Stock Exchange.

When I got to St. Louis I went to the hotel, washed up and went out to find the bucket shops. One was the J. G. Dolan Company, and the other was H. S. Teller & Co. ◁2.8▷ I knew I could beat them. I was going to play dead safe—carefully and conservatively. My one fear was that somebody might recognise me and give me away, because the bucket shops all over the country had heard of the Boy Trader. They are like gambling houses and get all the gossip of the profesh. ◁2.9▷

Dolan was nearer than Teller, and I went there first. I was hoping I might be allowed to do business a few days before they told me to take my trade somewhere else. I walked in. It was a whopping big place and there must have been at least a couple of hundred people there staring at the quotations. I was glad, because in such a crowd I stood a better chance of being unnoticed. I stood and watched the board and looked them over carefully until I picked out the stock for my initial play.

I looked around and saw the order-clerk at the window where you put down your money and get

2.7 ▷ Bucket shops first appeared in the Midwest in the late 1870s. Initially they were considered only as an incidental evil and had gained no strong foothold.[5] Soon they were booming as bountiful crops in 1879 enriched the region and speculation spread after a return to the gold standard further revived business confidence.

Naive small towns, far from the financial centers of New York and Boston, made easy targets for bucket shops, where "fraud, cheat and swindle are so transparent," according to an observer at the time. The ticker's promise of fortune was so strong that it was the subject of a lengthy 1879 editorial in the *Chicago Tribune* decrying the character of the customers who patronize them:

> Boys of larger growth and men, clerks, salesmen, bookkeepers, men in business, hackmen, teamsters, men on salaries, and men employed at day's work, stone cutters, blacksmiths and workmen of all wages and occupations; students and professors of colleges, reverend divines, dealers in theology, members of Christian Associations, members of societies for the prevention of cruelty to animals, and for the suppression of vice, gentlemen who war on saloons which permit minors to play pool, and teachers of Sunday schools, hard drinkers and temperate men, old men and young men—all, in person or by agent, purchase their 500 or 1,000 or 5,000 or 10,000 bushels, depositing their margins, and confidently hope to have their money back with 100, or even 500 per cent profit.[6]

These customers were the easy marks for the Midwest bucket shops. So imagine the shop owners' dismay when a shark of Livermore's ability entered their parlor. It was like a formidable Las Vegas poker champ sitting down at a card table in the outskirts of Reno. The odds had suddenly turned against them, and Livermore in this chapter bemoans their rude reaction.

2.8 ▷ Both of these companies, along with the Cosmopolitan Stock Brokerage Company mentioned earlier, appear to be fictitious stand-ins for real bucket shop operators. The two in St. Louis were most likely C. C. Christie and the Cella Commission Co., both of which had large operations focused on the Midwest.[7]

2.9 ▷ Livermore repeatedly refers to the bucket shops with the language of casinos. He complains here that bucket shop managers were on the lookout for him just like dealers in the gambling "profesh," or profession, make an effort to watch for notorious card counters at the blackjack tables.

2.10 ▶ The Chicago, St. Paul, Minneapolis and Omaha Railway, better known simply as the Omaha, was a popular stock at the time. The company was incorporated in 1880 and operated in Wisconsin, Minnesota, Iowa, Nebraska, and South Dakota. In 1882, control of the Omaha was turned over to the Chicago and North Western railroad. Eventually, in the 1990s, the Omaha was absorbed into the Union Pacific, which survives to this day.[8,9,10]

your ticket. He was looking at me so I walked up to him and asked, "Is this where you trade in cotton and wheat?"

"Yes, sonny," says he.

"Can I buy stocks too?"

"You can if you have the cash," he said.

"Oh, I got that all right, all right," I said like a boasting boy.

"You have, have you?" he says with a smile.

"How much stock can I buy for one hundred dollars?" I asked, peeved-like.

"One hundred; if you got the hundred."

"I got the hundred. Yes; and two hundred too!" I told him.

"Oh, my!" he said.

"Just you buy me two hundred shares," I said sharply.

"Two hundred what?" he asked, serious now. It was business.

I looked at the board again as if to guess wisely and told him, "Two hundred Omaha." **2.10**

"All right!" he said. He took my money, counted it and wrote out the ticket.

"What's your name?" he asked me, and I answered, "Horace Kent."

He gave me the ticket and I went away and sat down among the customers to wait for the roll to grow. I got quick action and I traded several times that day. On the next day too. In two days I made twenty-eight hundred dollars, and I was hoping they'd let me finish the week out. At the rate I was going, that wouldn't be so bad. Then I'd tackle the other shop, and if I had similar luck there I'd go back to New York with a wad I could do something with.

On the morning of the third day, when I went to the window, bashful-like, to buy five hundred B. R. T. the clerk said to me, "Say, Mr. Kent, the boss wants to see you." **2.11**

I knew the game was up. But I asked him, "What does he want to see me about?"

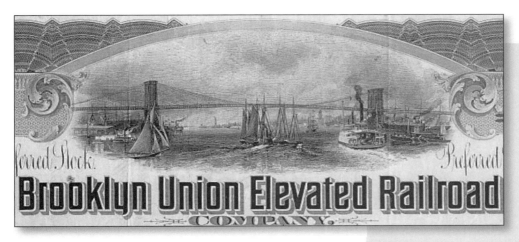

Brooklyn Union Elevated Railroad
COMPANY.

"I don't know."

"Where is he?"

"In his private office. Go in that way." And he pointed to a door.

I went in. Dolan was sitting at his desk. He swung around and said, "Sit down, Livingston."

He pointed to a chair. My last hope vanished. I don't know how he discovered who I was; perhaps from the hotel register.

"What do you want to see me about?" I asked him.

"Listen, kid. I ain't got nothin' agin yeh, see? Nothin' at all. See?"

"No, I don't see," I said.

He got up from his swivel chair. He was a whopping big guy. He said to me, "Just come over here, Livingston, will yeh?" and he walked to the door. He opened it and then he pointed to the customers in the big room.

"D' yeh see them?" he asked.

"See what?"

"Them guys. Take a look at 'em, kid. There's three hundred of 'em! Three hundred suckers! They feed me and my family. See? Three hundred suckers! Then yeh come in, and in two days yeh cop more than I get out of the three hundred in two weeks. That ain't business, kid—not for me! I ain't got nothin' agin yeh. Yer welcome to what ye've got. But yeh don't get any more. There ain't any here for yeh!"

"Why, I——"

2.11 ▶ The Brooklyn Rapid Transit (BRT), originally called the Brooklyn Union Elevated Railroad, was formed with $20 million in January 1896, to build and run railroads in the Brooklyn borough of New York. A month later, it took control of the bankrupt Long Island Traction Co. By 1900, it controlled nearly all of the streetcar lines east of Manhattan. Shares traded on the NYSE under the symbol B.

BRT shares were the focus of intense speculative attention during this period, which, based on Livermore's age of 22, is sometime in 1899. The stock rose rapidly from $35 in early 1898 to above $70 later that year, thanks to buying by ex-governor Roswell Flower (whom we will meet later) and a speculative fever set off by the U.S. war victory over Spain. In March 1899, BRT was the center of a major bull cycle on Wall Street as shares passed $136.

2.12 ▷ "Piece of cheese" is another slice of slang from card gambling. It refers to an unwanted card in poker that is destined for the "muck," or discard pile. By extension, it was used to refer to an undesirable person.

2.13 ▷ Teller was likely the Cella Commission Co., a real bucket shop that Livermore singles out for vengeance. The outfit was run by Louis and Angelo Cella, both of whom were actively involved in horse racing. Cella was based in St. Louis, had recently expanded to the eastern states, and was famous for closing out customer accounts "when they 'get right' with the market; that is, when they get on the winning side." In 1901, when cotton advanced, many of the customers of Cella's southern branches made a killing at its expense. The trades were closed and the offices abandoned.[11,12,13]

2.14 ▷ Shares topped out at $137 in April before plunging upon Flower's death in May. The company ultimately declared bankruptcy in 1919. Its rise and fall was very much like the Internet stocks of the late 1990s, which offered great promise and sold at astronomical multiples of sales when emotions ran high yet ultimately collapsed for lack of consistent earnings.

"That's all. I seen yeh come in day before yesterday, and I didn't like yer looks. On the level, I didn't. I spotted yeh for a ringer. I called in that jackass there"—he pointed to the guilty clerk—"and asked what you'd done; and when he told me I said to him: 'I don't like that guy's looks. He's a ringer!' And that piece of cheese says: ◁**2.12** 'Ringer my eye, boss! His name is Horace Kent, and he's a rah-rah boy playing at being used to long pants. He's all right!' Well, I let him have his way. That blankety-blank cost me twenty-eight hundred dollars. I don't grudge it yeh, my boy. But the safe is locked for yeh."

"Look here—" I began.

"You look here, Livingston," he said. "I've heard all about yeh. I make my money coppering suckers' bets, and yeh don't belong here. I aim to be a sport and yer welcome to what yeh pried off'n us. But more of that would make me a sucker, now that I know who yeh are. So toddle along, sonny!"

I left Dolan's place with my twenty-eight hundred dollars' profit. Teller's place was in the same block. I had found out that Teller was a very rich man who also ran up a lot of pool rooms. ◁**2.13** I decided to go to his bucket shop. I wondered whether it would be wise to start moderately and work up to a thousand shares or to begin with a plunge, on the theory that I might not be able to trade more than one day. They get wise mighty quick when they're losing and I did want to buy one thousand B. R. T. ◁**2.14** I was sure I could take four or five points out of it. But if they got suspicious or if too many customers were long of that stock they might not let me trade at all. I thought perhaps I'd better scatter my trades at first and begin small.

It wasn't as big a place as Dolan's, but the fixtures were nicer and evidently the crowd was of a better class. This suited me down to the ground and I decided to buy my one thousand B. R. T. So I stepped up to the proper window and said to the clerk, "I'd like to buy some B. R. T. What's the limit?"

"There's no limit," said the clerk. "You can buy all you please—if you've got the money."

"Buy fifteen hundred shares," I says, and took my roll from my pocket while the clerk starts to write the ticket.

Then I saw a red-headed man just shove that clerk away from the counter. He leaned across and said to me, "Say, Livingston, you go back to Dolan's. We don't want your business."

"Wait until I get my ticket," I said. "I just bought a little B. R. T."

"You get no ticket here," he said. By this time other clerks had got behind him and were looking at me. "Don't ever come here to trade. We don't take your business. Understand?"

There was no sense in getting mad or trying to argue, so I went back to the hotel, paid my bill and took the first train back to New York. It was tough. I wanted to take back some real money and that Teller wouldn't let me make even one trade.

I got back to New York, paid Fullerton his five hundred, and started trading again with the St. Louis money. I had good and bad spells, but I was doing better than breaking even. After all, I didn't have much to unlearn; only to grasp the one fact that there was more to the game of stock speculation than I had considered before I went to Fullerton's office to trade. I was like one of those puzzle fans, doing the crossword puzzles in the Sunday supplement. ◁2.15▷ He isn't satisfied until he gets it. Well, I certainly wanted to find the solution to my puzzle. I thought I was done with trading in bucket shops. But I was mistaken.

About a couple of months after I got back to New York an old jigger came into Fullerton's office. He knew A. R. Somebody said they'd once owned a string of race horses together. It was plain he'd seen better days. I was introduced to old McDevitt. He was telling the crowd about a bunch of Western racetrack crooks who had just pulled off some skin game out in St. Louis. The head devil, he said, was a poolroom owner by the name of Teller.

"What Teller?" I asked him.

"Hi Teller; H. S. Teller."

2.15 ▸ The action in this chapter takes place around 1900, but historians say the first crossword puzzle did not appear in a newspaper until December 1913. It was created by journalist Arthur Wynne of Liverpool, England, and it appeared on a Sunday in the *New York World*. Crosswords became a regular weekly feature in the *World*, and later the practice was picked up by the *Boston Globe* in 1917. Early crosswords were diamond shaped and had no internal black squares. Other newspapers began to run crosswords as they became a craze in the early 1920s, and that is when they took on their familiar rectangular shape and the use of black squares began.

Livermore refers positively to the time and effort it took to solve a crossword, but puzzles had many detractors, who considered them a silly fad. In an editorial titled "A Familiar Form of Madness," the *New York Times* complained of the "sinful waste in the utterly futile finding of words the letters of which will fit into a prearranged pattern, more or less complex. This is not a game at all, and it hardly can be called a sport; it merely is a new utilization of leisure by those for whom it otherwise would be empty and tedious. They get nothing out of it except a primitive form of mental exercise, and success or failure in any given attempt is equally irrelevant to mental development.[14] By 1942, the *Times* had finally determined crosswords were not a major threat to Western culture after all, and launched its own puzzle, which has become the pastime's benchmark.

WEEKLY BANK STATEMENT—NEW YORK CITY.

Banks	Capital	Surplus	Loans Average	Specie Average	Legals Average	Deposits Average	Per cent. Reserve
Bank of N. Y.	$2,000,000	$3,408,400	$20,729,000	$3,599,000	$1,354,000	$19,029,000	26.0
City	25,000,000	27,789,900	188,331,400	48,655,700	8,436,000	194,845,900	29.3
Merchants' Ex.	600,000	547,500	7,483,900	1,313,000	736,300	8,043,000	25.5
Pacific	500,000	864,800	3,978,300	751,500	522,500	4,045,000	31.4
Nassau	500,000	435,800	5,537,900	476,300	1,041,100	6,080,200	25.0
Copper	2,000,000	2,577,200	25,240,400	6,157,000	202,100	26,021,700	24.4
* *	* *	* *	* *	* *	* *	* *	* *
Totals, av'g	$126,350,000	$172,318,900	$1,338,224,100	$292,200,000	$77,884,200	$1,400,657,700	26.4

2.16 The cost and availability of credit have always been important to general market conditions because of the way they impact the capacity for corporate expansion and margin borrowing. Just as investors today watch the Federal Reserve's statements for insight into the movement of interest rates, in Livermore's era, prior to the establishment of the Federal Reserve System, traders would examine the weekly bank statement (see illustration) from the New York Clearinghouse. The NYCH was a member-owned association responsible for clearing checks between banks and brokers that offered assistance during financial panics; it also performed banking examinations as a sort of industry-run regulatory body.

Since the United States was on the gold standard at this time, credit conditions were regional in nature as gold bullion would need to be physically transported between banks. Thus, credit conditions for the NYSE were largely determined by the level of gold reserves within the New York area.

The statement Livermore is referring to was issued by the NYCH once a week, on Saturday at noon. If Saturday was a holiday, it was issued at 3 P.M. on Friday. The statement gave the conditions of all member banks; provided the weekly average amounts of loans, gold reserves, currency notes, and deposits; and listed gains and losses in each item compared to the previous week. Similar bank statements were made in other large cities, but the New York statement was taken as a proxy for the credit conditions of the country due to the city's importance as a financial center. The Bank of England issued a similar statement on Thursdays, which was also closely watched.

"I know that bird," I said.

"He's no good," said McDevitt.

"He's worse than that," I said, "and I have a little matter to settle with him."

"Meaning how?"

"The only way I can hit any of these short sports is through their pocketbook. I can't touch him in St. Louis just now, but some day I will." And I told McDevitt my grievance.

"Well," says old Mac, "he tried to connect here in New York and couldn't make it, so he's opened a place in Hoboken. The word's gone out that there is no limit to the play and that the house roll has got the Rock of Gibraltar faded to the shadow of a bantam flea."

"What sort of a place?" I thought he meant pool room.

"Bucket shop," said McDevitt.

"Are you sure it's open?"

"Yes; I've seen several fellows who've told me about it."

"That's only hearsay," I said. "Can you find out positively if it's running, and also how heavy they'll really let a man trade?"

"Sure, sonny," said McDevitt. "I'll go myself tomorrow morning, and come back here and tell you."

He did. It seems Teller was already doing a big business and would take all he could get. This was on a Friday. The market had been going up all that week—this was twenty years ago, remember—and it was a cinch the bank statement on Saturday would show a big decrease in the surplus reserve. ◀**2.16**▶ That would give the conventional excuse to the big room traders to jump on the market and try to shake out some of the weak commission-house accounts. There would be the usual reactions in the last half hour of the trading, particularly in stocks in which the public had been the most active. Those, of course, also would be the very stocks that Teller's customers would be most heavily long of, and the shop might be glad to see some short selling in them. There is nothing so nice as catching the suckers both ways; and nothing so easy—with one-point margins.

That Saturday morning I chased over to Hoboken to the Teller place. They had fitted up a big customers' room with a dandy quotation board and a full force of clerks and a special policeman in gray. There were about twenty-five customers.

I got talking to the manager. He asked me what he could do for me and I told him nothing; that a fellow could make much more money at the track on account of the odds and the freedom to bet your whole roll and stand to win thousands in minutes instead of piking for chicken feed in stocks and having to wait days, perhaps. He began to tell me how much safer the stock-market game was, and how much some of their customers made—you'd have sworn it was a regular broker who actually bought and sold your stocks on the Exchange— and how if a man only traded heavy he could make enough to satisfy anybody. He must have thought I was headed for some pool room and he wanted a whack at my roll before the ponies nibbled it away, for he said I ought to hurry up as the market closed at twelve o'clock on Saturdays. That would leave me free to devote the entire afternoon to other pursuits. I might have a bigger roll to carry to the track with me—if I picked the right stocks.

Livermore would have likely seen the initial results of the statement stream over the ticker. Not all the details would have been available, but he would have been able to see the total weekly changes in the various categories. The full statement was later copied by newspapers and financial magazines.[15,16]

I looked as if I didn't believe him, and he kept on buzzing me. I was watching the clock. At 11:15 I said, "All right," and I began to give him selling orders in various stocks. I put up two thousand dollars in cash, and he was very glad to get it. He told me he thought I'd make a lot of money and hoped I'd come in often.

It happened just as I figured. The traders hammered the stocks in which they figured they would uncover the most stops, and, sure enough, prices slid off. I closed out my trades just before the rally of the last five minutes on the usual traders' covering.

There was fifty-one hundred dollars coming to me. I went to cash in.

"I am glad I dropped in," I said to the manager, and gave him my tickets.

"Say," he says to me, "I can't give you all of it. I wasn't looking for such a run. I'll have it here for you Monday morning, sure as blazes."

"All right. But first I'll take all you have in the house," I said.

"You've got to let me pay off the little fellows," he said. "I'll give you back what you put up, and anything that's left. Wait till I cash the other tickets." So I waited while he paid off the other winners. Oh, I knew my money was safe. Teller wouldn't welsh with the office doing such a good business. And if he did, what else could I do better than to take all

2.17 Hoboken, New Jersey, was a thriving port city in the late 1890s and early 1900s, situated directly across the Hudson River from Manhattan, with major facilities for transatlantic shipping lines, such as Holland America and North American Lloyd. Most American troops shipping out to serve in World War I embarked for Europe there, giving rise to the hopeful phrase credited to General Pershing, "Heaven, Hell or Hoboken by Christmas." Leading financiers, such as John Jacob Astor, William Vanderbilt, and Jay Gould, entertained clients at Duke's House restaurant at the Hoboken ferry dock before it burned down in 1905.

he had then and there?
I got my own two thousand
dollars and about eight
hundred dollars besides,
which was all he had in
the office. I told him I'd
be there Monday morn-
ing. He swore the money
would be waiting for me.

I got to Hoboken a
little before twelve on
Monday. ‹2.17› I saw a fel-
low talking to the manager that I had seen in the
St. Louis office the day Teller told me to go back
to Dolan. I knew at once that the manager had
telegraphed to the home office and they'd sent up
one of their men to investigate the story. Crooks
don't trust anybody.

2.18▸ Gold notes or gold certificates were a paper currency
redeemable for gold coin and issued until the early 1930s.
Known as "yellow backs," they contrasted with greenbacks or
United States notes, which were a fiat currency not transferable
into precious metal on demand.

"I came for the balance of my money," I said
to the manager.

"Is this the man?" asked the St. Louis chap.

"Yes," said the manager, and took a bunch of
yellow backs from his pocket. ‹2.18›

"Hold on!" said the St. Louis fellow to him
and then turns to me, "Say, Livingston, didn't we
tell you we didn't want your business?"

"Give me my money first," I said to the manager, and he forked over two thousands, four five-
hundreds and three hundreds.

"What did you say?" I said to St. Louis.

"We told you we didn't want you to trade in
our place."

"Yes," I said; "that's why I came."

"Well, don't come any more. Keep away!"
he snarled at me. The private policeman in
gray came over, casual-like. St. Louis shook his
fist at the manager and yelled: "You ought to've
known better, you poor boob, than to let this
guy get into you. He's Livingston. You had your
orders."

2.19 ▶ Exchanges' efforts to destroy the bucket shops culminated in a landmark 1909 federal law banning them in the District of Columbia. This photo shows a crowd gathering outside the Mallers Building in Chicago during a police raid of a bucket shop in 1905. Sights like these would become increasingly common throughout the country in the years that followed. Justice Department special agent Bruce Bielaski used this new authority, along with evidence collected during the exchanges' three-decade campaign, to launch the final, fatal indictment of bucket shops. Over 10 weeks in early 1910, Bielaski sent investigators out to seven cities to examine operations of bucket shops with offices in Washington, D.C. The Justice Department noted that "substantially every bucket shop in the country has been put out of business as a result of this crusade." By the end of 1915, William Van Antwerp of the New York Stock Exchange declared the bucket shop dead.[17]

With the bucket shops closed, new business poured into the exchanges. In April 1916, the *New York Times* wrote of a "remarkable increase in the odd lot business" as thousands of old bucket shop customers, "practically all of whom were small speculators, have opened accounts with branches of Stock Exchange houses."[18]

"Listen, you," I said to the St. Louis man. "This isn't St. Louis. You can't pull off any trick here, like your boss did with Belfast Boy."

"You keep away from this office! You can't trade here!" he yells.

"If I can't trade here nobody else is going to," I told him. "You can't get away with that sort of stuff here."

Well, St. Louis changed his tune at once.

"Look here, old boy," he said, all fussed up, "do us a favor. Be reasonable! You know we can't stand this every day. The old man's going to hit the ceiling when he hears who it was. Have a heart, Livingston!"

"I'll go easy," I promised.

"Listen to reason, won't you? For the love of Pete, keep away! Give us a chance to get a good start. We're new here. Will you?"

"I don't want any of this high-and-mighty business the next time I come," I said, and left him talking to the manager at the rate of a million a minute. I'd got some money out of them for the way they treated me in St. Louis. There wasn't any sense in my getting hot or trying to close them up. I went back to Fullerton's office and told McDevitt what had happened. Then I told him that if it was agreeable to him I'd like to have him go to Teller's place and begin trading in twenty or thirty share lots, to get them used to him. Then, the moment I saw a good chance to clean up big, I'd telephone him and he could plunge.

I gave McDevitt a thousand dollars and he went to Hoboken and did as I told him. He got to be one of the regulars. Then one day when I thought I saw a break impending I slipped Mac the word and he sold all they'd let him. I cleared twenty-eight hundred dol-

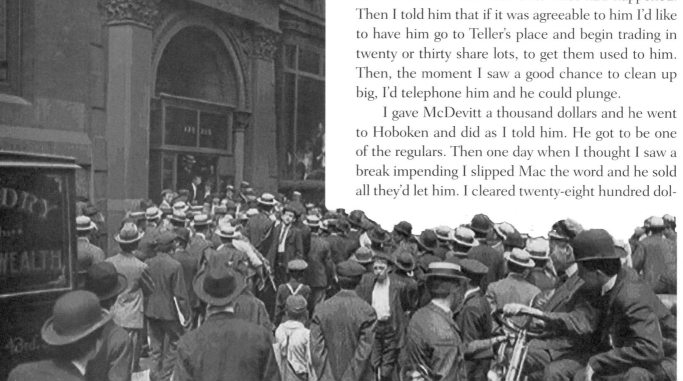

lars that day, after giving Mac his rake-off and paying expenses, and I suspect Mac put down a little bet of his own besides. Less than a month after that, Teller closed his Hoboken branch. The police got busy. And, anyhow, it didn't pay, though I only traded there twice. We ran into a crazy bull market when stocks didn't react enough to wipe out even the one-point margins, and, of course, all the customers were bulls and winning and pyramiding. No end of bucket shops busted all over the country. <2.19>

Their game has changed. Trading in the old-fashioned bucket shop had some decided advantages over speculating in a reputable broker's office. For one thing, the automatic closing out of your trade when the margin reached the exhaustion point was the best kind of stop-loss order. You couldn't get stung for more than you had put up, and there was no danger of rotten execution of orders, and so on. In New York the shops never were as liberal with their patrons as I've heard they were in the West. Here they used to limit the possible profit on certain stocks of the football order to two points. Sugar and Tennessee Coal and Iron were among these. <2.20> No matter if they moved ten points in ten minutes you could only make two on one ticket. They figured that otherwise the customer was getting too big odds; he stood to lose one dollar and to make ten. And then there were times when all the shops, including the biggest, refused to take orders on certain stocks. In 1900, on the day before Election Day, when it was a foregone conclusion that McKinley would win, not a shop in the land let its customers buy stocks. The election odds were 3 to 1 on McKinley. By buying stocks on Monday you stood to make from three to six points or more. A man could bet on Bryan and buy stocks and make sure money. <2.21> The bucket shops refused orders that day.

If it hadn't been for their refusing to take my business I never would have stopped trading in them. And then I never would have learned that there was much more to the game of stock speculation than to play for fluctuations of a few points.

2.20 Better known as TCI, the Tennessee Coal, Iron & Railroad Co. was a major U.S. steel manufacturer with assets in coal and iron ore mining as well as railways. The company was one of 12 that comprised the first Dow Jones Industrial Average index in 1896. It was a direct competitor to J. P. Morgan's massive United States Steel Corporation until he was able to secure control during the turmoil surrounding the Panic of 1907. At the time, TCI owned an estimated 800 million tons of iron ore and 2 billion tons of coal.[19]

2.21 William Jennings Bryan ran again unsuccessfully as a Democrat in the 1900 presidential election. Much of the same dynamic that played out in the 1896 contest between Bryan and William McKinley recurred. The economy was vibrant heading into the election. And America had won the brief Spanish-American War of 1898.

Bryan again ran on a "free silver" platform, but the message was not as popular as in 1896 due to the discovery of new gold deposits. Between 1900 and 1908, worldwide annual gold production surged from 425 tons to 736 tons, easing global monetary conditions by allowing more currency into circulation.[20] Gold proponents, who favored a "sound money" policy, cast Bryan's populist rhetoric as encouraging repudiation against the wealthy classes at best and full anarchy at worst.

Although Bryan's dream to restore the dollar to the pre-Civil War standard of convertibility into gold or silver never came to fruition, his desire to free the dollar from the constraints of gold was realized upon President Richard Nixon's order in 1971. Meanwhile, inflation raged: A dollar from 1900 would be worth $25.19 in 2009.

Livermore is referring in this passage to the belief that a McKinley win would be good for business conditions and great for stocks; a Bryan election would be good only for those wagering on his long-shot odds of victory. Bucket shops did best in volatile but trendless markets and worst in one-way markets, so they closed when the odds lined up against them.

Because most bucket shop operators refused to do business with Livermore and at any rate were fading from the scene, he next determines he must quit day-trading at them for short-term gain and learn how to use his intelligence, intuition, cunning, and agility to make larger, longer-lasting, more lucrative trades at legitimate brokerages.

ENDNOTES

1 Richard Wheatley, "The New York Stock Exchange," *Harper's Magazine* (November 1885).

2 Merrill A. Teague, "Bucket-Shop Sharks: Part II," *Everybody's Magazine* (July 1906): 38.

3 C. C. Christie, "Bucket-Shop vs. Board of Trade," *Everybody's Magazine* (November 1906): 707–713.

4 Ibid.

5 Charles H. Taylor, *History of the Board of Trade of the City of Chicago* (1917), 565, 585.

6 Ibid.

7 Teague, "Bucket-Shop Sharks: Part II," 43.

8 William H. Stennett, *A History of the Origin of the Place Names* (1908), 202.

9 "The Omaha Railroad; A Reorganization Under a Board of New Directors," *New York Times,* December 17, 1882, 14.

10 "Union Pacific," *New York Times,* April 26, 1995, D4.

11 "Arrest Cella for Perjury," *New York Times,* July 15, 1910, 16.

12 "Federal Raids on Bucket Shops," April 3, 1910.

13 Teague, "Bucket-Shop Sharks: Part II," 43.

14 "Topics of the Times," *New York Times*, November 17, 1924, 18.

15 John Thom Holdsworth, *Money and Banking* (1917), 274–275.

16 Edwin Griswold Nourse, *Brokerage* (1918), 225–227.

17 David Hochfelder, "'Where the Common People Could Speculate:' The Ticker, Bucket Shops, and the Origins of Popular Participation in Financial Markets, 1880–1920," *Journal of American History* (September 2006).

18 "Trading in Odd Lots New Market Force," *New York Times,* April 30, 1916, 21.

19 Robert F. Bruner and Sean D. Carr, *The Panic of 1907* (Hoboken, NJ: John Wiley & Sons, 2007), 118.

20 James Anderson Barnes, "Myths of the Bryan Campaign," *Mississippi Valley Historical Review* 34 (1947): 367–404.

It takes a man a long time to learn all the lessons of all his mistakes. They say there are two sides to everything. But there is only one side to the stock market; and it is not the bull side or the bear side, but the right side. It took me longer to get that general principle fixed firmly in my mind than it did most of the more technical phases of the game of stock speculation.

I have heard of people who amuse themselves conducting imaginary operations in the stock market to prove with imaginary dollars how right they are. Sometimes these ghost gamblers make millions. It is very easy to be a plunger that way. It is like the old story of the man who was going to fight a duel the next day.

His second asked him, "Are you a good shot?"

"Well," said the duelist, "I can snap the stem of a wineglass at twenty paces," and he looked modest.

"That's all very well," said the unimpressed second. "But can you snap the stem of the wineglass while the wineglass is pointing a loaded pistol straight at your heart?"

With me I must back my opinions with my money. My losses have taught me that I must not begin to advance until I am sure I shall not have to retreat. But if I cannot advance I do not move at all. I do not mean by this that a man should not limit his losses when he is wrong. He should. But that should not breed indecision. All my life I have made mistakes, but in losing money I have gained experience and accumulated a lot of valuable don'ts. I have been flat broke several times, but my loss has never been a total loss. Otherwise, I wouldn't be here now. I always knew I would have another chance and that I would not make the same mistake a second time. I believed in myself.

A man must believe in himself and his judgment if he expects to make a living at this game. That is why I don't believe in tips. If I buy stocks on Smith's tip I must sell those same stocks on Smith's tip. I am depending on him. Suppose Smith is away on a holiday when the selling time comes around? No, sir, nobody can make big money on what someone else tells him to do. I know from experience that nobody can give me a tip or a series of tips that will make more money for me than my own judgment. It took me five years to learn to play the game intelligently enough to make big money when I was right.

I didn't have as many interesting experiences as you might imagine. I mean, the process of learning how to speculate does not seem very dramatic at this distance. I went broke several times, and that is never pleasant, but the way I lost money is the way everybody loses money who loses money in Wall Street. Speculation is a hard and trying business, and a speculator must be on the job all the time or he'll soon have no job to be on.

My task, as I should have known after my early reverses at Fullerton's, was very simple: To look at speculation from another angle. But I didn't know that there was much more to the game than I could possibly learn in the bucket shops. There I thought I was beating the game when in reality I was only beating the shop. At the same time the tape-reading ability that trading in bucket shops developed in me and the training of my memory have been extremely valuable. Both of these things came easy to me. I owe my early success as a trader to them and not to brains or knowledge, because my mind was untrained and my ignorance was colossal. The game taught me the game. And it didn't spare the rod while teaching.

I remember my very first day in New York. I told you how the bucket shops, by refusing to take my business, drove me to seek a reputable commission house. One of the boys in the office where I got my first job was working for Harding Brothers, members of the New York Stock Exchange. I arrived in this city in the morning, and before one o'clock that same day I had opened an account with the firm and was ready to trade.

I didn't explain to you how natural it was for me to trade there exactly as I had done in the bucket shops, where all I did was to bet on fluctuations and catch small but sure changes in prices. Nobody offered to point out the essential differences or set me right. If somebody had told me my method would not work I nevertheless would have tried it out to make sure for myself, for when I am wrong only one thing convinces me of it, and that is, to lose money. And I am only right when I make money. That is speculating.

They were having some pretty lively times those days and the market was very active. That always cheers up a fellow. I felt at home right away. There was the old familiar quotation board in front of me, talking a language that I had learned before I was fifteen years old. There was a boy doing exactly the same thing I used to do in the first office I ever worked in. There were the customers—same old bunch—looking at the board or standing by the ticker calling out the prices and talking about the market. The machinery was to all appearances the same machinery that I was used to. The atmosphere was the atmosphere I had breathed since I had made my first stock-market money—$3.12 in Burlington. The same kind of ticker and the same kind of traders, therefore the same kind of game. And remember, I was only twenty-two. I suppose I thought I knew the game from A to Z. Why shouldn't I?

I watched the board and saw something that

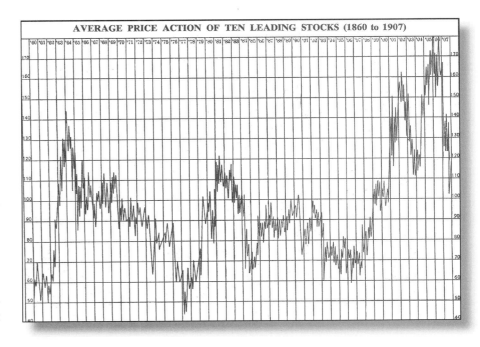

AVERAGE PRICE ACTION OF TEN LEADING STOCKS (1860 to 1907)

3.1 ► Although Livermore describes himself as a boy, he was about 24 years old. It had been 10 years since he arrived in Boston and first began studying the rhythm of prices. With some well-honed skills at his disposal, he was well positioned for the big bull market that lay ahead.

The 1901 market boom was fueled by the widespread economic prosperity the United States enjoyed at the beginning of the twentieth century. Factors included a succession of plentiful harvests, increased global gold production, an expanding trade surplus, and victory in the war against Spain. The situation was remarkable considering the nation's crippled financial state a short time earlier in 1894, when key industries were declining, big companies drifting toward bankruptcy, and the government was forced to borrow at high interest rates from Europe to maintain the public credit.[1]

The chart on page 37 shows the price action of the 10 leading stocks from 1860 to 1907. European crop failures increased demand for American wheat, boosting U.S. gold reserves from $44.5 million in 1896 to $254 million in 1898. This gold cache enabled legislation to be passed in March 1900 that officially put the United States back on the gold standard, ending the experiments with nonconvertible bills called greenbacks during the Civil War, and bimetallism—convertibility into both gold and silver—in the years that followed.

Companies and investors alike benefited from sounder monetary policy. But during the summer, as Democratic nominee William Jennings Bryan crisscrossed the country during the 1900 presidential campaign, business activity slowed as the country was gripped in an 1896-style "free-silver" scare. On August 22, only 86,000 shares traded on the New York Stock Exchange. On September 24, the Dow Jones Industrial Average set the year's closing low at 52.96.

Following President McKinley's reelection in November, stocks surged as gold poured into the United States from Europe once foreign investors were reassured of U.S. monetary stability. The Dow Jones Industrials leapt 34% from the summer low to close at 71.04 on December 27. The boom continued into 1901, and on January 7, the NYSE had its first 2-million-share day.

Veteran banker Henry Clews, who had helped finance the Civil War by cleverly marketing U.S. federal bonds to Europeans, captures the mood in his memoir:

> Wall Street changed with almost magical suddenness from depression and apprehension to confidence and buoyancy with the defeat of Bryan and his silver heresy. ... Large capitalists all over the country began to buy stocks and bonds on so heavy a scale that prices shot up rapidly... and very soon orders poured into the Stock Exchange

looked good to me. It was behaving right. I bought a hundred at 84. I got out at 85 in less than a half hour. Then I saw something else I liked, and I did the same thing; took three-quarters of a point net within a very short time. I began well, didn't I?

Now mark this: On that, my first day as a customer of a reputable Stock Exchange house, and only two hours of it at that, I traded in eleven hundred shares of stock, jumping in and out. And the net result of the day's operations was that I lost exactly eleven hundred dollars. That is to say, on my first attempt, nearly one-half of my stake went up the flue. And remember, some of the trades showed me a profit. But I quit eleven hundred dollars minus for the day.

It didn't worry me, because I couldn't see where there was anything wrong with me. My moves, also, were right enough, and if I had been trading in the old Cosmopolitan shop I'd have broken better than even. That the machine wasn't as it ought to be, my eleven hundred vanished dollars plainly told me. But as long as the machinist was all right there was no need to stew. Ignorance at twenty-two isn't a structural defect.

After a few days I said to myself, "I can't trade this way here. The ticker doesn't help as it should!" But I let it go at that without getting down to bed rock. I kept it up, having good days and bad days, until I was cleaned out. I went to old Fullerton and got him to stake me to five hundred dollars. And I came back from St. Louis, as I told you, with money I took out of the bucket shops there—a game I could always beat.

I played more carefully and did better for a while. As soon as I was in easy circumstances I began to live pretty well. I made friends and had a good time. I was not quite twenty-three, remember; all alone in New York with easy money in my pockets and the belief in my heart that I was beginning to understand the new machine.

I was making allowances for the actual execution of my orders on the floor of the Exchange, and moving more cautiously. But I was still sticking to the tape—that is, I was still ignoring general principles; and as long as I did that I could not spot the exact trouble with my game.

We ran into the big boom of 1901 and I made a great deal of money—that is, for a boy. **3.1** You remember those times? The prosperity of the country was unprecedented. We not only ran into an era of industrial consolidations and combinations of capital that beat anything we had had up to that time, but the public went stock mad. **3.2** In previous flush times, I have heard, Wall Street used to brag of two-hundred-and-fifty-thousand-share days, when securities of a par value of twenty-five million dollars changed hands. But in 1901 we had a three-million-share day. Everybody was making money. The steel crowd came to town, a horde of millionaires with no more regard for money than drunken sailors. The only game that satisfied them was the stock market. We had some of the biggest high rollers the Street ever saw: John W. Gates, of 'Bet-you-a-million' fame, and his friends, like John A. Drake, Loyal Smith, and the rest; the Reid-Leeds-Moore crowd, who sold part of their Steel holdings and with the proceeds bought in the open market the actual majority of the stock of the great Rock Island system; and Schwab and Frick and Phipps and the Pittsburgh coterie; to say nothing of scores of men who were lost in the shuffle but would have been called great plungers at any other time. **3.3** A fellow could buy and sell all the stock there was. Keene made a market for the U. S. Steel shares. **3.4** A broker sold one hundred thousand shares in a few minutes. A wonderful time! And there were some wonderful winnings. And no taxes to pay on stock sales! And no day of reckoning in sight.

Of course, after a while, I heard a lot of calamity howling and the old stagers said everybody—except themselves—had gone crazy. But everybody except themselves was making money. I knew, of course, there must be a limit to the advances and an end to

from people of smaller means everywhere, and a tremendous bull market for stocks resulted, with too many men staking, or ready to stake, their bottom dollar on the rise.[2]

3.2 As the United States attracted gold from around the world, *New York Times* financial editor Alexander Dana Noyes said the "reservoir of American capital seemed inexhaustible; it filled up on one side faster than it could be drained into these various enterprises on the other. It was then that the scheme of recapitalizing American industry was conceived."[3]

This was an era in which companies consolidated their power by obtaining controlling interests in rivals. Clews said observers "witnessed an unexampled rush to form combinations of industrial and railroad interests, or trusts, and generally to capitalize the concerns taken in for many times the amount of their previous capital or real value." Between 1895 and 1904, there were 319 mergers with a total capitalization of more than $6 billion, a massive number at the time.[4]

This behavior is similar to the 1980s and mid-2000s booms in leveraged buyouts and private equity acquisitions. In both eras, vast amounts of money were borrowed from gullible lenders to magnify returns. In the first decade of the twentieth century, consolidators would float new shares of equity, bid up the price through active price manipulation, and sell them to the new class of small investors being drawn from bucket shops into legitimate brokerage houses. As shares of new industrial combination were absorbed, public naïveté encouraged bankers to create new ones.

Wall Street enjoyed the greatest boom it had yet seen. Lefevre notes that "old timers perforce stopped bragging about the boom of '79 and '80."[5] He was referring to the booms of 1879 and 1880 brought about by passage of the Resumption Act, which allowed conversion of dollars into gold.

Although the Sherman Antitrust Act of 1890 had outlawed monopolies, this era did not end until passage of the Clayton Antitrust Act in 1914. The law allowed regulators to prevent acquisitions if they were intended to lessen competition or lay the groundwork to create a monopoly.

3.3 ▶ Livermore lists some of the biggest players of the day to show who he was up against in the market.

John A. Drake, the son of a former Iowa governor, was a banker and a member of the Chicago Board of Trade. He was also a well-known betting partner and business associate of John Gates. Drake was a pallbearer at Gates' funeral service, which was held at the Plaza Hotel in New York City in 1911. Drake afterward remained close to Gates' son, Charles, and at racetracks the two became known as the largest speculators of the time on the American turf. [6,7] He was equally keen on trading commodities. It was reported that once while his father was long wheat, Drake "resisted all invitations to come in at $60 and $70, but came in strong at $80, on the short side, to his own great advantage and papa's surprise."[8]

Loyal Smith was a successful real estate investor who made millions by buying properties in the toniest sections of Manhattan. The *New York Times* reported that Smith got his start as a "daring, determined, energetic, and shrewd young Yankee." Early in his career, he relocated to Chicago and fell in with Gates and Drake. He helped the group organize the American Steel & Wire Co., which landed Smith his first fortune of $1.6 million. Among the Chicago crowd, according to Lefevre, Smith was "one of the heaviest players of the bunch, bigger than John W. Gates himself." At the time of his death in 1908, at age 54, Smith was originally estimated to be worth $5 million. But losses incurred while speculating on stocks and coffee had in fact reduced his estate to around $1 million.[9]

The Reid-Leeds-Moore crowd were four men that dominated the tin-plating industry in this era, a business that was important both for its use in rust-proofing steel and for making cans and containers. They each had nicknames: "Tin Plate" William B. Leeds; "promoter extraordinary" Judge William H. Moore and his brother James H. Moore; and "Czar" Daniel Gray Reid. The group made a fortune when they sold their American Tin Plate holdings to U.S. Steel. [10,11,12]

The Rock Island system was formally known as the Chicago, Rock Island & Pacific Railway Company. It reached from Chicago to Denver, and was sold for $20 million in 1901. It is impossible to say what the actual profits were for the group. The *Kernel of Finance and Politics*, a monthly journal, wrote in 1914 that details of Rock Island's reorganization were still lacking and that bankers "of the highest talent are applying themselves to the work with full faith in eventual success."[13] When Reid was questioned on the matter, he claimed that he had "burned his books at the end of the month."[14]

3.4 ▶ James R. Keene was one of the "boldest and ablest operators that ever lived," according to Lefevre, who wrote about the trader many times in magazines. Keene specialized in manipulating stocks to attract investment interest from the masses. Lefevre compares the practice to labeling and advertising stocks to "coax and cajole outsiders to come into the market." In reality, it was a matter of supporting the market at critical moments to give the illusion of deep, sustained buying power. Once convinced, Lefevre said, the outside investors and speculators create a "dizzying upward whirl of security values" that would allow insiders to sell their substantial stakes profitably.

Keene's skills were instrumental in creating excitement in the initial sale of U.S. Steel shares, which will be explained in detail later.[15]

3.5 ▶ Northern Pacific was a railroad controlled by James J. Hill. Backed by J.P. Morgan, the tycoon also controlled the Great Northern railroad. Together the lines dominated transportation through Wisconsin, Minnesota, the Dakotas, Montana, Wyoming, Oregon and Washington. Hill also controlled the Illinois Central line, which paralleled the Mississippi River out of Louisiana before connecting to the major eastern railroads in Chicago. Hill's intention in cobbling together his system was to transport American cotton from the South to Japan by way of Seattle. "Little Nipper" was traders' nickname for Northern Pacific common stock due to its NP symbol. Its preferred shares were called "Big Nipper."

the crazy buying of A. O. T.—Any Old Thing—and I got bearish. But every time I sold I lost money, and if it hadn't been that I ran darn quick I'd have lost a heap more. I looked for a break, but I was playing safe—making money when I bought and chipping it out when I sold short—so that I wasn't profiting by the boom as much as you'd think when you consider how heavily I used to trade, even as a boy.

There was one stock that I wasn't short of, and that was Northern Pacific. My tape reading came in handy. I thought most stocks had been bought to a standstill, but Little Nipper behaved as if it were going still higher. **‹3.5›** We know now that both the common and the preferred were being steadily absorbed by the Kuhn-Loeb-Harriman combination. **‹3.6›** Well, I was long a thousand shares of Northern Pacific common, and held it against the advice of everybody in the office. When it got to about 110 I had thirty points profit, and I grabbed it. It made my balance at my brokers' nearly fifty thousand dollars, the greatest

3.6 ▶ The accumulation of Northern Pacific shares by Edward Henry Harriman and his bankers Kuhn, Loeb was a single strand in the most epic business battle of the new century. The fight resulted first in an explosive move higher for the market in which Livermore benefited, and then a panic that cost him a fortune. It will take a while to explain.

Harriman was a speculator, a railroad consolidator, and one of the dominant figures of the early twentieth century. Although his family was pedigreed, Harriman was born into poverty in 1848. His father, Orlando Harriman, struggled as the pastor of a church in Staten Island until an inheritance secured his family's finances.

Harriman's early education mirrors Livermore's: As a teen, he worked as a clerk in a Wall Street office. Success came quickly as he learned to speculate during the volatile years during and after the Civil War—a period marred not just by the battle between the states but also by President Lincoln's assassination, currency fluctuations, disputes over ownership of railroads, and attempts to corner the gold market.

By 1870, at age 22, Harriman had made enough to buy a seat on the New York Stock Exchange at a time when there were only 70 actively traded issues.[16] Through the aid of the richer branches of the Harriman family he soon formed the brokerage firm Harriman & Co. Lefevre, in a 1901 *American Magazine* article, wrote at length about Harriman's formative stage:

> He learned the routine of a broker's life; the ups and downs of stocks, panics and booms, gaining a knowledge of technical market conditions surpassed by few other operators big or little. The game of the Street he knew, and knows it still, from the sub-cellar to the gilt ball at the end of the flag pole, for he began at the bottom and has since climbed as high as any human being can climb in Wall Street.[17]

Harriman earned a reputation, which he would keep throughout his life, of being cold and detached. He had a great appetite for knowledge, dismissing the theory that the ticker's verdicts were determined by chance. The more he knew, the less he felt he needed to talk.

In 1883, through the influence of a friend and associate, Harriman was elected a director of the Illinois Central railroad. By 1887, he was vice president of the line. Focusing on exacting profit from all available angles, Harriman labored intensely—"literally burned the midnight oil mastering details," according to Lefevre.[18] He was cognizant of even the price of rail spikes so that contractors could not gain an advantage when submitting bids.

From 1890 to 1896, Harriman accumulated wealth through speculations and acquisitions, building his reputation for deal-making acumen among the rich men he would later need as allies. The economic downturn that followed the Panic of 1893 bankrupted many railroads, leaving a rich field of opportunity for ambitious men. Lefevre calls the deals that followed the "rungfinders and ladder-builders for Harriman" as he worked through his apprenticeship in the railways.

Harriman eventually took control of the Union Pacific, which he helped take out of bankruptcy in 1898. The railroad expanded rapidly through a string of acquisitions. First there was a pair of lines in Oregon, then the purchase of the large Southern Pacific system in February 1901. Soon Harriman's road dominated the territory west from Omaha, across the original Transcontinental Railroad through Wyoming and Utah before splitting south to San Francisco in California and north to Oregon and Washington.

Kuhn, Loeb & Co., led by Jacob Schiff (see photo on next page), became Harriman's banker. Together they formed a syndicate with capital backing from the Rockefellers of Standard Oil, the Vanderbilts, and the Goulds.[19]

A battle between Harriman and rival tycoon J.P. Morgan, who controlled Northern Pacific, and their proxies brewed for years as their competing rail networks wrestled for supremacy in the states west of the Mississippi River.

The first key rail fight that led to the Panic of 1901 was over the Chicago, Burlington & Quincy Railroad, which provided an entrance into Chicago and access to a feeder network of railways throughout the fertile Mississippi plain. If one wanted to control the shipment of American crops across the Pacific and the transshipment of Asian goods into America's heartland, the Burlington was a critical asset. Its president, Charles Perkins, had made the line the most efficient of the Midwestern railroads and was nearing retirement. Everyone knew the Burlington had to be sold.

Harriman moved first. In August 1899, at a luncheon he organized in Chicago, Harriman pulled aside a representative of the Burlington and wasted no words: He believed the Union Pacific and the Burlington should combine and wondered if Perkins would be interested. Perkins told Harriman that the Burlington was not for sale, but if it were, the price would be $200 a share.

(continued)

This was too rich for Harriman's taste, but he appreciated the challenge. In response, in mid-March, he made a dual counteroffer: $150 a share in cash or $200 a share in Union Pacific bonds. Perkins was unimpressed and firmly maintained that the price was $200 a share in cash.

Soon Harriman was distracted with the purchase of the Southern Pacific, which was labeled a "railway revolution" by the press (see table on the next page for a glimpse of the rising railroad stocks).[20] He did, however, form a pool to buy Burlington stock in the open market. If Perkins wanted to play tough, Harriman might as well strengthen his hand.[21]

Next, it was Morgan's turn. His ally, James Hill, was dispatched in February 1901 to propose a merger between the Great Northern and the Burlington through a stock swap. Perkins again maintained that the price was $200 a share in cash. At the same time, Hill's associates had been accumulating Burlington stock. In a meeting on February 24, Perkins and his top advisors decided that Morgan's Northern Pacific "would be a stronger and safer place for us to land."[22]

Unaware of Perkins's preference, and with rising suspicion as Burlington's stock soared, Harriman and Schiff paid a visit to Hill in late March to ask if he was trying to gain control of the Burlington. Schiff and Hill were old friends, both serving as directors on the board of Great Northern, so when Hill coldly replied that he was not buying and had no interest, Schiff believed him. Harriman made no mention of his intentions.

Having bought himself some time, Hill quickly set off for Boston to meet with Perkins to set terms for the sale

Jacob H. Schiff.

of the Burlington to Northern Pacific. After reporters spotted the two meeting on March 30 and the news went public, Harriman fumed. Schiff quickly arranged an audience with Hill on neutral ground. The air charged with tension, Hill apologized to Schiff but said it was necessary because of the banker's association with Harriman and Union Pacific. Harriman thought Hill had "paid a damned fool price for the Burlington," according to accounts of the meeting relayed to Lefevre, but nonetheless urged him to consider the interests of the Union Pacific and not close the deal until an agreement could be reached.

When Hill refused to do so, Harriman spewed forth with fury: "Then you will have to take the consequences."[23]

Schiff, who had started his career in the service of Morgan, went to the great banker's office in an attempt to avoid all-out war. He was quickly rebuffed as Morgan was preparing for his annual trip to Europe to restore his health after expending great energy in the U.S. Steel merger. Turning to Morgan's partner, Robert Bacon, Schiff proposed that the Union Pacific take a one-third interest in the Burlington. "It's too late," Bacon replied. "Nothing can be done." The Burlington was divided between the Great Northern and the Northern Pacific, with its shareholders tendering shares in exchange for $200 a share in bonds from the two Morgan-Hill roads. Hill and Morgan, who had been buying the Burlington from $100 up to $175 in large blocks, profited greatly.[24]

Harriman, with his "Napoleonic plans" for the railways, according to Lefevre, prepared to counter this direct challenge on his burgeoning empire.[25]

THE ECONOMIST. [May 4, 1901.

	This Week. $	A Year Ago. $	Rise. $	Highest and Lowest in 1900. $	$
Atchison	88 1/4	26 7/8	61 3/8	49 1/8	18 1/8
Do Pref.	106	72	34	91	59 3/4
Baltimore and Ohio	113 1/2	87	26 1/2	91 3/8	55
Chesapeake and Ohio	50 7/8	31 5/8	19 1/4	44	24 7/8
Chicago, Milwaukee, &c.	178 3/4	122 3/4	56	152	112
Denver Rio Grande	49 1/8	20 1/2	28 5/8	34 3/4	16 9/16
Do Pref.	99 1/8	72 7/8	26 1/4	89 3/8	66 3/4
Erie	42 3/8	13 5/8	28 3/4	26 3/4	10 3/4
Do 1st Pref.	73	48 7/8	32 1/4	60 1/4	31
Illinois Central	151 1/4	117 3/4	33 1/2	136 1/4	113 1/2
Louisville & Nashville	112 1/8	85	27 1/8	90 1/2	71
Missouri, Kansas, &c.	33 1/4	12 1/8	21 1/8	18 1/8	9 1/4
New York Central	171 1/2	137 3/4	33 3/4	150 1/8	129 1/4
New York, Ont., &c.	39 1/4	24 1/4	15	32 3/8	18 11/16
Norfolk and Western	56 1/8	39 3/8	16 3/4	46 3/4	22 1/8
Northern Pacific	118 7/8	60	58 7/8	87 5/8	47 3/8
Pennsylvania ($50)	80	70	10	77 1/2	63 3/4
Reading ($50)	22 5/8	9 7/8	12 3/4	13 5/8	7 1/4
Do 1st Pref ($50)	40 5/8	30 1/2	10 1/8	36 1/2	25 3/8
Southern	34 3/8	14 1/8	20 1/4	24 7/8	10 7/8
Do Pref.	89	59 1/2	29 1/2	74 7/8	50 5/8
Southern Pacific	58 1/2	38	20 1/2	47 1/2	31 1/4
Union Pacific	133	58	74 7/8	82 1/2	45
Do Pref.	100 1/2	77	23 1/2	86 3/4	72 3/4
Wabash Pref.	45 1/2	24	21 1/2	28 1/4	17

amount of money I had been able to accumulate up to that time. It wasn't so bad for a chap who had lost every cent trading in that selfsame office a few months before.

If you remember, the Harriman crowd notified Morgan and Hill of their intention to be represented in the Burlington-Great Northern-Northern Pacific combination, and then the Morgan people at first instructed Keene to buy fifty thousand shares of N. P. to keep the control in their possession. I have heard that Keene told Robert Bacon to make the order one hundred and fifty thousand shares and the bankers did. At all events, Keene sent one of his brokers, Eddie Norton, into the N. P. crowd and he bought one hundred thousand shares of the

3.7 The grand battle consumed the market in May 1901. It is important to understand the mood of the time. Ordinary investors had recently been worked into a frenzy as U.S. Steel shares were promoted and railroad stocks were rising fast on various rumors of insider accumulations and mergers. Lefevre recounts a "raging public speculation in stocks" while Clews talks of a "restless sea of reckless stock speculation that swept the American people into its vortex, with all its razzle-dazzle extravagance."

In this hyped-up environment, Harriman's attempt to retaliate against Morgan for grabbing the Burlington acted like a spark igniting a pool of gasoline. The resulting jump in prices, then panic, caused "intense excitement, demoralization, and confusion" that "convulsed the stock market in a way that alarmed money lenders, destroyed confidence, and caused a general rush to sell stocks which brought them down with a crash, involving many thousands in ruinous losses," according to Clews's account. [26]

With Burlington locked into the Great Northern and the Northern Pacific network, Harriman attacked Morgan with a daring raid: He bought Northern Pacific shares on the open market. The Northern Pacific was loosely controlled, with $80 million in common and $75 mil-

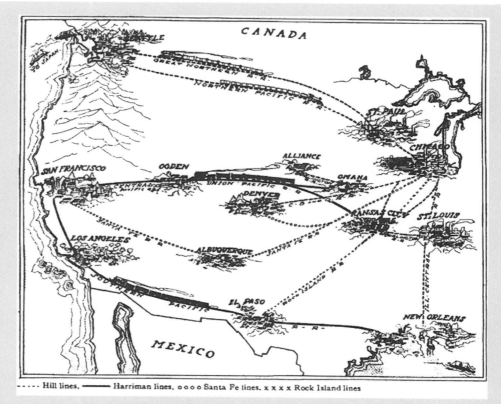

---- Hill lines. ——— Harriman lines. o o o o Santa Fe lines. x x x x Rock Island lines

stock. This was followed by another order, I think, of fifty thousand shares additional, and the famous corner followed. After the market closed on May 8, 1901, the whole world knew that a battle of financial giants was on. No two such combinations of capital had ever opposed each other in this country. Harriman against Morgan; an irresistible force meeting an immovable object. **3.7**

There I was on the morning of May ninth with nearly fifty thousand dollars in cash and no stocks. As I told you, I had been very bearish for some days, and here was my chance at last. I knew what would happen—an awful break and then some wonderful lion in preferred shares outstanding. Of this, James Hill and Morgan controlled only $35 million on the belief that no one was crazy enough to take down a $155 million railroad in the open market. But Harriman had the nerve, and the reserves, to "buy the mare to get the filly."[27]

The plan was bold. If he were to succeed, Harriman's Union Pacific would control two-thirds of the nation's railways and would relegate the Morgan-Hill system to a thin strip of land just under the Canadian border.

The market boiled as Harriman and his allies accumulated $42 million of Northern Pacific preferred (a majority) and $37 million of the common shares (which was 40,000 shares or so short of being a majority) by the end of April 1901. Large price rises in other railroads threw the market off the trail and set the rumor mill abuzz.

Meanwhile, Hill watched the ticker in his Seattle office with great unease as shares in his Northern Pacific steadily climbed. Something was amiss. With Morgan steaming for Europe, Hill felt it best to return to New York. He arrived on the afternoon of May 3 after riding a special express on the Great Northern line to St. Paul "with unlimited right of way over everything"—making it the fastest run to the Mississippi yet seen.[28]

As Hill went to see Jacob Schiff, traders were sending Union Pacific, Northern Pacific, and the rest of the list down on heavy profit taking. The *New York Times* wrote that since the boom that had started in November 1900, "nothing of this sort had intervened, though conservative advisors have been pointing out for weeks past that dangers were lurking in the market, that over-confidence and over-enthusiasm were inducing over-trading and inviting smashes."[29]

A dramatic scene played out in the Kuhn, Loeb & Co. offices after Schiff admitted his firm was buying Northern Pacific on Harriman's orders. "But you can't get control!" Hill cried in outrage. "That may be," Schiff replied, "but we've got a lot of it." After storming out, a shaken Hill immediately ordered Morgan's office to telegraph him in France for the authority to purchase at least $15 million worth of Northern Pacific stock to fight off Harriman.

Harriman's position was actually weaker than Schiff made it out to be. Although he maintained a majority of the preferred stock, he was still without a clear majority of the common. This was a problem since Northern Pacific's board had the authority to retire the preferred stock at any time after January 1, 1902. While he could elect his own board at the annual shareholders' meeting in October, Harriman feared that Morgan would somehow postpone the meeting until after the New Year.

Despite the assurances of legal counsel that a majority of the total stock was sufficient, Harriman wanted to leave nothing to chance. Bedridden with a cold, he decided that the final 40,000 shares should be purchased during the shortened Saturday trading session on May 4 to eliminate any weakness in the plan and ease his worries. Destiny foiled Harriman when he telephoned Kuhn, Loeb looking for Schiff, who was worshipping at a synagogue. A junior partner received the order, but the order was never filled. After much delay, Schiff was informed of Harriman's request, but he thought it unnecessary and ignored it.

Across the Atlantic, Morgan was enjoying a respite from trading when he received Hill's cable. Quickly dictating a reply, Morgan authorized his men to buy at any price all the Northern Pacific common stock needed to maintain control. But his message did not arrive in New York until the night of Sunday, May 5—too late if Harriman's order had been filled by Kuhn, Loeb.

(continued)

bargains. There would be a quick recovery and big profits—for those who had picked up the bargains. It didn't take a Sherlock Holmes to figure this out. We were going to have an opportunity to catch them coming and going, not only for big money but for sure money.

Everything happened as I had foreseen. I was dead right and—I lost every cent I had! I was wiped out by something that was unusual. If the unusual never happened there would be no difference in people and then there wouldn't be any fun in life. The game would become merely a matter of addition and subtraction. It would make of us a race

On Monday, Northern Pacific stock "came strong from London, and opened with a burst of activity"[30] as the Hill-Morgan brokers, led by James Keene, fanned across the exchange floor bidding for all the NP common shares to be had as the price rose from $110 to $133. Newspapers spoke of "wild scenes on the floor" as the day's action was "in some respects the most remarkable of any that Wall Street has yet seen." A total of 361,000 shares of Northern Pacific were traded, of which Keene's broker, Eddie Norton, bought 200,000— a new single-day record and slightly more than Livermore mentions.[31]

During the tumult, Harriman had phoned Kuhn, Loeb to ask why he received no confirmation on his 40,000-share order two days before. All he heard in reply was a lengthy, maddening silence before he was told of Schiff's decision to ignore the order. Schiff never explained why he made this decision but did maintain that the fault was his alone. Realizing that "the whole object of our work might be lost," Harriman pulled himself out of bed and down to Schiff's office to plan strategy.[32]

On Tuesday, Morgan's men ran Northern Pacific shares up to nearly $150 as they continued to buy heavily. Other stocks fell away as short sellers, who were questioning the legitimacy of the rise in the Northern Pacific, dunped other holdings to cover mounting losses. By the close of trading, Morgan and Hill had the shares they needed to maintain control.

The beginning of the end started Wednesday afternoon as stocks broke by 20 points; Northern Pacific zoomed from $143 to $200 and squeezed short sellers. That night, brokers crowded into the Waldorf hotel and filled the air with tobacco smoke and rumor. James Keene made an appearance but disclosed nothing despite the desperate pleas of traders.[33] Broker Bernard Baruch observed the scene: "One look inside the Waldorf that night was enough to bring home the truth of how little we differ from animals after all. From a palace the Waldorf had been transformed into the den of frightened men at bay."[34]

On Thursday, it became apparent that a corner was on, as more Northern Pacific had been sold short and contracted for delivery than could be bought or borrowed. Panic ensued when the price of Northern Pacific rose to $1,000 amid frantic attempts to cover shorts. The two big holders, Harriman and Morgan, were not interested in selling. Other stocks plummeted as the interest rate on short-term call loans went to 60%. For a few hours, based on the day's lows," a good part of Wall Street was technically insolvent."[35] Again, Baruch observes the chaos:

When one broker walked into the crowd, other traders, thinking he might have some Northern Pacific stock, charged him, banging him against the railing. "Let me go, will you?" he roared. "I haven't a share of the damned stock. Do you think I carry it in my clothes?"

Then, through the desperate crowd strode Al Stern, of Hertzfield & Stern, a young and vigorous broker. He had come as an emissary of Kuhn, Loeb & Company, which was handling Harriman's purchases of Northern Pacific. Stern blithely inquired: "Who wants to borrow Northern Pacific? I have a block to lend."

of bookkeepers with plodding minds. It's the guessing that develops a man's brain power. Just consider what you have to do to guess right.

The market fairly boiled, as I had expected. The transactions were enormous and the fluctuations unprecedented in extent. I put in a lot of selling orders at the market. When I saw the opening prices I had a fit, the breaks were so awful. My brokers were on the job. They were as competent and conscientious as any; but by the time they executed my orders the stocks had broken twenty points more. The tape was way behind the market and reports were slow in coming in by reason of the awful rush of business. When I found out that the stocks I had ordered sold when the tape said

The first response was a deafening shout. There was an infinitesimal pause and then the desperate brokers rushed at Stern. Struggling to get near enough to him to shout their bids, they kicked over stock tickers. Strong brokers thrust aside the weak ones. Hands were waving and trembling in the air.

Almost doubled over on a chair, his face close to a pad, Stern began to note his transactions. He would mumble to one man, "All right, you get it," and then complain to another, "For heaven's sake, don't stick your finger in my eye."

One broker leaned over and snatched Stern's hat, with which he beat a tattoo on Stern's head to gain attention. "Put back my hat!" shrieked Stern. "Don't make such a confounded excitement and maybe I can do better by you."

But the traders continue to push and fight and nearly climbed over one another's backs to get to Stern. They were like thirst-crazed men battling for water, with the biggest, strongest, and loudest faring best. Soon Stern had loaned the last of his stock. His face white, and his clothes disheveled, he managed to break away.[36]

Realizing the gravity of the situation, Harriman and Morgan joined forces to prevent catastrophe. Morgan, still in Europe, rushed to the Paris office of Morgan, Harjes & Co. as news of the panic reached him. Reporters swarmed as he frantically issued orders to New York. Cursing the newsmen as "idiots" and "rascals," and even threatening one with murder, Morgan famously stated when asked if some statement were not due the public: "I owe the public nothing."[37]

(continued)

the price was, say, 100 and they got mine off at 80, making a total decline of thirty or forty points from the previous night's close, it seemed to me that I was putting out shorts at a level that made the stocks I sold the very bargains I had planned to buy. The market was not going to drop right through to China. So I decided instantly to cover my shorts and go long.

My brokers bought; not at the level that had made me turn, but at the prices prevailing in the Stock Exchange when their floor man got my orders. They paid an average of fifteen points more than I had figured on. A loss of thirty-five points in one day was more than anybody could stand.

The ticker beat me by lagging so far behind the market. I was accustomed to regarding the tape as

	High-est.	Low-est.	Clos-ing.	Net Ch'g's.
N. Y. Central............	153¼	140	147¾	— 8¼
N. Y. C. & St. L.......	27	16	27	— 8
N. Y. C. & St. L. 2d pf.	55	50	50	— 25¾
N. Y., O. & W..........	32⅞	24	29⅝	— 3¾
Norfolk & Western....	51⅝	47½	50	+ 7
N. Amer., new.........	85	80	80	— 5½
Northern Pacific	1000	160	325	+165

Stern returned to the floor a few minutes before the 2:15 P.M. deadline for short sellers to deliver stock certificates (see photo, which is believed to depict Stern before a crowd during the May 9 panic). Mounting a chair and shouting to be heard, he announced his firm would not demand delivery of Northern Pacific shares sold short. Stern was followed by Eddie Norton, representing the Morgan forces, who also announced that his firm would not force delivery. Immediately, Northern Pacific sold off and closed at $325. The crisis was over.[38]

For Livermore, the May 1901 panic reinforced his earlier lessons about the difficulty of adapting his bucket shop trading strategy, which depended on instant fulfillment (since no actual stock transaction needs to occur), to actual purchases and sales on the New York Stock Exchange. Prices fell upward of 20 points between sales as the ticker lagged the action on the floor by 10 minutes. Livermore tried to compensate by placing limit orders but found that his orders simply went unfilled. As a result of this experience, Livermore learned the importance of capturing the big, secular movements in the stock market instead of the short-term undulations he had profited from in the past.[39] The stock table above shows the $840 swing in Little Nipper from a low of $160 to a high of $1000, and then the close at $325.

the best little friend I had because I bet according to what it told me. But this time the tape double-crossed me. The divergence between the printed and the actual prices undid me. It was the sublimation of my previous unsuccess, the selfsame thing that had beaten me before. It seems so obvious now that tape reading is not enough, irrespective of the brokers' execution, that I wonder why I didn't then see both my trouble and the remedy for it.

I did worse than not see it; I kept on trading, in and out, regardless of the execution. You see, I never could trade with a limit. I must take my chances with the market. That is what I am trying to beat—the market, not the particular price. When I think I should sell, I sell. When I think stocks will go up, I buy. My adherence to that general principle of speculation saved me. To have traded at limited prices simply would have been my old bucket-shop method inefficiently adapted for use in a reputable commission broker's office. I would never have learned to know what stock speculation is, but would have kept on betting on what a limited experience told me was a sure thing.

Whenever I did try to limit the prices in order to minimize the disadvantages of trading at the market when the ticker lagged, I simply found that the market got away from me. This happened so often that I stopped trying. I can't tell you how it came to take me so many years to learn that instead of placing piking bets on what the next few quotations were going to be, my game was to anticipate what was going to happen in a big way.

After my May ninth mishap I plugged along, using a modified but still defective method. If I hadn't made money some of the time I might have acquired market wisdom quicker. But I was making enough to enable me to live well. I liked friends and a good time. I was living down the Jersey Coast that summer, like hundreds of prosperous Wall Street men. My winnings were not quite enough to offset both my losses and my living expenses.

I didn't keep on trading the way I did through stubbornness. I simply wasn't able to state my own problem to myself, and, of course, it was utterly hopeless to try to solve it. I harp on this topic so much to show what I had to go through before I got to where I could really make money. My old shotgun and BB shot could not do the work of a high-power repeating rifle against big game.

Early that fall I not only was cleaned out again but I was so sick of the game I could no longer beat that I decided to leave New York and try something else some other place. I had been trading since my fourteenth year. I had made my first thousand dollars when I was a kid of fifteen, and my first ten thousand before I was twenty-one. I had made and lost a ten-thousand-dollar stake more than once. In New York I had made thousands and lost them. I got up to fifty thousand dollars and two days later that went. I had no other business and knew no other game. After several years I was back where I began. No—worse, for I had acquired habits and a style of living that required money; though that part didn't bother me as much as being wrong so consistently.

ENDNOTES

1 Alexander Dana Noyes, *Forty Years of American Finance* (New York: G. P. Putnam's Sons, 1909), 257.

2 Henry Clews, *Fifty Years in Wall Street* (New York: Irving Publishing Company, 1908), 156.

3 Noyes, *Forty Years of American Finance,* 286.

4 Clews, *Fifty Years in Wall Street,* 756.

5 Edwin Lefevre, "Boom Days in Wall Street," *Munsey's Magazine* (1901): 42.

6 *New York Times,* August 23, 1911, 7.

7 *New York Times,* January 3, 1917, 12.

8 E. M. Kingsbury, "John W. Gates: The Forgetful Man," *Everybody's Magazine* 10 (1904): 86.

9 *New York Times,* December 13, 1917. 22.

10 James Grant, *Bernard M. Baruch.* (New York: John Wiley & Sons, 1997), http://www.time.com/time/magazine/article/0,9171,753768,00.html.

11 *Time*, July 10, 1933.

12 *Kernel of Finance and Politics for Everybody,* April 1914.

13 Ibid.

14 *Railroad Age Gazette*, August 20, 1915.

15 Edwin Lefevre, "Boom Days in Wall Street," 40.

16 Peter Wyckoff, *Wall Street and the Stock Markets* (Philadelphia: Chilton Book Company, 1972), 18.

17 Edwin Lefevre, "Harriman," *American Magazine* (1907), 117–118.

18 Ibid., 118.

19 Ibid., 121.

20 "Vanderbilts' Great Deal," *New York Times,* October 26, 1900, 1.

21 Maury Klein, *Life and Legend of E. H. Harriman.* (Chapel Hill: The University of North Carolina Press, 2000), 216.

22 Ibid., 222.

23 Ibid., 223.

24 *New York Times,* April 26, 1901, 2.

25 Lefevre, Harriman, 123.

26 Clews, *Fifty Years in Wall Street,* 759

27 Matthew Josephson, *Robber Barons,* (New York: Harcourt, Brace and Company, 1934), 436.

28 Ibid., 438

29 *New York Times,* May 4, 1901, 3.

30 Josephson, *Robber Barons,* 439.

31 *New York Times,* May 8, 1901. 3.

32 Klein, *Life and Legend of E. H. Harriman,* 234.

33 "Night of Excitement in the Waldorf," *New York Times,* May 9, 1901, 1.

34 Ibid.

35 Noyes, *Forty Years of American Finance,* 307.

36 Bernard Baruch, *"Baruch: My Own Story* (Cutchogue, New York: Buccaneer Books, 1957), 143–144.

37 Josephson, *Robber Barons,* 441.

38 Leonard Louis Levinson, *Wall Street: A Pictorial History* (New York: Ziff-David Publishing, 1961), 202.

39 "Disaster and Ruin in Falling Market," *New York Times*, May 10, 1901, 1.

Well, I went home. But the moment I was back I knew that I had but one mission in life and that was to get a stake and go back to Wall Street. That was the only place in the country where I could trade heavily. Some day, when my game was all right, I'd need such a place. When a man is right he wants to get all that is coming to him for being right.

I didn't have much hope, but, of course, I tried to get into the bucket shops again. There were fewer of them and some of them were run by strangers. Those who remembered me wouldn't give me a chance to show them whether I had gone back as a trader or not. I told them the truth, that I had lost in New York whatever I had made at home; that I didn't know as much as I used to think I did; and that there was no reason why it should not now be good business for them to let me trade with them. But they wouldn't. And the new places were unreliable. Their owners thought twenty shares was as much as a gentleman ought to buy if he had any reason to suspect he was going to guess right.

I needed the money and the bigger shops were taking in plenty of it from their regular customers. I got a friend of mine to go into a certain office and trade. I just sauntered in to look them over. I again tried to coax the order clerk to accept a small order, even if it was only fifty shares. Of course he said no. I had rigged up a code with this friend so that he would buy or sell when and what I told him. But that only made me chicken feed. Then the office began to grumble about taking my friend's orders. Finally one day he tried to sell a hundred St. Paul and they shut down on him.

We learned afterward that one of the customers saw us talking together outside and went in and told the office, and when my friend went up to the order clerk to sell that hundred St. Paul the guy said:

4.1 From this casual introduction to cotton, an entirely new phase of Livermore's trading career would later unfold as the budding trader soon became disenchanted with stock exchanges and infatuated instead with the fast action and ample margin of commodity exchanges.

The New York Cotton Exchange was a commodity futures exchange founded in 1870 by a group of leading cotton merchants and brokers. The exchange initially helped market the southern U.S. cotton crop in the volatile years following the Civil War as trade routes reopened and prices fluctuated wildly. Later its auctions mainly offered a way for farmers and manufacturers to hedge price uncertainty and reduce risk. In time, its price quotes became the standard for all business conducted between textile mills and farmers.[1]

You can see the benefits of the exchange in the adjacent chart, which illustrates annual cotton price volatility from 1830 to 1909. After 1870, the NYCE helped reduce the magnitude of price movements, which helped farmers and textile makers alike. As an indication of the importance of the exchange, in 1916 the cost of membership was not far behind the cost of

DIAGRAM III
YEARLY RANGE OF COTTON PRICES AT NEW YORK 1830–1909

"We're not taking any selling orders in St. Paul, not from you."

"Why, what's the matter, Joe?" asked my friend.

"Nothing doing, that's all," answered Joe.

"Isn't that money any good? Look it over. It's all there." And my friend passed over the hundred—my hundred—in tens. He tried to look indignant and I was looking unconcerned; but most of the other customers were getting close to the combatants, as they always did when there was loud talking or the slightest semblance of a scrap between the shop and any customer. They wanted to get a line on the merits of the case in order to get a line on the solvency of the concern.

The clerk, Joe, who was a sort of assistant manager, came out from behind his cage, walked up to my friend, looked at him and then looked at me.

"It's funny," he said slowly—"it's damned funny that you never do a single thing here when your friend Livingston isn't around. You just sit and look at the board by the hour. Never a peep. But after he comes in you get busy all of a sudden. Maybe you are acting for yourself; but not in this office any more. We don't fall for Livingston tipping you off."

Well, that stopped my board money. But I had made a few hundred more than I had spent and I wondered how I could use them, for the need of making enough money to go back to New York with was more urgent than ever. I felt that I would do better the next time. I had had time to think calmly of some of my foolish plays; and then, one can see the whole better when one sees it from a little distance. The immediate problem was to make the new stake.

One day I was in a hotel lobby, talking to some fellows I knew, who were pretty steady traders. Everybody was talking stock market.

I made the remark that nobody could beat the game on account of the rotten execution he got from his brokers, especially when he traded at the market, as I did.

A fellow piped up and asked me what particular brokers I meant.

I said, "The best in the land," and he asked who might they be. I could see he wasn't going to believe I ever dealt with first-class houses.

But I said, "I mean, any member of the New York Stock Exchange. It isn't that they are crooked or careless, but when a man gives an order to buy at the market he never knows what that stock is going to cost him until he gets a report from the brokers. There are more moves of one or two points than of ten or fifteen. But the outside trader can't catch the small rises or drops because of the execution. I'd rather trade in a bucket shop any day in the week, if they'd only let a fellow trade big."

The man who had spoken to me I had never seen before. His name was Roberts. He seemed very friendly disposed. He took me aside and asked me if I had ever traded in any of the other exchanges, and I said no. He said he knew some houses that were members of the Cotton Exchange and the Produce Exchange and the smaller stock exchanges. 4.1, 4.2 These firms were very careful

a seat on the New York Stock Exchange.[2] Eventually, the NYCE created subsidiaries to trade in other commercial goods such as wool, citrus, tomatoes and financial instruments.

New York was a popular spot market for cotton well before the NYCE was founded. Middlemen would bring great quantities of bulk cotton north from southern states to resell to textile factories throughout the Northeast. The NYCE's formation and dominance of rival exchanges in places like New Orleans cemented the city's role in the transfer of the delicate fibers from field to factory.

Innovation drove the development of the cotton exchanges. During the Civil War, trade blockades made it difficult to get cotton bales through Confederate battle lines. As a result, large premiums were offered to merchants for "staple to arrive" contracts—the predecessor to the modern futures contract.[3] The concept caught on and it was quickly realized that there was a need to centralize and regulate the trading of contracts.

The NYCE got its start in small quarters at 142 Pearl Street and traded about 15,000 bales per week in 1870 before moving to larger quarters at 1 Hanover Square that still stand today. (One bale equals 500 pounds). It was here that Dickson G. Watts, who wrote "Speculation as a Fine Art" and is frequently quoted by both Livermore in this text and Lefevre in his other works, was president of the exchange for a short time.[4] The photo above shows the interior of the exchange circa 1900. Tufts of cotton litter the floor, as various grades of the actual product were displayed and assessed by traders each day.

In 1923, the exchange moved to a new 24-story building as volume increased to 500,000 bales per day.[5] In 1998 the NYCE and the Coffee, Sugar & Cocoa Exchange merged to create the New York Board of Trade. This entity eventually relocated to 4 World Trade Center, which was destroyed in the September 11, 2001 terrorist attacks. The New York Board of Trade was then purchased in 2006 by IntercontinentalExchange—an internet-based market maker.

4.2 The origins of the New York Produce Exchange can be traced back to the original New Amsterdam colony on Manhattan. Governor Peter Stuyvesant established what was known as the Monday market in the fall of 1618. According to a newspaper account in 1901, "a number of hardy old traders assembled and made 'puts' and 'calls' in much the same fashion as is done today" outside near present-day Bowling Green park.[6]

As the country grew and the trading volume expanded, the first Produce Exchange building was erected in 1860. There all manner of goods were traded, including butter, cheese, hops, tar, cornmeal, oatmeal, rye, flour, buckwheat, corn, oats, barley, beef, pork, seeds, sweet cured meats, liquors and high wines, beans, flaxseed, malt, tongues, and ham.[7]

As the membership roll swelled from 700 to 2,500 by 1880, more room was required. In 1884, the New Produce Exchange building was built at the corner of Beaver Street and Broadway.[8]

In Livermore's time, the pace of activity at the New York Produce Exchange was second only to the NYSE. It is likely that at some point, especially later in his career, as he began to heavily trade corn and wheat, Livermore ventured down to the bustling main exchange hall, as visitors were permitted if escorted by members. The hall, shown at left, was impressive to behold, measuring 220 feet by 144 feet, with a height of 60 feet. On one side, attached to pillars, were blackboards reporting the prices of refined petroleum at London, Antwerp, and Bremen and of naval stores, turpentine, and resin in London and Liverpool. Across the floor were long tables for merchants to display their goods for sample—one for flour, another for lard, and so on.[9]

Prices were determined in two places. In the pit, where futures contracts were traded, a reporter in the mid-1880s said buyers and sellers were "indiscriminately blended in the compact, throbbing, surging mass."[10] The scene is not unlike what you would find on any futures exchange today. Behind the pit was the call room, a 500-seat amphitheater where spot commodities were sold through an auctioneer. In was in these areas that the young "Napoleon of finance," Ferdinand Ward, who ruined Civil War hero and president Ulysses S. Grant in a Ponzi scheme, got his start.

The Produce Exchange failed in the aftermath of the Salad Oil Scandal of 1963. In this massive scam, wholesaler and commodity broker Anthony DeAngelis of New Jersey cornered the market for soybean oil—used in salad dressing—by fraudulently filling oil tanks held as collateral with water. When inspectors looked into the tanks, all they would see was oil, since it floated on top of the water. By inflating his true holdings, DeAngelis was able to secure additional lending and continue to buy futures contracts. Eventually, authorities were tipped off and the ruse collapsed.[11] As in Livermore's day, the smart money managed to exploit one victim's pain for a big gain: The scandal crushed the shares of DeAngelis's collateral backer, American Express, allowing a young Warren Buffett to grab a cheap 5% stake in the firm.

and paid special attention to the execution. He said that they had confidential connections with the biggest and smartest houses on the New York Stock Exchange and through their personal pull and by guaranteeing a business of hundreds of thousands of shares a month they got much better service than an individual customer could get.

"They really cater to the small customer," he said. "They make a specialty of out-of-town business and they take just as much pains with a ten-share order as they do with one for ten thousand. They are very competent and honest."

"Yes. But if they pay the Stock Exchange house the regular eighth commission, where do they come in?"

"Well, they are supposed to pay the eighth. But—you know!" He winked at me.

"Yes," I said. "But the one thing a Stock Exchange firm will not do is to split commissions. The governors would rather a member committed murder, arson and bigamy than to do business for outsiders for less than a kosher eighth. The very life of the Stock Exchange depends upon their not violating that one rule."

He must have seen that I had talked with Stock Exchange people, for he said, "Listen! Every now and then one of those pious Stock Exchange houses is suspended for a year for violating that rule, isn't it? There are ways and ways of rebating so nobody can squeal." He probably saw unbelief in my face, for he went on: "And besides, on certain kind of businesses we—I mean, these wire houses—charge a thirty-second extra, in addition to the eighth commission. They are very nice about it. They never charge the extra commission except in unusual cases, and then only if the customer has an inactive account. It wouldn't pay them, you know, otherwise. They aren't in business exclusively for their health."

By that time I knew he was touting for some phony brokers.

4.3 The New York Curb Exchange is being referred to here. It started as an outdoor, semiorganized venue for trading stocks that eventually grew into the American Stock Exchange. Although the two had long been fierce rivals, the American Stock Exchange was acquired by the parent company of the New York Stock Exchange in 2008 and today specializes in derivatives and exchange-traded funds.

The origins of the exchange date to the early 1820s, when NYSE board members who lost their seats mixed with outsiders to buy and sell securities and commodities. [12,13]

In Livermore's time, the curb market occupied a section of Broad Street just down the way from the NYSE. Brokers communicated with hand signals to men taking orders via telephones in adjacent office windows. Traders were supposed to remain inside a rope enclosure in the middle of the street, which would allow traffic to pass on either side. But during busy days, the action stretched from curb to curb. [14]

Until the formation of the New York Curb Agency in 1908, there was little government regulation of the market. Any securities could be traded by any broker. Brokers relied on reputation, as there was no official recording of sales and no ticker to track price changes. There was also no price advantage on the curb compared to the NYSE— the same one-eighth commission was charged to buy or sell. The main advantages of the curb were the extra trade liquidity it offered for listed securities and the ability to market securities that did not meet the NYSE's listing requirements.

One of the more famous swindles on the curb involved the Electric Car Coupler Co. in 1899. At the time, electric stocks were the focus of speculative excitement. Criminals created the company in name only, faking patent documents, renting an office, appointing directors, and printing engraved stock certificates. The gang fanned out across the Northeast to place orders with brokerage offices, placing $4,000 on margin to secure a purchase of $16,400 worth of the fictitious stock on the curb. The crooks happily fed their certificates to the curb brokers filling the out-of-town orders. Pocketing the $8,400 difference, the criminals made off with a fortune and were never caught. [15] Livermore thrived on the fringe of this environment, depending on his wits and experience.

"Do you know any reliable house of that kind?" I asked him.

"I know the biggest brokerage firm in the United States," he said. "I trade there myself. They have branches in seventy-eight cities in the United States and Canada. They do an enormous business. And they couldn't very well do it year in and year out if they weren't strictly on the level, could they?"

"Certainly not," I agreed. "Do they trade in the same stocks that are dealt in on the New York Stock Exchange?"

"Of course; and on the curb and on any other exchange in this country, or Europe. **4.3** They deal in wheat, cotton, provisions; anything you want. They have correspondents everywhere and memberships in all the exchanges, either in their own name or on the quiet."

I knew by that time, but I thought I'd lead him on.

"Yes," I said, "but that does not alter the fact that the orders have to be executed by somebody, and nobody living can guarantee how the market will be or how close the ticker's prices are to the actual prices on the floor of the Exchange. By the

time a man gets the quotation here and he hands in an order and it's telegraphed to New York, some valuable time has gone. I might better go back to New York and lose my money there in respectable company."

"I don't know anything about losing money; our customers don't acquire that habit. They make money. We take care of that."

"Your customers?"

"Well, I take an interest in the firm, and if I can turn some business their way I do so because they've always treated me white and I've made a good deal of money through them. If you wish I'll introduce you to the manager."

"What's the name of the firm?" I asked him.

He told me. I had heard about them. They ran ads in all the papers, calling attention to the great profits made by those customers who followed their inside information on active stocks. That was the firm's great specialty. They were not a regular bucket shop, but bucketeers, alleged brokers who bucketed their orders but nevertheless went through an elaborate camouflage to convince the world that they were regular brokers engaged in a legitimate business. They were one of the oldest of that class of firms. ⟨**4.4**⟩

They were the prototype at that time of the same sort of brokers that went broke this year by the dozen. The general principles and methods were the same, though the particular devices for fleecing the public differed somewhat, certain details having been changed when the old tricks became too well known.

These people used to send out tips to buy or sell a certain stock—hundreds of telegrams advising the instant purchase of a certain stock and hundreds recommending other customers to sell the same stock, on the old racing-tipster plan. Then orders to buy and sell would come in. The firm would buy and sell, say, a thousand of that stock through a rep-

4.4 ▶ The focus of this conversation was likely the Haight & Freese Co.—the largest of a particularly nasty breed of bucket shops that used a cloak of legitimacy to dupe small-time investors. The firm was large, well established, and famous for its complementary *Guide to Investors* that explained the finer points of speculation.

Bucketeers would join third-rate exchanges in cities like Philadelphia or St. Louis to give believability to their cover story of being legitimate brokers filling orders. Labeling their offices "bankers and brokers" in larger cities and "commissioned agent" in small towns, the bucketeers furnished their offices sumptuously with tickers, meals, cigars, and other comforts. Telegraph machines busily clacked in the corner, appearing to transmit customer orders to the trading floors of various exchanges.

In reality, the orders would go to central bookkeeping offices where orders would be "filled" at the next quotation that came over the ticker. Execution was completed by the initialing of the customer's order slip by the filling clerk, not an actual transaction. To complete the scam, a "confirmation" slip would be mailed to the customer.[16]

The trap was set. From there, the traditional bucket-shop game of small margin positions and wash sales wiped out the victims. According to Merrill Teague, who wrote a lengthy exposé against these practices in 1906, the

bucket-shop keeper has no purpose other than to steal all the money you have, or can beg or borrow or steal, and when he has done this, to steal the home that houses your family, to steal the dress your wife will need next year, and to steal the food your baby will require as it grows.[17]

Fortunately for Livermore, the bucketeers' system fit his method of trading perfectly. Since Haight & Freese wished to maintain an air of legitimacy, the company was not likely to limit his trading or kick him out for winning too frequently. Because traditional brokers benefit from additional commissions when their clients win, the bucketeers had to act the part. Moreover, since no actual transactions were taking place, Haight & Freese could tout their impressive order executions and promise fulfillment at the next quotation.

It is ironic that a system that was the source of so much misery and hardship for uninitiated investors was exactly what Livermore needed to get back on his feet.

utable Stock Exchange firm and get a regular report on it. This report they would show to any doubting Thomas who was impolite enough to speak about bucketing customers' orders.

They also used to form discretionary pools in the office and as a great favor allowed their customers to authorize them, in writing, to trade with the customer's money and in the customer's name, as they in their judgment deemed best. That way the most cantankerous customer had no legal redress when his money disappeared. They'd bull a stock, on paper, and put the customers in and then they'd execute one of the old-fashioned bucket-shop drives and wipe out hundreds of shoestring margins. They did not spare anyone, women, schoolteachers and old men being their best bet.

"I'm sore on all brokers," I told the tout. "I'll have to think this over," and I left him so he wouldn't talk any more to me.

I inquired about this firm. I learned that they had hundreds of customers and although there were the usual stories I did not find any case of a customer not getting his money from them if he won any. The difficulty was in finding anybody who had ever won in that office; but I did. Things seemed to be going their way just then, and that meant that they probably would not welsh if a trade went against them. Of course most concerns of that kind eventually go broke. There are times when there are regular epidemics of bucketeering bankruptcies, like the old-fashioned runs on several banks after one of them goes up. The customers of the others get frightened and they run to take their money out. But there are plenty of retired bucket-shop keepers in this country.

Well, I heard nothing alarming about the tout's firm except that they were on the make, first, last and all the time, and that they were not always truthful. Their specialty was trimming suckers who wanted to get rich quick. But they always asked their customers' permission, in writing, to take their rolls away from them.

One chap I met did tell me a story about seeing six hundred telegrams go out one day advising customers to get aboard a certain stock and six hundred telegrams to other customers strongly urging them to sell that same stock, at once. ◁4.5▷

"Yes, I know the trick," I said to the chap who was telling me.

"Yes," he said. "But the next day they sent telegrams to the same people advising them to close out their interest in everything and buy—or sell—another stock. I asked the senior partner, who was in the office, 'Why do you do that? The first part I understand. Some of your customers are bound to make money on paper for a while, even if they and the others eventually lose. But by sending out telegrams like this you simply kill them all. What's the big idea?'

"Well,' he said, 'the customers are bound to lose their money anyhow, no matter what they buy, or how or where or when. When they lose their money I lose the customers. Well, I might as well get as much of their money as I can—and then look for a new crop.'"

Well, I admit frankly that I wasn't concerned with the business ethics of the firm. I told you I felt sore on the Teller concern and how it tickled me to get even with them. But I didn't have any such feeling about this firm. They might be crooks or they might not be as black as they were painted. I did not propose to let them do any trading for me, or follow their tips or believe their lies. My one concern was with getting together a stake and returning to New York to trade in fair amounts in an office where you did not have to be afraid the police would raid the joint, as they did the bucket shops, or see the postal authorities swoop down and tie up your money so that you'd be lucky to get eight cents on the dollar a year and a half later.

4.5 ▶ The e-mail stock spam scandals of the early 2000s had their origin in the days of the telegraph. In both eras, criminal operators preyed via electronic communication on a gullible public eager to try to make a quick buck.

Anyhow, I made up my mind that I would see what trading advantages this firm offered over what you might call the legitimate brokers. I didn't have much money to put up as margin, and firms that bucketed orders were naturally much more liberal in that respect, so that a few hundred dollars went much further in their offices.

I went down to their place and had a talk with the manager himself. When he found out that I was an old trader and had formerly had accounts in New York with Stock Exchange houses and that I had lost all I took with me he stopped promising to make a million a minute for me if I let them invest my savings. He figured that I was a permanent sucker, the ticker-hound kind that always plays and always loses; a steady-income provider for brokers, whether they were the kind that bucket your orders or modestly content themselves with the commissions.

I just told the manager that what I was looking for was decent execution, because I always traded at the market and I didn't want to get reports that showed a difference of a half or a whole point from the ticker price.

He assured me on his word of honor that they would do whatever I thought was right. They wanted my business because they wanted to show me what high-class brokering was. They had in their employ the best talent in the business. In fact, they were famous for their execution. If there was any difference between the ticker price and the report it was always in favor of the customer, though of course they didn't guarantee that. If I opened an account with them I could buy and sell at the price which came over the wire, they were so confident of their brokers.

Naturally that meant that I could trade there to all intents and purposes as though I were in a bucket shop—that is, they'd let me trade at the next quotation. I didn't want to appear too anxious, so I shook my head and told him I guessed I wouldn't open an account that day, but I'd let him know. He urged me strongly to begin right away as it was a good market to make money in. It was—for them; a dull market with prices seesawing slightly, just the kind to get customers in and then wipe them out with a sharp drive in the tipped stock. I had some trouble in getting away.

I had given him my name and address, and that very same day I began to get prepaid telegrams and letters urging me to get aboard of some stock or other in which they said they knew an inside pool was operating for a fifty-point rise. **4.6**

I was busy going around and finding out all I could about several other brokerage concerns of the same bucketing kind. It seemed to me that if I could be sure of getting my winnings out of their clutches the only way of my getting together some real money was to trade in these near bucket-shops.

When I had learned all I could I opened accounts with three firms. I had taken a small office and had direct wires run to the three brokers.

I traded in a small way so they wouldn't get frightened off at the very start. I made money on balance and they were not slow in telling me that they expected real business from customers who had direct wires to their offices. They did not hanker for pikers. They figured that the more I did the more I'd lose, and the more quickly I was wiped out the more they'd make. It was a sound enough theory when you consider that these people necessarily dealt with averages and the average customer was never long-lived, financially speaking. A busted customer can't trade. A half-crippled customer can whine and insinuate things and make trouble of one or another kind that hurts business.

I also established a connection with a local firm that had a direct wire to its New York correspondent, who were also members of the New York Stock Exchange. I had a stock ticker put in and I began to trade conservatively. As I told you, it was

4.6 A telegram could be sent either collect, in which the receiver pays, or prepaid, in which the sender pays. The distinction was the focal point of frequent scams by telegraph messenger boys looking to pad their meager wages by unfairly charging recipients for prepaid messages. These telegrams were the equivalent of what traderslater would recognize as fax, text or social-media messages promoting penny stocks.[18]

pretty much like trading in bucket shops, only it was a little slower.

It was a game that I could beat, and I did. I never got it down to such a fine point that I could win ten times out of ten; but I won on balance, taking it week in and week out. I was again living pretty well, but always saving something, to increase the stake that I was to take back to Wall Street. I got a couple of wires into two more of these bucketing brokerage houses, making five in all—and, of course, my good firm.

There were times when my plans went wrong and my stocks did not run true to form, but did the opposite of what they should have done if they had kept up their regard for precedent. But they did not hit me very hard—they couldn't, with my shoestring margins. My relations with my brokers were friendly enough. Their accounts and records did not always agree with mine, and the differences uniformly happened to be against me. Curious coincidence—not! But I fought for my own and usually had my way in the end. They always had the hope of getting away from me what I had taken from them. They regarded my winnings as temporary loans, I think.

They really were not sporty, being in the business to make money by hook or by crook instead of being content with the house percentage. Since suckers always lose money when they gamble in stocks—they never really speculate—you'd think these fellows would run what you might call a legitimate illegitimate business. But they didn't. "Copper your customers and grow rich" is an old and true adage, but they did not seem ever to have heard of it and didn't stop at plain bucketing.

Several times they tried to double-cross me with the old tricks. They caught me a couple of times because I wasn't looking. They always did that when I had taken no more than my usual line. I accused them of being short sports or worse, but they denied it and it ended by my going back to trading as usual.

The beauty of doing business with a crook is that he always forgives you for catching him, so long as you don't stop doing business with him. It's all right as far as he is concerned. He is willing to meet you more than halfway. Magnanimous souls!

Well, I made up my mind that I couldn't afford to have the normal rate of increase of my stake impaired by crooks' tricks, so I decided to teach them a lesson. I picked out some stock that after having been a speculative favorite had become inactive. Water-logged. If I had taken one that never had been active they would have suspected my play. I gave out buying orders on this stock to my five bucketeering brokers. When the orders were taken and they were waiting for the next quotation to come out on the tape, I sent in an order through my Stock Exchange house to sell a hundred shares of that particular stock at the market. I urgently asked for quick action. Well, you can imagine what happened when the selling order got to the floor of the Exchange; a dull inactive stock that a commission house with out-of-town connections wanted to sell in a hurry. Somebody got cheap stock. But the transaction as it would be printed on the tape was the price that I would pay on my five buying orders. I was long on balance four hundred shares of that stock at a low figure. The wire house asked me what I'd heard, and I said I had a tip on it. Just before the close of the market I sent an order to my reputable house to buy back that hundred shares, and not waste any time; that I didn't want to be short under any circumstances; and I didn't care what they paid. So they wired to New York and the order to buy that hundred quick resulted in a sharp advance. I of course had put in selling orders for the five hundred shares that my friends had bucketed. It worked very satisfactorily.

Still, they didn't mend their ways, and so I worked that trick on them several times. I did not dare punish them as severely as they deserved, seldom more than a point or two on a hundred shares. But it helped to swell my little hoard that I was saving for my next Wall Street venture. I sometimes varied the process by selling some stock short, without overdoing it. I was satisfied with my six or eight hundred clear for each crack.

One day the stunt worked so well that it went far beyond all calculations for a ten-point swing. I wasn't looking for it. As a matter of fact it so happened that I had two hundred shares instead of my usual hundred at one broker's, though only a hundred in the four other shops. That was too much of a good thing—for them. They were sore as pups about it and they began to say things over the wires. So I went and saw the manager, the same man who had been so anxious to get my account, and so forgiving every time I caught him trying to put something over on me. He talked pretty big for a man in his position.

"That was a fictitious market for that stock, and we won't pay you a damned cent!" he swore.

"It wasn't a fictitious market when you accepted my order to buy. You let me in then, all right, and now you've got to let me out. You can't get around that for fairness, can you?"

"Yes, I can!" he yelled. "I can prove that somebody put up a job."

"Who put up a job?" I asked.

"Somebody!"

"Who did they put it up on?" I asked.

"Some friends of yours were in it as sure as pop," he said.

But I told him, "You know very well that I play a lone hand. Everybody in this town knows that. They've known it ever since I started trading in stocks. Now I want to give you some friendly advice: you just send and get that money for me. I don't want to be disagreeable. Just do what I tell you."

"I won't pay it. It was a rigged-up transaction," he yelled.

I got tired of his talk. So I told him: "You'll pay it to me right now and here."

Well, he blustered a little more and accused me flatly of being the guilty thimblerigger; but he finally forked over the cash. The others were not so rambunctious. In one office the manager had been studying these inactive-stock plays of mine and when he got my order he actually bought the stock for me and then some for himself in the Little Board, ◁**4.7**▷ and he made some money. These fellows didn't mind being sued by customers on charges of fraud, as they generally had a good technical legal defense ready. But they were afraid I'd attach the furniture—the money in the bank was not available because they took care not to have any funds exposed to that danger. It would not hurt them to be known as pretty sharp, but to get a reputation for welshing was fatal. For a customer to lose money at his broker's is no rare event. But for a customer to make money and then not get it is the worst crime on the speculators' statute books. ◁**4.8**▷

I got my money from all; but that ten-point jump put an end to the pleasing pastime of skinning skinners. They were on the lookout for the little trick that they themselves had used to defraud hundreds of poor customers. I went back to my regular trading; but the market wasn't always right for my system—that is, limited as I was by the size of the orders they would take, I couldn't make a killing.

I had been at it over a year, during which I used every device that I could think of to make money trading in those wire houses. I had lived very comfortably, bought an automobile and didn't limit myself about my expenses. I had to make a stake, but I also had to live while I was doing it. If my position on the market was right I couldn't spend as much as I made, so that I'd always be saving some. If I was wrong I didn't make any money and therefore couldn't spend. As I said, I had saved up a fair-sized

4.7 ▶ This is the nickname of the American Stock Exchange, which at the time was the New York Curb Exchange.

4.8 ▶ In 1905, Haight & Freese was forced into bankruptcy after authorities uncovered the company's illicit order room and it became clear that trade orders were not being filled legitimately. Members of the Consolidated Stock Exchange proved to be complicit in the scam. At the end of the trading day, Haight & Freese would send over a list of trading activity; insiders used those lists to forge the exchange's official documents to make it appear as if those orders had been taken to the trading floor.[19]

4.9 The early 1900s were an exciting period for young men with a fancy for speed. It was the dawn of the motoring era. In 1902, Ransom E. Olds—founder of the now-defunct Oldsmobile brand—made his Curved Dash model (which cost $650 at the time), the first mass-produced automobile. Henry Ford's Model T would not arrive until 1908. This was a considerable achievement since the first American-made self-propelled vehicle had been created just nine years earlier, in 1893, by the Duryea brothers.[20]

Livermore would have had the opportunity to select from the three different propulsion types that were in use at the time: steam, electric, and gasoline. Given his obvious preference for something sporty, he would have decided on a model with a gas engine. The benefits were longer range (important for a road trip from Boston to New York City), more power, and greater speed.

roll, and there wasn't so much money to be made in the five wire houses; so I decided to return to New York. **4.9**

I had my own automobile and I invited a friend of mine who also was a trader to motor to New York with me. He accepted and we started. We stopped at New Haven for dinner. At the hotel I met an old trading acquaintance, and among other things he told me there was a shop in town that had a wire and was doing a pretty good business.

We left the hotel on our way to New York, but I drove by the street where the bucket shop was to see what the outside looked like. We found it and couldn't resist the temptation to stop and have a look at the inside. It wasn't very sumptuous, but the old blackboard was there, and the customers, and the game was on.

The manager was a chap who looked as if he had been an actor or a stump speaker. He was very impressive. He'd say good morning as though he had discovered the morning's goodness after ten years of searching for it with a microscope and was making you a present of the discovery as well as of the sky, the sun and the firm's bank roll. He saw us come up in the sporty-looking automobile, and as both of us were young and careless—I don't suppose I looked twenty—he naturally concluded we were a couple of Yale boys. I didn't tell him we weren't. He didn't give me a chance, but began delivering a speech. He was very glad to see us. Would we have a comfortable seat? The market, we would find, was philanthropically inclined that morning; in fact, clamoring to increase the supply of collegiate pocket money, of which no intelligent undergraduate ever had a sufficiency since the dawn of historic time. But here and now, by the beneficence of the ticker, a small initial investment would return thousands. More pocket money than anybody could spend was what the stock market yearned to yield.

Well, I thought it would be a pity not to do as the nice man of the bucket shop was so anxious to have us do, so I told him I would do as he wished, because I had heard that lots of people made lots of money in the stock market.

I began to trade, very conservatively, but increasing the line as I won. My friend followed me.

We stayed overnight in New Haven and the next morning found us at the hospitable shop at five minutes to ten. The orator was glad to see us, thinking his turn would come that day. But I cleaned up within a few dollars of fifteen hundred. The next morning when we dropped in on the great orator, and handed him an order to sell five hundred Sugar he hesitated, but finally accepted it—in silence! The stock broke over a point and I closed out and gave him the ticket. There was exactly five hundred dollars coming to me in profits, and my five hundred dollar margin. He took twenty fifties from the safe, counted them three times very slowly, then he counted them again in front of me. It looked as if his fingers were sweating mucilage the way the notes seemed to stick to him, but finally he handed the money to me. He folded his arms, bit his lower lip, kept it bit, and stared at the top of a window behind me.

I told him I'd like to sell two hundred Steel. But he never stirred. He didn't hear me. I repeated my wish, only I made it three hundred shares. He turned his head. I waited for the speech. But all he did was to look at me. Then he smacked his lips and swallowed—as if he was going to start an attack on fifty years of political misrule by the unspeakable grafters of the opposition.

Finally he waved his hand toward the yellow-backs in my hand and said, "Take away that bauble!"

"Take away what?" I said. I hadn't quite understood what he was driving at.

"Where are you going, student?" He spoke very impressively.

E. F. HUTTON & CO.,
Members New York Stock Exchange.
Direct Wire to
San Francisco Office.   **33-35 New Street.**
Special attention given to Outside Securities.

4.10 ▷ As mentioned in Chapter 2, A. R. Fullerton was in reality Edward Francis Hutton. Born and raised in New York, Hutton eventually felt the gravitational pull of Wall Street. After rising from mailroom clerk to check writer at a brokerage, he tired of the mundane and enrolled in business school before purchasing a seat on the Consolidated Stock Exchange with friend Arthur Harris and starting Harris, Hutton & Co. in 1900.[21, 22] The Consolidated was located in an unimpressive little red building across New Street from the NYSE and its Big Board. In 1905, when a seat on the NYSE cost upward of $100,000, a seat on the Consolidated could be had for just $1,000. A secondary market, which depended in large part on the quotations that originated on the other side of the street and specialized in offering fraction-lot trades below the 100-share minimum required on the NYSE, the Consolidated still had enough volume to settle orders as large as 1,000 shares at a time.[23]

After falling in love with Blanche Horton, Hutton asked her father, H. L. Horton, an NYSE member, for his daughter's hand in marriage—only to be rebuffed due to his association with what one journalist called "a street bazaar for third-rate brokers." Hutton promptly dissolved his firm and sold his seat on the Consolidated before marrying Blanche in June 1902.

While honeymooning on the West Coast, Hutton was struck by the dismal quality of brokerage service in San Francisco. In a spark of entrepreneurial energy, he joined with his uncle William D. Hutton, another NYSE member, to start a new firm with the goal of stringing the nation's first privately leased transcontinental telegraph wire. As a result, the firm E. F. Hutton was born in October 1903. Offices were opened in April 1904 at 33 New Street, just one block from the NYSE. By December, a San Francisco office with direct service to the New York markets was opened. One of the first clients was none other than John "Bet-a-Million" Gates.[24]

The scarcity of historical evidence and the incongruity of many of the statements, dates, and ages given in *Reminiscences* make an exact reconstruction of all the steps and venues of Livermore's early years in Manhattan impossible. Livermore may have frequented the old Harris,

"New York," I told him.

"That's right," he said, nodding about twenty times. "That is exactly right. You are going away from here all right, because now I know two things—two, student! I know what you are not, and I know what you are. Yes! Yes! Yes!"

"Is that so?" I said very politely.

"Yes. You two—" He paused; and then he stopped being in Congress and snarled: "You two are the biggest sharks in the United States of America! Students? Ye-eh! You must be Freshmen! Ye-eh!"

We left him talking to himself. He probably didn't mind the money so much. No professional gambler does. It's all in the game and the luck's bound to turn. It was his being fooled in us that hurt his pride.

That is how I came back to Wall Street for a third attempt. I had been studying, of course, trying to locate the exact trouble with my system that had been responsible for my defeats in A. R. Fullerton & Co.'s office. **4.10** I was twenty when I made my first ten thousand, and I lost that. But I knew how and why—because I traded out of season all the time; because when I couldn't play according to my system, which was based on study and experience, I went in and gambled. I hoped to win, instead of knowing that I ought to win on form. When I was about twenty-two I ran up my stake to fifty thousand dollars; I lost it on May ninth. But I knew exactly why and how. It was the laggard tape and the unprecedented violence of the movements that awful day. But I didn't know why I had lost after my return from St. Louis or after the May ninth panic. I had theories—that is, remedies for some of the faults that I thought I found in my play. But I needed actual practice.

There is nothing like losing all you have in the world for teaching you what not to do. And when you know what not to do in order not to lose money, you begin to learn what to do in order to win. Did you get that? You begin to learn!

Hutton brokerage when he was first learning to trade on the exchanges between 1900 and 1901. It is also possible that Livermore started his account at W. E. Hutton & Co., a Cincinnati-based bond house run by Edward Hutton's cousin that got its start in 1886. W. E. Hutton had a seat on the NYSE, and E. F. Hutton worked at the firm's New York office for a time immediately after business school.[25]

What is clear is that Livermore had a close relationship with E. F. Hutton that eventually soured. In 1909, the *New York Times* wrote that Livermore had been missing for several weeks from "his accustomed place" at the E. F. Hutton offices at 35 New Street. His name had been erased from one of the inner office doors, and the reporter's inquiries about Livermore were met with impatience.[26] Over the next 70 years, E. F. Hutton became one of the largest and most respected brokerages on Wall Street, but it was brought down by a check-kiting scandal and losses associated with the stock market crash in 1987. It was sold to Shearson Lehman American Express, which ultimately spun it off to Primerica, which merged it with Smith Barney, which later itself became part of Citigroup.

ENDNOTES

1 United States House of Representatives, "Cotton Futures: Hearing before the Committee on Agriculture," February 13–14, 1922.

2 Melvin Thomas Copeland, The *Cotton Manufacturing Industry of the United States* (Cambridge, Massachusetts: Harvard University, 1912), 185-192.

3 Louis Guenther, *Investment and Speculation* (Chicago: LaSalle Extension University, 1916), 225.

4 "Business & Finance: New Cotton Exchange," *Time,* July, 30, 1923.

5 Edwin Lefevre, "Stock Manipulation," *Saturday Evening Post,* March 20, 1909, 5.

6 "The New York Produce Exchange," *New York Times,* September 22, 1901, magazine supplement.

7 Ibid.

8 Moses Smith, *Plain Truths about Stock Speculation* (Brooklyn, New York: E.V. Smith, 1887), 148–151.

9 Richard Wheatly, "The New York Produce Exchange," *Harper's Magazine* (June–September 1886): 191.

10 Ibid., 213.

11 Jerry W. Markham, *A Financial History of the United States* (2002), p. 332. Armonk, NY: M.E. Sharpe.

12 Robert Sobel, *The Curbstone Brokers* (2000), 17. New York: Beard Books.

13 Samuel Armstrong Nelson, *The ABC of Wall Street* (1900), 69.

14 Guenther, *Investment and Speculation,* 228–230.

15 Nelson, *ABC of Wall Street,* 72.

16 Merrill Teague, "Bucket-Shop Sharks," *Everybody's Magazine* (June 1906): 733.

17 Ibid., 734.

18 Gregory John Downey. "Telegraph Messenger Boys: Labor, Technology, and Geography, 1850–1950." (2002) 29.

19 "Haight & Freese Co. in Receiver's Hands," *New York Times,* May 10, 1905, 1.

20 Michael Berger, *The Automobile in American History and Culture* (Westport, Connecticut: Greenwood Press, 2002), xvii–xix.

21 Mark Stevens, *Sudden Death: The Rise and Fall of E. F. Hutton,* (New York: New American Library, 1989), 12.

22 "Stock Exchange News," *Wall Street Journal,* November 19, 1900, 6.

23 "The 'Little Board,'" *New York Times,* December 31, 1905, Business Section, 12.

24 Stevens, *Sudden Death,* 17.

25 Ibid., 13.

26 "Livermore's Office Vacant," *New York Times,* July 21, 1909, 1.

The average ticker hound—or, as they used to call him, tape-worm—goes wrong, I suspect, as much from overspecialization as from anything else. It means a highly expensive inelasticity. After all, the game of speculation isn't all mathematics or set rules, however rigid the main laws may be. Even in my tape reading something enters that is more than mere arithmetic. There is what I call the behavior of a stock, actions that enable you to judge whether or not it is going to proceed in accordance with the precedents that your observation has noted. If a stock doesn't act right don't touch it; because, being unable to tell precisely what is wrong, you cannot tell which way it is going. No diagnosis, no prognosis. No prognosis, no profit.

It is a very old thing, this of noting the behavior of a stock and studying its past performances. When I first came to New York there was a broker's office where a Frenchman used to talk about his chart. At first I thought he was a sort of pet freak kept by the firm because they were good-natured. Then I learned that he was a persuasive and most impressive talker. He said that the only thing that didn't lie because it simply couldn't was mathematics. By means of his curves he could forecast market movements. Also he could analyse them, and tell, for instance, why Keene did the right thing in his famous Atchison preferred bull manipulation, and later why he went wrong in his Southern Pacific pool. ◁ **5.1** ▷ At various times one or another of the professional traders tried the Frenchman's system—and then went back to their old unscientific methods of making a living. Their hit-or-miss system was cheaper, they said. I heard that the Frenchman said Keene admitted that the chart was

71

STOCK MANIPULATION

5.1 ▶ **Legendary stock operator James R. Keene** and market manipulations are two of Lefevre's favorite topics. The author frequently wrote about both in his regular articles for the *Saturday Evening Post* and other publications.

Lefevre said he believed that Keene, known as the Silver Fox of Wall Street, was "probably the greatest manipulator of stocks in our time" and knew the man well—frequently dropping by his office to chat about the news and the market.[1] Lefevre was not alone in praising Keene. Another operator, S. V. "Deacon" White, who we will meet later, said that of all the big operators on the exchange, "there never was one the equal of Keene, either for magnitude of operations or for brilliancy of execution."[2]

Keene, for his part, blamed Lefevre for popularizing "that hateful word" of manipulation and labeling him as one of the masters of the dark art. Keene's issue was that the public's belief that the manipulator was an arch-robber, "a picker of pockets by the thousand," was misinformed. Like the hedge fund managers and other market insiders of today, manipulators in Livermore's time were the frequent targets of public ire when amateur traders were duped out of their money.[3]

Manipulation, according to Lefevre, "consists in leading the stock market horse—otherwise known as the public—to water, and making him drink; or, as the case might be, in making the public believe the securities it holds are worthless and about to sell on that basis."[4] Most of the time, manipulation was used to advertise a certain stock by creating an illusion of deep trading interest through action on the ticker machine. Such action piqued the interest of the gambling, bucket-shop types who shunned statistics and earnings trends for the latest hot tip. It allowed insiders to distribute their holdings. Lefevre elaborates in a 1909 article:

> A newspaper advertisement, with illuminating statistics, sinks perhaps a thirty-second of an inch into the mind of the "discriminating investor." But advertising by means of the ticker is another thing. When a man sees a stock going up, up! UP! something goes to the very soul of the greed-stricken man, who visioning to himself a dazzling money-happiness, reaches out quivering fingers, clutches eagerly in the air for the fortune within his grasp. ... Men do not read the papers with their very soul; and that is the only way they reach the ticker. The mirage is so real! They buy and later, they curse the "manipulator" who deceived them.[5]

Manipulation also could be used to accumulate holdings. Two examples are tied to the events that precipitated the May 9, 1901, panic in Northern Pacific Railroad. James J. Hill and J. P. Morgan, after an initial disagreement, decided to pursue the St. Paul railroad and add it to their Great Northern and Northern Pacific empire. Hill stealthily started acquiring shares in the open market to keep the price down. When they had a healthy stake, Hill and Morgan approached the St. Paul insiders—with whom they would own a controlling stake—but were rejected. Then the men turned their attention to the Chicago, Burlington, and Quincy line.

This time, Hill loudly proclaimed his interest but revealed his intentions to the railroad's insiders. In the midst of a stock boom, the action in the Burlington was seen as another run on false rumors that was bound to reverse. Short sellers descended. At one point the price fell 10 points in a day. This increase in selling pressure helped Hill secure as many stock certificates as possible under $200 a share—the price that the Burlington management was demanding from potential acquirers.[6]

The Southern Pacific pool involved an attempt by Keene in 1901 to convince E. H. Harriman—who controlled the line—to join with him to boost the stock price.[7] Harriman declined. During this time, he preferred to keep dividends low and reinvest earnings to improve and expand his railroads—much to the chagrin of speculators looking for a quick rise.

Keene did not give up as his pool continued to accumulate shares. In 1902, after Harriman reiterated his position, Keene countered by leaking stories to the press and threatening to remove the Southern Pacific's management unless a 4% dividend was declared.[8] Harriman was irritated, just as today's executives are by activist investors, and "went gunning for Keene," according to Lefevre.[9] The battle was settled by a court ruling in 1903, resulting in heavy losses for Keene and his associates.[10]

Lefevre accounted for Keene's defeat this way: "Harriman was many things besides a stock operator, while Keene was only the greatest stock speculator that ever lived in the United States. Therefore, the man who was more than a stock speculator won."[11] In the end, as we will see in Chapter 6, the dividend was raised.

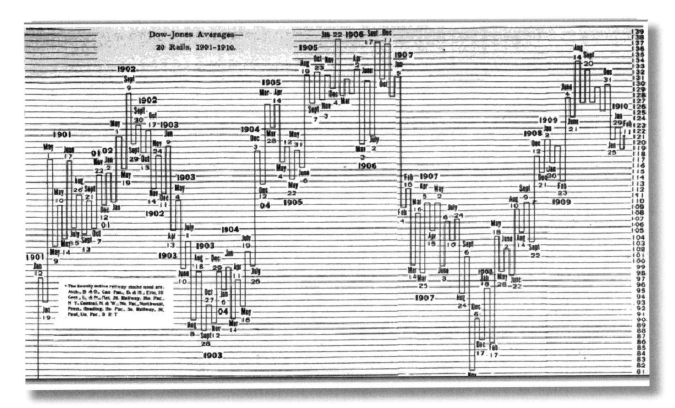

100 per cent right but claimed that the method was too slow for practical use in an active market. **5.2**

Then there was one office where a chart of the daily movement of prices was kept. It showed at a glance just what each stock had done for months. By comparing individual curves with the general market curve and keeping in mind certain rules the customers could tell whether the stock on which they got an unscientific tip to buy was fairly entitled to a rise. They used the chart as a sort of complementary tipster. To-day there are scores of commission houses where you find trading charts. They come ready-made from the offices of statistical experts and include not only stocks but commodities.

I should say that a chart helps those who can read it or rather who can assimilate what they read. The average chart reader, however, is apt to become obsessed with the notion that the dips and peaks and primary and secondary movements are all there

5.2 It is not clear exactly who the "Frenchman" is, but a number of different chart styles were beginning to appear in financial publications around this time. This illustration is an early chart of the Dow Jones Transportation Average.

5.3 ▶ Russell Sage was a stock operator who was a close associate of Jay Gould and also worked with James Keene for a time. He was also known as a miser in the company of big spenders, worrying about the cost of his suspenders, and he had a meagerly furnished office.[12] Sage, "who would always go about clad in the plainest of clothes, slightly bent and leaning on his rude cane—in appearance like a retired farmer," according to a biographer, died leaving a fortune in excess of $70 million.[13]

Born in 1816 in upstate New York, Sage got his start as an errand boy at a grocery store owned by his brother. By age 20, he became part owner and expanded into the wholesale business. He served in Congress as a member of the Whig party between 1853 and 1857. He made his first appearance in Wall Street in 1861. By 1874, he had his own seat on the New York Stock Exchange.[14]

Sage was an early innovator in options contracts, actively buying and selling puts and calls on stocks—called "privileges" at the time. This got him into trouble in May 1884, when the market broke badly following the Grant & Ward failure. Sage had written a large number of puts, and his loss was estimated to be roughly $7 million. As early as 8 A.M., the stairway to Sage's office at 71 Broadway, overlooking the Trinity churchyard, was jammed with creditors looking to collect on their paper profits. Journalist Will Payne describes the scene:

> When the door opened there was a bargain-day rush for the cashier's wicket. Payments were made for a time, with exceeding deliberation; then they stopped. The door was shut in the face of the crowd. One excited creditor undertook to kick it down. A sergeant of police and four patrolmen were required to convince the applicant that money could not be extorted from Mr. Sage by physical violence.[15]

Helped and advised by Gould, his old friend, Sage found the money needed to redeem his obligations. Having paid dearly for cheap stocks in the midst of panic and losing around $6.5 million, Sage eventually recovered as the market healed.

is to stock speculation. If he pushes his confidence to its logical limit he is bound to go broke. There is an extremely able man, a former partner of a well-known Stock Exchange house, who is really a trained mathematician. He is a graduate of a famous technical school. He devised charts based upon a very careful and minute study of the behaviour of prices in many markets—stocks, bonds, grain, cotton, money, and so on. He went back years and years and traced the correlations and seasonal movements—oh, everything. He used his charts in his stock trading for years. What he really did was to take advantage of some highly intelligent averaging. They tell me he won regularly—until the World War knocked all precedents into a cocked hat. I heard that he and his large following lost millions before they desisted. But not even a world war can keep the stock market from being a bull market when conditions are bullish, or a bear market when conditions are bearish. And all a man needs to know to make money is to appraise conditions.

I didn't mean to get off the track like that, but I can't help it when I think of my first few years in Wall Street. I know now what I did not know then, and I think of the mistakes of my ignorance because those are the very mistakes that the average stock speculator makes year in and year out.

After I got back to New York to try for the third time to beat the market in a Stock Exchange house I traded quite actively. I didn't expect to do as well as I did in the bucket shops, but I thought that after a while I would do much better because I would be able to swing a much heavier line. Yet, I can see now that my main trouble was my failure to grasp the vital difference between stock gambling and stock speculation. Still, by reason of my seven years' experience in reading the tape and a certain natural aptitude for the game, my stake was earning not indeed a fortune but a very high rate of interest. I won and lost as before, but I was winning on balance. The more I made the more I spent. This is the usual experience with most men. No, not necessarily with easy-money pickers, but with every human being who is not a slave of the hoarding instinct. Some men, like old Russell Sage, have the money-making and the money-hoarding instinct equally well developed, and of course they die disgustingly rich. ◁**5.3**]

The game of beating the market exclusively interested me from ten to three every day, and after three, the game of living my life. Don't misunderstand me. I never allowed pleasure to interfere with business. When I lost it was because I was wrong and not because I was suffering from dissipation or excesses. There never were any shattered nerves or rum-shaken limbs to spoil my game. I couldn't afford anything that kept me from feeling physically and mentally fit. Even now I am usually in bed by ten. As a young man I never kept late hours, because I could not do business properly on insufficient sleep. I was doing better than breaking even and that is why I didn't think there was any need to deprive myself of the good things of life. The market was always there to supply them. I was acquiring the confidence that comes to a man from a professionally dispassionate attitude toward his own method of providing bread and butter for himself.

The first change I made in my play was in the matter of time. I couldn't wait for the sure thing to come along and then take a point or two out of it as I could in the bucket shops. I had to start much

Sage—"quiet and simple in his habits," according to Henry Clews—was a famous accumulator of capital. "He is known as, in one sense, the largest capitalist on Wall Street, inasmuch as he keeps the largest cash balance," said Clews.[16] In 1903, it was said that only two or three of the greatest banks in New York City had more money "out on call" than Sage had.[17]

Some interesting trivia from the annals of history, which hearken to eccentric, voluble, media-friendly fund managers of today: Sage would arrive at his office at 9:30 A.M. and leave at 3:30 P.M. An apple and a bowl of crackers with milk constituted his lunch.[18] He never drank or smoked. His one apparent luxury was an occasional drive through Central Park. Sage was also quite friendly, freely speaking to reporters. He made a habit, even while talking to someone nearly his own age, of laying a hand on a man's shoulder and calling him "My son!" half a dozen times in the course of a conversation. He was also a generous provider of lucrative tips on insider information.[19]

5.4 ▶ The distinction between gambling and speculating was an important topic of this period. With the advent of popular participation in the financial markets and the rise of bucket shops, there was a great debate in polite circles about the benefits of these activities. Indeed, the fight against the bucket shops, and the reason they ultimately were shut down, was based on a clear line being drawn between gambling, which offers no larger benefits to society, and speculation, which helps finance business and efficiently sets prices.

Lefevre wrote on the subject in 1902:

For every investor in securities there are a hundred speculators; for every man who carefully calculated the value of a stock, and buys and locks his purchase in his strong box, content with the income which his investment yields him, there are a thousand who will buy with the hope of selling soon after at a profit. That is stock-gambling, which is no worse than any other form of gambling, though it is more insidious, since it masquerades as a legitimate business. It gratifies the craving of the gamester; it appears to a man's reason, to his knowledge of human nature, to his ability to read commercial, agricultural and political conditions; it induces visions of easily acquired wealth.[20]

For Livermore, it was a graduation of sorts as he climbed the ladder of respectability and potential profits by rounding out his technical trading prowess with fundamental knowledge of economic conditions and earnings trends.

earlier if I wanted to catch the move in Fullerton's office. In other words, I had to study what was going to happen; to anticipate stock movements. That sounds asininely commonplace, but you know what I mean. It was the change in my own attitude toward the game that was of supreme importance to me. It taught me, little by little, the essential difference between betting on fluctuations and anticipating inevitable advances and declines, between gambling and speculating. **5.4**

I had to go further back than an hour in my studies of the market—which was something I never would have learned to do in the biggest bucket shop in the world. I interested myself in trade reports and railroad earnings and financial and commercial statistics. Of course I loved to trade heavily and they called me the Boy Plunger; but I also liked to study the moves. I never thought that anything was irksome if it helped me to trade more intelligently. Before I can solve a problem I must state it to myself. When I think I have found the solution I must prove I am right. I know of only one way to prove it; and that is, with my own money.

Slow as my progress seems now, I suppose I learned as fast as I possibly could, considering that I was making money on balance. If I had lost oftener perhaps it might have spurred me to more continuous study. I certainly would have had more mistakes to spot. But I am not sure of the exact value of losing, for if I had lost more I would have lacked the money to test out the improvements in my methods of trading.

Studying my winning plays in Fullerton's office I discovered that although I often was 100 per cent right on the market—that is, in my diagnosis of conditions and general trend—I was not making as much money as my market "rightness" entitled me to. Why wasn't I?

There was as much to learn from partial victory as from defeat.

For instance, I had been bullish from the very start of a bull market, and I had backed my opinion by buying stocks. An advance followed, as I had clearly foreseen. So far, all very well. But what else did I do? Why, I listened to the elder statesmen and curbed my youthful impetuousness. I made up my mind to be wise and play carefully, conservatively. Everybody knew that the way to do that was to take profits and buy back your stocks on reactions. And that is precisely what I did, or rather what I tried to

5.5 One of Lefevre's key motivations for writing *Reminiscences* was to explain to the public that the stock market was a losing game even for many people who studied, lived, and breathed it. Livermore therefore spends a lot of time providing an ontology of suckerdom. In this passage, he lists various grades of chump: the absolute tyro who bets blindly; the "semisucker" who buys on dips and memorizes a set of rules; the Careful Mike who listens to too many experts and doesn't develop his own philosophy; and even the semipro who takes profits too quickly in a bull market.

He later explains that the only players who reliably win are ones who first determine if the primary trend is bullish or bearish; buy or short early in the firmly established new trend; sit patiently through any short-term countertrends; and then have a firm philosophy for determining when to exit on a change in the primary trend.

Connecticut-based trader Paul Tudor Jones, who is as close to the Livermore ideal as anyone operating today, recommends using the 200-day average as a guide for the primary trend. Nice and simple. If a stock or market is above the long-term moving average, then stick with it as a long until it falls below. See the chart of defense contractor General Dynamics, below, displayed with a 10-month average (dotted line). It started a new bullish trend in April 2003, and exited that trend in mid-2008. Over those five years were several multimonth corrections of 10% or more (shaded), but anyone exiting during those moves would have missed the terrific 150% gain in the stock. This is how Livermore believes you can take full advantage of your best ideas.

do; for I often took profits and waited for a reaction that never came. And I saw my stock go kiting up ten points more and I sitting there with my four-point profit safe in my conservative pocket. They say you never grow poor taking profits. No, you don't. But neither do you grow rich taking a four-point profit in a bull market.

Where I should have made twenty thousand dollars I made two thousand. That was what my conservatism did for me. About the time I discovered what a small percentage of what I should have made I was getting I discovered something else, and that is that suckers differ among themselves according to the degree of experience. **5.5**

The tyro knows nothing, and everybody, including himself, knows it. But the next, or second, grade thinks he knows a great deal and makes others feel that way too. He is the experienced sucker, who has studied—not the market itself but a few remarks about the market made by a still higher grade of suckers. The second-grade sucker knows how to keep from losing his money in some of the ways that get the raw beginner. It is this semisucker rather than the 100 per cent article who is the real all-the-year-round support of the commission houses. He lasts about three and a half years on an average, as compared with a single season of from three to thirty weeks, which is the usual Wall Street life of a first offender. It is naturally the semisucker who is always quoting the famous trading aphorisms and the various rules of the game. He knows all the don'ts that ever fell from the oracu-

GD (General Dynamics Corp.) NYSE © StockCharts.com
31-Dec-2008 4:00pm Last 56.37 Chg +5.79 (+11.46%) ▲
— GD (Monthly) 56.37
--MA(10) 75.34
General Dynamics, 2003-2008

lar lips of the old stagers—excepting the principal one, which is: Don't be a sucker!

This semisucker is the type that thinks he has cut his wisdom teeth because he loves to buy on declines. He waits for them. He measures his bargains by the number of points it has sold off from the top. In big bull markets the plain unadulterated sucker, utterly ignorant of rules and precedents, buys blindly because he hopes blindly. He makes most of the money—until one of the healthy reactions takes it away from him at one fell swoop. But the Careful Mike sucker does what I did when I thought I was playing the game intelligently—according to the intelligence of others. I knew I needed to change my bucket-shop methods and I thought I was solving my problem with any change, particularly one that assayed high gold values according to the experienced traders among the customers.

Most—let us call 'em customers—are alike. You find very few who can truthfully say that Wall Street doesn't owe them money. In Fullerton's there were the usual crowd. All grades! Well, there was one old chap who was not like the others. To begin with, he was a much older man. Another thing was that he never volunteered advice and never bragged of his winnings. He was a great hand for listening very attentively to the others. He did not seem very keen to get tips—that is, he never asked the talkers what they'd heard or what they knew. But when somebody gave him one he always thanked the tipster very politely. Sometimes he thanked the tipster again—when the tip turned out O.K. But if it went wrong he never whined, so that nobody could tell whether he followed it or let it slide by. It was a legend of the office that the old jigger was rich and could swing quite a line. But he wasn't donating much to the firm in the way of commissions; at least not that anyone could see. His name was Partridge, but they nicknamed him Turkey behind his back, because he was so thick-chested and had a habit of

5.6 Lefevre comes back to this phrase repeatedly because it was a central theme of Livermore's trading style. Lefevre believed that there were few techniques more important than trading in sync with the primary trend. In a bull market, he believed, you should trade with the bulls. In a bear market, you should trade with the bears. Later in this chapter he sums it up by stating "The big money was not in the individual fluctuations but in the main movements—that is, not in reading the tape but in sizing up the entire market and its trend." A little farther along, he adds, "In a bull market your game is to buy and hold until you believe that the bull market is near the end." The guidance is elegant in its timeless simplicity.

strutting about the various rooms, with the point of his chin resting on his breast.

The customers, who were all eager to be shoved and forced into doing things so as to lay the blame for failure on others, used to go to old Partridge and tell him what some friend of a friend of an insider had advised them to do in a certain stock. They would tell him what they had not done with the tip so he would tell them what they ought to do. But whether the tip they had was to buy or to sell, the old chap's answer was always the same.

The customer would finish the tale of his perplexity and then ask: "What do you think I ought to do?"

Old Turkey would cock his head to one side, contemplate his fellow customer with a fatherly smile, and finally he would say very impressively, "You know, it's a bull market!" **5.6**

Time and again I heard him say, "Well, this is a bull market, you know!" as though he were giving to you a priceless talisman wrapped up in a million-dollar accident-insurance policy. And of course I did not get his meaning.

One day a fellow named Elmer Harwood rushed into the office, wrote out an order and gave it to the clerk. Then he rushed over to where Mr. Partridge was listening politely to John Fanning's story of the time he overheard Keene give an order to one of his brokers and all that John made was a measly three points on a hundred shares and of course the stock had to go up twenty-four points in three days right after John sold out. It was at least the fourth time that John had told him that tale of woe, but old Turkey was smiling as sympathetically as if it was the first time he heard it.

Well, Elmer made for the old man and, without a word of apology to John Fanning, told Turkey, "Mr. Partridge, I have just sold my Climax Motors. My people say the market is entitled to a reaction and that I'll be able to buy it back cheaper. So you'd better do likewise. That is, if you've still got yours."

Elmer looked suspiciously at the man to whom he had given the original tip to buy. The amateur, or gratuitous, tipster always thinks he owns the receiver of his tip body and soul, even before he knows how the tip is going to turn out.

"Yes, Mr. Harwood, I still have it. Of course!" said Turkey gratefully. It was nice of Elmer to think of the old chap.

"Well, now is the time to take your profit and get in again on the next dip," said Elmer, as if he had just made out the deposit slip for the old man. Failing to perceive enthusiastic gratitude in the beneficiary's face Elmer went on: "I have just sold every share I owned!"

From his voice and manner you would have conservatively estimated it at ten thousand shares.

But Mr. Partridge shook his head regretfully and whined, "No! No! I can't do that!"

"What?" yelled Elmer.

"I simply can't!" said Mr. Partridge. He was in great trouble.

"Didn't I give you the tip to buy it?"

"You did, Mr. Harwood, and I am very grateful to you. Indeed, I am, sir. But———"

"Hold on! Let me talk! And didn't that stock go up seven points in ten days? Didn't it?"

"It did, and I am much obliged to you, my dear boy. But I couldn't think of selling that stock."

"You couldn't?" asked Elmer, beginning to look doubtful himself. It is a habit with most tip givers to be tip takers.

"No, I couldn't."

"Why not?" And Elmer drew nearer.

"Why, this is a bull market!" The old fellow said it as though he had given a long and detailed explanation.

"That's all right," said Elmer, looking angry because of his disappointment. "I know this is a bull market as well as you do. But you'd better slip them that stock of yours and buy it back on the reaction. You might as well reduce the cost to yourself."

"My dear boy," said old Partridge, in great distress—"my dear boy, if I sold that stock now I'd lose my position; and then where would I be?"

Elmer Harwood threw up his hands, shook his head and walked over to me to get sympathy: "Can you beat it?" he asked me in a stage whisper. "I ask you!"

I didn't say anything. So he went on: "I give him a tip on Climax Motors. He buys five hundred shares. He's got seven points' profit and I advise him to get out and buy 'em back on the reaction that's overdue even now. And what does he say when I tell him? He says that if he sells he'll lose his job. What do you know about that?"

"I beg your pardon, Mr. Harwood; I didn't say I'd lose my job," cut in old Turkey. "I said I'd lose my position. And when you are as old as I am and you've been through as many booms and panics as I have, you'll know that to lose your position is something nobody can afford; not even John D. Rockefeller. I hope the stock reacts and that you will be able to repurchase your line at a substantial concession, sir. But I myself can only trade in accordance with the experience of many years. I paid a high price for it and I don't feel like throwing away a second tuition fee. But I am as much obliged to you as if I had the money in the bank. It's a bull market, you know." And he strutted away, leaving Elmer dazed.

What old Mr. Partridge said did not mean much to me until I began to think about my own numerous failures to make as much money as I ought to when I was so right on the general market. The more I studied the more I realized how wise that old chap was. He had evidently suffered from the same defect in his young days and knew his own human weaknesses. He would not lay himself open to a temptation that experience had taught him was hard to resist and had always proved expensive to him, as it was to me.

I think it was a long step forward in my trading education when I realized at last that when old Mr. Partridge kept on telling the other customers, "Well, you know this is a bull market!" he really meant to tell them that the big money was not in the individual fluctuations but in the main movements—that is, not in reading the tape but in sizing up the entire market and its trend.

And right here let me say one thing: After spending many years in Wall Street and after making and losing millions of dollars I want to tell you this: It never was my thinking that made the big money for me. It always was my sitting. Got that? My sitting tight! It is no trick at all to be right on the market. You always find lots of early bulls in bull markets and early bears in bear markets. I've known many men who were right at exactly the right time, and began buying or selling stocks when prices were at the very level which should show the greatest profit. And their experience invariably matched mine—that is, they made no real money out of it. Men who can both be right and sit tight are uncommon. I found it one of the hardest things to learn. But it is only after a stock operator has firmly grasped this that he can make big money. It is literally true that millions come easier to a trader after he knows how to trade than hundreds did in the days of his ignorance. ⟨**5.7**⟩

The reason is that a man may see straight and clearly and yet become impatient or doubtful when the market takes its time about doing as he figured it must do. That is why so

5.7 Livermore expends a lot of ink trying to drive home the point that it does no good to be right about buying at the start of a bull market, or shorting at the start of a bear market, if you take profits too soon. "Men who can both be right and sit tight are uncommon," he says, even for traders who are "not at all in the sucker class."

The bear market of 2007–2009 served up a prime example. The S&P 500 Index fell below its 10-month average (dotted line) in December 2007, and was ultimately cut in half over the next year and a half. Within that decline were numerous 10%+ countertrend advances that encouraged many shortsellers to cover. But the big money was in sitting tight and letting the entire move play out, covering only on a move back above the 10-month average, which occurred in May 2009.

Livermore laments, in a comment familiar to traders of every era, "Disregarding the big swing and trying to jump in and out was fatal to me. Nobody can catch all the fluctuations." His development as a pro reached its apex only once he learned to chill out and not overtrade. "It was never my thinking that made the big money for me," he says. "It always was my sitting."

$SPX (S&P 500 Large Cap Index) INDX   © StockCharts.com
1-Jun-2009   Close 942.87 Volume 5.2B Chg +23.73 (+2.58%) ▲
$SPX (Weekly)

S&P 500: Dec '07 – Jun '09
Primary trend down 40% over 16 months, arrow to arrow.

5.8 Despite all of the knowledge that he gained in bucket shops, the stock market and the commodity pits, Livermore blew his entire fortune several times—and ultimately killed himself when he had done it one too many times. Prudent money management was not his strong suit.

The newspaper article shown here was published in the *New York Times* on February 18, 1915, when he was 38. The article recalls that Livermore's first big coup came in 1906 when he sold short the Union Pacific and Reading railroads, and made a fortune in the crash of 1907. The following August, it says, he made another "big killing" by shorting cotton in Liverpool, and by 1908 was worth up to $3 million. But it says his luck turned south in August 1908, when he was caught long 60,000 bales of October cotton and the price broke down 67 points, costing him $1 million. This bankruptcy, however, occurred five years later as a result of losses incurred in 1913 and 1914.

Reminiscences was published almost a decade later, so you can see that Livermore was nothing if not resilient, as he accepted every setback as a course in what he calls "a very efficient educational agency." He survived because he learned to "capitalize" his mistakes, he says, by determining the reason for each loss and adding it to his "schedule of assets."

COTTON 'KING' A BANKRUPT.

Jesse L. Livermore Loses Millions He Made in Wall Street.

Jesse L. Livermore, whose spectacular rise to fortune during the panic of 1907, and whose equally startling losses in cotton a few months later, made him one of the well-known characters in Wall Street, filed yesterday a voluntary petition in bankruptcy in the Federal District Court. He gave Bretton Hall, Broadway and Eighty-sixth Street, as his residence. He said he owed $102,474, and the value of his assets were unknown.

His debts are the results of stock transactions during 1913 and 1914, his principal creditors being Mitchell & Co., $27,463; Murray Mitchell, $10,000; Chapman & Seaman, $7,207; H. F. Bachman & Co., $9,740; Dickerson & C——

many men in Wall Street, who are not at all in the sucker class, not even in the third grade, nevertheless lose money. The market does not beat them. They beat themselves, because though they have brains they cannot sit tight. Old Turkey was dead right in doing and saying what he did. He had not only the courage of his convictions but the intelligent patience to sit tight.

Disregarding the big swing and trying to jump in and out was fatal to me. Nobody can catch all the fluctuations. In a bull market your game is to buy and hold until you believe that the bull market is near its end. To do this you must study general conditions and not tips or special factors affecting individual stocks. Then get out of all your stocks; get out for keeps! Wait until you see—or if you prefer, until you think you see—the turn of the market; the beginning of a reversal of general conditions. You have to use your brains and your vision to do this; otherwise my advice would be as idiotic as to tell you to buy cheap and sell dear. One of the most helpful things that anybody can learn is to give up trying to catch the last eighth—or the first. These two are the most expensive eighths in the world. They have cost stock traders, in the aggregate, enough millions of dollars to build a concrete highway across the continent.

Another thing I noticed in studying my plays in Fullerton's office after I began to trade less unintelligently was that my initial operations seldom showed me a loss. That naturally made me decide to start big. It gave me confidence in my own judgment before I allowed it to be vitiated by the advice of others or even by my own impatience at times. Without faith in his own judgment no man can go very far in this game. That is about all I have learned—to study general conditions, to take a position and stick to it. I can wait without a twinge of impatience. I can see a setback without being shaken, knowing that it is only temporary. I have been short one hundred thousand shares and I have seen a big rally coming. I have figured—and figured correctly—that such a rally as I felt was inevitable, and even wholesome, would make a difference of one million dollars in my paper profits. And I nevertheless have stood pat and seen half my paper profit wiped out, without once considering the advisability of covering my shorts to put them out again on the rally. I knew that if I did I might lose my position and with it the certainty of a big killing. It is the big swing that makes the big money for you.

If I learned all this so slowly it was because I learned by my mistakes, and some time always elapses between making a mistake and realizing it, and more time between realizing it and exactly determining it. But at the same time I was faring pretty comfortably and was very young, so that I made up in other ways. Most of my winnings were still made in part through my tape reading because the kind of markets we were having lent themselves fairly well to my method. I was not losing either as often or as irritatingly as in the beginning of my New York experiences. It wasn't anything to be proud of, when you think that I had been broke three times in less than two years. And as I told you, being broke is a very efficient educational agency. ⟨**5.8**⟩

I was not increasing my stake very fast because I lived up to the handle all the time. I did not deprive myself of many of the things that a fellow of my age and tastes would want. I had my own automobile and I could not see any sense in skimping on living when I was taking it out of the market. The ticker only stopped Sundays and holidays, which was as it should be. Every time I found the reason for a loss or the why and how of another mistake, I added a brand-new Don't! to my schedule of assets. And the nicest way to capitalize my increasing assets was by not cutting down on my living expenses. Of course I had some amusing experiences and some that were not so amusing, but if I told them all in detail I'd never finish. As a matter of fact, the only incidents that I remember without special effort are those that taught me something of definite value to me in my trading; something that added to my store of knowledge of the game—and of myself!

ENDNOTES

1 Edwin Lefevre, "Stock Manipulation," *Saturday Evening Post,* March 20, 1909, 33.

2 Edwin Lefevre, "The Unbeatable Game of Stock Speculation." *Saturday Evening Post,* September 4, 1915, 5.

3 Lefevre, "Stock Manipulation."

4 Edwin Lefevre, "James Robert Keene," *Cosmopolitan* 34 (November 1902– April 1903): 92.

5 Lefevre, "Stock Manipulation," 35.

6 Ibid., 36.

7 Maury Klein, *The Life & Legend of E. H. Harriman* (Chapel Hill: University of North Carolina Press, 2000), 280–281.

8 Ibid.

9 Lefevre, "Unbeatable Game of Stock Speculation."

10 Klein, *Life & Legend of E. H. Harriman,"* 281.

11 Lefevre, "Unbeatable Game of Stock Speculation."

12 William Peter Hamilton, *The Stock Market Barometer* (1922), 96.

13 Robert N. Burnett, "Russell Sage," *Cosmopolitan* (1903): 344.

14 Paul Sarnoff, *Russell Sage, the Money King* (1965).

15 Will Payne, "The Mere Incident of Failure," *Everybody's Magazine* 16 (January–June 1907): 24.

16 Henry Clews, *Fifty Years in Wall Street* (New York: Irving Publishing Company, 1908), 671.

17 Burnett, "Russell Sage," 342.

18 "Little Stories of People and Things," *Everybody's Magazine* 7 (July– December 1902): 99.

19 Laura Carter Holloway, *Famous American Fortunes and the Men who Have Made Them* (1884), 593–596.

20 Lefevre, "James Robert Keene," 91.

In the spring of 1906 I was in Atlantic City for a short vacation. I was out of stocks and was thinking only of having a change of air and a nice rest. By the way, I had gone back to my first brokers, Harding Brothers, and my account had got to be pretty active. I could swing three or four thousand shares. That wasn't much more than I had done in the old Cosmopolitan shop when I was barely twenty years of age. But there was some difference between my one-point margin in the bucket shop and the margin required by brokers who actually bought or sold stocks for my account on the New York Stock Exchange.

You may remember the story I told you about that time when I was short thirty-five hundred Sugar in the Cosmopolitan and I had a hunch something was wrong and I'd better close the trade? Well, I have often had that curious feeling. As a rule, I yield to it. But at times I have pooh-poohed the idea and have told myself that it was simply asinine to follow any of these sudden blind impulses to reverse my position. I have ascribed my hunch to a state of nerves resulting from too many cigars or insufficient sleep or a torpid liver or something of that kind. When I have argued myself into disregarding my impulse and have stood pat I have always had cause to regret it. A dozen instances occur to me when I did not sell as per hunch, and the next day I'd go downtown and the market would be strong, or perhaps even advance, and I'd tell myself how silly it would have been to obey the blind impulse to sell. But on the following day there would be a pretty bad drop. Something had broken loose somewhere and I'd have made money by not being so wise and logical. The reason plainly was not physiological but psychological.

6.1 At the turn of the century, Atlantic City was the seaside resort a short train ride from Manhattan where upper-middle-class urbanites of New York, New Jersey, and Pennsylvania went to relax, enjoy luxury hotels, take in the ocean air, and see a show. In the spring of 1906 when Livermore was visiting, upbeat songs from Broadway musicals like "You're a Grand Old Flag" by George Cohan were popular, as was piano music like "Frog Legs Rag" by James Scott.

The earliest version of the game "Monopoly" was created around this time, known later to historians as the Progressive Era, by a Quaker woman who used Atlantic City street names to help people understand the evils of property concentration. Streets running parallel to the ocean are named after major bodies of water, such as the Baltic and Pacific, while east-west streets are named after the states. The first decade of the 1900s featured an explosion of luxury hotel construction there, and Livermore would have stayed at one of the grand resorts such as the Marlborough-Blenheim (pictured), the Shelburne, the Traymore, or the Brighton. A wooden boardwalk traversed the front of the oceanfront hotels to prevent guests from tramping sand into lobbies, and there were branches of New York brokerages along the way for those who wished to make a trade while on vacation.[1]

There is no record of a Harding Brothers brokerage in New York or New Jersey. This name may have been a pseudonym for Lehman Brothers because the firm was active in cotton trading—Livermore's favorite commodity. In 1906, Lehman was just getting started in underwriting equities, and brought General Cigar (maker of the Macanudo and Cohiba brands) and Sears, Roebuck & Co. to market that year. In mid-April 1906, the stock market was trading around the same level as at the start of the year, but had risen 115% over the prior two years, giving bulls a lot of confidence.

I want to tell you only about one of them because of what it did for me. It happened when I was having that little vacation in Atlantic City in the spring of 1906. **6.1** I had a friend with me who also was a customer of Harding Brothers. I had no interest in the market one way or another and was enjoying my rest. I can always give up trading to play, unless of course it is an exceptionally active market in which my commitments are rather heavy. It was a bull market, as I remember it. The outlook was favorable for general business and the stock market had slowed down but the tone was firm and all indications pointed to higher prices.

One morning after we had breakfasted and had finished reading all the New York morning papers, and had got tired of watching the sea gulls picking up clams and flying up with them twenty feet in the air and dropping them on the hard wet sand to open them for their breakfast, my friend and I started up the Boardwalk. That was the most exciting thing we did in the daytime.

It was not noon yet, and we walked up slowly to kill time and breathe the salt air. Harding Brothers had a branch office on the Boardwalk and we used to drop in every morning and see how they'd opened. It was more force of habit than anything else, for I wasn't doing anything.

The market, we found, was strong and active. My friend, who was quite bullish, was carrying a moderate line purchased several points lower. He began to tell me what an obviously wise thing it was to hold stocks for much higher prices. I wasn't paying enough attention to him to take the trouble to agree with him. I was looking over

the quotation board, noting the changes—they were mostly advances—until I came to Union Pacific. I got a feeling that I ought to sell it. I can't tell you more. I just felt like selling it. I asked myself why I should feel like that, and I couldn't find any reason whatever for going short of UP.

I stared at the last price on the board until I couldn't see any figures or any board or anything else, for that matter. All I knew was that I wanted to sell Union Pacific and I couldn't find out why I wanted to.

I must have looked queer, for my friend, who was standing alongside of me, suddenly nudged me and asked, "Hey, what's the matter?"

"I don't know," I answered.

"Going to sleep?" he said.

"No," I said. "I am not going to sleep. What I am going to do is to sell that stock." I had always made money following my hunches.

I walked over to a table where there were some blank order pads. My friend followed me. I wrote out an order to sell a thousand Union Pacific at the market and handed it to the manager. He was smiling when I wrote it and when he took it. But when he read the order he stopped smiling and looked at me.

"Is this right?" he asked me. But I just looked at him and he rushed it over to the operator.

"What are you doing?" asked my friend.

"I'm selling it!" I told him.

"Selling what?" he yelled at me. If he was a bull how could I be a bear? Something was wrong.

"A thousand UP," I said.

"Why?" he asked me in great excitement.

I shook my head, meaning I had no reason. But he must have thought I'd got a tip, because he took me by the arm and led me outside into the hall, where we could be out of sight and hearing of the other customers and rubbering chairwarmers.

"What did you hear?" he asked me.

He was quite excited. UP was one of his pets and he was bullish on it because of its earnings and its prospects. But he was willing to take a bear tip on it at second hand.

"Nothing!" I said.

"You didn't?" He was skeptical and showed it plainly.

"I didn't hear a thing."

"Then why in blazes are you selling?"

"I don't know," I told him. I spoke gospel truth.

"Oh, come across, Larry," he said.

He knew it was my habit to know why I traded. I had sold a thousand shares of Union Pacific. I must have a very good reason to sell that much stock in the face of the strong market.

"I don't know," I repeated. "I just feel that something is going to happen."

"What's going to happen?"

"I don't know. I can't give you any reason. All I know is that I want to sell that stock. And I'm going to let 'em have another thousand."

I walked back into the office and gave an order to sell a second thousand. If I was right in selling the first thousand I ought to have out a little more.

"What could possibly happen?" persisted my friend, who couldn't make up his mind to follow my lead. If I'd told him that I had heard UP was going down he'd have sold it without asking me from whom I'd heard it or why. "What could possibly happen?" he asked again.

"A million things could happen. But I can't promise you that any of them will. I can't give you any reasons and I can't tell fortunes," I told him.

"Then you're crazy," he said. "Stark crazy, selling that stock without rime or reason. You don't know why you want to sell it?"

"I don't know why I want to sell it. I only know I do want to," I said. "I want to, like everything." The urge was so strong that I sold another thousand.

That was too much for my friend. He grabbed me by the arm and said, "Here! Let's get out of this place before you sell the entire capital stock."

I had sold as much as I needed to satisfy my feeling, so I followed him without waiting for a report on the last two thousand shares. It was a pretty good jag of stock for me to sell even with the best of reasons. It seemed more than enough to be short of without any reason whatever, particularly when the entire market was so strong and there was nothing in sight to make anybody think of the bear side. But I remembered that on previous occasions when I had the same urge to sell and didn't do it I always had reasons to regret it. ◁6.2▷

I have told some of these stories to friends, and some of them tell me it isn't a hunch but the subconscious mind, which is the creative mind, at work. That is the mind which makes artists do things without their knowing how they came to do them. Perhaps with me it was the cumulative effect of a lot of little things individually insignificant but collectively powerful. Possibly my friend's unintelligent bullishness aroused a spirit of contradiction and I picked on UP because it had been touted so much. I can't tell you what the cause or motive for hunches may be. All I know is that I went out of the Atlantic City branch office of Harding Brothers short three thousand Union Pacific in a rising market, and I wasn't worried a bit.

I wanted to know what price they'd got for my last two thousand shares. So after luncheon we walked up to the office. I had the pleasure of seeing that the general market was strong and Union Pacific higher.

"I see your finish," said my friend. You could see he was glad he hadn't sold any.

The next day the general market went up some more and I heard nothing but cheerful remarks from my friend. But I felt sure I had done right to sell UP, and I never get impatient when I feel I am right. What's the sense? That afternoon Union Pacific stopped climbing, and toward the end of the day it began to go off. Pretty soon it

6.2 ▷ By this time in his life, Livermore has come to think of himself as a pro who carefully studied general conditions before making trades, then acted when the odds of success were clearly in his favor. And yet he is fascinated by the notion that he could also act on a hunch, which is a precognitive impulse—a "feeling" rather than a conscious decision evolved from hard data.

Hunches mostly have a bad reputation because they are believed to arise from emotions rather than reason. But that may not be the case. Brett Steenbarger, a Chicago-based clinical psychiatry professor who provides counseling services to traders, has studied the thought processes of thousands of investors in a quest to understand what makes the best ones successful. He believes Livermore's hunches actually came from his tape-reading experience rather than from his gut.[2]

After years of looking at stocks' trading sequences, Livermore had internalized probability outcomes to an extent that did not need to be verbalized. Psychologists call this "implicit learning," or the ability to know something without knowing you know it. The key is immersion, or repeated concentrated exposure. For someone who doesn't watch the markets every day, a hunch about a stock would be random and a less-than-50/50 bet. For someone who watches stock movements tick by tick, day after day, as a profession, a hunch about a stock emerges from a deep level of pattern recognition. In this case, then, what Livermore calls following through on a "hunch" was actually a matter of acting intuitively and decisively based on his experience after observing UP quotes at the boardwalk brokerage. It was an important step in his development as a major Wall Street operator.

6.3 In the predawn mist of Wednesday, April 18, 1906, a massive rupture in the San Andreas Fault rocked San Francisco with a 8.3 magnitude earthquake that lasted 42 seconds. The young city withstood the initial tremor remarkably well but was devastated by the fires that followed. The majority of San Francisco's buildings were made of wood, rather than the brick used in eastern cities at the time, due to its booming lumber trade and proximity to coastal forests.

About 1,000 of the city's 375,000 residents died as more than four square miles, roughly half the city, burned to the ground. Because the quake damaged water mains, firefighters were stymied.

Property damage estimates ranged from $350 million to $500 million, on which roughly $235 million in insurance policies were held. Losses represented 1.5% of U.S. economic output for the year. Livermore anticipated damage to companies ranging from railroads to banks, and he was right.

Since most buildings had fire insurance but not earthquake insurance, many policyholders set their damaged homes ablaze during the resulting chaos. As you will see later, insurance payouts resulting from this disaster played a huge role in the financial crisis that followed.[3]

The news spread quickly throughout the United States, eventually affecting the financial markets in London and New York. On April 26, the *New York Times* reported that the San Francisco disaster resulted in a plunge of 12.5% on the New York Stock Exchange, wiping out $1 billion in market capitalization.

British insurers were particularly hard hit by the disaster, as shares of leading underwriters, such as London & Lancashire, fell as much as 30%. Even before the transcontinental railroad was built in 1869, San Francisco was an international trade hub connecting California's mining and

got down to a point below the level of the average of my three thousand shares. I felt more positive than ever that I was on the right side, and since I felt that way I naturally had to sell some more. So, toward the close, I sold an additional two thousand shares.

There I was, short five thousand shares of UP on a hunch. That was as much as I could sell in Harding's office with the margin I had up. It was too much stock for me to be short of, on a vacation; so I gave up the vacation and returned to New York that very night. There was no telling what might happen and I thought I'd better be Johnny-on-the-spot. There I could move quickly if I had to.

The next day we got the news of the San Francisco earthquake. **6.3** It was an awful disaster. But the market opened down only a couple of points.

The bull forces were at work, and the public never is independently responsive to news. You see that all the time. If there is a solid bull foundation, for instance, whether or not what the papers call bull manipulation is going on at the same time, certain news items fail to have the effect they would have if the Street was bearish. It is all in the state of sentiment at the time. In this case the Street did not appraise the extent of the catastrophe because it didn't wish to. Before the day was over prices came back.

I was short five thousand shares. The blow had fallen, but my stock hadn't. My hunch was of the first water, but my bank account wasn't growing; not even on paper. ◁**6.4** The friend who had been in Atlantic City with me when I put out my short line in UP. was glad and sad about it.

He told me: "That was some hunch, kid. But, say, when the talent and the money are all on the bull side what's the use of bucking against them? They are bound to win out."

"Give them time," I said. I meant prices. I wouldn't cover because I knew the damage was enormous and the Union Pacific would be one of the worst sufferers. But it was exasperating to see the blindness of the Street.

"Give 'em time and your skin will be where all the other bear hides are stretched out in the sun, drying," he assured me.

"What would you do?" I asked him. "Buy UP on the strength of the millions of dollars of damage suffered by the Southern Pacific and other lines? Where are the earnings for dividends going to come from after they pay for all they've lost? The best you can say is that the trouble may not be as bad as it is painted. But is that a reason for buying the stocks of the roads chiefly affected? Answer me that."

agricultural resources to the rest of the world. Most of the exports destined for Europe were financed through the San Francisco offices of British banks. Looking for new sources of revenue, and taking advantage of the pre-1907 California law allowing insurers to underwrite both marine and fire insurance, London's financial firms decided to diversify at exactly the wrong time. By the turn of the century, nearly half of all fire insurance policies in the city were carried by British firms.[4]

British banks were caught so off guard because San Francisco's boom had clouded their judgment. In the days that followed the quake, the *New York Times* commented, "San Francisco had been so thoroughly free from fire for years" that nearly all the large insurers were very active there. The frequency of earthquakes and the possibility for one natural disaster spurring another were not adequately factored into actuarial tables, a fault that short sellers were able to exploit.[5]

6.4 ▷ The slang term "of the first water" was used primarily in this era in a sarcastic sense, as in "he was a swindler of the first water." But it originated among jewel merchants, who rate the quality and brilliance of diamonds in terms of waters: first water, second water, and so on. *First water* diamonds are flawless and perfectly clear.[6]

6.5 ▶ **James Fisk Jr.** was a speculator associated with Daniel Drew and Jay Gould. A man of many nicknames, including Prince Erie, Jim Jubilee, and Diamond Jim, Fisk was made famous through his involvement with the Erie War and the gold corner attempt that resulted in the Black Friday panic of 1869. He was also involved with William "Boss" Tweed and the Tammany Hall political machine that corrupted the New York politics of the era.

Fisk was one of the most colorful men of the post-Civil War years—an era marked by fantastic economic growth. These were the wild days of capitalism. Regulation was lax. Confidence men, scam artists, prospectors, and speculators mixed with legitimate businessmen, old-money dynasties, and politicians. And yet Fisk stands out above all the other big personalities. Meade Minnigerode brings him to life in a 1927 study:

He was a big, burly, blond creature with "kiss curls" who looked like a butcher, jovial and quick witted, with the manners and gaudy habits of a publican; he was a swindler and a bandit, a destroyer of law and an apostle of fraud; he was a clown in velvet waistcoats and spurious admiral's uniforms, a fatuous fat man who never grew up, playing with railroads and steamboats, canary birds and ballerinas; his private life was to many a public dismay, his public conduct to some a private scorn; he was, for a while, the most successful, the most conspicuous, the most significant figure in the sinister business world of New York. And to the hundreds of his fellow citizens—thousands, as was shown when his funeral train passed by—he was charitable, light-hearted, open-handed big Jim Fisk; a community which loathed Jay Gould adored him; and when he died they adored him with ballads. The America of the Sixties produced him, and nowhere perhaps, except in the America of 1870, could he have existed.[7]

The son of a country peddler, a common sight before the spread of railroads, Fisk was born in Vermont on April Fool's Day, 1835. The young man got his start as a hotel waiter before joining the circus as a sweeper, animal keeper, and ticket collector. He returned home to join his father on his peddling trips but soon tired of his conservative style. Fisk wanted more. He wanted gaudy, flashy carts pulled by fast horses that could be seen from afar. He wanted to drive through unsuspecting villages at 10 miles an hour, throwing out candy and pennies to the children. Soon Jim was out on his own, according to Minnigerode, as a "jobber in silks, shawls, dress goods, jewelry, silver ware and Yankee notions."[8] The conspicuous circus man found success with multiple carts covering multiple routes and eventually bought out his father.[9]

Fisk rose quickly once he turned his attention to big business. Jordan, Marsh & Company, his supplier in Boston, offered him a job in its store. Fisk became a partner as the firm bought and erected several mills to begin manufacturing its own goods. To boost profitability near the start of the Civil War, Fisk illegally broke the southern blockade and started running cotton up through the Confederate lines. At the time, cotton was selling at 12 cents a pound in the South compared to $2 in the North. Fisk became too big, too successful, and was bought out of the partnership. He started his own firm, but it failed.

Finally, in 1864, he went to New York to become a broker. He opened richly festooned offices on Broad Street and treated his fellow speculators to the best liquors. But he was new to the Wall Street game; a "lamb fraternizing with wolves," according to a biographer.[10] He jumped boldly into all the leading stocks but was cut down by a sudden bear raid. He hatched a plan to get another stake: He would

But all my friend said was: "Yes, that listens fine. But I tell you, the market doesn't agree with you. The tape doesn't lie, does it?"

"It doesn't always tell the truth on the instant," I said.

"Listen. A man was talking to Jim Fisk **6.5** a little before Black Friday, **6.6** giving ten good reasons why gold ought to go down for keeps. He send a man to London on a fast steamer to short Confederate bonds upon the South's defeat. With the Atlantic telegraphic cable not yet laid, it took news eight full days to cross the Atlantic on the mail ship. Fisk's man did it in six and a half and collected a great profit. But in short order, Fisk was ruined again and returned home to Boston.

It was here that he forged a long-lasting friendship with veteran Wall Street operator Daniel Drew. Drew, who was 68

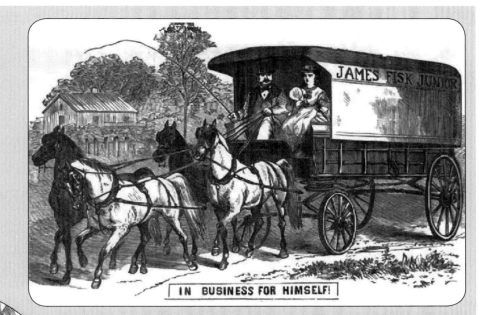

IN BUSINESS FOR HIMSELF!

at the time, shared Fisk's love for the circus since he grew up in Carmel, New York, a common winter camp for traveling acts.[11] He became Drew's broker during the Erie War, which enabled all the events that made Fisk famous.

Fisk would go on to run a railroad, which resulted in an episode of rival trains charging each other on the same disputed piece of track. He paid the debts of the Ninth Regiment of the New York National Guard and was made an honorary colonel. He was admiral of the Narragansett Steamship Company. And he bought Pike's Opera House, where he would host spectacular shows "in which blondes and brunettes appears on alternate evenings," according to an ad.

In the end, Fisk met a tragic fate: He was shot dead at age 37 in 1872 by a former business associate and boyfriend of his favored mistress, Helen Mansfield. The *New York Times* reported his body lay in state with military honors at his opera house before the funeral, and the outpouring of grief outside led to the assembly of one of the largest crowds in the city's history to date.[13]

got so encouraged by his own words that he ended by telling Fisk that he was going to sell a few million. And Jim Fisk just looked at him and said, "Go ahead! Do! Sell it short and invite me to your funeral.'"

"Yes," I said; "and if that chap had sold it short, look at the killing he would have made! Sell some UP yourself."

6.6 Of all the frauds, scams, and other blemishes on America's financial history, the gold corner attempt of 1869, masterminded by Jay Gould and Jim Fisk, ranks near the top. The plot, which involved political corruption at the highest level of government, initially blew the value of gold sky-high before it crashed, creating such a singular example of misdirected prices that it was still a topic of casual conversation 35 years later.

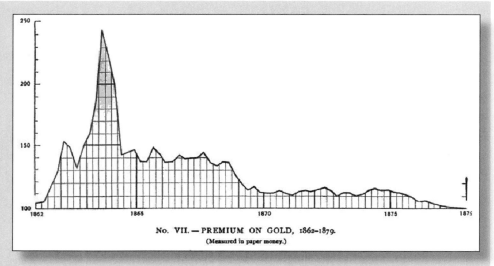

No. VII. — PREMIUM ON GOLD, 1862–1879.
(Measured in paper money.)

The groundwork for the corner attempt was laid a decade before it occurred in the financing of the Civil War. The government of Abraham Lincoln had issued millions of dollars' worth of "greenbacks," or paper money not redeemable into precious metal, to pay its bills. They were backed by bonds sold in Europe. Naturally this new policy of issuing a fiat currency was considered inflationary, so citizens hoarded gold as a store of value. Gold began trading at a premium to the dollar, with the spread fluctuation based on the fortunes of the Union Army. Traders figured that if the North were defeated, greenbacks would become worthless. In contrast, they believed victory by the Union Army would bring the resumption of the gold standard and greenback redemption at face value.

Volume in the gold market charged higher during the Civil War as traders bet on its outcome, but also for commercial reasons: Foreigners would make payments to U.S. merchants in dollars but demand gold for the settlement of debt. An early exchange was formed in 1862, and soon gold speculators hired agents in both the Union and Confederate camps to alert them of the outcome of battles via private telegraph wires. At one point, Lincoln asked Pennsylvania governor Andrew Curtin: "What do you think of those fellows in Wall Street who are gambling in gold at such a time as this?" Curtin's terse reply: "For my part, I wish every one of them had his devilish head shot off."[14]

The center of the action was the New York Gold Room on New Street, where traders surrounded a fountain in the center of the floor and confronted each other through a water spray. During heated moments, traders reached down to splash water on their faces. Up above was a large mechanical sign displaying the current price of gold. A similar indicator was placed on the building's facade for the entertainment of those outside. Writing in 1873, William Worthington Fowler described the scene:

> The gold room was like a cavern, full of dank and noisome vapors, and the deadly carbonic acid was blended with the fumes of stale smoke and vinous breaths. But the stifling gases engendered in that low-browed cave of evil enchanters, never seemed to depress the energies of the gold-dealers; from "morn to dewy eve" the drooping ceiling and bistre-colored walls reechoed with the sounds of all kinds of voices while an up reared forest of arms was swayed furiously by the storms of a swiftly rising and falling market.[15]

Gould's convoluted plan, hatched four years after the Civil War ended, was to boost the price of gold, thereby cheapening the cost of American grain in dollar terms and increasing exports. Not only would Gould profit from his gold holdings as the price rose, but his Wabash Railroad would benefit from higher volumes as more grain was moved to eastern ports for shipment to Europe. The only trouble was that President Ulysses S. Grant and the U.S. Treasury held some $80 million of gold and could enter the market as a seller if prices rose dramatically. For the scheme to work, Grant had to be convinced that higher gold prices were in the nation's best interest.

After launching his corner attempt in August 1869, Gould personally appealed to Grant, arguing that elevated gold prices would bring economic prosperity. Figuring that he needed help on the inside, Gould co-opted Abel Corbin, an old speculator who had married Grant's sister, to lobby the president. But Grant was no simpleton. After listening to the tycoon's plea and suspecting a con, he told advisors: "It seems to me that there's a good deal of fiction in all this talk about prosperity. The bubble may as well be pricked one way or another."[16]

Gould did not give up, through, and persuaded Corbin and others to try to manipulate the president's view in new ways. Reported financier Henry Clews in his own account of the affair: "President Grant began to think that the opinion of almost everybody he talked with on this subject was on the same side, and must, therefore, be correct."[17]

Gould initially had limited success. He was able to push the price up only two points, to $136.50, between August 31 and September 14 despite his purchases of more than $50 million in gold contracts. Moreover, Gould's syndicate started to weaken as corrupted brokers broke ranks and began to sell into the advance. Gould needed a big event to scare off the bears, create panic, and send gold higher. He called on celebrated stock operator Jim Fisk for help (see illustration of the meeting).

After being assured everything was in order for the corner, Fisk entered the Gold Room on the morning of September 23 with great flourish, causing the bears to fear for their financial safety and prices to rise to $144.50.[18] Although it seemed as if the plot was proceeding according to plan, a critical error made by Fisk a few days earlier had already doomed the play. He was so eager to make sure Grant didn't foil their plan that he had Corbin send the president another letter, this time hand-delivered by special

PLOTTING THE GREAT GOLD RING OF '69.

messenger, recommending no gold sales. Recounts Clews:

"He read the letter, and had his suspicions at once aroused. He said laconically to the messenger, 'It is satisfactory; there is no answer.' Grant then told his sister to instruct her husband to have nothing more to do with the Gould-Fisk gang."[19]

Corbin, upon hearing the news, demanded his fee. Gould then realized it was only hours before the New York Treasury would sell gold and break the corner attempt. But to switch to the bear side, he would need to cross Fisk. So while Fisk was buying on Thursday, Gould was secretly selling to him. He said later: "I was a seller of gold that day. . . . I purchased merely enough to make believe I was a bull."[20]

Pandemonium was unleashed the next day as bears believed that Fisk was buying at any price and predicted gold's eventual rise to $200 or more. Prices moved to $155 as ambulances carried fainting short sellers to hospitals and crowds started to gather outside Gould's office (see illustration). In Philadelphia, a clocklike indicator of gold prices could no longer keep pace with the action in New York. Finally, according to one account, "a black flag with a skull and crossbones was thrown over its face."[21] Prices on the stock exchanges collapsed as speculators sold other securities to help cover their short gold positions. In the final climactic moment around noon, the price reached $160 with no bidders.

BLACK FRIDAY.

Then one of Fisk's brokers bid $161, an offer that was met with maddening silence. He lifted the bid by fractions, the staccato of each successive bid driving stakes into the hearts of the bears. When he reached $161.375, James Brown, a Scots banker known to represent several European groups, sold $1 million in gold at that price. The Fisk coterie was stunned and lowered the bid to $161. Brown sold again. The corner was over.

The room buzzed that a large bear syndicate organized in Europe was ready to dump tens of millions of dollars in gold on the market as needed to restore order. At around this time, news of Grant's order to sell the U.S. Treasury's gold reached inside the trading area courtesy of James Garfield, a future president. In the chaos that ensued, Fisk's men were still bidding $160 in one corner of the Gold Room while the bid was $135 in another. The afternoon ended with gold at $131.25. Gould had made a fortune, though not exactly the way he intended, and reimbursed Fisk and his men before all went their separate ways.

That session would become known over the years as Black Friday, its facts embellished as the legend grew. A congressional investigation followed, but no one went to jail.[22]

"Not I! I'm the kind that thrives best on not rowing against wind and tide."

On the following day, when fuller reports came in, the market began to slide off, but even then not as violently as it should. Knowing that nothing under the sun could stave off a substantial break I doubled up and sold five thousand shares. Oh, by that time it was plain to most people, and my brokers were willing enough. It wasn't reckless of them or of me, not the way I sized up the market. On the day following, the market began to go for fair. There was the dickens to pay. Of course I pushed my luck for all it was worth. I doubled up again and sold ten thousand shares more. It was the only play possible.

I wasn't thinking of anything except that I was right—100 per cent right—and that this was a heaven-sent opportunity. It was up to me to take advantage of it. I sold more. Did I think that with such a big line of shorts out, it wouldn't take much of a rally to wipe out my paper profits and possibly my principal? I don't know whether I thought of that or not, but if I did it didn't carry much weight with me. I wasn't plunging recklessly. I was really playing conservatively. There was nothing that anybody could do to undo the earthquake, was there? They couldn't restore the crumpled buildings overnight, free, gratis, for nothing, could they? All the money in the world couldn't help much in the next few hours, could it?

I was not betting blindly. I wasn't a crazy bear. I wasn't drunk with success or thinking that because Frisco was pretty well wiped off the map the entire country was headed for the scrap heap. No, indeed! I didn't look for a panic. Well, the next day I cleaned up. I made two hundred and fifty thousand dollars. It was my biggest winnings up to that time. It was all made in a few days. The Street paid no attention to the earthquake the first day or two. They'll tell you that it was because the first despatches were not so alarming, but I think it was because it took so long to change the point of view of the public toward the securities markets. Even the professional traders for the most part were slow and shortsighted.

I have no explanation to give you, either scientific or childish. I am telling you what I did, and why, and what came of it. I was much less concerned with the mystery of the hunch than with the fact that I got a quarter of a million out of it. It meant that I could now swing a much bigger line than ever, if or when the time came for it.

That summer I went to Saratoga Springs. **6.7** It was supposed to be a vacation for me, but I kept an eye on the market. To begin with, I wasn't so tired that it bothered me to think about it. And then, everybody I knew up there had or had had an active interest in it. We naturally talked about it. I have noticed that there is quite a difference between talking and trading. Some of these chaps remind you of the bold clerk who talks to his cantankerous employer as to a yellow dog—when he tells you about it.

Harding Brothers had a branch office in Saratoga. Many of their customers were there. But the real reason, I suppose, was the advertising value. Having a branch office in a resort is simply high-class billboard advertising. I used to drop in and sit around with the rest of the crowd. The manager was a very nice chap from the New York office who was there to give the glad hand to friends and strangers and, if possible, to get business. It was a wonderful place for tips—all kinds of tips, horse-race, stock-market, and waiters'. The office knew I didn't take any, so the manager didn't come and whisper confidentially in my ear what he'd just got on the q. t. from the New York office. He simply passed over the telegrams, saying, "This is what they're sending out," or something of the kind.

Of course I watched the market. With me, to look at the quotation board and to read the signs is one process. My good friend Union Pacific, I no-

6.7 Saratoga Springs in upstate New York, about 45 minutes from Albany, was one of the liveliest resorts in America for high society in the Gilded Age and the first few decades of the 20th century. It was best known for the Saratoga Race Course, which was co-founded in 1863 by Wall Street titan William R. Travers, and continues today as the oldest continuously operated Thoroughbred track in the United States.[23]

The natural mineral springs, believed to have medicinal powers, were the main draw initially in the 1860s and 1870s, and a Baedeker guidebook published in Europe at the time described the city's hotels as the largest in the world, with enormous ballrooms and plazas. Vacationers were entertained by street performance artists, traveling circuses, carnival troupes, lecturers, musicians, and tableaux vivants, which were costumed actors posed motionlessly and silently to represent paintings or historical events.[24]

By the time Livermore would have visited in this passage around 1907, all of these amusements were still plentiful, though it was primarily a place for the Manhattan elite to get away from the heat of the city and bet on the ponies. Of course there were brokerage offices where professional traders like Livermore and Travers rubbed elbows with the dilettante public to gossip and trade ideas without the usual frenetic pace of the stock exchange floor. One of the vacationers' favorite places to stay was the Grand Union Hotel.

ticed, looked like going up. The price was high, but the stock acted as if it were being accumulated. I watched it a couple of days without trading in it, and the more I watched it the more convinced I became that it was being bought on balance by somebody who was no piker, somebody who not only had a big bank roll but knew what was what. Very clever accumulation, I thought.

As soon as I was sure of this I naturally began to buy it, at about 160. It kept on acting all hunky, and so I kept on buying it, five hundred shares at a clip. The more I bought the stronger it got, without any spurt, and I was feeling very comfortable. I couldn't see any reason why that stock shouldn't go up a great deal more; not with what I read on the tape.

All of a sudden the manager came to me and said they'd got a message from New York—they had a direct wire of course—asking if I was in the office, and when they answered yes, another came saying: "Keep him there. Tell him Mr. Harding wants to speak to him."

I said I'd wait, and bought five hundred shares more of UP. I couldn't imagine what Harding could have to say to me. I didn't think it was anything about business. My margin was more than ample for what I was buying. Pretty soon the manager came and told me that Mr. Ed Harding wanted me on the long-distance telephone.

"Hello, Ed," I said.

But he said, "What the devil's the matter with you? Are you crazy?"

"Are you?" I said.

"What are you doing?" he asked.

"What do you mean?"

"Buying all that stock."

"Why, isn't my margin all right?"

"It isn't a case of margin, but of being a plain sucker."

"I don't get you."

"Why are you buying all that Union Pacific?"

"It's going up," I said.

"Going up, hell! Don't you know that the insiders are feeding it out to you? You're just about the easiest mark up there. You'd have more fun losing it on the ponies. Don't let them kid you."

"Nobody is kidding me," I told him. "I haven't talked to a soul about it."

But he came back at me: "You can't expect a miracle to save you every time you plunge in that stock. Get out while you've still got a chance," he said. "It's a crime to be long of that stock at this level—when these highbinders are shoveling it out by the ton."

"The tape says they're buying it," I insisted.

"Larry, I got heart disease when your orders began to come in. For the love of Mike, don't be a sucker. Get out! Right away. It's liable to bust wide open any minute. I've done my duty. Good-by!" And he hung up.

Ed Harding was a very clever chap, unusually well-informed and a real friend, disinterested and kind-hearted. And what was even more, I knew he was in position to hear things. All I had to go by, in my purchases of UP., was my years of studying the behaviour of stocks and my perception of certain symptoms which experience had taught me usually accompanied a substantial rise. I don't know what happened to me, but I suppose I must have concluded that my tape reading told me the stock was being absorbed simply because very clever manipulation by the insiders made the tape tell a story that wasn't true. Possibly I was impressed by the pains Ed Harding took to stop me from making what he was so sure would be a colossal mistake on my part. Neither his brains nor his motives were to be questioned. Whatever it was that made me decide to follow his advice, I cannot tell you; but follow it, I did.

I sold out all my Union Pacific. Of course if it was unwise to be long of it it was equally unwise not to be short of it. So after I got rid of my long stock

6.8 ▶ Upon President McKinley's assassination in September 1901, Theodore Roosevelt assumed the presidency and began responding to public criticism of the concentration of power and wealth among a small class of capitalists.[25]

Roosevelt's first target was the Northern Securities Co. This entity, formed in the aftermath of the May 1901 battle between J. P. Morgan and E. H. Harriman, had the sole purpose of holding shares of the disputed Northern Pacific railroad and the parallel Great Northern system. In February 1902, the government attacked the $400 million corporation as a virtual merger of two competing transcontinental lines, Harriman's Union Pacific system and Morgan's Great Northern and Northern Pacific, by which a monopoly of former competitors would be created. In 1904, after an appeal to the Supreme Court, it was found in a 5 to 4 ruling that the mere existence of Northern Securities, and the power it wielded, "constitute a menace to, and a restraint upon, that freedom of commerce which Congress intended to recognize and protect."[26]

Harriman, after receiving his share of the Northern Pacific and Great Northern stock, proceeded to sell it to the public at a healthy profit thanks to the booming stock market in 1905 and 1906. By June 30, 1906, Union Pacific held nearly $56 million in cash compared to just $7 million in the previous year. Harriman went east, where his system had no tracks, and bought shares of railways including the New York Central, Atchison Topeka & Santa Fe, and Baltimore & Ohio. Not content with his cash hoard, Harriman had the Union Pacific's management borrow another $75 million—bringing his total railroad investments between June 1906 and February 1907 to nearly $132 million.

As a result of the dividend income from these investments and increased revenue in its own business, Union Pacific's net profit went from $12.6 million in 1900 to nearly $32 million in 1906. Such a dramatic rise in fortune was not ignored by the speculators amassing in brokerage houses across the country: The stock went from a low of $16⅛ in 1898 to a high of $195⅜ during 1906. Wall Street was eager for a dividend increase, as Harriman conservatively kept the rate at 4%, despite the jump in earnings, to help fund the expansion of his empire. Eventually, the rate was increased to 5% in 1905 and again to 6% in March 1906.[27]

Finally, in August, Harriman presented Union Pacific's board with financial statements showing a surplus of $25 million. Based on this, the dividend was bumped to 10%, and the New York Stock Exchange erupted. On August 18, the *New York Times* breathlessly reported: "Not since the day for the Northern Pacific 'corner,' with its accompanying panic, has the Stock Exchange witnessed so mad a scene as followed the announcement after the market's open-

I sold four thousand shares short. I put out most of it around 162.

The next day the directors of the Union Pacific Company declared a 10 per cent dividend on the stock. **6.8** At first nobody in Wall Street believed it. It was too much like the desperate manœuvre of cornered gamblers. All the newspapers jumped on the directors. But while the Wall Street talent hesitated to act the market boiled over. Union Pacific led, and on huge transactions made a new high-record price. Some of the room traders made fortunes in an hour and I remember later hearing about a rather dull-witted specialist who made a mistake that put three hundred and fifty thousand dollars in his pocket. He sold his seat the following week and became a gentleman farmer the following month.

Of course I realised, the moment I heard the news of the declaration of that unprecedented 10 per cent dividend, that I got what I deserved for disregarding the voice of experience and listening to the voice of a tipster. My own convictions I had set aside for the suspicions of a friend, simply because he was disinterested and as a rule knew what he was doing.

As soon as I saw Union Pacific making new high records I said to myself, "This is no stock for me to be short of."

All I had in the world was up as margin in Harding's office. I was neither cheered nor made stubborn by the knowledge of that fact. What was plain was that I had read the tape accurately and that I had been a ninny to let Ed Harding shake my own resolution. There was no sense in recriminations, because I had no time to lose; and besides, what's done is done. So I gave an order to take in my shorts. The stock was around 165 when I sent in that order to buy in the four thousand UP at the market. I had a three-point loss on it at that figure. Well, my brokers paid 172 and 174 for some of it before they were through. I found when I got my reports that Ed Harding's kindly intentioned interference cost me forty thousand dollars. A low price for a man to pay for not having the courage of his own convictions! It was a cheap lesson.

I wasn't worried, because the tape said still higher prices. It was an unusual move and there were no precedents for the action of the directors, but I did this time what I thought I ought to do. As soon as I had given the first order to buy four thousand shares to cover my shorts I decided to profit by what the tape indicated and so I went along. I bought four thousand shares and held that stock until the next morning. Then I got out. I not only made up the forty thousand dollars I had lost but about fifteen thousand besides. If Ed Harding hadn't tried to save me money I'd have made a killing. But he did me a very great service, for it was the lesson of that episode that, I firmly believe, completed my education as a trader. ◁ 6.9

It was not that all I needed to learn was not to take tips but follow my own inclination. It was that I gained confidence in myself and I was able finally to shake off the old method of trading. That Saratoga experience was my last haphazard, hit-or-miss operation. From then on I began to think of basic conditions instead of individual stocks. I promoted myself to a higher grade in the hard school of speculation. It was a long and difficult step to take.

ing." Yet again, shorts were caught in a squeeze and were forced to cover as the "tickers were minutes behind the trading on the floor, quotations of $167½ appearing on the tape in brokerage offices when on the Exchange brokers were fighting to get the stock at $171."[28]

Livermore mentions that the directors, namely Harriman, were criticized by the media for initially withholding news of the dividend increase. The decision was made on August 15, but Harriman delayed the release until August 17 to ensure that all directors were briefed and because he wished the announcement be made during New York trading hours. According to Harriman scholar Maury Klein, "More than one observer labeled the episode a throwback to the days of Gould, Fisk, and Drew."[29]

6.9 One reason that *Reminiscences* resonates with professional traders is that they have all had the experience of making the mistakes that Livermore makes, both here and elsewhere. In this case, the sin is changing your mind on a position after receiving well-meaning, persuasive but erroneous guidance from a friend or colleague. Being flexible is a valuable trait, but taking advice in the form of a tip without any new underlying data is dangerous. Learning to trust his own instincts and play a lone hand based on his own judgment of fundamental conditions and evidence from trading patterns was a milestone in Livermore's development—though this was certainly not the last time he would have to take this lesson.

ENDNOTES

1 Vicki Gold Levi and Lee Eisenberg, *Atlantic City: 125 Years of Ocean Madness*, (Ten Speed Press, 1979).

2 Interview with Brett Steenbarger by Jon Markman, September 25, 2009.

3 Leonard Wildman,. "Memorandum," *Virtual Museum of San Fransico* (2009). www.sfmuseum.org/1906.2/arson.html.

4 *The Economist,* May 5, 1906, 767.

5 "Enormous Losses of Fire Companies," *New York Times,* April 20, 1906, 4.

6 Betty Kirkpatrick. "Clichés: over 1500 phrases explored and explained." (New York: St. Martin's Press, 1996).

7 Meade Minnigerode, *Certain Rich Men* (1927), 192–193.

8 Ibid., p. 194.

9 S. A. Swanberg, *Jim Fisk: The Career of an Improbable Rascal* (1959), p. 15.

10 Ibid., 20.

11 Ibid., 24.

12 Minnigerode, *Certain Rich Men,* 201.

13 "The Fisk Murder. Imposing and Elaborate Funeral Services Yesterday". *New York Times*, January 9, 1872.

14 Robert Sobel, *Panic on Wall Street* (1968), 136.

15 William Worthington Fowler, *Ten Years in Wall Street* (1873), 411–412.

16 Sobel, *Panic on Wall Street,* 140.

17 Henry Clews, *Fifty Years in Wall Street* (New York: Irving Publishing Company, 1908), 192.

18 Sobel, *Panic on Wall Street,* 145.

19 Clews, *Fifty Years in Wall Street,* 196.

20 Kenneth D. Ackerman, *The Gold Ring* (1988), 164.

21 Matthew Josephson, *Robber Barons* (New York: Harcourt, Brace and Company, 1934), 146.

22 Sobel, *Panic on Wall Street,* 147–149.

23 "Saratoga Springs: A Historical Portrait." Timothy A. Holmes and Martha Stonequist. 2000. Arcadia Publishing

24 "First Resorts." John Sterngrass. 2001. Johns Hopkins University Press.

25 Miller Center of Public Affairs, University of Virginia, "First Annual Message" by Theodore Roosevelt to Congress, December 3, 1901, http://millercenter.org/scripps/archive/speeches/detail/3773.

26 Alexander Dana Noyes, *Forty Years of American Finance* (1909), 347.

27 Maury Klein, *Union Pacific: 1894–1969* (2006), 153.

28 "Harriman Dividend Amazes Wall Street," *New York Times,* August 18, 1906, 1.

29 Klein, *Union Pacific,* 154.

I never hesitate to tell a man that I am bullish or bearish. But I do not tell people to buy or sell any particular stock. In a bear market all stocks go down and in a bull market they go up. I don't mean of course that in a bear market caused by a war, ammunition shares do not go up. I speak in a general sense. But the average man doesn't wish to be told that it is a bull or a bear market. What he desires is to be told specifically which particular stock to buy or sell. He wants to get something for nothing. He does not wish to work. He doesn't even wish to have to think. It is too much bother to have to count the money that he picks up from the ground.

Well, I wasn't that lazy, but I found it easier to think of individual stocks than of the general market and therefore of individual fluctuations rather than of general movements. I had to change and I did.

People don't seem to grasp easily the fundamentals of stock trading. I have often said that to buy on a rising market is the most comfortable way of buying stocks. Now, the point is not so much to buy as cheap as possible or go short at top prices, but to buy or sell at the right time. When I am bearish and I sell a stock, each sale must be at a lower level than the previous sale. When I am buying, the reverse is true. I must buy on a rising scale. I don't buy long stock on a scale down, I buy on a scale up.

Let us suppose, for example, that I am buying some stock. I'll buy two thousand shares at 110. If the stock goes up to 111 after I buy it I am, at least temporarily, right in my operation, because it is a point higher; it shows me a profit. Well, because I am right I go in and buy another two thousand shares. If the market is still rising I buy a third lot of two thousand shares. Say the price goes to 114. I think it is enough for the time being. I now have a trading basis to work from. I am long six thousand shares at an average of 111¾, and

7.1 ▶ **"Deacon" White** was one of the more honorable and upstanding of the Wall Street operators of this era. He was a director for Western Union and the Lackawanna railroad. Henry Clews calls him a "bold, dashing operator in stocks, and in Wall Street has met with considerable success." Clews goes on to say: "He is a ready and forcible speaker, full of vim and fire."[1]

Stephen Van Cullen White was born in North Carolina in 1831. His family maintained a small farm, and in the winter months the boy turned to trapping, selling the skins of the animals he captured. He endeavored to become a lawyer and enrolled in the prep school of Knox College in Galesburg, Illinois.

White practiced law until 1865, when he moved to New York, joined the New York Stock Exchange, and worked as a banker and broker. He went bankrupt over a $1 million loss in 1891 but was released from his obligations to trade again with $200,000 after promising to repay his debts in full. In less than a year, he did just that and was readmitted to the NYSE in 1892. He would go on to fail a few more times but always repaid his creditors.[2, 3] In 1886, he was elected to Congress from Brooklyn.[4]

Although White was a member of Plymouth Church in Brooklyn for many years, this was not the source of his nickname. According to a *Munsey's Magazine* profile in January 1894, White said the sobriquet came from a newspaper reporter in a case of mistaken identity.

White was also a poet, renowned Latin translator, classical scholar, and astronomer. He was sympathetic to antislavery advocates and helped build a house for African Americans near his home in Illinois.[5]

Despite his many good works, S. V. White was not above making trouble. His most famous exploit was the Lackawanna corner in 1883, called "the only really successful corner in Wall Street since Commodore Vanderbilt's time."[6] The operation netted the lawyer $2 million in profits. White also tried to corner corn in 1891 but failed after accumulating 10 million bushels at 48cents. The price went up but dropped before the Deacon could unload his position.[7] In total, though, he was held up as one of the few operators of the time with an ethical backbone.

White crossed paths with a young E. H. Harriman in 1874 while attempting to corner the so-called anthracite stocks. These were railroads responsible for hauling coal. Harriman, a commission broker at the time, noted the rise in these stocks and, according to his biographer, "felt sure someone was trying to monopolize them for speculative purposes. He did not believe that the shares were intrinsically worth the prices that were being offered for them, and when the rise seemed to have reached its culmination, he sold them short."[8] White was not able to get enough shares to secure the corner, and in the resulting sell-off, Harriman cleared $150,000.

Edwin Lefevre also wrote of White, who died in 1913, in a *Saturday Evening Post* series warning against stock speculation in 1915. He said:

Of the older men of the generation that preceded [Bet-a-Million] Gates the most picturesque that I have known personally was Stephen Van Cullen White. He tried to beat the game. He made millions—and lost them. He was three times a millionaire and he died poor....He had a remarkable mind; he distinguished between what was impossible as few other men; he had courage without rashness; patience and genius for striking at the right moment. Over and above all this he had character in the highest degree. Yet he died poor, because the game he tried to beat, beat him.[9]

the stock is selling at 114. I won't buy any more just then. I wait and see. I figure that at some stage of the rise there is going to be a reaction. I want to see how the market takes care of itself after that reaction. It will probably react to where I got my third lot. Say that after going higher it falls back to 112¼, and then rallies. Well, just as it goes back to 113¾ I shoot an order to buy four thousand—at the market of course. Well, if I get that four thousand at 113¾

I know something is wrong and I'll give a testing order—that is, I'll sell one thousand shares to see how the market takes it. But suppose that of the order to buy the four thousand shares that I put in when the price was 113¾ I get two thousand at 114 and five hundred at 114½ and the rest on the way up so that for the last five hundred I pay 115½. Then I know I am right. It is the way I get the four thousand shares that tells me whether I am right in buying that particular stock at that particular time— for of course I am working on the assumption that I have checked up general conditions pretty well and they are bullish. I never want to buy stocks too cheap or too easily.

I remember a story I heard about Deacon S. V. White ⟨7.1⟩ when he was one of the big operators of the Street. He was a very fine old man, clever as they make them, and brave. He did some wonderful things in his day, from all I've heard.

It was in the old days when Sugar was one of the most continuous purveyors of fireworks in the market. H. O. Havemeyer, president of the company, was in the heyday of his power. ⟨7.2⟩ I gather from talks with the old-timers that H. O. and his following had all the resources of cash and clever-

7.2 ▷ **Henry Osborne Havemeyer** founded the American Sugar Refining Co. in 1891 after inheriting a small refinery business. In the mold of the Standard Oil Trust, a string of consolidations allowed American Sugar to dominate its industry. A profit margin of 1.1 cents per pound held in all seasons. The stock produced big annual dividend yields: 9% in 1892, 22% in 1893, and 12% in 1894 through 1899. According to Matthew Josephson in 1934, "H.O. Havemeyer would quietly raise the price of the American breakfast: 'Who cares for a quarter of a cent a pound?' he would say blandly."[10, 11] At left is his Manhattan mansion, where he and his wife amassed a legendary collection of European art.

7.3 The American Sugar Refining Co. was the crown jewel in the network of companies known as the Sugar Trust, all controlled by the Havemeyers. The company operated four refineries in Boston, Jersey City, Brooklyn, and New Orleans. Combined, these four facilities maintained about 70% of the nation's total capacity.[12] There were only six other refineries, and one of these, in San Francisco, was effectively controlled by the Sugar Trust. By the mid-1890s, the company controlled all but one of these competing facilities and increased its share of the market to 98%.

In the years that followed, budding competitors tried to grab some of the profits the Sugar Trust enjoyed as it expanded the margin between raw and refined sugar. Many, such as the United States Sugar Refining Company, never even got a chance to get started. The company was incorporated for the purpose of building a refinery in Camden, New Jersey. Before the plant was ready to open, American Sugar purchased all of its stock; as a result, the plant was never finished.[13]

7.4 This refers to the debate within Congress over free trade with Cuba in 1902 and the reduction or elimination of an import tariff. It was important to the sugar industry because of the potential for fierce competition with the island nation's tropical climate and ideal growing conditions for sugar cane compared to the less desirable sugar beets grown in the northeastern United States.

Beet sugar producers were represented at the time by Henry Oxnard and the American Beet-Sugar Association. Oxnard said at the time:

> Stripped of sentimentality and all extraneous considerations, and reducing the Cuban demands for free or freer sugar to its simplest equation, it is this: Shall the United States, through its agriculturists, produce its raw sugar, and in its factories scattered from the Atlantic to the Pacific, refine its products, or shall it permit foreign lands to export to it the raw material and content itself merely with the refining?[14]

The sugar beet interests attacked the Sugar Trust and accused it of being in league with foreign producers. From American Sugar's perspective, additional competition for raw sugar would boost the profitability of its large refining operations. The Sugar Trust was also accused of controlling the Cuban sugar crop.[15]

In the end, the Congress passed the Reciprocity Treaty of 1903, which granted Cuba a 20% discount on full sugar import tariffs. In the years that followed, Cuban producers came to be the major supplier of sugar to the United States: From less than 15% in 1900, Cuba's share of the U.S. sugar market fluctuated between 50% and 70% during the 1920s.[16]

ness necessary to put through successfully any deal in their own stock. They tell me that Havemeyer trimmed more small professional traders in that stock than any other insider in any other stock. As a rule, the floor traders are more likely to thwart the insiders' game than help it.

One day a man who knew Deacon White rushed into the office all excited and said, "Deacon, you told me if I ever got any good information to come to you at once with it and if you used it you'd carry me for a few hundred shares." He paused for breath and for confirmation.

The deacon looked at him in that meditative way he had and said, "I don't know whether I ever told you exactly that or not, but I am willing to pay for information that I can use."

"Well, I've got it for you."

"Now, that's nice," said the deacon, so mildly that the man with the info swelled up and said, "Yes, sir, deacon." Then he came closer so nobody else would hear and said, "H. O. Havemeyer is buying Sugar." **7.3**

"Is he?" asked the deacon quite calmly.

It peeved the informant, who said impressively: "Yes, sir. Buying all he can get, deacon."

"My friend, are you sure?" asked old S. V.

"Deacon, I know it for a positive fact. The old inside gang are buying all they can lay their hands on. It's got something to do with the tariff **7.4** and there's going to be a killing in the common. It will cross the preferred. And that means a sure thirty points for a starter."

"D' you really think so?" And the old man looked at him over the top of the old-fashioned silver-rimmed spectacles that he had put on to look at the tape.

"Do I think so? No, I don't think so; I know so. Absolutely! Why, deacon, when H. O. Havemeyer and his friends buy Sugar as they're doing now they're never satisfied with anything less than forty points net. I shouldn't be surprised to see the market get away from them any minute and shoot up before they've got their full lines. There ain't as much of it kicking around the brokers' offices as there was a month ago."

"He's buying Sugar, eh?" repeated the deacon absently.

"Buying it? Why, he's scooping it in as fast as he can without putting up the price on himself."

"So?" said the deacon. That was all.

But it was enough to nettle the tipster, and he said, "Yes, sir-ree! And I call that very good information. Why, it's absolutely straight."

"Is it?"

"Yes; and it ought to be worth a whole lot. Are you going to use it?"

"Oh, yes. I'm going to use it."

"When?" asked the information bringer suspiciously.

"Right away." And the deacon called: "Frank!" It was the first name of his shrewdest broker, who was then in the adjoining room.

"Yes, sir," said Frank.

"I wish you'd go over to the Board and sell ten thousand Sugar."

"Sell?" yelled the tipster. There was such suffering in his voice that Frank, who had started out at a run, halted in his tracks.

"Why, yes," said the deacon mildly.

"But I told you H. O. Havemeyer was buying it!"

"I know you did, my friend," said the deacon calmly; and turning to the broker: "Make haste, Frank!"

The broker rushed out to execute the order and the tipster turned red.

"I came in here," he said furiously, "with the best information I ever had. I brought it to you because I thought you were my friend, and square. I expected you to act on it——"

"I am acting on it," interrupted the deacon in a tranquillising voice.

7.5 The notion that sugar could be the basis for an exciting stock that traded with great volatility in large size is hard to grasp today. But the reality is that sugar was one of the most important crops in the development of industry and world trade in the seventeenth through early twentieth centuries, and has a bittersweet history.

While sugar was first grown commercially in India, and then dispersed through Europe and the rest of the world by Muslim refiners and traders, it was not cultivated on a massive scale until the opening of the New World by European merchant farmers. Most of the slave trade in the 1700s and 1800s was focused on transporting Africans to the Caribbean and South America to work sugar cane fields on plantations graced with the tremendous amount of rainfall the crop requires. On the plus side, the industrial base of the Caribbean and Brazil was built to refine sugar and its derivatives.

By the early twentieth century, sugar had already become inexpensive enough to satisfy the sweet tooth of the middle class at the breakfast table, providing the Havemeyer clan with its billions—but new commercial food products and techniques would soon bring sugar to the masses in the form of candy, cookies, and soda pop, ramping demand exponentially.

In 1900, Milton S. Hershey created the first milk chocolate bar, shown here, in his home town of Derry Church, Pennsylvania, which would later be renamed Hershey. In 1902, the National Biscuit Co., later renamed Nabisco, created its iconic circus wagon box for animal crackers, with a string attached so it could be hung on Christmas trees. Caleb Bradham, a North Carolina pharmacist, invented a competitor to Coca-Cola for sale in his drugstore in 1893, flavored with vanilla and pepsin, but didn't trademark the name for the commercial distribution of Pepsi-Cola until 1903. In 1904, the ice cream cone was invented at the St. Louis World's Fair. In 1905, Frank Epperson invented the Popsicle, though it was originally named the Epsicle. Around 1909, Nabisco debuted the Oreo cookie. And by 1910, the government estimated that there were over 80,000 soda fountains in the United States.

Trading in the commodity was tough even for insiders. Pepsi-Cola went bankrupt in 1923 after Bradham gambled on a big increase in the cost of sugar during World War 1. Prices actually fell in value, leaving Pepsi with an overpriced sugar inventory that crippled the firm. It was purchased out of bankruptcy and revived in the Depression with branding focused on low cost.

In the background all the while were traders like the White and Livermore providing liquidity for Sugar's shares.

"But I told you H. O. and his gang were buying!"

"That's right. I heard you."

"Buying! Buying! I said buying!" shrieked the tipster.

"Yes, buying! That is what I understood you to say," the deacon assured him. He was standing by the ticker, looking at the tape.

"But you are selling it."

"Yes; ten thousand shares." And the deacon nodded. "Selling it, of course." **7.5**

He stopped talking to concentrate on the tape and the tipster approached to see what the deacon saw, for the old man was very foxy. While he was looking over the deacon's shoulder a clerk came in with a slip, obviously the report from Frank. The deacon barely glanced at it. He had seen on the tape how his order had been executed.

It made him say to the clerk, "Tell him to sell another ten thousand Sugar."

"Deacon, I swear to you that they really are buying the stock!"

"Did Mr. Havemeyer tell you?" asked the deacon quietly.

"Of course not! He never tells anybody anything. He would not bat an eyelid to help his best friend make a nickel. But I know this is true."

"Do not allow yourself to become excited, my friend." And the deacon held up a hand. He was looking at the tape. The tip-bringer said, bitterly:

"If I had known you were going to do the opposite of what I expected I'd never have wasted your time or mine. But I am not going to feel glad when you cover that stock at an awful loss. I'm sorry for you, deacon. Honest! If you'll excuse me I'll go elsewhere and act on my own information."

"I'm acting on it. I think I know a little about the market; not as much, perhaps, as you and your friend H. O. Havemeyer, but still a little. What I am doing is what my experience tells me is the wise thing to do with the information you brought me. After a man has been in Wall Street as long as I have he is grateful for anybody who feels sorry for him. Remain calm, my friend."

The man just stared at the deacon, for whose judgment and nerve he had great respect.

Pretty soon the clerk came in again and handed a report to the deacon, who looked at it and said: "Now tell him to buy thirty thousand Sugar. Thirty thousand!"

The clerk hurried away and the tipster just grunted and looked at the old gray fox.

"My friend," the deacon explained kindly, "I did not doubt that you were telling me the truth as you saw it. But even if I had heard H. O. Havemeyer tell you himself, I still would have acted as I did. For there was only one way to find out if anybody was buying the stock in the way you said H. O. Havemeyer and his friends were buying it, and that was to do what I did. The first ten thousand shares went fairly easily. It was not quite conclusive. But the second ten thousand was absorbed by a market that did not stop rising. The way the twenty thousand shares were taken by somebody proved to me that somebody was in truth willing to take all the stock that was offered. It doesn't particularly matter at this point who that particular somebody may be. So

I have covered my shorts and am long ten thousand shares, and I think that your information was good as far as it went."

"And how far does it go?" asked the tipster.

"You have five hundred shares in this office at the average price of the ten thousand shares," said the deacon. "Good day, my friend. Be calm the next time."

"Say, deacon," said the tipster, "won't you please sell mine when you sell yours? I don't know as much as I thought I did."

That's the theory. That is why I never buy stocks cheap. Of course I always try to buy effectively—in such a way as to help my side of the market. When it comes to selling stocks, it is plain that nobody can sell unless somebody wants those stocks.

If you operate on a large scale you will have to bear that in mind all the time. A man studies conditions, plans his operations carefully and proceeds to act. He swings a pretty fair line and he accumulates a big profit—on paper. Well, that man can't sell at will. You can't expect the market to absorb fifty thousand shares of one stock as easily as it does one hundred. He will have to wait until he has a market there to take it. There comes the time when he thinks the requisite buying power is there. When that opportunity comes he must seize it. As a rule he will have been waiting for it. He has to sell when he can, not when he wants to. To learn the time, he has to watch and test. It is no trick to tell when the market can take what you give it. But in starting a movement it is unwise to take on your full line unless you are convinced that conditions are exactly right. Remember that stocks are never too high for you to begin buying or too low to begin selling. But after the initial transaction, don't make a second unless the first shows you a profit. Wait and watch. That is where your tape reading comes in—to enable you to decide as to the proper time for beginning. Much depends upon beginning at exactly the right time. It took me years to realize the importance of this. It also cost me some hundreds of thousands of dollars. **7.6**

I don't mean to be understood as advising persistent pyramiding. A man can pyramid and make big money that he couldn't make if he didn't pyramid; of course. But what I meant to say was this: Suppose a man's line is five hundred shares of stock. I say that he ought not to buy it all at once; not if he is speculating. If he is merely gambling the only advice I have to give him is, don't!

Suppose he buys his first hundred, and that promptly shows him a loss. Why should he go to work and get more stock? He ought to see at once that he is in wrong; at least temporarily.

7.6 Livermore reveals some tradecraft here, explaining with a colorful story that it's not enough to simply take a bullish tip from a source: It's important to test the idea against the market. If there's ample demand for the stock when it's first sold, or shorted, then there's probably enough buying power to drive it higher. But to take a recommendation blindly leaves the tip taker in the position of being the lowest level of sucker, or at best a gambler.

He also stresses two other big themes: Stocks are never too high to be bought or too low to be shorted, and a well-trained speculator never purchases the full amount that he wishes to apportion to a new position at the start of his buying.

After much trial and error in the early part of his career, Livermore has discovered that even if a stock like Sugar has already doubled in the past six months it can double again—but you won't know exactly how it trades, and how much money to put into it, until you own the shares yourself and become more intimately familiar with its volatility. If your first purchase results in a loss, he believes, you're not early, you're just wrong—so don't add more until, by rising, it shows that you are right. If your first purchase results in a gain, he recommends, then add more as it rises and it fulfills your expectations.

ENDNOTES

1 Henry Clews, *Fifty Years in Wall Street* (New York, Irving Publishing Company, 1908), 661–662.

2 *The Cyclopædia of American Biography,* vol. 5 (1897), 478.

3 John W. Leonard, "Albert Nelson Marquis," *Who's Who in America* (1901–1902), 1225.

4 Edward G. Riggs, Charles J. Rosebault, and C. J. Fitzgerald, "Wall Street," *Munsey's Magazine* (January, 1894): 360.

5 Ibid., 361.

6 Ibid.

7 "Banking and Financial News," *Banker's Magazine* 65 (July–December 1902): 1030.

8 George Kennan, *E. H. Harriman* (1922), 17.

9 Edwin Lefevre, "The Unbeatable Game of Stock Speculation," *Saturday Evening Post,* September 4, 1915, 29.

10 Matthew Josephson, *The Robber Barons* (New York: Harcourt, Brace and Company, 1934), 381.

11 Ibid.

12 Eliot Jones, *The Trust Problem in the United States* (1921), 93.

13 Ibid., 96.

14 "The Cuban Tariff Hearings," *Public Opinion,* January 30, 1902, 4.

15 *Public Opinion,* May 1, 1902, 1.

16 Alan Dye, *Cuban Sugar in the Age of Mass Production* (1998), 53.

The Union Pacific incident in Saratoga in the summer of 1906 made me more independent than ever of tips and talk—that is, of the opinions and surmises and suspicions of other people, however friendly or however able they might be personally. Events, not vanity, proved for me that I could read the tape more accurately than most of the people about me. I also was better equipped than the average customer of Harding Brothers in that I was utterly free from speculative prejudices. The bear side doesn't appeal to me any more than the bull side, or vice versa. My one steadfast prejudice is against being wrong.

Even as a lad I always got my own meanings out of such facts as I observed. It is the only way in which the meaning reaches me. I cannot get out of facts what somebody tells me to get. They are my facts, don't you see? If I believe something you can be sure it is because I simply must. When I am long of stocks it is because my reading of conditions has made me bullish. But you find many people, reputed to be intelligent, who are bullish because they have stocks. I do not allow my possessions—or my prepossessions either—to do any thinking for me. That is why I repeat that I never argue with the tape. To be angry at the market because it unexpectedly or even illogically goes against you is like getting mad at your lungs because you have pneumonia.

I had been gradually approaching the full realization of how much more than tape reading there was to stock speculation. Old man Partridge's insistence on the vital importance of being continuously bullish in a bull market doubtless made my mind dwell on the need above all other things of determining the kind of market a man is trading in. I began to realize that the big money must necessarily be in the big swing. Whatever might seem to give a big swing its initial impulse, the fact is that its continuance is not the result of manipulation by pools or artifice by financiers, but depends upon basic conditions. And no matter who opposes it, the swing must inevitably run as far and as fast and as long as the impelling forces determine.

After Saratoga I began to see more clearly—perhaps I should say more maturely—that since the entire list moves in accordance with the main current there was not so much need as I had imagined to study individual plays or the behaviour of this or the other stock. Also, by thinking of the swing a man was not limited in his trading. He could buy or sell the entire list. In certain stocks a short line is dangerous after a man sells more than a certain percentage of the capital stock, the amount depending upon how, where and by whom the stock is held. But he could sell a million shares of the general list—if he had the price—without the danger of being squeezed. A great deal of money used to be made periodically by insiders in the old days out of the shorts and their carefully fostered fears of corners and squeezes.

Obviously the thing to do was to be bullish in a bull market and bearish in a bear market. Sounds silly, doesn't it? But I had to grasp that general principle firmly before I saw that to put it into practice really meant to anticipate probabilities. It took me a long time to learn to trade on those lines. But in justice to myself I must remind you that up to then I had never had a big enough stake to speculate that way. A big swing will mean big money if your line is big, and to be able to swing a big line you need a big balance at your broker's.

I always had—or felt that I had—to make my daily bread out of the stock market. It interfered with my efforts to increase the stake available for the more profitable but slower and therefore more immediately expensive method of trading on swings.

But now not only did my confidence in myself grow stronger but my brokers ceased to think of me as a sporadically lucky Boy Plunger. They had made a great deal out of me in commissions, but now I was in a fair way to become their star customer and as such to have a value beyond the actual volume of my trading. A customer who makes money is an asset to any broker's office.

The moment I ceased to be satisfied with merely studying the tape I ceased to concern myself exclusively with the daily fluctuations in specific stocks, and when that happened I simply had to study the game from a different angle. I worked back from the quotation to first principles; from price fluctuations to basic conditions.

Of course I had been reading the daily dope 8.1 regularly for a long time. All traders do. But much of it was gos-

8.1 Livermore kept abreast of political and market conditions by being a voracious reader of trade and financial publications. Many of the resources available more than 100 years ago would be familiar to modern investors, including the *New York Times*, the *Economist*, and the *Wall Street Journal*. But many popular publications of this era have passed into history, most prominently the *Ticker and Investment Digest*, the *Magazine of Wall Street*, the *Kernel of Finance and Politics for Everybody*, *Dun's Review*, and the excellent *Commercial & Financial Chronicle*, which failed in the aftermath of the Black Monday crash of 1987.

THE TICKER INVESTMENT DIGEST

Investment: The placing of capital in a more or less permanent way, mainly for the income to be derived therefrom.	Speculation: Operations wherein intelligent foresight is employed for the purpose of deriving a profit from price changes.

Vol. 7   **NOVEMBER, 1910**   No. 1

What Makes the Market?

Article II.   Influence of Gold Production on Stock Prices

By G. C. Selden.

THE Commercial & Financial Chronicle

Entered according to Act of Congress, in the year 1899, by the WILLIAM B. DANA COMPANY, in the office of the Librarian of Congress.]

VOL. 68.   SATURDAY, JANUARY 7, 1899.   NO. 1750.

CLEARING HOUSE RETURNS.

For the month of December the clearings are the heaviest on record for any month. All but nineteen of the cities included in our statement show gains over the corresponding month of 1897, and in the aggregate for the whole country the excess reaches 23·4 per cent. For the twelve months the increase over the same period of a year ago is 20·2 p. c.

The week's total for all cities shows a gain of 24·7 per cent over 1897. The increase over 1896 is 62·6 per cent and the excess over 1895 is 33·4 per cent. Outside of New York the increase compared with 1897 is 13·6 per cent, the gain over 1896 is 32·7 per cent, and the increase over 1895 reaches 10·0 p. c

	Week ending December 31.				
Clearings at—	1898.	1897.	1898. P. Cent.	1896.	1895.
New York..........	975,590,275	789,557,262	+81·9	525,831,466	645,073,289

December.			Twelve Months.		
1898,	1897,	P. Ct.	1898,	1897,	P. Ct.

8.2 Livermore refers here to the flow and quantity of gold specie available to fund economic activity and investment. Between 1870 and 1914, much of the developed world was on the gold standard, in which paper currency was redeemable into measures of gold on demand. Therefore, money supply growth was limited to the success of gold mining operations and the cross-border flow of gold reserves. In short, countries shared a finite supply of money.

Simple economics controlled the supply of gold stocks. As an example, a sudden outflow of gold would cause a tightening of the money supply, a rise in interest rates, and a reduction in the general price level as the economy slowed. The increased competitiveness of cheap exports and more attractive interest rates would cause gold to flow back into the country and restore the previous equilibrium. Central bankers of the period operated according to these rules, expanding and contracting the money supply and raising or lowering interest rates accordingly.

With large policy exposures to the 1906 San Francisco earthquake and fire, foreign insurers, especially British firms, began sending gold to California to pay off claims. Between late April and May 1906 nearly $50 million of gold poured into the United States from Germany, France, the Netherlands, and England (whose contribution alone amounted to $30 million). Of these flows, 80% went directly to San Francisco. The city that staked its existence and prosperity on the mining and export of gold now was receiving huge amounts of gold back with which to replenish ashen wreckage.[1]

Other factors contributed to unusual supply constraints on gold during this period, which increased the price of money. The first was the Boer War that Livermore mentions. Officially known as the Second Boer War, and waged between 1899 and 1902, it was a conflict fought between the British Empire and two independent Boer republics in present-day South Africa upon the discovery of massive gold deposits. Not only was money put to nonproductive use buying arms and other war supplies, but full gold production did not resume until 1905—dampening the influx of new capital at a time of feverish speculation and capital investment. (Photo on page 119 shows *London Morning Post* war correspondent Winston Churchill, far right, after being captured by Boers in 1899 and held in Pretoria. His heroism during an ambush of a British army unit he was covering helped launch his political career.)

Another development was the outbreak of war between Russia and Japan in 1904, following a previous conflict between 1884 and 1885 over competing claims on Manchuria and Korea. To fund the war, both Japan and Russia tapped the credit markets of neutral nations—Russian

sip, some of it deliberately false, and the rest merely the personal opinion of the writers. The reputable weekly reviews when they touched upon underlying conditions were not entirely satisfactory to me. The point of view of the financial editors was not mine as a rule. It was not a vital matter for them to marshal their facts and draw their conclusions from them, but it was for me. Also there was a vast difference in our appraisal of the element of time. The analysis of the week that had passed was less important to me than the forecast of the weeks that were to come.

For years I had been the victim of an unfortunate combination of inexperience, youth and insufficient capital. But now I felt the elation of a discoverer. My new attitude toward the game explained my repeated failures to make big money in New York. But now with adequate resources, experience and confidence, I was in such a hurry to try the new key that I did not notice that there was another lock on the door—a time lock! It was a perfectly natural oversight. I had to pay the usual tuition—a good whack per each step forward.

I studied the situation in 1906 and I thought that the money outlook was particularly serious. **8.2** Much actual wealth the world over had been destroyed. Everybody must sooner or later feel the pinch, and therefore nobody would be in position to help anybody. It would not be the kind of hard times that comes from the swapping of a house worth ten thousand dollars for a carload of race horses worth eight thousand dollars. It was the complete destruction of the house by fire and of most of the horses by a railroad wreck. It was good hard cash that went up in cannon smoke in the Boer War, and the millions spent for feeding nonproducing soldiers in South Africa meant no help from British investors as in the past. Also, the earthquake and the fire in San Francisco and other disasters touched everybody—manufacturers, farmers, merchants, labourers and millionaires. The railroads must suffer greatly. I figured that nothing could stave off one peach of a smash. Such being the case there was but one thing to do—sell stocks!

I told you I had already observed that my initial transaction, after I made up my mind which way I was going to trade, was apt to show me a profit. And now when I decided to sell I plunged. Since we undoubtedly were entering upon a genuine bear market I was sure I should make the biggest killing of my career.

The market went off. Then it came back. It shaded off and then it began to advance steadily. My paper profits vanished and my paper losses grew. One day it looked as if not a bear would be left to tell the tale of the strictly genuine bear market. I couldn't stand the gaff. I covered. It was just as well. If I hadn't I wouldn't have had enough left to buy a postal card. I lost most of my fur, but it was better to live to fight another day.

I had made a mistake. But where? I was bearish in a bear market. That was wise. I had sold stocks short. That was proper. I had sold them too soon. That was costly. My position was right but my play was wrong. However, every day brought the market nearer to the inevitable smash. So I waited and when the rally began to falter and pause I let them have as much stock as my sadly diminished margins permitted. I was right this time—for exactly one whole day, for on the next there was another rally. Another big bite out of yours truly! So I read the tape and covered and waited. In due course I sold again—and again they went down promisingly and then they rudely rallied.

bonds were floated in Paris while Japanese issues were sold in London and New York. Overall, historian Alexander Dana Noyes estimated that neutral markets spent roughly $1 billion on "pure waste; it does not return to the channels of industry, and it diminishes the world's reserve of capital."

Before 1913, the United States lacked a central bank that could temper the economic volatility associated with gold flows. Indeed, historians argue that unusual gold movements were responsible for most financial crises and economic downturns in the pre-Federal Reserve era. Complications in the United States associated with gold flows set the stage for the defining moment of Livermore's early trading career: the Panic of 1907.

8.3 As gold specie flowed from London to San Francisco to settle fire insurance claims following the earthquake, a liquidity crisis began. The huge outflow of wealth tightened monetary conditions in England to such an extent that the Bank of England was forced to double its discount rate in an attempt to attract foreign gold. The situation was so dire that the Bank of France was forced to help by forwarding some £3 million worth of gold to "take some share in the international burden," according to Hartley Withers, financial editor of the *Times* of London.[2]

Eventually, the Bank of England retaliated by instituting a discriminatory policy against capital flows to the United States. This effectively cut off exports of gold, turned England from an exporter to an importer of capital, and pushed the American economy into recession. With gold no longer flowing from London, the New York financial markets were extremely vulnerable as interest rates were raised in an effort to restock depleted gold reserves.

The global economy was also booming. "Everything is in motion," wrote Noyes; "railways, steamers, factories, harbors, docks; it is evident that so gigantic a development of trade and industry could not fail to have a marked influence upon the positions of the international money market."[3] Surpassing what was seen in 1901, a flood of speculation further increased demand on bank deposits and gold reserves as stock traders went on margin to profit from rising prices.

This fever was by no means limited to the United States. The cessation of hostilities in Japan in the summer of 1905 was followed by what the government described as a "fever of enterprise" in which "prices of securities rose higher and higher."[4] The German central bank raised its discount rate from 5% to 6% in late 1905, the highest level reached except during financial panics, in an attempt to curb the speculative mania. In Egypt between 1905 and 1907, stock and land speculation reached a point that the chairman of the Bank of Egypt described as meaning that the "people were apparently mad; I do not know what other word to use; they seemed to think that every company that came out was worth double its value before it had even started business."[5]

The pressure on the banking system grew until on November 11, 1905, the reserves of New York banks fell below the 25% ratio to deposits required by the National Bank Act. As a result, the rates for demand loans on Wall Street increased to 25%, but stocks continued to rise. On December 28, the rate reached 125%. A few days later, Jacob Schiff told the New York Chamber of Commerce, "If the currency conditions of this country are not changed materially, I predict that you will have such a panic in this country as will make all previous panics look like child's play."[6]

It looked as if the market were doing its best to make me go back to my old and simple ways of bucket-shop trading. It was the first time I had worked with a definite forward-looking plan embracing the entire market instead of one or two stocks. I figured that I must win if I held out. Of course at that time I had not developed my system of placing my bets or I would have put out my short line on a declining market, as I explained to you the last time. I would not then have lost so much of my margin. I would have been wrong but not hurt. You see, I had observed certain facts but had not learned to co-ordinate them. My incomplete observation not only did not help but actually hindered.

I have always found it profitable to study my mistakes. Thus I eventually discovered that it was all very well not to lose your bear position in a bear market, but that at all times the tape should be read to determine the propitiousness of the time for operating. If you begin right you will not see your profitable position seriously menaced; and then you will find no trouble in sitting tight.

Of course to-day I have greater confidence in the accuracy of my observations—in which neither hopes nor hobbies play any part—and also I have greater facilities for verifying my facts as well as for variously testing the correctness of my views. But in 1906 the succession of rallies dangerously impaired my margins.

I was nearly twenty-seven years old. I had been at the game twelve years. But the first time I traded because of a crisis that was still to come I found that I had been using a telescope. Between my first glimpse of the storm cloud and the time for cashing in on the big break the stretch was evidently so much greater than I had thought that I began to wonder whether I really saw what I thought I saw so clearly. We had had many warnings and sensational ascensions in call-money rates. **8.3** Still some of the great financiers talked hopefully—at least to newspaper reporters—and the ensuing rallies in the stock market gave the lie to the calamity howlers. Was I fundamentally wrong in being bearish or merely temporarily wrong in having begun to sell short too soon?

I decided that I began too soon, but that I really couldn't help it. Then the market began to sell off. That was my opportunity. I sold all I could, and then stocks rallied again, to quite a high level.

It cleaned me out.

There I was—right and busted!

I tell you it was remarkable. What happened was this: I looked ahead and saw a big pile of dollars. Out of it stuck a sign. It had "Help yourself," on it, in huge letters. Beside it stood a cart with "Lawrence Livingston Trucking Corporation" painted on its side. I had a brand-new shovel in my hand. There was not another soul in sight, so I had no competition in the gold-shoveling, which is one beauty of seeing the dollar-heap ahead of others. The people who might have seen it if they had stopped to look were just then looking at baseball games instead, or motoring or buying houses to be paid for with the very dollars that I saw. ◁**8.4**] That was the first time that I had seen big money ahead, and I naturally started toward it on the run. Before I could reach the dollar-pile my wind went back on me and I fell to the ground. The pile of dollars was still there, but I had lost the shovel, and the wagon was gone. So much for sprinting too soon! I was too eager to prove to myself that I had seen real dollars and not a mirage. I saw, and knew that I saw. Thinking about the reward for my excellent sight kept me from considering the distance to the dollar-heap. I should have walked and not sprinted.

That is what happened. I didn't wait to determine whether or not the time was right for plunging on the bear side. On the one occasion when I should have invoked the aid of my tape-reading I didn't do it. That is how I came to learn that even when one is properly bearish at the very beginning

8.4 Baseball was the nation's most popular professional sport in the 1890s and early 1900s. In 1906, the Chicago Cubs lost in the World Series to the Chicago White Sox. The Cubs were led by the famed infield combination of Joe Tinker, Johnny Evers, and Frank Chance; their best pitcher was "Three Finger" Mordecai Brown, who went 26-6 with a 1.04 earned run average. New York had two teams: the Highlanders in the American League, which would change its name to the Yankees seven years later, and the Giants in the National League. In 1907, the Chicago Cubs beat the Detroit Tigers in the World Series. Future Hall of Famer Ty Cobb led the Tigers' attack, and in August that year, he got the first professional hit, a bunt single, off another future Hall of Famer, fire-balling pitcher Walter "Big Train" Johnson.

8.5 With monetary conditions tightening, James Hill wanted to lock up the capital needed to maintain and expand his rail network before it became unavailable. For illustration, look at the situation with the Northern Pacific. From 1898 to 1907, net earnings more than doubled, from $13 million to $33 million, as track mileage went from 4,350 to 5,444. Some $87 million in capital expenditures were made during this period. Wrote University of California at Berkeley business professor Stuart Daggett at the time:

> Grades have been reduced, lines straightened, new branches built, real estate acquired, track re-laid and ballasted, bridges strengthened and renewed, equipment rebuilt and increased in amount, and other similar betterments undertaken. It is a work which all the great American systems have carried on.[7]

Due to the need to continue these efforts, shareholders voted to issue new common stock. The proceeds were aimed at improvements previously made out of cash flow.[8] Clearly, the directors were looking to hoard capital and protect dividend payments as the economic situation deteriorated.

The stock market situation warranted the change. In late 1905 to early 1906, there was a big boom in railroad stocks as years of fierce competition, reorganizations, and consolidations paved the way for increased profitability. In the fall of 1905, the Great Northern raised $25 million in equity capital and, corroborating Livermore's account of events, "gave to its stockholders the privilege of subscribing to the new issue at par."[9] Soon afterward, the Northern Pacific was bid up to $232.50 a share while the Great Northern zoomed to $348 compared to par values of $100.

8.6 To fully understand Livermore's reaction to the share offering on what amounted to an installment plan, one must understand how new the concept was at that time. For instance, the modern automobile loan was not created until 1919 by General Motors. Until then, people would enroll in savings plans, socking away a few dollars a week until they had enough to purchase a car with cash.[10] Thus, a move to an installment payment plan was a clear sign of desperation.

In December 1906, the Great Northern offered $60 million in new stock at par, raising its capital to $210 million with payment extended over 16 months to April 1908. The Northern Pacific railway also offered $93 million in new stock at par, increasing its capital to $250 million with the last payment not required until January 1909.[11] An interest rate of 5% was charged on unpaid balances.[12]

Prices then broke badly, mainly because of tight money and the large new capital dilutions announced by Great

of a bear market it is well not to begin selling in bulk until there is no danger of the engine backfiring.

I had traded in a good many thousands of shares at Harding's office in all those years, and, moreover, the firm had confidence in me and our relations were of the pleasantest. I think they felt that I was bound to be right again very shortly and they knew that with my habit of pushing my luck all I needed was a start and I'd more than recover what I had lost. They had made a great deal of money out of my trading and they would make more. So there was no trouble about my being able to trade there again as long as my credit stood high.

The succession of spankings I had received made me less aggressively cocksure; perhaps I should say less careless, for of course I knew I was just so much nearer to the smash. All I could do was wait watchfully, as I should have done before plunging. It wasn't a case of locking the stable after the horse was stolen. I simply had to be sure, the next time I tried. If a man didn't make mistakes he'd own the world in a month. But if he didn't profit by his mistakes he wouldn't own a blessed thing.

Well, sir, one fine morning I came downtown feeling cocksure once more. There wasn't any doubt this time. I had read an advertisement in the financial pages of all the newspapers that was the high sign I hadn't had the sense to wait for before plunging. It was the announcement of a new issue of stock by the Northern Pacific and Great Northern roads. **8.5** The payments were to be made on the installment plan for the convenience of the stockholders. This consideration was something new in Wall Street. It struck me as more than ominous. **8.6**

For years the unfailing bull item on Great Northern preferred had been the announcement that another melon was to be cut, said melon consisting of the right of the lucky stockholders to subscribe at par to a new issue of Great Northern stock. These rights were valuable, since the market price was always way above par. But now the money market was such that the most powerful banking houses in the country were none too sure the stockholders would be able to pay cash for the bargain. And Great Northern preferred was selling at about 330! ⟨**8.7**⟩

As soon as I got to the office I told Ed Harding, "The time to sell is right now. This is when I should have begun. Just look at that ad, will you?"

He had seen it. I pointed out what the bankers' confession amounted to in my opinion, but he couldn't quite see the big break right on top of us. He thought it better to wait before putting out a very big short line by reason of the market's habit of having big rallies. If I waited prices might be lower, but the operation would be safer.

"Ed," I said to him, "the longer the delay in starting the sharper the break will be when it does start. That ad is a signed confession on the part of the bankers. What they fear is what I hope. This is a sign for us to get aboard the bear wagon. It is all we needed. If I had ten million dollars I'd stake every cent of it this minute."

I had to do some more talking and arguing. He wasn't content with the only inferences a sane man could draw from that amazing advertisement. It was enough for me, but not for most of the people in the office. I sold a little; too little.

A few days later St. Paul very kindly came out with an announcement of an issue of its own; either stock or notes, I forget which. ⟨**8.8**⟩ But that doesn't matter. What mattered then was that I noticed the moment I read it that the date of payment was set ahead of the Great Northern and Northern Pacific payments, which had been announced earlier. It was as plain as though they had used a megaphone that grand old St. Paul was trying to beat the two other railroads to what little money there was floating around in Wall Street.

Northern, Northern Pacific, and the Milwaukee & St. Paul railroads.[13] Prices also reversed at times and squeezed the short sellers—especially after the New York Central line increased its dividend by a quarter of a point—but the overall movement was down.

8.7 Preferred shares are a slightly different class of equity from common shares. Before dividends can be paid to common shareholders, preferred holders must receive a set dividend. After that, preferred holders are not entitled to additional disbursements of earnings. In this way, preferred stock has features of both debt and common equity.

In the case of Great Northern, the dividend on preferred shares was set at 7%, and James Hill "announced it as his opinion that 7% is a high enough dividend on any railroad stock,"[14] according to a newspaper report. To close the gap with other, higher-yielding railroad issues, Hill and a few other railroad men offered valuable subscription rights on new issuances of stock, which effectively boosted the dividend rate. In 1905, Great Northern preferred holders received rights valued at $33. Spread over a period of six years, this boosted the dividend yield to a whopping 12.5%.

8.8 The Milwaukee & St. Paul offered at par some $100 million to build its Pacific Coast extension through Montana, Idaho, and Washington from its hub on the shores of Lake Michigan. The last installment payment was not due till March 1909. Along with the offering from James Hill's railroads, the *Banker's Magazine* wrote in January: "It is not often that in one month so many large issues of securities are offered to the public or are announced as in contemplation as was the case last month."

8.9 This phrase arose from a popular comic strip, *Alphonse and Gaston,* that first appeared in the *New York Journal,* a newspaper owned by William Randolph Hearst, in September 1901. The strip, by Frederick Burr Opper, followed a pair of klutzy Frenchmen depicted as overly polite. The lines "After you, my dear Alphonse!" and "No, you first, my dear Gaston!" entered into the language as catchphrases that have endured to describe a situation in which an individual is courteous to a fault.

8.10 The Great Northern preferred shares hit a high of $348 on February 9, 1906, before sliding to a low of $178 on December 26.

The St. Paul's bankers quite obviously feared that there wasn't enough for all three and they were not saying, "After you, my dear Alphonse!" **8.9** If money already was that scarce—and you bet the bankers knew—what would it be later? The railroads needed it desperately. It wasn't there. What was the answer?

Sell 'em! Of course! The public, with their eyes fixed on the stock market, saw little—that week. The wise stock operators saw much—that year. That was the difference.

For me, that was the end of doubt and hesitation. I made up my mind for keeps then and there. That same morning I began what really was my first campaign along the lines that I have since followed. I told Harding what I thought and how I stood, and he made no objections to my selling Great Northern preferred at around 330, and other stocks at high prices. **8.10** I profited by my earlier and costly mistakes and sold more intelligently.

My reputation and my credit were reestablished in a jiffy. That is the beauty of being right in a broker's office, whether by accident or not. But this time I was cold-bloodedly right, not because of a hunch or from skilful reading of the tape, but as the result of my analysis of conditions affecting the stock market in general. I wasn't guessing. I was anticipating the inevitable. It did not call for any courage to sell stocks. I simply could not see anything but lower prices, and I had to act on it, didn't I? What else could I do?

The whole list was soft as mush. Presently there was a rally and people came to me to warn me that the end of the decline had been reached. The big fellows, knowing the short interest to be enormous, had decided to squeeze the stuffing out of the bears, and so forth. It would set us pessimists back a few millions. It was a cinch that the big fellows would have no mercy. I used to thank these kindly counsellors. I wouldn't even argue, because then they would have thought that I wasn't grateful for the warnings.

The friend who had been in Atlantic City with me was in agony. He could understand the hunch that was followed by the earthquake. He couldn't disbelieve in such agencies, since I had made a quarter of a million by intelligently obeying my blind impulse to sell Union Pacific. He even said it was Providence working in its mysterious way to make me sell stocks when he himself was bullish. And he could understand my second UP trade in Saratoga because he could understand any deal that involved one stock, on which the tip definitely fixed the movement in advance, either up or down. But this thing of predicting that all stocks were bound to go down used to exasperate him. What good did that kind of dope do anybody? How in blazes could a gentleman tell what to do?

I recalled old Partridge's favourite remark—"Well, this is a bull market, you know"—as though that were tip enough for anybody who was wise enough; as in truth it was. It was very curious how, after suffering tremendous losses from a break of fifteen or twenty points, people who were still hanging on, welcomed a three-point rally and were certain the bottom had been reached and complete recovery begun.

One day my friend came to me and asked me, "Have you covered?"

"Why should I?" I said.

"For the best reason in the world."

"What reason is that?"

"To make money. They've touched bottom and what goes down must come up. Isn't that so?"

"Yes," I answered. "First they sink to the bottom. Then they come up; but not right away. They've got to be good and dead a couple of days. It isn't time for these corpses to rise to the surface. They are not quite dead yet."

An old-timer heard me. He was one of those chaps that are always reminded of something. He

8.11 The Philadelphia & Reading Railroad operated throughout Delaware, Maryland, New Jersey, and Pennsylvania and was brought out of bankruptcy by J. P. Morgan in the aftermath of the Panic of 1893. The float on Reading—or the shares available for trade—was relatively small because of the tight control insiders maintained.[15] In December 1906, when Livermore likely was operating in the stock, it fell from $152 to $129 in two weeks. These figures do not match up with those given, but the story behind them remains intact. At right is a Philadelphia & Reading train in 1897.

said that William R. Travers, who was bearish, once met a friend who was bullish. They exchanged market views and the friend said, "Mr. Travers, how can you be bearish with the market so stiff?" and Travers retorted, "Yes! Th-the s-s-stiffness of d-death!" It was Travers who went to the office of a company and asked to be allowed to see the books. The clerk asked him, "Have you an interest in this company?" and Travers answered, "I sh-should s-say I had! I'm sh-short t-t-twenty thousand sh-shares of the stock!"

Well, the rallies grew feebler and feebler. I was pushing my luck for all I was worth. Every time I sold a few thousand shares of Great Northern preferred the price broke several points. I felt out weak spots elsewhere and let 'em have a few. All yielded, with one impressive exception; and that was Reading. **8.11**

When everything else hit the toboggan slide Reading stood like the Rock of Gibraltar. Everybody said the stock was cornered. It certainly acted like it. They used to tell me it was plain suicide to sell Reading short. There were people in the office who were now as bearish on everything as I was. But when anybody hinted at selling Reading they shrieked for help. I myself had sold some short and was standing pat on it. At the same time I naturally preferred to seek and hit the soft spots instead of attacking the more strongly protected specialties. My tape reading found easier money for me in other stocks.

I heard a great deal about the Reading bull pool. It was a mighty strong pool. To begin with they had a lot of low-priced stock, so that their average was actually below the prevailing level, according to friends who told me. Moreover, the principal members of the pool had close connections of the friendliest character with the banks whose money they were using to carry their huge holdings of Reading. As long as the price stayed up the bankers' friendship was staunch and steadfast. One pool member's paper profit was upward of three millions. That allowed for some decline without causing fatalities. No wonder the stock stood up and defied the bears. Every now and then the room traders looked at the price, smacked their lips and proceeded to test it with a thousand shares or two. They could not dislodge a share, so they covered and went looking elsewhere for easier money. Whenever I looked at it I also sold a little more—just enough to convince myself that I was true to my new trading principles and wasn't playing favourites.

In the old days the strength of Reading might have fooled me. The tape kept on saying, "Leave it alone!" But my reason told me differently. I was anticipating a general break, and there were not going to be any exceptions, pool or no pool.

I have always played a lone hand. I began that way in the bucket shops and have kept it up. It is the way my mind works. I have to do my own seeing and my own thinking. But I can tell you after the market began to go my way I felt for the first time in my life that I had allies—the strongest and truest in the world: underlying conditions. They were helping me with all their might. Perhaps they were a trifle slow at times in bringing up the reserves, but they were dependable, provided I did not get too impatient. I was not pitting my tape-reading knack or my hunches against chance. The inexorable logic of events was making money for me.

The thing was to be right; to know it and to act accordingly. General conditions, my true allies, said "Down!" and Reading disregarded the command. It was an insult to us. It began to annoy me to see Reading holding firmly, as though everything were serene. It ought to be the best short sale in the entire list because it had not gone down and the pool was carrying a lot of stock that it would not be able to carry when the money stringency grew more pronounced. Some day the bankers' friends would fare no better than the friendless public. The stock must go with the others. If Reading didn't decline, then my theory was wrong; I was wrong; facts were wrong; logic was wrong.

I figured that the price held because the Street was afraid to sell it. So one day I gave to two brokers each an order to sell four thousand shares, at the same time.

You ought to have seen that cornered stock, that it was sure suicide to go short of, take a headlong dive when those competitive orders struck it. I let 'em have a few thousand more. The price was 111 when I started selling it. Within a few minutes I took in my entire short line at 92.

I had a wonderful time after that, and in February of 1907 I cleaned up. **8.12** Great Northern preferred had gone down sixty or seventy points, and other stocks in proportion. I had made a good bit, but the reason I cleaned up was that I figured that the decline had discounted the immediate future. I looked for a fair recovery, but I wasn't bullish

8.12 Market weakness that started in December 1906 continued throughout 1907. The Great Northern preferred shares recovered slightly to $189.75 on January 2 before sliding all the way to $107.50 in October. The *Financial Review* wrote at the time: "The stock market was very much depressed during January, and there was a large and almost continuous decline in prices, with only fitful rallies except at the very close, when a somewhat more substantial recovery ensured. The disposition was to take a very unfavorable view of things."[16]

Railroad stocks continued to recover somewhat into the early part of February. We can imagine that Livermore, having successfully timed the steep decline of December and January thanks to his new approach to the market, cautiously closed out his positions during this reactionary move to protect his profits, with the sting of recent failures in mind.

Although Livermore made a small fortune on his short positions in the rails, they would remain among the most popular and successful stocks for decades. And they were not just owned by the tycoons in the bull pool that Livermore fretted about. In 1908, the *New York Times* ran a magazine cover story titled "Two Million Partners Own the Corporations," in which it complained about the "bitter warfare" that President Theodore Roosevelt was waging on large companies.

The *Times* said: "Who owns the corporations? The man in the street, whose financial education is gained from newspaper headlines and campaign cartoons, is forced to believe that a little coterie of Falstaffian gentlemen carry the ownership of the corporations around in their waistcoat pockets. But the hard, cold facts, as shown on the stock books of the great railroads and industrials of the country, show that there are 2,000,000 partners in American corporate enterprise, and that there are 20,000,000 persons whose savings are invested in these companies."[17]

Illustrated with the table below, the article continues, "The misinformed speak of the Sugar Trust and the Havemeyers as though they were interchangeable names for the same thing, but no stock is more widely distributed than Sugar. The Havemeyers have 20,000 partners. Mr. Harriman has 30,000 partners in his Western railway empire, nearly 12,000 of whom have joined him since the Government opened fire on him."

The article mounts the same defense for the Guggenheims before adding, with evident approval, that the public was defying the government's anti-trust crusade by putting its money into stocks at a pace "as never before in history."[17]

The next decade and a half would not be kind to investors who adhered to a buy-and-hold strategy. The month the article ran, the Dow Jones Industrial Average closed at 83. Despite considerable volatility along the way, it would still be trading at the same level in 1922, 14 years later.

THE PUBLIC'S INTERESTS IN PROMINENT STOCKS.

Stock.	Stock.	Shareholders.	Average Share Holdings.	Income Per Shareholder.
American Sugar	$90,000,000	20,000	45	$315
Pennsylvania	314,000,000	59,200	55	330
Pullman	100,000,000	13,500	75	600
Bell Telephone	180,000,000	24,100	75	600
Steel	868,000,000	110,000	79	320
New York Central	178,000,000	22,100	80	400
Amalgamated Copper	154,000,000	18,000	85	170
Atchison	217,000,000	25,000	87	435
Smelters	100,000,000	9,400	106	580
Southern Pacific	148,000,000	15,000	99	620
St. Paul	133,000,000	10,000	133	930
Erie	176,000,000	10,000	176	..
Union Pacific	295,000,000	15,000	196	1,560
Standard Oil	98,000,000	5,500	178	7,120
	$3,031,000,000	356,800	85	$580

*Exclusive of stock owned by Union Pacific.

enough to play for a turn. I wasn't going to lose my position entirely. The market would not be right for me to trade in for a while. The first ten thousand dollars I made in the bucket shops I lost because I traded in and out of season, every day, whether or not conditions were right. I wasn't making that mistake twice. Also, don't forget that I had gone broke a little while before because I had seen this break too soon and started selling before it was time. Now when I had a big profit I wanted to cash in so that I could feel I had been right. The rallies had broken me before. I wasn't going to let the next rally wipe me out. Instead of sitting tight I went to Florida. I love fishing and I needed a rest. I could get both down there. And besides, there are direct wires between Wall Street and Palm Beach.

ENDNOTES

1 Kerry A. Odell and Marc D. Weidenmier, "Real Shock, Monetary Aftershock: The 1906 San Francisco Earthquake and the Panic of 1907," *Journal of Economic History* (September 2002): 1002–1027.

2 Charles Kindleberger, *Manias, Panics, and Crashes* (1978), 189.

3 Alexander Dana Noyes, *Forty Years of American Finance* (New York: G.P. Putnam's Sons, 1909), 324.

4 Ibid., 325.

5 Ibid.

6 Ibid., 329.

7 Stuart Daggett, *Railroad Reorganization* (1908), 309.

8 Ibid.

9 George Kennan, *E. H. Harriman* (1922), 395.

10 Public Radio International, "Culture of Debt Driven by GM," March 9, 2000. http://marketplace.publicradio.org/display/web/2009/03/09/pm_gmac/.

11 "Retrospect," *Financial Review* (1907): 26.

12 "The Financial Situation," *New York Times*, December 17, 1906, 12.

13 Ibid.

14 "Subscription Rights as Extra Dividends," *New York Times*, August 27, 1906, 11.

15 "Topics in Wall Street," *New York Times*, November 4, 1905, 13.

16 "Retrospect." *Financial Review.* (1908) "Two Million Partners of Corporations." *New York Times Magazine*, SM1.

17 "Two Million Partners of Corporations." Oct. 4, 1908. *New York Times Magazine*, SM1.

I cruised off the coast of Florida. The fishing was good. I was out of stocks. My mind was easy. I was having a fine time. One day off Palm Beach some friends came alongside in a motor boat. One of them brought a newspaper with him. I hadn't looked at one in some days and had not felt any desire to see one. I was not interested in any news it might print. But I glanced over the one my friend brought to the yacht, and I saw that the market had had a big rally; ten points and more.

I told my friends that I would go ashore with them. Moderate rallies from time to time were reasonable. But the bear market was not over; and here was Wall Street or the fool public or desperate bull interests disregarding monetary conditions 〈9.1〉 and marking up prices beyond reason or letting somebody else do it. It was too much for me. I simply had to take a look at the market. I didn't know what I might or might not do. But I knew that my pressing need was the sight of the quotation board.

9.1 ▶ More than 14 years had passed since the last serious banking panic in 1893. The business community grew more confident after the return to the gold standard quelled the threat of inflation. A flurry of consolidation activity in major industries followed, which helped reduce competition and boost profitability. As a result, a speculative fever of rare magnitude dominated the public consciousness and redirected desperately needed funds from credit markets to the stock exchanges. The titans of banking and industry actively encouraged this in order to unload inside positions and cash out at the top.

But it was an unsustainable situation. Lefevre wrote of these conditions in a magazine article in 1908:

Aside from spasms of speculation in stocks and staples and metals, there has been unprecedented activity and expansion in industries and manufactures, not only in the United States but also in Germany and England and France. In our country, because of the national optimism, the expansion has been extraordinary, the volume of business simply colossal; our industries have grown at such a rate that we have been unable properly to finance that growth....We have had too much prosperity for the money; more than we could promptly pay for.[1]

This prosperity complicated the tight monetary conditions that prevailed in the wake of the 1906 San Francisco earthquake, the Boer War, and the war between Russia and Japan. All of these events increased the demand for gold just as its production was starting to wane worldwide. Interest rates rose as governments fought over what liquid capital remained.[2]

Add to this the advent of the trust company, which collected deposits and resembled a bank but undertook much more speculative investments and operated without regulatory oversights, and the financial system was left in a very vulnerable state. As a result, as Lefevre describes it:

[O]ne cloudy day somebody asked for a dollar, and, not getting it promptly enough, very promptly squealed. That squeal was the signal for the chorus to join—the chorus of the entire world, which also wanted Money! Money! MONEY! It is sad to want money and not get it. But to ask for your own money and not get it is the civilized man's hell.[3]

9.2 The beautiful resort town of Palm Beach, Florida, got its start after Standard Oil magnate Henry Morrison Flagler built two magnificent hotels in the area: the Royal Poinciana and the Breakers. Flagler also operated the Florida East Coast Railway, which served the town via an impressive overwater viaduct. Livermore's broker, E. F. Hutton, also had interests in the area.

Hutton and his wife, Marjorie Post—heiress of the Post Cereals fortune—built their huge Mar-a-Lago estate on Palm Beach Island. The grounds were later transformed into the Mar-a-Lago Club, a private resort complex renovated and owned by Donald Trump, a real estate developer who would have been at home in the wheeler-dealer days of the early 1900s.

In Livermore's time, the resorts were buzzing with the electricity and energy of the nation's new prosperity. Business tycoons, financers, and royalty could be seen in hotel lobbies, on the white-sand beaches, and in the dining halls of Flagler's impressive hotels.

My brokers, Harding Brothers, had a branch office in Palm Beach. **9.2** When I walked in I found there a lot of chaps I knew. Most of them were talking bullish. They were of the type that trade on the tape and want quick action. Such traders don't care to look ahead very far because they don't need to with their style of play. I told you how I'd got to be known in the New York office as the Boy Plunger. Of course people always magnify a fellow's winnings and the size of the line he swings. The fellows in the office had heard that I had made a killing in New York on the bear side and they now expected that I again would plunge on the short side. They themselves thought the rally would go to a good deal further, but they rather considered it my duty to fight it.

I had come down to Florida on a fishing trip. I had been under a pretty severe strain and I needed my holiday. But the moment I saw how far the re-

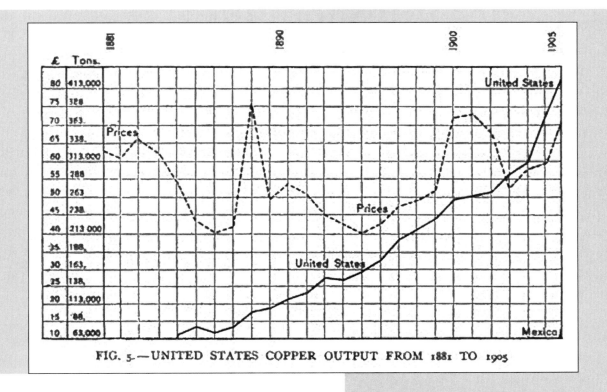

FIG. 5.—UNITED STATES COPPER OUTPUT FROM 1881 TO 1905

covery in prices had gone I no longer felt the need of a vacation. I had not thought of just what I was going to do when I came ashore. But now I knew I must sell stocks. I was right, and I must prove it in my old and only way—by saying it with money. To sell the general list would be a proper, prudent, profitable and even patriotic action.

The first thing I saw on the quotation board was that Anaconda **9.3** was on the point of crossing 300. It had been going up by leaps and bounds and there was apparently an aggressive bull party in it. It was an old trading theory of mine that when a stock crosses 100 or 200 or 300 for the first time the price does not stop at the even figure but goes a good deal higher, so that if you buy it as soon as it crosses the line it is almost certain to show you a profit. Timid people don't like to buy a stock at a new high record. But I had the history of such movements to guide me.

9.3 Copper plays an important role in the Panic of 1907, as an attempt to corner the stock of United Copper was the catalyst for numerous bank failures and a stock market crash.

The Anaconda Copper Mining Co. was founded by Marcus Daly in 1881 when he bought a small silver mine near Butte, Montana. After discovering a large deposit of copper, Daly sought outside investment to expand operations. First the Rothschild family got involved, purchasing stock in Anaconda. Then H. H. Rogers and William Rockefeller of Standard Oil formed the Amalgamated Copper Company in 1899 and purchased a majority share of Anaconda, thereby taking control of the company. From an initial stake of 75%, Amalgamated's share of Anaconda dropped to less than 40% by 1904.[4] The two companies were traded separately on the New York Stock Exchange.

By 1887, Anaconda was the largest, most productive copper mine in the world.[5] Like now, the late 1800s and early 1900s were a time of great industrial progress. The red metal was in high demand since it was used in electrical wiring and plumbing—both of which were important in the construction of everything from passenger railcars and ocean liners to office buildings and residences. Therefore, copper stocks were closely followed by traders and very sensitive to the economic outlook.

9.4 The par or face value of a share is an archaic concept that has little relevance to modern stock traders. Originally used to set a minimum price during the initial public offer process, the par value would be printed on the stock certificate. Today, most stocks are "no-par" issues or have a par value set at an extremely low value.

The concept of par value, however, is still used in relation to bond prices to describe the amount that the issuer will pay to the bondholder at maturity. When a bond is issued, it is described as being sold at a discount if the price is below its face value. Conversely, a bond sold for more than its face value is said to be trading at a premium.

In Benjamin Graham's classic *Security Analysis*, lowering the par value of the shares, as was the case with Anaconda, was described as being equivalent to a share split or a stock dividend. All of these actions would reduce the market value of the stock to better appeal to retail investors.[6]

Anaconda was only quarter stock—that is, the par of the shares was only twenty-five dollars. **9.4** It took four hundred shares of it to equal the usual one hundred shares of other stocks, the par value of which was one hundred dollars. I figured that when it crossed 300 it ought to keep on going and probably touch 340 in a jiffy.

I was bearish, remember, but I was also a tape-reading trader. I knew Anaconda, if it went the way I figured, would move very quickly. Whatever moves fast always appeals to me. I have learned patience and how to sit tight, but my personal preference is for fleet movements, and Anaconda certainly was no sluggard. My buying it because it crossed 300 was prompted by the desire, always strong in me, of confirming my observations.

Just then the tape was saying that the buying was stronger than the selling, and therefore the general rally might easily go a bit further. It would be prudent to wait before going short. Still I might as well pay myself wages for waiting. This would be accomplished by taking a quick thirty points out of Anaconda. Bearish on the entire market and bullish on that one stock! So I bought thirty-two thousand shares of Anaconda—that is, eight thousand full shares. It was a nice little flyer but I was sure of my premises and I figured that the profit would help to swell the margin available for bear operations later on.

On the next day the telegraph wires were down on account of a storm up North or something of the sort. I was in Harding's office waiting for news. The crowd was chewing the rag and wondering all sorts of things, as stock traders will when they can't trade. Then we got a quotation—the only one that day: Anaconda, 292.

There was a chap with me, a broker I had met in New York. He knew I was long eight thousand full shares and I suspect that he had some of his own, for when we got that one quotation he certainly had a fit. He couldn't tell whether the stock at that very moment had gone off another ten points or not. The way Anaconda had gone up it wouldn't have been anything unusual for it to break twenty points. But I said to him, "Don't you worry, John. It will be all right to-morrow." That was really the way I felt. But he looked at me and shook his head. He knew better. He was that kind. So I laughed, and I waited in the office in case some quotation trickled through. But no, sir. That one was all we got: Anaconda, 292. It meant a paper loss to me of nearly one hundred thousand dollars. I had wanted quick action. Well, I was getting it.

The next day the wires were working and we got the quotations as usual. Anaconda opened at 298 and went up to 302¾, but pretty soon it began to fade away. Also, the rest of the market was not acting just right for a further rally. I made up my mind that if Anaconda went back to 301 I must consider the whole thing a fake movement. On a legitimate advance the price should have gone to 310 without stopping. If instead it reacted it meant that precedents had failed me and I was wrong; and the only thing to do when a man is wrong is to be right by ceasing to be wrong. I had bought eight thousand full shares in expectation of a thirty or forty point rise. It would not be my first mistake; nor my last.

Sure enough, Anaconda fell back to 301. The moment it touched that figure I sneaked over to the telegraph operator—they had a direct wire to the New York office—and I said to him, "Sell all my Anaconda, eight thousand full shares." I said it in a low voice. I didn't want anybody else to know what I was doing.

He looked up at me almost in horror. But I nodded and said, "All I've got!"

"Surely, Mr. Livingston, you don't meant at the market?" and he looked as if he was going to lose a couple of millions of his own through bum execu-

9.5 Long-distance messages were transmitted in this era by Morse code, a rhythm-based communication system named for Samuel Morse, inventor of telegraphy. An intimate knowledge of Morse code would have allowed Ollie Black—a pseudonym, by the way, for a trader whose identity Livermore wished to hide—to translate Livermore's order by sound alone.

Black's eavesdropping technique would soon be obsolete. Manual tap entry was replaced by keyboard entry machines and automatic telegraphy equipment in the years after 1910. Telegram transmission reached a peak in 1919 when some 82 million messages were transmitted.[7] By 1969, it was down to eight million. In 2006, Western Union delivered its last telegram.

tion by a careless broker. But I just told him, "Sell it! Don't argue about it!"

The two Black boys, Jim and Ollie, were in the office, out of hearing of the operator and myself. They were big traders who had come originally from Chicago, where they had been famous plungers in wheat, and were now heavy traders on the New York Stock Exchange. They were very wealthy and were high rollers for fair.

As I left the telegraph operator to go back to my seat in front of the quotation board Oliver Black nodded to me and smiled.

"You'll be sorry, Larry," he said.

I stopped and asked him, "What do you mean?"

"To-morrow you'll be buying it back."

"Buying what back?" I said. I hadn't told a soul except the telegraph operator.

"Anaconda," he said. "You'll be paying 320 for it. That wasn't a good move of yours, Larry." And he smiled again.

"What wasn't?" And I looked innocent.

"Selling your eight thousand Anaconda at the market; in fact, insisting on it," said Ollie Black.

I knew that he was supposed to be very clever and always traded on inside news. But how he knew my business so accurately was beyond me. I was sure the office hadn't given me away.

"Ollie, how did you know that?" I asked him.

He laughed and told me: "I got it from Charlie Kratzer." That was the telegraph operator.

"But he never budged from his place," I said.

"I couldn't hear you and him whispering," he chuckled. "But I heard every word of the message he sent to the New York office for you. I learned telegraphy years ago after I had a big row over a mistake in a message. **9.5** Since then when I do what you did just now—give an order by word of mouth to an operator—I want to be sure the operator sends the message as I give it to him. I know what he sends in my name. But you will be sorry you sold that Anaconda. It's going to 500."

"Not this trip, Ollie," I said.

He stared at me and said, "You're pretty cocky about it."

"Not I; the tape," I said. There wasn't any ticker there so there wasn't any tape. But he knew what I meant.

"I've heard of those birds," he said, "who look at the tape and instead of seeing prices they see a railroad time-table of the arrival and departure of stocks. But they were in padded cells where they couldn't hurt themselves."

I didn't answer him anything because about that time the boy brought me a memorandum. They had sold five thousand shares at 299¾. I knew our quotations were a little behind the market. The price on the board at Palm Beach when I gave the operator the order to sell was 301. I felt so certain that at that very moment the price at which the stock was actually selling on the Stock Exchange in New York was less, that if anybody had offered to take the stock off my hands at 296 I'd have been tickled to death to accept. What happened shows you that I am right in never trading at limits. Suppose I had limited my selling price to 300? I'd never have got it off. No, sir! When you want to get out, get out.

Now, my stock cost me about 300. They got off five hundred shares—full shares, of course—at 299¾. The next thousand they sold at 299⅝. Then a hundred at ½; two hundred at ⅜ and two hundred at ¼. The last of my stock went at 298¾. It took Harding's cleverest floor man fifteen minutes to get rid of that last one hundred shares. They didn't want to crack it wide open.

The moment I got the report of the sale of the last of my long stock I started to do what I had really come ashore to do—that is, to sell stocks. I simply had to. There was the market after its outrageous rally, begging to be sold. Why, people were

9.6 ▶ As seen elsewhere in the book, Lefevre gives an account of stock prices that differs somewhat from the historical record. Anaconda's shares reached a high of $300 on February 13, 1906, before falling to $223.50 in May and ending the year at $290.[8] The motivation for the big move was reports from Montana that "ore veins of incredible richness" had been discovered in the company's mines.[9] As a result, Anaconda's dividend was increased from 14% to 24%.

The *New York Times* reported that F. Augustus Heinze, who had sold his copper smelting interests in Montana to the Amalgamated Copper Co. for $10.5 million in early 1906, was largely responsible for Anaconda's advance to $300.[10] No doubt this was done to maximize the purchase price of his assets. Heinze was likely behind the "aggressive bull party" that Livermore mentions.

9.7 ▶ In Chapter VIII, Livermore said:

The market went off. Then it came back. It shaded off and then it began to advance steadily. My paper profits vanished and my paper losses grew....I couldn't stand the gaff. I covered....If it hadn't I wouldn't have had enough left to buy a postal card. I lost most of my fur, but it was better to live to fight another day.

beginning to talk bullish again. The course of the market, however, told me that the rally had run its course. It was safe to sell them. It did not require reflection.

The next day Anaconda opened below 296. **9.6** Oliver Black, who was waiting for a further rally, had come down early to be Johnny-on-the-spot when the stock crossed 320. I don't know how much of it he was long of or whether he was long of it at all. But he didn't laugh when he saw the opening prices, nor later in the day when the stock broke still more and the report came back to us in Palm Beach that there was no market for it at all.

Of course that was all the confirmation any man needed. My growing paper profit kept reminding me that I was right, hour by hour. Naturally I sold some more stocks. Everything! It was a bear market. They were all going down. The next day was Friday, Washington's Birthday. I couldn't stay in Florida and fish because I had put out a very fair short line, for me. I was needed in New York. Who needed me? I did! Palm Beach was too far, too remote. Too much valuable time was lost telegraphing back and forth.

I left Palm Beach for New York. On Monday I had to lie in St. Augustine three hours, waiting for a train. There was a broker's office there, and naturally I had to see how the market was acting while I was waiting. Anaconda had broken several points since the last trading day. As a matter of fact, it didn't stop going down until the big break that fall.

I got to New York and traded on the bear side for about four months. The market had frequent rallies as before, and I kept covering and putting them out again. I didn't, strictly speaking, sit tight. Remember, I had lost every cent **9.7** of the three hundred thousand dollars I made out of the San Francisco earthquake break. I had been right, and nevertheless had gone broke. I was now playing safe—because after being down a man enjoys being up, even if he doesn't quite make the top. The way to make money is to make it. The way to make big money is to be right at exactly the right time. In this business a man has to think of both theory and practice. A speculator must not be merely a student, he must be both a student and a speculator.

I did pretty well, even if I can now see where my campaign was tactically inadequate. When summer came the market got dull. It was a cinch that there would be nothing doing in a big way until well along in the fall. Everybody I knew had gone or was going to Europe. I thought that would be a good move for me. So I cleaned up. When I sailed for Europe I was a trifle more than three-quarters of a million to the good. To me that looked like some balance.

I was in Aix-les-Bains ⟨9.8⟩ enjoying myself. I had earned my vacation. It was good to be in a place like that with plenty of money and friends and acquaintances and everybody intent upon having a good time. Not much trouble about having that, in Aix. Wall Street was so far away that I never thought about it, and that is more than I could say of any resort in the United States. I didn't have to listen to talk about the stock market. I didn't need to trade. I had enough to last me quite a long time, and besides, when I got back I knew what to do to make much more than I could spend in Europe that summer.

One day I saw in the Paris *Herald* a dispatch from New York that Smelters had declared an extra dividend. They had run up the price of the stock and the entire market had come back quite strong. Of course that changed everything for me in Aix. The news simply meant that the bull cliques were still fighting desperately against conditions—against common sense and against common honesty, for they knew what was coming and were resorting to such schemes to put up the market in order to unload stocks before the storm struck them. It is possible they really did not believe the danger was as serious or as close at hand as I thought. The big

9.8 Located in southeastern France, Aix-les-Bains was a popular vacation destination for American financiers and businessmen, including J. P. Morgan. Morgan frequently "took the waters," as they said at the time, and bathed in the area's natural hot sulfur springs for his health. It was here, where Morgan was accompanied by "a Frenchwoman of title and quality," that word of E. H. Harriman's assault on the Northern Pacific reached the banker in 1901—forcing him to relocate to Paris.[11]

9.9 ▶ Livermore is likely referring to the Smelters Security Corp., which was formed in 1905 by Jacob Schiff of Kuhn, Loeb for the purpose of controlling the American Smelting & Refining Co.[12, 13] The latter was founded in 1899 by Standard Oil tycoons H. H. Rogers and William Rockefeller. In June, after reporting strong results for the end of its fiscal year, American Smelting increased its annual dividend from 7% to 8%.[14]

9.10 ▶ After much delay, tight credit conditions finally began to be felt. The Bank of England increased its lending rate from 4% to 6% in October to stem the outflow of gold and warned London's investment houses to curtail the extension of credit to the United States on threat of an increase in rates to 7%. According to historian Alexander Dana Noyes, in both March and August, there occurred stock sales "so enormous, and at such sacrifice of values, as to convince the experienced Wall Street man, despite official denials, that forced liquidation by the largest financiers was under way."[15]

Lefevre wrote of the slump and its aftermath in *Everybody's Magazine*: "In Newport, Tuxedo, and Westchester County were heard voices ordering horses to be sold and stablemen to be dismissed; automobile repair-bills were angrily sent back for revision, and itemized accounts were insisted upon and extensions of time asked for."[16]

The financial contagion was truly global. Markets in Egypt, then Japan, were thrown into turmoil. Brokerages in Germany succumbed to the pressure of 10% call money. Banks were forced to close in Chile. Holland and Denmark suffered a "formidable convulsion of their credit markets, with numerous banking failures."[17] New York was next.

men of the Street are as prone to be wishful thinkers as the politicians or the plain suckers. I myself can't work that way. In a speculator such an attitude is fatal. Perhaps a manufacturer of securities or a promoter of new enterprises can afford to indulge in hope-jags.

At all events, I knew that all bull manipulation was foredoomed to failure in that bear market. The instant I read the dispatch I knew there was only one thing to do to be comfortable, and that was to sell Smelters ◀**9.9** short. Why, the insiders as much as begged me on their knees to do it, when they increased the dividend rate on the verge of a money panic. It was as infuriating as the old "dares" of your boyhood. They dared me to sell that particular stock short.

I cabled some selling orders in Smelters and advised my friends in New York to go short of it. When I got my report from the brokers I saw the price they got was six points below the quotations I had seen in the Paris *Herald*. It shows you what the situation was.

My plans had been to return to Paris at the end of the month and about three weeks later sail for New York, but as soon as I received the cabled reports from my brokers I went back to Paris. The same day I arrived I called at the steamship offices and found there was a fast boat leaving for New York the next day. I took it.

There I was, back in New York, almost a month ahead of my original plans, because it was the most comfortable place to be short of the market in. I had well over half a million in cash available for margins. My return was not due to my being bearish but to my being logical.

I sold more stocks. As money got tighter call-money rates went higher and prices of stocks lower. ◀**9.10** I had foreseen it. At first, my foresight broke me. But now I was right and prospering. However, the real joy was in the consciousness that as a trader I was at last on the right track. I still had much to learn but I knew what to do. No more floundering, no more half-right methods. Tape reading was an important part of the game; so was beginning at the right time; so was sticking to your position. But my greatest discovery was that a man must study general conditions, to size them so as to be able to anticipate probabilities. In short, I had learned that I had to work for my money. I was no longer betting blindly or concerned with mastering the technic of the game, but with earning my successes by hard study and clear thinking. I also had found out that nobody was immune from the danger of making sucker plays. And for a sucker play a man gets sucker pay; for the paymaster is on the job and never loses the pay envelope that is coming to you.

Our office made a great deal of money. My own operations were so successful that they began to be talked about and, of course, were greatly exaggerated. I was credited with starting the breaks in various stocks. People I didn't know by name used to come and congratulate me. They all thought the most wonderful thing was the money I had made. They did not say a word about the time when I first talked bearish to them and they thought I was a crazy bear with a stock-market loser's vindictive grouch. That I had foreseen the money troubles was nothing. That my brokers' bookkeeper had used a third of a drop of ink on the credit side of the ledger under my name was a marvellous achievement to them.

Friends used to tell me that in various offices the Boy Plunger in Harding Brothers' office was quoted as making all sorts of threats against the bull cliques that had tried to mark up prices of various stocks long after it was plain that the market was bound to seek a much lower level. To this day they talk of my raids.

From the latter part of September on, the money market was megaphoning warnings to the entire world. But a belief in miracles kept people

9.11 The Panic of 1907 began like so many other financial crises of this era: through an ill-fated exercise in unrestrained greed. At the center was Frederick Augustus Heinze. Born in Brooklyn and educated at Columbia University's graduate school of business, he made a mess of the Standard Oil crowd and their attempt to gain a foothold in the Montana copper business at the tender age of 36. Heinze bought judges, corrupted politicians, and made himself a populist hero by paying higher wages than his competitors. His main avenue of attack was a provision of federal mining legislation called the apex law—which allowed him to claim that his veins of copper ran beneath Amalgamated Copper's property.

After being paid millions to leave Montana, Heinze took his fortune to Wall Street, hooked up with "a little barrel-shaped man named Charles W. Morse" who built a monopoly in the ice business, and started buying small to midsize banks and trusts with the eventual goal of cornering copper stocks.[18] By controlling these institutions, Heinze and Morse could "command ready funds with which to play the market, and there wasn't a finer gambling game in the world," Lefevre wrote in a magazine article.[19]

Morse already controlled the Bank of North America. He used the bank's funds to buy the Mercantile National Bank, which in turn allowed him to buy the Knickerbocker Trust Co. in a process dubbed "chain banking," which involved the use of ownership shares as loan collateral.[20]

It was with these funds that Heinze and Morse started accumulating shares and options in the United Copper Co.—a firm Heinze had founded in 1902. Its Butte properties were sold to Amalgamated before Heinze used the company to acquire new mining assets in Nevada and British Columbia. No one really knew what was going on behind closed doors. As late as August, shareholders were worried about where Heinze was getting the money for United's generous dividend payments.[21] The Standard Oil crowd was watching, waiting for Heinze to overstep so they could exact their revenge.

They got their chance on October 14, 1907, when United Copper went from $37.50 to $60 while all other important mining stocks declined. The next morning, the *New York Times* reported a "Skyrocket Jump" as the stock blasted higher in the first 15 minutes of trading.[22] Heinze had started his short squeeze believing he controlled enough of the shares to effectively corner it. He did not.

The next morning shares collapsed to $38 as other shareholders—who likely included H. H. Rogers and William Rockefeller—sold into the rise and supplied short sellers with the stock certificates they needed to repay their loans. Also contributing to the slide was a bungled execution of Heinze's call options, negative stories about United

from selling what remained of their speculative holdings. Why, a broker told me a story the first week of October that made me feel almost ashamed of my moderation.

You remember that money loans used to be made on the floor of the Exchange around the Money Post. Those brokers who had received notice from their banks to pay call loans knew in a general way how much money they would have to borrow afresh. And of course the banks knew their position so far as loanable funds were concerned, and those which had money to loan would send it to the Exchange. This bank money was handled by a few brokers whose principal business was time loans. At about noon the renewal rate for the day was posted. Usually this represented a fair average of the loans made up to that time. Business was as a rule transacted openly by bids and offers, so that everyone knew what was going on. Between noon and about two o'clock there was ordinarily not much business done in money, but after delivery time—namely, 2:15 P.M.—brokers would know exactly what their cash position for the day would be, and they were able either to go to the Money Post and lend the balances that they had over or to borrow what they required. This business also was done openly.

Well, sometime early in October the broker I was telling you about came to me and told me that brokers were getting so they didn't go to the Money Post when they had money to loan. The reason was that members of a couple of well-known commission houses were on watch there, ready to snap up any offerings of money. Of course no lender who offered money publicly could refuse to lend to these firms. They were solvent and the collateral was good enough. But the trouble was that once these firms borrowed money on call there was no prospect of the lender getting that money back. They simply said they couldn't pay it back and the lender would willy-nilly have to renew the loan. So any Stock Exchange house that had money to loan to its fellows used to send its men about the floor instead of to the Post, and they would whisper to good friends, "Want a hundred?" meaning, "Do you wish to borrow a hundred thousand dollars?" The money brokers who acted for the banks presently adopted the same plan, and it was a dismal sight to watch the Money Post. Think of it!

Why, he also told me that it was a matter of Stock Exchange etiquette in those October days for the borrower to make his own rate of interest. You see, it fluctuated between 100 and 150 per cent per annum. I suppose by letting the borrower fix the rate the lender in some strange way didn't feel so much like a usurer. But you bet he got as much as the rest. The lender naturally did not dream of not paying a high rate. He played fair and paid whatever the others did. What he needed was the money and was glad to get it.

Things got worse and worse. Finally there came the awful day of reckoning for the bulls and the optimists and the wishful thinkers and those vast hordes that, dreading the pain of a small loss at the beginning, were now about to suffer total amputation without anæsthetics. A day I shall never forget, October 24, 1907. ◁9.11▷

Reports from the money crowd early indicated that borrowers would have to pay whatever the lenders saw fit to ask. There wouldn't be enough to go around. That day the money crowd was much larger than usual. When delivery time came that afternoon there must have been a hundred brokers around the Money Post, each hoping to borrow the money that his firm urgently needed. Without money they must sell what stocks they were carrying on margin—sell at any price they could get in a market where buyers were as scarce as money—and just then there was not a dollar in sight.

in newspapers controlled by the Rockefellers, and the calling of Heinze-Morse loans made by Rockefeller-influenced banks.[23] Heinze and Morse were forced to sell into the declining market to protect their banks' cash reserves. By October 16, United was selling at $10 a share.

The scheme collapsed, pulling down the brokerage houses of Gross & Kleeburg and Otto Heinze & Company. Bank runs began on the three institutions whose managements and directors were involved with the corner attempt and who were forced to resign: Mercantile National Bank, New Amsterdam Bank, and the Bank of North America. The crisis burgeoned as depositor uncertainty spread. There was a run on the Knickerbocker Trust on Tuesday, October 22, after its president, Charles T. Barney, was found to be involved; other banks stopped clearing its checks. Knickerbocker failed the next day as a line of depositors formed outside the Trust Company of America.

By October 24, the panic reached its zenith. J. P. Morgan had been recalled from a church convention and was busily organizing a response. Old friends and rivals—including James R. Keene, E. H. Harriman, and the Rockefellers—were seen at Morgan's opulent private library at 33 East 36th Street "as if they were visiting the Vatican,"[24] according to one account. Morgan decided that the line would be drawn at the Trust Company of America after his men examined its books and found it solvent: "Then, this is the place to stop the trouble,"[25] he said. By pooling the resources of the U.S. government as well as stronger financial institutions, Morgan was able to restore confidence in the banking system and end the crisis.

Heinze left Wall Street for the western frontier for a few years before he was sued in 1914 by Edwin Gould, son of Jay Gould, for $1.25 million in damages related to the sale of Mercantile National Bank stock. The jury awarded Gould the money, but he never collected. Heinze died, penniless, that November. Morse left town soon after the trial and was never heard from again. Charles Barney appealed to J. P. Morgan to save him from certain ruin but was rebuffed. Distraught, with his name tarnished, Barney died from a gunshot wound to the abdomen, an apparent suicide.[26, 27]

9.12 Prior to 1869, borrowing and lending activity in support of the trading on the exchange floor was done from office to office. Messenger boys would scurry up and down the muddied streets carrying stock certificates to be pledged as collateral. Banks demanded the highest rate and were the last to be asked for loans. In those days, brokers would rather ask their peers for a loan on more favorable terms. The atmosphere was collegial among the members of the New York Stock Exchange.

As transaction volumes grew, the old way of doing business became unwieldy. The "Loan Crowd" was given its own room inside the NYSE. Eventually, starting in 1878, the cohort by then known as the Loan Market was given a post to mark its place on the trading floor. The original was made of wood. This was replaced by one made of iron in 1881 that was probably still in use in 1907. But throughout its history, the Money Post always carried the number 10.[28]

My friend's partner was as bearish as I was. The firm therefore did not have to borrow, but my friend, the broker I told you about, fresh from seeing the haggard faces around the Money Post, came to me. ◁**9.12** He knew I was heavily short of the entire market.

He said, "My God, Larry! I don't know what's going to happen. I never saw anything like it. It can't go on. Something has got to give. It looks to me as if everybody is busted right now. You can't sell stocks, and there is absolutely no money in there."

"How do you mean?" I asked.

But what he answered was, "Did you ever hear of the classroom experiment of the mouse in a glass-bell when they begin to pump the air out of the bell? You can see the poor mouse breathe faster and faster, its sides heaving like overworked bellows, trying to get enough oxygen out of the decreasing supply in the bell. You watch it suffocate till its eyes almost pop out of their sockets, gasping, dying. Well, that is what I think of when I see the crowd at the Money Post! No money anywhere, and you can't liquidate stocks because there is nobody to buy them. The whole Street is broke at this very moment, if you ask me!"

It made me think. I had seen a smash coming, but not, I admit, the worst panic in our history. It might not be profitable to anybody—if it went much further.

Finally it became plain that there was no use in waiting at the Post for money. There wasn't going to be any. Then hell broke loose.

The president of the Stock Exchange, Mr. R. H. Thomas, so I heard later in the day, knowing that every house in the Street was headed for disaster, went out in search of succour. He called on James Stillman, president of the National City Bank, the richest bank in the United States. Its boast was that it never loaned money at a higher rate than 6 per cent.

Stillman heard what the president of the New York Stock Exchange had to say. Then he said, "Mr. Thomas, we'll have to go and see Mr. Morgan about this."

The two men, hoping to stave off the most disastrous panic in our financial history, went together to the office of J. P. Morgan & Co. and saw Mr. Morgan. Mr. Thomas laid the case before him. The moment he got through speaking Mr. Morgan said, "Go back to the Exchange and tell them that there will be money for them."

"Where?"

"At the banks!"

So strong was the faith of all men in Mr. Morgan in those critical times that Thomas didn't wait for further details but rushed back to the floor of the Exchange to announce the reprieve to his death-sentenced fellow members.

Then, before half past two in the afternoon, J. P. Morgan sent John T. Atterbury, of Van Emburgh & Atterbury, who was known to have close relations with J. P. Morgan & Co., into the money crowd. My friend said that the old broker walked quickly to the Money Post. He raised his hand like an exhorter at a revival meeting. The crowd, that at first had been calmed down somewhat by President Thomas' announcement, was beginning to fear that the relief plans had miscarried and the worst was still to come. But when they looked at Mr. Atterbury's face and saw him raise his hand they promptly petrified themselves.

In the dead silence that followed, Mr. Atterbury said, "I am authorized to lend ten million dollars. Take it easy! There will be enough for everybody!"

Then he began. Instead of giving to each borrower the name of the lender he simply jotted down the name of the borrower and the amount of the loan and told the borrower, "You will be told where your money is." He meant the name of

9.13 Thomas originally suggested that the stock exchange be closed until a more moderate tone prevailed. J. P. Morgan would not have it, since he believed that would only further damage confidence in the financial system. Immediately following his conversation with Thomas, Morgan had a telephone message sent to the presidents of all the banks in the area. At two o'clock, they all gathered at his office. Morgan's biographer, Herbert Satterlee, describes what happened next:

> When they had gathered in his room he explained the situation, which was that the Stock Exchange houses needed in the aggregate at least $25,000,000, and unless that sum could be raised within the next quarter of an hour he feared that at lease fifty firms would go under. Mr. Stillman was the first to speak up and said that the National City Bank would furnish $5,000,000 to loan on the Exchange before closing time. Mr. Morgan called on each of the other men present to state how much his bank would lend, and in turn they said, "$500,000," "$1,000,000," or "One-half million"; and Perkins took down the figures. Some of them kept quiet, and Mr. Morgan had to speak to them pretty plainly before they announced their contributions to the fund. However, in not more than five minutes $27,000,000 was at Mr. Morgan's command to loan to the Stock Exchange at 10 percent."[29]

the bank from which the borrower would get the money later.

I heard a day or two later that Mr. Morgan simply sent word to the frightened bankers of New York that they must provide the money the Stock Exchange needed.

"But we haven't got any. We're loaned up to the hilt," the banks protested.

"You've got your reserves," snapped J. P. **9.13**

"But we're already below the legal limit," they howled

"Use them! That's what reserves are for!" And the banks obeyed and invaded the reserves to the extent of about twenty million dollars. It saved the stock market. The bank panic didn't come until the following week. He was a man, J. P. Morgan was. They don't come much bigger.

That was the day I remember most vividly of all the days of my life as a stock operator. It was the day when my winnings exceeded one million dollars. It marked the successful ending of my first deliberately planned trading campaign. What I had foreseen had come to pass. But more than all these things was this: a wild dream of mine had been realised. I had been king for a day!

I'll explain, of course. After I had been in New York a couple of years I used to cudgel my brains trying to determine the exact reason why I couldn't beat in a Stock Exchange house in New York the game that I had beaten as a kid of fifteen in a bucket shop in Boston. I knew that some day I would find out what was wrong and I would stop being wrong. I would then have not alone the will to be right but the knowledge to insure my being right. And that would mean power.

Please do not misunderstand me. It was not a deliberate dream of grandeur or a futile desire born of overweening vanity. It was rather a sort of feeling that the same old stock market that so baffled me in Fullerton's office and in Harding's would one day eat out of my hand. I just felt that such a day would come. And it did—October 24, 1907.

The reason why I say it is this: That morning a broker who had done a lot of business for my brokers and knew that I had been plunging on the bear side rode down in the company of one of the partners of the foremost banking house in the Street. My friend told the banker how heavily I had been trading, for I certainly pushed my luck to the limit. What is the use of being right unless you get all the good possible out of it?

Perhaps the broker exaggerated to make his story sound important. Perhaps I had more of a following than I knew. Perhaps the banker knew far better than I how critical the situation was. At all events, my friend said to me: "He listened with great interest to what I told him you said the market was going to do when the real selling began, after another push or two. When I got through he said he might have something for me to do later in the day."

When the commission houses found out there was not a cent to be had at any price I knew the time had come. I sent brokers into the various crowds. Why, at one time there wasn't a single bid for Union Pacific. Not at any price! Think of it! And in other stocks the same thing. No money to hold stocks and nobody to buy them.

I had enormous paper profits and the certainty that all that I had to do to smash prices still more was to send in orders to sell ten thousand shares each of Union Pacific and of a half dozen other good dividend-paying stocks and what would follow would be simply hell. It seemed to me that the panic that would be precipitated would be of such an intensity and character that the board of governors would deem it advisable to close the Exchange, as was done in August, 1914, when the World War broke out.

It would mean greatly increased profits on paper. It might also mean an inability to convert those

9.14 While Livermore was enjoying himself, rightfully proud of his accomplishments, it was a time of extreme duress for the rest of Wall Street and for the average man. Perhaps empathy, and not just cold-blooded calculation, played into his decision to turn and go long as the panic deepened. In this photo we see a common sight during the panic: Depositors lined up outside the Nineteenth Ward Bank in New York, hoping to secure a share of their savings.

profits into actual cash. But there were other things to consider, and one was that a further break would retard the recovery that I was beginning to figure on, the compensating improvement after all that bloodletting. Such a panic would do much harm to the country generally.

I made up my mind that since it was unwise and unpleasant to continue actively bearish it was illogical for me to stay short. So I turned and began to buy. **9.14**

It wasn't long after my brokers began to buy in for me—and, by the way, I got bottom prices—that the banker sent for my friend.

"I have sent for you," he said, "because I want you to go instantly to your friend Livingston and say to him that we hope he will not sell any more stocks to-day. The market can't stand much more pressure. As it is, it will be an immensely difficult task to avert a devastating panic. Appeal to your friend's patriotism. This is a case where a man has to work for the benefit of all. Let me know at once what he says."

My friend came right over and told me. He was very tactful. I suppose he thought that having planned to smash the market I would consider his request as equivalent to throwing away the chance to make about ten million dollars. He knew I was sore on some of the big guns for the way they had acted trying to land the public with a lot of stock when they knew as well as I did what was coming.

As a matter of fact, the big men were big sufferers and lots of the stocks I bought at the very bottom were in famous financial names. I didn't know it at the time, but it did not matter. I had practically covered all my shorts and it seemed to me there was a chance to buy stocks cheap and help the needed recovery in prices at the same time—if nobody hammered the market.

So I told my friend, "Go back and tell Mr. Blank that I agree with them and that I fully realised the gravity of the situation even before he sent for you. I not only will not sell any more stocks to-day, but I am going in and buy as much as I can carry." And I kept my word. I bought one hundred thousand shares that day, for the long account. I did not sell another stock short for nine months.

That is why I said to friends that my dream had come true and that I had been king for a moment. The stock market at one time that day certainly was at the mercy of anybody who wanted to hammer it. I do not suffer from delusions of grandeur; in fact you know how I feel about being accused of raiding the market and about the way my operations are exaggerated by the gossip of the Street.

I came out of it in fine shape. The newspapers said that Larry Livingston, the Boy Plunger, had made several millions. Well, I was worth over one million after the close of business that day. But my biggest winnings were not in dollars but in the intangibles: I had learned what a man must do in order to make big money; I was permanently out of the gambler class; I had at last learned to trade intelligently in a big way. It was a day of days for me.

ENDNOTES

1 Edwin Lefevre, "The Game Got Them," *Everybody's Magazine* (January 1908): 7–8.

2 Robert Sobel, *Panic on Wall Street* (1968), 301.

3 Lefevre, "Game Got Them," 9.

4 John Moody, "The Truth About the Trusts," 1904. 3.

5 Horace J. Stevens and Walter Harvey Weed, *The Copper Handbook* (1911), 19.

6 Benjamin Graham, and David Le Fevre Dodd. "*Security Analysis.*" 441. 1934.

7 Beauchamp, K.G. "History of Telegraphy," 2001, 399.

8 "Retrospect," *Financial Review* (1907): 12.

9 "Topics in Wall Street." *New York Times,* October 17, 1906, 13.

10 Ibid.

11 Matthew Josephson, *The Robber Barons* (1934), 436.

12 Debi Unger, *The Guggenheims* (2005), 80.

13 "Some Smelted Finance," *New York Times,* May 14, 1905, 15.

14 "Smelting & Refining Co.'s Earnings Show Large Gain," *Wall Street Journal,* June 7, 1907, 5.

15 Alexander Dana Noyes, *Forty Years of American Finance* (1909), 358.

16 Lefevre, "The Game Got Them," 9.

17 Ibid., 363.

18 Frederick Lewis Allen, *The Lords of Creation* (1935), 115–116.

19 Ibid.

20 Noyes, *Forty Years of American Finance,* 365.

21 "Light on Heinze Mining Schemes," *New York Times,* August 1, 1907, 11.

22 "Skyrocket Jump in United Copper," *New York Times,* October 15, 1907, 11.

23 Sobel, *Panic on Wall Street,* 308.

24 Robert Sobel, *The Big Board* (1965), 193.

25 Ibid., 194.

26 Sobel, *Panic on Wall Street,* 321.

27 Robert F. Bruner and Sean D. Carr, *The Panic of 1907* (Hoboken: John Wiley & Sons, 2007), ix–xiii.

28 Stedman, Edmund Clarence. "The New York Stock Exchange," 1905, 448.

29 Satterlee, Herbert L. "J. Pierpont Morgan," 1940, 468–472.

The recognition of our own mistakes should not benefit us any more than the study of our successes. But there is a natural tendency in all men to avoid punishment. When you associate certain mistakes with a licking, you do not hanker for a second dose, and, of course, all stock-market mistakes wound you in two tender spots—your pocketbook and your vanity. But I will tell you something curious: A stock speculator sometimes makes mistakes and knows that he is making them. And after he makes them he will ask himself why he made them; and after thinking over it cold-bloodedly a long time after the pain of punishment is over he may learn how he came to make them, and when, and at what particular point of his trade; but not why. And then he simply calls himself names and lets it go at that.

Of course, if a man is both wise and lucky, he will not make the same mistake twice. But he will make any one of the ten thousand brothers or cousins of the original. The Mistake family is so large that there is always one of them around when you want to see what you can do in the fool-play line.

To tell you about the first of my million-dollar mistakes I shall have to go back to this time when I first became a millionaire, right after the big break of October, 1907. As far as my trading went, having a million merely meant more reserves. Money does not give a trader more comfort, because, rich or poor, he can make mistakes and it is never comfortable to be wrong. And when a millionaire is right his money is merely one of his several servants. Losing money is the least of my troubles. A loss never bothers

10.1 This is another key tenet of Livermore's style of trading, which he repeats several times in the book and has become a central theme of modern trading as well: Take losses quickly, and let your winners run.

10.2 Kentucky native Dickson G. Watts moved to New York at age 35. He joined the New York Cotton Exchange in 1870 and was twice elected president, with his last stint from 1878 to 1880.[1] He was a well-regarded trader of the era, and in fact, Livermore states that Watts "wrote the book on speculating," and quotes him repeatedly.

Watts's famed book, *Speculation as a Fine Art and Thoughts on Life*, is really a small pamphlet of epigrams, and only the first 15 pages focus on the markets. The story relayed here about a cotton trader who cannot sleep because he is worried about a large position is an embellished version of Watts's fourth "absolute" law. Watts argues that "when the mind is not satisfied with the position taken, or the interest is too large for safety," a trader should "sell down to a sleeping point."[2]

Watts's other laws show up elsewhere in *Reminiscences*. Watts argues that, contrary to popular opinion, "It is better to 'average up' than to 'average down,' " and explains why with a math exercise. He later argues that one should "never completely and at once reverse a position" from long to short, or vice versa, because it can be psychologically "very hazardous." The reason: Should the market reverse and go back to its original direction, "complete demoralization ensues." Instead, he says, change in the original position should be made "cautiously, thus keeping the judgment clear and preserving the balance of mind."

Elsewhere in his book, Watts declares that traders should not get too hung up on economic numbers because they obscure a comprehensive view of a market situation. He states: "Those who confine themselves too closely to statistics are poor guides" and then quotes British statesman George Canning's comment: "There is nothing so fallacious as facts, except figures."

Here are two more Watts's epigrams that show up in Livermore's words in *Reminiscences*: "When in doubt, do nothing. Don't enter the market on half-convictions." And: "A man must think for himself and follow his own convictions. A man cannot have another man's ideas any more than he can another man's soul or another man's body."[3]

me after I take it. **10.1** I forget it overnight. But being wrong—not taking the loss—that is what does the damage to the pocketbook and to the soul. You remember Dickson G. Watts' story about the man who was so nervous that a friend asked him what was the matter. **10.2**

"I can't sleep," answered the nervous one.

"Why not?" asked the friend.

"I am carrying so much cotton that I can't sleep thinking about it. It is wearing me out. What can I do?"

"Sell down to the sleeping point," answered the friend.

As a rule a man adapts himself to conditions so quickly that he loses the perspective. He does not feel the difference much—that is, he does not vividly remember how it felt not to be a millionaire. He only remembers that there were things he could not do that he can do now. It does not take a reasonably young and normal man very long to lose the habit of being poor. It requires a little longer to forget that he used to be rich. I suppose that is because money creates needs or encourages their multiplication. I mean that after a man makes money in the stock market he very quickly loses the habit of not spending. But after he loses his money it takes him a long time to lose the habit of spending.

After I took in my shorts and went long in October, 1907, I decided to take it easy for a while. I bought a yacht and planned to go off on a cruise in Southern waters. **10.3** I am crazy about fishing and I was due to have the time of my life. I looked forward to it and expected to go any day. But I did not. The market wouldn't let me.

I always have traded in commodities as well as in stocks. I began as a youngster in the bucket shops. I studied those markets for years, though perhaps not so assiduously as the stock market. As a matter of fact, I would rather play commodities than stocks. **10.4** There is no question about their greater legitimacy, as it were. It partakes more of the nature of a commercial venture than trading in stocks does. A man can approach it as he might any mercantile problem. It may be possible to use fictitious arguments for or against a certain trend in a commodity market; but success will be only temporary, for in the end the facts are bound to prevail, so that a trader gets dividends on study and observation, as he does in a regular business. He can watch and weigh conditions and he knows as much about it as anyone else. He need not guard against inside cliques. Dividends are not unexpectedly passed or increased overnight in the cotton market or in wheat or corn. In the long run commodity prices are governed but by one law—the economic law of demand and supply. The business of the trader in commodities is simply to get facts about the demand and the supply, present and prospective. He does not indulge in guesses about a dozen things as he does in stocks. It always appealed to me—trading in commodities.

Of course the same things happen in all speculative markets. The message of the tape is the same. That will be perfectly plain to anyone who will take the trouble to think. He will find if he asks himself questions and considers conditions, that the answers will supply themselves directly. But people never take the trouble to ask questions, leave alone seeking answers. The average American is from Missouri everywhere and at all times except when he goes to the brokers' offices and looks at the tape, whether it is stocks or commodities. The one game of all games that really requires study before making a play is the one he goes into without his usual highly intelligent preliminary and precautionary doubts. He will risk half his fortune in the stock market with less reflection than he devotes to the selection of a medium-priced automobile.

This matter of tape reading is not so complicated as it appears. Of course you need experience. But it is even more important to keep certain funda-

10.3 The period from 1880 to 1905 is considered to be the golden age of yachting, and all the market luminaries of the time, including the Astors, Vanderbilts, Morgans, Jay Gould, and William Randolph Hearst, tried to outdo each other by spending lavish sums on sail- and steam-powered boats with palatial interiors. Gould's biggest, the *Atlanta*, was 233 feet long and run by a crew of 52. William K. Vanderbilt had a 291-foot steamer called *Valiant* that had 20 staterooms for friends and family.[4]

The purchase of smaller yachts was well within the means of successful traders, who used them to go fishing out of marinas in Fort Myers, Miami, and Palm Beach.

10.4 Livermore prefers commodities because prices were less prone to manipulation. In arguing that commodities respond mainly to the laws of supply and demand, he further reveals his exasperation with what he calls "inside cliques."

10.5 In this chapter, Livermore provides the most extended explanation of his trading philosophy. It is one that any technical trader today would recognize: "Prices... move along the line of least resistance." He energetically explains that speculators should not worry whether a stock looks too cheap or too dear but only if it is more likely to go up or down.

Livermore further observes that stocks should be bought on breakouts and shorted on breakdowns; stocks are never too high to buy or too low to sell; a speculator must keep an open mind on fundamentals and focus primarily on price action; trends appear before news is published; bearish news is ignored in bull cycles, and vice versa; losing trades should never be added to, because "there is no profit in being wrong"; and a speculator's chief enemies are always the natural impulses of his own human nature. Echoing the words of Dickson Watts in laying down his "laws," Livermore adds that his views on trading are "incontrovertible statements" regardless of what anybody says to the contrary.

mentals in mind. To read the tape is not to have your fortune told. The tape does not tell you how much you will surely be worth next Thursday at 1:35 P.M. The object of reading the tape is to ascertain, first, how and, next, when to trade—that is, whether it is wiser to buy than to sell. It works exactly the same for stocks as for cotton or wheat or corn or oats.

You watch the market—that is, the course of prices as recorded by the tape—with one object: to determine the direction—that is, the price tendency. Prices, we know, will move either up or down according to the resistance they encounter. For purposes of easy explanation we will say that prices, like everything else, move along the line of least resistance. **10.5** They will do whatever comes easiest, therefore they will go up if there is less resistance to an advance than to a decline; and vice versa.

Nobody should be puzzled as to whether a market is a bull or a bear market after it fairly starts. The trend is evident to a man who has an open mind and reasonably clear sight, for it is never wise for a speculator to fit his facts to his theories. Such a man will, or ought to, know whether it is a bull or a bear market, and if he knows that he knows whether to buy or to sell. It is therefore at the very inception of the movement that a man needs to know whether to buy or to sell.

Let us say, for example, that the market, as it usually does in those between-swings times, fluctuates within a range of ten points; up to 130 and down to 120. It may look very weak at the bottom; or, on the way up, after a rise of eight or ten points, it may look as strong as anything. A man ought not to be led into trading by tokens. He should wait until the tape tells him that the time is ripe. As a matter of fact, millions upon millions of dollars have been lost by men who bought stocks because they looked cheap or sold them because they looked dear. The speculator is not an investor. His object is not to secure a steady return on his money at a good rate of interest, but to profit by either a rise or a fall in the price of whatever he may be speculating in. Therefore the thing to determine is the speculative line of least resistance at the moment of trading; and what he should wait for is the moment when that line defines itself, because that is his signal to get busy.

Reading the tape merely enables him to see that at 130 the selling had been stronger than the buying and a reaction in the price logically followed. Up to the point where the selling prevailed over the buying, superficial students of the tape may conclude that the price is not going to stop short of 150, and they buy. But after the reaction begins they hold on, or sell out at a small loss, or they go short and talk bearish. But at 120 there is stronger resistance to the decline. The buying prevails over the selling, there is a rally and the shorts cover. The public is so often whipsawed that one marvels at their persistence in not learning their lesson.

Eventually something happens that increases the power of either the upward or the downward force and the point of greatest resistance moves up or down—that is, the buying at 130 will for the first time be stronger than the selling, or the selling at 120 be stronger than the buying. The price will break through the old barrier or movement-limit and go on. As a rule, there is always a crowd of traders who are short at 120 because it looked so weak, or long at 130 because it looked so strong, and, when the market goes against them they are forced, after a while, either to change their minds and turn or to close out. In either event they help to define even more clearly the price line of least resistance. Thus the intelligent trader who has patiently waited to determine this line will enlist the aid of fundamental trade conditions and also of the force of the trading of that part of the community that happened to guess wrong and must now rectify mistakes. Such corrections tend to push prices along the line of least resistance.

And right here I will say that, though I do not give it as a mathematical certainty or as an axiom of speculation, my experience has been that accidents—that is, the unexpected or unforeseen—have always helped me in my market position whenever the latter has been based upon my determination of the line of least resistance. Do you remember that Union Pacific episode at Saratoga that I told you about? Well, I was long because I found out that the line of least resistance was upward. I should have stayed long instead of letting my broker tell me that insiders were selling stocks. It didn't make any difference what was going on in the directors' minds. That was something I couldn't possibly know. But I could and did know that the tape said: "Going up!" And then came the unexpected raising of the dividend rate and the thirty-point rise in the stock. At 164 prices looked mighty high, but as I told you before, stocks are never too high to buy or too low to sell. The price, per se, has nothing to do with establishing my line of least resistance.

You will find in actual practice that if you trade as I have indicated any important piece of news given out between the closing of one market and the opening of another is usually in harmony with the line of least resistance. The trend has been established before the news is published, and in bull markets bear items are ignored and bull news exaggerated, and vice versa. Before the war broke out the market was in a very weak condition. There came the proclamation of Germany's submarine policy. ◁10.6▷ I was short one hundred and fifty thousand shares of stock, not because I knew the news was coming, but because I was going along the line of least resistance. What happened came out of a clear sky, as far as my play was concerned. Of course I took advantage of the situation and I covered my shorts that day.

It sounds very easy to say that all you have to do is to watch the tape, establish your resistance points and be ready to trade along the line of least resistance as soon as you have determined it. But in actual practice a man has to guard against many things, and most of all against himself—that is, against human nature. That is the reason why I say that the man who is right always has two forces working in his favor—basic conditions and the men who are wrong. In a bull market bear factors are ignored. That is human nature, and yet human beings profess astonishment at it. People will tell you that the wheat crop has gone to pot because there has been bad weather in one or two sections and some farmers have been ruined. When the entire crop is gathered and all the farmers in all the wheat-growing sections begin to take their wheat to the elevators the bulls are surprised at the smallness of the damage. They discover that they merely have helped the bears.

When a man makes his play in a commodity market he must not permit himself set opinions. He must have an open mind and flexibility. It is not wise to disregard the message of the tape, no matter what your opinion of crop conditions or of

10.6 Germany pioneered the development of submarines and their use in naval warfare, starting with the *Brandtaucher* in 1850. The Karp class of U-boats, called the U-1s, were the first submarines specifically built for the German navy; they were powered with a kerosene engine and armed with one torpedo tube. Diesel engines were added in 1912.

At the start of World War I, Germany had 29 subs in service. They were used to sink British warships that had little defense against underwater attack. At first, the Germans avoided attacking British merchant ships, but by February 1915, fighting escalated and the kaiser proclaimed the area around the British Isles a war zone—ordering his captains to attack civilian commercial ships without warning. This naturally hit the world's financial markets hard, allowing Livermore to take profits on short sales he had set in motion amid an already weak market.

President Woodrow Wilson then declared that he would hold Germany "to a strict accountability" for the loss of American lives and would take all steps necessary to safeguard American citizens' rights on the high seas. The kaiser countered by declaring that neutral vessels entering the war zone would themselves bear responsibility for any "unfortunate accidents" that might occur.[5]

On May 7, 1915, a German U-20 sank the *Lusitania* with a torpedo, taking 1,198 lives, including the lives of 128 U.S. civilians. The American government severed diplomatic relations with Germany over the incident, and the German navy backed off attacking merchant ships for a while before announcing unrestricted submarine warfare in 1917. On March 17 of that year, U-boats sank three U.S. merchant ships. The United States declared war on Germany in April.[6]

10.7 Livermore devotes much of his 1940 book, *How to Trade in Stocks*, to what he calls "the pivotal point"—his name for critical support and resistance levels. In addition to referring to the limits of a trading range, he believes a pivotal point can also be whole number milestones such as $50, $100, or $200. As he does frequently in *Reminiscences*, Livermore makes reference to his experiences with Anaconda to convey this point.

In the age long before computer analytics or online stock charts, Livermore used a complex system of notation written in red ink, black ink, and pencil on custom-printed pages of graph paper. With dates running down the left-hand column, prices would be recorded in one of six columns depending on the nature of the current movement: secondary rally, natural rally, upward trend, downward trend, natural reaction, and secondary reaction.

In the chart from his book, you can see the stock prices of both U.S. Steel and Bethlehem Steel are listed along with a "Key Price" entry. Here, Livermore would combine the movements of individual stocks to generate a trend for the group. This would protect him from false movements in individual stocks that would mask the actual trend. A modern interpretation of Livermore's system would be to use sector-level indexes or exchange-traded funds to monitor the price behavior of industries.

CHART ONE

	U.S. STEEL						BETHLEHEM STEEL						KEY PRICE					
1938 DATE	Sec. Rally	Nat. Rally	Upward Trend	Downward Trend	Nat. Reaction	Sec. Reaction	Sec. Rally	Nat. Rally	Upward Trend	Downward Trend	Nat. Reaction	Sec. Reaction	Sec. Rally	Nat. Rally	Upward Trend	Downward Trend	Nat. Reaction	Sec. Reaction
		53		48½				59		45¼				122½	91¾	128			
		62⅛		48⁴			56⅞			50⅜							98⅜	
MAR 23			47						50⁴						97¼			
24																		
25			44¾						46						91½			
SAT 26			44						46						90			
28			45⅝												89¾			
29			39⅞						43						82⅞			
30			39						42⅝						81⅝			
31			38						40						78			
APR 1																		
SAT 2	43½						46⅜						89¾					
4																		
5																		
6																		
7																		
8																		
SAT 9	46½						49¾						96¼					
11																		
12																		
13	47¾												97½					
14	47½												97¼					
SAT 16	49						52						101					
18																		
19																		
20																		
21																		
22																		
SAT 23																		
25																		
26																		
27																		
28			43															
29			42⅝							45						87⅞		
SAT 30																		
MAY 2			41½							44¼						85¾		
3																		
4																		

103

the probable demand may be. I recall how I missed a big play just by trying to anticipate the starting signal. I felt so sure of conditions that I thought it was not necessary to wait for the line of least resistance to define itself. I even thought I might help it arrive, because it looked as if it merely needed a little assistance.

I was very bullish on cotton. It was hanging around twelve cents, running up and down within a moderate range. It was in one of those in-between places and I could see it. I knew I really ought to wait. **10.7** But I got to thinking that if I gave it a little push it would go beyond the upper resistance point.

I bought fifty thousand bales. Sure enough, it moved up. And sure enough, as soon as I stopped buying it stopped going up. Then it began to settle back to where it was when I began buying it. I got out and it stopped going down. I thought I was now much nearer the starting signal, and presently I thought I'd start it myself again. I did. The same thing happened. I bid it up, only to see it go down when I stopped. I did this four or five times until I finally quit in disgust. It cost me about two hundred thousand dollars. I was done with it. It wasn't very long after that when it began to go up and never stopped till it got to a price that would have meant a killing for me—if I hadn't been in such a great hurry to start.

This experience has been the experience of so many traders so many times that I can give this rule: In a narrow market, when prices are not getting anywhere to speak of but move within a narrow range, there is no sense in trying to anticipate what the next big movement is going to be—up or down. The thing to do is to watch the market, read the tape to determine the limits of the get-nowhere prices, and make up your mind that you will not take an interest until the price breaks through the limit in either direction. A speculator must concern himself with making money out of the market and not with insisting that the tape must agree with him. Never argue with it or ask it for reasons or explanations. Stock-market post-mortems don't pay dividends.

Not so long ago I was with a party of friends. They got to talking wheat. Some of them were bullish and others bearish. Finally they asked me what I thought. Well, I had been studying the market for some time. I knew they did not want any statistics or analyses of conditions. So I said: "If you want to make some money out of wheat I can tell you how to do it."

They all said they did and I told them, "If you are sure you wish to make money in wheat just you watch it. Wait. The moment it crosses $1.20 buy it and you will get a nice quick play in it!"

"Why not buy it now, at $1.14?" one of the party asked.

"Because I don't know yet that it is going up at all."

"Then why buy it at $1.20? It seems a mighty high price."

10.8 ▶ Manitoba was a major center of wheat production in North America, and the Winnipeg Commodity Exchange, established in 1887 and shown below, was a force in setting world prices in wheat futures after 1904. It is now the only agricultural commodities exchange in Canada.[7]

"Do you wish to gamble blindly in the hope of getting a great big profit or do you wish to speculate intelligently and get a smaller but much more probable profit?"

They all said they wanted the smaller but surer profit, so I said, "Then do as I tell you. If it crosses $1.20 buy."

As I told you, I had watched it a long time. For months it sold between $1.10 and $1.20, getting nowhere in particular. Well, sir, one day it closed at above $1.19. I got ready for it. Sure enough the next day it opened at $1.20½, and I bought. It went to $1.21, to $1.22, to $1.23, to $1.25, and I went with it.

Now I couldn't have told you at the time just what was going on. I didn't get any explanations about its behaviour during the course of the limited fluctuations. I couldn't tell whether the breaking through the limit would be up through $1.20 or down through $1.10, though I suspected it would be up because there was not enough wheat in the world for a big break in prices.

As a matter of fact, it seems Europe had been buying quietly and a lot of traders had gone short of it at around $1.19. Owing to the European purchases and other causes, a lot of wheat had been taken out of the market, so that finally the big movement got started. The price went beyond the $1.20 mark. That was all the point I had and it was all I needed. I knew that when it crossed $1.20 it would be because the upward movement at last had gathered force to push it over the limit and something had to happen. In other words, by crossing $1.20 the line of least resistance of wheat prices was established. It was a different story then.

I remember that one day was a holiday with us and all our markets were closed. Well, in Winnipeg wheat opened up six cents a bushel. ◀**10.8** When our market opened on the following day, it also was up six cents a bushel. The price just went along the line of least resistance.

What I have told you gives you the essence of my trading system as based on studying the tape. I merely learn the way prices are most probably going to move. I check up my own trading by additional tests, to determine the psychological moment. I do that by watching the way the price acts after I begin.

It is surprising how many experienced traders there are who look incredulous when I tell them that when I buy stocks for a rise I like to pay top prices and when I sell I must sell low or not at all. It would not be so difficult to make money if a trader always stuck to his speculative guns—that is, waited for the line of least resistance to define itself and began buying only when the tape said up or selling only when it said down. He should accumulate his line on the way up. Let him buy one-fifth of his full line. If that does not show him a profit he must not increase his holdings because he has obviously begun wrong; he is wrong temporarily and there is no profit in being wrong at any time. The same tape that said up did not necessarily lie merely because it is now saying not yet.

In cotton I was very successful in my trading for a long time. I had my theory about it and I absolutely lived up to it. Suppose I had decided that my line would be forty to fifty thousand bales. Well, I would study the tape as I told you, watching for an opportunity either to buy or to sell. Suppose the line of least resistance indicated a bull movement. Well, I would buy ten thousand bales. After I got through buying that, if the market went up ten points over my initial purchase price, I would take on another ten thousand bales. Same thing. Then, if I could get twenty points' profit, or one dollar a bale, I would buy twenty thousand more. That would give me my line—my basis for my trading. But if after buying the first ten or twenty thousand bales, it showed me a loss, out I'd go. I was wrong. It might be I was only temporarily wrong. But as

10.9 In Lefevre's view, Livermore traveled in a sea of colorful characters from whom he learned his trade a day at a time. In *Reminiscences*, Lefevre leans on the literary device of having these characters tell stories to Livermore so he can liven the narrative with new voices. In this section, he introduces a nameless old codger who tells Livermore about Pat Hearne, a "nervy chap" and professional gambler who deployed a system of pyramiding up a winning market bet while keeping a trailing stop in place one point below the price of his last purchase.

Hearne illustrates an important facet of Livermore's game: He was not after tips for big 20-point advances but just sure money in sufficient quantities to provide him with a good living. He was a speculator who viewed the stock market as a game of chance that would yield to a sound betting method. Hearne would never directly answer tip seekers who asked about the wisdom of a prospective play and would instead relate a horse-racing maxim: "You can't tell till you bet." This was a succinct description of Livermore's own philosophy.

I have said before it doesn't pay to start wrong in anything.

What I accomplished by sticking to my system was that I always had a line of cotton in every real movement. In the course of accumulating my full line I might chip out fifty or sixty thousand dollars in these feeling-out plays of mine. This looks like a very expensive testing, but it wasn't. After the real movement started, how long would it take me to make up the fifty thousand dollars I had dropped in order to make sure that I began to load up at exactly the right time? No time at all! It always pays a man to be right at the right time.

As I think I also said before, this describes what I may call my system for placing my bets. It is simple arithmetic to prove that it is a wise thing to have the big bet down only when you win, and when you lose to lose only a small exploratory bet, as it were. If a man trades in the way I have described, he will always be in the profitable position of being able to cash in on the big bet.

Professional traders have always had some system or other based upon their experience and governed either by their attitude toward speculation or by their desires. I remember I met an old gentleman in Palm Beach whose name I did not catch or did not at once identify. I knew he had been in the Street for years, way back in Civil War times, and somebody told me that he was a very wise old codger who had gone through so many booms and panics that he was always saying there was nothing new under the sun and least of all in the stock market.

The old fellow asked me a lot of questions. When I got through telling him about my usual practice in trading he nodded and said, "Yes! Yes! You're right. The way you're built, the way your mind runs, makes your system a good system for you. It comes easy for you to practice what you preach, because the money you bet is the least of your cares. I recollect Pat Hearne. ◁ **10.9**▷ Ever hear of him? Well, he was a very well-known sporting man and he had an account with us. Clever chap and nervy. He made money in stocks, and that made people ask him for advice. He would never give any. If they asked him point-blank for his opinion about the wisdom of their commitments he used a favourite race-track maxim of his: 'You can't tell till you bet.' He traded in our office. He would buy one hundred shares of some active stock and when, or if, it went up 1 per cent he would buy another hundred. On another point's advance, another hundred shares; and so on. He used to say he wasn't playing the game to make money for others and therefore he would put in a stop-loss order one point below the price of his last purchase. When the price kept going up he simply moved up his stop with it. On a 1 per cent reaction he was stopped out. He declared he did not see any sense in losing more than one point, whether it came out of his original margin or out of his paper profits.

"You know, a professional gambler is not looking for long shots, but for sure money. Of course long shots are fine when they come in. In the stock market Pat wasn't after tips or playing to catch twenty-points-a-week advances, but sure money in sufficient quantity to provide him with a good living. Of all the thousands of outsiders that I have run across in Wall Street, Pat Hearne was the only one who saw in stock speculation merely a game of chance like faro or roulette, but, nevertheless, had the sense to stick to a relatively sound betting method.

"After Hearne's death one of our customers who had always traded with Pat and used his system made over one hundred thousand dollars in Lackawanna. Then he switched over to some other stock and because he had made a big stake he thought he need not stick to Pat's way. When a reaction came,

10.10 **William R. Travers** was a very successful speculator and bon vivant in the post–Civil War era who played the market primarily as a short seller. He was also an avid horseman who cofounded the Saratoga Race Course in upstate New York; the track's Travers Stakes, named for him, is the oldest Thoroughbred race in America. He was also a longtime president of the New York Athletic Club.

In his book, *Fifty Years in Wall Street*, financier Henry Clews devotes all of Chapter 33 to Travers, lauding his kind nature, inexhaustible supply of sparkling humor, and fondness for sports—personality traits that seemed more fitting a bull than a bear. The chapter is peppered with references to Travers's stutter and wit. In one, a fellow transplant from Maryland tells the trader that he seems to stutter a great deal more than when he lived in Baltimore. "W-h-y, y-e-s," replied Mr. Travers, darting a look of surprise at his friend; "of course I do. This is a d-d-damned sight b-b-bigger city."[8]

instead of cutting short his losses he let them run— as though they were profits. Of course every cent went. When he finally quit he owed us several thousand dollars.

"He hung around for two or three years. He kept the fever long after the cash had gone; but we did not object as long as he behaved himself. I remember that he used to admit freely that he had been ten thousand kinds of an ass not to stick to Pat Hearne's style of play. Well, one day he came to me greatly excited and asked me to let him sell some stock short in our office. He was a nice enough chap who had been a good customer in his day and I told him I personally would guarantee his account for one hundred shares.

"He sold short one hundred shares of Lake Shore. That was the time Bill Travers hammered the market, in 1875. **10.10** My friend Roberts put out that Lake Shore at exactly the right time and kept selling it on the way down as he had been wont to do in the old successful days before he forsook Pat Hearne's system and instead listened to hope's whispers.

"Well, sir, in four days of successful pyramiding, Roberts' account showed him a profit of fifteen thousand dollars. Observing that he had not put in a stop-loss order I spoke to him about it and he told me that the break hadn't fairly begun and he wasn't going to be shaken out by any one-point reaction. This was in August. Before the middle of September he borrowed ten dollars from me for a baby carriage—his fourth. He did not stick to his own proved system. That's the trouble with most of them," and the old fellow shook his head at me.

And he was right. I sometimes think that speculation must be an unnatural sort of business, because I find that the average speculator has arrayed against him his own nature. The weaknesses that all men are prone to are fatal to success in speculation—usually those very weaknesses that make him likable to his fellows or that he himself particularly guards against in those other ventures of his where they are not nearly so dangerous as when he is trading in stocks or commodities.

The speculator's chief enemies are always boring from within. It is inseparable from human nature to hope and to fear. In speculation when the market goes against you you hope that every day will be the last day—and you lose more than you should had you not listened to hope—to the same ally that is so potent a success-bringer to empire builders and pioneers, big and little. And when the market goes your way you become fearful that the next day will take away your profit, and you get out—too soon. Fear keeps you from making as much money as you ought to. The successful trader has to fight these two deep-seated instincts. He has to reverse what you might call his natural impulses. Instead of hoping he must fear; instead of fearing he must hope. He must fear that his loss may develop into a much bigger loss, and hope that his profit may become a big profit. It is absolutely wrong to gamble in stocks the way the average man does.

I have been in the speculative game ever since I was fourteen. It is all I have ever done. I think

I know what I am talking about. And the conclusion that I have reached after nearly thirty years of constant trading, both on a shoe-string and with millions of dollars back of me, is this: A man may beat a stock or a group at a certain time, but no man living can beat the stock market! A man may make money out of individual deals in cotton or grain, but no man can beat the cotton market or the grain market. It's like the track. A man may beat a horse race, but he cannot beat horse racing.

If I knew how to make these statements stronger or more emphatic I certainly would. It does not make any difference what anybody says to the contrary. I know I am right in saying these are incontrovertible statements.

ENDNOTES

1 "Funeral of Dickson G. Watts," *New York Times,* February 2, 1902.

2 Dickson G. Watts, *Speculation as a Fine Art and Thoughts on Life* (Traders Press, 1965), 11.

3 Ibid., 8.

4 Ed Holm, *Yachting's Golden Age: 1880–1905* (New York: Knopf).

5 Charles Downer Hazen, *Fifty Years of Europe, 1870–1919* (New York: H. Holt & Co., 1919).

6 Ibid.

7 Michael Atkin, *Agricultural Commodity Markets: A Guide to Futures Trading* (Routledge, 1989).

8 Henry Clews, *Fifty Years in Wall Street,* Part 1 (New York: Irving Publishing Company, 1908), 407.

And now I'll get back to October, 1907. I bought a yacht and made all preparations to leave New York for a cruise in Southern waters. I am really daffy about fishing and this was the time when I was going to fish to my heart's content from my own yacht, going wherever I wished whenever I felt like it. Everything was ready. I had made a killing in stocks, but at the last moment corn held me back. **11.1**

I must explain that before the money panic which gave me my first million I had been trading in grain at Chicago. **11.2** I was short ten million

11.1 Livermore quickly became something of a celebrity after his exploits from the Panic of 1907 netted him more than $3 million over six weeks. The *Chicago Daily Tribune* wrote that this "beardless fortune hunter of 28" had "waited five years to make money in this bewildering way."[1]

The *Boston Daily Globe* said that "young Livermore read the signs of the big slump in stocks" and "hit market right." Livermore gave one of the first in a long line of interviews to newspapermen. "I prefer not to discuss my personal affairs," he said. "Few men in Wall St. know me, and I prefer not to be known. When a man has been successful down there, Wall St. is looking for him. There are those who have won fortunes in the markets and heralded their success. I prefer to enjoy my gains as quietly as I won them."[2]

11.2 Livermore is referring to the Chicago Board of Trade, which was founded in 1848 and is the world's oldest futures exchange. Although he could have traded in grains in New York through the Produce Exchange, trading volume in Chicago soon eclipsed that of New York due to its proximity to the Midwestern growing region and its importance as a railroad hub. Also key: the ability to ship product for export south to New Orleans via the Mississippi River or north out of the Great Lakes through the St. Lawrence River, avoiding the Erie Canal or the overland route to the port of New York.

Throughout 1907, there was great excitement in Chicago as commodity prices rose. Starting in February, unfavorable crop reports from Argentina helped push up wheat, corn, and oats contracts. The rise accelerated as shorts were forced to cover on reports that Russia was conserving its grain to fight famine within its borders. Then over the spring came word of insect ravages and idled farm acreage, resulting in more short covering. As prices continued to advance, the market was "one of the wildest, largest and most excited and well sustained the Board of Trade has ever known," according to Charles Taylor's memoirs from 1917.[3]

It was at this time that Livermore saw his opportunity to go short. According to Taylor, most of the excited buying was coming from the public—not professional traders. By May, the "market was almost in a state of hysteria, there was wild cheering when September wheat passed the coveted $1 mark, women in the gallery wept and shouted without knowing exactly why and traders were overwhelmed....It seemed that the whole world was in the market buying wheat."[4]

11.3 "Stratton" appears to be a pseudonym for **James A. Patten,** a notorious Chicago speculator. Patten was born in a farming community in 1852, and got his start as a clerk in a country store before receiving an appointment as a clerk in the office of the State Grain Inspector's office in Chicago. Later he started, along with his brother, the brokerage firm of Patten Brothers, which attracted international attention.[5]

In one high-profile spat in 1909, Patten exchanged jibes through the newspaper with the U.S. secretary of agriculture, James Wilson. At issue was Patten's manipulation of wheat prices during a corner earlier that year, which Wilson claimed artificially raised prices despite plentiful supply. Patten was soon blamed for inciting bread riots, and bomb threats forced him to hire two bodyguards. Preachers called him "the God of Get."[6] Later, in 1911, he tried cornering cotton and was mobbed in Liverpool at the height of a panic.[7]

Just before embarking on his corn corner, Patten went west in July 1907 to study crop conditions firsthand.[8]

bushels of wheat and ten million bushels of corn. I had studied the grain markets for a long time and was as bearish on corn and wheat as I had been on stocks.

Well, they both started down, but while wheat kept on declining the biggest of all the Chicago operators—I'll call him Stratton—took it into his head to run a corner in corn. **11.3** After I cleaned up in stocks and was ready to go South on my yacht I found that wheat showed me a handsome profit, but in corn Stratton had run up the price and I had quite a loss.

I knew there was much more corn in the country than the price indicated. The law of demand and supply worked as always. But the demand came chiefly from Stratton and the supply was not coming at all, because there was an acute congestion in the movement of corn. I remember that I used to pray for a cold spell that would freeze the impassable roads and enable the farmers to bring their corn into the market. But no such luck.

There I was, waiting to go on my joyously planned fishing trip and that loss in corn holding me back. I couldn't go away with the market as it was. Of course Stratton kept pretty close tabs on the short interest. He knew he had me, and I knew it quite as well as he did. But, as I said, I was hoping I might convince the weather that it ought to get busy and help me. Perceiving that neither the weather nor any other kindly wonder-worker was paying any attention to my needs I studied how I might work out of my difficulty by my own efforts.

I closed out my line of wheat at a good profit. But the problem in corn was infinitely more difficult. If I could have covered my ten million bushels at the prevailing prices I instantly and gladly would have done so, large though the loss would have been. But, of course, the moment I started to buy in my corn Stratton would be on the job as squeezer in chief, and I no more relished running up the price on myself by reason of my own purchases than cutting my own throat with my own knife.

Strong though corn was, my desire to go fishing was even stronger, so it was up to me to find a way out at once. I must conduct a strategic retreat. I must buy back the ten million bushels I was short of and in so doing keep down my loss as much as I possibly could.

It so happened that Stratton at that time was also running a deal in oats and had the market pretty well sewed up. I had kept track of all the grain markets in the way of crop news and pit gossip, and I heard that the powerful Armour interests were not friendly, marketwise, to Stratton. ◁**11.4** Of course I knew that Stratton would not let me have the corn I needed except at his own price, but the moment I heard the rumors about Armour being against Stratton it occurred to me that I might look to the Chicago traders for aid. The only way in which they could possibly help me was for them to sell me the corn that Stratton wouldn't. The rest was easy.

11.4 While Patten was running a corner in corn, **Jonathan Ogden Armour**—better known as J. Ogden—was running a parallel corner in wheat.[9] The Armour family operated the large Armour & Co. meatpacking business that was the inspiration for Upton Sinclair's exposé of the industry, *The Jungle*. The company was criticized for furnishing rotten meat to soldiers during the Spanish-American War. J. Ogden's father, Philip D. Armour, started the company in the mid-1800s after driving cattle, mining gold, and shorting pork just as the Civil War was coming to an end—netting $2 million from all his endeavors with which to expand his meatpacking empire.[10]

From this early adventure in speculation, the Armours developed something of a family tradition. The senior Armour went on to corner pork three separate times. To explain the practice, banker and historian Henry Clews wrote: "A campaign against the bears in pork or meats he calls protecting his cellars."[11] Philip Armour made millions in grain speculation, and dabbled in railroads after purchasing the St. Paul railroad on the open market for $4 million.

After the deaths of his father and brother, J. Ogden took the reins of Armour & Co. in 1901 and expanded its business greatly. The company collapsed in the economic downturn that followed World War I. As a result, along with losses on his other investments, J. Ogden lost his family's fortune, which was estimated at the time to be the world's second largest. He bravely declared: "I do not mind the loss, for I have regained my health." But fate was cruel. Within a few months, he lost that too, dying of heart failure.[12]

11.5 ▶ The record shows unusually active speculation in commodities in Chicago throughout October. There were "fierce battles in the corn pit, both corn and wheat being upheld by the heavy buying by Patten," according to a historian.[13] For delivery in December, wheat contracts fell from $107¾ to $94⅝ while corn fell from $64⅞ to $55 and oats collapsed from $56 to $44. However, the drop "stimulated an active export demand for grain" as overseas crops were ravaged by bad weather, causing prices to recover.[14]

Until the corners were complete the following May, Patten and Armour were locked in a running battle: Armour caught Patten short in wheat; Patten similarly caught Armour, who was one of the largest shorts in the corn market.[15] The two corners ended on May 29 upon the expiration of May futures contracts without a crash or panic. Both reaped large profits by the two deals, with Patten's winnings estimated at $2 million.[16]

11.6 ▶ **Addison Cammack**, was a great Wall Street bear of the Civil War era. On occasion, he would team with Jay Gould and James Keene. He was close to William Travers, with whom he shared an office on 23rd Street in Manhattan.[17]

Cammack was born in 1826 in Kentucky in what was then America's western frontier. His father was of Scottish descent and had grown tobacco in Virginia before becoming a gentleman farmer. At the age of 16, Cammack went to New Orleans to become an office boy. By 1861, he had become a senior partner in the firm, which changed its name to Cammack & Converse. During the Civil War, the firm relocated its headquarters to Havana and controlled a fleet of blockade runners that penetrated the Union navy's

First, I put in orders to buy five hundred thousand bushels of corn every eighth of a cent down. After these orders were in I gave to each of four houses an order to sell simultaneously fifty thousand bushels of oats at the market. That, I figured, ought to make a quick break in oats. Knowing how the traders' minds worked, it was a cinch that they would instantly think that Armour was gunning for Stratton. Seeing the attack opened in oats they would logically conclude that the next break would be in corn and they would start to sell it. If that corner in corn was busted, the pickings would be fabulous.

My dope on the psychology of the Chicago traders was absolutely correct. When they saw oats breaking on the scattered selling they promptly jumped on corn and sold it with great enthusiasm. I was able to buy six million bushels of corn in the next ten minutes. The moment I found that their selling of corn ceased I simply bought in the other four million bushels at the market. Of course that made the price go up again, but the net result of my manœuvre was that I covered the entire line of ten million bushels within one-half cent of the price prevailing at the time I started to cover on the traders' selling. The two hundred thousand bushels of oats that I sold short to start the traders' selling of corn I covered at a loss of only three thousand dollars. That was pretty cheap bear bait. The profits I had made in wheat offset so much of my deficit in corn that my total loss on all my grain trades that time was only twenty-five thousand dollars. Afterwards corn went up twenty-five cents a bushel. Stratton undoubtedly had me at his mercy. If I had set about buying my ten million bushels of corn without bothering to think of the price there is no telling what I would have had to pay. ◀ **11.5**

A man can't spend years at one thing and not acquire a habitual attitude towards it quite unlike that of the average beginner. The difference distinguishes the professional from the amateur. It is

REMINISCENCES OF A STOCK OPERATOR

the way a man looks at things that makes or loses money for him in the speculative markets. The public has the dilettante's point of view toward his own effort. The ego obtrudes itself unduly and the thinking therefore is not deep or exhaustive. The professional concerns himself with doing the right thing rather than with making money, knowing that the profit takes care of itself if the other things are attended to. A trader gets to play the game as the professional billiard player does—that is, he looks far ahead instead of considering the particular shot before him. It gets to be an instinct to play for position.

I remember hearing a story about Addison Cammack that illustrates very nicely what I wish to point out. 11.6 From all I have heard, I am inclined to think that Cammack was one of the ablest stock traders the Street ever saw. He was not a chronic bear as many believe, but he felt the greater appeal of trading on the bear side, of utilising in his behalf the two great human factors of hope and fear. He is credited with coining the warning: "Don't sell stocks when the sap is running up the trees!" and the old-timers tell me that his biggest winnings were made on the bull side, so that it is plain he did not play prejudices but conditions. At all events, he was a consummate trader. It seems that once—this was way back at the tag end of a bull market—Cammack was bearish, and J. Arthur Joseph, the financial writer and raconteur, knew it. The market, however, was not only strong but still rising, in response to prodding by the bull leaders and optimistic reports by the newspapers. Knowing what use a trader like Cammack could make of bearish information, Joseph rushed to Cammack's office one day with glad tidings.

"Mr. Cammack, I have a very good friend who is a transfer clerk in the St. Paul office and he has just told me something which I think you ought to know."

"What is it?" asked Cammack listlessly.

defenses with varying degrees of success in an attempt to smuggle war provisions.

After the war, Cammack moved to New York City to run a whisky distribution business before leaving for Europe in 1867 for three years. Upon his return, he formed and ran the brokerage Osborne & Cammack for a short time, of which Jay Gould was a special partner, before it was dissolved in 1873. After studying the art of stock brokering, Cammack was ready to take on Wall Street as an operator.

He joined the NYSE in 1875 and quickly earned the Latin nickname "Ursa Major," or great bear. According to the *New York Times*, Cammack's successes in the 1880s came from his methodical research and careful planning: "Few Wall Street men have had his thorough knowledge of railroad matters. He often had the figures of railroad earnings before they reached the offices of the companies."[18]

Cammack sold his exchange seat in 1897 and retired to the embrace of his family. His fortune was estimated to be $1.2 million at the time. He died in 1901 from kidney problems.[19] When asked for the keys to his success, Cammack would answer: "Luck, sir; chiefly luck. Perhaps caution, too. I never overtrade and don't like big losses. I don't think I ever took a big loss in my life. Then again I don't spend much. My habits are very quiet and inexpensive. That is about all, sir."[20]

Lefevre, writing in the *Saturday Evening Post* in 1915, used Cammack as an example of his view that the speculation game was unwinnable:

The late Addison Cammack, the great bear operator in Wall Street, after many years of battling and after some spectacular successes and unadvertised failures, did not leave an estate that consisted of the winnings on the bear side. One of his intimate friends told me that if it had not been for fortunate investments Cammack would not have died rich.[21]

That was pretty uncharitable. The *New York Times* reported in 1909 that S. V. White said Cammack had left his widow a rather sizable annual income of $50,000 from a fortune earned on both the long and the short sides of the market.[22]

11.7 W. B. Wheeler was one of the most active brokerages on Wall Street in the 1880s and early 1890s. Its founder, William B. Wheeler, was called a "bold and successful" operator in his own right, and Addison Cammack thought enough of his "pluck and judgment," according to the *New York Times*, that he traded a joint account with him.

Wheeler, said to have a "genial disposition," preferred trading on his own to dealing on behalf of customers, primarily on the short side of the market. He got in trouble in 1895 when he shorted a declining market heavily and then saw stocks rebound rapidly before he could cover. His resources "became practically exhausted," according to the *Times*, so he had to borrow money from another dealer and a relative. When he couldn't pay a margin call, the fragility of his position was exposed to his clients—and they shunned his firm. He was forced to close the brokerage in April 1896.

Wheeler was one of the early corporate backers of the New York Giants, the baseball team that later moved to San Francisco. The *Times* reported that "it was his habit to take his office force and enough others to make a good party to every game at the Polo Grounds."

"You've turned, haven't you? You are bearish now?" asked Joseph, to make sure. If Cammack wasn't interested he wasn't going to waste precious ammunition.

"Yes. What's the wonderful information?"

"I went around to the St. Paul office to-day, as I do in my news-gathering rounds two or three times a week, and my friend there said to me: 'The Old Man is selling stock.' He meant William Rockefeller. 'Is he really, Jimmy?' I said to him, and he answered, 'Yes; he is selling fifteen hundred shares every three-eighths of a point up. I've been transferring the stock for two or three days now.' I didn't lose any time, but came right over to tell you."

Cammack was not easily excited, and, moreover, was so accustomed to having all manner of people rush madly into his office with all manner of news, gossip, rumors, tips and lies that he had grown distrustful of them all. He merely said now, "Are you sure you heard right, Joseph?"

"Am I sure? Certainly I am sure! Do you think I am deaf?" said Joseph.

"Are you sure of your man?"

"Absolutely!" declared Joseph. "I've known him for years. He has never lied to me. He wouldn't! No object! I know he is absolutely reliable and I'd stake my life on what he tells me. I know him as well as I know anybody in this world—a great deal better than you seem to know me, after all these years."

"Sure of him, eh?" And Cammack again looked at Joseph. Then he said, "Well, you ought to know." He called his broker, W. B. Wheeler. **11.7** Joseph expected to hear him give an order to sell at least fifty thousand shares of St. Paul. William Rockefeller was disposing of his holdings in St. Paul, taking advantage of the strength of the market. Whether it was investment stock or speculative holdings was irrelevant. The one important fact was that the best stock trader of the Standard Oil crowd was getting out of St. Paul. What would the average man have done if he had received the news from a trustworthy source? No need to ask.

But Cammack, the ablest bear operator of his day, who was bearish on the market just then, said to his broker, "Billy, go over to the board and buy fifteen hundred St. Paul every three-eighths up." The stock was then in the nineties.

"Don't you mean sell?" interjected Joseph hastily. He was no novice in Wall Street, but he was thinking of the market from the point of view of the newspaper man and, incidentally, of the general public. The price certainly ought to go down on the news of inside selling. And there was no better inside selling than Mr. William Rockefeller's. The Standard Oil getting out and Cammack buying! It couldn't be!

"No," said Cammack; "I mean buy!"

"Don't you believe me?"

"Yes!"

"Don't you believe my information?"

"Yes."

"Aren't you bearish?"

"Yes."

"Well, then?"

"That's why I'm buying. Listen to me now: You keep in touch with that reliable friend of yours and the moment the scaled selling stops, let me know. Instantly! Do you understand?"

"Yes," said Joseph, and went away, not quite sure he could fathom Cammack's motives in buying William Rockefeller's stock. It was the knowledge that Cammack was bearish on the entire market that made his manœuvre so difficult to explain. However, Joseph saw his friend the transfer clerk and told him he wanted to be tipped off when the Old Man got through selling. Regularly twice a day Joseph called on his friend to inquire.

One day the transfer clerk told him, "There isn't any more stock coming from the Old Man." Joseph

11.8 Grangers were railroads whose principal business was carrying farmers' produce to market. Examples include the Milwaukee & St. Paul, the Burlington & Quincey, and the Chicago & Alton.

thanked him and ran to Cammack's office with the information.

Cammack listened attentively, turned to Wheeler and asked, "Billy, how much St. Paul have we got in the office?" Wheeler looked it up and reported that they had accumulated about sixty thousand shares.

Cammack, being bearish, had been putting out short lines in the other Grangers as well as in various other stocks, even before he began to buy St. Paul. **11.8** He was now heavily short of the market. He promptly ordered Wheeler to sell the sixty thousand shares of St. Paul that they were long of, and more besides. He used his long holdings of St. Paul as a lever to depress the general list and greatly benefit his operations for a decline.

St. Paul didn't stop on that move until it reached forty-four and Cammack made a killing in it. He played his cards with consummate skill and profited accordingly. The point I would make is his habitual attitude toward trading. He didn't have to reflect. He saw instantly what was far more important to him than his profit on that one stock. He saw that he had providentially been offered an opportunity to begin his big bear operations not only at the proper time but with a proper initial push. The St. Paul tip made him buy instead of sell because he saw at once that it gave him a vast supply of the best ammunition for his bear campaign.

To get back to myself. After I closed my trade in wheat and corn I went South in my yacht. I cruised about in Florida waters, having a grand old time. The fishing was great. Everything was lovely. I didn't have a care in the world and I wasn't looking for any.

One day I went ashore at Palm Beach. I met a lot of Wall Street friends and others. They were all talking about the most picturesque cotton speculator of the day. A report from New York had it that Percy Thomas had lost every cent. It wasn't a commercial bankruptcy; merely the rumor of the world-famous operator's second Waterloo in the cotton market. ◁ 11.9

I had always felt a great admiration for him. The first I ever heard of him was through the newspapers at the time of the failure of the Stock Exchange house of Sheldon & Thomas, when Thomas tried to corner cotton. Sheldon, who did not have the vision or the courage of his partner, got cold feet on the very verge of success. At least, so the Street said at the time. At all events, instead of making a killing they made one of the most sensational failures in years. I forget how many millions. The firm was wound up and Thomas went to work alone. He devoted himself exclusively to cotton and it was not long before he was on his feet again. He paid off his creditors in full with interest—debts he was not legally obliged to discharge—and withal had a million dollars left for himself. His comeback in the cotton market was in its way as remarkable as Deacon S. V. White's famous stock-market exploit of paying off one million dollars in one year. Thomas' pluck and brains made me admire him immensely.

Everybody in Palm Beach was talking about the collapse of Thomas' deal in March cotton. You know how the talk goes—and grows; the amount of misinformation and exaggeration and improvements that you hear. Why, I've seen a rumor about myself grow so that the fellow who started it did not recognise it when it came back to him in less than twenty-four hours, swollen with new and picturesque details.

The news of Percy Thomas' latest misadventure turned my mind from the fishing to the cotton market. I got files of the trade papers and read them to get a line on conditions. When I got back to New York I gave myself up to studying the market. Everybody was bearish and everybody was selling July cotton. You know how people are. I suppose it is the

11.9 The cotton crop was plentiful in 1908. Some 13.5 million bales of 500 pounds each were harvested in the United States. At an average price of 9.2 cents a pound, the entire crop was worth more than $625 million.[23]

contagion of example that makes a man do something because everybody around him is doing the same thing. Perhaps it is some phase or variety of the herd instinct. In any case it was, in the opinion of hundreds of traders, the wise and proper thing to sell July cotton—and so safe too! You couldn't call that general selling reckless; the word is too conservative. The traders simply saw one side to the market and a great big profit. They certainly expected a collapse in prices.

I saw all this, of course, and it struck me that the chaps who were short didn't have a terrible lot of time to cover in. The more I studied the situation the clearer I saw this, until I finally decided to buy July cotton. I went to work and quickly bought one hundred thousand bales. I experienced no trouble in getting it because it came from so many sellers. It seemed to me that I could have offered a reward of one million dollars for the capture, dead or alive, of a single trader who was not selling July cotton and nobody would have claimed it.

I should say this was in the latter part of May. I kept buying more and they kept on selling it to me until I had picked up all the floating contracts and I had one hundred and twenty thousand bales. A couple of days after I had bought the last of it it began to go up. Once it started the market was kind enough to keep on doing very well indeed—that is, it went up from forty to fifty points a day.

One Saturday—this was about ten days after I began operations—the price began to creep up. I did not know whether there was any more July cotton for sale. It was up to me to find out, so I waited until the last ten minutes. At that time, I knew, it was usual for those fellows to be short and if the market closed up for the day they would be safely hooked. So I sent in four different orders to buy five thousand bales each, at the market, at the same time. That ran the price up thirty points and the shorts were doing their best to wriggle away.

11.10 ▶ The advent of organized exchanges made it unnecessary for mills, which were concentrated in New England and Europe, to deal directly with cotton growers in America's southern states. This was important in the years following the Civil War, when prices fluctuated dramatically and the transportation networks were undeveloped.

There were a number of smaller exchanges in Houston, Texas, and Mobile, Alabama, but a majority of the trading volume was relegated to the cotton exchanges in New Orleans and in New York City. Global trade was concentrated at the Liverpool Cotton Exchange, shown at right, which handled nearly all foreign trade in the fiber.[24] Liverpool was a key transaction point for American exports headed to textile mills in nearby Manchester in the northern reaches of England.

Because of the large quantities of cotton dealt with in Liverpool, and the fact that the market absorbed surplus production, global cotton prices tended to gravitate toward the price in Liverpool. Said one observer: "If…every producing country has a large crop, Liverpool does not have to pay much to attract wheat. If, on the other hand, all producers have small crops, Liverpool must pay exorbitantly."[25] Like Chicago, Liverpool was an active center for the exchange of all types of commodities.

The Liverpool Cotton Exchange was formed after the so-called cotton famine of the 1860s, when exports from America were curtailed because of the Civil War and the Union navy's blockade of southern ports. According to a cotton industry historian, the origin of the organization can be traced to a Sir George Drinkwater who, in September 1766, "sold a quantity of damaged cotton saved of the *Molly*, from Granada, which vessel was accidentally set on fire in the river, owing to the carelessness of the Excise officers, who had gone into the hold to rummage with a lighted candle."[26]

LIVERPOOL COTTON ASSOCIATION, LIMITED.

[*Face*]   CONTRACT FORM I.

CONTRACT NOTE FOR SPOT COTTON (" FIXED PRICE ").

(1st *June*, 1912.)

Liverpool,................19

Messrs...

Dear Sirs,
We have this day ....

....
the following COTTON :—

Mark.	Number of Bales.	Description.	Ship.	Price.	

The market closed at the top. All I did, remember, was to buy that last twenty thousand bales.

The next day was Sunday. But on Monday, Liverpool was due to open up twenty points to be on a parity with the advance in New York. ◀**11.10** Instead, it came fifty points higher. That meant that Liverpool had exceeded our advance by 100 per cent. I had nothing to do with the rise in that market. This showed me that my deductions had been sound and that I was trading along the

11.11 ▶ With this move, which cleared him some $2 million, Livermore added to his notoriety.[27]

Just as Livermore describes, July cotton was very weak in the spring of 1908. The *New York Times* wrote on April 8 that cotton was "active on continued weakness —closes 12 to 21 points down" on poor trade reports, good weather in the South, and rumors of an increase in planted acreage.[28] By mid-May, the situation reversed as Livermore put out his line. A "big rise in July cotton" was reported.[29] Traders at the New York Cotton Exchange no doubt scratched their heads in wonderment as the July contracts "kept climbing…and eventually the entire list felt its strength."[30]

The move continued. On May 14, newspapers wrote of a $2.50-per-bale advance in July cotton—bringing the total rise from the recent low to $9.90. The market started to get suspicious, according to a reporter: "The advance was called a 'corner,' made possible by the strength of the Southern market."[31] The next day, Livermore was fingered as possibly being responsible for the rise. The market in Liverpool became active as spinners, who had let their raw cotton stocks dwindle to dangerously low levels, were forced to make bids on fears "spot and nearby delivery had been cornered."[32] It is at this point that Livermore is said to have started unloading his position.

By the end of June, after Livermore had gone back to cash, July cotton collapsed. Prices moved down to $6.40 per bale as a bull clique in New Orleans was rumored to have been routed: "Selling by the coterie of brokers who have been credit with creating practically a corner in July cotton in this market, was explained by a picturesque story that the sudden illness of one of the operators had thrown his associates into a panic and started them selling out on one another."[33] We will never know if there is some truth to this, or if Livermore was just throwing the bears off his scent.

line of least resistance. At the same time I was not losing sight of the fact that I had a whopping big line to dispose of. A market may advance sharply or rise gradually and yet not possess the power to absorb more than a certain amount of selling.

Of course the Liverpool cables made our own market wild. But I noticed the higher it went the scarcer July cotton seemed to be. I wasn't letting go any of mine. Altogether that Monday was an exciting and not very cheerful day for the bears; but for all that, I could detect no signs of an impending bear panic; no beginnings of a blind stampede to cover. And I had one hundred and forty thousand bales for which I must find a market.

On Tuesday morning as I was walking to my office I met a friend at the entrance of the building.

"That was quite a story in the *World* this morning," he said with a smile.

"What story?" I asked.

"What? Do you mean to tell me you haven't seen it?"

"I never see the *World*," I said. "What is the story?"

"Why, it's all about you. It says you've got July cotton cornered." **11.11**

"I haven't seen it," I told him and left him. I don't know whether he believed me or not. He probably thought it was highly inconsiderate of me not to tell him whether it was true or not.

When I got to the office I sent out for a copy of the paper. Sure enough, there it was, on the front page, in big headlines:

JULY COTTON CORNERED
BY LARRY LIVINGSTON

Of course I knew at once that the article would play the dickens with the market. If I had deliberately studied ways and means of disposing of my one hundred and forty thousand bales to the best advantage I couldn't have hit upon a better plan.

It would not have been possible to find one. That article at that very moment was being read all over the country either in the *World* or in other papers quoting it. It had been cabled to Europe. That was plain from the Liverpool prices. That market was simply wild. No wonder, with such news.

Of course I knew what New York would do, and what I ought to do. The market here opened at ten o'clock. At ten minutes after ten I did not own any cotton. I let them have every one of my one hundred and forty thousand bales. For most of my line I received what proved to be the top prices of the day. The traders made the market for me. All I really did was to see a heaven-sent opportunity to get rid of my cotton. I grasped it because I couldn't help it. What else could I do?

The problem that I knew would take a great deal of hard thinking to solve was thus solved for me by an accident. If the *World* had not published that article I never would have been able to dispose of my line without sacrificing the greater portion of my paper profits. Selling one hundred and forty thousand bales of July cotton without sending the price down was a trick beyond my powers. But the *World* story turned it for me very nicely.

Why the *World* published it I cannot tell you. I never knew. I suppose the writer was tipped off by some friend in the cotton market and he thought he was printing a scoop. I didn't see him or anybody from the *World*. I didn't know it was printed that morning until after nine o'clock; and if it had not been for my friend calling my attention to it I would not have known it then.

Without it I wouldn't have had a market *big* enough to unload in. That is one trouble about trading on a large scale. You cannot sneak out as you can when you pike along. You cannot always sell out when you wish or when you think it wise. You have to get out when you can; when you have a market that will absorb your entire line. Failure to grasp the opportunity to get out may cost you millions. You cannot hesitate. If you do you are lost. Neither can you try stunts like running up the price on the bears by means of competitive buying, for you may thereby reduce the absorbing capacity. And I want to tell you that perceiving your opportunity is not as easy as it sounds. A man must be on the lookout so alertly that when his chance sticks in its head at his door he must grab it.

Of course not everybody knew about my fortunate accident. In Wall Street, and, for that matter, everywhere else, any accident that makes big money for a man is regarded with suspicion. When the accident is unprofitable it is never considered an accident but the logical outcome of your hoggishness or of the swelled head. But when there is a profit they call it loot and talk about how well unscrupulousness fares, and how ill conservatism and decency.

It was not only the evil-minded shorts smarting under punishment brought about by their own recklessness who accused me of having deliberately planned the coup. Other people thought the same thing.

One of the biggest men in cotton in the entire world met me a day or two later and said, "That was certainly the slickest deal you ever put over, Livingston. I was wondering how much you were going to lose when you came to market that line of yours. You knew this market was not big enough to take more than fifty or sixty thousand bales without selling off, and how you were going to work off the rest and not lose all your paper profits was beginning to interest me. I didn't think of your scheme. It certainly was slick."

"I had nothing to do with it," I assured him as earnestly as I could.

But all he did was to repeat: "Mighty slick, my boy. Mighty slick! Don't be so modest!"

It was after that deal that some of the papers referred to me as the Cotton King. But, as I said, I really was not entitled to that crown. It is not necessary to tell you that there is not enough money in the United States to buy the columns of the New York *World* ◁**11.12**▷ or enough personal pull to secure the publication of a story like that. It gave me an utterly unearned reputation that time.

But I have not told this story to moralize on the crowns that are sometimes pressed down upon the brows of undeserving traders or to emphasize the need of seizing the opportunity, no matter when or how it comes. My object merely was to account for the vast amount of newspaper notoriety that came to me as the result of my deal in July cotton. If it hadn't been for the newspapers I never would have met that remarkable man, Percy Thomas.

11.12 ▷ The New York *World* was one of the most popular newspapers of the era. Founded in 1860, it was purchased by Joseph Pulitzer in 1883 and became an innovator of many of the forms of journalism practiced today. One of its most famous journalists at the time was Nellie Bly, who was one of the first investigative reporters in the late 1880s. The paper's headquarters, the New York World Building, shown below, was the tallest office tower in the world when completed in 1890. It was torn down in 1955 to build a new ramp to the Brooklyn Bridge.

The *World* became one of the first papers to run color in 1896, and its Yellow Kid cartoon lent its name to the term "yellow journalism," which means sensationalism. The paper earned that sobriquet amid a series of fierce circulation battles with its archrival, the New York *Journal American*, owned by William Randolph Hearst. Pulitzer was best known for running stories that encouraged the thriving new immigrant community to read his paper, and many had great social impact, particularly its campaign against unsafe tenements. It actively covered the exploits of flashy traders like Livermore, alternately making them out to be folk heroes or villains, depending on editors' reading of the public mood.

ENDNOTES

1 "Wins $3,000,000 in Six Weeks," *Chicago Daily Tribune,* November 12, 1907, 5.

2 "Hit Market Right," *Boston Daily Globe,* November 12, 1907, 7.

3 Charles Henry Taylor, *History of the Board of Trade of the City of Chicago* (1917), 1118.

4 Ibid., 1119.

5 John William Leonard, ed., *Who's Who in Finance, Banking, and Insurance* (1911), 154.

6 David Greising and Laurie Morse, *Brokers, Bagmen, and Moles* (1991), 54.

7 "Who's Who in Finance," *Moody's Magazine* (March 1913): 197.

8 Taylor, *History of the Board of Trade of the City of Chicago,* 1123.

9 "Grain Corners End," *New York Times,* May 29, 1908, 1.

10 Henry Clews, *Fifty Years in Wall Street* (New York: Irving Publishing Company, 1908), 664.

11 Ibid.

12 "Death of Armour," *Time,* August 29, 1927.

13 Taylor, *History of the Board of Trade of the City of Chicago,* 1125.

14 William B. Dana Company, *The Financial Review* (1908), 28–30.

15 "Corn Soars to 79 in the Chicago Pit," *New York Times,* May 20, 1908, 9.

16 "Grain Corners End."

17 Edmund Clarence Stedman,ed., *The New York Stock Exchange* (1908), 308.

18 "Mr. Cammack's Retirement," *New York Times,* February 7, 1897, 4.

19 "Addison Cammack Dead," *New York Times,* February 6, 1901, 9.

20 Edward G.Riggs, "Wall Street," *Munsey's Magazine* (1894): 368–370.

21 Edwin Lefevre, "The Unbeatable Game of Stock Speculation," *Saturday Evening Post,* September 4, 1915, 3.

22 "Deacon White Gives It Up," *New York Times,* April 9, 1909, 6.

23 Edwin Griswold Nourse, *Brokerage* (1910), 154.

24 Ibid., 155.

25 Albert William Atwood, *The Exchanges and Speculation* (1917), 208.

26 Thomas Ellison, *The Cotton Trade of Great Britain* (1886), 166.

27 "Young Broker Raids Cotton," *Los Angeles Times,* August 6, 1908, 11.

28 "The Cotton Market," *New York Times,* April 8, 1908, 8.

29 "Grain Market," *Boston Daily Globe,* May 12, 1908, 7.

30 Ibid.

31 "Big Jump in July Cotton," *New York Times,* May 14, 1908, 16.

32 "Cotton Up and Down," *New York Times,* May 15, 1908, 16.

33 "Cotton Corner Collapses," *New York Times,* June 24, 1908, 12.

XII

Not long after I closed my July cotton deal more successfully than I had expected I received by mail a request for an interview. The letter was signed by Percy Thomas. ◁**12.1** Of course I immediately answered that I'd be glad to see him at my office at any time he cared to call. The next day he came.

I had long admired him. His name was a household word wherever men took an interest in growing or buying or selling cotton. In Europe as well as all over this countrypeople quoted Percy Thomas'

12.1 **Percy Thomas** appears to be a pseudonym for Theodore Hazeltine Price, a southern cotton expert and financier with deep-rooted American lineage. Born in 1861, he was a descendant of John Price, who traveled from Bristol, England, to Virginia in 1720. His grandfather fought in the Revolutionary War, and his father was an early member of the New York Cotton Exchange.

Price got his start in the cotton business in 1882. His skill as a speculator and insights into market conditions were lauded by many: "To a remarkable knowledge of the great staple, he added brilliancy, daring, and an extraordinary grasp of affairs. He wrote well, and his letters to the trade were real contributions to cotton literature,"[1] wrote one admirer. An example was his presentation, at the 1904 convention of the New England Cotton Manufacturers' Association, on the state the industry. He discussed both America's rising appetite for cotton and the progress of cotton production and manufacturing in China and India.[2]

Price was a member of the cotton firm Eure, Farrar & Price of Norfolk, Virginia. Later he was head of Price, Reid & Co. in New York City, which eventually merged with a competitor to become Price, McCormick & Company. In 1899 and 1900, Price attempted the largest cotton corner to date, but it failed and bankrupted his firm, leaving more than $13 million in liabilities.[3] This is likely the failure Livermore mentions.

Price had good reason to engage in that corner attempt. According to contemporary reports, he was the first man to recognize the crop failure of 1899.[4] In August of that year, prices were low, at around 6 cents per pound. Despite some resistance from the Liverpool market and contrary predictions from London trading houses, Price pushed prices up to 7.5 cents per pound.

(continued)

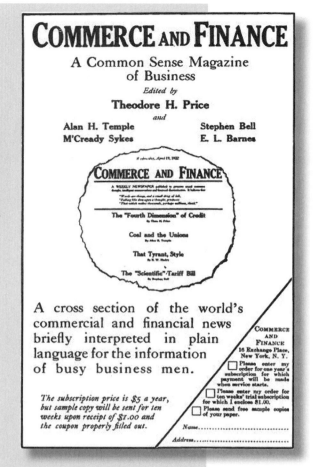

Satisfied with his accomplishment, Price started selling the market short early the next year. Prices wavered for a day or two, but soon the crop deficiency became apparent and a journalist reported "the price moved irresistibly upward."[5] Price quickly switched back to the bull side, but his profits were already lost and he was unable to secure the corner. In following years, cotton prices remained very volatile, allowing Price to conduct profitable trading operations. In the end, he was able to personally repay every dollar his firm's creditors owed in the bankruptcy.

In his later years, Price focused more heavily on his writing, becoming a commentator on economic and financial matters. He was also editor and owner of the *Commerce and Finance*, a widely read financial newspaper, where he penned columns on topics including foreign trade with Europe, the effects of World War I, speculation, and credit conditions.

opinions to me. I remember once at a Swiss resort talking to a Cairo banker who was interested in cotton growing in Egypt in association with the late Sir Ernest Cassel. ◁**12.2** When he heard I was from New York he immediately asked me about Percy Thomas, whose market reports he received and read with unfailing regularity.

Thomas, I always thought, went about his business scientifically. He was a true speculator, a thinker with the vision of a dreamer and the courage of a fighting man—an unusually well-informed man, who knew both the theory and the practice of trading in cotton. He loved to hear and to express ideas and theories and abstractions, and at

12.2 **Sir Ernest Cassel** was a financier and philanthropist who advised King Edward VII. The *New York Times* reported in his obituary that the "banker loaned money to nations and had vast enterprises on every continent."[6] He was born in 1852 in Cologne, Germany, where his father, Jacob, was a banker.

Cassel followed his father's example. He went to England at 16 to complete his education before working as a clerk for a group of grain dealers in Liverpool. By 1871, he joined the London banking house of Bischoffsheim & Gold-smid, where he was said to have "displayed his financial genius in straightening out the tangled affairs of one of the largest firms in the city."[7] At the time, Bischoffsheim was actively involved in the building of British railroads, a business in which lawsuits were often unavoidable.[8] Cassel's tough negotiating—"even lawyers feared him,"[9] said a royal biographer—secured favorable settlements and kept his firm out of court.

Eventually, Cassel founded his own firm and focused on extending his reach to distant corners of the globe. Upon his retirement at the age of 58, he had accumulated one of the largest fortunes in England. One of his first achievements in international finance was to come to the aid of Argentina in 1890 when its finances collapsed.

This was followed by transactions in Mexico, Sweden, Egypt, and the United States. He helped direct a loan to China after its first war with Japan. His knighthood, bestowed by Queen Victoria, was in response to his work in financing the Aswan Dam in Egypt. Over the opposition of France and Turkey, Cassel secured an agreement from the Egyptian government to allow British firms to dam the Nile River. He also assisted in the creation of the National Bank of Egypt and the Agricultural Bank of Egypt.[10]

Contemporary accounts describe Cassel as reserved and cool. He rarely shared his feelings with others. But he certainly had a deep concern for his fellow man, as according to a biographer, "London institutions received more than a million pounds from his bounty, cancer research, hospitals, and education coming in for his especial benevolence."[11]

the same time there was mighty little about the practical side of the cotton market or the psychology of cotton traders that he did not know, for he had been trading for years and had made and lost vast sums.

After the failure of his old Stock Exchange firm of Sheldon & Thomas he went it alone. Inside of two years he came back, almost spectacularly. I remember reading in the *Sun* that the first thing he did when he got on his feet financially was to pay off his old creditors in full, and the next was to hire an expert to study and determine for him how he had best invest a million dollars. This expert examined the properties and analysed the reports of several

12.3 The Delaware & Hudson was originally chartered in 1823 to build canals between New York City and the coal fields of eastern Pennsylvania. The company was one of the earliest adopters of rail technology in the United States. When it was decided that a particular 16-mile section was too mountainous for a canal, Delaware & Hudson built a railway instead. On it the *Stourbridge Lion*, the first steam locomotive to operate in North America, was tested.[12] (The locomotive, named for the town in England where it was built, never actually ran commercially on the D&H track because the rails were built for machines weighing four tons or less, and it weighed in at 7.5 tons. A replica of the *Lion* is shown below.) During Livermore's time, the company had expanded to become an important bridge railroad that provided other railroad systems with a connection between New York and Montreal, Canada.

companies and then recommended the purchase of Delaware & Hudson stock. ◁12.3⟩

Well, after having failed for millions and having come back with more millions, Thomas was cleaned out as the result of his deal in March cotton. There wasn't much time wasted after he came to see me. He proposed that we form a working alliance. Whatever information he got he would immediately turn over to me before passing it on to the public. My part would be to do the actual trading, for which he said I had a special genius and he hadn't.

That did not appeal to me for a number of reasons. I told him frankly that I did not think I could run in double harness and wasn't keen about trying to learn. But he insisted that it would be an ideal combination until I said flatly that I did not want to have anything to do with influencing other people to trade.

"If I fool myself," I told him, "I alone suffer and I pay the bill at once. There are no drawn-out payments or unexpected annoyances. I play a lone hand by choice and also because it is the wisest and cheapest way to trade. I get my pleasure out of matching my brains against the brains of other traders—men whom I have never seen and never talked to and never advised to buy or sell and never expect to meet or know. When I make money I make it backing my own opinions. I don't sell them or capitalise them. If I made money in any other way I would imagine I had not earned it. Your proposition does not interest me because I am interested in the game only as I play it for myself and in my own way."

He said he was sorry I felt the way I did, and tried to convince me that I was wrong in rejecting his plan. But I stuck to my views. The rest was a pleasant talk. I told him I knew he would "come back" and that I would consider it a privilege if he would allow me to be of financial assistance to him. But he said he could not accept any loans from me. Then he asked me about my July deal and I told him all about it; how I had gone into it and how much cotton I bought and the price and other details. We chatted a little more and then he went away.

When I said to you some time ago that a speculator has a host of enemies, many of whom successfully bore from within, I had in mind my many mistakes. I have learned that a man may possess an original mind and a lifelong habit of independent thinking and withal be vulnerable to attacks by a persuasive personality. I am fairly immune from the commoner speculative ailments, such as greed and fear and hope. But being an ordinary man I find I can err with great ease.

I ought to have been on my guard at this particular time because not long before that I had had an experience that proved how easily a man may be talked into doing something against his judgment and even against his wishes. It happened in Harding's office. I had a sort of private office—a room that they let me occupy by myself—and nobody was supposed to get to me during market hours without my consent. I didn't wish to be bothered and, as I was trading on a very large scale and my account was fairly profitable, I was pretty well guarded.

One day just after the market closed I heard somebody say, "Good afternoon, Mr. Livingston."

I turned and saw an utter stranger—a chap of about thirty or thirty-five. I could not understand how he'd got in, but there he was. I concluded his business with me had passed him. But I didn't say anything. I just looked at him and pretty soon he

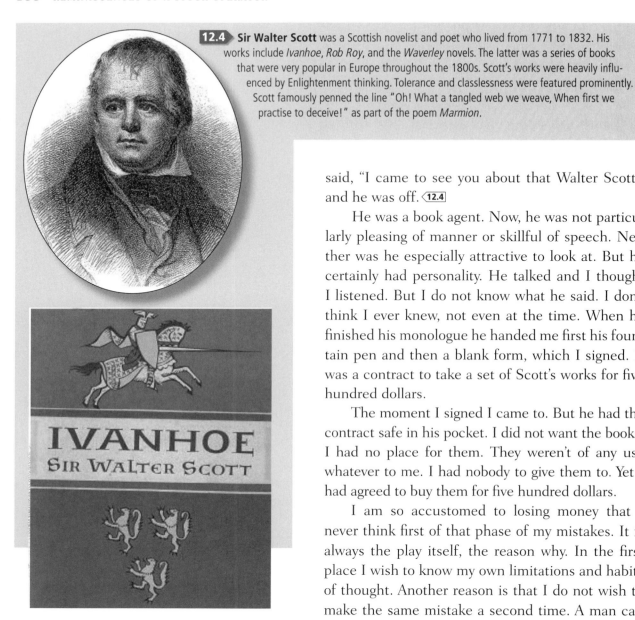

12.4 ▶ **Sir Walter Scott** was a Scottish novelist and poet who lived from 1771 to 1832. His works include *Ivanhoe*, *Rob Roy*, and the *Waverley* novels. The latter was a series of books that were very popular in Europe throughout the 1800s. Scott's works were heavily influenced by Enlightenment thinking. Tolerance and classlessness were featured prominently. Scott famously penned the line "Oh! What a tangled web we weave, When first we practise to deceive!" as part of the poem *Marmion*.

said, "I came to see you about that Walter Scott," and he was off. ◀**12.4**

He was a book agent. Now, he was not particularly pleasing of manner or skillful of speech. Neither was he especially attractive to look at. But he certainly had personality. He talked and I thought I listened. But I do not know what he said. I don't think I ever knew, not even at the time. When he finished his monologue he handed me first his fountain pen and then a blank form, which I signed. It was a contract to take a set of Scott's works for five hundred dollars.

The moment I signed I came to. But he had the contract safe in his pocket. I did not want the books. I had no place for them. They weren't of any use whatever to me. I had nobody to give them to. Yet I had agreed to buy them for five hundred dollars.

I am so accustomed to losing money that I never think first of that phase of my mistakes. It is always the play itself, the reason why. In the first place I wish to know my own limitations and habits of thought. Another reason is that I do not wish to make the same mistake a second time. A man can excuse his mistakes only by capitalising them to his subsequent profit.

Well, having made a five-hundred dollar mistake but not yet having localised the trouble, I just looked at the fellow to size him up as a first step. I'll be hanged if he didn't actually smile at me—an understanding little smile! He seemed to read my thoughts. I somehow knew that I did not have to explain anything to him; he knew it without my telling him. So I skipped the explanations and the preliminaries and asked him, "How much commission will you get on that five hundred dollar order?"

He promptly shook his head and said, "I can't do it! Sorry!"

"How much do you get?" I persisted.

"A third. But I can't do it!" he said.

"A third of five hundred dollars is one hundred and sixty-six dollars and sixty-six cents. I'll give you two hundred dollars cash if you give me back that signed contract." And to prove it I took the money out of my pocket.

"I told you I couldn't do it," he said.

"Do all your customers make the same offer to you?" I asked.

"No," he answered.

"Then why were you so sure that I was going to make it?"

"It is what your type of sport would do. You are a first-class loser and that makes you a first-class business man. I am much obliged to you, but I can't do it."

"Now tell me why you do not wish to make more than your commission?"

"It isn't that, exactly," he said. "I am not working just for the commission."

"What are you working for then?"

"For the commission and the record," he answered.

"What record?"

"Mine."

"What are you driving at?"

"Do you work for money alone?" he asked me.

"Yes," I said.

"No." And he shook his head. "No, you don't. You wouldn't get enough fun out of it. You certainly do not work merely to add a few more dollars to your bank account and you are not in Wall Street because you like easy money. You get your fun some other way. Well, same here."

12.5 ▶ Although it may seem strange that a traveling salesman would show up in a brokerage office to hawk a set of Sir Walter Scott books, this was not an unfamiliar phenomenon at the time.

Itinerant peddlers were common in the United States as early as the pre-Revolutionary War era, but the concept of salesmen working on commission for a large company really only developed in the post–Civil War era. Called "canvassers" or "drummers," traveling salesmen depended on their wits and shrewd insights into human nature at first. But by the 1860s, companies were marking out sales territories, setting commission rates, and developing scripts to help their men wrestle their wares past the objections of lonely, fretful, and poor farmers and shopkeepers.

Traveling sellers of book subscriptions, sets or volumes, who were called "agents," received elaborate instruction kits on how to talk to prospects that soon leveraged a canon of rules and tips that would be recognizable today for its emphasis on persuasion rather than content.[13] Religious, self-help and history books were common, as customers worried about their souls and status.

The first important book sold by agents was *Birds of America*, written and illustrated by John James Audubon in the 1820s. Fifty years later, Mark Twain used subscriptions exclusively to sell his first books, including *Innocents Abroad* in 1869 and *The Adventures of Tom Sawyer* in 1876, and got heavily involved in the marketing campaigns—right down to writing out proposed patter.[14] And in the 1880s, Twain persuaded Ulysses S. Grant to let his sales force take on the task of hawking the dying ex-president's memoirs door to door around the country. A pamphlet titled, "How to Introduce the Personal Memoirs of U.S. Grant" outlined sales arguments. Grant's fortune had been nearly wiped out in a Wall Street swindle in 1884, so salesmen used sympathy for his impoverishment as a tactic to persuade veterans to buy the book. The Twain campaign was ultimately a tremendous success, netting Grant's family at least $450,000—around $8 million today.[15]

Many titans of twentieth-century sales got their starts as door-to-door book agents, including David Hall McConnell, who went on to start the California Perfume Co., and later transformed that into Avon Products, the industry standard.[16] Other early-century entrepreneurs and inventors who also went door to door to sell their ideas were future chewing gum magnate William Wrigley Jr., cereal titan C. W. Post, adding machine pioneer William S. Burroughs, and ketchup king Henry Heinz.[17]

So the insightful salesman of Scott books with whom Livermore tangled was part of a rich tradition in the era before marketers could use radio and television to market on a much broader scale. (Ad seeking traveling book salesmen, at left, appeared in *Publishers Weekly* in 1910.)

I did not argue but asked him, "And how do you get your fun?"

"Well," he confessed, "we've all got a weak spot."

"And what's yours?"

"Vanity," he said.

"Well," I told him, "you succeeded in getting me to sign on. Now I want to sign off, and I am paying you two hundred dollars for ten minutes' work. Isn't that enough for your pride?"

"No," he answered. "You see, all the rest of the bunch have been working Wall Street for months and failed to make expenses. They said it was the fault of the goods and the territory. So the office sent for me to prove that the fault was with their salesmanship and not with the books or the place. They were working on a 25 per cent commission. I was in Cleveland, where I sold eighty-two sets in two weeks. I am here to sell a certain number of sets not only to people who did not buy from the other agents but to people they couldn't even get to see. That's why they give me 33⅓ per cent." [12.5]

"I can't quite figure out how you sold me that set."

"Why," he said consolingly, "I sold J. P. Morgan a set."

"No, you didn't," I said.

He wasn't angry. He simply said, "Honest, I did!"

"A set of Walter Scott to J. P. Morgan, who not only has some fine editions but probably the original manuscripts of some of the novels as well?"

"Well, here's his John Hancock." And he promptly flashed on me a contract signed by J. P. Morgan himself. It might not have been Mr. Morgan's signature, but it did not occur to me to doubt it at the time. Didn't he have mine in his pocket? All I felt was curiosity. So I asked him, "How did you get past the librarian?"

"I didn't see any librarian. I saw the Old Man himself. In his office."

"That's too much!" I said. Everybody knew that it was much harder to get into Mr. Morgan's private office empty handed than into the White House with a parcel that ticked like an alarm clock.

But he declared, "I did."

"But how did you get into his office?"

"How did I get into yours?" he retorted.

"I don't know. You tell me," I said.

"Well, the way I got into Morgan's office and the way I got into yours are the same. I just talked to the fellow at the door whose business it was not to let me in. And the way I got Morgan to sign was the same way I got you to sign. You weren't signing a contract for a set of books. You just took the fountain pen I gave you and did what I asked you to do with it. No difference. Same as you."

"And is that really Morgan's signature?" I asked him, about three minutes late with my skepticism.

"Sure! He learned how to write his name when he was a boy."

"And that's all there's to it?"

"That's all," he answered. "I know exactly what I am doing. That's all the secret there is. I am much obliged to you. Good day, Mr. Livingston." And he started to go out.

"Hold on," I said. "I'm bound to have you make an even two hundred dollars out of me." And I handed him thirty-five dollars.

He shook his head. Then: "No," he said. "I can't do that. But I can do this!" And he took the contract from his pocket, tore it in two and gave me the pieces.

I counted two hundred dollars and held the money before him, but he again shook his head.

"Isn't that what you meant?" I said.

"No."

"Then, why did you tear up the contract?"

"Because you did not whine, but took it as I would have taken it myself had I been in your place."

"But I offered you the two hundred dollars of my own accord," I said.

"I know; but money isn't everything."

Something in his voice made me say, "You're right; it isn't. And now what do you really want me to do for you?"

"You're quick, aren't you?" he said. "Do you really want to do something for me?"

"Yes," I told him, "I do. But whether I will or not depends what it is you have in mind."

"Take me with you into Mr. Ed Harding's office and tell him to let me talk to him three minutes by the clock. Then leave me alone with him."

I shook my head and said, "He is a good friend of mine."

"He's fifty years old and a stock broker," said the book agent.

That was perfectly true, so I took him into Ed's office. I did not hear anything more from or about that book agent. But one evening some weeks later when I was going uptown I ran across him in a Sixth Avenue L train. He raised his hat very politely and I nodded back. He came over and asked me, "How do you do, Mr. Livingston? And how is Mr. Harding?"

"He's well. Why do you ask?" I felt he was holding back a story.

"I sold him two thousand dollars' worth of books that day you took me in to see him."

"He never said a word to me about it," I said.

"No; that kind doesn't talk about it."

"What kind doesn't talk?"

"The kind that never makes mistakes on account of its being bad business to make them. That kind always knows what he wants and nobody can tell him different. That is the kind that's educating my children and keeps my wife in good humor. You did me a good turn, Mr. Livingston. I expected it when I gave up the two hundred dollars you were so anxious to present to me."

"And if Mr. Harding hadn't given you an order?"

"Oh, but I knew he would. I had found out what kind of man he was. He was a cinch."

"Yes. But if he hadn't bought any books?" I persisted.

"I'd have come back to you and sold you something. Good day, Mr. Livingston. I am going to see the mayor." And he got up as we pulled up at Park Place.

"I hope you sell him ten sets," I said. His Honor was a Tammany man. ◁**12.6**

"I'm a Republican, too," he said, and went out, not hastily, but leisurely, confident that the train would wait. And it did.

I have told you this story in such detail because it concerned a remarkable man who made me buy what I did not wish to buy. He was the first man who did that to me. There never should have been a

12.6 ▷ Tammany Hall was a Democratic Party political machine that played a role in New York City politics from the late 1700s through the 1960s. Founded in 1789 as the Tammany Society, originally envisaged as a fraternal organization, the group became increasingly politicized under Aaron Burr.[18] In Livermore's time, the organization was synonymous with the corruption of New York politics under William "Boss" Tweed in the mid-1800s. Tweed was in league with speculators Jim Fisk and Jay Gould and helped arrange favorable legislation for them.

At the time Livermore's story likely takes place, in 1907 or 1908, the mayor of New York was George Brinton McClellan Jr. Although McClellan was a Democrat affiliated with Tammany Hall, he actually battled the organization upon reelection in 1905 after promising an independent administration during the campaign.[19]

second, but there was. You can never bank on there being but one remarkable salesman in the world or on complete immunization from the influence of personality.

When Percy Thomas left my office, after I had pleasantly but definitely declined to enter into a working alliance with him, I would have sworn that our business paths would never cross. I was not sure I'd ever even see him again. But on the very next day he wrote me a letter thanking me for my offers of help and inviting me to come and see him. I answered that I would. He wrote again. I called.

I got to see a great deal of him. It was always a pleasure for me to listen to him, he knew so much and he expressed his knowledge so interestingly. I think he is the most magnetic man I ever met.

We talked of many things, for he is a widely read man with an amazing grasp of many subjects and a remarkable gift for interesting generalization. The wisdom of his speech is impressive; and as for plausibility, he hasn't an equal. I have heard many people accuse Percy Thomas of many things, including insincerity, but I sometimes wonder if his remarkable plausibility does not come from the fact that he first convinces himself so thoroughly as to acquire thereby a greatly increased power to convince others.

Of course we talked about market matters at great length. I was not bullish on cotton, but he was. I could not see the bull side at all, but he did. He brought up so many facts and figures that I ought to have been overwhelmed, but I wasn't. I couldn't disprove them because I could not deny their authenticity, but they did not shake my belief in what I read for myself. But he kept at it until I no longer felt sure of my own information as gathered from the trade papers and the dailies. That meant I couldn't see the market with my own eyes. A man cannot be convinced against his own convictions, but he can be talked into a state of uncertainty and indecision, which is even worse, for that means that he cannot trade with confidence and comfort.

I cannot say that I got all mixed up, exactly, but I lost my poise; or rather, I ceased to do my own thinking. I cannot give you in detail the various steps by which I reached the state of mind that was to prove so costly to me. I think it was his assurances of the accuracy of his figures, which were exclusively his, and the undependability of mine, which were not exclusively mine, but public property. He harped on the utter reliability, as proved time and again, of all his ten thousand correspondents throughout the South. In the end I came to read conditions as he himself read them—because we were both reading from the same page of the same book, held by him before my eyes. He has a logical mind. Once I accepted his facts it was a cinch that my own conclusions, derived from his facts, would agree with his own.

When he began his talks with me about the cotton situation I not only was bearish but I was short of the market. Gradually, as I began to accept his facts and figures, I began to fear I had been basing my previous position on misinformation. Of course I could not feel that way and not cover. And once I had covered because Thomas made me think I was wrong, I simply had to go long. It is the way my mind works. You know, I have done nothing in my life but trade in stocks and commodities. I naturally think that if it is wrong to be bearish it must be right to be a bull. And if it is right to be a bull it is imperative to buy. As my old Palm Beach friend said Pat Hearne used to say, "You can't tell till you bet!" I must prove whether I am right on the market or not; and the proofs are to be read only in my brokers' statements at the end of the month.

I started in to buy cotton and in a jiffy I had my usual line, about sixty thousand bales. It was the most asinine play of my career. Instead of standing

12.7 Given Livermore's preference for staying close to Wall Street when he has a large position out, his likely destination was the Raritan Bayshore region of New Jersey. The shoreline of Sandy Hook, which is the barrier spit that separates Lower New York Bay from the Atlantic Ocean, would have been a good spot for him to walk by the water and collect his thoughts.

12.8 Initially, it appeared as if Livermore was about to strike gold again. On August 6, the *Los Angeles Times* reported: "The entire supply of cotton stored in New York City and vicinity…has been cornered by J.L. Livermore, the young broker, who last May made more than $2,000,000 in a corner on the July options."[20] The price had advanced by $3.50 a bale over the previous two weeks as the short sellers became more concerned about the tenability of their positions. Said the *Times*: "An enormous quantity of October contracts have been sold short in New York because of the general belief…that an enormous croup will be gathered."[21]

The *Chicago Daily Tribune* also covered the story through its local bureau:

> A fair haired, beardless man of 31, younger looking by ten years than his age, who sits in a back room of a brokerage house and issues orders to a score of busy clerks in a gently modulated voice, has possessed himself of every bale of cotton not under contract in the warehouses of Greater New York, and is smilingly watching the painful contortions of a group of grizzled bears on the New York cotton exchange.[22]

Soon it was apparent something went terribly wrong for the Boy Plunger. On August 13, the *New York Times* reported that the "bull interests in the cotton market, who have had to fight to maintain their position in the market within the last few days, were forced to meet a still heavier onset of the bears yesterday," which knocked prices down $4.25 a bale below the highs reached the previous week.[23] Ominously, most of the selling was done by an "operator, who has been supposed to be in harmony with the bull leader."[24]

On August 20, the market broke badly, sending cotton down $5 per bale compared to the previous week as members of the bull pool were credited with selling some 75,000 bales just within the first hour of trading. The day before, Theodore Price sent out a market letter that seemed to confirm the rumor that he was an active member of the bull party. A reporter asked Livermore about the heavy losses being credited to him. "I keep my own books," he said in response. "I am not publishing them to the Street."[25]

or falling by my own observation and deductions I was merely playing another man's game. It was eminently fitting that my silly plays should not end with that. I not only bought when I had no business to be bullish but I didn't accumulate my line in accordance with the promptings of experience. I wasn't trading right. Having listened, I was lost.

The market was not going my way. I am never afraid or impatient when I am sure of my position. But the market didn't act the way it should have acted had Thomas been right. Having taken the first wrong step I took the second and the third, and of course it muddled me all up. I allowed myself to be persuaded not only into not taking my loss but into holding up the market. That is a style of play foreign to my nature and contrary to my trading principles and theories. Even as a boy in the bucket shops I had known better. But I was not myself. I was another man—a Thomasized person.

I not only was long of cotton but I was carrying a heavy line of wheat. That was doing famously and showed me a handsome profit. My fool efforts to bolster up cotton had increased my line to about one hundred and fifty thousand bales. I may tell you that about this time I was not feeling very well. I don't say this to furnish an excuse for my blunders, but merely to state a pertinent fact. I remember I went to Bayshore for a rest. **12.7**

While there I did some thinking. It seemed to me that my speculative commitments were overlarge. I am not timid as a rule, but I got to feeling nervous and that made me decide to lighten my load. To do this I must clean up either the cotton or the wheat.

It seems incredible that knowing the game as well as I did and with an experience of twelve or fourteen years of speculating in stocks and commodities I did precisely the wrong thing. The cotton showed me a loss and I kept it. The wheat showed me a profit and I sold it out. It was an ut-terly foolish play, but all I can say in extenuation is that it wasn't really my deal, but Thomas'. Of all speculative blunders there are few greater than trying to average a losing game. My cotton deal proved it to the hilt a little later. Always sell what shows you a loss and keep what shows you a profit. That was so obviously the wise thing to do and was so well known to me that even now I marvel at myself for doing the reverse.

And so I sold my wheat, deliberately cut short my profit in it. After I got out of it the price went up twenty cents a bushel without stopping. If I had kept it I might have taken a profit of about eight million dollars. And having decided to keep on with the losing proposition I bought more cotton!

I remember very clearly how every day I would buy cotton, more cotton. And why do you think I bought it? To keep the price from going down! If that isn't a supersucker play, what is? I simply kept on putting up more and more money—more money to lose eventually. My brokers and my intimate friends could not understand it; and they don't to this day. Of course if the deal had turned out differently I would have been a wonder. More than once I was warned against placing too much reliance on Percy Thomas' brilliant analyses. To this I paid no heed, but kept on buying cotton to keep it from going down. I was even buying it in Liverpool. I accumulated four hundred and forty thousand bales before I realised what I was doing. And then it was too late. So I sold out my line.

I lost nearly all that I had made out of all my other deals in stocks and commodities. I was not completely cleaned out, but I had left fewer hundreds of thousands than I had millions before I met my brilliant friend Percy Thomas. ◁12.8▷ For me of all men to violate all the laws that experience had taught me to observe in order to prosper was more than asinine.

Price had double-crossed Livermore by participating in the rise before switching to the short side and trapping the trader as he was forced to close his large position. A Boston newspaper reported: "It is known that Theodore H. Price, who was in the original deal with Mr. Livermore, has been bearish for more than a week. Mr. Price is supposed to have been short of the market on the slump, and to have made a handsome profit on the decline. Mr. Price is reputed to have sold out all of his long cotton in the recent rise."[26]

Livermore had overreached. He was betting on a pledge from the cotton farmers' union to not sell cotton for less than 10 cents a pound. But when push came to shove as an abundant crop threatened their livelihood, the union ignored the price floor and quickly took the best available offer. Livermore, said the paper, had been "opposed by a score of old operators on the exchange, who have had much longer experience. . . . They knew the temperament of the southern planter better than their young adversary."[27]

Livermore quickly bounced back. By October, he reportedly cleared $500,000 as a result of increases in his equity positions in Union Pacific, Southern Pacific, and Reading and St. Paul railroads. It was said at the time that his operations in the stock and cotton markets were reportedly "heavier than those of any other speculator."[28]

12.9 ▶ A woodbine is a climbing vine much like a honeysuckle, with yellow flowers. "Twineth" is an old-fashioned version of the verb "twine," meaning to become twisted or entangled.

According to a biography of James Fisk Jr., this strange locution has its origins in the congressional investigation of the Black Friday panic. When asked later what he meant by this phrase, which had become a part of the financier's legend, he explained that he had used it as a euphemism: "You see I was before that learned and dignified body, the Committee on Banking and Currency, and when Garfield asked me where the money got by Corbin went to, I could not make a vulgar reply, and say 'up a spout,' but observing, while peddling through New England, that every spout of house or cottage had a woodbine twining about it, I said, naturally enough, 'where the woodbine twineth.'"

His biographer then added: "His famous reply when asked where the money had gone—'Gone where the woodbine twineth'—will be remembered as long as the memorable panic itself will."[29]

So why was "up the spout" considered vulgar? The New York Times in 1871 wasn't quite sure, so on September 3 it published a 1,115 word essay on what editors called "that remarkable sentence."[30] The paper concluded that Fisk didn't realize the term came from England and meant an item had been pawned, apparently because of the spout-like device pawnbrokers used to send new items into storage.

But there was another definition that the prim *Times* editors may not have known about. Dictionaries of 19th Century slang report that it was used to describe the condition of a young, unmarried woman who had become pregnant, and thus "ruined."[31] This may well have been the meaning the bawdy trader had in mind.

12.10 ▶ Livermore needed to raise this cash to defend his brother-in-law, vaudeville performer Chester S. Jordan, after he was accused of murdering his wife.[32] Jordan was eventually sentenced to death for his crime despite an appeal to the United States Supreme Court on the grounds that one of his jurors went insane as a result of the trial.[33]

To learn that a man can make foolish plays for no reason whatever was a valuable lesson. It cost me millions to learn that another dangerous enemy to a trader is his susceptibility to the urgings of a magnetic personality when plausibly expressed by a brilliant mind. It has always seemed to me, however, that I might have learned my lesson quite as well if the cost had been only one million. But Fate does not always let you fix the tuition fee. She delivers the educational wallop and presents her own bill, knowing you have to pay it, no matter what the amount may be. Having learned what folly I was capable of I closed that particular incident. Percy Thomas went out of my life.

There I was, with more than nine-tenths of my stake, as Jim Fisk used to say, gone where the woodbine twineth—up the spout. **12.9** I had been a millionaire rather less than a year. My millions I had made by using brains, helped by luck. I had lost them by reversing the process. I sold my two yachts and was decidedly less extravagant in my manner of living.

But that one blow wasn't enough. Luck was against me. I ran up first against illness and then against the urgent need of two hundred thousand dollars in cash. **12.10** A few months before that sum would have been nothing at all; but now it meant almost the entire remnant of my fleet-winged fortune. I had to supply the money and the question was: Where could I get it? I didn't want to take it out of the balance I kept at my brokers' because if I did I wouldn't have much of a margin left for my own trading; and I needed trading facilities more than ever if I was to win back my millions quickly. There was only one alternative that I could see, and that was to take it out of the stock market!

Just think of it! If you know much about the average customer of the average commission house you will agree with me that the hope of making the stock market pay your bill is one of the most prolific sources of loss in Wall Street. You will chip out all you have if you adhere to your determination.

Why, in Harding's office one winter a little bunch of high flyers spent thirty or forty thousand dollars for an overcoat—and not one of them lived to wear it. It so happened that a prominent floor trader—who since has become world-famous as one of the dollar-a-year men—came down to the Exchange wearing a fur overcoat lined with sea otter. 12.11 In those days, before furs went up sky high, that coat was valued at only ten thousand dollars. Well, one of the chaps in Harding's office, Bob Keown, decided to get a coat lined with Russian sable. He priced one uptown. The cost was about the same, ten thousand dollars.

"That's the devil of a lot of money," objected one of the fellows.

"Oh, fair! Fair!" admitted Bob Keown amiably. "About a week's wages—unless you guys promise to present it to me as a slight but sincere token of the esteem in which you hold the nicest man in the office. Do I hear the presentation speech? No? Very well. I shall let the stock market buy it for me!"

"Why do you want a sable coat?" asked Ed Harding.

"It would look particularly well on a man of my inches," replied Bob, drawing himself up.

"And how did you say you were going to pay for it?" asked Jim Murphy, who was the star tip-chaser of the office.

"By a judicious investment of a temporary character, James. That's how," answered Bob, who knew that Murphy merely wanted a tip.

Sure enough, Jimmy asked, "What stock are you going to buy?"

"Wrong as usual, friend. This is no time to buy anything. I propose to sell five thousand Steel. It ought to go down ten points at the least. I'll just

12.11 Dollar-a-year men were business executives who were inspired by the moral righteousness of America's role in World War I to enter government service in their areas of expertise. Because U.S. law forbade the government from accepting free services, they accepted $1 a year for their work, plus expenses.

The term was later used again in World War II, and was used to distinguish high-level businessmen who came to work for the government in difficult jobs like materiel procurement from middle managers who needed a real wage while serving as reservists in disciplines like logistics. Dollar-a-year men were often accused of favoring their old business loyalties when private and public interests came into conflict, such as when ordering a new blast furnace to make steel for arms might take resources away from commercial interests.

take two and a half points net. That is conservative, isn't it?"

"What do you hear about it?" asked Murphy eagerly. He was a tall thin man with black hair and a hungry look, due to his never going out to lunch for fear of missing something on the tape.

"I hear that coat's the most becoming I ever planned to get." He turned to Harding and said, "Ed, sell five thousand U.S. Steel common at the market. To-day, darling!"

He was a plunger, Bob was, and liked to indulge in humorous talk. It was his way of letting the world know that he had an iron nerve. He sold five thousand Steel, and the stock promptly went up. Not being half as big an ass as he seemed when he talked, Bob stopped his loss at one and a half points and confided to the office that the New York climate was too benign for fur coats. They were unhealthy and ostentatious. The rest of the fellows jeered. But it was not long before one of them bought some Union Pacific to pay for the coat. He lost eighteen hundred dollars and said sables were all right for the outside of a woman's wrap, but not for the inside of a garment intended to be worn by a modest and intelligent man.

After that, one after another of the fellows tried to coax the market to pay for that coat. One day I said I would buy it to keep the office from going broke. But they all said that it wasn't a sporting thing to do; that if I wanted the coat for myself I ought to let the market give it to me. But Ed Harding strongly approved of my intention and that same afternoon I went to the furrier's to buy it. I found out that a man from Chicago had bought it the week before.

That was only one case. There isn't a man in Wall Street who has not lost money trying to make the market pay for an automobile or a bracelet or a motor boat or a painting. I could build a huge hospital with the birthday presents that the tight-fisted stock market has refused to pay for. In fact, of all hoodoos in Wall Street ◁12.12▷ I think the resolve to induce the stock market to act as a fairy godmother is the busiest and most persistent.

Like all well-authenticated hoodoos this has its reason for being. What does a man do when he sets out to make the stock market pay for a sudden need? Why, he merely hopes. He gambles. He therefore runs much greater risks than he would if he were speculating intelligently, in accordance with opinions or beliefs logically arrived at after a dispassionate study of underlying conditions. To begin with, he is after an immediate profit. He cannot afford to wait. The market must be nice to him at once if at all. He flatters himself that he is not asking more than to place an even-money bet. Because he is prepared to run quick—say, stop his loss at two points when all he hopes to make is two points—he hugs the fallacy that he is merely taking a fifty-fifty chance. Why, I've known men to lose thousands of dollars on such trades, particularly on purchases made at the height of a bull market just before a moderate reaction. It certainly is no way to trade.

Well, that crowning folly of my career as a stock operator was the last straw. It beat me. I lost what little my cotton deal had left me. It did even more harm, for I kept on trading—and losing. I persisted in thinking that the stock market must perforce make money for me in the end. But the only end in sight was the end of my resources. I went into debt, not only to my principal brokers but to other houses that accepted business from me without my putting up an adequate margin. I not only got in debt but I stayed in debt from then on.

12.12 Hoodoo is a form of folk magic that developed in the southern United States in the 1800s as a blend of African, Native American, and Christian cultures. It was originally used to described a magic spell, but also was used to describe a conjurer or witch, or objects that hoodoo practitioners created to cast a spell. The term could also refer to itinerant healers who traveled the countryside in the 1800s dispensing folk remedies, charms, and herbal potions aimed at helping people enlist supernatural forces for help with luck, money or love. [34]

Hoodoos used anything at hand to create their spells, including, according to one account, chicken feathers, earthworms, red peppers, coffee grounds, nails, beef tongues, oils, powders and graveyard dirt.[35] A hoodoo named Julia Jackson was said to have devised this formula to kill someone: "Catch a rattlesnake, kill it, hang it in the sun to dry. Write the person's name on a piece of paper and put it in the snake's mouth. Just like that snake dry up the person gonna dry up too. If you keep that snake in the sun long enough the person's gonna die."[36]

Traders have long used the term sardonically to mean paranormal beings or enchantments that prevent them from enjoying success. Livermore had a lot of personal superstitions, and one of the most closely held was that traders should not expect the market to deliver the money to pay for a specific expensive item, like a car or a fur coat. He believed that the notion cursed traders' thought processes, making them short-term oriented and wishful when they should be analytical.

ENDNOTES

1 Isaac F. Marcosson, "The Perilous Game of Cornering a Crop," *Munsey's Magazine* (November 1910): 239.

2 "Cotton Manufacturers' Conventions," *Dun's Review* (March 1904): 48.

3 *The National Cyclopaedia of American Biography* (1910), 281.

4 Marcosson, "Perilous Game of Cornering a Crop."

5 Ibid.

6 "Sir Ernest Cassel Dead in London," *New York Times*, September 23, 1921, 12.

7 Ibid.

8 Sidney Lee, *King Edward VII: A Biography Part II* (1927), 60.

9 Ibid.

10 "Foreign Banking and Finance," *Banker's Magazine* (1911): 392.

11 Lee, *King Edward VII.*

12 John H. White, *A History of the American Locomotive* (1979), 239.

13 Birth of a Salesman: The transformation of selling in America. Walter A. Friedman. Harvard University Press. 2004. 36.

14 Ibid.

15 Ibid.

16 Ibid.

17 Ibid.

18 Gustavus Myers, *The History of Tammany Hall* (1917), 13.

19 Ibid., 324.

20 "Young Broker Raids Cotton," *Los Angeles Times*, August 6, 1908, 11.

21 Ibid.

22 "Corner in Cotton by a Lamb of 31," *Chicago Daily Tribune*, August 10, 1908, 9.

23 "Bears Raid Cotton and Smash Prices," *New York Times,* August 13, 1908, 8.

24 Ibid.

25 "Bull Pool in Cotton Smashed by Bears," *New York Times,* August 21, 1908, 14.

26 "Cotton Bulls in Big Panic," *Boston Daily Globe,* August 21, 1908, 11.

27 Ibid.

28 "$500,000 to the Good," *Boston Daily Globe*, October 31, 1908, 9.

29 Edward L. Stokes, *The Life of Col. James Fisk Jr.* (H.S. Goodspeed & Co., 1872), 69.

30 "Up the Spout," *New York Times*, p. 5, September 3, 1871.

31 The Routledge Dictionary of Historical Slang. Eric Partridge and Jacqueline Simpson. 1973. 894

32 "Wife Slayer Aided by Cotton Plunger," *New York Times,* September 5, 1908, 2.

33 "Question Murder Juror's Sanity," *New York Times,* February 1, 1911, 7.

34 Herbal Magick: A Witch's Guide to Herbal Folklore and Enhantments. Gerina Dunwich. Career Press. 2002.

35 Joseph E. Holloway, Africanisms in American Culture. (Indiana University Press), 144.

36 Ibid., 145.

There I was, once more broke, which was bad, and dead wrong in my trading, which was a sight worse. I was sick, nervous, upset and unable to reason calmly. That is, I was in the frame of mind in which no speculator should be when he is trading. Everything went wrong with me. Indeed, I began to think that I could not recover my departed sense of proportion. Having grown accustomed to swinging a big line—say, more than a hundred thousand shares of stock—I feared I would not show good judgment trading in a small way. It scarcely seemed worth while being right when all you carried was a hundred shares of stock. After the habit of taking a big profit on a big line I wasn't sure I would know when to take my profit on a small line. I can't describe to you how weaponless I felt.

Broke again and incapable of assuming the offensive vigorously. In debt and wrong! After all those long years of successes, tempered by mistakes that really served to pave the way for greater successes, I was now worse off than when I began in the bucket shops. I had learned a great deal about the game of stock speculation, but I had not learned quite so much about the play of human weaknesses. There is no mind so machinelike that you can depend upon it to function with equal efficiency at all times. I now learned that I could not trust myself to remain equally unaffected by men and misfortunes at all times.

Money losses have never worried me in the slightest. But other troubles could and did. I studied my disaster in detail and of course found no difficulty in seeing just where I had been silly. I spotted the exact time and place. A man must know himself thoroughly if he is going to make a good job out of trading in the speculative markets. To know what I was capable of in the line of folly was a long educational step. I sometimes think that no price is too high for a speculator to

13.1 Chicago had been around for only about 70 years by the time Livermore arrived in the early 1910s. It had been incorporated in 1833 with a population of 350 and boundaries that extended only half a square mile. By 1840, the population had risen to 4,000, but a real influx of trade didn't arrive until the Illinois & Michigan Canal opened in 1848 to permit shipping from the Great Lakes through Chicago to the Mississippi River and beyond to the Gulf of Mexico.

Soon after that the first railroad arrived—and by the 1860s the city was the ninth most populous city in the nation and the main transportation hub of the region then known as the Northwest, connecting grains and mills of the Great Plains to the cities of the eastern seaboard. In the first year of the decade, the Republican National Convention took place in the city and nominated for president a fiery orator, attorney, and state politician named Abraham Lincoln.

Modern Chicago grew out of a tragedy: In 1871, a massive fire leveled the city, destroying nearly 20,000 wooden buildings and leaving a third of the 300,000 residents homeless. Because the lakeside ground was too unstable to rebuild on with masonry, architects innovated with steel and invented the skyscraper. A building boom emerged that created a dense, modern city with innovative architecture on par with New York, and the first underground sewage system. By 1900, the city had grown at an astonishing rate to house 1.7 million people, including tens of thousands of European immigrants and migrants from the southern United States.

The city grew to dominate the livestock and grain trades, which is what attracted commodity traders like Livermore; the beautiful art deco style Chicago Board of Trade Building opened in 1930, and was the city's tallest building until 1965. The CBOT merged with the Chicago Mercantile Exchange in 2007 and the New York Mercantile Exchange in 2008, becoming the commodity and financial futures powerhouse known now as the CME Group.

pay to learn that which will keep him from getting the swelled head. A great many smashes by brilliant men can be traced directly to the swelled head—an expensive disease everywhere to everybody, but particularly in Wall Street to a speculator.

I was not happy in New York, feeling the way I did. I didn't want to trade, because I wasn't in good trading trim. I decided to go away and seek a stake elsewhere. The change of scene could help me to find myself again, I thought. So once more I left New York, beaten by the game of speculation. I was worse than broke, since I owed over one hundred thousand dollars spread among various brokers.

I went to Chicago and there found a stake. **13.1** It was not a very substantial stake, but that merely meant that I would need a little more time to win back my fortune. A house that I once had done business with had faith in my ability as a trader and they were willing to prove it by allowing me to trade in their office in a small way.

I began very conservatively. I don't know how I might have fared had I stayed there. But one of the most remarkable experiences in my career cut short my stay in Chicago. It is an almost incredible story.

One day I got a telegram from Lucius Tucker. I had known him when he was the office manager of a Stock Exchange firm that I had at times given some business to, but I had lost track of him. The telegram read:

> Come to New York at once.
> L. TUCKER.

I knew that he knew from mutual friends how I was fixed and therefore it was certain he had something up his sleeve. At the same time I had no money to throw away on an unnecessary trip to New York; so instead of doing what he asked me to do I got him on the long distance.

"I got your telegram," I said. "What does it mean?"

"It means that a big banker in New York wants to see you," he answered.

"Who is it?" I asked. I couldn't imagine who it could be.

"I'll tell you when you get to New York. No use otherwise."

"You say he wants to see me?"

"He does."

"What about?"

"He'll tell you that in person if you give him a chance," said Lucius.

"Can't you write me?"

"No."

"Then tell me more plainly," I said.

"I don't want to."

"Look here, Lucius," I said, "just tell me this much: Is this a fool trip?"

"Certainly not. It will be to your advantage to come."

"Can't you give me an inkling?"

"No," he said. "It wouldn't be fair to him. And besides, I don't know just how much he wants to do for you. But take my advice: Come, and come quick."

"Are you sure it is I that he wishes to see?"

"Nobody else but you will do. Better come, I tell you. Telegraph me what train you take and I'll meet you at the station."

"Very well," I said, and hung up.

I didn't like quite so much mystery, but I knew that Lucius was friendly and that he must have a good reason for talking the way he did. I wasn't far-

13.2 This appears to be a pseudonym for **Charles E. Pugh**, who died in 1914 after a long career in railroads.[1] Pugh was born in 1841 and got his start in the railroad business in 1859 as a station agent for the Pennsylvania Railroad. He climbed the ranks, with successive turns as passenger conductor, train dispatcher, and general agent before becoming president of the Baltimore, Chesapeake & Atlantic Railway and vice president of the Pennsylvania system. Pugh was also on the board of various banking and insurance institutions, including the Manor Real Estate and Trust Co., Centennial National Bank, Mutual Fire, and the Marina and Inland Insurance Co.[2]

ing so sumptuously in Chicago that it would break my heart to leave it. At the rate I was trading it would be a long time before I could get together enough money to operate on the old scale.

I came back to New York, not knowing what would happen. Indeed, more than once during the trip I feared nothing at all would happen and that I'd be out my railroad fare and my time. I could not guess that I was about to have the most curious experience of my entire life.

Lucius met me at the station and did not waste any time in telling me that he had sent for me at the urgent request of Mr. Daniel Williamson, of the well-known Stock Exchange house of Williamson & Brown. Mr. Williamson told Lucius to tell me that he had a business proposition to make to me that he was sure I would accept since it would be very profitable for me. Lucius swore he didn't know what the proposition was. The character of the firm was a guaranty that nothing improper would be demanded of me.

Dan Williamson was the senior member of the firm, which was founded by Egbert Williamson way back in the '70's. There was no Brown and hadn't been one in the firm for years. The house had been very prominent in Dan's father's time and Dan had inherited a considerable fortune and didn't go after much outside business. They had one customer who was worth a hundred average customers and that was Alvin Marquand, ◁**13.2** Williamson's brother-in-law, who in addition to being a director in a dozen banks and trust companies was the president of the great Chesapeake and Atlantic Railroad system. He was the most picturesque personality in the railroad world after James J. Hill, and was the spokesman and dominant member of the powerful banking coterie known as the Fort Dawson gang.◁**13.3** He was worth from fifty million to five hundred million dollars, the estimate depending upon the state of the speaker's liver.

13.3 **James Hill**, nicknamed the "Empire Builder" by the media, was an ally of J. P. Morgan and a rival of E. H. Harriman and the Standard Oil crowd in the infamous Northern Pacific corner of 1901.[3] Born in 1836 in a village outside of Toronto, Canada, Hill immigrated to Minnesota in 1856 after his father died and ultimately built a $75 million fortune. His decision to leave home is the stuff of legend:

According to the story, a way-worn traveler stopped at the Hill farm for dinner, leaving his horse tied at the gate. The boy saw that the animal was tired and carried it a pail of water. The stranger was pleased at his thoughtfulness, and as he rode off tossed him a newspaper from the United States and called out gravely, "Go there young man. That country needs youngsters of your spirit."[4]

After studying the paper carefully and finding it rich with stories of opportunities and success, Hill decided to investigate. He traveled to St. Paul, which was then a frontier town of 5,000. Hill got a job as a stevedore and clerk with a local river transportation company. By 1865, after studying the finer points of his business and realizing the great potential to service the unsettled Northwest interior, Hill became an agent of the Northwest Packet Co. before becoming a representative of the St. Paul and Pacific Railroad. In 1869, he started his own transportation and fuel firm, notable for being the first to bring coal to the St. Paul area.

This was period of intense growth for the railroad industry. The promise of a new technology encouraged overinvestment not unlike the Internet technology bubble of the late 1990s. At the time, St. Paul was having its first experience with railroads. It was unsuccessful, with 100 miles of track built "into space which were said to begin and end nowhere,"[5] according to one account. After the venture went bankrupt for debts of $30 million and "a few streaks of rust and a right of way" as its only assets, Hill swooped in and acquired the property in 1878 for $100,000.[6] So was born the railroad that would eventually become the Great Northern.

Within five years, Hill was elected president of the Great Northern and immediately began work to fulfill his dream of building a transportation network that reached over the Pacific Ocean to Asia via steamships. It was this ambition that put him in league with Morgan and resulted in the confrontation with E.H. Harriman that ended in the May 1901 panic. At that time, he was described as "[s]omewhat below the average height but built like a buffalo, with a prodigious chest and neck and head; his arms long, sinewy, powerful; his feet large and firm planted and his legs as solid as steel columns—truly a massive, imposing figure of a man."[7]

In April 1907, Hill retired as president of the Great Northern, then resigned from the board of directors five years later. In the interim he wrote a book, *Highways of Progress*. In it, besides discussing the importance of resource conservation and railroad operations, he notes the importance of global trade to American farmers and businessmen: "Chinese and Japanese could be made customers for our flour in increasing quantity. A people once accustomed to wheat are slow to give it up. And the dense population would make consumption large."[8] Hill died in 1916 at the age of 77 at home in St. Paul.

When he died they found out that he was worth two hundred and fifty million dollars, all made in Wall Street. So you see he was some customer.

Lucius told me he had just accepted a position with Williamson & Brown—one that was made for him. He was supposed to be a sort of circulating general business getter. The firm was after a general commission business and Lucius had induced Mr. Williamson to open a couple of branch offices, one in one of the big hotels uptown and the other in Chicago. I rather gathered that I was going to be offered a position in the latter place, possibly as office

13.4 ▶ President of the National City Bank, precursor to today's Citigroup, James Stillman was a close friend of both E. H. Harriman and J. P. Morgan, had ties to William Rockefeller and the Standard Oil crowd, and played a role in the Northern Pacific corner of 1901, the Panic of 1907, and the public offering of Amalgamated Copper securities. In fact, Stillman's two daughters married two of William Rockefeller's sons.[9]

Stillman was a small, dark man who dressed immaculately and was described by a contemporary as "a perfect example of the well-built man of the world, sartorially correct, soft spoken, with a tendency toward cynical humor, and with tongue capable of devastating sarcasms."[10]

Stillman was born in 1850 in Brownsville, Texas. His father, Charles Stillman, a native of Connecticut, built a business empire stretching from New York to Texas and Mexico. His businesses included silver and lead mines, real estate, a cotton brokerage, shipping, textile factories, and retail outlets. During the Civil War, Charles helped smuggle Confederate cotton south to his cotton mills in Monterrey and north to the Cotton Exchange in Manhattan.[11]

At 18, Stillman got his start as a clerk at the cotton merchant house of Smith, Woodward & Stillman in New York. Within two years, he became a full partner and the firm was reincorporated as Woodward & Stillman. Relationships between his firm and National City Bank brought Stillman in close contact with bank president Moses Taylor. Eventually, he was made a bank director and in 1891 succeeded Taylor as president.[12] These were tumultuous years, according to a biographer:

The world was ripe for a fall. The Baring panic, the crisis of 1893, the free-silver collapse, lay just beyond the hill where man's eyes could not see them. By chance, Mr. Stillman took the presidency. The storm broke. He showed himself the master mariner, quiet, skilful, courageous, cold as an iceberg in panic, intuitive as a woman in the hour of action. And so he came to his inheritance.[13]

Livermore mentions Stillman's ability to embrace silence. Reporters of the day called Stillman "the coldest proposition in America."[14] Historian Maury Klein said that few "rivaled the glacial façade of Stillman. Laughter came to his lips with the frequency of leap years. He was an iceberg whose smooth, pleasant features revealed absolutely nothing of the dark complexities swimming beneath their surface."[15]

Accomplished Wall Street operator and statesman Bernard Baruch, who was also a friend of Livermore's, told a story about Stillman returning from a trip to Europe and running into George Perkins, a J. P. Morgan partner. "I see you're back," Perkins remarked. When Stillman merely stared, Perkins quipped, "Oh you need not confirm it."[16] At home he required his family to sit silently through two-hour formal dinners.[17]

Stillman retired from his post as president of National City Bank in 1908. Soon after, he reportedly tried to convince E. H. Harriman, J. P. Morgan, and William Rockefeller that all four should retire for the good of the country. The idea was to put an end to the government's campaign against the "Money Trusts" and quell the public's apprehension about the great concentration of wealth and power controlled by these four men. Soon Stillman got his wish. Harriman died a year later. Morgan paid less and less attention to business affairs and became better known as an art collector and traveler. Rockefeller suffered from ill health and was forced to retire. Stillman died in the spring of 1918.[18]

manager, which was something I would not accept. I didn't jump on Lucius because I thought I'd better wait until the offer was made before I refused it.

Lucius took me into Mr. Williamson's private office, introduced me to his chief and left the room in a hurry, as though he wished to avoid being called as witness in a case in which he knew both parties. I prepared to listen and then to say no.

Mr. Williamson was very pleasant. He was a thorough gentleman, with polished manners and a kindly smile. I could see that he made friends easily and kept them. Why not? He was healthy and therefore good-humored. He had slathers of money and therefore could not be suspected of sordid motives. These things, together with his education and social training, made it easy for him to be not only polite but friendly, and not only friendly but helpful.

I said nothing. I had nothing to say and, besides, I always let the other man have his say in full before I do any talking. Somebody told me that the late James Stillman, ◁**13.4** president of the National City Bank ◁**13.5**—who, by the way, was an intimate friend of Williamson's—made it his practice to listen in silence, with an impassive face, to anybody who brought a proposition to him. After the man got through Mr. Stillman continued to look at him, as though the man had not finished. So the man, feeling urged to say something more, did so. Simply by looking and listening Stillman often made the man offer terms much more advantageous to the bank than he had meant to offer when he began to speak.

I don't keep silent just to induce people to offer a better bargain, but because I like to know all the facts of the case. By letting a man have his say in full you are able to decide at once. It is a great time-saver. It averts debates and prolonged discussions that get nowhere. Nearly every business proposition that is brought to me can be settled, as far as my participation in it is concerned, by my saying yes or no. But I cannot say yes or no right off unless I have the complete proposition before me.

Dan Williamson did the talking and I did the listening. He told me he had heard a great deal about my operations in the stock market and how he regretted that I had gone outside of my bailiwick and come a cropper in cotton. Still it was to my bad luck that he owed the pleasure of that interview with me. He thought my forte was the stock market, that I was born for it and that I should not stray from it.

13.5 National City Bank, or City Bank as it was popularly called, was chartered in 1812 by the New York Legislature and reorganized as a national bank in 1865. Moses Taylor held the office of president for 34 years, until his death. The original capitalization of $1 million rose to $25 million by 1904.[19]

When James Stillman took the reins of City Bank, he pushed the firm into investment banking, then the fastest-growing and most profitable area of finance.[20] Although Morgan dominated the business of security underwriting and marketing, Stillman was able to secure a foothold by teaming with Jacob Schiff of Kuhn, Loeb. One of their first efforts together was to help E. H. Harriman reorganize Union Pacific Railroad in 1895.

Soon Stillman focused on building City Bank into an institution that could provide any service that the new large corporations needed. He also notably expanded the bank's reach into foreign markets, especially South America, with branches in Rio de Janeiro and Buenos Aires. In 1907, Stillman wrote to his associate:

I firmly believe…that the most successful banks will be the ones that can do something else than the mere receiving and loaning of money. That does not require a very high order of ability, but devising methods of serving people and [of] attracting business without resorting to unconservative or unprofitable methods, that opens limited fields for study, ability and resourcefulness and few only will be found to do it.[21]

In 1955, National City Bank merged with the First National Bank of New York to form Citibank. After merging with Travelers Insurance in 1998, Citigroup was formed. Before nearly collapsing in the credit crisis of 2007–2009, Citigroup was America's largest financial institution for decades.

"And that is the reason, Mr. Livingston," he concluded pleasantly, "why we wish to do business with you."

"Do business how?" I asked him.

"Be your brokers," he said. "My firm would like to do your stock business."

"I'd like to give it to you," I said, "but I can't."

"Why not?" he asked.

"I haven't any money," I answered.

"That part is all right," he said with a friendly smile. "I'll furnish it." He took out a pocket check book, wrote out a check for twenty-five thousand dollars to my order, and gave it to me.

"What's this for?" I asked.

"For you to deposit in your own bank. You will draw your own checks. I want you to do your trading in our office. I don't care whether you win or lose. If that money goes I will give you another personal check. So you don't have to be so very careful with this one. See?"

I knew that the firm was too rich and prosperous to need anybody's business, much less to give a fellow the money to put up as margin. And then he was so nice about it! Instead of giving me a credit with the house he gave me the actual cash, so that he alone knew where it came from, the only string being that if I traded I should do so through his firm. And then the promise that there would be more if that went! Still, there must be a reason.

"What's the idea?" I asked him.

"The idea is simply that we want to have a customer in this office who is known as a big active trader. Everybody knows that you swing a big line on the short side, which is what I particularly like about you. You are known as a plunger."

"I still don't get it," I said.

"I'll be frank with you, Mr. Livingston. We have two or three very wealthy customers who buy and sell stocks in a big way. I don't want the Street to suspect them of selling long stock every time we sell ten or twenty thousand shares of any stock. If the Street knows that you are trading in our office it will not know whether it is your short selling or the other customers' long stock that is coming on the market."

I understood at once. He wanted to cover up his brother-in-law's operations with my reputation as a plunger! It so happened that I had made my biggest killing on the bear side a year and a half before, and, of course, the Street gossips and the stupid rumor mongers had acquired the habit of blaming me for every decline in prices. To this day when the market is very weak they say I am raiding it. ◁**13.6**

I didn't have to reflect. I saw at a glance that Dan Williamson was offering me a chance to come back and come back quickly. I took the check, banked it, opened an account with his firm and began trading. It was a good active market, broad enough for a man not to have to stick to one or two specialties. I had begun to fear, as I told you, that I had lost the knack of hitting it right. But it seems I hadn't. In three weeks' time I had made a profit of one hundred and twelve thousand dollars out of the twenty-five thousand that Dan Williamson lent me.

I went to him and said, "I've come to pay you back that twenty-five thousand dollars."

"No, no!" he said and waved me away exactly as if I had offered him a castor-oil cocktail. "No, no, my boy. Wait until your account amounts to something. Don't think about it yet. You've only got chicken feed there."

There is where I made the mistake that I have regretted more than any other I ever made in my Wall Street career. It was responsible for long and dreary years of suffering. I should have insisted on his taking the money. I was on my way to a bigger fortune than I had lost and walking pretty fast. For three weeks my average profit was 150 per cent per week. From then on my trading would be on a steadily increasing scale. But instead of freeing my-

13.6 ▶ The problem of Livermore being identified with every market swoon became so extreme that in 1929 he was forced to hire a bodyguard. A former policeman, Frank Gorman, stayed in Livermore's mansion after several anonymous death threats were made against the speculator.[22]

There was a lot of property to protect in years when he wasn't flat broke. Patricia Livermore, the trader's daughter-in-law, gave a rundown of the family's lifestyle in a 1990 documentary about the 1929 crash. She said in part:[23]

"[The Livermores] lived in utter splendor, typical of the '20s when society was showy and wealth was displayed. They had a beautiful place on 76th Street in Manhattan on the West Side, off Central Park.... They had a house in Great Neck. They had a summer house in Lake Placid. They had a house in Palm Beach. They had a private railroad car, two yachts. The only yacht that was bigger was J. P. Morgan's. And they used one of them, the big one, very frequently when they went to Europe. They lived very comfortably....

"Jesse Livermore had a ticker tape in every home that he owned, on his railway cars, on his yachts....They had several Rolls Royces, lots of chauffeurs. They had a staff of about 20 or 25 and in each place, in each house, see, and with the exception of [his wife's] personal maid, they did not take their staffs with them. They simply kept them year-round in all their establishments....Oh, they lived. They really lived. Mrs. Livermore was a spender. And, of course, she loved to buy. She spent her days buying and buying and buying."

13.7 Known formally as the Baltimore, Chesapeake and Atlantic Railroad, the company was the result of an 1868 merger between the Virginia Central and the Covington & Ohio systems. In 1899, the Pennsylvania Railroad purchased a majority interest in the company.[24] The railroad operated from the Atlantic shores of Virginia and over the Appalachian Mountains into Illinois, Michigan, and Canada. Eventually, the line joined with a number of smaller railroads to form today's CSX Transportation.[25]

self from all obligation I let him have his way and did not compel him to accept the twenty-five thousand dollars. Of course, since he didn't draw out the twenty-five thousand dollars he had advanced me I felt I could not very well draw out my profit. I was very grateful to him, but I am so constituted that I don't like to owe money or favours. I can pay the money back with money, but the favours and kindnesses I must pay back in kind—and you are apt to find these moral obligations mighty high priced at times. Moreover there is no statute of limitations.

I left the money undisturbed and resumed my trading. I was getting on very nicely. I was recovering my poise and I was sure it would not be very long before I should get back into my 1907 stride. Once I did that, all I'd ask for would be for the market to hold out a little while and I'd more than make up my losses. But making or not making the money was not bothering me much. What made me happy was that I was losing the habit of being wrong, of not being myself. It had played havoc with me for months but I had learned my lesson.

Just about that time I turned bear and I began to sell short several railroad stocks. Among them was Chesapeake & Atlantic. **13.7** I think I put out a short line in it; about eight thousand shares.

One morning when I got downtown Dan Williamson called me into his private office before the market opened and said to me: "Larry, don't do anything in Chesapeake & Atlantic just now. That was a bad play of yours, selling eight thousand short. I covered it for you this morning in London and went long."

I was sure Chesapeake & Atlantic was going down. The tape told it to me quite plainly; and besides I was bearish on the whole market, not violently or insanely bearish, but enough to feel comfortable with a moderate short line out. I said to Williamson, "What did you do that for? I am bearish on the whole market and they are all going lower."

But he just shook his head and said, "I did it because I happen to know something about Chesapeake & Atlantic that you couldn't know. My advice to you is not to sell that stock short until I tell you it is safe to do so."

What could I do? That wasn't an asinine tip. It was advice that came from the brother-in-law of the chairman of the board of directors. Dan was not only Alvin Marquand's closest friend but he had been kind and generous to me. He had shown his faith in me and confidence in my word. I couldn't do less than to thank him. And so my feelings again won over my judgment and I gave in. To subordinate my judgment to his desires was the undoing of me. Gratitude is something a decent man can't help feeling, but it is for a fellow to keep it from completely tying him up. The first thing I knew I not only had lost all my profit but I owed the firm one hundred and fifty thousand dollars besides. I felt pretty badly about it, but Dan told me not to worry.

"I'll get you out of this hole," he promised. "I know I will. But I can only do it if you let me. You will have to stop doing business on your own hook. I can't be working for you and then have you completely undo all my work in your behalf. Just you lay off the market and give me a chance to make some money for you. Won't you, Larry?"

Again I ask you: What could I do? I thought of his kindliness and I could not do anything that might be construed as lacking in appreciation. I had grown to like him. He was very pleasant and friendly. I remember that all I got from him was encouragement. He kept on assuring me that everything would come out O.K. One day, perhaps six months later, he came to me with a pleased smile and gave me some credit slips.

"I told you I would pull you out of that hole," he said, "and I have." And then I discovered that not only had he wiped out the debt entirely but I had a small credit balance besides.

13.8 Livermore is likely referring to the Atlantic Coast Line Railroad that operated from New York City down along the Atlantic seaboard to Tampa, Florida. It was formed through combination of smaller lines in 1869 by William Walters, a produce merchant from Baltimore. In addition to transporting vacationers to the tropical waters of the Gulf of Mexico, the Southern Atlantic moved fresh fruit and vegetables in refrigerator cars to northern cities. In the late 1950s, the railroad merged with its old rival, the Seaboard Coast Line, before becoming part of CSX.[26]

I think I could have run that up without much trouble, for the market was right, but he said to me, "I have bought you ten thousand shares of Southern Atlantic." **13.8** That was another road controlled by his brother-in-law, Alvin Marquand, who also ruled the market destinies of the stock.

When a man does for you what Dan Williamson did for me you can't say anything but "Thank you"—no matter what your market views may be. You may be sure you're right, but as Pat Hearne used to say: "You can't tell till you bet!" and Dan Williamson had bet for me—with his money.

Well, Southern Atlantic went down and stayed down and I lost, I forget how much, on my ten thousand shares before Dan sold me out. I owed him more than ever. But you never saw a nicer or less importunate creditor in your life. Never a whimper from him. Instead, encouraging words and admonitions not to worry about it. In the end the loss was made up for me in the same generous but mysterious way.

He gave no details whatever. They were all numbered accounts. Dan Williamson would just say to me, "We made up your Southern Atlantic loss with profits on this other deal," and he'd tell me how he had sold seventy-five hundred shares of some other stock and made a nice thing out of it. I can truthfully say that I never knew a blessed thing about those trades of mine until I was told that the indebtedness was wiped out.

After that happened several times I began to think, and I got to look at my case from a different angle. Finally I tumbled. It was plain that I had been used by Dan Williamson. It made me angry to think it, but still angrier that I had not tumbled to it quicker. As soon as I had gone over the whole thing in my mind I went to Dan Williamson, told him I was through with the firm, and I quit the office of Williamson & Brown. I had no words with him or any of his partners. What good would that have done me? But I will admit that I was sore—at myself quite as much as at Williamson & Brown.

The loss of the money didn't bother me. Whenever I have lost money in the stock market I have always considered that I have learned something; that if I have lost money I have gained experience, so that the money really went for a tuition fee. A man has to have experience and he has to pay for it. But there was something that hurt a whole lot in that experience of mine in Dan Williamson's office, and that was the loss of a great opportunity. The money a man loses is nothing; he can make it up. But opportunities such as I had then do not come every day.

The market, you see, had been a fine trading market. I was right; I mean, I was reading it accurately. The opportunity to make millions was there. But I allowed my gratitude to interfere with my play. I tied my own hands. I had to do what Dan Williamson in his kindness wished done. Altogether it was more unsatisfactory than doing business with a relative. Bad business!

And that wasn't the worst thing about it. It was that after that there was practically no opportunity for me to make big money. The market flattened out. Things drifted from bad to worse. I not only lost all I had but got into debt again—more heavily than ever. Those were long lean years, 1911, 1912, 1913 and 1914. **‹13.9›** There was no money to be made. The opportunity simply wasn't there and so I was worse off than ever.

It isn't uncomfortable to lose when the loss is not accompanied by a poignant vision of what might have been. That was precisely what I could not keep my mind from dwelling on, and of course it unsettled me further. I learned that the weaknesses to which a speculator is prone are almost numberless. It was proper for me as a man to act the way I did in Dan Williamson's office, but it was improper and unwise for me as a speculator to allow myself

13.9 After the excitement of the preceding decade, the years running up to the beginning of World War I were rather dull. It was a period marked by investigations and regulations in the aftermath of the Panic of 1907 and the populism of the administration of Theodore Roosevelt. In 1911, the Supreme Court ordered both Standard Oil and American Tobacco dissolved. The Dow Jones Industrials added less than 1% for the year to close at 81.68. The Dow Jones Transportation Average added 2.4% to close at 116.83.

The year 1912 brought the sinking of the *Titanic*, a panic on the Paris Bourse, the country's first minimum wage statute, and the Pujo Anti-Trust Committee. The Dow Industrials gained 7.6% while the Dow Transports were essentially unchanged. In 1913, the New York Stock Exchange waged war against stock manipulation and excessive margins, federal income taxes began, and the Federal Reserve System was established. The Dow Industrials lost 10.3% while the Dow Transports fell 11.2%.

Unfortunately, 1914 continued the downward trend. World War I broke out after Archduke Franz Ferdinand was assassinated in Austria. On July 31, the war in Europe prompted the NYSE to close for four months: the first time it had closed at all since 1873. The Curb Market also closed. Wall Street feared that a liquidation of European accounts, which were valued at $2.4 billion, would cause a panic. Over the summer, the situation in Europe deteriorated as Germany declared war on France and Russia before attacking Belgium. England reciprocated by declaring war on Germany.

On December 1, the San Francisco Stock and Bond Exchange became the first exchange to reopen. On December 12, trading resumed with restrictions on the NYSE. The Dow Industrials fell 30.7% to a level not seen since just after the Panic of 1907—erasing seven years of growth. The Dow Transports fell 17.2%.[27]

to be influenced by any consideration to act against my own judgment. *Noblesse oblige*—but not in the stock market, because the tape is not chivalrous and moreover does not reward loyalty. I realise that I couldn't have acted differently. I couldn't make myself over just because I wished to trade in the stock market. But business is business always, and my business as a speculator is to back my own judgment always.

It was a very curious experience. I'll tell you what I think happened. Dan Williamson was perfectly sincere in what he told me when he first saw me. Every time his firm did a few thousand shares in any one stock the Street jumped at the conclusion that Alvin Marquand was buying or selling. He was the big trader of the office, to be sure, and he gave this firm all his business; and he was one of the best and biggest traders they have ever had in Wall Street. Well, I was to be used as a smoke screen, particularly for Marquand's selling.

Alvin Marquand fell sick shortly after I went in. His ailment was early diagnosed as incurable, and Dan Williamson of course knew it long before Marquand himself did. That is why Dan covered my Chesapeake & Atlantic stock. He had begun to liquidate some of his brother-in-law's speculative holdings of that and other stocks.

Of course when Marquand died the estate had to liquidate his speculative and semispeculative lines, and by that time we had run into a bear market. By tying me up the way he did, Dan was helping the estate a whole lot. I do not speak boastfully when I say that I was a very heavy trader and that I was dead right in my views on the stock market. I know that Williamson remembered my successful operations in the bear market of 1907 and he couldn't afford to run the risk of having me at large. Why, if I had kept on the way I was going I'd have made so much money that by the time he was trying to liquidate part of Alvin Marquand's estate I would have been trading in hundreds of thousands of shares. As an active bear I would have done damage running into the millions of dollars to the Marquand heirs, for Alvin left only a little over a couple of hundred millions.

It was much cheaper for them to let me get into debt and then to pay off the debt than to have me in some other office operating actively on the bear side. That is precisely what I would have been doing but for my feeling that I must not be outdone in decency by Dan Williamson. ◁**13.10**]

I have always considered this the most interesting and most unfortunate of all my experiences as a stock operator. As a lesson it cost me a disproportionately high price. It put off the time of my recovery several years. I was young enough to wait with patience for the strayed millions to come back. But five years is a long time for a man to be poor. Young or old, it is not to be relished. I could do without the yachts a great deal easier than I could without a market to come back on. The greatest opportunity of a lifetime was holding before my very nose the purse I had lost. I could not put out my hand and reach for it. A very shrewd boy, that Dan Williamson; as slick as they make them; farsighted, ingenious, daring. He is a thinker, has imagination, detects the vulnerable spot in any man and can plan cold-bloodedly to hit it. He did his own sizing up and soon doped out just what to do to me in order to reduce me to complete inoffensiveness in the market. He did not actually do me out of any money. On the contrary, he was to all appearances extremely nice about it. He loved his sister, Mrs. Marquand, and he did his duty toward her as he saw it.

13.10 ▷ There is no historical record of Williamson or his firm, so it is likely that this was another pseudonym to cover the identity of an individual who Livermore did not wish to openly name. Pugh retired in 1911, which coincides roughly with the timeline given here. It makes sense that Williamson, whoever he was, wanted to rein in Livermore's bear operations to maximize the value of Pugh's estate—especially in a trendless market.[28]

ENDNOTES

1 "Obituary," *Railway World* (1913), 388.

2 John William Leonard, *Who's Who in Finance, Banking, and Insurance* (1911), 859.

3 "J.J. Hill Dead," *New York Times,* May 30, 1916, 1.

4 Ibid.

5 Ibid.

6 Ibid.

7 Ibid.

8 James Jerome Hill, *Highways of Progress* (1910), 160.

9 Henry Morgenthau, *All in a Life-Time* (1922), 77.

10 Maury Klein, *The Life & Legend of E.H. Harriman,* 163

11 "Charles Stillman," *Handbook of Texas Online,* accessed June 24, 2009: www.tshaonline.org/handbook/online/articles/SS/fst57.html.

12 Mitchell Charles Harriman, *Prominent and Progressive Americans* (1902), 321–323.

13 C. M. Keys, "The Money-Kings," *The World's Work: A History of Our Time* (1907), 9520.

14 Maury Klein, *The Life & Legend of E.H. Harriman* (2000), 163.

15 Ibid.

16 Bernard Baruch, *My Own Story* (1957), 261.

17 Celia McGee, "A Wasp's Buzz," *New York,* August 1, 1994, 38.

18 "James Stillman, Head of City Bank, Dies Suddenly," *New York Times,* March 16, 1918, 1.

19 Thomas William Lawson, *Frenzied Finance* (1906), 52–53.

20 Klein, *The Life & Legend of E.H. Harriman,* 165.

21 Robert F. Bruner and Sean D. Carr, *The Panic of 1907* (Hoboken, NJ: John Wiley & Sons, 2007), 186.

22 "Livermore Has Bodyguard." *New York Times.* December 21, 1929. 5.

23 "The American Experience: The Crash of 1929," WGBH. 1990

24 "News of the Railroads," *New York Times,* September 5, 1899, 4.

25 John F. Stover and Mark Christopher Carnes, *The Routledge Historical Atlas of American Railroads* (1999), 82–83.

26 Ibid., 78.

27 Peter Wyckoff, *Wall Street and the Stock Markets* (1972), 50–54.

28 "Pugh Leaves Pennsylvania," *New York Times,* February 25, 1911, 8.

XIV

It has always rankled in my mind that after I left Williamson & Brown's office the cream was off the market. We ran smack into a long moneyless period; four mighty lean years. There was not a penny to be made. As Billy Henriquez once said, "It was the kind of market in which not even a skunk could make a scent."

It looked to me as though I was in Dutch with destiny. It might have been the plan of Providence to chasten me, but really I had not been filled with such pride as called for a fall. I had not committed any of those speculative sins which a trader must expiate on the debtor side of the account. I was not guilty of a typical sucker play. What I had done, or, rather, what I had left undone, was something for which I would have received praise and not blame—north of Forty-second Street. In Wall Street it was absurd and costly. But by far the worst thing about it was the tendency it had to make a man a little less inclined to permit himself human feelings in the ticker district.

I left Williamson's and tried other brokers' offices. In every one of them I lost money. It served me right, because I was trying to force the market into giving me what it didn't have to give—to wit, opportunities for making money. I did not find any trouble in getting credit, because those who knew me had faith in me. You can get an idea of how strong their confidence was when I tell you that when I finally stopped trading on credit I owed well over one million dollars.

The trouble was not that I had lost my grip but that during those four wretched years the opportunities for making money simply didn't exist. Still I plugged along, trying to make a stake and succeeding only in increasing my indebtedness. After I ceased trading on my own hook because I wouldn't owe my friends any more money I made a living handling accounts for people who believed I knew the game well enough to beat it even in a dull market. For my services I received a percentage of the profits—when there were any. That is how I lived. Well, say that is how I sustained life.

Of course, I didn't always lose, but I never made enough to allow me materially to reduce what I owed. Finally, as things got worse, I felt the beginnings of discouragement for the first time in my life.

Everything seemed to have gone wrong with me. I did not go about bewailing the descent from millions and yachts to debts and the simple life. ◁14.1▷ I didn't enjoy the situation, but I did not fill up with self-pity. I did not propose to wait patiently for time and Providence to bring about the cessation of my discomforts. I therefore studied my problem. It was plain that the only way out of my troubles was by making money. To make money I needed merely to trade successfully. I had so traded before and I must do so once more. More than once in the past I had run up a shoe string into hundreds of thousands. Sooner or later the market would offer me an opportunity.

I convinced myself that whatever was wrong was wrong with me and not with the market. Now what could be the trouble with me? I asked myself that question in the same spirit in which I always study the various phases of my trading problems. I thought about it calmly and came to the conclusion that my main trouble came from worrying over the money I owed. I was never free from the mental discomfort of it. I must explain to you that it was not the mere consciousness of my indebtedness. Any business man contracts debts in the course of his regular business. Most of my debts were really

14.1 Livermore actually owned two steam yachts during this period, the *Venetia* and the *Anita*.[1] The *Venetia* was originally purchased in 1908 from Morton F. Plant, a yachtsman, railroad man, and financier. Plant's father had established the Plant System of railroads that were eventually absorbed into the Atlantic Coast Line, an early predecessor of CSX Transportation.[2, 3]

The *Venetia* displaced 580 tons and stretched 310 feet long with a beam of 51 feet. Its crew consisted of "eight sailors, three engineers, one ice plant man, two oilers, two firemen, two coal passers and one electrician,"[4] according to one account. The ship had eight staterooms, four bathrooms, a smoking room, a dining room, and a pantry and galley.[5]

The *Venetia* had witnessed a number of adventures by the time Livermore acquired it. In 1905, it sailed through the Strait of Gibraltar and cruised the Mediterranean Sea before returning home via the Bermuda Islands.[6] During that trip, the *Venetia* came to the rescue of the French schooner *St. Antonie de Padua* in the Gulf of Bougie on the north coast of Africa. Although the *Venetia* suffered some damage, it saved the other ship from certain loss.[7]

The *Anita* was previously owned by John H. Flagler, founder of the National Tube Co. (which was eventually merged into J. P. Morgan's U.S. Steel).[8] The yacht was 202 feet long.

Although Livermore loved both of his yachts, he would not own them for long. Because of the losses he suffered in cotton speculation with Theodore Price, Livermore turned over the *Anita* to cover a $50,000 brokerage account.[9] By 1910, the *Venetia* had passed to John D. Spreckels of San Francisco, whose fortune originated in the Hawaiian sugar business.[10] The *Venetia* was commandeered by the U.S. Navy in 1917 and, after being armed with three-inch guns and depth charges, served with distinction in World War I against German submarines.[11] Photos show the *Venetia* when owned by Livermore, top, and when outfitted for World War I subchasing, below.

The strain on Livermore at this time was severe, but his family tried to cover for him. In July 1909, reporters tracked down Livermore's wife at her father's house in the Washington, D.C., area. In her words, "The stories emanating from New York that, because Mr. Livermore is absent from his offices there, he is financially embarrassed, are all bosh."[12] She went on to claim that he was out west on mining business.

14.2 Livermore was not the only one to compare stock speculators with merchants. Chicago commodity trader Arthur W. Cutten, one of the most successful and notorious grain pool operators and individual investors of the era, had a few words to say about it:

> The chief temperamental distinction I think between a merchant and a speculator is that when a merchant has a small profit, his fingers itch to take it. All his training inspires him to keep turning over his capital. Sometimes as I have observed merchants engaged in speculation, they have seemed to be most daring when they thought they were being cautious.[13]

A fragile, uptight, childless speculator partial to wearing pince-nez glasses, stiff collars and going to bed early, Cutten was one of Livermore's most bitter nemeses during the 1920s.[14, 15] Born in a farming community in eastern Ontario, he had a natural affinity for trading agricultural products, and became wealthy trading wheat and other grains by 1906. He built a large fortune during the boom years of the 1920s before losing $50 million in the 1929 crash.[16] But ever nimble, he turned bearish in 1930 and restored his fortune.[17]

Cutten was vilified in the 1930s by the media, which had turned against speculators not long after it had been lionizing them, and was hounded by regulators and prosecutors over accusations of market manipulation and tax evasion.[18] He was exonerated of the manipulation charges in a landmark Supreme Court decision and died with a net worth of $50 million to $100 million.[19]

nothing but business debts, due to what were unfavourable business conditions for me, and no worse than a merchant suffers from, for instance, when there is an unusually prolonged spell of unseasonable weather. **14.2**

Of course as time went on and I could not pay I began to feel less philosophical about my debts. I'll explain: I owed over a million dollars—all of it stock-market losses, remember. Most of my creditors were very nice and didn't bother me; but there were two who did bedevil me. They used to follow me around. Every time I made a winning each of them was Johnny-on-the-spot, wanting to know all about it and insisting on getting theirs right off. One of them, to whom I owed eight hundred dollars, threatened to sue me, seize my furniture, and so forth. I can't conceive why he thought I was concealing assets, unless it was that I didn't quite look like a stage hobo about to die of destitution.

As I studied the problem I saw that it wasn't a case that called for reading the tape but for reading my own self. I quite cold-bloodedly reached the conclusion that I would never be able to accomplish anything useful so long as I was worried, and it was equally plain that I should be worried so long as I owed money. I mean, as long as any creditor had the power to vex me or to interfere with my coming back by insisting upon being paid before I could get a decent stake together. This was all so obviously true that I said to myself, "I must go through bankruptcy." What else could relieve my mind?

It sounds both easy and sensible, doesn't it? But it was more than unpleasant, I can tell you. I hated to do it. I hated to put myself in a position to be misunderstood or misjudged. I myself never cared much for money. I never thought enough of it to consider it worth while lying for. But I knew that everybody didn't feel that way. Of course I also knew that if I got on my feet again I'd pay everybody off, for the obligation remained. But unless I was able to trade in the old way I'd never be able to pay back that million.

I nerved myself and went to see my creditors. It was a mighty difficult thing for me to do, for all that most of them were personal friends or old acquaintances.

I explained the situation quite frankly to them. I said: "I am not going to take this step because I don't wish to pay you but because, in justice to both myself and you, I must put myself in a position to make money. I have been thinking of this solution off and on for over two years, but I simply didn't have the nerve to come out and say so frankly to you. It would have been infinitely better for all of us if I had. It all simmers down to this: I positively cannot be my old self while I am harassed or upset by these debts. I have decided to do now what I should have done a year ago. I have no other reason than the one I have just given you."

What the first man said was to all intents and purposes what all of them said. He spoke for his firm.

"Livingston," he said, "we understand. We realise your position perfectly. I'll tell you what we'll do: we'll just give you a release. Have your lawyer prepare any kind of paper you wish, and we'll sign it."

That was in substance what all my big creditors said. That is one side of Wall Street for you. It wasn't merely careless good nature or sportsmanship. It was also a mighty intelligent decision, for it was clearly good business. I appreciated both the good will and the business gumption.

These creditors gave me a release on debts amounting to over a million dollars. But there were the two minor creditors who wouldn't sign off. One of them was the eight-hundred-dollar man I told you about. I also owed sixty thousand dollars to a brokerage firm which had gone into bankruptcy, and the receivers, who didn't know me from Adam, were

14.3 In February 1915, a *New York Times* headline blared, "Cotton 'King' a Bankrupt."[20] The article explained that as a result of stock-transaction losses from 1913 to 1914, Livermore was voluntarily filing for bankruptcy with debts of $102,474. His main creditor was the brokerage firm Mitchell & Co. Livermore's assets included 5,600 shares of the West Tonopah Consolidated Mining Co., 15 shares of Long Island Motor Parkway preferred, and 7 shares of the common.

By June, Livermore's debts had been discharged. It was said that his creditors "did not press him for payment of his debts, because in most instances he had previously paid many times the sums concerned in commissions."[21] None of his creditors contested his discharge from bankruptcy.

14.4 Still reeling from the aftermath of the Panic of 1907 and a serious recession in 1913, the financial markets suffered through the short but painful Panic of 1914, spurred by the outbreak of war in Europe. Foreign investors rapidly sold American securities and repatriated the profits, resulting in gold exports and a tightening of money. Complicating matters was the recent formation of the Federal Reserve System. New Federal Reserve notes were not ready to be placed in circulation.

New York Times financial editor and historian Alexander Dana Noyes believed the United States avoided catastrophe by closing the New York Stock Exchange between July and December 1914:

> *Therefore the question of how great the decline of prices would have been with the market open, the whole world in a panic, Stock Exchange prices crumbling and the banks calling loans and throwing the collateral on the market, is a matter of pure conjecture. If New York had continued to provide an open stock market during financial Europe's bewilderment…it is not impossible that foreign selling would have driven down…the already very low prices of securities. That might very possibly have forced… widespread insolvency of private bankers or of the banks themselves.*[22]

There were problems in the real economy too. Concerns that Europe would be unable to accept the U.S. crop resulted in plummeting commodity prices. The U.S. Treasury and the Federal Reserve reacted by securing a cotton loan fund of $100 million from commercial banks to assist farmers pinched by price declines. Moreover, to help ease worries over German submarines and the effect on shipping volumes, the Treasury created a war-risk insurance plan.

Meanwhile, steel ingot production dropped from 2.5 million tons in March 1914 to just 1.6 million tons in No-

on my neck early and late. Even if they had been disposed to follow the example set by my largest creditors I don't suppose the court would have let them sign off. At all events my schedule of bankruptcy amounted to only about one hundred thousand dollars; though, as I said, I owed well over a million.

It was extremely disagreeable to see the story in the newspapers. **14.3** I had always paid my debts in full and this new experience was most mortifying to me. I knew I'd pay off everybody some day if I lived, but everybody who read the article wouldn't know it. I was ashamed to go out after I saw the report in the newspapers. But it all wore off presently and I cannot tell you how intense was my feeling of relief to know that I wasn't going to be harried any more by people who didn't understand how a man must give his entire mind to his business—if he wishes to succeed in stock speculation.

My mind now being free to take up trading with some prospect of success, unvexed by debts, the next step was to get another stake. The Stock Exchange had been closed from July thirty-first to the middle of December, 1914, and Wall Street was in the dumps. **14.4** There hadn't been any business whatever in a long time. I owed all my friends. I couldn't very well ask them to help me again just because they had been so pleasant and friendly to me, when I knew that nobody was in a position to do much for anybody.

It was a mighty difficult task, getting a decent stake, for with the closing of the Stock Exchange there was nothing that I could ask any broker to do for me. **14.5** I tried in a couple of places. No use.

Finally I went to see Dan Williamson. This was in February, 1915. I told him that I had rid myself of the mental incubus of debt and I was ready to trade as of old. You will recall that when he needed me he offered me the use of twenty-five thousand dollars without my asking him.

Now that I needed him he said, "When you see something that looks good to you and you want to buy five hundred shares go ahead and it will be all right."

I thanked him and went away. He had kept me from making a great deal of money and the office had made a lot in commissions from me. I admit I was a little sore to think that Williamson & Brown didn't give me a decent stake. I intended to trade conservatively at first. It would make my financial recovery easier and quicker if I could begin with a line a little better than five hundred shares. But, anyhow, I realised that, such as it was, there was my chance to come back.

I left Dan Williamson's office and studied the situation in general and my own problem in particular. It was a bull market. That was as plain to me as it was to thousands of traders. But my stake consisted merely of an offer to carry five hundred shares for me. That is, I had no leeway, limited as I was. I couldn't afford even a slight setback at the beginning. I must build up my stake with my very first play. That initial purchase of mine of five hundred shares must be profitable. I had to make real money. I knew that unless I had sufficient trading capital I would not be able to use good judgment. Without adequate margins it would be impossible to take the cold-blooded, dispassionate attitude toward the game that comes from the ability to afford a few minor losses such as I often incurred in testing the market before putting down the big bet.

I think now that I found myself then at the most critical period of my career as a speculator. If I failed this time there was no telling where or when, if ever, I might get another stake for another try. It was very clear that I simply must wait for the exact psychological moment.

I didn't go near Williamson & Brown's. I mean, I purposely kept away from them for six long weeks of steady tape reading. I was afraid that if I went to

vember. Employment at U.S. Steel dropped from 228,000 to 179,000. Economist Charles Gilbert wrote:

So suddenly did the impact of war make itself felt that export trade was, in August 1914, completely demoralized. Trade with our principal European customers, Germany, France, and the United Kingdom, was completely cut off by both the collapse of the foreign exchange market and credits, and the lack of ocean transportation. The situation was extremely serious.[23]

14.5 Livermore had called in more than a few favors from the brokers he frequented. It was not just the $500 loan from E. F. Hutton. The *New York Sun* wrote in 1910 that "Jesse Livermore…got help from his brokers more than once when he had sustained reverses."[24] This was not an unusual occurrence; the newspaper added, "Brokers with whom big operators have done business often interpose to save these operators from complete loss when the market goes against them."[25] This was done, of course, to protect a valuable source of commission revenue.

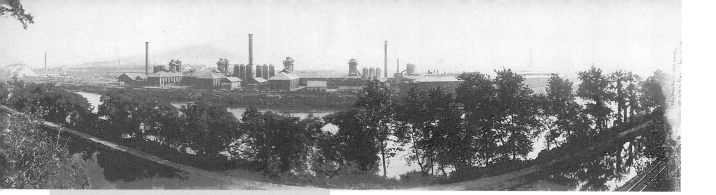

14.6 As World War I raged, it became increasingly clear that a prolonged conflict would dramatically increase the demand for steel. Gun barrels had to be forged. Battleships had to be built. In this context, the steel stocks were due for an advance. Bethlehem Steel, based in eastern Pennsylvania, would be one of them.

The company's history dated to 1857. But the company of Livermore's era was really born when former U.S. Steel president Charles Schwab bought majority ownership in 1901 and started to revitalize the company. According to Schwab biographer Robert Hessen: "Bethlehem Steel had been a small, specialty producer; within a decade after Schwab took control he had made it into the second largest and most diversified steel company in America."[26]

Bethlehem began a close relationship with the U.S. Navy in 1887 when the company was awarded a large contract for expensive heavy forgings to be used for naval guns and armor. In fact, in 1896, it completely dismantled its rail production machinery to focus exclusively on forgings. (Photo above shows Bethlehem Steel plant in 1896.) In 1904, Schwab took his first official tour of Bethlehem's properties. He told a reporter: "I shall make the Bethlehem plant the greatest armor plate and gun factory in the world."[27]

In addition to its steel works, Bethlehem owned a number of shipyards, the most important one being the Union Iron Works in San Francisco. Clearly, the outbreak of a world war would be very profitable for Bethlehem's operations. But building American warships was not what made the company famous.

Structural steel, better known as the modern I-beam, was the company's claim to fame. It was invented by Henry Grey in 1897, first put into production in 1902 in Luxembourg, and embraced by Bethlehem in 1906.[28] Bethlehem Steel would go on to provide the steel for much of America's iconic structures, including the Golden Gate Bridge, the George Washington Bridge, the Hoover Dam, and the Chrysler Building. The company went bankrupt during the 2001 recession. Its assets were sold to International Steel Group, owned by conglomerateur Wilbur Ross, which went on to merge with Mittal Steel of India in 2005; that business then went on to merge with Arcelor of Luxembourg to become the world's largest steelmaker in 2006.

the office, knowing that I could buy five hundred shares, I might be tempted into trading at the wrong time or in the wrong stock. A trader, in addition to studying basic conditions, remembering market precedents and keeping in mind the psychology of the outside public as well as the limitations of his brokers, must also know himself and provide against his own weaknesses. There is no need to feel anger over being human. I have come to feel that it is as necessary to know how to read myself as to know how to read the tape. I have studied and reckoned on my own reactions to given impulses or to the inevitable temptations of an active market, quite in the same mood and spirit as I have considered crop conditions or analysed reports of earnings.

So day after day, broke and anxious to resume trading, I sat in front of a quotation-board in another broker's office where I couldn't buy or sell as much as one share of stock, studying the market, not missing a single transaction on the tape, watching for the psychological moment to ring the full-speed-ahead bell.

By reason of conditions known to the whole world the stock I was most bullish on in those critical days of early 1915 was Bethlehem Steel. **14.6** I was morally certain it was going way up, but in order to make sure that I would win on my very first play, as I must, I decided to wait until it crossed par.

I think I have told you it has been my experience that whenever a stock crosses 100 or 200 or 300 for the first time, it nearly always keeps going up for 30 to 50 points—and after 300 faster than after 100 or 200. One of my first big coups was in Anaconda, which I bought when it crossed 200 and sold a day later at 260. My practice of buying a stock just after it crossed par dated back to my early bucket-shop days. It is an old trading principle.

You can imagine how keen I was to get back to trading on my old scale. I was so eager to begin that I could not think of anything else; but I held myself in leash. I saw Bethlehem Steel climb, every day, higher and higher, as I was sure it would, and yet there I was checking my impulse to run over to Williamson & Brown's office and buy five hundred shares. I knew I simply had to make my initial operation as nearly a cinch as was humanly possible.

Every point that stock went up meant five hundred dollars I had not made. The first ten points' advance meant that I would have been able to pyramid, and instead of five hundred shares I might now be carrying one thousand shares that would be earning for me one thousand dollars a point. But I sat tight and instead of listening to my loud-mouthed hopes or to my clamorous beliefs I heeded only the level voice of my experience and the counsel of common sense. Once I got a decent stake together I could afford to take chances. But without a stake, taking chances, even slight chances, was a luxury utterly beyond my reach. Six weeks of patience—but, in the end, a victory for common sense over greed and hope!

I really began to waver and sweat blood when the stock got up to 90. Think of what I had not made by not buying, when I was so bullish. Well, when it got to 98 I said to myself, "Bethlehem is going through 100, and when it does the roof is going to blow clean off!" The tape said the same thing more than plainly. In fact, it used a megaphone. I tell you, I saw 100 on the tape when the ticker was only printing 98. And I knew that wasn't the voice of my hope or the sight of my desire, but the assertion of my tape-reading instinct. So I said to myself, "I can't

14.7 ▸ The sinking of the *Lusitania* on May 7, 1915, sent waves of concern through the trading floors. The *New York Times* wrote: "Panic conditions reigned in the stock market…following receipt of dispatches confirming earlier reports that the *Lusitania* had been sunk. Stocks of all classes were thrown overboard."[29] Panic conditions lasted only half an hour before a strong rally reversed some of the losses. Bethlehem Steel fell from a high of $159 to a low of $130 before recovering to close at $145. The day's trading resulted in the largest percentage losses for the Dow Jones Industrial Average and the Dow Jones Transportation Average for all of 1915 at −4.5% and −1.9% respectively.[30]

Although we do not know the circumstances of Livermore's misfortunes during this episode, he surely was not alone. The *New York Times* reported:

The news came out of a clear sky when many stocks were close to the top of a sudden rise, and the downward movement of some of the specialties not only ignored fractions but skipped whole points. It was small wonder that seasoned office managers and floor members lost their heads and made mistakes, especially as the ticker was so far behind the market that quotations were a poor measure of what was happening at the time on the Exchange.[31]

wait until it gets through 100. I have to get it now. It is as good as gone through par."

I rushed to Williamson & Brown's office and put in an order to buy five hundred shares of Bethlehem Steel. The market was then 98. I got five hundred shares at 98 to 99. After that she shot right up, and closed that night, I think, at 114 or 115. I bought five hundred shares more.

The next day Bethlehem Steel was 145 and I had my stake. But I earned it. Those six weeks of waiting for the right moment were the most strenuous and wearing six weeks I ever put in. But it paid me, for I now had enough capital to trade in fair-sized lots. I never would have got anywhere just on five hundred shares of stock.

There is a great deal in starting right, whatever the enterprise may be, and I did very well after my Bethlehem deal—so well, indeed, that you would not have believed it was the selfsame man trading. As a matter of fact I wasn't the same man, for where I had been harassed and wrong I was now at ease and right. There were no creditors to annoy and no lack of funds to interfere with my thinking or with my listening to the truthful voice of experience, and so I was winning right along.

All of a sudden, as I was on my way to a sure fortune, we had the *Lusitania* break. ◂**14.7** Every once in a while a man gets a crack like that in the solar plexus, probably that he may be reminded of the sad fact that no human being can be so uniformly right on the market as to be beyond the reach of unprofitable accidents. I have heard people say that no professional speculator need have been hit very hard by the news of the torpedoing of the *Lusitania*, and they go on to tell how they had it long before the Street did. I was not clever enough to escape by means of advance information, and all I can tell you is that on account of what I lost through the *Lusitania* break and one or two other reverses that I wasn't wise enough to foresee,

I found myself at the end of 1915 with a balance at my brokers' of about one hundred and forty thousand dollars. That was all I actually made, though I was consistently right on the market throughout the greater part of the year.

I did much better during the following year. I was very lucky. I was rampantly bullish in a wild bull market. Things were certainly coming my way so that there wasn't anything to do but to make money. It made me remember a saying of the late H. H. Rogers, of the Standard Oil Company, to the effect that there were times when a man could no more help making money than he could help getting wet if he went out in a rainstorm without an umbrella. It was the most clearly defined bull market we ever had. It was plain to everybody that the Allied purchases of all kinds of supplies here made the United States the most prosperous nation in the world. We had all the things that no one else had for sale, and we were fast getting all the cash in the world. I mean that the wide world's gold was pouring into this country in torrents. **14.8** Inflation was inevitable, and, of course, that meant rising prices for everything.

All this was so evident from the first that little or no manipulation for the rise was needed. That was the reason why the preliminary work was so much less than in other bull markets. And not only was the war-bride boom more naturally developed than all others but it proved unprecedentedly profitable for the general public. That is, the stock-market winnings during 1915 were more widely distributed than in any other boom in the history of Wall Street. **14.9** That the public did not turn all their paper profits into good hard cash or that they did not long keep what profits they actually took was merely history repeating itself. Nowhere does history indulge in repetitions so often or so uniformly as in Wall Street. When you read contemporary accounts of booms or panics the one thing that strikes you most forcibly is how little either stock speculation or stock specula-

14.8 In 1915 and 1916, the United States received some $950 million in gold as demand for exports swelled. The yellow metal came from a number of sources. The Russian Imperial Bank sent $340 million of its gold reserves. The British diverted the total production of its South African mines in these two years—totaling some $500 million—to America. The Bank of England and the Bank of France were responsible for the remainder.[32]

By April 1917, when the United States entered the war, the allied powers had purchased $7 billion worth of American food and war materiel. By the end of the war in 1918, U.S. exports had nearly tripled while imports merely doubled. The difference, net exports, was directly responsible for the rapid economic growth of this period. The Federal Reserve Board's Index of Industrial Production, which reached a low of 39 in November 1914, reached 54 in May 1915 and jumped to 75 the following year.[33] Financial historian Margaret Myers wrote:

Employment rapidly increased, unemployment was almost eliminated, and new workers were added to the workforce. The increased buying power of the workers, and the smaller volume of consumer goods in the market, as production was shifted from consumer goods to war goods, were significant factors in the price increases which soon appeared.[34]

14.9 The stock market enjoyed an incredible year in 1915. After a long streak of bad luck, Livermore had caught a break. The Dow Jones Industrial Average gained 82% to close at 99.15. The Dow Transports added 22% to end the year at 108.05.[35]

14.10 The Dow Industrials ran to a high of 110.15 on November 21, 1916, before sliding to close the year at 95. The Dow Transports hit a high of 108.28 on October 4 before falling to 105.15.[36]

tors to-day differ from yesterday. The game does not change and neither does human nature.

I went along with the rise in 1916. **14.10** I was as bullish as the next man, but of course I kept my eyes open. I knew, as everybody did, that there must be an end, and I was on the watch for warning signals. I wasn't particularly interested in guessing from which quarter the tip would come and so I didn't stare at just one spot. I was not, and I never have felt that I was, wedded indissolubly to one or the other side of the market. That a bull market has added to my bank account or a bear market has been particularly generous I do not consider sufficient reason for sticking to the bull or the bear side after I receive the get-out warning. A man does not swear eternal allegiance to either the bull or the bear side. His concern lies with being right.

And there is another thing to remember, and that is that a market does not culminate in one grand blaze of glory. Neither does it end with a sudden reversal of form. A market can and does often cease to be a bull market long before prices generally begin to break. My long expected warning came to me when I noticed that, one after another, those stocks which had been the leaders of the market reacted several points from the top and—for the first time in many months—did not come back. Their race evidently was run, and that clearly necessitated a change in my trading tactics.

It was simple enough. In a bull market the trend of prices, of course, is decidedly and definitely upward. Therefore whenever a stock goes against the general trend you are justified in assuming that there is something wrong with that particular stock. It is enough for the experienced trader to perceive that something is wrong. He must not expect the tape to become a lecturer. His job is to listen for it to say "Get out!" and not wait for it to submit a legal brief for approval.

As I said before, I noticed that stocks which had been the leaders of the wonderful advance had ceased to advance. They dropped six or seven points and stayed there. At the same time the rest of the market kept on advancing under new standard bearers. Since nothing wrong had developed with the companies themselves, the reason had to be sought elsewhere. Those stocks had gone with the current for months. When they ceased to do so, though the bull tide was still running strong, it meant that for those particular stocks the bull market was over. For the rest of the list the tendency was still decidedly upward.

There was no need to be perplexed into inactivity, for there were really no cross currents. I did not turn bearish on the market then, because the tape didn't tell me to do so. The end of the bull market had not come, though it was within hailing distance. Pending its arrival there was still bull money to be made. Such being the case, I merely turned bearish on the stocks which had stopped advancing and as the rest of the market had rising power behind it I both bought and sold.

The leaders that had ceased to lead I sold. I put out a short line of five thousand shares in each of them; and then I went long of the new leaders. The stocks I was short of didn't do much, but my long stocks kept on rising. When finally these in turn ceased to advance I sold them out and went short—five thousand shares of each. By this time I was more bearish than bullish, because obviously the next big money was going to be made on the down side. While I felt certain that the bear market had really begun before the bull market had really ended, I knew the time for being a rampant bear was not yet. There was no sense in being more royalist than the king; especially in being so too soon. The tape merely said that patrolling parties from the main bear army had dashed by. Time to get ready.

I kept on both buying and selling until after about a month's trading I had out a short line of sixty thousand shares—five thousand shares each in a dozen different stocks which earlier in the year

14.11 ▶ Rumors plagued the stock exchange throughout 1916. There was not a fear of war but a fear of peace and the consequences for the booming economy. This was a curious development compared to the reactions to previous conflicts, such as the Russo-Japanese War of 1904, the Boer War, and the Civil War. In all those cases, the concern was that the wars would continue to interfere with normal trade flows and consume productive capital. Peace used to be the bulls' weapon.

What changed all this was the unique position of the United States to profit from the hostilities by attracting new gold inflows. Because of the appreciation of security and commodity prices, as well as the intense capital investments made by American businesses, peace would bring about a damaging bout of deflation. As a result, when peace rumors floated around Wall Street in March and again in October, violent declines of up to 20% resulted.

In December, President Wilson asked the warring nations to state their purposes so that "some common ground" could be found to "get together and arrange the settlement," according to a State Department note sent to all the involved parties.[37] As a result, Noyes said, "something like a panic occurred in speculative markets—not only on the Stock Exchange, where the decline in prices was the most violent of the whole war period, but in the grain market also."[38] But these peace overtures were short-lived.

The December break was when Livermore really came back big. There were, however, questions surrounding the leaking of information about Wilson's letter to Wall Street. Livermore's old broker, E. F. Hutton, was forced to testify before Congress concerning a wire he received from his correspondent in Washington. According to a *Wall Street Journal* report of the hearing, Hutton received a telegram to the effect that "a highly important message had been issued from Washington to belligerents and neutrals."[39] Eventually, the proceedings ended with no charges filed.

As part of the investigation, Livermore's profits were exposed through the statements of his broker Oliver Harriman, of Harriman & Co., who was an uncle of E. H. Harriman. He said that at the time of the break, his customer was short some $7 million worth of shares. The resulting profits were estimated to be between $800,000 and $1 million. The *New York Times* wrote:

> Mr. Harriman said he had rather not give the name of the operator, but from the signature "J.L.L." to telegrams sent over the Harriman wire to Washington on the peace situation it was surmised that he was Jesse L. Livermore, who is known to have been recently a "short" trader. Mr. Harriman said his customer was in the south. Mr. Livermore is at Palm Beach, Fla.[40]

had been the public's favourites because they had been the leaders of the great bull market. It was not a very heavy line; but don't forget that neither was the market definitely bearish.

Then one day the entire market became quite weak and prices of all stocks began to fall. When I had a profit of at least four points in each and every one of the twelve stocks that I was short of, I knew that I was right. The tape told me it was now safe to be bearish, so I promptly doubled up.

I had my position. I was short of stocks in a market that now was plainly a bear market. There wasn't any need for me to push things along. The market was bound to go my way, and, knowing that, I could afford to wait. After I doubled up I didn't make another trade for a long time. About seven weeks after I put out my full line, we had the famous "leak," and stocks broke badly. It was said that somebody had advance news from Washington that President Wilson was going to issue a message that would bring back the dove of peace to Europe in a hurry. Of course the war-bride boom was started and kept up by the World War, and peace was a bear item. When one of the cleverest traders on the floor was accused of profiting by advance information he simply said he had sold stocks not on any news but because he considered that the bull market was overripe. I myself had doubled my line of shorts seven weeks before.

On the news the market broke badly and I naturally covered. **14.11** It was the only play possible. When something happens on which you did not count when you made your plans it behooves you to utilise the opportunity that a kindly fate offers you. For one thing, on a bad break like that you have a big market, one that you can turn around in, and that is the time to turn your paper profits into real money. Even in a bear market a man cannot always cover one hundred and twenty thousand shares of stock without putting up the price on himself. He must wait for the market that will allow him to buy that much at no damage to his profit as it stands him on paper.

I should like to point out that I was not counting on that particular break at that particular time for that particular reason. But, as I have told you before, my experience of thirty years as a trader is that such accidents are usually along the line of least resistance on which I base my position in the market. Another thing to bear in mind is this: Never try to sell at the top. It isn't wise. Sell after a reaction if there is no rally.

I cleared about three million dollars in 1916 by being bullish as long as the bull market lasted and then by being bearish when the bear market started. As I said before, a man does not have to marry one side of the market till death do them part.

That winter I went South, to Palm Beach, as I usually do for a vacation, because I am very fond of salt-water fishing. I was short of stocks and wheat, and both lines showed me a handsome profit. There wasn't anything to annoy me and I was having a good time. Of course unless I go to Europe I cannot really be out of touch with the stock or commodities markets. For instance, in the Adirondacks I have a direct wire from my broker's office to my house. 14.12

In Palm Beach I used to go to my broker's branch office regularly. I noticed that cotton, in which I had no interest, was strong and rising. About that time—this was in 1917—I heard a great deal about the efforts that President Wilson was making to bring about peace. The reports came from Washington, both in the shape of press dispatches and private advices to friends in Palm Beach. That is the reason why one day I got the notion that the course of the various markets reflected confidence in Mr. Wilson's success. With peace supposedly close at hand, stocks and wheat ought to go down and cotton up. I was all set as far as stocks and wheat went, but I had not done anything in cotton in some time.

14.12 Livermore bought a house on Lake Placid, in the Adirondack Mountains of upstate New York, around this time. In August 1925, the *New York Times* reported that Livermore had begun "conducting his operations" in stocks from his lodge in Lake Placid after having been out of the market for a year following heavy losses the summer before.[41] He had been short stocks in anticipation of the election of Calvin Coolidge, but the market soared 30% that year. The *Times* said he took a 50,000-share position in U.S. Steel at his Lake Placid retreat, and an "important position" in White Motors.[42]

14.13 By December, after Wilson had narrowly won reelection, the Allied Powers jointly rebuffed Germany's compromise proposal and stated terms that Germany in turn rejected two weeks later. Finally, in January 1917, German diplomats warned the United States that it would adopt a policy of "forcibly preventing … in a zone around Great Britain, France, Italy and in the Eastern Mediterranean, all navigation, that of neutrals included," adding that "all ships met within the zone will be sunk."[43]

In early February the market broke badly on word that relations with Germany were souring quickly and the United States might be forced to enter the war. As a result of its unrestricted submarine policy, American ships were hunted in the open sea. Further complicating American neutrality were Berlin's overtures to the Mexican government, encouraging it join with the Central Powers and attack the United States to reclaim its lost territory. By April, Congress had voted to declare war on Germany.

At 2:20 that afternoon I did not own a single bale, but at 2:25 my belief that peace was impending made me buy fifteen thousand bales as a starter. I proposed to follow my old system of trading—that is, of buying my full line—which I have already described to you.

That very afternoon, after the market closed, we got the Unrestricted Warfare note. There wasn't anything to do except to wait for the market to open the next day. I recall that at Gridley's that night one of the greatest captains of industry in the country was offering to sell any amount of United States Steel at five points below the closing price that afternoon. There were several Pittsburgh millionaires within hearing. Nobody took the big man's offer. They knew there was bound to be a whopping big break at the opening.

Sure enough, the next morning the stock and commodity markets were in an uproar, as you can imagine. Some stocks opened eight points below the previous night's close. **14.13** To me that meant a heaven-sent opportunity to cover all my shorts profitably. As I said before, in a bear market it is always wise to cover if complete demoralisation suddenly develops. That is the only way, if you swing a good-sized line, of turning a big paper profit into real money both quickly and without regrettable reductions. For instance, I was short fifty thousand shares of United States Steel alone. Of course I was short of other stocks, and when I saw I had the market to cover in, I did. My profits amounted to about one and a half million dollars. It was not a chance to disregard.

Cotton, of which I was long fifteen thousand bales, bought in the last half hour of the trading the previous afternoon, opened down five hundred points. Some break! It meant an overnight loss of three hundred and seventy-five thousand dollars. While it was perfectly clear that the only wise play in stocks and wheat was to cover on the break I was not so clear as to what I ought to do in cotton. There were various things to consider, and while I always take my loss the moment I am convinced I am wrong, I did not like to take that loss that morning. Then I reflected that I had gone South to have a good time fishing instead of perplexing myself over the course of the cotton market. And, moreover, I had taken such big profits in my wheat and in stocks that I decided to take my loss in cotton. I would figure that my profit had been a little more than one million instead of over a million and a half. It was all a matter of bookkeeping, as promoters are apt to tell you when you ask too many questions.

If I hadn't bought that cotton just before the market closed the day before, I would have saved that four hundred thousand dollars. It shows you how quickly a man may lose big money on a moderate line. My main position was absolutely correct and I benefited by an accident of a nature diametrically opposite to the considerations that led me to take the position I did in stocks and wheat. Observe, please, that the speculative line of least resistance again demonstrated its value to a trader. Prices went as I expected, notwithstanding the unexpected market factor introduced by the German note. If things had turned out as I had figured I would have been 100 per cent right in all three of my lines, for with peace stocks and wheat would have gone down and cotton would have gone kiting up. I would have cleaned up in all three. Irrespective of peace or war, I was right in my position on the stock market and in wheat and that is why the unlooked-for event helped. In cotton I based my play on something that might happen outside of the market—that is, I bet on Mr. Wilson's success in his peace negotiations. It was the German military leaders who made me lose the cotton bet.

When I returned to New York early in 1917 I paid back all the money I owed, which was over a million dollars. ◁**14.14** It was a great pleasure to me to pay my debts. I might have paid it back a few months earlier, but I didn't for a very simple reason. I was trading actively and successfully and I needed

14.14 ▶ In January, Livermore was proudly telling reporters how he "came back" and that he was no longer a gambler but a "business speculator."[44] Although he did not confirm or deny a rumor that he had cleared $3.5 million recently, he explained how he earned his new stake and offered some advice:

> I must have made a very large amount, for I have paid in full for my mistakes of the past, and they cost me $2,000,000. I did not make this new fortune as I made my former one. It was not a case of gambling all on one turn. I made this fortune on several issues—cotton, grain and "war brides." This Wall Street game is a psychological one.
>
> The first requisite to success is confidence in one's self. I never lost my nerve. Usually a man buys and then, when the stock goes up a few points, he is fearful that it will go down again and he will lose the little he had made. That is the wrong time to fear. He should know that the very fact that the stock has gone up proves he is right, and he should hold on. But he sells through fear. Don't try to scalp the market. It does not pay. Buy one issue. Don't pyramid, for by doing that you wipe out your profit percentage. Apply just the same principles to the market that you would to a business. Go on your own judgment.[45]

Livermore immediately returned to his spendthrift ways. In February, he bought his wife a $120,000 emerald ring and a fast speedboat that he called the "submarine catcher."[46] He also hired a train from Jacksonville to Palm Beach after the scheduled train had no berths on its lower level. He did not want to climb into the upper berth.[47]

all the capital I had. I owed it to myself as well as to the men I considered my creditors to take every advantage of the wonderful markets we had in 1915 and 1916. I knew that I would make a great deal of money and I wasn't worrying because I was letting them wait a few months longer for money many of them never expected to get back. I did not wish to pay off my obligations in driblets or to one man at a time, but in full to all at once. So as long as the market was doing all it could for me I just kept on trading on as big a scale as my resources permitted.

I wished to pay interest, but all those creditors who had signed releases positively refused to accept it. The man I paid off the last of all was the chap I owed the eight hundred dollars to, who had made my life a burden and had upset me until I couldn't trade. I let him wait until he heard that I had paid off all the others. Then he got his money. I wanted to teach him to be considerate the next time somebody owed him a few hundreds.

And that is how I came back.

After I paid off my debts in full I put a pretty fair amount into annuities. I made up my mind I wasn't going to be strapped and uncomfortable and minus a stake ever again. Of course, after I married I put some money in trust for my wife. And after the boy came I put some in trust for him. ◁14.15▷

The reason I did this was not alone the fear that the stock market might take it away from me, but because I knew that a man will spend anything he can lay his hands on. By doing what I did my wife and child are safe from me.

More than one man I know has done the same thing, but has coaxed his wife to sign off when he needed the money, and he has lost it. But I have fixed it up so that no matter what I want or what my wife wants, that trust holds. It is absolutely safe from all attacks by either of us; safe from my market needs; safe even from a devoted wife's love. I'm taking no chances!

14.15 This was actually Livermore's second marriage. His first wife was Nettie Jordan, a girl from Indianapolis that he met during his time in St. Louis.[48] Livermore and Jordan were wed in Boston in 1900.[49] He liked say it was Nettie that first made him famous: "The first time I ever got in print was when my wife came back from Europe in 1901 with $12,000 in jewels in her handbag. I had to pay $7,200 duty, and the customs took the jewels and held them overnight."[50]

Later, Livermore spent a large sum trying to help Nettie's brother, Chester Jordan, a vaudeville performer, avoid the electric chair for the brutal murder and dismemberment of his wife. After the happy days in 1908, cruising about the *Venetia* after winning big in July cotton, Livermore's relationship with Nettie quickly soured. He neglected her as he struggled to recover from the disastrous operation with Theodore Price, being suckered by the protectors of Charles E. Pugh's estate, and the flat market in the years preceding World War I. A separation was long in coming. Nettie told the *Lake Placid News* in the fall of 1917 that despite Livermore's absence, she wanted to fight to make it work:

> As for me, I will never divorce him. He may harass me and hurt me, but I shall never stoop to divorce....If Mr. Livermore has some other woman in mind whom he should like to marry, he will find that idea hard to carry out. It will be quite impossible for I shall never release him. He may torment me and humiliate me, but I shall stick by him.[51]

Eventually, Nettie realized that Livermore's heart had moved on. In November 1918, she filed for divorce in Reno, Nevada.[52] A month later, he married showgirl and cabaret singer Dorothy Fox Wendt of Brooklyn.[53] He had spent considerable time with the young girl "of rare beauty" during the previous summer at Lake Placid in the Adirondacks.[54] At the time of their marriage, Livermore was 41 years old. His new wife was just 23. After the ceremony at the St. Regis Hotel in New York City, the two honeymooned in Atlantic City. Inside her wedding band read a vow: "Dotsie, for ever and ever, J.L."[55] On September 19, 1919, Jesse Livermore Jr. was born.[56] Paul Livermore followed in 1921.

ENDNOTES

1 "Yachts at Port Jefferson," *New York Sun*, January 10, 1909, 13.

2 "Morton F. Plant Dies," *New York Times*, November 5, 1918, 13.

3 "Henry B. Plant Dead," *New York Times*, June 24, 1899, 1.

4 "Quartermaster of Plant's Yacht," *Pensacola Journal*, March 31, 1906, 3.

5 "Elkins Yacht Sold," *New York Times*, September 30, 1910, 9.

6 "America Has 3,389 Yachts," New York Times, June 4, 1905, 21.

7 "Saved by Mr. Plant's Yacht," *New York Times*, February 1905, 1.

8 "John H. Flagler, Capitalist, Dies," *New York Times*, September 9, 1922, 9.

9 "His Boat, His Security," *Boston Daily Globe*, August 8, 1909, 9.

10 "Elkins Yacht Sold," *New York Times*, September 30, 1910, 9.

11 "War Raider Venetia Sold," *New York Times*, November 8, 1939, 4.

12 "Mrs. Livermore Says Husband Is in the West on Mining Business," *Washington Times*, July 22, 1909.

13 Richard Wycoff, *Stock Market Technique: Number Two*, (1989), 38.

14 John Brooks, *Once in Goldonda: A True Drama of Wall Street 1920–1938*, (New York: John Wiley & Sons, 1969), 78.

15 Kenneth L. Fisher, 100 Minds *That Made the Market*, (New York: John Wiley & Sons, 1993), 330.

16 Edwin C. Sims, *Capitalism in Spite of It All*, (Gordon & Breach Science Publishers, 1969).

17 Kenneth L. Fisher, *100 Minds That Made the Market*, (New York: John Wiley & Sons, 1993), 332.

18 "Cutten Is Indicted Over $414,525 Tax." *New York Times*. March 11, 1936, 6.

19 Kenneth L. Fisher, *100 Minds That Made the Market*, (New York: John Wiley & Sons, 1993), 330.

20 "Cotton 'King' a Bankrupt," *New York Times*, February 18, 1915, 5.

21 "Livermore's Slate Clean," *New York Times*, June 8, 1915, 9.

22 Alexander D. Noyes, *The War Period of American Finance: 1908–1925* (1926), 59–60.

23 Charles Gilbert, *American Financing of World War I* (1970), 23.

24 "Gossip of Wall Street," *New York Sun*, February 9, 1910, 11.

25 Ibid.

26 Robert Hessen, *Steel Titan: The Life of Charles M. Schwab* (1975), 163.

27 Ibid., 167.

28 Ibid., 173.

29 "Stocks Collapse on Lusitania News," *New York Times*, May 8, 1915, 3.

30 Peter Wyckoff, *Wall Street and the Stock Markets* (1972), 193.

31 "Topics in Wall Street," *New York Times*, May 8, 1915, 3.

32 William J. Shultz and M. R. Caine, *Financial Development of the United States* (1937), 506–507.

33 Gilbert, *American Financing of World War I*, 34.

34 Margaret G. Myers, *A Financial History of the United States* (1970), 272.

35 Wyckoff, *Wall Street and the Stock Markets*, 176.

36 Ibid.

37 Noyes, *War Period of American Finance*.

38 Ibid.

39 "Advance News on Message Sent from Washington," *Wall Street Journal*, February 1, 1917, 2.

40 "'Leak' Hunt Closed; Bolling Quits Firm," *New York Times*, February 16, 1917, 5.

41 "Livermore Trading Again." *New York Times*, August 26, 1925, Business Section, 24.

42 Ibid.

43 Noyes, *The War Period of American Finance*.

44 "Jesse L. Livermore in the Swim Again," *Boston Daily Globe*, January 11, 1917, 16.

45 Ibid.

46 "Livermore Buys Emerald," *New York Times*, February 24, 1917, 3.

47 "Livermore Hires a Train," *New York Times*, February 16, 1917, 11.

48 Maury Klein, *Rainbow's End: The Crash of 1929* (2001), 65.

49 "Says She Will Not Sue for Divorce," *Lake Placid News*, September 14, 1917, 2.

50 "Jesse Livermore Ends Life in Hotel," *New York Times*, November 29, 1940, 1.

51 "Says She Will Not Sue for Divorce."

52 "Jesse Livermore Weds," *Lake Placid News*, December 6, 1918, 1.

53 "Report Jesse Livermore Has Married Actress," *Boston Daily Globe*, December 4, 1918, 7.

54 "Jesse Livermore Weds."

55 Richard Smitten, Jesse Livermore: *World's Greatest Stock Trader* (2001), 126.

56 "The Cradle," *Lake Placid News*, September 19, 1919, 6.

Among the hazards of speculation the happening of the unexpected—I might even say of the unexpectable—ranks high. There are certain chances that the most prudent man is justified in taking—chances that he must take if he wishes to be more than a mercantile mollusk. Normal business hazards are no worse than the risks a man runs when he goes out of his house into the street or sets out on a railroad journey. When I lose money by reason of some development which nobody could foresee I think no more vindictively of it than I do of an inconveniently timed storm. Life itself from the cradle to the grave is a gamble and what happens to me because I do not possess the gift of second sight I can bear undisturbed. But there have been times in my career as a speculator when I have both been right and played square and nevertheless I have been cheated out of my earnings by the sordid unfairness of unsportsmanlike opponents.

Against misdeeds by crooks, cowards and crowds a quick-thinking or far-sighted business man can protect himself. I have never gone up against downright dishonesty except in a bucket shop or two because even there honesty was the best policy; the big money was in being square and not in welshing. I have never thought it good business to play any game in any place where it was necessary to keep an eye on the dealer because he was likely to cheat if unwatched. But against the whining welsher the decent man is powerless. Fair play is fair play. I could tell you a dozen instances where I have been the victim of my own belief in the sacredness of the pledged word or of the inviolability of a gentlemen's agreement. I shall not do so because no useful purpose can be served thereby.

15.1 Lefevre has a virtually inexhaustible supply of synonyms for *swindle*. "Boodle" was primarily slang for bribes or illicit payments. According to *A New Dictionary of Americanisms*, published in 1902, it was a Dutch-derived word that was also popular in the thieving community for counterfeit money.[1] An 1875 book about the U.S. Secret Service refers to passers of fake U.S. money as "boodle carriers" and to a "boodle game" as a "cheating process."[2]

Market manipulation and unfair trading practices were a key focus of Lefevre as a journalist, but he shows Livermore as a righteous actor who played fair and rarely blamed losses on fraud.

15.2 The move toward basing market views on observed facts rather than tips or gut instinct was an important step in Livermore's development. This statement most likely also reflected a hot debate in the 1910s over the mutability of truth. The new pragmatist approach of popular philosopher William James—which held that the value of any truth was dependent on its use to the person who held it—was gaining acceptance and discussed avidly in the media.

The battle between philosophies of truth—objective, intrinsic, deductive, relative, or religious—came to a boil a decade later during the Scopes trial in Tennessee. Former presidential candidate and congressman William Jennings Bryan, in testimony for the prosecution, challenged the scientific process by calling evolution "millions of guesses strung together."

The debate over what constitutes reliable information for investors continues to rage today. Proponents of the efficient market hypothesis—the consensus paradigm of stock behavior of the 1970s and 1980s—believe that prices on traded assets reflect all known knowledge and quickly change to reflect new data. In other words, they believe that price always tells the truth. A new school of thought, called behavioral economics, upended that view in the 1990s by asserting that investors regularly hold false beliefs due to cognitive biases such as overconfidence, overreaction, and improper use of linear reasoning.

It is likely that Livermore would have leaned toward the latter camp, as he believed his role as a thinking speculator was to find people who held false beliefs about price and trade against them.

Fiction writers, clergymen and women are fond of alluding to the floor of the Stock Exchange as a boodlers' battlefield and to Wall Street's daily business as a fight. ◁**15.1**

It is quite dramatic but utterly misleading. I do not think that my business is strife and contest. I never fight either individuals or speculative cliques. I merely differ in opinion—that is, in my reading of basic conditions. What playwrights call battles of business are not fights between human beings. They are merely tests of business vision. I try to stick to facts and facts only, and govern my actions accordingly. ◁**15.2** That is Bernard M. Baruch's recipe for success in wealth-winning. ◁**15.3** Sometimes I do not see the facts—all the facts—clearly enough or early enough; or else I do not reason logically. Whenever any of these things happen I lose. I am wrong. And it always costs me money to be wrong.

No reasonable man objects to paying for his mistakes. There are no preferred creditors in mistake-making and no exceptions or exemptions. But I object to losing money when I am right. I do not mean, either, those deals that have cost me money because of sudden changes in the rules of some particular exchange. I have in mind certain hazards of speculation that from time to time remind a man that no profit should be counted safe until it is deposited in your bank to your credit.

After the Great War broke out in Europe there began the rise in the prices of commodities that was to be expected. It was as easy to foresee that as to foresee war inflation. Of course the general advance continued as the war prolonged itself. As you may remember, I was busy "coming back" in 1915. The boom in stocks was there and it was my duty to utilise it. My safest, easiest and quickest big play was in the stock market, and I was lucky, as you know.

By July, 1917, I not only had been able to pay off all my debts but was quite a little to the good besides.

Bernard Mannes Baruch is probably known today for his role as a trusted advisor to President Franklin Roosevelt. But in the first two decades of the twentieth century, he was admired both as a cunning speculator who made a fortune before age 30 and as a war advisor to President Woodrow Wilson.

Baruch was born in Camden, South Carolina, in 1870. His father was a Prussia-born Jew who immigrated to the United States to escape military service, found work as a book-keeper in a rural South Carolina general store, went to medical school under the sponsorship of his boss, Mannes Baum, and served as a Confederate Army surgeon during the Civil War. Baruch's mother, Belle, was the daughter of a Jewish plantation owner, Sailing Wolfe, who lost a fortune when his estate was burned to the ground and his slaves were freed by General Sherman of the Union Army.[3]

At left, Bernard Baruch in 1919. Above, seated at far right during the Versailles Peace Conference, he served as an advisor to President Wilson. To his left are Louis Loucheur, Winston Churchill and David Lloyd George.

Dr. Baruch's medical practice was slow to grow in war-ravaged Camden, but the family was still among the most prosperous in town. The area was too backwoods for his wife, though, so after the dueling death of a close friend, the family moved to the lightly populated Upper East Side of New York in 1880. Dr. Baruch soon developed a successful new medical practice from scratch and became a leading advocate for clean water.[4] By the late 1890s, the family was successful enough to afford servants, although they were not considered truly rich.[5]

Baruch had his heart set on attending Yale University but his mother wanted him close to home, so he started at City College of New York at age 14. After his graduation in 1889, his mother helped him get a job with a friend who had a seat on the stock exchange. He started as an unpaid apprentice and was soon learning about speculation, arbitrage, and foreign exchange; it was not long before he became useful enough to earn the princely sum of $3 a week.[6] A year later, he took off for Colorado to try to strike it rich in the new gold and silver mines, completing the last leg of the trip by stagecoach. He gambled and boxed in his spare time and later liked to quote British ring champion Bob Fitzsimmons, who watched him beat a taller opponent after several tough early rounds. The quip was appropriate for his later career as a speculator. "A fight is never over until one man is out," said Fitzsimmons. "As long as you ain't that man you have a chance. To be a champion you have to learn to take it or you can't give it."[7]

Baruch, who never lost his southern accent, ultimately returned home to work on Wall Street again and became an analyst and gofer for legendary tycoon James Keene. Speculating on his own, using margin because of his small capital base, he made and lost hundreds of thousands of dollars as he learned his craft. He became a broker and partner at A. A. Housman & Co., and started a brokerage after gaining a reputation as "the Lone Wolf on Wall Street" because of his preference, like Livermore later, to play his own hand.

After becoming a millionaire speculating in sugar and stocks and emerging as a role model for younger traders like Livermore, Baruch would serve President Wilson during World War I as a national defense consultant and later as an advisor at the Versailles Peace Conference. He prospered during the 1920s, did not lose his fortune in the 1929 crash, and played a key role as an advisor to President Roosevelt during the New Deal and World War II. He later became an expert on nuclear disarmament in the Truman administration and died at age 94 in 1965. With a life experience spanning from the Civil War to the Cold War, he certainly did merit Livermore's early admiration.

15.4 ▶ Livermore's yearlong adventure with coffee in 1917 amply illustrates four of his main themes: the benefits of anticipation and patience; the unfairness of manipulation; the fact that government interference in commodity prices never lasts; and the need to expect the "unexpectable." He says, "I object to losing money when I am right" not as sour grapes but as just one more lesson learned. He added later that postmortems in speculation are a waste of time but observed that this episode—in which he was correct to think that U.S. coffee prices would soar during World War I but never made a dime because importers lobbied the government to set price limits—at least had educational value.

This meant that I now had the time, the money and the inclination to consider trading in commodities as well as in stocks. For many years I have made it my practice to study all the markets. The advance in commodity prices over the pre-war level ranged from 100 to 400 per cent. There was only one exception, and that was coffee. Of course there was a reason for this. The breaking out of the war meant the closing up of European markets and huge cargoes were sent to this country, which was the one big market. That led in time to an enormous surplus of raw coffee here, and that, in turn, kept the price low. Why, when I first began to consider its speculative possibilities coffee was actually selling below pre-war prices. If the reasons for this anomaly were plain, no less plain was it that the active and increasingly efficient operation by the German and Austrian submarines must mean an appalling reduction in the number of ships available for commercial purposes. This eventually in turn must lead to dwindling imports of coffee. With reduced receipts and an unchanged consumption the surplus stocks must be absorbed, and when that happened the price of coffee must do what the prices of all other commodities had done, which was, go way up. ◁**15.4**

It didn't require a Sherlock Holmes to size up the situation. Why everybody did not buy coffee I cannot tell you. When I decided to buy it I did not consider it a speculation. It was much more of an investment. I knew it would take time to cash in, but I knew also that it was bound to yield a good profit. That made it a conservative investment operation—a banker's act rather than a gambler's play.

I started my buying operations in the winter of 1917. I took quite a lot of coffee. The market, however, did nothing to speak of. It continued inactive and as for the price, it did not go up as I had expected. The outcome of it all was that I simply carried my line to no purpose for nine long months. My contracts expired then and I sold out all my options. I took a whopping big loss on that deal and yet I was sure my views were sound. I had been clearly wrong in the matter of time, but I was confident that coffee must advance as all commodities had done, so that no sooner had I sold out my line than I started in to buy again. I bought three times as much coffee as I had so unprofitably carried during those nine disappointing months. Of course I bought deferred options—for as long a time as I could get.

I was not so wrong now. As soon as I had taken on my trebled line the market began to go up. People everywhere seemed to realise all of a sudden what was bound to happen in the coffee market. It began to look as if my investment was going to return me a mighty good rate of interest.

The sellers of the contracts I held were roasters, mostly of German names and affiliations, who had bought the coffee in Brazil confidently expecting to bring it to this country. But there were no ships to bring it, and presently they found themselves in the uncomfortable position of having no end of coffee down there and being heavily short of it to me up here.

Please bear in mind that I first became bullish on coffee while the price was practically at a pre-war level, and don't forget that after I bought it I carried it the greater part of a year and then took a big loss on it. The punishment for being wrong is to lose money. The reward for being right is to make money. Being clearly right and carrying a big line, I was justified in expecting to make a killing. It would not take much of an advance to make my profit satisfactory to me, for I was carrying several hundred thousand bags. I don't like to talk about my operations in figures because sometimes they sound rather formidable and people might think I was boasting. As a matter of fact I trade in accordance to my means and always leave myself an ample margin of safety. In this instance I was conservative enough.

15.5 Lefevre's distaste for coffee industry insiders who demanded price controls on their product when they were short the commodity is evident in this highly sarcastic remark. Of course he means they were neither philanthropic nor patriotic but rather out for their own interests when they appealed to the government for a limit on prices.

President Wilson set up the War Industries Board in July 1917, four months after the country's late entrance into World War I, to unify the federal government's relationship with strategic industries and ensure the availability of key raw materials at reasonable prices. This was a first for the country, and his advisors squabbled among themselves and with Congress about how to mobilize.

Congress gave the president power to control food and fuel supplies and fix a minimum price for wheat and other commodities, even though most U.S. production was already committed to the French and British, who had been at war with Germany for three years. Prices were set for sales to the government—not at retail—for everything ranging from aluminum, iron, and cement to jam and beer. The program initially suffered from a lack of cooperation from manufacturers, though, so Wilson appointed Bernard Baruch to whip it into shape.

The Price Fixing Committee was added in March 1918, but because it lacked compulsory power, originally its effectiveness was limited. Baruch tried to gain industrial chiefs' voluntary cooperation through patriotic appeals at first, but they were disdainful of the effort and not fond of being told what to do by an ex-banker. Baruch gained their help only after threatening to bring down the force of the federal government on them.[8] In the end, the committee did keep inflation low in the last year of the war, and the board ensured that the War Department got the materials it needed on time. Just as Livermore says, coffee had the smallest price increase of all food commodities during the war by a wide margin.[9]

A decade and a half later, President Roosevelt used the War Industries Board as a model for adjusting the forces of industrial supply and demand during the Great Depression and then re-created the board during World War II.[10] The concept that the government should command the economy during wartime was one of Baruch's chief intellectual contributions to Roosevelt's approach.

The reason I bought options so freely was because I couldn't see how I could lose. Conditions were in my favour. I had been made to wait a year, but now I was going to be paid both for my waiting and for being right. I could see the profit coming—fast. There wasn't any cleverness about it. It was simply that I wasn't blind.

Coming sure and fast, that profit of millions! But it never reached me. No; it wasn't side-tracked by a sudden change in conditions. The market did not experience an abrupt reversal of form. Coffee did not pour into the country. What happened? The unexpectable! What had never happened in anybody's experience; what I therefore had no reason to guard against. I added a new one to the long list of hazards of speculation that I must always keep before me. It was simply that the fellows who had sold me the coffee, the shorts, knew what was in store for them, and in their efforts to squirm out of the position into which they had sold themselves, devised a new way of welshing. They rushed to Washington for help, and got it.

Perhaps you remember that the Government had evolved various plans for preventing further profiteering in necessities. You know how most of them worked. Well, the philanthropic coffee shorts appeared before the Price Fixing Committee of the War Industries Board—I think that was the official designation—and made a patriotic appeal to that body to protect the American breakfaster. **15.5** They asserted that a professional speculator, one Lawrence Livingston, had cornered, or was about to corner, coffee. If his speculative plans were not brought to naught he would take advantage of the conditions created by the war and the American people would be forced to pay exorbitant prices for their daily coffee. It was unthinkable to the patriots who had sold me cargoes of coffee they couldn't find ships for, that one hundred millions of Americans, more or less, should pay tribute to

15.6 The New York Coffee Exchange was founded to trade coffee futures in 1882. It sat opposite the Cotton Exchange at the corner of William and Beaver streets in Manhattan and became the world's first coffee trading organization of national proportions. Up to that time, coffee was traded primarily in port cities in an uncoordinated manner. Soon after, national coffee exchanges opened in Germany, the Netherlands, Great Britain, Italy, and Brazil.[11]

Coffee was a big turn-of-the-century business: In 1900, 99 companies imported green coffee from Brazil and Central America to New York, and there were 6 more importers in Philadelphia, 28 in San Francisco, and 12 in New Orleans. By 1920, there were 216 in New York, 31 in San Francisco, and 15 in New Orleans.[12] Moreover, the 1919 census counted 769 coffee shops across the country. Outside New York, the states with the most coffee shops were Pennsylvania, California, Missouri, Illinois, and Texas.[13]

The exchange added sugar futures in 1914, then merged with the New York Cocoa Exchange in 1979. In 1998, that group merged with the New York Cotton Exchange and became units of the New York Board of Trade, which itself merged with the Intercontinental Exchange in 2006.

conscienceless speculators. They represented the coffee trade, not the coffee gamblers, and they were willing to help the Government curb profiteering actual or prospective.

Now I have a horror of whiners and I do not mean to intimate that the Price Fixing Committee was not doing its honest best to curb profiteering and wastefulness. But that need not stop me from expressing the opinion that the committee could not have gone very deeply into the particular problem of the coffee market. They fixed on a maximum price for raw coffee and also fixed a time limit for closing out all existing contracts. This decision meant, of course, that the Coffee Exchange would have to go out of business. **15.6** There was only one thing for me to do and I did it, and that was to sell out all my contracts. Those profits of millions that I had deemed as certain to come my way as any I ever made failed completely to materialise. I was and am as keen as anybody against the profiteer in the necessaries of life, but at the time the Price Fixing Committee made their ruling on coffee, all other commodities were selling at from 250 to 400 per cent above pre-war prices while raw coffee was actually below the average prevailing for some years before the war.

I can't see that it made any real difference who held the coffee. The price was bound to advance; and the reason for that was not the operations of conscienceless speculators, but the dwindling surplus for which the diminishing importations were responsible, and they in turn were affected exclusively by the appalling destruction of the world's ships by the German submarines. The committee did not wait for coffee to start; they clamped on the brakes.

As a matter of policy and of expediency it was a mistake to force the Coffee Exchange to close just then. If the committee had let coffee alone the price undoubtedly would have risen for the reasons I have already stated, which had nothing to do with any alleged corner. But the high price—which need not have been exorbitant—would have been an incentive to attract supplies to this market. I have heard Mr. Bernard M. Baruch say that the War Industries Board took into consideration this factor—the insuring of a supply—in fixing prices, and for that reason some of the complaints about the high limit on certain commodities were unjust. When the Coffee Exchange resumed business, later on, coffee sold at twenty-three cents. The American people paid that price because of the small supply, and the supply was small because the price had been fixed too low, at the suggestion of philanthropic shorts, to make it possible to pay the high ocean freights and thus insure continued importations.

I have always thought that my coffee deal was the most legitimate of all my trades in commodities. I considered it more of an investment than a speculation. I was in it over a year. If there was any gambling it was done by the patriotic roasters with German names and ancestry. ◁**15.7**▷ They had coffee in Brazil and they sold it to me in New York. The Price Fixing Committee fixed the price of the only commodity that had not advanced. They

15.7 **Hermann Sielcken**, a German who claimed American citizenship, was known as the Coffee King in the 1890s and 1910s. A biographer said he ruled the coffee markets of the world as an absolute dictator with a commanding presence. Born in Hamburg to a family in the bakery business in 1847, Sielcken shipped out to Costa Rica to work for a German firm at 21, moved on to work as a shipping clerk and then a wool buyer in San Francisco in the late 1860s, was almost killed in a stagecoach wreck in Oregon, and moved to New York to recuperate, landing a job as a clerk for a glassware importer.[14]

Sielcken next found work with a merchandiser specializing in South American imports, leveraging his facility with languages. After prowling around Brazil, he drummed up enough business to earn a partnership at the firm W. H. Crossman & Bro., which later changed its name to Crossman & Sielcken. At that point, according to his biographer, Sielcken became a "human dynamo" of self-education and deal making in Brazil, the United States, and Germany who pushed the trading firm into world prominence in the coffee trade. Newspapers claimed he made the bulk of his fortune in a 1907 coffee futures corner,[15] although he always denied creating corners to advance his own positions.

When coffee trading grew tedious, Sielcken branched out into the trading of steel and railroads stocks, where he crossed horns with John W. Gates, E. H. Harriman, and railroad magnate George J. Gould, son of the notorious speculator Jay Gould. After his first wife died, he married the daughter of Paul Isenberg, a wealthy sugar planter in the Hawaiian Islands, and the couple divided their time between a suite at the Waldorf-Astoria in New York and a lavish 200-acre estate near Baden-Baden, Germany, that was renowned for its 168 varieties of roses and its pine trees imported from Oregon.[16] He was said to love regaling guests with tales of his adventures on stagecoaches in the Wild West and in shipwrecks in South America.

Sielcken died in 1917, the year of Livermore's coffee exploits, but his partners carried on. Livermore's account reveals that he disliked the German-born coffee importers intensely and deplored their ability to persuade the U.S. government to limit prices. A biographer says Sielcken's policy in coffee "was one of blood and iron," he was "silent and uncommunicative," exploded in rage under stress, was ruthless in dealing with men and governments, but avoided the limelight. You can just imagine the duel of wits as the crafty import house battled with the cunning speculator. Sielcken's firm won in the end, although after the war, prices did explode higher, as Livermore had forecast.

protected the public against profiteering before it started, but not against the inevitable higher prices that followed. Not only that, but even when green coffee hung around nine cents a pound, roasted coffee went up with everything else. It was only the roasters who benefited. If the price of green coffee had gone up two or three cents a pound it would have meant several millions for me. And it wouldn't have cost the public as much as the later advance did.

Post-mortems in speculation are a waste of time. They get you nowhere. But this particular deal has a certain educational value. It was as pretty as any I ever went into. The rise was so sure, so logical, that

15.8 Livermore was regularly amused to find himself the subject of newspaper stories during big market movements, but he understood that reporters needed to provide readers with explanations for mysterious events. He dismisses the idea that "some plunger's operations" were responsible for big moves, observing instead that the larger forces at work were supply and demand imbalances. He believed that stories about speculators' raids were essentially ghost stories that brokers told clients to keep them in the dark about their losses from what he considered "blind gambling."

I figured that I simply couldn't help making several millions of dollars. But I didn't.

On two other occasions I have suffered from the action of exchange committees making rulings that changed trading rules without warning. But in those cases my own position, while technically right, was not quite so sound commercially as in my coffee trade. You cannot be dead sure of anything in a speculative operation. It was the experience I have just told you that made me add the unexpectable to the unexpected in my list of hazards.

After the coffee episode I was so successful in other commodities and on the short side of the stock market, that I began to suffer from silly gossip. The professionals in Wall Street and the newspaper writers got the habit of blaming me and my alleged raids for the inevitable breaks in prices. **15.8** At times my selling was called unpatriotic—whether I was really selling or not. The reason for exaggerating the magnitude and the effect of my operations, I suppose, was the need to satisfy the public's insatiable demand for reasons for each and every price movement.

As I have said a thousand times, no manipulation can put stocks down and keep them down. There is nothing mysterious about this. The reason is plain to everybody who will take the trouble to think about it half a minute. Suppose an operator raided a stock—that is, put the price down to a level below its real value—what would inevitably happen? Why, the raider would at once be up against the best kind of inside buying. The people who know what a stock is worth will always buy it when it is selling at bargain prices. If the insiders are not able to buy, it will be because general conditions are against their free command of their own resources, and such conditions are not bull conditions. When people speak about raids the inference is that the raids are unjustified; almost criminal. But selling a stock down to a price much below what it is worth is mighty dangerous business. It is well to bear in mind that a raided stock that fails to rally is not getting much inside buying and where there is a raid—that is, unjustified short selling—there is usually apt to be inside buying; and when there is that, the price does not stay down. I should say that in ninety-nine cases out of a hundred, so-called raids are really legitimate declines, accelerated at times but not primarily caused by the operations of a professional trader, however big a line he may be able to swing.

The theory that most of the sudden declines or particular sharp breaks are the results of some plunger's operations probably was invented as an easy way of supplying reasons to those speculators who, being nothing but blind gamblers, will believe anything that is told them rather than do a little thinking. The raid excuse for losses that unfortunate speculators so often receive from brokers and financial gossipers is really an inverted tip. The difference lies in this: A bear tip is distinct, positive advice to sell short. But the inverted tip—that is, the explanation that does not explain—serves merely to keep you from wisely selling short. The natural tendency when a stock breaks badly is to sell it. There is a reason—an unknown reason but a good reason; therefore get out. But it is not wise to get out when the break is the result of a raid by an operator, because the moment he stops the price must rebound. Inverted tips! ◁**15.9**▷

15.9 ▷ This section provides a great illustration of the symbiotic relationship between Livermore and Lefevre in the creation of *Reminiscences*. The chapter begins as an opportunity for Livermore to explain his well-reasoned but ill-fated decision to buy coffee futures during World War I. It was a great idea that went awry due to the treachery of German-born roasters and the misguided naïveté of government price regulators. The one-time bucket shop gambler wants to make sure we know that he had ascended to the ranks of sophisticated, long-term investors.

Then he gets a shot in against those who think short sellers like himself can push a stock down that doesn't deserve it. He points out that if a bear raid smashes the price of a commodity or company well below its intrinsic value, insiders who understand the business will swoop in and push it back up to fair value. In short he says that any stock or commodity that goes down and stays down deserves its fate, and the public's losses should not be blamed on short sellers.

In the last few paragraphs, though, the discussion swerves over to one of Lefevre's favorite topics, which is that the public should close their ears to stock tips. The narrator suggests that there are two kinds of bad advice on the short side of the market. A regular "bear tip" is a recommendation to sell short, usually on the theory that some famous plunger and his clique are about to gang up on a stock. An "inverted" bear tip is one that actually comes from the evil plunger himself and could be intended either to get the public to short a stock just before it rebounds so they can be wiped out on a reversal, or as a recommendation to buy just as the plunger intends to short heavily again.

Lefevre's implicit message is: Just say no to all tips, because they're usually a poisoned gift. By the same token, he would warn that all fund managers' remarks in the media today are conflicted, and should be ignored. No doubt he would be appalled by financial cable television.

ENDNOTES

1 Sylva Clapin, *A New Dictionary of Americanisms* (1902), 66.

2 George O. Waitt, *Three Years with Counterfeiters, Smugglers and Boodle Carriers* (1875), 9.

3 James Grant, *Bernard Baruch: The Adventures of a Wall Street Legend* (New York: John Wiley & Sons, 1997), 2.

4 Ibid.

5 Ibid.

6 Ibid.

7 Bernard Baruch, *Baruch: My Own Story* (Cutchoge, NY: Buccaneer Books, 1957), 65.

8 William O'Neill, *A Democracy at War* (Cambridge, MA: Harvard University Press, 1995).

9 Simon Litman, *Prices and Price Controls in Great Britain and the United States during the World War.* (1920), 102.

10 O'Neill, *Democracy at War.*

11 William Harrison Ukers, *All About Coffee* (New York: Tea & Coffee Trade Journal Co., 1922), 491.

12 Ibid.

13 Ibid., 516.

14 Ibid., 518.

15 "Herman Sielcken Reported to Be Dead," *New York Times,* November 23, 1917.

16 Ukers, *All About Coffee,* 521.

XVI

ips! How people want tips! They crave not only to get them but to give them. There is greed involved, and vanity. It is very amusing, at times, to watch really intelligent people fish for them. And the tip-giver need not hesitate about the quality, for the tip-seeker is not really after good tips, but after any tip. If it makes good, fine! If it doesn't, better luck with the next. I am thinking of the average customer of the average commission house. There is a type of promoter or manipulator that believes in tips first, last and all the time. A good flow of tips is considered by him as a sort of sublimated publicity work, the best merchandising dope in the world, for, since tip-seekers and tip-takers are invariably tip-passers, tip-broadcasting becomes a sort of endless-chain advertising. The tipster-promoter labours under the delusion that no human being breathes who can resist a tip if properly delivered. He studies the art of handing them out artistically.

I get tips by the hundreds every day from all sorts of people. I'll tell you a story about Borneo Tin. 〈16.1〉 You remember when the stock was brought out? It was at the height of the boom. The promoter's pool had taken the advice of a very clever banker and decided to float the new company in the open market at once instead of letting an underwriting syndicate take its time about it. It was good advice. The only mistake the members of the pool made came from inexperience. They did not know what the stock market

16.1 Tin was an important commodity during this period because of its flexibility as a retail packaging material. Most of the metal was mined in the Malay Peninsula as well as the Borneo, Sulawesi, and Java islands of Indonesia.[1] Borneo Tin appears to be a fictitious company. However, in late 1914, a new tin can company called Continental Can was incorporated and combined the interests of the Export & Domestic Can Co. and the Standard Tin Plate Co. Goldman Sachs and Lehman Brothers handled the underwriting of the new securities and acquired an interest in the new concern. The company was capitalized with $17.5 million.[2] The classic three-piece, soldered-seam tin can was ultimately replaced in the 1950s and 1960s in the consumer market by aluminum and steel alloy cans that were lighter and less expensive to transport and retained cold temperatures better.

was capable of doing during a crazy boom and at the same time they were not intelligently liberal. They were agreed on the need of marking up the price in order to market the stock, but they started the trading at a figure at which the traders and the speculative pioneers could not buy it without misgivings.

By rights the promoters ought to have got stuck with it, but in the wild bull market their hoggishness turned out to be rank conservatism. The public was buying anything that was adequately tipped. Investments were not wanted. The demand was for easy money; for the sure gambling profit. Gold was pouring into this country through the huge purchases of war material. They tell me that the promoters, while making their plans for bringing out Borneo stock, marked up the opening price three different times before their first transaction was officially recorded for the benefit of the public.

I had been approached to join the pool and I had looked into it but I didn't accept the offer because if there is any market manœuvring to do, I like to do it myself. I trade on my own information and follow my own methods. When Borneo Tin was brought out, knowing what the pool's resources were and what they had planned to do, and also knowing what the public was capable of, I bought ten thousand shares during the first hour of the first day. Its market début was successful at least to that extent. As a matter of fact the promoters found the demand so active that they decided it would be a mistake to lose so much stock so soon. They found out that I had acquired my ten thousand shares about at the same time that they found out that they would probably be able to sell every share they owned if they merely marked up the price twenty-five or thirty points. They therefore concluded that the profit on my ten thousand shares would take too big a chunk out of the millions they felt were already as good as banked. So they actually ceased their bull operations and tried to shake me out. But I simply sat tight. They gave me up as a bad

16.2 Gridley's is a pseudonym for Bradley's Beach Club casino in Florida, which Livermore frequented for years. Its owner, Edward R. Bradley, was a well-regarded racehorse owner and gambler. His steeds would go on to win four Kentucky Derbies. The man had a colorful past: He was a former army scout who helped hunt down Geronimo. He was also acquainted with Wild West legends like Billy the Kid and Wyatt Earp. Livermore used to tell his sons about how Bradley would lend Billy the Kid money to bet on Indian horse races.

Like Livermore, Bradley was a quiet and reserved. Although his operation was considered the longest-running illegal casino in U.S. history, it was a classy establishment that fed off traffic brought in by Henry Flagler's railroads and hotels. After 7 P.M., tuxedos were required. Security was tight, the clientele was exclusive, and the limits were high. Games available included hazard, chemin de fer, and roulette.[3]

In May 1933, *Time* magazine reported that "Beat Bradley and take the pot," had become a Louisville axiom for Kentucky Derby hopefuls. Then a Bradley-owned horse won the celebrated race for the fourth time, by a nose, much to the delight of the crowd, which included financier Bernard Baruch. The winning horse's name: Broker's Tip.[4]

job because they didn't want the market to get away from them, and then they began to put up the price, without losing any more stock than they could help.

They saw the crazy height that other stocks rose to and they began to think in billions. Well, when Borneo Tin got up to 120 I let them have my ten thousand shares. It checked the rise and the pool managers let up on their jacking-up process. On the next general rally they again tried to make an active market for it and disposed of quite a little, but the merchandising proved to be rather expensive. Finally they marked it up to 150. But the bloom was off the bull market for keeps, so the pool was compelled to market what stock it could on the way down to those people who love to buy after a good reaction, on the fallacy that a stock that has once sold at 150 must be cheap at 130 and a great bargain at 120. Also, they passed the tip first to the floor traders, who often are able to make a temporary market, and later to the commission houses. Every little helped and the pool was using every device known. The trouble was that the time for bulling stocks had passed. The suckers had swallowed other hooks. The Borneo bunch didn't or wouldn't see it.

I was down in Palm Beach with my wife. One day I made a little money at Gridley's **16.2** and when I got home I gave Mrs. Livingston a five-hundred-dollar bill out of it. It was a curious coincidence, but that same night she met at a dinner the presi-

16.3 Just as Borneo Tin is a made-up name, so is Mr. Wisenstein. The character primarily illustrates one of the many varieties of tip-givers to avoid. But the name did not come out of thin air.

The considerable time Livermore spent in Chicago would have made him familiar with the work of George Ade, a popular *Morning News* and *Record-Herald* columnist and humorist in the 1890s to 1920s. Ade, shown below, specialized in the comedy of manners, satirizing social climbers and others who tried to take advantage of the common man. In 1916, around the same time of the action described in *Reminiscences*, Ade produced a popular silent movie[5] titled, "The Fable of How Wisenstein Did Not Lose Out to Buttinsky" based on a short story of the same title. [6]

Lefevre or Livermore may well have had this smooth but pushy character in mind for an anecdote meant to showcase a conniving stock-pool operator who tried to take advantage of Mrs. Livermore through flattery and false camaraderie. The moral of the Ade story—"Beware of the friend who tells you how good you are"—is appropriate in this context.

dent of the Borneo Tin Company, a Mr. Wisenstein, who had become the manager of the stock pool. We didn't learn until some time afterward that this Wisenstein deliberately manœuvred so that he sat next to Mrs. Livingston at dinner. **16.3**

He laid himself out to be particularly nice to her and talked most entertainingly. In the end he told her, very confidentially, "Mrs. Livingston, I'm going to do something I've never done before. I am very glad to do it because you know exactly what it means." He stopped and looked at Mrs. Livingston anxiously, to make sure she was not only wise but discreet. She could read it on his face, plain as print. But all she said was, "Yes."

"Yes, Mrs. Livingston. It has been a very great pleasure to meet you and your husband, and I want to prove that I am sincere in saying this because I hope to see a great deal of both of you. I am sure I don't have to tell you that what I am going to say is strictly confidential!" Then he whispered, "If you will buy some Borneo Tin you will make a great deal of money."

"Do you think so?" she asked.

"Just before I left the hotel," he said, "I received some cables with news that won't be known to the public for several days at least. I am going to gather in as much of the stock as I can. If you get some at the opening to-morrow you will be buying it at the same time and at the same price as I. I give you my word that Borneo Tin will surely advance. You are the only person that I have told this to. Absolutely the only one!"

She thanked him and then she told him that she didn't know anything about speculating in stocks. But he assured her it wasn't necessary for her to know any more than he had told her. To make sure she heard it correctly he repeated his advice to her:

"All you have to do is to buy as much Borneo Tin as you wish. I can give you my word that

if you do you will not lose a cent. I've never before told a woman—or a man, for that matter—
to buy anything in my life. But I am so sure the
stock won't stop this side of 200 that I'd like you
to make some money. I can't buy all the stock myself, you know, and if somebody besides myself is
going to benefit by the rise I'd rather it was you
than some stranger. Much rather! I've told you in
confidence because I know you won't talk about
it. Take my word for it, Mrs. Livingston, and buy
Borneo Tin!"

He was very earnest about it and succeeded
in so impressing her that she began to think she
had found an excellent use for the five hundred
dollars I had given her that afternoon. That money
hadn't cost me anything and was outside of her
allowance. In other words, it was easy money to
lose if the luck went against her. But he had said
she would surely win. It would be nice to make
money on her own hook—and tell me all about it
afterwards.

Well, sir, the very next morning before the market opened she went into Harding's office and said
to the manager:

"Mr. Haley, I want to buy some stock, but I don't
want it to go in my regular account because I don't
wish my husband to know anything about it until
I've made some money. Can you fix it for me?"

Haley, the manager, said, "Oh, yes. We can
make it a special account. What's the stock and how
much of it do you want to buy?"

She gave him the five hundred dollars and told
him, "Listen, please. I do not wish to lose more than
this money. If that goes I don't want to owe you anything; and remember, I don't want Mr. Livingston to
know anything about this. Buy me as much Borneo
Tin as you can for the money, at the opening."

Haley took the money and told her he'd never
say a word to a soul, and bought her a hundred shares
at the opening. I think she got it at 108. The stock

was very active that day and closed at an advance of three points. Mrs. Livingston was so delighted with her exploit that it was all she could do to keep from telling me all about it.

It so happened that I had been getting more and more bearish on the general market. The unusual activity in Borneo Tin drew my attention to it. I didn't think the time was right for any stock to advance, much less one like that. I had decided to begin my bear operations that very day, and I started by selling about ten thousand shares of Borneo. If I had not I rather think the stock would have gone up five or six points instead of three.

On the very next day I sold two thousand shares at the opening and two thousand shares just before the close, and the stock broke to 102.

Haley, the manager of Harding Brothers' Palm Beach Branch, was waiting for Mrs. Livingston to call there on the third morning. She usually strolled in about eleven to see how things were, if I was doing anything.

Haley took her aside and said, "Mrs. Livingston, if you want me to carry that hundred shares of Borneo Tin for you you will have to give me more margin."

"But I haven't any more," she told him.

"I can transfer it to your regular account," he said.

"No," she objected, "because that way L. L. would learn about it."

"But the account already shows a loss of——" he began.

"But I told you distinctly I didn't want to lose more than the five hundred dollars. I didn't even want to lose that," she said.

"I know, Mrs. Livingston, but I didn't want to sell it without consulting you, and now unless you authorise me to hold it I'll have to let it go."

"But it did so nicely the day I bought it," she said, "that I didn't believe it would act this way so soon. Did you?"

"No," answered Haley, "I didn't." They have to be diplomatic in brokers' offices.

"What's gone wrong with it, Mr. Haley?"

Haley knew, but he could not tell her without giving me away, and a customer's business is sacred. So he said, "I don't hear anything special about it, one way or another. There she goes! That's low for the move!" and he pointed to the quotation board.

Mrs. Livingston gazed at the sinking stock and cried: "Oh, Mr. Haley! I didn't want to lose my five hundred dollars! What shall I do?"

"I don't know, Mrs. Livingston, but if I were you I'd ask Mr. Livingston."

"Oh, no! He doesn't want me to speculate on my own hook. He's told me so. He'll buy or sell stock for me, if I ask him, but I've never before done trading that he did not know all about. I wouldn't dare tell him."

"That's all right," said Haley soothingly. "He is a wonderful trader and he'll know just what to do." Seeing her shake her head violently he added devilishly: "Or else you put up a thousand or two to take care of your Borneo."

The alternative decided her then and there. She hung about the office, but as the market got weaker and weaker she came over to where I sat watching the board and told me she wanted to speak to me. We went into the private office and she told me the whole story. So I just said to her: "You foolish little girl, you keep your hands off this deal."

She promised that she would, and so I gave her back her five hundred dollars 16.4 and she went away happy. The stock was par by that time.

I saw what had happened. Wisenstein was an astute person. He figured that Mrs. Livingston would

16.4 ▶ Livermore inadvertently funded his wife's misadventure with a $500 bill. That places the time at 1918 or later, as the first $500 bill was issued that year. The bill featured an engraving of pioneering Virginian John Marshall, who was secretary of state under President John Adams, then a Congressman, and later chief justice of the Supreme Court from 1801 to 1835. On the back was pictured the Spanish explorer Hernando de Soto discovering the Mississippi in 1541. In 1928, another $500 bill went into circulation featuring President William McKinley.

Bills over $100 were removed from circulation in 1969 by order of President Richard Nixon as part of a broad effort to battle the Mafia. Other high-denomination bills formerly in circulation included the $1,000 (featuring Grover Cleveland), $5,000 (James Madison), $10,000 (Salmon P. Chase), and $100,000 (Woodrow Wilson). Although the last high-denomination bill was printed in 1945, there are still plenty in collectors' hands, including more than 100,000 $1,000s. For years, Binion's casino in Las Vegas displayed a hundred $1,000 bills in a well-guarded horseshoe display.

McKinley $500 bills were listed for sale by collectors in 2009 for $800 to $10,000, depending on condition and issuer (e.g., Federal Reserve Bank of New York, Boston. or San Francisco), and are still accepted as legal tender.

tell me what he had told her and I'd study the stock. He knew that activity always attracted me and I was known to swing a pretty fair line. I suppose he thought I'd buy ten or twenty thousand shares.

It was one of the most cleverly planned and artistically propelled tips I've ever heard of. But it went wrong. It had to. In the first place, the lady had that very day received an unearned five hundred dollars and was therefore in a much more venture-some mood than usual. She wished to make some money all by herself, and womanlike dramatised the temptation so attractively that it was irresistible. She knew how I felt about stock speculation as practised by outsiders, and she didn't dare mention the matter to me. Wisenstein didn't size up her psychology right.

He also was utterly wrong in his guess about the kind of trader I was. I never take tips and I was bearish on the entire market. The tactics that he thought would prove effective in inducing me to buy Borneo—that is, the activity and the three-point rise—were precisely what made me pick Borneo as a starter when I decided to sell the entire market.

After I heard Mrs. Livingston's story I was keener than ever to sell Borneo. Every morning at the opening and every afternoon just before closing I let him have some stock regularly, until I saw a chance to take in my shorts at a handsome profit.

It has always seemed to me the height of damfoolishness to trade on tips. I suppose I am not built the way a tip-taker is. I sometimes think that tip-takers are like drunkards. There are some who can't resist the craving and always look forward to those jags which they consider indispensable to their happiness. It is so easy to open your ears and let the tip in. To be told precisely what to do to be happy in such a manner that you can easily obey is the next nicest thing to being happy—which is a mighty long first step toward the fulfilment of your heart's desire. It is not so much greed made blind by eagerness as it is hope bandaged by the unwillingness to do any thinking.

And it is not only among the outside public that you find inveterate tip-takers. The professional trader on the floor of the New York Stock Exchange is quite as bad. I am definitely aware that no end of them cherish mistaken notions of me because I never give anybody tips. If I told the average man, "Sell yourself five thousand Steel!" he would do it on the spot. But if I tell him I am quite bearish on the entire market and give him my reasons in detail, he finds trouble in listening and after I'm done talking he will glare at me for wasting his time expressing my views on general conditions instead of giving him a direct and specific tip, like a real philanthropist of the type that is so abundant in Wall Street—the sort who loves to put millions into the pockets of friends, acquaintances and utter strangers alike.

The belief in miracles that all men cherish is born of immoderate indulgence in hope. There are people who go on hope sprees periodically and we all know the chronic hope drunkard that is held up before us as an exemplary optimist. Tip-takers are all they really are.

I have an acquaintance, a member of the New York Stock Exchange, who was one of those who thought I was a selfish, cold-blooded pig because I never gave tips or put friends into things. One day— this was some years ago—he was talking to a newspaper man who casually mentioned that he had had it from a good source that G. O. H. was going up. My broker friend promptly bought a thousand shares and saw the price decline so quickly that he was out thirty-five hundred dollars before he could stop his loss. He met the newspaper man a day or two later, while he still was sore.

"That was a hell of a tip you gave me," he complained.

16.5 Jim Hickey was a term first widely used during the Civil War era to mean an exceptional person or thing, much like Jim Dandy.[7] It was usually rendered as "jimhickey," and appears most notably that way in Stephen Crane's classic Civil War novel, *The Red Badge of Courage*.[8]

"Coppering" was one of many terms in *Reminiscences* that comes from the slang of gamblers. Coppering in the game faro means making a reverse bet. Players of the game could place a copper token, usually a penny, on top of a standard wager to reverse it. A "coppered" bet won on the first losing card drawn and lost on the first winning card—the opposite of a regular bet.[9, 10] So when Gates says he coppered Westlake's tips, it was a real gambling man's insult.

"What tip was that?" asked the reporter, who did not remember.

"About G. O. H. You said you had it from a good source."

"So I did. A director of the company who is a member of the finance committee told me."

"Which of them was it?" asked the broker vindictively.

"If you must know," answered the newspaper man, "it was your own father-in-law, Mr. Westlake."

"Why in Hades didn't you tell me you meant him!" yelled the broker. "You cost me thirty-five hundred dollars!" He didn't believe in family tips. The farther away the source the purer the tip.

Old Westlake was a rich and successful banker and promoter. He ran across John W. Gates one day. Gates asked him what he knew. "If you will act on it I'll give you a tip. If you won't I'll save my breath," answered old Westlake grumpily.

"Of course I'll act on it," promised Gates cheerfully.

"Sell Reading! There is a sure twenty-five points in it, and possibly more. But twenty-five absolutely certain," said Westlake impressively.

"I'm much obliged to you," and Bet-you-a-million Gates shook hands warmly and went away in the direction of his broker's office.

Westlake had specialized on Reading. He knew all about the company and stood in with the insiders so that the market for the stock was an open book to him and everybody knew it. Now he was advising the Western plunger to go short of it.

Well, Reading never stopped going up. It rose something like one hundred points in a few weeks. One day old Westlake ran smack up against John W. in the Street, but he made out he hadn't seen him and was walking on. John W. Gates caught up with him, his face all smiles and held out his hand. Old Westlake shook it dazedly.

"I want to thank you for that tip you gave me on Reading," said Gates.

"I didn't give you any tip," said Westlake, frowning.

"Sure you did. And it was a Jim Hickey ◁**16.5**▷ of a tip too. I made sixty thousand dollars."

"Made sixty thousand dollars?"

"Sure! Don't you remember? You told me to sell Reading; so I bought it! I've always made money coppering your tips, Westlake," said John W. Gates pleasantly. "Always!"

Old Westlake looked at the bluff Westerner and presently remarked admiringly, "Gates, what a rich man I'd be if I had your brains!"

The other day I met Mr. W. A. Rogers, the famous cartoonist, whose Wall Street drawings brokers so greatly admire. His daily cartoons in the New York *Herald* for years gave pleasure to thousands. Well, he told me a story. It was just before we went to war with Spain. ◁**16.6**▷ He was spending an evening with a broker friend. When he left he picked up his derby hat from the rack, at least he thought it was his hat, for it was the same shape and fitted him perfectly.

The Street at that time was thinking and talking of nothing but war with Spain. Was there to be one or not? If it was to be war the market would go down; not so much on our own selling as on pressure from European holders of our securities. If peace, it would be a cinch to buy stocks, as there had been considerable declines prompted by the sensational clamorings of the yellow papers. ◁**16.7**▷ Mr. Rogers told me the rest of the story as follows:

"My friend, the broker, at whose house I had been the night before, stood in the Exchange the next day anxiously debating in his mind which side of the market to play. He went over the pros and cons, but it was impossible to distinguish which were rumours and which were facts. There was no

16.6 ▷ The Spanish-American War began in the spring of 1898. At the center of the conflict was Cuba's fight for independence from Spain, its colonial master. Upon the sinking of the USS *Maine* in Havana Harbor in February, believed to be the result of a Spanish mine, the "yellow papers"—especially those owned by William Randolph Hearst—sensationalized the accident and enraged the American public. Soon American troops were entering Cuba to assist the independence fighters. In April, Spain declared war on the United States.

Called a "splendid little war" by a friend of war hero and future president Theodore Roosevelt, the conflict allowed the United States to secure former Spanish territories as war prizes.[11] The Treaty of Paris, signed in December 1898, gave the United States control of Puerto Rico, islands in the West Indies, Guam, and the Philippines.

16.7 ▷ "Yellow papers" is a slang term for a type of journalism more concerned with selling papers than adhering to the truth. The term was coined in 1896 and was used during Livermore's time to describe the fight for New York City circulation between William Randolph Hearst and Joseph Pulitzer. Part of the battle focused on having dramatic front-page illustrations that grabbed the reader's attention. The paper titans held nothing back: When artist R. F. Outcault, creator of the popular Yellow Kid cartoon, left Pulitzer's paper to join with Hearst, his replacement was told to create rival Yellow Kid characters. This feud over the stories of a "jug-eared child of the New York City tenements" was emblematic of the broader struggle. Since then, the term has been used to describe people and papers that sacrifice journalistic integrity in the pursuit of profits.[12]

16.8 According to biographer Richard Smitten, Livermore told an entirely different version of this story to his sons at the dinner table one night. In the alternate version, a WAR premonition spurred him to sell stocks on the eve of the United States entering World War I. Here's Paul Livermore's account of his father telling the tale, by way of Smitten:

> I was seeing some friends off at the Grand Central Station. I walked with them to my private railway car, which I was loaning to them, to take them down to Palm Beach. The porter walked beside us pushing the trolley with their luggage. When we got to the car, my friend reached over to pick up his wife's jewelry case from the trolley, and his hat fell off and rolled under the car. The porter reached under the car to pick up the Stetson homburg from the tracks, and he handed it to me to give to my friend. I looked down at the upturned hat. In the hatband there were the initials in gold, "W.A.R.," for Warren Augustus Reed, my friend's initials.
>
> Well, that was a message to me, boys, a sign, and I raced back to the office and started selling in earnest. I already was short the market, but now there was no question in my mind, war was coming to the United States.[13]

16.9 This is a fictitious name that could be a stand-in for either the Atlantic Coast Line or the Southern Railway. Another possibility is the Atlantic & Pacific, which was acquired by the Santa Fe in 1881.[14]

authentic news to guide him. At one moment he thought war was inevitable, and on the next he almost convinced himself that it was utterly unlikely. His perplexity must have caused a rise in his temperature, for he took off his derby to wipe his fevered brow. He couldn't tell whether he should buy or sell.

"He happened to look inside of his hat. There in gold letters was the word WAR. **16.8** That was all the hunch he needed. Was it not a tip from Providence via my hat? So he sold a raft of stock, war was duly declared, he covered on the break and made a killing." And then W. A. Rogers finished, "I never got back that hat!"

But the prize tip story of my collection concerns one of the most popular members of the New York Stock Exchange, J. T. Hood. One day another floor trader, Bert Walker, told him that he had done a good turn to a prominent director of the Atlantic & Southern. **16.9** In return the grateful insider told him to buy all the A. & S. he could carry. The directors were going to do something that would put the stock up at least twenty-five points. All the directors were not in the deal, but the majority would be sure to vote as wanted.

Bert Walker concluded that the dividend rate was going to be raised. He told his friend Hood and they each bought a couple of thousand shares of A. & S. The stock was very weak, before and after they bought, but Hood said that was obviously intended to facilitate accumulation by the inside clique, headed by Bert's grateful friend.

On the following Thursday, after the market closed, the directors of the Atlantic & Southern met and passed the dividend. The stock broke six points in the first six minutes of trading Friday morning.

Bert Walker was sore as a pup. He called on the grateful director, who was broken-hearted about it and very penitent. He said that he had forgotten that he had told Walker to buy. That was the reason he had neglected to call him up to tell him of a change in the plans of the dominant faction in the board. The remorseful director was so anxious to make up that he gave Bert another tip. He kindly explained that a couple of his colleagues wanted to get cheap stock and against his judgment resorted to coarse work. He had to yield to win their votes. But now that they all had accumulated their full lines there was nothing to stop the advance. It was a double-riveted, lead-pipe cinch to buy A. & S. now.

Bert not only forgave him but shook hands warmly with the high financier. Naturally he hastened to find his friend and fellow-victim, Hood, to impart the glad tidings to him. They were going to make a killing. The stock had been tipped for a rise before and they bought. But now it was fifteen points lower. That made it a cinch. So they bought five thousand shares, joint account.

As if they had rung a bell to start it, the stock broke badly on what quite obviously was inside selling. Two specialists cheerfully confirmed the suspicion. Hood sold out their five thousand shares. When he got through Bert Walker said to him, "If that blankety-blank blanker hadn't gone to Florida day before yesterday I'd lick the stuffing out of him. Yes, I would. But you come with me."

"Where to?" asked Hood.

"To the telegraph office. I want to send that skunk a telegram that he'll never forget. Come on."

Hood went on. Bert led the way to the telegraph office. There, carried away by his feelings—they had taken quite a loss on the five thousand shares—he composed a masterpiece of vituperation. He read it to Hood and finished, "That will come pretty near to showing him what I think of him."

He was about to slide it toward the waiting clerk when Hood said, "Hold on, Bert!"

"What's the matter?"

"I wouldn't send it," advised Hood earnestly.

16.10 **The Rothschilds** are a German Jewish family dynasty that has deep roots in international finance and investment banking dating back to the late 1700s. Many members of the family, including its patriarch, Mayer Amschel Rothschild, were ennobled by the European royalty they served. The family's fortune was based in part on the money King George III of England paid for the use of 17,000 Hessian mercenaries in the war against George Washington and the Colonial Army.[15] Amschel, based in Frankfurt, had five sons and commanded that they equally divide and share profits: Anselm succeeded his father in Germany; Solomon went to Vienna; Nathan Mayer to London; Charles to Naples; and James to Paris. In this passage, Livermore is referring to Nathan Rothschild, the first Baron Rothschild and grandson of Nathan Mayer Rothschild. Baron Rothschild was born in 1840 and died in 1915. He was a partner at the NM Rothschild & Sons investment bank his grandfather founded in 1811.

"Why not?" snapped Bert.

"It will make him sore as the dickens."

"That's what we want, isn't it?" said Bert, looking at Hood in surprise.

But Hood shook his head disapprovingly and said in all seriousness, "We'll never get another tip from him if you send that telegram!"

A professional trader actually said that. Now what's the use of talking about sucker tip-takers? Men do not take tips because they are bally asses but because they like those hope cocktails I spoke of. Old Baron Rothschild's **16.10** recipe for wealth winning applies with greater force than ever to speculation. Somebody asked him if making money in the Bourse was not a very difficult matter, and he replied that, on the contrary, he thought it was very easy.

"That is because you are so rich," objected the interviewer.

"Not at all. I have found an easy way and I stick to it. I simply cannot help making money. I will tell you my secret if you wish. It is this: I never buy at the bottom and I always sell too soon."

Investors are a different breed of cats. Most of them go in strong for inventories and statistics of earnings and all sorts of mathematical data, as though that meant facts and certainties. The human factor is minimised as a rule. Very few people like to buy into a one-man business. But the wisest investor I ever knew was a man who began by being a Pennsylvania Dutchman and followed it up by coming to Wall Street and seeing a great deal of Russell Sage.

He was a great investigator, an indefatigable Missourian. He believed in asking his own questions and in doing his seeing with his own eyes. He had no use for another man's spectacles. This was years ago. It seems he held quite a little Atchison. Presently he began to hear disquieting reports about the company and its management. He was told that Mr. Reinhart, the president, instead of being the marvel he was credited with being, in reality was a most extravagant manager whose recklessness was fast pushing the company into a mess. There would be the deuce to pay on the inevitable day of reckoning.

This was precisely the kind of news that was as the breath of life to the Pennsylvania Dutchman. He hurried over to Boston to interview Mr. Reinhart and ask him a few questions. The questions consisted of repeating the accusations he had heard and then asking the president of the Atchison, Topeka & Santa Fe Railroad ◁**16.11**] if they were true.

Mr. Reinhart not only denied the allegations emphatically but said even more: He proceeded to prove by figures that the allegators were malicious liars. The Pennsylvania Dutchman had asked for exact information and the president gave it to him, showing him what the company was doing and how it stood financially, to a cent.

The Pennsylvania Dutchman thanked President Reinhart, returned to New York and promptly sold all his Atchison holdings. A week or so later he used his idle funds to buy a big lot of Delaware, Lackawanna & Western.

Years afterward we were talking of lucky swaps and he cited his own case. He explained what prompted him to make it.

16.11 ▶ The Santa Fe Railroad got its start in 1863 in Kansas. Its founder, Cyrus Holliday, received a land grant from the state to build a line west from Atchison to the Colorado border. Eventually, the company expanded to New Mexico in 1878 before building to the Pacific Ocean via Los Angeles and San Diego in 1887. Later, lines were built to Chicago and down to the Gulf of Mexico in Texas. In 1995, the company merged with the Burlington Northern, creating the Burlington Northern Santa Fe Corporation.[16]

16.12 The Delaware, Lackawanna & Western Railroad was organized in 1850 from a combination of smaller lines to connect the rich coal-mining territory of Pennsylvania with Hoboken, New Jersey. Lackawanna was famous for using cleaner-burning anthracite that it mined from its own properties. As a result, Lackawanna's riders were spared the soot covering that accompanied passage on a regular coal-fired train. The company created the "Phoebe Snow" character—a beautiful woman clad in white linen—for use in its print advertisements to illustrate this advantage.[17]

In the 1960s, the company merged with the Erie Railroad before falling into bankruptcy in 1972 and eventually becoming part of CSX Transportation.[18]

"You see," he said, "I noticed that President Reinhart, when he wrote down figures, took sheets of letter paper from a pigeonhole in his mahogany roll-top desk. It was fine heavy linen paper with beautifully engraved letterheads in two colors. It was not only very expensive but worse—it was unnecessarily expensive. He would write a few figures on a sheet to show me exactly what the company was earning on certain divisions or to prove how they were cutting down expenses or reducing operating costs, and then he would crumple up the sheet of the expensive paper and throw it in the waste-basket. Pretty soon he would want to impress me with the economies they were introducing and he would reach for a fresh sheet of the beautiful notepaper with the engraved letterheads in two colors. A few figures—and bingo, into the waste-basket! More money wasted without a thought. It struck me that if the president was that kind of a man he would scarcely be likely to insist upon having or rewarding economical assistants. I therefore decided to believe the people who had told me the management was extravagant instead of accepting the president's version and I sold what Atchison stock I held.

"It so happened that I had occasion to go to the offices of the Delaware, Lackawanna & Western <16.12 a few days later. Old Sam Sloan was the president. His office was the nearest to the entrance and his door was wide open. It was always open. Nobody could walk into the general offices of the D. L. & W. in those days and not see the president of the company seated at his desk. Any man could walk in and do business with him right off, if he had any business to do. The financial reporters used to tell me that they never had to beat about the bush with old Sam Sloan, but would ask their questions and get a straight yes or no from him, no matter what the stock-market exigencies of the other directors might be.

"When I walked in I saw the old man was busy. I thought at first that he was opening his mail, but after I got inside close to the desk I saw what he was doing. I learned afterwards that it was his daily custom to do it. After the mail was sorted and opened, instead of throwing away the empty envelopes he had them gathered up and taken to his office. In his leisure moments he would rip the envelope all around. That gave him two bits of paper, each with one clean blank side. He would pile these up and then he would have them distributed about, to be used in lieu of scratch pads for such figuring as Reinhart had done for me on engraved notepaper. No waste of empty envelopes and no waste of the president's idle moments. Everything utilised.

"It struck me that if that was the kind of man the D. L. & W. had for president, the company was managed economically in all departments. The president would see to that! Of course I knew the company was paying regular dividends and had a good property. I bought all the D. L. & W. stock I could. Since that time the capital stock has been doubled and quadrupled. My annual dividends amount to as much as my original investment. I still have my D. L. & W. And Atchison went into the hands of a receiver a few months after I saw the president throwing sheet after sheet of linen paper with engraved letterheads in two colors into the waste-basket to prove to me with figures that he was not extravagant."

And the beauty of that story is that it is true and that no other stock that the Pennsylvania Dutchman could have bought would have proved to be so good an investment as D. L. & W. ◁**16.13**▷

16.13 ▷ Lefevre never explicitly says so, but it is clear he meant to end this chapter about the perils of lazy tip-taking with an anecdote that provides an exemplar of the opposite tack: hard work.

Livermore describes the adventures of an unnamed Pennsylvanian Dutchman—an appellation that suggests thrift—who personally investigates companies and their managers. He also calls this investor an "indefatigable Missourian" to suggest he was always in "show me" mode.

Livermore gives this investor his highest accolade: "He believed in asking his own questions and in doing his seeing with his own eyes. He had no use for another man's spectacles."

Here he concludes the story by showing that prudence and discipline brought the ultimate reward: "No other stock...would have proved to be so good an investment."

The construction of this chapter is thus different than the rest of the book, working much like one of George Ade's parables. It is a narration intended to illustrate a moral lesson to indolent gamblers among the public who he terms "chronic hope drunkards": Don't take tips; do your own research.

ENDNOTES

1 "Big Jump in Tin Imports," *New York Times,* June 16, 1918, 48.

2 "Organizing New Can Co.," *New York Times,* December 11, 1912, 17.

3 Richard Smitten, *Jesse Livermore: World's Greatest Stock Trader* (2001), 81–82.

4 "At Churchill Downs," *Time,* May 15, 1933.

5 Purdue University Libraries. List of George Ade films. http://www.lib.purdue.edu/spcol/fa/html/ade/index.htm#d0e9939.

6 George Ade, *The Girl Proposition: A Bunch of He and She Fables* (R. H. Russell Publishing. 1902), 69.

7 John D. Wright, *The Language of the Civil War* (Oryx Press, 2001), 163.

8 Stephen Crane, *The Red Badge of Courage* (D. Appleton & Co., 1895).

9 Richard L. Frey, *According to Hoyle: The Rules of Games* (Random House. 1970), 212.

10 Mark Howard, "Bucking the Tiger: The Traditional Game of Faro," Barbary Coast Vigilance Committee. 2004, www.bcvc.net/faro/.

11 Hugh Thomas, *Cuba, or, the Pursuit of Freedom* (1998), 404.

12 W. Joseph Campbell, *Yellow Journalism* (2003), 25.

13 Smitten, *Jesse Livermore,* 114.

14 John F. Stover, *Historical Atlas of the American Railroads* (1999), 90.

15 Henry Clews, *Fifty Years in Wall Street* (New York: Irving Publishing Company, 1908), 398.

16 Ibid.

17 Roger H. Grant, *Erie Lackawanna* (1996), 80.

18 John F. Stover, *Historical Atlas of the American Railroads* (1999), 71.

XVII

One of my most intimate friends is very fond of telling stories about what he calls my hunches. He is forever ascribing to me powers that defy analysis. He declares I merely follow blindly certain mysterious impulses and thereby get out of the stock market at precisely the right time. His pet yarn is about a black cat that told me, at his breakfast-table, to sell a lot of stock I was carrying, and that after I got the pussy's message I was grouchy and nervous until I sold every share I was long of. I got practically the top prices of the movement, which of course strengthened the hunch theory of my hard-headed friend.

I had gone to Washington ◁17.1 to endeavor to convince a few Congressmen that there was no wisdom in taxing us to death and I wasn't paying much attention to the stock market. My decision to sell out my line came suddenly, hence my friend's yarn.

I admit that I do get irresistible impulses at times to do certain things in the market. It doesn't matter whether I am long or short of stocks. I must get out. I am uncomfortable until I do. I myself think that what happens is that I see a lot of warning-signals. Perhaps not a single one may be sufficiently clear or powerful to afford me a positive, definite reason for doing what I suddenly feel like doing. Probably that is all there is to what they call "ticker-sense" that old traders say

17.1 ▷ Livermore was dragged in front of a Senate committee in late 1923 to discuss market manipulations and the commissions earned by pool operators.[1]

269

17.2 Lefevre wrote an article about Keene in 1909 that reveals a lot about both the trader's agility and the author's view of journalists' role in the reporting process. The piece captures Keene's reaction to news that the United States would intervene in an 1895 boundary dispute between British Guiana and Venezuela after the discovery of gold in a remote area between the two countries.

Richard Olney, secretary of state under President Grover Cleveland, sent a strongly worded message to his British counterpart, Lord Salisbury, that invoked the Monroe Doctrine barring intervention in the Western Hemisphere by European powers. After being rebuffed by the British government, which contended that the Monroe Doctrine was not international law, Cleveland turned to Congress for authorization to create a boundary commission to settle the dispute. He proposed that its findings be enforced "by every means," which was taken to mean military force. The measure was passed and talk of war began to circulate in the press.

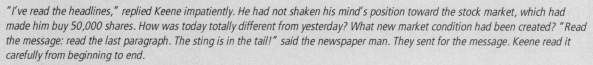

Lefevre wrote:

At the time the stock market was bullish. Wall Street read the message and thought nothing of it. A newspaper man, who happened to be calling on James R. Keene, expressed his surprise that the Street took it so calmly. Mr. Keene was long about 50,000 shares in various stocks. He asked why the President's message should have any effect. The newspaper man looked at the great stock speculator in blank amazement and asked: "Have you read it?"

"I've read the headlines," replied Keene impatiently. He had not shaken his mind's position toward the stock market, which had made him buy 50,000 shares. How was today totally different from yesterday? What new market condition had been created? "Read the message: read the last paragraph. The sting is in the tail!" said the newspaper man. They sent for the message. Keene read it carefully from beginning to end.

"Well?" he said, his mind still clinging to its previous position.

"Well? You mean 'hell' don't you? That's what will break loose tomorrow when London begins to sell American stocks by the ship-load! You'll see nothing but WAR!! in the English papers tomorrow. And the same here!"

Still, Keene hesitated. Think of it! A man of his temperament and experience and imagination hesitated! But the more he thought the more he realized that a new market condition had been created. He began selling out of the stocks he held. Freed from the handicap of his market commitments, which so often fetter the minds of operators, he then and only then grasped the situation clearly. And then, and only then, did he begin to sell short. From bull to nothing, from nothing to bear. Even the great Keene had to take these two steps. All that day he sold and sold, up to the close of the market. From being long 50,000 shares in the morning he went home at three o'clock short 73,000 shares. And the next day hell broke loose first in the newspapers, then on the Stock Exchange. And Keene made a fortune.[2]

James R. Keene ⟨**17.2**⟩ had so strongly developed and other operators before him. Usually, I confess, the warning turns out to be not only sound but timed to the minute. But in this particular instance there was no hunch. The black cat had nothing to do with it. What he tells everybody about my getting up so grumpy that morning I suppose can be explained— if I in truth was grouchy—by my disappointment. I knew I was not convincing the Congressman I talked to and the Committee did not view the problem of

taxing Wall Street as I did. I wasn't trying to arrest or evade taxation on stock transactions but to suggest a tax that I as an experienced stock operator felt was neither unfair nor unintelligent. I didn't want Uncle Sam to kill the goose that could lay so many golden eggs with fair treatment. Possibly my lack of success not only irritated me but made me pessimistic over the future of an unfairly taxed business. But I'll tell you exactly what happened.

At the beginning of the bull market I thought well of the outlook in both the Steel trade and the copper market and I therefore felt bullish on stocks of both groups. So I started to accumulate some of them. I began by buying 5,000 shares of Utah Copper **17.3** and stopped because it didn't act right. That is, it did not behave as it should have behaved to make me feel I was wise in buying it. I think the price was around 114. I also started to buy United

17.3 Utah Copper's colorful history began when Enos Wall purchased low-grade copper deposits around Bingham Canyon just south of Salt Lake City in 1887. Steam shovels were brought in to work the mountain in 1906, and developed it into one of the most productive mines in the world, now almost a mile deep and three miles wide. Kennecott Mines Co. of Alaska bought a 25% stake in the company in 1915, and then purchased the rest in 1936. After World War II, copper prices dropped sharply and the Utah company's assets were sold to a succession of oil companies, starting with Standard Oil of Ohio and ending with British Petroleum. A predecessor of Australian mining conglomerate Rio Tinto bought and reincorporated the company in 1989 and operates the Bingham mine now again as its Kennecott Utah Copper unit.[3]

17.4 This narrative appears to describe the spring of 1923, when the economy was recovering from a post-World War I recession thanks to interest rate cuts by the Federal Reserve. The business expansion kicked off the epic bull market of the "Roaring Twenties," which peaked in a speculative frenzy in the final summer of the decade and ended with the October 1929 crash.

The business contraction that preceded this period was brief but very severe. It's perhaps no surprise that Lefevre skips the post–World War I era in his narrative. Deflation ravaged asset values as industrial production slowed. Wholesale prices fell 56% from May 1920 to June 1921. The only comparable deflation occurred during the War of 1812 and the Civil War.[4] It was also a period of social strife punctuated with labor strikes and race riots. A horse-drawn wagon bomb that detonated outside the J. P. Morgan building on Wall Street, shown below, killed 38 people and wounded 300 on September 16, 1920.[5] (The case was never solved, though Italian anarchists were suspected.[6])

The Dow Jones Industrial Average rose 28% in the year after World War I ended in November 1918, but then sank 30% over the next two years. Stocks then gradually worked their way higher until July 1924, when the new boom ensued.

You can see how the favorable conditions Livermore describes would have acted as a power tailwind for stocks as the world struggled to recover from the horrors and destruction of the world war. In 1921, the Federal Reserve slashed U.S. short-term rates to 4.5% from 7%, helping the recovery gain momentum. Historian Robert Sobel writes that inventories had reached such low levels that "companies were forced to place new orders or go out of business." The economy briefly tipped back into recession from May 1923 to July 1924, but industry and stocks then shifted into overdrive and never looked back for the next five years as the Dow Jones Industrials soared 270%.[7]

States Steel at almost the same price. I bought in all 20,000 shares the first day because it did act right. I followed the method I have described before.

Steel continued to act right and I therefore continued to accumulate it until I was carrying 72,000 shares of it in all. But my holdings of Utah Copper consisted of my initial purchase. I never got above the 5,000 shares. Its behaviour did not encourage me to do more with it.

Everybody knows what happened. We had a big bull movement. **17.4** I knew the market was going up. General conditions were favourable. Even after stocks had gone up extensively and my paper-profit was not to be sneezed at, the tape kept trumpeting: Not yet! Not yet! When I arrived in Washington the tape was still saying that to me. Of course, I had no intention of increasing my line at that late day, even though I was still bullish. At the same time, the market was plainly going my way and there was no occasion for me to sit in front of a quotation board all day, in hourly expectation of getting a tip to get out. Before the clarion call to retreat came—barring an utterly unexpected catastrophe, of course—the market would hesitate or otherwise prepare me for a reversal of the speculative situation. That was the reason why I went blithely about my business with my Congressmen.

At the same time, prices kept going up and that meant that the end of the bull market was drawing nearer. I did not look for the end on any fixed date. That was something quite beyond my power to determine. But I needn't tell you that I was on the watch for the tip-off. I always am, anyhow. It has become a matter of business habit with me.

I cannot swear to it but I rather suspect that the

day before I sold out, seeing the high prices made me think of the magnitude of my paper-profit as well as of the line I was carrying and, later on, of my vain efforts to induce our legislators to deal fairly and intelligently by Wall Street. That was probably the way and the time the seed was sown within me. The subconscious mind worked on it all night. In the morning I thought of the market and began to wonder how it would act that day. When I went down to the office I saw not so much that prices were still higher and that I had a satisfying profit but that there was a great big market with a tremendous power of absorption. I could sell any amount of stock in that market; and, of course, when a man is carrying his full line of stocks, he must be on the watch for an opportunity to change his paper profit into actual cash. He should try to lose as little of the profit as possible in the swapping. Experience has taught me that a man can always find an opportunity to make his profits real and that this opportunity usually comes at the end of the move. That isn't tape-reading or a hunch.

Of course, when I found that morning a market in which I could sell out all my stocks without any trouble I did so. When you are selling out it is no wiser or braver to sell fifty shares than fifty thousand; but fifty shares you can sell in the dullest market without breaking the price and fifty thousand shares of a single stock is a different proposition. I had seventy-two thousand shares of U.S. Steel. This may not seem a colossal line, but you can't always sell that much without losing some of that profit that looks so nice on paper when you figure it out and that hurts as much to lose as if you actually had it safe in bank.

I had a total profit of about $1,500,000 and I grabbed it while the grabbing was good. But that wasn't the principal reason for thinking that I did the right thing in selling out when I did. The market proved it for me and that was indeed a source

17.5 On April 20, 1923, Livermore warned that the "technical position of the stock market is weak because of undigested securities." Immediately there was a backlash as newspapers reported that bankers conspired to "teach him a lesson" and speculated that a "squeeze might shortly be engineered against him if it were found that he were short of stocks" after issuing his dire prediction.[8] By October, Livermore was turning bullish once more, telling the *Christian Science Monitor*, "I have no intention of staying out of the stock market permanently."[9]

of satisfaction to me. It was this way: I succeeded in selling my entire line of seventy-two thousand shares of U.S. Steel at a price which averaged me just one point from the top of the day and of the movement. **17.5** It proved that I was right, to the minute. But when, on the very same hour of the very same day I came to sell my 5,000 Utah Copper, the price broke five points. Please recall that I began buying both stocks at the same time and that I acted wisely in increasing my line of U.S. Steel from twenty thousand shares to seventy-two thousand, and equally wisely in not increasing my line of Utah from the original 5,000 shares. The reason why I didn't sell out my Utah Copper before was that I was bullish on the copper trade and it was a bull market in stocks and I didn't think that Utah would hurt me much even if I didn't make a killing in it. But as for hunches, there weren't any.

The training of a stock trader is like a medical education. The physician has to spend long years learning anatomy, physiology, materia medica and collateral subjects by the dozen. He learns the theory and then proceeds to devote his life to the practice. He observes and classifies all sorts of pathological phenomena. He learns to diagnose. If his diagnosis is correct—and that depends upon the accuracy of his observation—he ought to do pretty well in his prognosis, always keeping in mind, of course, that human fallibility and the utterly unforeseen will keep him from scoring 100 per cent of bull's-eyes. And then, as he gains in experience, he learns not only to do the right thing but to do it instantly, so that many people will think he does it instinctively. It really isn't automatism. It is that he has diagnosed the case according to his observations of such cases during a period of many years; and, naturally, after he has diagnosed it, he can only treat it in the way that experience has taught him is the proper treatment. You can transmit knowledge—that is, your particular collection of card-indexed facts—but not your experience. A man may know what to do and lose money—if he doesn't do it quickly enough.

Observation, experience, memory and mathematics—these are what the successful trader must depend on. He must not only observe accurately but remember at all times what he has observed. He cannot bet on the unreasonable or on the unexpected, however strong his personal convictions may be about man's unreasonableness or however certain he may feel that the unexpected happens very frequently. He must bet always on probabilities—that is, try to anticipate them. ◁**17.6** Years of practice at the game, of constant study, of always remembering, enable the trader to act on the instant when the unexpected happens as well as when the expected comes to pass.

A man can have great mathematical ability and an unusual power of accurate observation and yet fail in speculation unless he also possesses the experience and the memory. And then, like the physician who keeps up with the advances of science, the wise trader never ceases to study general conditions, to keep track of developments everywhere that are likely to affect or influence the course of the various markets. After years at the game it becomes a habit to keep posted. He acts almost automatically. He acquires the invaluable professional attitude and that enables him to beat the game—at times! This difference between the professional and the amateur or occasional trader cannot be overemphasised. I find, for instance, that memory and mathematics help me very much. Wall Street makes its money on a mathematical basis. I mean, it makes its money by dealing with facts and figures.

When I said that a trader has to keep posted to the minute and that he must take a purely professional attitude toward all markets and all developments, I merely meant to emphasise again that hunches and the mysterious ticker-sense haven't

17.6 ▷ Anticipation was a very important theme for Livermore, one he expressed again and again to reporters who sought out his secrets. Today we would recognize the concept by the phrase "Buy the rumor and sell the news."

William Hamilton, the fourth editor of the *Wall Street Journal*, wrote in 1922:

> Jesse Livermore was quoted in the columns of Barron's as saying that "all market movements are based on sound reasoning. Unless a man can anticipate future events his ability to speculate successfully is limited." And he went on to add: "Speculation is a business. It is neither guesswork nor a gamble. It is hard work and plenty of it."[10]

Separately, Livermore described his methods to Richard Wyckoff, who founded the *Magazine of Wall Street*:

> My principal method is to study the effect of present and future conditions on the earning power of the various companies engaged in different lines of industry. Anticipation of coming events is the whole thing. When I have my mind made up about this, I wait for the psychological moment. I do not deal promiscuously; instead, I decide how much I will trade in, and how much money I will risk on that trade, and then I buy or sell the whole quantity at once.[11]

And finally, there is a testimony Livermore gave to the Federal Trade Commission in 1922 during a hearing on grain exporters:

> Every successful player has to anticipate. If he anticipates right, see, there will come a time in the next period of two or three months that his judgment is going to be proved right by the action of the market. You see what I mean? It is going to be so plain then that everyone is going to think at some time in the future what he is thinking today, and when the time comes that everyone gets thinking, it is very plain, and the papers begin to talk and everything else, and the government agencies, and say there is going to be a scarcity of wheat, as they did last spring, and come out with a lot of misinformation and excite the public—the successful man who anticipated the situation three months previous, he would not be successful very long if he did not take advantage and sell out at that time.[12]

Hedge fund manager Michael Steinhardt succinctly described this process as the need to develop a "variant perception."[13] In these comments, as well as in Lefevre's narrative, the speculator's art is defined less by the purely technical expectation of price movements than by a forecast of future news and market participants' reaction to it.

17.7 Railway shopmen walked off the job between July and September 1922 to protest against wage reductions. Coal miners went on strike throughout the year in response to mining company efforts to establish separate wage contracts.

so very much to do with success. Of course, it often happens that an experienced trader acts so quickly that he hasn't time to give all his reasons in advance—but nevertheless they are good and sufficient reasons, because they are based on facts collected by him in his years of working and thinking and seeing things from the angle of the professional, to whom everything that comes to his mill is grist. Let me illustrate what I mean by the professional attitude.

I keep track of the commodities markets, always. It is a habit of years. As you know, the Government reports indicated a winter wheat crop about the same as last year and a bigger spring wheat crop than in 1921. The condition was much better and we probably would have an earlier harvest than usual. When I got the figures of condition and I saw what we might expect in the way of yield—mathematics—I also thought at once of the coal miners' strike and the railroad shopmen's strike. **17.7** I couldn't help thinking of them because my mind always thinks of all developments that have a bearing on the markets. It instantly struck me that the strike which had already affected the movement of freight everywhere must affect wheat prices adversely. I figured this way: There was bound to be considerable delay in moving winter wheat to market by reason of the strike-crippled transportation facilities, and by the time those improved the Spring wheat crop would be ready to move. That meant that when the railroads were able to move wheat in quantity they would be bringing in both crops together—the delayed winter and the early spring wheat—and that would mean a vast quantity of wheat pouring into the market at one fell swoop. Such being the facts of the case—the obvious probabilities—the traders, who would know and figure as I did, would not bull wheat for a while. They would not feel like buying it unless the price declined to such figures as made the purchase of wheat a good investment. With no buying power in the market, the price ought to go down. Thinking the way I did I must find whether I was right or not. As old Pat Hearne used to remark, "You can't tell till you bet." Between being bearish and selling there is no need to waste time.

Experience has taught me that the way a market behaves is an excellent guide for an operator to follow. It is like taking a patient's temperature and pulse or noting the colour of the eyeballs and the coating of the tongue.

Now, ordinarily a man ought to be able to buy or sell a million bushels of wheat within a range of ¼ cent. On this day when I sold the 250,000 bushels to test the market for timeliness, the price went down ¼ cent. Then, since the reaction did not definitely tell me all I wished to know, I sold another quarter of a million bushels. I noticed that it was taken in driblets; that is, the buying was in lots of 10,000 or 15,000 bushels instead of being taken in two or three transactions which would have been the normal way. In addition to the homeopathic buying the price went down 1 ¼ cents on my selling. Now, I need not waste time pointing out that the way in which the market took my wheat and the disproportionate decline on my selling told me that there was no buying power there. Such being the case, what was the only thing to do? Of course, to sell a lot more. Following the dictates of experience may possibly fool you, now and then. But not following them invariably makes an ass of you. So I sold 2,000,000 bushels and the price went down some more. A few days later the market's behaviour practically compelled me to sell an additional 2,000,000 bushels and the price declined further still; a few days later wheat started to break badly ◁**17.8** and slumped off 6 cents a bushel. And it didn't stop there. It has been going down, with short-lived rallies.

Now, I didn't follow a hunch. Nobody gave me a tip. It was my habitual or professional mental attitude toward the commodities markets that gave

17.8 ▷ The railroad strike created a supply overhang at a time when the U.S. economy was already suffering from price deflation in the wake of the economic distress of World War I. Also complicating matters was a large influx of grain from European nations as reconstruction of their fields and transportation infrastructure started to take hold. World wheat production swelled from nearly 3 million bushels in 1919 to more than 3.7 million.[14] From a high of $1.07 a bushel, wheat fell as low as 96.5 cents per bushel in Chicago.[15]

Besides the reasons given here, there was also a rumor floating around Wall Street that Livermore believed wheat would sell at 75 cents a bushel following government hearings on the grain exchanges. As a result, the *New York Times* reported: "Several millions of bushels of long wheat went overboard, and the break was assisted by selling by houses that usually act for Livermore."[16]

17.9 The Crucible Steel Co. of America was founded in 1900 from a combination of 13 smaller companies. It produced 95% of the country's total supply of crucible steel and was at the time the world's largest producer.[17] Sales offices were located all around the world, including Seattle, Boston, Berlin, London, Petrograd, and Paris.[18]

In 1968, Crucible was bought by Colt Industries. In 1985, the company regained its independence after a group of employees bought it. The years that followed featured labor strikes, modernization initiatives, and increased reliance on the automobile industry. In May 2009, Crucible filed for bankruptcy protection.[19]

The company took its name from crucible steel, which is a high-quality metal formed under high temperatures within a crucible to increase its carbon content. In the 1830s, the United States imported all of its crucible steel for use in tools and saws from England. After a large clay deposit was discovered in West Virginia, suitable for the construction of crucibles, American manufacturers began experimenting with the process. By the 1860s, Hussey, Wells & Co. of Pittsburgh was the first to find "complete financial as well as mechanical success in this difficult department of American manufacturing enterprise."[20] Eventually, the firm would become part of Crucible Steel. The method survives today but was largely supplanted in the mid twentieth century by the faster, lower-cost Bessemer process for mass-market steel making.

17.10 Republic Iron and Steel Co. was founded in 1899 and based in Youngstown, Ohio. Republic was combined with a few smaller competitors in 1927 to become the third largest steel producer in the United States behind Bethlehem and U.S. Steel. Eventually, the firm became part of International Steel Group, which in turn was purchased by Luxembourg-based global steelmaker ArcelorMittal.[21]

me the profit and that attitude came from my years at this business. I study because my business is to trade. The moment the tape told me that I was on the right track my business duty was to increase my line. I did. That is all there is to it.

I have found that experience is apt to be steady dividend payer in this game and that observation gives you the best tips of all. The behaviour of a certain stock is all you need at times. You observe it. Then experience shows you how to profit by variations from the usual, that is, from the probable. For example, we know that all stocks do not move one way together but that all the stocks of a group will move up in a bull market and down in a bear market. This is a commonplace of speculation. It is the commonest of all self-given tips and the commission houses are well aware of it and pass it on to any customer who has not thought of it himself; I mean, the advice to trade in those stocks which have lagged behind other stocks of the same group. Thus, if U.S. Steel goes up, it is logically assumed that it is only a matter of time when Crucible **17.9** or Republic **17.10** or Bethlehem will follow suit. Trade conditions and prospects should work alike with all stocks of a group and the prosperity should be shared by all. On the theory, corroborated by experience times without number, that every dog has his day in the market, the public will buy A. B. Steel because it has not advanced while C. D. Steel and X. Y. Steel have gone up.

I never buy a stock even in a bull market, if it doesn't act as it ought to act in that kind of market. I have sometimes bought a stock during an undoubted bull market and found out that other stocks in the same group were not acting bullishly and I have sold out my stock. Why? Experience tells me that it is not wise to buck against what I may call the manifest group-tendency. I cannot expect to play certainties only. I must reckon on probabilities—and anticipate them. An old broker once said to me: "If I am walking along a railroad track and I see a train coming toward me at sixty miles an hour, do I keep on walking on the ties? Friend, I side-step. And I do not even pat myself on the back for being so wise and prudent."

Last year, after the general bull movement was well under way, I noticed that one stock in a certain group was not going with the rest of the group, though the group with that one exception was going with the rest of the market. I was long a very fair amount of Blackwood Motors. Everybody knew that the company was doing a very big business. The price was rising from one to three points a day and the public was coming in more and more. This naturally centered attention on the group and all the various motor stocks began to go up. One of them, however, persistently held back and that was Chester. It lagged behind the others so that it was not long before it made people talk. The low price of Chester and its apathy was contrasted with the strength and activity in Blackwood and other motor stocks and the public logically enough listened to the touts and tipsters and wiseacres and began to buy Chester on the theory that it must presently move up with the rest of the group.

Instead of going up on this moderate public buying, Chester actually declined. Now, it would have been no job to put it up in that bull market, considering that Blackwood, a stock of the same group, was one of the sensational leaders of the general advance and we were hearing nothing but the wonderful improvement in the demand for automobiles of all kinds and the record output. ◁17.11▷

It was thus plain that the inside clique in Chester were not doing any of the things that inside cliques invariably do in a bull market. For this failure to do the usual thing there might be two reasons. Perhaps the insiders did not put it up because they wished to accumulate more stock before advancing the price. But this was an untenable theory if you analysed the volume and character of the trading in Chester. The other reason was that they did not put it up because they were afraid of getting stock if they tried to.

17.11 There is no record of auto companies Blackwood or Chester, but the car industry was rising at this time to a prominence that it would hold for another six decades. Indeed, the distinguishing characteristic of economic expansion of the 1920s was the way it improved the standard of living of the average American.

This was a function of two developments: a rapid expansion of credit and of advertising. Historian Sobel writes: "The magazines, newspapers, and radio were glutted with appeals to buy, to consume, to 'enhance your status,' with the statement, 'easy credit arranged' appended."[22]

At the center of the action for Jazz Age urbanites was the automobile. Production increased sharply as the age of the railroad was eclipsed: From 1.5 million units in 1921, the industry churned out 3.6 million units by 1925.

The period was quite similar to the mortgage-fueled consumerism of the 1990s and 2000s. Sobel, speaking of the depression that was to follow, wrote: "All of these purchases took massive amounts of credit, and involved the mortgage of tomorrow for today. The American consumer was willing to make this deal, and he traded a decade of unemployment and hunger for a decade of tinsel, much like the man who sold his soul to the devil."[23]

17.12 Guiana Gold was likely a pseudonym for a stock known as Engineer's Gold. Shares traded on the Curb Exchange and jumped over $100 a share from $55 in 1925.[24]

17.13 Livermore bought a seat on the New York Curb Market in 1920 for $5,000. It was not until 1922 that he got around to using it, as traditionally he operated out of the backrooms of brokerages or out of his private office. Livermore's appearance at the market caused quite a stir. He walked over to the Mexico Oil post, which was the first oil stock to be listed at the rival New York Stock Exchange board, and started buying, according to a newspaper account:

"Four and five-sixteenths for 1,000 Mexico," Livermore cried. He got it. "Same for another 1,000," he said. "Sold," said Jimmy Lee, Tammany broker. So the game went for the hour between 11 and 12 o'clock, during which Livermore had bid for 10,000 shares and came off with a new 5,000 shares to his credit.[25]

When the men who ought to want a stock don't want it, why should I want it? I figured that no matter how prosperous other automobile companies might be, it was a cinch to sell Chester short. Experiences had taught me to beware of buying a stock that refuses to follow the group-leader.

I easily established the fact that not only there was no inside buying but that there was actually inside selling. There were other symptomatic warnings against buying Chester, though all I required was its inconsistent market behaviour. It was again the tape that tipped me off and that was why I sold Chester short. One day, not very long afterward, the stock broke wide open. Later on we learned—officially, as it were—that insiders had indeed been selling it, knowing full well that the condition of the company was not good. The reason, as usual, was disclosed after the break. But the warning came before the break. I don't look out for the breaks; I look out for the warnings. I didn't know what was the trouble with Chester; neither did I follow a hunch. I merely knew that something must be wrong.

Only the other day we had what the newspapers called a sensational movement in Guiana Gold. ◁**17.12**▷ After selling on the Curb ◁**17.13**▷ at 50 or close to it, it was listed on the Stock Exchange. It started there at around 35, began to go down and finally broke 20.

Now, I'd never have called that break sensational because it was fully to be expected. If you had asked you could have learned the history of the company. No end of people knew it. It was told to me as follows: A syndicate was formed consisting of a half dozen extremely well-known capitalists and a prominent banking-house. One of the members was the head of the Belle Isle Exploration Company, which advanced Guiana over $10,000,000 cash and received in return bonds and 250,000 shares out of a total of one million shares of the Guiana Gold Mining Company. The stock went on a dividend basis and it was mighty well advertised. The Belle Isle people thought it well to cash in and they gave a call on their 250,000 shares to the bankers, who arranged to try to market that stock and some of their own holdings as well. They thought of entrusting the market manipulation to a professional whose fee was to be one third of the profits from the sale of the 250,000 shares above 36. I understand that the agreement was drawn up and ready to be signed but at the last moment the bankers decided to undertake the marketing themselves and save the fee. So they organized an inside pool. The bankers had a call on the Belle Isle holdings of 250,000 at 36. They put this in at 41. That is, insiders paid their own banking colleagues a 5-point profit to start with. I don't know whether they knew it or not.

It is perfectly plain that to the bankers the operation had every semblance of a cinch. We had run into a bull market and the stocks of the group to which Guiana Gold belonged were among the market leaders. The company was making big profits and paying regular dividends. This together with the high character of the sponsors made the public regard Guiana almost as an investment stock. I was told that about 400,000 shares were sold to the public all the way up to 47.

The gold group was very strong. But presently Guiana began to sag. It declined ten points. That was all right if the pool was marketing stock. But pretty soon the Street began to hear that things were not altogether satisfactory and the property was not bearing out the high expectations of the promoters. Then, of course, the reason for the decline became plain. But before the reason was known I had the warning and had taken steps to test the market for Guiana. The stock was acting pretty much as Chester Motors did. I sold Guiana. The price went down. I sold more. The price went still lower. The stock was repeating the performance of Chester and of a dozen other stocks whose clinical history I remembered. The tape plainly told me that there was something wrong—something that kept insiders from buying it—insiders who knew exactly why they should not buy their own stock in a bull market. On the other hand, outsiders, who did not know, were now buying because having sold at 45 and higher the stock looked cheap at 35 and lower. The dividend was still being paid. The stock was a bargain.

Then the news came. It reached me, as important market news often does, before it reached the public. But the confirmation of the reports of striking barren rock instead of rich ore merely gave me the reason for the earlier inside selling. I myself didn't sell on the news. I had sold long before, on the stock's behaviour. My concern with it was not philosophical. I am a trader and therefore looked for one sign: Inside buying. There wasn't any. I didn't have to know why the insiders did not think enough of their own stock to buy it on the decline. It was enough that their market plans plainly did not include further manipulation for the rise. That made it a cinch to sell the stock short. The public had bought almost a half million shares and the only change in ownership possible was from one set of ignorant outsiders who would sell in the hope of stopping losses to another set of ignorant outsiders who might buy in the hope of making money.

I am not telling you this to moralise on the public's losses through their buying of Guiana or on my profit through my selling of it, but to emphasise how important the study of group-behaviourism is and how its lessons are disregarded by inadequately equipped traders, big and little. And it is not only in the stock market that the tape warns you. It blows the whistle quite as loudly in commodities.

I had an interesting experience in cotton. I was bearish on stocks and put out a moderate short line. At the same time I sold cotton short; 50,000 bales. My stock deal proved profitable and I neglected my cotton. The first thing I knew I had a loss of $250,000

REMINISCENCES OF A STOCK OPERATOR

on my 50,000 bales. As I said, my stock deal was so interesting and I was doing so well in it that I did not wish to take my mind off it. Whenever I thought of cotton I just said to myself: "I'll wait for a reaction and cover." The price would react a little but before I could decide to take my loss and cover the price would rally again, and go higher than ever. So I'd decide again to wait a little and I'd go back to my stock deal and confine my attention to that. Finally I closed out my stocks at a very handsome profit and went away to Hot Springs <17.14> for a rest and a holiday.

That really was the first time that I had my mind free to deal with the problem of my losing deal in cotton. The trade had gone against me. There were times when it almost looked as if I might win out. I noticed that whenever anybody sold heavily there was a good reaction. But almost instantly the price would rally and make a new high for the move.

Finally, by the time I had been in Hot Springs a few days, I was a million to the bad and no let up in the rising tendency. I thought over all I had done and had not done and I said to myself: "I must be wrong!" With me to feel that I am wrong and to decide to get out are practically one process. So I covered, at a loss of about one million.

17.14 This is most likely Hot Springs, Virginia, a resort town featuring natural springs and luxury hotels. Livermore probably stayed at the Homestead Hotel, which was visited by President Taft, President Wilson, and President Coolidge during this period.

17.15 In the 1920s, cotton futures were one of the most avidly traded commodities by big Wall Street players, much as oil and copper would be decades later. Newspapers carried detailed daily reports on prices and kept close tabs on the positions held by Livermore, Cutten, and others.

Livermore in this passage shares his view that his success in the cotton market did not come from hunches, but from close observation of the way the market accepted his supply if he was selling, or reacted to his demand if he was buying. If he dumped 10,000 bales on the market and there was no rally, he felt comfortable short-selling more lots because it showed that bulls were scarce.

The fiber, which grows in a puff known as a "boll," requires a lot of water, so cotton traders try to forecast rainfall and flooding prospects by tracking weather trends, as well as the public's demand for new clothing. Most of the cotton in the United States at the time was produced in the Mississippi delta and north Texas areas, so traders tried to gain an edge on each other by determining if conditions were exceptionally dry or wet, which would impair the size of the crop and lift prices.

Although cotton was grown and traded in the Middle East, India and Africa in the earliest years of recorded history, it did not become part of an important manufactured good until Eli Whitney invented the cotton gin to mechanize cleaning in 1793, and factory-scale looms emerged during the Industrial Revolution in England. The British empire grew strong on textile exports, and while the crown merchants originally imported their cotton from India they later turned to their former American colonies due to the superior plant grown in the South and the low cost of slave labor.

After emancipation during the Civil War and well into Livermore's era, impecunious sharecroppers and small farmers from east Georgia to west Texas continued to produce the cotton that provided lavish fortunes to traders on Wall Street by processing, pressing, and baling it at plantations, then shipping it north to textile mills on riverboats. Above is the steamer *Chas. P. Chouteau* in Natchez, Mississippi, stuffed with 7,818 bales in 1878.

The next morning I was playing golf and not thinking of anything else. I had made my play in cotton. I had been wrong. I had paid for being wrong and the receipted bill was in my pocket. I had no more concern with the cotton market than I have at this moment. When I went back to the hotel for luncheon I stopped at the broker's office and took a look at the quotations. I saw that cotton had gone off 50 points. That wasn't anything. But I also noticed that it had not rallied as it had been in the habit of doing for weeks, as soon as the pressure of the particular selling that had depressed it eased up. This had indicated that the line of least resistance was upward and it had cost me a million to shut my eyes to it. **17.15**

Now, however, the reason that had made me cover at a big loss was no longer a good reason since there had not been the usual prompt and vigorous rally. So I sold 10,000 bales and waited. Pretty soon the market went off 50 points. I waited a little while longer. There was no rally. I had got pretty hungry by now, so I went into the dining-room and ordered my luncheon. Before the waiter could serve it, I jumped up, went to the broker's office, I saw that there had been no rally and so I sold 10,000 bales more. I waited a little and had the pleasure of seeing the price decline 40 points more. That showed me I was trading correctly so I returned to the dining-room, ate my luncheon and went back to the broker's. There was no rally in cotton that day. That very night I left Hot Springs.

It was all very well to play golf but I had been wrong in cotton in selling when I did and in covering when I did. So I simply had to get back on the job and be where I could trade in comfort. The way the market took my first ten thousand bales made me sell the second ten thousand, and the way the market took the second made me certain the turn had come. It was the difference in behaviour.

Well, I reached Washington and went to my brokers' office there, which was in charge of my old friend Tucker. While I was there the market went down some more. I was more confident of being right now than I had been of being wrong before. So I sold 40,000 bales and the market went off 75 points. It showed that there was no support there. That night the market closed still lower. The old buying power was plainly gone. There was no telling at what level that power would again develop, but I felt confident of the wisdom of my position. The next morning I left Washington for New York by motor. There was no need to hurry.

When we got to Philadelphia I drove to a broker's office. I saw that there was the very dickens to pay in the cotton market. Prices had broken badly and there was a small-sized panic on. I didn't wait to get to New York. I called up my brokers on the long distance and I covered my shorts. As soon as I got my reports and found that I had practically made up my previous loss, I motored on to New York without having to stop en route to see any more quotations.

Some friends who were with me in Hot Springs talk to this day of the way I jumped up from the luncheon table to sell that second lot of 10,000 bales. But again that clearly was not a hunch. It was an impulse that came from the conviction that the time to sell cotton had now come, however great my previous mistake had been. I had to take advantage of it. It was my chance. The subconscious mind probably went on working, reaching conclusions for me. The decision to sell in Washington was the result of my observation.

My years of experience in trading told me that the line of least resistance had changed from up to down.

I bore the cotton market no grudge for taking a million dollars out of me and I did not hate myself for making a mistake of that calibre any more than I felt proud for covering in Philadelphia and making up my loss. My trading mind concerns itself with trading problems and I think I am justified in asserting that I made up my first loss because I had the experience and the memory.

ENDNOTES

1 "Livermore Before Senate Committee," *Boston Daily Globe,* December 22, 1923, 5.

2 Edwin Lefevre, "Stock Manipulation," *Saturday Evening Post,* March 20, 1909, 32.

3 Charles M. Goodsell, *The Manual of Statistics* (1914), 851.

4 Milton Friedman and Anna Jacobson Schwartz, *A Monetary History of the United States 1867–1960* (1963), 232.

5 Robert Sobel, *The Big Board.* (1965), 224.

6 Federal Bureau of Investigation Archives, http://www.fbi.gov/page2/sept07/wallstreet091307.htm

7 Peter Wyckoff, *Wall Street and the Stock Markets* (1972), 63.

8 "Wall Street News," *Los Angeles Times,* April 24, 1923, I12.

9 "Livermore Is to Re-Enter Market," *Christian Science Monitor,* October 10, 1923, 12.

10 W. P. Hamilton, *The Stock Market Barometer* (1922), 63–65.

11 Richard Wyckoff, *Wall Street Ventures and Adventures through Forty Years* (1930), 254.

12 Federal Trade Commission, "Report of the Federal Trade Comission on Methods and Operations of Grain Exporters, Volume 1," May 16, 1922, 14.

13 Michael Steinhardt, *No Bull: My Life in and out of Markets* (New York: John Wiley & Sons, 2001).

14 Alexander D. Noyes, *The War Period of American Finance* (1926), 435.

15 Ibid.

16 "Wheat Liquidation Causes Heavy Drop," *New York Times,* June 21, 1923, 29.

17 Mira Wilkins, *The History of Foreign Investment in the United States to 1914* (1989), 255.

18 American Iron and Steel Institute, *Directory of the Iron and Steel Works of the United States and Canada* (1916), 111–112.

19 Charley Hannagan, "Will Bankruptcy Give Crucible Materials Corp. Enough Breathing Room?" *The Post-Standard,* May 7, 2009.

20 Kevin Hillstrom and Laurie Collier Hillstrom, *Industrial Revolution in America,* vol. 1 (2005), 73–75.

21 "Business & Finance: Catalyst in Steel," *Time,* December 30, 1929.

22 Robert Sobel, *The Big Board.* (1965), 231.

23 Ibid., 230.

24 "Excited Trading in Gold Mine Stock," *New York Times,* July 9, 1925, 32.

25 "Livermore Makes Curb Market Gasp," *Boston Daily Globe,* April 7, 1922, 19.

XVIII

History repeats itself all the time in Wall Street. Do you remember a story I told you about covering my shorts at the time Stratton had corn cornered? Well, another time I used practically the same tactics in the stock market. The stock was Tropical Trading. I have made money bulling it and also bearing it. It always was an active stock and a favourite with adventurous traders. The inside coterie has been accused time and again by the newspapers of being more concerned over the fluctuations in the stock than with encouraging permanent investment in it. The other day one of the ablest brokers I know asserted that not even Daniel Drew 18.1

18.1 Known as the Old Man of the Street, **Daniel Drew** was born in New York in 1797 to a family of poor farmers and became one of the fiercest stock operators of the mid-1800s. He locked horns with Cornelius Vanderbilt, was alternately friends and enemies with Jim Fisk and Jay Gould, and used his directorship of the Erie Railroad to manipulate its stock.

Drew's intense and hardnosed attitude was on display early in his life. In 1814, he sold himself as a military service stand-in for $100. After a few months, he mustered out and started an illegal "bob veal" business. He would buy sickly newborn calves and rush them to market before they died.[1]

With bankruptcy imminent in the early 1820s, Drew fled his creditors—joining the circus before returning to the livestock business as a drover taking cattle over the treacherous Allegheny Mountains from Ohio to market in lower Manhattan. It was here that Drew originated the term "watering stocks." He would deny his cows water until just before they were to be sold. Then he would give them salt and let them drink, boosting their weight and their sale price.

Despite his sketchy ethics, Drew had the fear of God in him after hearing a revivalist preacher warn of hell's fires and eternal damnation. Later in life, he would donate significant sums to the Methodist church. Historian Robert Sobel describes him: "This was young Daniel Drew—part circus clown, part religious zealot, but primarily shrewd speculator."[2]

Drew became a bar owner and money lender before getting into the emerging steamship business in 1834. After railroads threatened his naval ambitions, along with competition from Vanderbilt, he turned to Wall Street in 1844 to speculate, participating in many of the big market swings that preceded the 1857 panic. According to Henry Clews, "Daniel Drew, at one time, could command more ready cash at short notice than any man in Wall Street, or probably than any man in America."[3] At his peak, he was worth $30 million.

In 1876, Drew went bankrupt. He tried to return home to spend the rest of his days with his grandchildren but said he was beset by old debts: "I was troubled with visitors, some of 'em well on to 100 years old. Some of them said I bought cattle from them when I was young, on credit, and they wanted their bills. I kept no books, and how was I to know I owed 'em for them critters?"[4] His bankruptcy schedule listed these assets: Watch and chain, $150; sealskin coat, $150; clothing, $100; bible and hymn books, $130. Drew died in 1879.[5]

287

18.2 Early in his career as a speculator, Daniel Drew realized the benefits that direct control of a railroad would afford. Foreshadowing the operations of E. H. Harriman, Drew knew that insider knowledge and access to the company treasury would provide him with an unbeatable informational edge. With this in mind, he set his sights on the dilapidated New York & Erie Railway.

Granted a state charter in 1832, the Erie eventually connected New York City to Chicago via Pennsylvania, Ohio, and Indiana, and was for a time the longest railroad in the world. In these early days, before standardized track widths, Erie's first president, Eleazor Lord, chose a unique six-foot gauge. This, combined with a poorly chosen route through sparsely populated areas, resulted in the railroad's bankruptcy in 1859. It was then that Drew, Jim Fisk, and Jay Gould took control and battled with Cornelius Vanderbilt by selling him 150,000 counterfeit shares.

Before this, in 1852, Drew secured a directorship through underhanded means. First, he started giving the rival New York Central railway preferential rates on his steamboats. Then he took control of the steamers that operated on Lake Erie and served the New York & Erie Railway. Finally, he bought another rival, the Buffalo & State Line Railroad. With the "Erie completely bottled up," according to historian Meade Minnigerode, shareholders had no choice but to make Drew a director.[6]

But Drew wanted more control. So, when the Erie sought to build a line into Jersey City by tunneling through Bergen Hill, Drew did all in his power to obstruct the undertaking without actually preventing it.[7] There were rumors on Wall Street about the instability of the tunnel. There was trouble in the state capital over the Erie's charter. Eventually, as its shares dropped, the company was forced to take a loan from Drew—who in return became its treasurer.

It was then that the real scam began as Drew manipulated the stock and made a fortune. His most famous exploit was his corner in 1866. The Erie needed a loan of $3.5 million. In exchange, Drew received 28,000 shares of unissued stock and $3 million in convertible bonds. The market was strong and rising that spring as Drew started selling short. Erie shares became scarcer, and the price kept rising. It looked as if Drew would be the victim of a corner. Henry Clews, writing in 1886, describes what happened next:

> Mr. Drew had a large number of contracts to fill, and operators were wondering where he would get the stock to settle. Many of them were laughing in their sleeves at his impending embarrassment, as they had done on a former occasion, and were in ecstasies of delight at the idea of the terrific "squeeze" which the old man was about to experience. When he seemed on the very horns of this dilemma, upon which the rampant bulls thought they would successfully impale him, he converted his bonds into an equivalent amount of stock, threw 58,000 shares on the market, met all his contracts, and fed the voracious bulls all they wanted.

> Hungry as the Street had been for Erie, this was an overdose that it was utterly incapable of digesting. The bulls were paralyzed, and before they could rally their broken ranks from the demoralizing effects of this unexpected sortie from the stronghold of Erie, the stock had declined from 95 to 50, wiping out the broadest margins and putting the whole army of bulls, reserve forces and all, to utter rout.[8]

Eventually, the Erie merged with the Delaware, Lackawanna & Western Railroad before becoming part of Conrail in 1976.[9]

in Erie ◁**18.2** or H. O. Havemeyer in Sugar ◁**18.3** developed so perfect a method for milking the market for a stock as President Mulligan and his friends have done in Tropical Trading. ◁**18.4** Many times they have encouraged the bears to sell TT short and then have proceeded to squeeze them with business-like thoroughness. There was no more vindictiveness about the process than is felt by a hydraulic press—or no more squeamishness, either.

Of course, there have been people who have spoken about certain "unsavory incidents" in the market career of TT stock. But I dare say these critics were suffering from the squeezing. Why do the room traders, who have suffered so often from the loaded dice of the insiders, continue to go up against the game? Well, for one thing they like action and they certainly get it in Tropical Trading. No prolonged spells of dulness. No reasons asked or given. No time wasted. No patience strained by waiting for the tipped movement to begin. Always enough stock to go around—except when the short interest is big enough to make the scarcity worth while. One born every minute!

It so happened some time ago that I was in Florida on my usual winter vacation. I was fishing and enjoying myself without any thought of the markets excepting when we received a batch of newspapers. One morning when the semi-weekly mail came in I looked at the stock quotations and saw that Tropical Trading was selling at 155. The last time I'd seen a quotation in it, I think, was around 140. My opinion was that we were going into a bear market and I was biding my time before going short of stocks. But there was no mad rush. That was why I was fishing and out of hearing of the ticker. I knew that I'd be back home when the real call came. In the meanwhile nothing that I did or failed to do would hurry matters a bit.

The behaviour of Tropical Trading was the outstanding feature of the market, according to the

18.3 ▷ I will let Lefevre, writing in 1909 in the *Saturday Evening Post*, elaborate on Havemeyer—the fearsome Sugar King—in his artful way, capturing the cynical mood of the time. We see in his comments the connection with James Keene as well as more on the topic of stock manipulation:

> When the Sugar Trust was formed the common stock was a speculative football. The Street said that nobody could make money out of it excepting Mr. H.O. Havemeyer and his brother. But, even at that, it was made evident that either the Havemeyers did not make enough or that they had made so much that they wished to make their holders of Sugar common a good solid investment for themselves. To achieve this object they had to make it a good investment for the public. The sugar business itself was very profitable, especially after unprofitable competition was eliminated.

> There remained for the Trust's stock to be "distributed," to be marketed among investors; to find a final resting place among widows and orphans who wanted a large return on their investment and reasonable assurance as to the stability of the dividends. To "distribute" the stock properly they felt compelled to "manipulate" it. They did not know how. After trying unsuccessfully, Mr. Theodore Havemeyer finally entrusted the manipulation of the stock to a man who had not long before lost many millions in speculation, but who was nevertheless a genius—the best manipulator of all.

> And so Mr. Keene undertook it and succeeded. He made a fortune for himself; a bigger one for the Havemeyer crowd. By establishing a market for Sugar stock he made investors buy it. And the way it was done was not by appealing first, last and all the time to the investors but also by paying especial attention to the speculator and the gambler. It did not become a popular investment until after Mr. Keene had made it a popular gamble! And that is the way it has always been because of the preponderance of gambling in the stock market: first load up the Street; then from the Street pass it gradually into the strong boxes of investors.[10]

18.4 ▷ Tropical Trading and President Mulligan appear to be fictitious names. There was a Tropical Trading Co., but it was sold to the United Fruit banana empire in 1899. A Mr. Mulligan is not mentioned in this context in any newspaper, magazine, or book accounts of the time.

newspapers I got that morning. It served to crystal-
lise my general bearishness because I thought it particularly asinine for the insiders to run up the price
of TT in the face of the heaviness of the general list.
There are times when the milking process must be
suspended. What is abnormal is seldom a desirable
factor in a trader's calculations and it looked to me as
if the marking up of that stock were a capital blunder.
Nobody can make blunders of that magnitude with
impunity; not in the stock market.

After I got through reading the newspapers I
went back to my fishing but I kept thinking of what
the insiders in Tropical Trading were trying to do.
That they were bound to fail was as certain as that
a man is bound to smash himself if he jumps from
the roof of a twenty-story building without a para-
chute. I couldn't think of anything else and finally
I gave up trying to fish and sent off a telegram to
my brokers to sell 2,000 shares of TT at the market.
After that I was able to go back to my fishing. I did
pretty well.

That afternoon I received the reply to my telegram by special courier. My brokers reported that
they had sold the 2,000 shares of Tropical Trading at
153. So far so good. I was selling short on a declining market, which was as it should be. But I could
not fish any more. I was too far away from a quotation board. I discovered this after I began to think
of all the reasons why Tropical Trading should go
down with the rest of the market instead of going up
on inside manipulation. I therefore left my fishing
camp and returned to Palm Beach; or, rather, to the
direct wire to New York.

The moment I got to Palm Beach and saw what
the misguided insiders were still trying to do, I let
them have a second lot of 2,000 TT. Back came the
report and I sold another 2,000 shares. The market
behaved excellently. That is, it declined on my selling. Everything being satisfactory I went out and
had a chair ride. **18.5** But I wasn't happy. The more I

thought the unhappier it made me to think that I hadn't sold more. So back I went to the broker's office and sold another 2,000 shares.

I was happy only when I was selling that stock. Presently I was short 10,000 shares. Then I decided to return to New York. I had business to do now. My fishing I would do some other time.

When I arrived in New York I made it a point to get a line on the company's business, actual and prospective. What I learned strengthened my conviction that the insiders had been worse than reckless in jacking up the price at a time when such an advance was not justified either by the tone of the general market or by the company's earnings.

18.5 Livermore is likely referring to the wicker pedicabs that were a frequent sight in the oceanfront resorts in places like Atlantic City and Palm Beach. We can imagine Livermore, after contemplating his short trade, going for a ride to clear his head in the cool Atlantic breeze. In a photo of the era, we see a model pushed by a walking attendant. Given Livermore's preference for fast boats and Rolls-Royces, he likely requested a brisk pace.

The rise, illogical and ill-timed though it was, had developed some public following and this doubtless encouraged the insiders to pursue their unwise tactics. Therefore I sold more stock. The insiders ceased their folly. So I tested the market again and again, in accordance with my trading methods, until finally I was short 30,000 shares of the stock of the Tropical Trading Company. By then the price was 133.

I had been warned that the TT insiders knew the exact whereabouts of every stock certificate in the Street and the precise dimensions and identity of the short interest as well as other facts of tactical importance. They were able men and shrewd traders. Altogether it was a dangerous combination to go up against. But facts are facts and the strongest of all allies are conditions.

Of course, on the way down from 153 to 133 the short interest had grown and the public that buys on reactions began to argue as usual: That stock had been considered a good purchase at 153 and higher.

18.6 Watts considered five qualities as "essential to the equipment of a speculator." They were self-reliance, judgment, courage, prudence, and pliability or the ability to change an opinion. As for courage, Watts quotes French Revolution luminary Honoré Mirabeau: "Be bold, still be bold, always be bold."[11]

Now 20 points lower, it was necessarily a much better purchase. Same stock; same dividend rate; same officers; same business. Great bargain!

The public's purchases reduced the floating supply and the insiders, knowing that a lot of room traders were short, thought the time propitious for a squeezing. The price was duly run up to 150. I daresay there was plenty of covering but I stayed pat. Why shouldn't I? The insiders might know that a short line of 30,000 shares had not been taken in but why should that frighten me? The reasons that had impelled me to begin selling at 153 and keep at it on the way down to 133, not only still existed but were stronger than ever. The insiders might desire to force me to cover but they adduced no convincing arguments. Fundamental conditions were fighting for me. It was not difficult to be both fearless and patient. A speculator must have faith in himself and in his judgment. The late Dickson G. Watts, **18.6** ex-President of the New York Cotton Exchange and famous author of "Speculation as a Fine Art," says that courage in a speculator is merely confidence to act on the decision of his mind. With me, I cannot fear to be wrong because I never think I am wrong until I am proven wrong. In fact, I am uncomfortable unless I am capitalising my experience. The course of the market at a given time does not necessarily prove me wrong. It is the character of the advance—or of the decline—that determines for me the correctness or the fallacy of my market position. I can only rise by knowledge. If I fall it must be by my own blunders.

There was nothing in the character of the rally from 133 to 150 to frighten me into covering and presently the stock, as was to be expected, started down again. It broke 140 before the inside clique began to give it support. Their buying was coincident with a flood of bull rumors about the stock. The company, we heard, was making perfectly fabulous profits, and the earnings justified an increase in the regular dividend rate. Also, the short interest was said to be perfectly huge and the squeeze of the century was about to be inflicted on the bear party in general and in particular on a certain operator who was more than over-extended. I couldn't begin to tell you all I heard as they ran the price up ten points.

The manipulation did not seem particularly dangerous to me but when the price touched 149 I decided that it was not wise to let the Street accept as true all the bull statements that were floating around. Of course, there was nothing that I or any other rank outsider could say that would carry conviction either to the frightened shorts or to those credulous customers of commission houses that trade on hearsay tips. The most effective retort courteous is that which the tape alone can print. People will believe that when they will not believe an affidavit from any living man, much less one from a chap who is short 30,000 shares. So I used the same tactics that I did at the time of the Stratton corner in corn, when I sold oats to make the traders bearish on corn. Experience and memory again.

When the insiders jacked up the price of Tropical Trading with a view to frightening the shorts I didn't try to check the rise by selling that stock. I was already short 30,000 shares of it which was as big a percentage of the floating supply as I thought wise to be short of. I did not propose to put my head into the noose so obligingly held open for me—the second rally was really an urgent invitation. What I did when TT touched 149 was to sell about 10,000 shares of Equatorial Commercial Corporation. This company owned a large block of Tropical Trading.

Equatorial Commercial, which was not as active a stock as TT, broke badly on my selling, as I had foreseen; and, of course, my purpose was achieved. When the traders—and the customers of the commission houses who had listened to the uncontradicted bull dope on TT—saw that the rise in Tropical synchronised with heavy selling and a sharp break in Equatorial, they naturally concluded that the strength of TT was merely a smoke-screen—a manipulated advance obviously designed to facilitate inside liquidation in Equatorial Commercial, which was the largest holder of TT stock. It must be both long stock and inside stock in Equatorial, because no outsider would dream of selling so much short stock at the very moment when Tropical Trading was so very strong. So they sold Tropical Trading and checked the rise in that stock, the insiders very properly not wishing to take all the stock that was pressed for sale. The moment the insiders took away their support the price of TT declined. The traders and principal commission houses now sold some Equatorial also and I took in my short line in that at a small profit. I hadn't sold it to make money out of the operation but to check the rise in TT.

Time and again the Tropical Trading insiders and their hard-working publicity man flooded the Street with all manner of bull items and tried to put up the price. And every time they did I sold Equatorial Commercial short and covered it with TT and carried EC with it. It took the wind out of the manipulators' sails. The price of TT finally went down to 125 and the short interest really grew so big that the insiders were enabled to run it up 20 or 25 points. This time it was a legitimate enough drive against an over-extended short interest; but while I foresaw the rally I did not cover, not wishing to lose my position. Before Equatorial Commercial could advance in sympathy with the rise in TT I sold a raft of it short—with the usual results. This gave the lie to the bull talk in TT which had got quite boisterous after the latest sensational rise.

By this time the general market had grown quite weak. As I told you, it was the conviction that we were in a bear market that started me selling TT short in the fishing-camp in Florida. I was short of quite a few other stocks but TT was my pet. Finally, general conditions proved too much for the inside clique to defy and TT hit the toboggan slide. It went below 120 for the first time in years; then below 110; below par; and still I did not cover. One day when the entire market was extremely weak Tropical Trading broke 90 and on the demoralisation I covered. Same old reason! I had the opportunity—the big market and the weakness and the excess of sellers over buyers. I may tell you, even at the risk of appearing to be monotonously bragging of my cleverness, that I took in my 30,000 shares of TT at practically the lowest prices of the movement. But I wasn't thinking of covering at the bottom. I was intent on turning my paper profits into cash without losing much of the profit in the changing.

I stood pat throughout because I knew my position was sound. I wasn't bucking the trend of the market or going against basic conditions but the reverse, and that was what made me so sure of the failure of an over-confident inside clique. What they tried to do others had tried before and it had always failed. The frequent rallies, even when I knew as well as anybody that they were due, could not frighten me. I knew I'd do much better in the end by staying pat than by trying to cover to put out a new short line at a higher price. By sticking to the position that I felt was right I made over a million dollars. I was not indebted to hunches or to skilful tape reading or to stubborn courage. It was a dividend declared by my faith in my judgment and not by my cleverness or by my vanity. Knowledge is power and power need not fear lies—not even when the tape prints them. The retraction follows pretty quickly.

A year later, TT was jacked up again to 150 and hung around there for a couple of weeks. The entire market was entitled to a good reaction for it had risen uninterruptedly and it did not bull any longer. I know because I tested it. Now, the group to which TT belonged 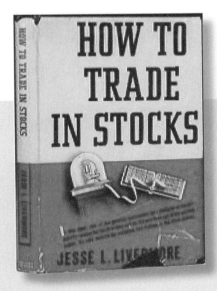 had been suffering from very poor business and I couldn't see anything to bull those stocks on anyhow, even if the rest of the market were due for a rise, which it wasn't. So I began to

18.7 In his 1940 book *How to Trade in Stocks*, Livermore discusses at length his method of monitoring and analyzing the movement of groups of stocks to detect the overall trend. He describes a situation in the late 1920s in which the copper and auto stocks moved lower, but he mistakenly took that as a cue to sell the entire market short. He says, "I should hate to tell you the amount of money I lost by acting upon that premise."

He stresses the lesson to be learned from his folly:

What I wish to impress upon you is the fact that when you clearly see a move coming in a particular group, act upon it. But do not let yourself act in the same way in some other group, until you plainly see signs that the second group is in a position to follow suit. Have patience and wait. In time you will get the same tip-off in other groups that you received in the first group.[12]

sell Tropical Trading. I intended to put out 10,000 shares in all. The price broke on my selling. I couldn't see that there was any support whatever. Then suddenly, the character of the buying changed.

I am not trying to make myself out a wizard when I assure you that I could tell the moment support came in. It instantly struck me that if the insiders in that stock, who never felt a moral obligation to keep the price up, were now buying the stock in the face of a declining general market there must be a reason. They were not ignorant asses nor philanthropists nor yet bankers concerned with keeping the price up to sell more securities over the counter. The price rose notwithstanding my selling and the selling of others. At 153 I covered my 10,000 shares and at 156 I actually went long because by that time the tape told me the line of least resistance was upward. I was bearish on the general market but I was confronted by a trading condition in a certain stock and not by a speculative theory in general. The price went out of sight, above 200. It was the sensation of the year. I was flattered by reports spoken and printed that I had been squeezed out of eight or nine millions of dollars. As a matter of fact, instead of being short I was long of TT all the way up. In fact, I held on a little too long and let some of my paper profits get away. Do you wish to know why I did? Because I thought the TT insiders would naturally do what I would have done had I been in their place. But that was something I had no business to think because my business is to trade—that is, to stick to the facts before me and not to what I think other people ought to do.

ENDNOTES

1 Robert Sobel, *Panic on Wall Street* (1969), 122.

2 Ibid., 123.

3 Henry Clews, *Fifty Years in Wall Street* (New York: Irving Publishing Company, 1908), 119.

4 Ibid., 152.

5 Ibid., 153.

6 Meade Minnigerode, *Certain Rich Men* (1927), 91.

7 Ibid.

8 Clews, *Fifty Years in Wall Street*, 127–128.

9 John F. Stover, *Historical Atlas of the American Railroads* (1999), 71.

10 Edwin Lefevre, "Stock Manipulation," *Saturday Evening Post*, March 27, 1909, 13.

11 Dickson G. Watts, *Speculation as a Fine Art and Thoughts on Life* (1965), 8.

12 Jesse Livermore, *How to Trade in Stocks* (1940), 32–33.

XIX

I do not know when or by whom the word "manip-ulation" was first used in connection with what really are no more than common merchandising processes applied to the sale in bulk of securities on the Stock Exchange. Rigging the market to facilitate cheap purchases of a stock which it is desired to accumulate is also manipulation. But it is different. It may not be necessary to stoop to illegal practices, but it would be difficult to avoid doing what some would think illegitimate. How are you going to buy a big block of a stock in a bull market without put-ting up the price on yourself? That would be the problem. How can it be solved? It depends upon so many things that you can't give a general solu-tion unless you say: possibly by means of very adroit manipulation. For instance? Well, it would depend upon conditions. You can't give any closer answer than that.

I am profoundly interested in all phases of my business, and of course I learn from the experience of others as well as from my own. But it is very dif-ficult to learn how to manipulate stocks to-day from such yarns as are told of an afternoon in the brokers' offices after the close. Most of the tricks, devices and expedients of bygone days are obsolete and fu-tile; or illegal and impracticable. Stock Exchange rules and conditions have changed, ◁19.1 and the

19.1 In the 1800s and early 1900s, securities law did not offer investors much security and there was not much law. Most states required railroad securities to be registered starting in the 1850s, but rules were loose and fraud was rampant. By the late 1890s, states began to clamp down on sales of worthless securities in dubious gold mines, oil wells, and elixir makers that were said to promise "blue skies" but had no real assets.

By the mid-1910s, the time frame of this chapter, Mid-western states, led by Kansas and its pioneering banking commissioner, Joseph Norman Dolley, went a step further in barring the sale of securities of companies whose busi-ness was unfair, unjust, inequitable, or oppressive, or did not promise a fair return. The new statutes required regis-tration of new securities and securities salespeople. New issues of shares also had to be accompanied by detailed financial statements. Government officials would have final say on which securities could be offered to the public.[1]

The state laws were challenged on constitutional grounds, as business owners complained that the rules lacked enough definition, usurped federal government authority, and amounted to an unfair hurdle to capital formation. The first major case, *Hall v. Geiger-Jones Co.*, was heard by the U.S. Supreme Court in 1917. The opinion, written by Justice Joseph McKenna, stated in part, "The prevention of deception is within the competency of government."[2]

Most of the modern regulatory system as we recognize it today was created in the 1930s and 1940s following the 1929 stock market crash, putting an end to the law of the jungle that prevailed in the earliest years of Livermore's campaigns.

19.2 ▶ The first "Great Bear of Wall Street," **Jacob Little,** had nothing when he first arrived in New York in 1817 at age 20 from his hometown of Newburyport, Massachusetts. The son of a shipbuilder used his guile to win an apprenticeship with Jacob Barker, then the largest banker in New York, from 1817 to 1822. He eventually left banking to trade securities on his own, and became a member of an early form of the New York Stock Exchange. After opening his small office in a Wall Street basement, he became known for hard work and keen business insight. Historian Matthew Hale Smith wrote: "Caution, self-reliance, integrity, and a far-sightedness beyond his years, marked his early career. For 12 years he worked in his little den as few men work. His ambition was to hold the foremost place on Wall Street. Eighteen hours a day he devoted to business—twelve hours to his office."[3]

Little caught a big break in the Panic of 1837 before going on to make and lose nine fortunes during his peak years, 1838 to 1846. Said one biographer: "He would reign the king of the market, fight a dozen pitched battles, suffer defeat, abdicate, and then once more ascend the throne, all in the space of six months."[4] Finally, Little failed for good during the Civil War, says his biographer, when he "remained a bear on the rising tide of currency inflation following the outbreak of the war, and was submerged and wiped out."[5]

Little is credited with inventing the "manipulated short sale"—selling short and floating rumors of the company's financial woes.[6] He also claimed to be the inventor of the convertible bond, which he used to great effect to break Daniel Drew's attempt to corner him in Erie stock in 1855. Reported a journalist three decades later:

He had sold large blocks of Erie, seller's option, at six and twelve months. The "happy family," composed of the most eminent members of the board, combined against him. The day of settlement came, Erie shares had been run up to a high figure. At 2 p.m. the brokers prophesied that the Napoleon of finance would meet his Waterloo. At 1 p.m. he stepped into the Erie office, presented a mass of convertible bonds that he had quietly purchased in England, and demanded the instantaneous exchange of share equivalents for them. The requisition was met. Little returned to his office, fulfilled his contracts, broke the corner, and was Wellington and Napoleon in one. The convertibles were his Blucher and night.[7]

A "Blucher" is a bid to win all the tricks in a hand of a British card game called Napoleon, and that was an appropriate reference because Little was described by a biographer as a "master of every kind of game played in stocks, rings, corners, sleight-of-hand, beggar your neighbor, bluff, lock-up and bar-out, straddling two horses going different ways, he had the skill as well as the nerve to play them all, and for the most part came out the winner."[8]

The beginning of the end for Little came in the run-up to the Panic of 1857, which resulted from a credit bubble following the discovery of gold in California. Paper money in circulation doubled between 1849 and 1857 on the promise of new gold coin. But a trade deficit with Europe sent the gold away, so bankers withdrew currency, and trade and speculation collapsed. Little was short 100,000 shares of Erie, expecting a crash, but a last advance before the decline overextended him. He lost his position and failed for want of $10 million on December 5, 1856.[9]

Little died poor on March 28, 1865, leaving a widow but no children.[10] He once said: "I care more for the game than the results, and, winning or losing, I like to be in it!"[11] This energy was on display in his latter years, as described by William Fowler:

Still clinging to the objects of a pursuit which was to him a passion, his face bearing the marks of the fierce struggles of his life, a broken weird looking old man, he haunted the Board Room [in the New York Stock Exchange] like a spectre where he had once reigned as a king, offering small lots of shares of the same stock, the whole capital whereof he had once controlled. Where then were the piled millions which that cunning hand and scheming brain had rolled up? Where the prestige of his victories on 'change? Gone, scattered, lost. Poor and unnoticed, he passed away from the scene, and left nothing behind him but the shadow of what was once a great Wall Street reputation.[12]

story—even the accurately detailed story—of what Daniel Drew or Jacob Little ◀**19.2** or Jay Gould could do fifty or seventy-five years ago is scarcely worth listening to. The manipulator to-day has no more need to consider what they did and how they did it than a cadet at West Point need study archery as practiced by the ancients in order to increase his working knowledge of ballistics.

On the other hand there is profit in studying the human factors—the ease with which human beings believe what it pleases them to believe; and how they allow themselves—indeed, urge themselves—to be influenced by their cupidity or by the dollar-cost of the average man's carelessness. Fear and hope remain the same; therefore the study of the psychology of speculators is as valuable as it ever was. Weapons change, but strategy remains strategy, on the New York Stock Exchange as on the battlefield. I think the clearest summing up of the whole thing was expressed by Thomas F. Woodlock ◁**19.3**◻ when he declared: "The principles of successful stock speculation are based on the supposition that people will continue in the future to make the mistakes that they have made in the past."

In booms, which is when the public is in the market in the greatest numbers, there is never any need of subtlety, so there is no sense of wasting time discussing either manipulation or speculation during such times; it would be like trying to find the difference in raindrops that are falling synchronously on the same roof across the street. The sucker has always tried to get something for nothing, and the appeal in all booms is always frankly to the gambling instinct aroused by cupidity and spurred by a pervasive prosperity. People who look for easy money invariably pay for the privilege of proving conclusively that it cannot be found on this sordid earth. At first, when I listened to the accounts of old-time deals and devices I used to think that people were more gullible in the 1860's and '70's than in the 1900's. But I was sure to read in the newspapers that very day or the next something about the latest Ponzi ◁**19.4**◻ or the bust-up of some bucketing broker and about the millions of sucker money gone to join the silent majority of vanished savings.

19.3 ▶ Born in Ireland in 1866, Thomas Woodlock was "one of the leading financial writers of this country, and he had held that position for half a century," according to the *New York Times*.[13,14] He was editor of the *Wall Street Journal* from 1902 to 1905 and a columnist at the paper from 1930 until his death in 1945. At the age of 28, he wrote *The Anatomy of a Railroad Report*, a book meant to help investors who do not "take the trouble to make themselves acquainted with the actual condition of their property… obtain a clear idea of the state of his investment, for great and important changes in railroad conditions are in progress."[15]

Woodlock worked as a broker in both London and New York. He was a member of the U.S. Interstate Commerce Commission and active in the Catholic Church. His morality, depth of knowledge, and command of history impressed his peers. According to the *Times*, "He might illustrate a point in economics by quoting some thirteenth-century pope, or some scrap of wisdom from some obscure figure in the eighteenth century."[16]

19.4 ▶ Charles Ponzi's scheme in 1919–1920 to defraud gullible Bostonians was so extreme that his name has entered the English lexicon. Ponzi's promise was to pay investors 50% returns in 45 days through investment in international reply coupons (IRCs).[17] The coupons were created in 1906 to facilitate global shipping by the Universal Postal Union, and were redeemable into country-specific postage. Ponzi claimed that by arbitraging postage rate—buying IRCs cheaply and exchanging them for more expensive stamps in other countries—he could provide unbelievable returns. In reality he was merely paying old investors the proceeds from new deposits. The scam collapsed after being exposed in a Pulitzer Prize-winning series by the *Boston Post* in August 1920. Ponzi served 10 years in prison before being deported to Italy; he died blind and poor in Brazil in 1949.

A similar scheme ruined ex-President Ulysses S. Grant in the 1880s after he partnered with his son and a speculator named Ferdinand Ward, who was said to have "a born genius for evil."[18] Ward befriended Grant's son, and together they persuaded the former Civil War general to lend his credibility to create a brokerage called Grant & Ward in 1883.[19] The brokerage took investors' money but never actually invested it, paying out new deposits to old customers as dividends. The scheme collapsed on May 9, 1884, after the firm overdrew its account at the Marine National Bank, causing both companies to fail. A week later, a second wave of bank failures led to the Panic of 1884. Ward served 6 years in prison.[20] Grant's family was left destitute until the tarnished hero's memoirs earned a fortune a few years later.

19.5 These were cons in which bucket shop operators would place legitimate orders on the actual exchanges to move the price of underlying stocks against the positions of their patrons. They were an example of the adversarial relationship between bucket shops and their customers. In contrast, legitimate brokers benefited from their customers' good fortune through larger trades and more commissions. In 1895 and again in 1900, the Chicago Board of Trade launched investigations into its members' telegraph wire connections. During the crackdown, 6 members were expelled and 13 were suspended. Fearful of further investigations, other brokers soon refused to fill orders from bucket shop owners.[21]

When I first came to New York there was a great fuss made about wash sales ◁**19.5** and matched orders, for all that such practices were forbidden by the Stock Exchange. At times the washing was too crude to deceive anyone. The brokers had no hesitation in saying that "the laundry was active" whenever anybody tried to wash up some stock or other, and, as I have said before, more than once they had what were frankly referred to as "bucket-shop drives," when a stock was offered down two or three points in a jiffy just to establish the decline on the tape and wipe up the myriad shoe-string traders who were long of the stock in the bucket shops. As for matched orders, they were always used with some misgivings by reason of the difficulty of coördinating and synchronising operations by brokers, all such business being against Stock Exchange rules. A few years ago a famous operator canceled the selling but not the buying part of his matched orders, and the result was that an innocent broker ran up the price twenty-five points or so in a few minutes, only to see it break with equal celerity as soon as his buying ceased. The original intention was to create an appearance of activity. Bad business, playing with such unreliable weapons. You see, you can't take your best brokers into your confidence—not if you want them to remain members of the New York Stock Exchange. Then also, the taxes have made all practices involving fictitious transactions much more expensive than they used to be in the old times.

The dictionary definition of manipulation includes corners. Now, a corner might be the result of manipulation or it might be the result of competitive buying, as, for instance, the Northern Pacific corner on May 9, 1901, which certainly was not manipulation. The Stutz corner ◁**19.6** was expensive to everybody concerned, both in money and in prestige. And it was not a deliberately engineered corner, at that.

Renowned for speedy appearance as well as performance, this 1915 Stutz Bearcat was one of the most popular sport models of its day.

From **STUTZ** Bearcat

19.6 In 1920, Thomas F. Ryan cornered the stock of the Stutz Motor Car Co.—the last great corner on the New York Stock Exchange, which historian Robert Sobel calls "a forerunner of the Livermore and Cutten operations of a few years later."[22] Stutz was a maker of legendary sports cars, such as the 1915 Bearcat. Ryan was one of its largest investors.

Thomas's father, Allan A. Ryan, had turned over his NYSE seat to his son at the age of 25. The young man became known to contemporaries as a "powerful and clever bull operator" with a talent for squeezing short sellers. For the most part, the wind was at his back: There was an explosive bull market in 1919 after the armistice that ended World War I was signed. In response, the Federal Reserve issued a warning about what it called the "speculative tendency of the times."[23]

The mood was subdued in 1920, which makes Ryan's achievement all the more impressive. Prohibition had started. Interest rates were on the rise. Anarchists exploded a deadly bomb outside the offices of J .P. Morgan & Co. By the end of the year, prices on the NYSE were 33% below their April peak.

Stutz was in excellent business shape when its stock started rising from $100 a share in January to more than $134 on February 2. Ryan was told that short sellers, many of whom were leading members of the NYSE, were readying a bear raid. Observer John Brooks describes Ryan's predicament, since many of the bears were acquaintances:

In the course of making a killing in Stutz they might maim the company and separate Ryan from much of his fortune—or, contrariwise, their maneuver might end up costing them their own shirt—but in either case the antagonists would be supposed to take it all in good part and continue the joking and bantering during the contest and after it. Such was the code.[24]

Ryan, who was sick in bed with pneumonia, returned to Wall Street with nurse in tow to do battle. His goal was to buy all the stock offered for sale at increasing prices to squeeze the shorts. This, of course, required lots of cash. Ryan turned to banks and friends, putting up his family's possessions as collateral. In early March, things looked bleak for Ryan as Stutz dropped back to $100. He persevered, at risk of losing his wife's furs, and by March 24, the price was up to $282. By the end of the week it was at $391. Other shareholders took advantage of the rise to capture profits, but Ryan kept buying.

More short sellers descended. They would borrow shares from Ryan before selling them back to him since, according to a historian, "there was no longer anyone else who had any."[25] Slowly, as shares became scarce, the bears realized they had been overpowered. They could either pay an exorbitant sum to buy shares back from Ryan to settle their loan of stock certificates, or they could go to jail. The corner was in effect.

Instead, the bears chose a third way. Using their committee positions on the NYSE, they summoned Ryan to explain the gyrations in Stutz. After telling them matter-of-factly that he owned more shares than were in existence, he demanded $750 per share to settle. The NYSE insiders then threatened to throw Ryan out of the exchange. Ryan was defiant: His offer rose to $1,000 per share. The exchange responded by voiding Ryan's contracts and de-listing Stutz shares. He resigned from his seat and published the names of some of the short sellers in the *New York World*. Confidence in the integrity of the exchange waned, and there was talk of increased government regulation.

In the end, the NYSE blinked and the shorts were settled at $550 per share. It was a Pyrrhic victory for Ryan. Since the exchange had delisted Stutz, there was no market for Ryan to sell into. To make matters worse, the bears were mad with desire for revenge and started raiding Ryan's other holdings. And bankers were closing in as well. On July 21, 1922, Ryan filed for bankruptcy, listing debts of over $32 million and assets of $643,533. Stutz Motors stock was sold at public auction for $20 a share. The company eventually failed in 1937. Ryan never recovered and died in 1940.

19.7 **Cornelius Vanderbilt** was born in 1794 into a Staten Island farming family that sailed its produce to market in Manhattan. After earning a small sum from his mother for fieldwork, Vanderbilt bought himself a two-masted, flat-bottomed sailboat with which he carried passengers and freight across the bay. Two years later, during the War of 1812, Vanderbilt was awarded a U.S. Army contract to supply posts around New York. Later, with the advent of the steamship, Vanderbilt sold his military supply business interests and became the captain of another man's steamer.

From this inauspicious start, Vanderbilt built a vast empire of riverboats, steamships, and railroads. He dominated shipping routes up and down the Atlantic seaboard, to Europe, and to California. In fact, it is said that he moved more men to the gold fields of California than anyone else. Sobel describes him:

> The Commodore was tall and aristocratic….He had a large nose, piercing eyes, and an expression of utter contempt on his face that frightened friends as well as enemies. When he spoke a stream of colorful, profane language would emerge from imperious lips…. He was not the sort of man that one crossed twice.

Yet that is exactly what Daniel Drew and his associates did on several occasions. In the aftermath of the Erie shenanigans described earlier, Vanderbilt sent the local sheriff to arrest Drew, Fisk, and Gould. The men caught wind of this and, with the Erie's ledgers and $8 million from its treasury, sailed through the fog to New Jersey, where they barricaded themselves in the lobby of a hotel. Fisk hired gangs of men for protection, ultimately organizing a ramshackle navy of rowboats bristling with rifles. Twelve-pound cannons were mounted on a dock. A sensational display of political corruption ensued as the two sides battled to win over judges and legislators.

Eventually, Vanderbilt wrote to his old foe and occasional ally: "Drew: I'm sick of the whole damned business. Come and see me. Vanderbilt."[26] Drew was sympathetic. He did not care for New Jersey or for the antics of Gould and Fisk. The two men met and reminisced about their old days on the river. A peace was forged: The Erie treasury would buy the illegitimate shares sold to Vanderbilt.

DANIEL DREW.   CORNELIUS VANDERBILT.

L. W. JEROME.   JACOB LITTLE.

CELEBRITIES OF WALL STREET.

As a matter of fact very few of the great corners were profitable to the engineers of them. Both Commodore Vanderbilt's `19.7` Harlem corners paid big, but the old chap deserved the millions he made out of a lot of short sports, crooked legislators and aldermen who tried to double-cross him. `19.8` On the other hand, Jay Gould lost in his Northwestern corner. `19.9` Deacon S. V. White made a million in his Lackawanna corner, but Jim Keene dropped a million `19.10` in the Hannibal & St. Joe deal. The financial success of a corner of course depends upon the marketing of the accumulated holdings at higher than cost, and the short interest has to be of some magnitude for that to happen easily.

I used to wonder why corners were so popular among the big operators of a half-century ago. They were men of ability and experience, wide-awake and not prone to childlike trust in the philanthropy of their fellow traders. Yet they used to get stung with an astonishing frequency. A wise old broker told me that all the big operators of the '60's and '70's had one ambition, and that was to work a corner. In many cases this was the offspring of vanity; in others, of the desire for revenge. At all events, to be pointed out as the man who had successfully cornered this or the other stock was in reality recognition of brains, boldness and boodle. It gave the cornerer the right to be haughty. He accepted the plaudits of his fellows as fully earned. It was more than the prospective money profit that prompted the engineers of corners to do their damnedest. It was the vanity complex asserting itself among cold-blooded operators.

Dog certainly ate dog in those days with relish and ease. I think I told you before that I have managed to escape being squeezed more than once, not because of the possession of a mysterious ticker-sense but because I can generally tell the moment the character of the buying in the

19.8 The most famous example of this occurred when Vanderbilt returned from a trip to Europe to find that the Nicaragua Transit Co., to which he had turned over his shipping trade in Nicaragua, had "failed to give him what he thought should be a proper accounting."[27] Vanderbilt wrote one of the few letters he ever sent in his own hand. It was barely legible but the message was clear. It read: "Gentlemen: You have undertaken to cheat me. I won't sue you, for the law is too slow. I will ruin you. Yours truly, Cornelius Vanderbilt."[28] Within two years, the company was gone.

19.9 In 1872, Gould and two collaborators successfully bid up the shares of Chicago & NorthWestern Railroad from $95 to $230 over a two-day period—yet they were reported to have made nothing from the advance.[29] Henry Clews says the rise went from $80 to $280 before falling back to $80 again, in the process "pretty near crushing" Gould "in spite of his incomparable capacity for wriggling out of a tight place."[30]

19.10 In 1881, just after President Garfield had been shot, a corner attempt was made in Hannibal & St. Joseph Railroad shares. The line ran from Hannibal, Missouri, on the Mississippi River to St. Joseph on the Kansas River. After a marked decline in revenue, the company was suffering financial distress. Dividends on common shares amounted to only 1.5%. Like vultures scouting a meal, short sellers began to descend. Meanwhile, the firm's vice president had left the city and given his broker, William Hutchinson, written instructions to use discretion when managing his large fortune.

Hutchinson started to buy all the stock the bears would sell. On Monday, September 5, the price moved over $97. The following day, the situation became clear as the shorts tried to cover and the price of Hannibal & St. Joe soared to close at $137. On Wednesday, the price reached $200.

Luckily for the bears, Thursday was a holiday: The New York governor had called for a day of prayer to help President Garfield recover from his wounds. (He died a few days later.) A break in the action allowed shorts to plot an exit strategy. On Friday, the company's president, William Dowd, was accused of conspiracy to corner the stock by an operative of the bear pool. Meanwhile, the price continued to rise and peaked at $350 a week later.

In the end, the accusation was settled out of court. It turned out that Hutchinson was surreptitiously making side bets for himself on the short side and was using his position to ensure the price sank as the shorts settled. When that was uncovered, he was expelled from the exchange for what observers called "obvious fraud."[31]

19.11 Many of the great business tycoons and speculators of this time lacked a formal education. Drew came from a modest background but possessed what Henry Clews called a steadfast ability to attain "great success by stubbornly following up one idea, and one line of thought and purpose."[32] Clews said of both Drew and Vanderbilt:

Everybody who knew these two men were of the opinion that with a fair or liberal education they would never have cut a prominent figure as financiers.... Perhaps it might have been impossible for any teacher to make Drew pronounce the word shares otherwise than "sheers." Or convince Vanderbilt that the part of a locomotive in which steam is generated should not be spelt phonetically, "boylar."[33]

stock makes it imprudent for me to be short of it. This I do by common-sense tests, which must have been tried in the old times also. Old Daniel Drew used to squeeze the boys with some frequency and make them pay high prices for the Erie "sheers" **19.11** they had sold short to him. He was himself squeezed by Commodore Vanderbilt in Erie, and when old Drew begged for mercy the Commodore grimly quoted the Great Bear's own deathless distich:

He that sells what isn't hisn
Must buy it back or go to prisn.

CELEBRITIES OF WALL STREET.

19.12 **Addison** and his eight siblings were collectively known as the Jerome Brothers. Speculation ran in their genes. Leonard Jerome was a partner with William Travers in the brokerage house Travers & Jerome and had previously been appointed consul to the Austrian Empire by President Millard Fillmore. Jerome and Travers were successful on the short side of the market. Another brother, while studying theology at Princeton, "took a flier in the memorable mulberry tree speculation and made $40,000,"[34] according to the *New York Times*.

Addison got his start in the dry goods business before he amassed a fortune and earned a reputation as "the Napoleon of the Open Board" in 1863 through a series of speculative exploits.[35] He was worth $3 million after successfully cornering four railroad stocks but lost it all in an attempt to manipulate the Old Southern, ending his nine-month reign. At the time, the Open Board was a major competitor to the New York Stock Exchange. The two institutions were merged in 1869 in the wake of the Erie War.

Addison was a "middle-sized, quiet-looking man, with a bluish gray eye, and a slight stoop," according to William Fowler's excellent *Ten Years in Wall Street*. He was a big operator who inspired confidence in observers and was watched closely for clues during the Open Board's stock auctions. Fowler holds Jerome's achievements during the spring and summer of 1863 in high regard, labeling him a "bull-leader." He defines the term at length in a way that could be applied in any era:

Wall Street, considered as an aggregation of human-forces and money-forces, without bull-leaders, would be a flock of sheep without a bell-wether, a mob without a spokesman, an army without a commander. It is the bull-leader who organizes and compacts those forces, brings them under his banner and leads them to victory or—ruin.[36]

And ruin was where Jerome ended. Clews wrote that Jerome "displayed great ability in the conduct of speculative campaigns, but he went beyond his depth and the end was financial shipwreck."[37]

19.13 Called **"William the Silent"** in an homage to rebel sixteenth-century Dutch nobleman William I, Prince of Orange, who earned the nickname for his quiet circumspection, Keep rose to prominence after being born in a poorhouse and running away from his foster parents as a youth. He never returned to them, and instead made a living by gathering Canadian currency for 20 cents in the United States and running it north to collect 25 cents. Eventually, he opened an exchange office in a small town and eloped with the daughter of a townsman who had sworn to shoot him.[38]

Keep was the first to master the blind pool, in which several speculators would provide capital to manage a corner and would share in the profits or losses proportionally. Keep was so trusted that participants often accepted unfavorable terms. Said one historian: "So as to prevent any one member from using information gained during the meetings to secretly work against his fellows at the market, no one was to know when the stock would be bought or sold, how the corner would be accomplished, or even which stock was chosen for the manipulation."[39]

At the peak of his influence, Keep could raise $1 million in a week. One participant netted over $2 million through a $100,000 investment. At one point, the Michigan Southern & Northern Indiana Railroad, nicknamed "Old Southern," became his favorite stock. Fowler recalls watching Keep snap up shares:

> I remember, in the spring of 1863, seeing him stand behind his broker in the street-crowd and pull his coat-tail, as a signal to buy. His broker after buying one thousand shares of Old Southern stopped, when he felt his coat-tail jerked again, violently, and he commenced buying until after seven successive jerks he had bought eight thousand shares, all for the account of the quiet man in the rear, who thereupon relaxed his grasp, and retired to his office without saying a word. He believed in the proverb, "Speech is silver; silence is golden."[40]

Keep eventually ascended to a directorship at Old Southern. When Jerome launched his corner attempt, Keep turned bearish and authorized the issuance of 14,000 shares of stock. He planned to use the high prices to enrich his company's treasury as well as his own pocket. To ensure success, Keep borrowed shares from the Jerome ring and sold into the market—creating the illusion of a rising and vulnerable short interest. When the U.S. Treasury borrowed $35 million from Wall Street in September 1863, monetary conditions tightened and stocks began to fall. The trap was set. Keep used all 14,000 shares to repay borrowed stock, and Fowler said, "Old Southern came down like an avalanche."[41]

Jerome lost his fortune and died of a heart attack in 1864. Keep died wealthy in 1869, leaving his family $4.5 million. He once told a friend:

> Would you like to know how I made my money? I did it by cooping the chickens; I did not wait till the whole brood was hatched. I caught the first little chicken that chipped the shell, and put it in the coop. I then went after more. If there were no more chickens, I had one safe at least. I never despised small gains. What I earned, I took care of. I never periled what I had, for the sake of grasping what I had not secured.[42]

Wall Street remembers very little of an operator who for more than a generation was one of its Titans. His chief claim to immortality seems to be the phrase "watering stock."

Addison G. Jerome ◁**19.12** was the acknowledged king of the Public Board in the spring of 1863. His market tips, they tell me, were considered as good as cash in bank. From all accounts he was a great trader and made millions. He was liberal to the point of extravagance and had a great following in the Street—until Henry Keep, ◁**19.13** known as William the Silent, squeezed him out of all his millions in the Old Southern corner. Keep, by the way, was the brother-in-law of Gov. Roswell P. Flower.

19.14 The New York & Harlem Railroad was chartered in 1831 and never grew more than 132 miles long. It possessed one great asset: the right of direct access to the east side of Manhattan. The line constructed its railway from Harlem to lower Manhattan through what would become Park Avenue. At first, passengers in open carriages were pulled by horse teams. Later, as it expanded, the Harlem decided on an inland route to avoid antagonizing the powerful steamboat interests on the Hudson.

Financial difficulties befell the Harlem in the early 1860s. It canceled its dividend payment, and its shares tumbled to just $9. In 1862, Vanderbilt accumulated 55,000 shares with an idea of improving the railroad and reaping a profit. Clews notes that this came 30 years after Vanderbilt originally had been asked to join the railroad, to which he had responded: "I'm a steamboat man, a competitor of these steam contrivances that you tell us will run on dry land. Go ahead. I wish you well, but I never shall have anything to do with 'em."[43]

Vanderbilt pushed for a new streetcar line franchise for Harlem from the Common Council of the City of New York of which Daniel Drew was a member. Harboring resentment from their prior battles, Drew conspired to sell Harlem short, bribe his fellow council members to vote against Vanderbilt, and watch as Harlem's anticipatory rise was reversed.

On June 25, the council denied the Harlem's request. Shares fell from $110 to $72. But Vanderbilt and his allies continued to buy. Imagine Drew's surprise as the Harlem leveled off and began slowly to rise.[44] Prices continued to advance past $150 as the shorts started to sweat. Vanderbilt eventually settled with the shorts at $180 a share—a loss to Drew of $70 a share. Besides the monetary reward and the satisfaction for foiling an old adversary, Vanderbilt had gained control of his first railroad.

Later in 1864, the same thing happened again when the New York state legislature was discussing whether to allow Vanderbilt to merge the Harlem and the Hudson River Railroad. It occurred to some of the legislators that there was money to be made by selling Harlem short and then defeating the measure. Drew had had the same idea."[45] The politicians mortgaged their houses and properties to get money to sell Harlem short. It was, according to Clews, an example of the old maxim, "Whom the gods devote to destruction, they first make mad."[46]

Later, after he defeated the bears in the same manner as before, Vanderbilt remarked that he had "busted the whole legislature, and scores of the honorable members had to go home without paying their board bills."[47]

In most of the old corners the manipulation consisted chiefly of not letting the other man know that you were cornering the stock which he was variously invited to sell short. It therefore was aimed chiefly at fellow professionals, for the general public does not take kindly to the short side of the account. The reasons that prompted these wise professionals to put out short lines in such stocks were pretty much the same as prompts them to do the same thing to-day. Apart from the selling by faith-breaking politicians in the Harlem corner **19.14** of the Commodore, I gather from the stories I have read that the professional traders sold the stock because it was too high. And the reason they thought it was too high was that it never before had sold so high; and that made it too high to buy; and if it was too high to buy it was just right to sell. That sounds pretty modern, doesn't it? They were thinking of the price, and the Commodore was thinking of the value! And so, for years afterwards, old-timers tell me that people used to say, "He went short of Harlem!" whenever they wished to describe abject poverty.

Many years ago I happened to be speaking to one of Jay Gould's **19.15** old brokers. He assured me earnestly that Mr. Gould not only was a most unusual man—it was of him that old Daniel Drew shiveringly remarked, "His touch is Death!"—but that he was head and shoulders above all other manipulators past and present. He must have been a financial wizard indeed to have done what he did; there can be no question of that. Even at this distance I can see that he had an amazing knack for adapting himself to new conditions, and that is valuable in a trader. He varied his methods of attack and defense without a pang because he was more concerned with the manipulation of properties than with stock speculation. He manipulated for investment rather than for a market turn. He early saw that the big money was in owning the railroads instead of rigging their securities on the floor of the

19.15 Of all the men mentioned in these pages, Jay Gould is probably the best example of a wild speculator on Wall Street during the Civil War era. Gould was born in 1836 into a poor dairy-farming family in upstate New York. His given name was Jason, but he liked Jay better. As a boy, Gould tended his father's 20 cows barefoot, suffering from painful thistles. He saved some money, went to a local seminary school, and wrote an essay entitled "Honesty Is the Best Policy."

Later, Gould worked in a country store and as a land surveyor. He got his break when he started selling his own maps and went to New York to try to sell a mousetrap he invented. There he befriended a local businessman with interests in tanneries. After the

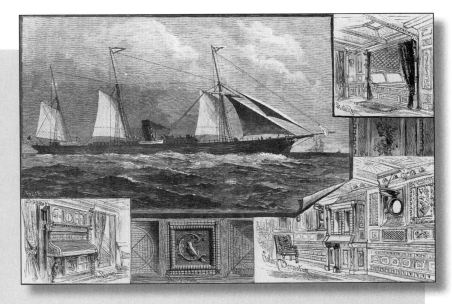

owner shot himself during the Panic of 1857, Gould hired a squad of several hundred men to storm the tannery and push out the other partner. For a while, Gould was strictly a leather merchant. But soon he started dabbling in Wall Street via a little brokerage business.

Naturally, that meant an interest in railroads, which eventually led to an association with Daniel Drew and his broker Jim Fisk. By 1867, both Gould and Fisk joined Drew on the board of the Erie Railroad. All the pieces were in place for Gould to embark on his most famous exploits, which included the Black Friday gold corner attempt and the Erie War against Vanderbilt.

Called the "Wizard of Wall Street," Gould was a man of great contrasts. On the outside, he was a timid, short, frail, and sickly man who rarely looked anyone in the eye and was rather effeminate. On the inside, he was a ruthless, smart, cold-blooded predator who would extract his profit with indifference from friend or foe. What his physique lacked, his intellect and spirit provided in abundance: He was endowed with a rare "courage, grit, insight, foresight, tireless energy, and indomitable will,"[48] according to a biographer.

Meade Minnigerode writes of Gould's public persona:

"He played the great game of speculative finance for all it could be made to yield without disguise or apology—a stranger to honesty and good faith; a personality of alarming cunning deprived of all feeling, scornful of any consideration or rectitude. An operator who always played with loaded dice; an administrator whose only interest lay in the accumulation of selfish profits; a genius whose talents were completely devoted to the limited spheres of his own enrichment; a parasite of disaster, an instrument of calamity, a destroyer."[49]

Yet Gould was also a loving, charitable man to his inner circle. Jim Fisk's wife wrote that Gould was the only friend who still responded to her after her husband's death. Gould lived a clean life free of extravagance except for his private, luxuriously appointed railcar and his yacht *Atalanta*, shown above. He was a lover of flowers and a noted orchid collector. He was also a gifted writer, penning a 426-page history of his home entitled *History of Delaware County* before he was 20. A work based on Drew's diary references Gould's accomplishment:

Jay would do most of the writer-work. "Jay, you're the ink slinger," Jimmy [Fisk] would say to him, and would pull him up to the table and slap a pen in his hand. He would do it so rough that Jay, who is a slip of a man, would wince. . . . As I started to say, Jay has a high and noble way of stringing words together—a knack which I never could get.[50]

Here is a sample from the opening chapter of his book:

History with the more and more extensive meaning acquired by the advancement of civilization, by the diffusion of education, and by the elevation of the standard of human liberty, has expanded into a grand and beautiful science. It treats of man in all his social relations, whether civil, religious, or literary, in which he has had intercourse with his fellows. The study of history, to a free government like the one in which we live, is an indispensable requisite to the improvement and elevation of the human race. It leads us back through the ages that have succeeded each other in time past; it exhibits the condition of the human race at each respective period, and by following down its pages over the vast empires and mighty cities now engulfed in oblivion, but which the faithful historian presents in a living light before us, we are enabled profitably to compare and form a more correct appreciation of our own relative position.[51]

In 1874, Gould was sued and eventually forced from the Erie board by British shareholders who did not approve of his buccaneering ways. He agreed to return $6 million in company funds and retire provided all pending suits against him were dropped. His final days were plagued by dyspepsia and insomnia. On December 2, 1892, Gould died, leaving $72 million to his family. Said Minnigerode: "And when it was announced, the stocks of all his corporations rose in a rejoicing market."[52]

19.16 **Collis P. Huntington** was one of the men responsible for building the Central Pacific Railroad, which joined with the Union Pacific at Promontory Summit in Utah to form the First Transcontinental Railroad. Afterward, Huntington would work with a number of other railroads, including the Southern Pacific and the Chesapeake & Ohio. Born in Connecticut in 1821, he sailed for San Francisco in 1849 and operated a general store out of a tent. Later, his business grew to be one of the most prosperous on the Pacific coast.

It was then that Huntington devised the idea for a railroad to the East. He went to Washington to lobby for the passage of the Pacific Railroad bill that provided land grants and monetary support to the constructors of the railway. However, during the construction of the first 50 miles of Central Pacific track, funds ran dry, forcing Huntington and his associates to use their private wealth to keep 800 workers on the job and ensure the project's success. Clews says that Huntington was "one of the few men in this country who have shown themselves more than a match for Jay Gould."[53]

Stock Exchange. He utilised the stock market of course. But I suspect it was because that was the quickest and easiest way to quick and easy money and he needed many millions, just as old Collis P. Huntington [19.16] was always hard up because he always needed twenty or thirty millions more than the bankers were willing to lend him. Vision without money means heartaches; with money, it means achievement; and that means power; and that means money; and that means achievement; and so on, over and over and over.

Of course manipulation was not confined to the great figures of those days. There were scores of minor manipulators. I remember a story an old broker told me about the manners and morals of the early '60's. He said:

"The earliest recollection I have of Wall Street is of my first visit to the financial district. My father had some business to attend to there and for some reason or other took me with him. We came down Broadway and I remember turning off at Wall Street. We walked down Wall and just as we came to Broad or, rather, Nassau Street, to the corner

19.17 Shylock is a fictional Jewish character from Shakespeare's *Merchant of Venice*. Shylock's character lends money to his Christian rival Antonio and sets the price of the loan at a pound of his flesh. After Antonio goes bankrupt, Shylock demands his pound of flesh in revenge for Antonio's previous insults against him.

Shylock's image and name were commonly used to air anti-Semitic feelings during this period. A cartoon from 1840 shows a well-dressed Shylock grabbing a man by his throat and demanding "Pay me what thou owest" while his victim pleads for patience. The cartoon was drawn in protest of a failure by Congress to pass a national bankruptcy law.

where the Bankers' Trust Company's building now stands, I saw a crowd following two men. The first was walking eastward, trying to look unconcerned. He was followed by the other, a red-faced man who was wildly waving his hat with one hand and shaking the other fist in the air. He was yelling to beat the band: 'Shylock! Shylock! What's the price of money? Shylock! Shylock!' **19.17** I could see heads sticking out of windows. They didn't have skyscrapers in those days, but I was sure the second- and third-story rubbernecks would tumble out. My father asked what was the matter, and somebody answered something I didn't hear. I was too busy keeping a death clutch on my father's hand so that the jostling wouldn't separate us. The crowd was growing, as street crowds do, and I wasn't comfortable. Wild-eyed men came running down from Nassau Street and up from Broad as well as east and west on Wall Street. After we finally got out of the jam my father explained to me that the man who was shouting 'Shylock!' was So-and-So. I have forgotten the name, but he was the biggest operator in clique stocks in the city and was understood

19.18 ▶ It is likely that this old broker, if he is indeed a real person, might be referring to the efforts of Daniel Drew, Jim Fisk, and Jay Gould to "constrict the money arteries by locking up greenbacks,"[54] In Fowler's words. It worked like this: Checks for large amounts were drawn up from various banks by heavy depositors. The banks then certified the checks as good. Then the certified amount would be removed from the banks' surplus fund reserve, as illustrated to the right.

Here is the kicker: The conspirator would use the checks as collateral for new currency loans, the proceeds of which would then be locked away. As a result, money became scarce, interest rates rose, and stocks fell.

In October 1868, the Erie coterie possessed some $14 million after selling a bogus batch of the railroad's shares. The group proceeded as outlined with the goal of driving down the stock's price—which they had sold short with the intention of buying it back at a lower price. The effect of such a sudden withdrawal of funds was dramatic. Minnigerode said loans were called, money "became almost unobtainable, and whoever had borrowed money on stocks was compelled to sell to pay off his loans and trade throughout the country was brought to a perfect standstill. ... It required the strong arm of the Treasury to prevent the panic from spreading all over the country."[55]

Drew, Fisk, and Gould reaped huge profits and immediately went about making more, according to the historian:

"With the money so obtained they had run up the price of gold and made another large profit; they had then again advanced the price of Erie ... and made a larger profit than ever. In the course of these operations they had ruined hundreds ... had arrested the whole business of the country ... had brought the banks to the verge of suspension and seriously threatened the national credit.[56]

But all did not end well. Drew became worried about a public backlash. After coming to the assistance of his old friend Henry Keep, who was loaded down with a long position and needed $2 million, Drew distanced himself from the scheme while privately continuing to sell Erie short. Fisk, who had a gift for colorful epithets, called the old man "Turn Tail" and "Danny Cold Feet."

Drew, who was not warned when Fisk and Gould turned bullish, was caught in the fangs of a short squeeze. Not only did Fisk and Gould start buying Erie, but they unleashed their hoard of greenbacks. Stocks boiled higher. When Drew went to see his compatriots to ask for more time to deliver his shares, he was laughed at and told that "he was the last man who ought to whine over any position in which he has placed himself in regard to Erie."[57]

Drew, it seemed, was beyond rescue. However, as Erie's price soared, a special British issue of stock certificates appeared in New York. With just five minutes to spare, Drew was able to meet his commitments for a loss of roughly $500,000. As a consequence, Gould and Fisk suffered losses of several millions in the broken corner attempt.

to have made—and lost—more money than any other man in Wall Street with the exception of Jacob Little. I remember Jacob Little's name because I thought it was a funny name for a man to have. The other man, the Shylock, was a notorious locker-up of money. His name has also gone from me. But I remember he was tall and thin and pale. In those days the cliques used to lock up money by borrowing it or, rather, by reducing the amount available to Stock Exchange borrowers. They would borrow it and get a certified check. They wouldn't actually take the money out and use it. Of course that was rigging. It was a form of manipulation, I think." ◀**19.18**

I agree with the old chap. It was a phase of manipulation that we don't have nowadays.

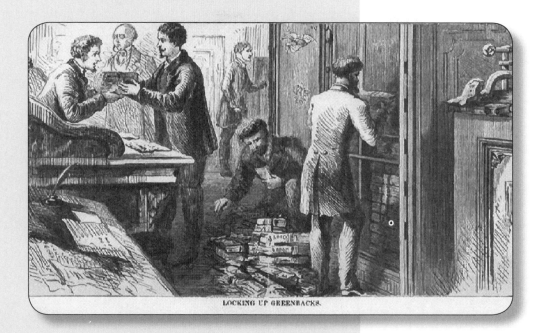

LOCKING UP GREENBACKS.

ENDNOTES

1 Paul Mahoney, "The Origins of the Blue Sky Laws," *Journal of Law and Economics* (April 2003), 229–253.

2 Richard I. Alvarez and Mark J. Astarita, "Introduction to the Blue Sky Laws," SECLaw.com, 1.

3 Matthew Hale Smith, *Sunshine and Shadow* (1869), 462.

4 William Worthington Fowler, *Ten Years in Wall Street* (1870), 92.

5 Henry Clews, *Fifty Years in Wall Street* (New York: Irving Publishing Company, 1908), 728.

6 Edwin G. Burrows and Mike Wallace, *Gotham* (2000), 568–569.

7 Richard Wheatley, "The New York Stock Exchange," *Harper's Monthly* (November 1885): 848.

8 Fowler, *Ten Years in Wall Street,* 93.

9 Walter Werner and Steven T. Smith, *Wall Street* (1991), 56.

10 "Obituary. Mr. Jacob Little," *New York Times*, March 29, 1865, 4.

11 Clews, *Fifty Years in Wall Street*, 730.

12 Fowler, *Ten Years in Wall Street,* 117.

13 "Thomas F. Woodlock," *New York Times*, August 27, 1945, 18.

14 Ibid.

15 Thomas F. Woodlock, *The Anatomy of a Railroad Report* (1895), 3.

16 "Woodlock," *New York Times.*

17 "National Affairs: Take My Money!" *Time,* January 31, 1949.

18 Clews, *Fifty Years in Wall Street,* 35.

19 "Ferdinand Ward Married Again," *New York Times,* March 22, 1894, 1.

20 "The Quicksands of Wall Street," *New York Times,* June 25, 1905, magazine section.

21 David Hochfelder, "Where the Common People Could Speculate: The Ticker, Bucket Shops, and the Origins of Popular Participation in Financial Markets, 1880–1920," *Journal of American History* (September 2006), 353.

22 Robert Sobel, *The Big Board* (1965), 263.

23 Peter Wyckoff, *Wall Street and the Stock Markets* (1972), 59.

24 John Brooks, *Once in Golconda: A True Drama of Wall Street 1920–1938* (New York: John Wiley & Sons, 1969), 26.

25 *Vanderbilt,* Ibid. 134.

26 Richard Barry, "The Vanderbilts," *Pearson's Magazine* (1911): 715.

27 Ibid., 125.

28 Fowler, *Ten Years in Wall Street,* 333.

29 Clews, *Fifty Years in Wall Street,* 93.

30 Edmund Clarence Stedman, ed., *The New York Stock Exchange* (1905), 297–298.

31 Clews, *Fifty Years in Wall Street,* 117.

32 Ibid.

33 Ibid.

34. "Leonard W. Jerome Dead." *New York Times,* March 5, 1891, 8.

35 Sobel, *Panic on Wall Street,* 120.

36 Fowler, *Ten Years in Wall Street,* 159.

37 Clews, *Fifty Years in Wall Street,* 666.

38 Matthew Hale Smith, *Bulls and Bears of New York* (1875), 486.

39 Sobel, *Panic on Wall Street,* 120.

40 Fowler, *Ten Years in Wall Street,* 259.

41 Ibid., 261.

42 Smith, *Bulls and Bears of New York,* 547.

43 Clews, *Fifty Years in Wall Street,* 110.

44 Kurt C. Schlichting, *Grand Central Terminal* (2001), 14.

45 Meade Minnigerode, *Certain Rich Men* (1927), 124.

46 Clews, *Fifty Years in Wall Street,* 114.

47 Minnigerode, *Certain Rich Men.*

48 Ibid., 186.

49 Ibid.

50 Bouck White, *The Book of Daniel Drew* (1910), 3–4.

51 Jay Gould, *History of Delaware County* (1856), 1.

52 Minnigerode, *Certain Rich Men,* 187.

53 Clews, *Fifty Years in Wall Street,* 453.

54 Fowler, *Ten Years in Wall Street,* 504.

55 Minnigerode, *Certain Rich Men,* 180.

56 Ibid., 181.

57 Ibid., 182.

I myself never spoke to any of the great stock manipulators that the Street still talks about. I don't mean leaders; I mean manipulators. They were all before my time, although when I first came to New York, James R. Keene, ◁20.1 greatest of them all, was in his prime. But I was a mere youngster then, exclusively concerned with duplicating, in a reputable broker's office, the success I had enjoyed in the bucket shops of my native city. And, then,

20.1 **James Robert Keene**, known as the Silver Fox for his ashen features and formidable cunning, had an improbable start in the mines of California and Nevada. He was born in London in 1838, and his family moved to Virginia when he was a boy. As a young man, he studied law before he went west in search of fortune and opportunity. He took turns as a cowboy, mill hand, and teacher before he became editor of a newspaper in Shasta, California.[1] Later, he became a miner on the Comstock Lode, the first major U.S. silver deposit. Lefevre, who knew Keene well and peppered *Reminiscences* with his exploits, as you have seen amply by now, describes what happened next:

> *From Virginia City, Nevada, he went to San Francisco with $10,000 and an accurate knowledge of the mines and mining conditions in the great lode. He ran his stake up to $150,000 in a few months, speculating in mining stocks. Remember, he was a man with a remarkable mind and born speculator, besides being a specialist in the mines of the Comstock Lode, a man who knew what he was buying and selling. Within two years he had lost all he had made and a great deal more besides; but arranged with his creditors to be allowed to join the Mining Exchange, and before long he was the leading mining-stock broker of San Francisco. Within a few years he was a millionaire with a national reputation.*
>
> *In 1876 he came East. He was worth $6,000,000 and was on his way to Europe for his health. He told me this himself, and there is no reason to doubt it. On his trip across the continent he saw with his own eyes what made him a bear on railroad stocks. He didn't go to Europe but remained in New York to speculate.[2]*

Rumor had it that Keene went east to "bust" Jay Gould, but in reality the two joined forces for a time before Keene was betrayed. He should have known better, according to financier-historian William Fowler: "Now the late James Fisk, Jr., was wont to say in his sportive way, 'If you sleep in the same bed with Jay and take the inside, you will be sure to wake up and find him next to the wall, and no matter how cold the night he will plant his clammy feet in the small of your back and land you on the floor.'"[3]

Keene quickly recovered from his rocky relationship with Gould. He did not limit himself to just stocks or mines; he also dealt in lard, opium, and fast horses. He shorted coal stocks with great success. His confidence grew until, in 1878, he attempted to corner wheat with disastrous results. Henry Clews describes Keene's persona: "In an evil hour Mr. Keene was induced to spread himself out all over creation, while he still retained his immense interest in stocks. He was so flushed with successive victories that he began to regard failure impossible, and thought he was a man of destiny in speculation, such as Napoleon considered himself in war."[4]

too, at the time Keene was busy with the U.S. Steel stocks—his manipulative masterpiece—I had no experience with manipulation, no real knowledge of it or of its value or meaning, and, for that matter, no great need of such knowledge. If I thought about it at all I suppose I must have regarded it as a well-dressed form of thimble-rigging, of which the lowbrow form was such tricks as had been tried on me in the bucket shops. Such talk as I since have heard on the subject has consisted in great part of surmises and suspicions; of guesses rather than intelligent analyses.

More than one man who knew him well has told me that Keene was the boldest and most brilliant operator that ever worked in Wall Street. That is saying a great deal, for there have been some great traders. Their names are now all but forgotten, but nevertheless they were kings in their day—for a day! They were pulled up out of obscurity into the sunlight of financial fame by the ticker tape—and the little paper ribbon didn't prove strong enough to keep them suspended there long enough for them to become historical fixtures. At all events Keene was by all odds the best manipulator of his day—and it was a long and exciting day.

He capitalized his knowledge of the game, his experience as an operator and his talents when he sold his services to the Havemeyer brothers, who wanted him to develop a market for the Sugar stocks. ⟨**20.2**⟩ He was broke at the time or he would have continued to trade on his own hook; and he was some plunger! He was successful with Sugar; made the shares trading favourites, and that made them easily vendible. After that, he was asked time and again to take charge of pools. I am told that in these pool operations he never asked or accepted a fee, but paid for his share like the other members of the pool. The market conduct of the stock, of

20.2 ▶ H. O. Havemeyer, leader of the Sugar Trust, was the first to offer Keene a fresh start in the wake of his crippling losses in wheat. Keene moved on to equities, then considered a less important trading vehicle. Lefevre wrote: "The stock had never established itself as a speculative favorite. Mr. Keene made it that, and marketed much of it. It placed him on his feet, financially, and from then on he became a power in the street, a free lance, the greatest market strategist living."[5]

20.3 **William Collins Whitney** was a politician, speculator, and scion of the prominent family that included cotton gin inventor Eli Whitney. Born in 1841, William was trained as a lawyer and dabbled on Wall Street in the mid-1880s before becoming U.S. Navy Secretary under President Grover Cleveland. He was instrumental in the modernization of the Navy through advancements in plate armor and heavy guns. Whitney was also a famous breeder of racehorses and competed heartily with Keene's stable.

His business partner, **Thomas F. Ryan**, was born in 1851 and orphaned at age five. Ryan started out as a dry goods merchant before he went to Wall Street, was taken under Whitney's wing, and started a brokerage house. Investments in public transit and tobacco followed, including the formation of the American Tobacco Co. Later in life, he diversified into coalfields and insurance, and even developed diamond mines in Africa for King Leopold II of Belgium.[6] Ryan was also a frequent rival to E. H. Harriman. The *New York Times* wrote that he "was born in poverty and died one of the world's wealthiest men."[7] His son, Allan Ryan, was the man behind the Stutz Motors corner, for which he was expelled from the New York Stock Exchange.

As for the feud between Keene and Whitney-Ryan, the group had earlier operated together in the whisky pool engineered by Keene that ended disastrously. The target was the stock of the Distilling and Cattle Feeding Co., better known as the Whisky Trust. The company was an original member of the Dow Jones Industrial Average that at its peak controlled two-thirds of the nation's spirits output.[8] The stock had been run up to $73, said a 1910 report, but "opened one sad morning at $55, and dropped to $10 before it stopped."[9]

They had also joined forces in the American Tobacco pool, another troubled venture; after the price soared, one pool member turned bearish and broke the market. Keene blamed Whitney. Whitney blamed Keene. But when shares finally bottomed, it was Keene who was discovered to be heavily short. The Whitney crew retaliated and bulled the stock to $200. The episode created a permanent rift between the Whitney-Ryan group and Keene and presaged clashes over transit stocks a few years later.

Whitney died in 1904 from complications after an appendectomy. Ryan died in 1928 after troubles with his gallbladder.

course, was exclusively in his charge. Often there was talk of treachery—on both sides. His feud with the Whitney-Ryan clique **20.3** arose from such accusations. It is not difficult for a manipulator to be misunderstood by his associates. They don't see his needs as he himself does. I know this

20.4 As J. P. Morgan's new billion-dollar steel trust was slowly coming together in the spring of 1901, Keene sneered: "The thing is impossible, because, for one reason, you never could sell the stock. There would be too much of it and too many people would be trying to sell at the same time."[10] Yet it was Keene who was tasked with the impossible after Morgan entrusted him to make a market for U.S. Steel's capitalization of $500 million common and $500 million preferred stock.

With no risk to himself in the case of failure and rich rewards if he was successful, Keene enthusiastically went about the work even though he privately harbored doubts. Armed with a paltry sum of $25 million with which to conduct his operation, the situation was not hopeless.[11] The broad market was bounding higher in a wave of speculative mania unmatched to that time. In addition, the U.S. Steel flotation had been heavily advertised the world over and was eagerly anticipated by the working classes eager to share in the profits of what newspapers called the "captains of industry"—men like John Gates, Andrew Carnegie, and Morgan.

The formation of U.S. Steel was the defining moment for American industry at the dawn of the twentieth century. Lefevre described Keene's role as "marvelous," adding:

It was the greatest work of his lifetime; not the most picturesque, nor, possibly, the most captivating, but certainly the most important. Imagine a Napoleon, after commanding a brigade for years, being placed in command of a huge army. Mr. Keene could now go ahead, backed not only by his genius and his own resources but by practically unlimited capital. It was the most remarkable manipulation that ever has been, and perhaps ever will be witnessed in Wall Street.[12]

20.5 Taylor was born in Baltimore, Maryland, in 1865, a descendant of a prestigious Southern family. He apprenticed in Baltimore banks before going into real estate. His story might have ended there, but he caught the eye of young Jessica Keene, James Keene's only daughter, who at the time was living in Baltimore. They wed in 1892. Soon Taylor had direct access to one of the greatest speculators on Wall Street. By 1893, he became a broker and bought a seat on the New York Stock Exchange. Taylor's ties to Keene grew when Taylor offered the older man's son, Foxhall Keene, a partnership interest in his business.

from my own experience. It is a matter of regret that Keene did not leave an accurate record of his greatest exploit—the successful manipulation of the U.S. Steel shares **20.4** in the spring of 1901. As I understand it, Keene never had an interview with J. P. Morgan about it. Morgan's firm dealt with or through Talbot J. Taylor & Co., at whose office Keene made his headquarters. **20.5** Talbot Taylor was Keene's son-in-law. I am assured that Keene's fee for his work consisted of the pleasure he derived from the work. That he made millions trading in the market he helped to put up that spring is well known. He told a friend of mine that in the course of a few weeks he sold in the open market for the underwriters' syndicate more than seven hundred and fifty thousand shares. Not bad when you consider two things: That they were new and untried stocks of a corporation whose capitalization was greater than the entire debt of the United States at that time; and second, that men like D. G. Reid, W. B. Leeds, the Moore brothers, Henry Phipps, H. C. Frick and the other Steel magnates **20.6** also sold hundreds of thousands of shares to the public at the same time in the same market that Keene helped to create.

Of course, general conditions favoured him. Not only actual business but sentiment and his unlimited financial backing made possible his success. What we had was not merely a big bull market but a boom and a state of mind not likely to be seen again. The undigested-securities panic came later, when Steel common, which Keene had marked up to 55 in 1901, sold at 10 in 1903 and at 8⅞ in 1904.

We can't analyse Keene's manipulative campaigns. His books are not available; the adequately detailed record is nonexistent. For example, it would be interesting to see how he worked in

20.6 ▶ **Henry Phipps** and **Henry Frick,** along with **Charles Schwab,** were lieutenants of Andrew Carnegie and worked for his Carnegie Steel Co. in Pittsburgh. Born in 1851 and first working for Carnegie in 1879, Schwab rose "from the bottom," according to Clews, to become president of Carnegie Steel at the tender age of 35.[13] He helped negotiate Carnegie Steel's incorporation into J. P. Morgan's U.S. Steel in 1901 and, upon the completion of the merger, became the new company's president. He built the largest private residence ever seen in Manhattan and went on to run Bethlehem Steel.

Mr. and Mrs. Henry Phipps (top), Charles M. Schwab (right), Henry Clay Frick (below)

Henry Clay Frick, born in 1849, made his fortune in coke — the coal derivative used in the steelmaking process. The grandson of a successful rye whiskey distiller, Frick got his start at the Overholt distillery in western Pennsylvania. He launched his own business by actively purchasing acreage in that area after learning it was endowed with a rich seam of coal; he knew that the iron and steel trade was exploding, and would increase demand for coke.

After the Panic of 1873 bankrupted competitors, Frick, who had added foreclosed mining properties to his own, eventually controlled 80% of the coal in the region that was a critical supplier to the steel plants in Pittsburgh. As demand recovered, Frick raised the price of coke from 90 cents a ton to $5. At age 30, he was a millionaire and Carnegie was his largest customer. Impressed with Frick's business acumen and managerial talent while at the same time recognizing the threat he presented, Carnegie joined forces with his supplier in 1883 by purchasing a 50% stake in the coke company.[14]

Henry Phipps was born in 1839 and grew up in Pittsburgh as Andrew Carnegie's childhood neighbor and friend. Phipps had been "the plodder, the bookkeeper, the economizer, the man who had an eye for microscopic details,"[15] according to a biographer. Next to his boss, Phipps was the largest owner of Carnegie Steel.[16]

After selling the proceeds of his stake in the combined U.S. Steel Corporation, Phipps formed the Bessemer Trust in 1907, named after the Bessemer steel process, to manage his family's wealth. The firm still operates as an asset management advisor based in New York.

20.7 ▶ In the spring of 1903, Keene found himself in another slump. He was hard up for cash and mostly out of the market. And yet again, the call to manipulate a market for others won him a new stake. When the "Rich Man's Panic" of 1903 subsided—it had been the result of the excessive speculation in 1901 and 1902—Keene lingered in the shadows. He did not get back into the game until the stock market boom of 1905, when Henry H. Rogers asked him to bull Amalgamated Copper.

Keene carried the stock to $90 before he announced that the top had been reached and ended his manipulation. Rogers believed otherwise. He called on another man to push Amalgamated still higher until prices reached $180.[17] By Keene's own admission, such a manipulation was possible only because the basic conditions of the market were favorable.[18]

Thomas Lawson, an Amalgamated insider who wrote an exposé in *Everybody's Magazine*, describes what happened:

> Once again Amalgamated was in all mouths. Keene's hand was everywhere. Wall and State Streets began to sizzle with sales…and the price mounted rapidly. So well was the manipulation screened, so cleverly was the buying conducted, that the world took the activity as a genuine revival of interest in the property. Of course it was merely the magic of the stock market operator at work, for all this eager movement was the result of wash sales.[19]

Amalgamated Copper. ◀**20.7** H. H. Rogers and William Rockefeller ◀**20.8** had tried to dispose of their surplus stock in the market and had failed. Finally they asked Keene to market their line, and he agreed. ◀**20.9** Bear in mind that H. H. Rogers was one of the ablest business men of his day in Wall Street and that William Rockefeller was the boldest speculator of the entire Standard Oil coterie. They had practically unlimited resources and vast prestige as well as years of experience in the stock-market game. And yet they had to go to Keene. I mention this to show you that there are some tasks which it requires a specialist to perform. Here was a widely touted stock, sponsored by America's greatest capitalists, that could not be sold except at a great sacrifice of money and prestige. Rogers and Rockefeller were intelligent enough to decide that Keene alone might help them.

Keene began to work at once. He had a bull market to work in and sold two hundred and twenty thousand shares of Amalgamated at around par. After he disposed of the insiders' line the public kept on buying and the price went ten points higher. Indeed the insiders got bullish on the stock they had sold when they saw how eagerly the public was taking it. There was a story that Rogers actually advised Keene to go long of Amalgamated. It is scarcely credible that Rogers meant to unload on Keene. He was too shrewd a man not to know that Keene was no bleating lamb. Keene worked as he always did—that is, doing his big selling on the way down after the big rise. Of course his tactical moves were directed by his needs and by the minor currents that changed from day to day. In the stock market, as in warfare, it is well to keep in mind the difference between strategy and tactics. One of Keene's confidential men—he is the best fly fisherman I know—told me only the other day that during the Amalgamated campaign Keene would find himself almost out of stock one day—

20.8 On November 6, 1906, the New York Times wrote "the four most powerful figures … are E.H. Harriman, H.C. Frick, H.H. Rogers, and William Rockefeller." Along with J. P. Morgan, they represented the great captains of industry of the era.[20]

Rockefeller, of course, was a co-founder of Standard Oil along with older brother John D. Rockefeller. Henry Huttleston Rogers was an early competitor to the Rockefellers before he sold his firm to them and joined forces. He was widely recognized as the brains behind many of Standard Oil's strategic decisions. As a large shareholder, he benefited greatly from the relationship, and left a $75 million fortune upon his death.

In addition to his business acumen, Rogers was a close friend of Mark Twain. After a trip on Rogers's steamer one day, Twain held his friend's arm and was reported by the *New York Times* to have quipped, "Birds of a feather. … You know the rest of it," before bursting into laughter.[21]

Pictured from left are Henry H. Rogers and William Rockefeller.

that is, out of the stock he had been forced to take in marking up the price; and on the next day he would buy back thousands of shares. On the day after that, he would sell on balance. Then he would leave the market absolutely alone, to see how it would take care of itself and also to accustom it to do so. When it came to the actual marketing of the line he did what I told you: he sold it on the way down. The trading public is always looking for a rally, and, besides, there is the covering by the shorts.

The man who was closest to Keene during that deal told me that after Keene sold the Rogers-Rockefeller line for something like twenty or twenty-five million dollars in cash Rogers sent him a check for two hundred thousand. This reminds you of the millionaire's wife who gave the Metropolitan Opera House scrub-woman fifty cents

20.9 The *Times* wrote in 1905:

Nearly everybody in Wall Street knows that Mr. Keene did distribute 220,000 shares of Amalgamated Copper for Mr. Rogers.… By this achievement Mr. Keene earned the respect and admiration of Mr. Rogers or that division of the so-called Standard Oil crowd which Mr. Rogers represents, and probably holds both still.[22]

20.10 Opera has had a rich history in New York City dating to 1825. The art form got a new home with the opening of the Academy of Music theater in 1854. The venue quickly became a gathering place for the city's social elite. The *New York Times*, when reporting its opening, was sure to mention the clever armchairs with spring seats—"so that they fold up when not in use"—a new invention at the time.[23] With the academy's membership dominated by families that had been wealthy since colonial times, the new capitalists of the age—men like Vanderbilt and Morgan—decided to open a new opera house.

Historian Henry Edward Krehbiel wrote: "It had become plain that the Academy of Music could not accommodate all the representatives of the two elements in fashionable society, who, for one reason or another, wished to own or occupy the boxes which were the visible sign of wealth and social position."[24] Thus, the Metropolitan Opera House was born in 1883. Vicious competition between the two theaters ended when the academy abandoned its opera season in 1886.

Following a fire in 1892, the Met underwent extensive renovations for a decade that resulted in its distinctive red and gold interior. The building was finally demolished in 1967 after a new, larger facility was built.

reward for finding the one-hundred-thousand-dollar pearl necklace. **20.10** Keene sent the check back with a polite note saying he was not a stock broker and that he was glad to have been of some service to them. They kept the check and wrote him that they would be glad to work with him again. Shortly after that it was that H. H. Rogers gave Keene the friendly tip to buy Amalgamated at around 130!

A brilliant operator, James R. Keene! His private secretary told me that when the market was going his way Mr. Keene was irascible; and those who knew him say his irascibility was expressed in sardonic phrases that lingered long in the memory of his hearers. But when he was losing he was in the best of humour, a polished man of the world, agreeable, epigrammatic, interesting.

He had in superlative degree the qualities of mind that are associated with successful speculators anywhere. That he did not argue with the tape is plain. He was utterly fearless but never reckless. He could and did turn in a twinkling, if he found he was wrong.

Since his day there have been so many changes in Stock Exchange rules and so much more rigorous enforcement of old rules, so many new taxes on stock sales and profits, and so on, that the game seems different. Devices that Keene could use with skill and profit can no longer be utilised. Also, we are assured, the business morality of Wall Street is on a higher plane. Nevertheless it is fair to say that in any period of our financial history Keene would have been a great manipulator because he was a great stock operator and knew the game of speculation from the ground up. He achieved what he did because conditions at the time permitted him to do so. He would have been as successful in his undertakings in 1922 as he was in 1901 or in 1876, when he first came to New York from California and made nine million dollars in two years. There are men whose gait is far quicker than the mob's. They are bound to lead—no matter how much the mob changes.

As a matter of fact, the change is by no means as radical as you'd imagine. The rewards are not so great, for it is no longer pioneer work and therefore it is not pioneer's pay. But in certain respects manipulation is easier than it was; in other ways much harder than in Keene's day.

There is no question that advertising is an art, and manipulation is the art of advertising through the medium of the tape. The tape should tell the story the manipulator wishes its readers to see. The truer the story the more convincing it is bound to be, and the more convincing it is the better the advertising is. A manipulator to-day, for instance, has not only to make a stock look strong but also to make it be strong. Manipulation therefore must be based on sound trading principles. That is what made Keene such a marvellous manipulator; he was a consummate trader to begin with.

The word "manipulation" has come to have an ugly sound. It needs an alias. I do not think there is anything so very mysterious or crooked about the process itself when it has for an object the selling of a stock in bulk, provided, of course, that such operations are not accompanied by misrepresentation. There is little question that a manipulator necessarily seeks his buyers among speculators. He turns to men who are looking for big returns on their capital and are therefore willing to run a greater than normal business risk. I can't have much sympathy for the man who, knowing this, nevertheless blames others for his own failure to make easy money. He is a devil of a clever fellow when he wins. But when he loses money the other fellow was a crook; a manipulator! In such moments and from such lips the word connotes the use of marked cards. But this is not so.

Usually the object of manipulation is to develop marketability—that is, the ability to dispose of fair-sized blocks at some price at any time. Of course a

20.11 **Jay Gould** realized the potential of controlling a telegraph system early in his career. Railroads depended on the technology. Long-distance communication was being revolutionized. His target was Western Union, which dominated the nation's telegraph network after it was created out of various smaller companies in the 1850s. Gould described his motivation, which sounds a lot like investors' interest in Internet investments more than a century later: "The telegraph and the railroad systems go hand in hand, as it were, integral parts of a great civilization. I naturally became acquainted with the telegraph business and gradually became interested in it. I thought well of it as an investment, and I kept increasing my interests."[25]

For his first strike, Gould teamed with James Keene and Russell Sage to push down shares of Western Union. This netted the bears $1 million apiece while Western Union directors, including the son of frequent Gould-Fisk-Drew rival Commodore Vanderbilt, grew concerned. They had good reason.

In addition to his market manipulations, Gould began to build telegraph lines along his railroad tracks—creating the Atlantic & Pacific Co. and engaging in cutthroat rate warfare. Through his ownership of the *New York World* newspaper, Gould turned public opinion against Western Union by labeling it a monopoly. And finally, Gould purchased the rights to Thomas Edison's high-speed automatic telegraph as well as his quadruplex telegraph technology, which allowed four messages to be passed simultaneously along a single wire.

Gould's antics severely reduced the Western Union's business. With no other choice, the directors bought his A&P for a large sum.[26] Josephson writes: "But no sooner had he sold, and all were heaving a sigh of relief, than Jay Gould struck again, tirelessly."[27] He formed another competitor, the American Union Telegraph Co. A second rate war ensued, causing another bitter capitulation from Western Union. Gould then promised to start no more telegraph companies. But this did not preclude him from causing more trouble.

Gould organized a third bear campaign by calling on the skills and nerves of Keene, Sage, and Cammack. Using "every trick and art of Stock Exchange manipulation," according to a historian, Gould and company again forced down Western Union's stock and took millions in short-selling profits.[28] Keene, in a bloodlust, extended his line until it became apparent that someone was absorbing Western Union as fast as he was selling it. Just as he had done to Jim Fisk on Black Friday and Daniel Drew in the Erie War, Jay Gould had turned on his partners. Seeking full control of Western Union, Gould had turned bullish. Prices recovered, and the bears were trapped.

One of the men in the pool, a Major Selover, had served in the Mexican-American and Civil wars and was offered the position of postmaster general of San Francisco by President Franklin Pierce before going to Wall Street. A longtime friend of Keene, he sought revenge against Gould over the Western Union deal through physical violence one afternoon in New York in 1877.[29] Henry Clews describes the scene:

> The Major and Keene met one morning at the rear entrance of the Stock Exchange, in New Street, and interchanged intelligent glances on the subject.... Selover walked down the street with blood in his eye, and meeting Mr. Gould on the corner of New Street and Exchange Place, caught him up by the collar of the coat and a part of his pants and dropped him in the areaway of a barber's shop. The little man promptly picked himself up, went quietly to his office, and made a transaction by which Selover lost $15,000 more. This was his method of retaliation.[30]

Later, according to historian Maury Klein, a broker smirked that "It is characteristic of Mr. Gould that he landed on his feet."[31] As a result of his unethical gambit, Gould gained control of Western Union and soon moved into its modern, fortresslike offices in Manhattan.

Speaking of Gould's treachery, Russell Sage said: "Gould gave us his contract. That was no good. He gave us his word, and that was no good."[32] As for Keene, his anger was palpable: "Gould is nothing to me, and I don't care what he does or says as far as I am concerned....I can say this—that I have lost nothing by Mr. Gould's maneuvering and have no apprehension of doing so."[33] Selover, for his part, continued to spew venom:

> It would exhaust the capacity of the English language to fittingly characterize the meanness, the duplicity, and the treachery with which this scoundrel has treated me. For weeks and months he has lied to me in the most varied and persistent manner....He has all the time pretended to be my friend, and yet in secret he has been constantly plotting my overthrow.[34]

pool, by reason of a reversal of general market conditions, may find itself unable to sell except at a sacrifice too great to be pleasing. They then may decide to employ a professional, believing that his skill and experience will enable him to conduct an orderly retreat instead of suffering an appalling rout.

You will notice that I do not speak of manipulation designed to permit considerable accumulation of a stock as cheaply as possible, as, for instance, in buying for control, because this does not happen often nowadays.

When Jay Gould wished to cinch his control of Western Union ‹20.11› and decided to buy a big block of the stock, Washington E. Connor, ‹20.12› who had not been seen on the floor of the Stock Exchange for years, suddenly showed up in person at the Western Union post. He began to bid for Western Union. The traders to a man laughed—at his stupidity in thinking them so simple—and they cheerfully sold him all the stock he wanted to buy. It was too raw a trick, to think he could put up the price by acting as though Mr. Gould wanted to buy Western Union. Was that manipulation? I think I can only answer that by saying "No; and yes!"

In the majority of cases the object of manipulation is, as I said, to sell stock to the public at the best possible price. It is not alone a question of selling but of distributing. It is obviously better in every way for a stock to be held by a thousand people than by one man—better for the market in it. So it is not alone the sale at a good price but the character of the distribution that a manipulator must consider.

There is no sense in marking up the price to a very high level if you cannot induce the public to take it off your hands later. Whenever inexperienced manipulators try to unload at the top and fail, old-timers look mighty wise and tell you that you can lead a horse to water but you cannot make him drink. Original devils! As a matter of fact, it is well to remember a rule of manipulation, a rule that Keene and his able

20.12 **Washington Connor, along with William Belden and William Heath,** was Gould's main broker after the assassination of Jim Fisk. Connor first appeared on Wall Street as a clerk at William Belden & Co., where Fisk was once a partner. Through his relationship with Gould, Connor received directorships from Western Union and the Union Pacific. He is described by Henry Clews as "a natural leader in speculation—cool, quick and adroit."[35] It was said that Gould admired Connor for his "shrewdness, adroitness, persistency, and audacity in financial matters."[36]

20.13 ▸ **Keene's transition** from lone wolf operator to market manipulator extraordinaire was driven by the tragic wheat corner attempt mentioned earlier. His misfortune provides a prime example of how one can accurately analyze conditions and predict the path of prices yet still be felled by outsiders. Perhaps it was because of this experience with loose lips, deception, and intrigue that Keene embraced tactics like rumor mongering and tip giving in his manipulative efforts.

It started in October 1878 when wheat had reached its lowest price in six years. A severe yellow fever epidemic in the South, along the Mississippi River, depressed demand at a time of heavy supply. Inventories grew rapidly. Grain elevators and warehouses became overwhelmed as a few fell two days behind in issuing receipts. Keene sensed an opportunity, according to historian Charles Taylor:

In December began the great buying movement of which Keene, the New York speculator, was the head. He believed that wheat was destined to go much higher, and he bought largely with the intention of holding.... The movement stimulated all markets, and was the chief feature of trading during the first half of 1879.[37]

People started to pay attention. The *Chicago Tribune* published a poem on December 7 entitled "Jim Keene's Song of the Wheat." Keene began to boast, according to journalist Isaac Marcosson, that "I'll carry away the Chicago Board of Trade in my vest-pocket."[38] Like lions stalking a herd, Keene's enemies began to gather. Addison Cammack went to Gould and told him that Keene was too extended, his position too vulnerable. Historian Matthew Josephson writes:

Now, in a sudden devastating bear raid, Cammack and Gould fell upon Keene when his guard was down, and began selling everything he held. Bankers became timid, brokers began demanding more margin, loans were called, prices crashed. In the jungle of the stock market one beast of prey was tearing

predecessors well knew. It is this: Stocks are manipulated to the highest point possible and then sold to the public on the way down. ◂**20.13**

Let me begin at the beginning. Assume that there is some one—an underwriting syndicate or a pool or an individual—that has a block of stock which it is desired to sell at the best price possible. It is a stock duly listed on the New York Stock Exchange. The best place for selling it ought to be the open market, and the best buyer ought to be the general public. The negotiations for the sale are in charge of a man. He—or some present or former associate—has tried to sell the stock on the Stock Exchange and has not succeeded. He is—or soon becomes—sufficiently familiar with stock-market operations to realise that more experience and greater aptitude for the work are needed than he possesses. He knows personally or by hearsay several men who have been successful in their handling of similar deals, and he decides to avail himself of their professional skill. He seeks one of them as he would seek a physician if he were ill or an engineer if he needed that kind of expert.

Suppose he has heard of me as a man who knows the game. Well, I take it that he tries to find out all he can about me. He then arranges for an interview, and in due time calls at my office.

Of course, the chances are that I know about the stock and what it represents. It is my business to know. That is how I make my living. My visitor tells me what he and his associates wish to do, and asks me to undertake the deal.

It is then my turn to talk. I ask for whatever information I deem necessary to give me a clear understanding of what I am asked to undertake. I determine the value and estimate the market possibilities of that stock. That and my reading of current conditions in turn help me to gauge the likelihood of success for the proposed operation.

If my information inclines me to a favourable view I accept the proposition and tell him then and there what my terms will be for my services. If he in turn accepts my terms—the honorarium and the conditions—I begin my work at once.

I generally ask and receive calls on a block of stock. I insist upon graduated calls as the fairest to all concerned. The price of the call begins at a little below the prevailing market price and goes up; say, for example, that I get calls on one hundred thousand shares and the stock is quoted at 40. I begin with a call for some thousands of shares at 35, another at 37, another at 40, and at 45 and 50, and so on up to 75 or 80.

If as the result of my professional work—my manipulation—the price goes up, and if at the highest level there is a good demand for the stock so that I can sell fair-sized blocks of it I of course call the stock. I am making money; but so are my clients making money. This is as it should be. If my skill is what they are paying for they ought to get value. Of course, there are times when a pool may be wound up at a loss, but that is seldom, for I do not undertake the work unless I see my way clear to a profit. This year I was not so fortunate in one or two deals, and I did not make a profit. There are reasons, but that is another story, to be told later—perhaps. ⟨20.14⟩

The first step in a bull movement in a stock is to advertise the fact that there is a bull movement on. Sounds silly, doesn't it? Well, think a moment. It isn't as silly as it sounded, is it? The most effective way to advertise what, in effect, are your honourable intentions is to make the stock active and strong. After all is said and done, the greatest publicity agent in the wide world is the ticker, and by far the best advertising medium is the tape. I do not need to put out any literature for my clients. I do not have to inform the daily press as to the value of the stock or to work the financial reviews for notices about the company's prospects. Neither do I have to get a following. I accomplish all these highly desirable things by merely making the stock active. When there is activity there is a synchronous demand for

another to pieces. Keene, who had grown to believe himself infallible, was shorn, like the veriest lamb, of seven millions and turned adrift, a bankrupt. It was a grievous lesson.[39]

Keene struggled to recover. Efforts to recapture lost profits only resulted in further misfortune. According to Clews, "Disaster followed disaster, and as he became desperate in his efforts to get back something, his losses became constantly greater, until nearly the whole of his immense pile was buried in fruitless efforts to recover a portion of it."[40]

It was in the aftermath of this failure that Keene earned a new stake by marketing stocks for others. Although he was penniless, Keene was still well respected on Wall Street. There was an outpouring of sympathy for Keene. And soon, men like Havemeyer from the Sugar Trust, William Rockefeller and H. H. Rogers of Standard Oil fame, and J. P. Morgan came to call on his services.

Lefevre held Keene in high regard, and said he had "uncommon foresight, lighting rapidity of perception, a strong grasp of essential facts and an unerring judgment of the capacity of his stock-market opponents."[41] It is said that his early reverses made him more cautious in his later exploits.

In addition to his stock market forays, Keene was a renowned racehorse owner. He died on January 3, 1915, after a failed operation for stomach troubles. The *New York Times* lamented the loss of "the last of his race, the sporting men of Wall Street."[42]

20.14 One of Livermore's most notorious operations came in shares of Piggly Wiggly, a Tennessee-based supermarket chain that was notable for being the first to offer self-service stores, shown below. In 1923, company founder Clarence Saunders asked Livermore to form a bull pool to boost the price of a secondary offering of shares. Livermore launched his operation in tandem with Frank Bliss, a trading floor veteran.[43] Within a month, Livermore had pushed the once-moribund shares from $40 to $120. On March 20 alone, the stock jumped $52 amid frantic short covering. A reporter said, "Fully one-third of the brokers on the floor were crowded about the Piggly Wiggly post."[44]

So far, so good. But soon Livermore learned that Saunders had an ulterior motive: The eccentric grocer wanted to corner the stock in an effort to punish short sellers who had targeted the company. Bears had apparently targeted Piggly Wiggly because of the failure of a similarly named but unrelated company in the East. Determined to protect his creation, Saunders vowed to "beat Wall Street professionals at their own game."[45]

Livermore backed away from the operation after learning Saunders' true motivation, as punishment was bad business, but Saunders pressed on. And he almost won. Yet just when he had his enemies on the run after reportedly acquiring 160,000 of the 200,000 shares oustanding, NYSE governors took the unusual step of suspending trading in Piggly Wiggly shares for five days. That gave bears extra time to find shares to cover their shorts, and ended the corner.

Saunders, who originally believed he could wrest $20 million from the bears, was ruined. Historian Robert Sobel writes: "It is fitting that the first major corner of the [1920s] bull market began with a Livermore-Bliss victory, the wreck of a businessman, an avoidance of responsibility on the part of the Exchange—all in connection with a stock named after a pig."

Livermore emerged from the deal untarnished, and although Saunders was forced to declare bankruptcy he later came back. In 1928 he started a new grocery chain called the Clarence Saunders, Sole Owner of My Name Stores Inc., which busted in the Depression.[46] Later he started another automated discount grocery chain called the Keedoozle, about which he said, according to *Time* magazine, "It can't miss. It's the biggest thing I've ever had."[47] It busted too, but still Saunders was undaunted and tried again with another chain that never got off the ground, called Foodelectric. He died in 1953 at age 72.

explanations; and that means, of course, that the necessary reasons—for publication—supply themselves without the slightest aid from me.

Activity is all that the floor traders ask. They will buy or sell any stock at any level if only there is a free market for it. They will deal in thousands of shares wherever they see activity, and their aggregate capacity is considerable. It necessarily happens that they constitute the manipulator's first crop of buyers. They will follow you all the way up and they thus are a great help at all the stages of the operation. I understand that James R. Keene used habitually to employ the most active of the room traders, both to conceal the source of the manipulation and also because he knew that they were by far the best business-spreaders and tip-distributors. He often gave calls to them—verbal calls—above the market, so that they might do some helpful work before they could cash in. He made them earn their profit. To get a professional following I myself have never had to do more than to make a stock active. Traders don't ask for more. It is well, of course, to remember that these professionals on the floor of the Exchange buy stocks with the intention of selling them at a profit. They do not insist on its being a big profit; but it must be a quick profit.

I make the stock active in order to draw the attention of speculators to it, for the reasons I have given. I buy it and I sell it and the traders follow suit. The selling pressure is not apt to be strong where a man has as much speculatively held stock sewed up—in calls—as I insist on having. The buying, therefore, prevails over the selling, and the public follows the lead not so much of the manipulator as of the room traders. It comes in as a buyer. This highly desirable demand I fill—that is, I sell stock on balance. If the demand is what it ought to be it will absorb more than the amount of stock I was compelled to accumulate in the earlier stages of the manipulation; and when this happens I sell the stock short—that is, technically. In other words, I sell more stock than I actually hold. It is perfectly safe for me to do so since I am really selling against my calls. Of course, when the demand from the public slackens, the stock ceases to advance. Then I wait.

Say, then, that the stock has ceased to advance. There comes a weak day. The entire market may develop a reactionary tendency or some sharp-eyed trader my perceive that there are no buying orders to speak of in my stock, and he sells it, and his fellows follow. Whatever the reason may be, my stock starts to go down. Well, I begin to buy it. I give it the support that a stock ought to have if it is in good odour with its own sponsors. And more: I am able to support it without accumulating it—that is, without increasing the amount I shall have to sell later on. Observe that I do this without decreasing my financial resources. Of course what I am really doing is covering stock I sold short at higher prices when the demand from the public or from the traders or from both enabled me to do it. It is always well to make it plain to the traders—and to the public, also—that there is a demand for the stock on the way down. That tends to check both reckless short selling by the professionals and liquidation by frightened holders—which is the selling you usually see when a stock gets weaker and weaker, which in turn is what a stock does when it is not supported. These covering purchases of mine constitute what I call the stabilising process.

As the market broadens I of course sell stock on the way up, but never enough to check the rise. This is in strict accordance with my stabilising plans. It is obvious that the more stock I sell on a reasonable and orderly advance the more I encourage the conservative speculators, who are more numerous than the reckless room traders; and in addition the more support I shall be able to give to the stock on the inevitable weak days. By always being short I always am in a position to support the stock without danger to myself. As a rule I begin my selling at a price that will show me a profit. But I often sell without having a profit, simply to create or to increase what I may call my riskless buying power. My business is not alone to put up the price or to sell a big block of stock for a client but to make money for myself. That is why I do not ask any clients to finance my operations. My fee is contingent upon my success.

Of course what I have described is not my invariable practice. I neither have nor adhere to an inflexible system. I modify my terms and conditions according to circumstances. ◁20.15▷

20.15 In this chapter, Lefevre has laid out his most explicit explanation of exactly how manipulation campaigns by operators like Keene and Livermore worked. The passage provides a brilliant primer for investors of any era on exactly how brokerages, underwriters, promoters, and major institutional investors use an increase in volume and volatility to call attention to a stock they wish to strong-arm higher, and then distribute to the unsuspecting public on the way down. "It is perfectly astonishing how much stock a man can get rid of on a decline," Livermore says through Lefevre. True enough.

A few notable examples of Livermore's manipulative efforts include the one million dollars he made on a stock called Computing Tabulator (predecessor to IBM) and the successful manipulation of Mammoth Oil Company, a subsidiary of Sinclair.

MAMMOTH STOCK SOLD.

Block Offered by Jesse L. Livermore Is Oversubscribed.

Jesse L. Livermore, who made his début in a new role when he offered a block of stock of the Mammoth Oil Company, announced yesterday at the close

A stock which it is desired to distribute should be manipulated to the highest possible point and then sold. I repeat this both because it is fundamental and because the public apparently believes that the selling is all done at the top. Sometimes a stock gets waterlogged, as it were; it doesn't go up. That is the time to sell. The price naturally will go down on your selling rather further than you wish, but you can generally nurse it back. As long as a stock that I am manipulating goes up on my buying I know I am all hunky, and if need be I buy it with confidence and use my own money without fear—precisely as I would any other stock that acts the same way. It is the line of least resistance. You remember my trading theories about that line, don't you? Well, when the price line of least resistance is established I follow it, not because I am manipulating that particular stock at that particular moment but because I am a stock operator at all times.

When my buying does not put the stock up I stop buying and then proceed to sell it down; and that also is exactly what I would do with that same stock if I did not happen to be manipulating it. The principal marketing of the stock, as you know, is done on the way down. It is perfectly astonishing how much stock a man can get rid of on a decline.

I repeat that at no time during the manipulation do I forget to be a stock trader. My problems as a manipulator, after all, are the same that confront me as an operator. All manipulation comes to an end when the manipulator cannot make a stock do what he wants it to do. When the stock you are manipulating doesn't act as it should, quit. Don't argue with the tape. Do not seek to lure the profit back. Quit while the quitting is good—and cheap.

ENDNOTES

1 Marc M. Reynolds, "Men and Movements of Finance: The Hocking Pool and James R. Keene," *Moody's Magazine* (1910): 89.

2 Edwin Lefevre, "The Unbeatable Game of Stock Speculation," *Saturday Evening Post*, September 4, 1915, 5.

3 William Worthington Fowler, *Twenty Years in Wall Street* (1880), 555.

4 Henry Clews, *Fifty Years in Wall Street* (New York: Irving Publishing Company, 1908), 234.

5 Edwin Lefevre, "James Robert Keene," *Cosmopolitan* (1903): 94.

6 "Business & Finance: Death of Ryan," *Time*, December 3, 1928.

7 "How Ryan Rose in Wall Street," *New York Times*, November 24, 1928.

8 Peter Caldwell, "Amalgamation or Trust: Anglo-Scottish and American Comparative Legal Institutions and How the Shaped the Nations' Whiskey Industries, 1870–1900," Department of Business and Economics: Eastern Nazarene College, 7.

9 "James R. Keene," *New York Times,* January 30, 1910, Sunday magazine.

10 John Parr, "The Stock Yards of New York," *Everybody's Magazine* (March 1909): 300.

11 C. Norman Fry, "Plain Tales from Chicago: The Stock Exchange and the Trusts," *Outlook* (1909): 593.

12 Lefevre, "James Robert Keene," 94–95.

13 Clews, *Fifty Years in Wall Street,* 801.

14 Matthew Josephson, *The Robber Barons,* 260–264.

15 Burton Jesse Hendrick, *The Age of Big Business* (1919), 70.

16 Henry George Jr., "Modern Methods of 'Finance,'" *Pearson's Magazine,* 58.

17 "James R. Keene," *New York Times,* January 30, 1910.

18 William Peter Hamilton and Charles Henry Dow, *The Stock Market Barometer* (1922), 35.

19 Thomas W. Lawson, "Frenzied Finance," *Everybody's Magazine* (1905): 370.

20 "Topics in Wall Street," *New York Times,* November 16, 1906, 13.

21 "Twain and Rogers Back from Bermuda," *New York Times,* April 14, 1908, 9.

22 "That Third Avenue Deal," *New York Times,* September 17, 1905, 15.

23 "Musical: Opening of the Academy of Music," *New York Times,* October 3, 1854, 4.

24 Henry Edward Krehbiel, *Chapters of Opera* (1908), 85.

25 Josephson, *The Robber Barons,* 205.

26 Maury Klein, *The Life and Legend of Jay Gould* (1986), 204.

27 Josephson, *The Robber Barons,* 206.

28 bid.

29 "Mr. Jay Gould Assaulted," *New York Times,* August 3, 1877, 1.

30 Clews, *Fifty Years in Wall Street,* 232–233.

31 Klein, *The Life and Legend of Jay Gould,* 206.

32 "Mr. Jay Gould Assaulted."

33 Ibid.

34 Ibid.

35 Clews, *Fifty Years in Wall Street,* 730.

36 "Wall Street," *Munsey's Magazine* 10 (October 1893–March 1894): 375–376.

37 Taylor, Charles Henry, *History of the Board of Trade of the City of Chicago* (1917), 564.

38 Isaac F. Marcosson, "The Perilous Game of Cornering a Crop." *Munsey's Magazine* (August 1909), 624.

39 Josephson, *Robber Barons,* 208.

40 Clews, *Fifty Years in Wall Street,* 235.

41 Lefevre, "Unbeatable Game of Stock Speculation," 5.

42 "James R. Keene." *New York Times.* January 5, 1913, 16.

43 Edwin C. Sims, *Capitalism, in Spite of It All.* (1989). 235.

44 "Bar Piggly Wiggly After 52-Point Rise." *New York Times,* March 21, 1923, 1.

45 Ibid.

46 "Annals of Finance: A Corner in Piggly Wiggly," *New Yorker,* June 6, 1959.

47 "The Keedoozle," *Time,* August 30, 1948.

I am well aware that all these generalities do not sound especially impressive. Generalities seldom do. Possibly I may succeed better if I give a concrete example. I'll tell you how I marked up the price of a stock 30 points, and in so doing accumulated only seven thousand shares and developed a market that would absorb almost any amount of stock.

It was Imperial Steel. ◁ 21.1 ▷ The stock had been brought out by reputable people and it had been fairly well tipped as a property of value. About 30 per cent of the capital stock was placed with the general public through various Wall Street houses, but there had been no significant activity in the shares after they were listed. From time to time somebody would ask about it and one or another insider—members of the original underwriting syndicate—would say that the company's earnings were better than expected and the prospects more than encouraging. This was true enough and very good as far as it went, but not exactly thrilling. The speculative appeal was absent, and from the investor's point of view the price stability and dividend permanency of the stock were not yet demonstrated. It was a stock that never behaved sensationally. It was so gentlemanly that no corroborative rise ever followed the insiders' eminently truthful re-

21.2 In most of *Reminiscences*, Lefevre depicts Livermore in his role as a trader. But in Chapters 21, 22, and 23, we see Livermore in a role he took on later in life: as an "operator," a polite term for "manipulator." We learn in great detail how corporate insiders and outside financiers pooled their shares in a company that was not moving fast enough for their liking and hired pros like Livermore to sell them to the public at higher prices.

Livermore takes pains to explain that he would not manipulate a stock unless he believed it was financially sound. He explains that he demanded call options on the stock as a fee so that his interests were aligned with those of his customers, as he could sell his shares at a low, preset price once he had manipulated them higher. Livermore would order the pool shareholders to put their stock in an escrow account so that they could not interfere with his manipulation by selling at the wrong time. He often funded the manipulation himself for the same reason: He did not want anyone, even his customers, to know what he was doing.

There were no regulations prohibiting manipulation in the early 1900s, and it was not considered illegal unless false statements were made. Pools also were not permitted to buy and sell stock among themselves to make it look as if it were more active, a practice called "wash sales."

ports. On the other hand, neither did the price decline.

Imperial Steel remained unhonoured and unsung and untipped, content to be one of those stocks that don't go down because nobody sells and that nobody sells because nobody likes to go short of a stock that is not well distributed; the seller is too much at the mercy of the loaded-up inside clique. Similarly, there is no inducement to buy such a stock. To the investor Imperial Steel therefore remained a speculation. To the speculator it was a dead one—the kind that makes an investor of you against your will by the simple expedient of falling into a trance the moment you go long of it. The chap who is compelled to lug a corpse a year or two always loses more than the original cost of the deceased; he is sure to find himself tied up with it when some really good things come his way.

One day the foremost member of the Imperial Steel syndicate, acting for himself and associates, came to see me. They wished to create a market for the stock, of which they controlled the undistributed 70 per cent. They wanted me to dispose of their holdings **21.2** at better prices than they thought they would obtain if they tried to sell in the open market. They wanted to know on what terms I would undertake the job.

I told him that I would let him know in a few days. Then I looked into the property. I had experts go over the various departments of the company—industrial, commercial and financial. They made reports to me which were unbiased. I wasn't looking for the good or the bad points, but for the facts, such as they were.

The reports showed that it was a valuable property. The prospects justified purchases of the stock at the prevailing market price—if the investor were willing to wait a little. Under the circumstances an advance in the price would in reality be the commonest and most legitimate of all market movements—to wit, the process of discounting the future. There was therefore no reason that I could see why I should not conscientiously and confidently undertake the bull manipulation of Imperial Steel.

I let my man know my mind and he called at my office to talk the deal over in detail. I told him what my terms were. For my services I asked no cash, but calls on one hundred thousand shares of the Imperial Steel stock. The price of the calls ran up from 70 to 100. That may seem like a big fee to some. But they should consider that the insiders were certain they themselves could not sell one hundred thousand shares, or even fifty thousand shares, at 70. There was no market for the stock. All the talk about wonderful earnings and excellent prospects had not brought in buyers, not to any great extent. In addition, I could not get my fee in cash without my clients first making some millions of dollars. What I stood to make was not an exorbitant selling commission. It was a fair contingent fee.

Knowing that the stock had real value and that general market conditions were bullish and therefore favourable for an advance in all good stocks, I figured that I ought to do pretty well. My clients were encouraged by the opinions I expressed, agreed to my terms at once, and the deal began with pleasant feelings all around.

I proceeded to protect myself as thoroughly as I could. The syndicate owned or controlled about 70 per cent of the outstanding stock. I had them deposit their 70 per cent under a trust agreement. I didn't propose to be used as a dumping ground for the big holders. With the majority holdings thus securely tied up, I still had 30 per cent of scattered holdings to consider, but that was a risk I had to take. Experienced speculators do not expect ever to engage in utterly riskless ventures. As a matter of fact, it was not much

21.3 As a trader who had been around the block a few times, Livermore was a natural choice for pools looking for a manipulator. It was also relatively sure money, which traders who lived on the edge welcomed. He approached the job of pushing a stock higher with the perspective of his target audience in his mind, ensuring that traders would believe the path of least resistance was higher.

As Chapters 21 and 22 make clear, Livermore was leery of his pool partners; he feared that he would be double-crossed and left holding stocks at untenable prices. But when he leaned into the task, contemporary accounts suggest that his manipulations had the mark of artistry, as he painted the tape to make it look as if there were higher-than-natural demand for a stock—buying just enough to pique the unsuspecting public's interest.

He would also sometimes let shares fall just enough below certain levels on high volume to entice a heavy round of short selling, then would pull the chain to force bears to cover, propelling the stock much higher. He makes clear that his efforts were oriented toward shoving a stock toward a predetermined top by any legal means and then selling the pool's shares on the way down into a falling market. He did this by letting the price sink off the top and then buying just enough to make the public think it was witnessing a mere correction off the high.

The public's attempt to buy this manufactured dip would then create a second, equivalent high—familiar to traders as a "double top"—that he would sell into with high volume. This is why old highs become formidable barriers: They represent a lot of supply overhang. And of course this was a key reason that Livermore says he liked to buy new highs, as they were largely possible only when a stock was free from the gravity of oversupply.

more likely that all the untrusteed stock would be thrown on the market at one fell swoop than that all the policyholders of a life-insurance company would die at the same hour, the same day. There are unprinted actuarial tables of stock-market risks as well as of human mortality.

Having protected myself from some of the avoidable dangers of a stock-market deal of that sort, I was ready to begin my campaign. **21.3** Its objective was to make my calls valuable. To do this I must put up the price and develop a market in which I could sell one hundred thousand shares—the stock in which I held options.

The first thing I did was to find out how much stock was likely to come on the market on an advance. This was easily done through my brokers, who had no trouble in ascertaining what stock was for sale at or a little above the market. I don't know whether the specialists told them what orders they had on their books or not. The price was nominally 70, but I could not have sold one thousand shares at that price. I had no evidence of even a moderate demand at that figure or even a few points lower. I had to go by what my brokers found out. But it was enough to show me how much stock there was for sale and how little was wanted.

As soon as I had a line on these points I quietly took all the stock that was for sale at 70 and higher. When I say "I" you will understand that I mean my brokers. The sales were for account of some of the minority holders because my clients naturally had cancelled whatever selling orders they might have given out before they tied up their stock.

I didn't have to buy very much stock. Moreover, I knew that the right kind of advance would bring in other buying orders—and, of course, selling orders also.

I didn't give bull tips on Imperial Steel to anybody. I didn't have to. My job was to seek directly to influence sentiment by the best possible kind of publicity. I do not say that there should never be bull propaganda. It is as legitimate and indeed as desirable to advertise the value of a new stock as to advertise the value of woolens or shoes or automobiles. Accurate and reliable information should be given to the public. But what I meant was that the tape did all that was needed for my purpose. As I said before, the reputable newspapers always try to print explanations for market movements. It is news. Their readers demand to know not only what happens in the stock market but why it happens. Therefore without the manipulator lifting a finger the financial writers will print all the available information and gossip, and also analyse the reports of earnings, trade condition and outlook; in short, whatever may throw light on the advance. Whenever a newspaperman or an acquaintance asks my opinion of a stock and I have one I do not hesitate to express it. I do not volunteer advice and I never give tips, but I have nothing to gain in my operations from secrecy. At the same time I realise that the best of all tipsters, the most persuasive of all salesmen, is the tape.

When I had absorbed all the stock that was for sale at 70 and a little higher I relieved the market of that pressure, and naturally that made clear for trading purposes the line of least resistance in Imperial Steel. It was manifestly upward. The moment that fact was perceived by the observant traders on the floor they logically assumed that the stock was in for an advance the extent of which they could not know; but they knew enough to begin buying. Their demand for Imperial Steel, created exclusively by the obviousness of the stock's rising tendency—the tape's infallible bull tip!—I promptly filled. I sold to the traders the stock that I had bought from the tired-out holders at the beginning. Of course this selling was judiciously done; I contented myself with supplying the demand. I was not forcing my stock on the market and I did not want too rapid an advance. It wouldn't have been good business to sell out the half of my one hundred thousand shares at that stage of the proceedings. My job was to make a market on which I might sell my entire line.

But even though I sold only as much as the traders were anxious to buy, the market was temporarily deprived of my own buying power, which I had hitherto exerted steadily. In due course the traders' purchases ceased and the price stopped rising. As soon as that happened there began the selling by disappointed bulls or by those traders whose reasons for buying disappeared the instant the rising tendency was checked. But I was ready for this selling, and on the way down I bought back the stock I had sold to the traders a couple of points higher. This buying of stock I knew was bound to be sold in turn checked the downward course; and when the price stopped going down the selling orders stopped coming in.

I then began all over again. I took all the stock that was for sale on the way up—it wasn't very much—and the price began to rise a second time; from a higher starting point than 70. Don't forget that on the way down there are many holders who wish to heaven they had sold theirs but won't do it three or four points from the top. Such speculators always vow they will surely sell out if there is a rally. They put in their orders to sell on the way up, and then they change their minds with the change in the stock's price-trend. Of course there is always profit taking from safe-playing quick runners to whom a profit is always a profit to be taken.

All I had to do after that was to repeat the process; alternately buying and selling; but always working higher.

Sometimes, after you have taken all the stock that is for sale, it pays to rush up the price sharply, to have what might be called little bull flurries in the stock you are manipulating. It is excellent advertising, because it makes talk and also brings in both the professional traders and that portion of the speculating public that likes action. 21.4 It is, I think, a large portion. I did that in Imperial Steel, and whatever demand was created by those spurts I supplied. My selling always kept the upward movement within bounds both as to extent and as to speed. In buying on the way down and selling on the way up I was doing more than marking up the price: I was developing the marketability of Imperial Steel.

After I began my operations in it there never was a time when a man could not buy or sell the stock freely; I mean by this, buy or sell a reasonable amount without causing over-violent fluctuations in the price. The fear of being left high and dry if he bought, or squeezed to death if he sold, was gone. The gradual spread among the professionals and the public of a belief in the permanence of the market for Imperial Steel had much to do with creating confidence in the movement; and, of course, the activity also put an end to a lot of other objections. The result was that after buying and selling a good many thousands of shares I succeeded in making the stocks sell at par. At one hundred dollars a share everybody wanted to buy Imperial Steel. Why not? Everybody now knew that it was a good stock; that it had been and still was a bargain. The proof was the rise. A stock that could go thirty points from 70 could go up thirty more from par. That is the way a good many argued.

In the course of marking up the price those thirty points I accumulated only seven thousand shares. The price on this line averaged me almost exactly 85. That meant a profit of fifteen points on it; but, of course, my entire profit, still on paper, was much more. It was a safe enough profit, for I had a market for all I wanted to sell. The stock would sell higher on judicious manipulation and I had graduated calls on one hundred thousand shares beginning at 70 and ending at 100.

21.4 Creating "bull flurries" was a common strategy for pool operators and market manipulators, and you can still see it occur today. Traders are always attracted by shiny objects, just like fish are attracted to silvery lures.

Keene famously used this technique with U.S. Steel, as historian Frederick Lewis Allen writes: "Keene's manipulative operations were fulfilling the triple function of providing a steadying influence for the market price, of advertising Steel common on the ticker tape and in brokers' offices and on financial pages and wherever speculators and investors gathered, and of providing plenty of buyers for those who had been allotted stock and wished to unload and gather in their cash."[1]

Circumstances prevented me from carrying out certain plans of mine for converting my paper profits into good hard cash. It had been, if I do say so myself, a beautiful piece of manipulation, strictly legitimate and deservedly successful. The property of the company was valuable and the stock was not dear at the higher price. One of the members of the original syndicate developed a desire to secure the control of the property—a prominent banking house with ample resources. The control of a prosperous and growing concern like the Imperial Steel Corporation is possibly more valuable to a banking firm than to individual investors. At all events, this firm made me an offer for all my options on the stock. It meant an enormous profit for me, and I instantly took it. I am always willing to sell out when I can do so in a lump at a good profit. I was quite content with what I made out of it.

Before I disposed of my calls on the hundred thousand shares I learned that these bankers had employed more experts to make a still more thorough examination of the property. Their reports showed enough to bring me in the offer I got. I kept several thousand shares of the stock for investment. I believe in it.

There wasn't anything about my manipulation of Imperial Steel that wasn't normal and sound. As long as the price went up on my buying I knew I was O.K. The stock never got waterlogged, as a stock sometimes does. When you find that it fails to respond adequately to your buying you don't need any better tip to sell. You know that if there is any value to a stock and general market conditions are right you can always nurse it back after a decline, no matter if it's twenty points. But I never had to do anything like that in Imperial Steel.

In my manipulation of stocks I never lose sight of basic trading principles. Perhaps you wonder why I repeat this or why I keep on harping on

21.5 **Colonel John Wing Prentiss**, a senior partner in the prominent New York brokerage Hornblower & Weeks, became notorious for offering Henry Ford $1 billion three separate times from 1924 to 1927 for control of the Ford Motor Co.[2]

Born in Maine in 1875 and a graduate of Phillips Academy and Harvard University, he was described by the *New York Times* as a young man who attracted the attention of firm owner John W. Weeks for his strength as a bond salesman in Boston "at a time when the general public knew nothing and cared less about bond issues."[3] Prentiss handled financing for Dodge, Chevrolet, General Motors, and Hudson Motors, and his daring attempt to capture Ford at a time when it was down on its luck was considered a spectacular, if ultimately unsuccessful, raid.

Weeks, who later became a U.S. senator from Massachusetts and served as secretary of war under presidents Warren Harding and Calvin Coolidge, described Prentiss's application for his first job in this way:

When Prentiss came into our office I told him there wasn't a chance, because we had twice as many young men in the office as we could use. He said he didn't care about salary, and when I asked him how soon he could go to work if we found a place for him he answered, "right now," and took off his coat and hung it up. I had to give him a job.[3]

Prentiss served in the U.S. Army as a logistics aide during World War I and was discharged as a lieutenant colonel. After the crash of 1929, the avid golfer and squash player served on many committees tasked with determining ways to improve Wall Street practices and help New York Stock Exchange members who had become unemployed. He was particularly noted for his role in unwinding the mess left after the Stutz Motor Co. pool was crushed.

Livermore's diatribe against Prentiss in *Reminiscences* for exhibiting naïveté as a pool operator is indicative of the veteran trader's contempt for the Wall Street establishment. It is a rare passage in which Livermore directly airs his side of a bitter grievance over a failed deal.

the fact that I never argue with the tape or lose my temper at the market because of its behaviour. You would think—wouldn't you?—that shrewd men who have made millions in their own business and in addition have successfully operated in Wall Street at times would realise the wisdom of playing the game dispassionately. Well, you would be surprised at the frequency with which some of our most successful promoters behave like peevish women because the market does not act the way they wish it to act. They seem to take it as a personal slight, and they proceed to lose money by first losing their temper.

There has been much gossip about a disagreement between John Prentiss 21.5 and myself. People have been led to expect a dramatic narrative of a stock-market deal that went wrong or some double-crossing that cost me—or him—millions; or something of that sort. Well, it wasn't.

> **21.6** Many small petroleum companies began popping up around this time in the wake of the breakup of the Standard Oil monopoly. Examples include King Petroleum, Cushing Petroleum, and Mexican Petroleum. Traders would affectionately abbreviate the names to "Pete" for convenience.
>
> Although there is no record of a Petroleum Products Co., Livermore was famously involved in a pool focused on the shares of Mammoth Oil, a subsidiary of Sinclair Oil. The company was embroiled a short while later in the Teapot Dome scandal, which brought down the Harding administration's secretary of the interior on a bribery conviction. Livermore told a Senate committee that he "made a market" by buying and selling $10 million worth of stock.[4]

312   CURB MARKET.

1920—(Continued)

COMPANY	Par	Sales No. Shares	Open	Low	High	Last Sale	COMPANY	Par	Sales No. Shares	Open	Low	High	Last Sale
OTHER OIL STOCKS—(Con)							**OTHER OIL STOCKS**—(Concl.)						
Canadian American Oil & Gas...1		44,200	¾	⅜	⅝	⅜	Steiner Oil Corporation....(no par)		25,240	15	3	15¼	4⅝
Carib Syndicate		770,400	53	5¾	53	7	Texas Oil & Refining............1		4,600	7-16		7-16	
Carib Trading		5,148	85	18	85	20½	Texas Atlantic Oil...........		15,700	1¾	1⅜	1¾	1⅜
Casa Oil		6,4 C	2	1¼	4	2	Texas Chief Oil.............10		65,300			47⅛	11
Central Amer Petrol Corp. (no par)		80,600	31	15	35	31	Texas Company new........26		317,600	55½	43¾	59¾	49¾
Central Petroleum common........5		2,100	34	30	35	31	Texas Pacific Coal & Oil.....10		104,200	139	58	139	47½
Preferred.........100		3,800	71	66	79	72	Texas Ranger Prod & Refining...		253,500	1¼	1-16	1¼	1-1⅜
Central States Oil..........1		11,600	2		2¼		Texas-Kentucky Oil Corp.....5		66,150	3¼	¾	4¼	
Circle Oil		29,100	4½	3	5¾	3¾	Texon Oil & Land..........		2,037,500	½	¼	1¼	¾
Continental Refining.........10		38,700	4	3	5¼		Thraman Oil..............		35,800	2¾	⅜	3¾	1⅜
Cosden & Co common........		243,700	9¼	3	10¾	8¼	Trinity Oil..............		79,950		⅜	1¼	1¼
Creole Syndicate..........		16,900	7¾		7¾	1½	Tropical Oil.............26		203,700	21	15	23¾	18
Cushing Petroleum..........		776,300		¼	3	⅜	Union Oil of California......100		525	177	177	182	182
Del-Tex Petroleum..........		82,100	1½	⅜	3	1½	United Texas Petroleum...		640,200	1¼	⅜	1¼	

Prentiss and I had been friendly for years. He had given me at various times information that I was able to utilise profitably, and I had given him advice which he may or may not have followed. If he did he saved money.

He was largely instrumental in the organisation and promotion of the Petroleum Products Company. **21.6** After a more or less successful market début general conditions changed for the worse and the new stock did not fare as well as Prentiss and his associates had hoped. When basic conditions took a turn for the better Prentiss formed a pool and began operations in Pete Products.

I cannot tell you anything about his technique. He didn't tell me how he worked and I didn't ask him. But it was plain that notwithstanding his Wall Street experience and his undoubted cleverness, whatever it was he did proved of little value and it didn't take the pool long to find out that they couldn't get rid of much stock. He must have tried everything he knew, because a pool manager does not ask to be superseded by an outsider unless he feels unequal to the task, and that is the last thing the average man likes to admit. At all events he came to me and after some friendly preliminaries he said he wanted me to take charge of the market for Pete Products and dispose of the pool's holdings, which amounted to a little over one hundred thousand shares. The stock was selling at 102 to 103.

The thing looked dubious to me and I declined his proposition with thanks. But he insisted that I accept. He put it on personal grounds, so that in the end I consented. I constitutionally dislike to identify myself with enterprises in the success of which I cannot feel confidence, but I also think a man owes something to his friends and acquaintances. I said I would do my best, but I told him I did not feel very cocky about it and I enumerated the adverse factors that I would have to contend with. But all Prentiss said to that was that he wasn't asking me to guarantee millions in profits to the pool. He was sure that if I took hold I'd make out well enough to satisfy any reasonable being.

Well, there I was, engaged in doing something against my own judgment. I found, as I feared, a pretty tough state of affairs, due in great measure to Prentiss' own mistakes while he was manipulating the stock for account of the pool. But the chief factor against me was time. I was convinced that we were rapidly approaching the end of a bull swing and therefore that the improvement in the market, which had so encouraged Prentiss, would prove to be merely a short-lived rally. I feared that the market would turn definitely bearish before I could accomplish much with Pete Products. However, I had given my promise and I decided to work as hard as I knew how.

I started to put up the price. I had moderate success. I think I ran it up to 107 or thereabouts, which was pretty fair, and I was even able to sell a little stock on balance. It wasn't much, but I was glad not to have increased the pool's holdings. There were a lot of people not in the pool who were just waiting for a small rise to dump their stock, and I was a godsend to them. Had general conditions been better I also would have done better. It was too bad that I wasn't called in earlier. All I could do now, I felt, was to get out with as little loss as possible to the pool.

I sent for Prentiss and told him my views. But he started to object. I then explained to him why I took the position I did. I said: "Prentiss, I can feel very plainly the pulse of the market. There is no follow-up in your stock. It is no trick to see just what the public's reaction is to my manipulation. Listen: When Pete Products is made as attractive to traders as possible and you give it all the support needed at all times and notwithstanding all that you find that the public leaves it alone you may be sure that there is something wrong, not with the stock but with the market. There is absolutely no use in trying to force matters. You are bound to lose if you do. A pool manager should be willing to buy his own stock when he has company. But when he is the only buyer in the market he'd be an ass to buy it. For every five thousand shares I buy the public ought to be willing or able to buy five thousand more. But I certainly am not going to do all the buying. If I did, all I would succeed in doing would be to get soaked with a lot of long stock that I don't want. There is only one thing to do, and that is to sell. And the only way to sell is to sell."

"You mean, sell for what you can get?" asked Prentiss.

"Right!" I said. I could see he was getting ready to object. "If I am to sell the pool's stock at all you can make up your mind that the price is going to break through par and——"

"Oh, no! Never!" he yelled. You'd have imagined I was asking him to join a suicide club. ◁**21.7**▷

21.7 ▶ The term was popularized in 1878 by a series of macabre detective fiction from Scottish novelist Robert Louis Stevenson called, "The Suicide Club." In the stories, the characters of Prince Florizel of Bohemia and sidekick Colonel Geraldine sneak into a secret society of people who are set on killing themselves but don't have to courage to do it themselves. Set in the gas-lit streets of Victorian-era London, the work begins with the characters dining at an oyster bar when a man starts handing out cream tarts for free. Intrigued by such odd behavior, the two protagonists invite the man to dinner, whereupon they learn of the suicide club.

Lefevre actually wrote about the stories in the context of the stock boom of 1901. In an article for *Munsey's Magazine,* he said: "Stevenson, you remember, had a coward in his 'Suicide Club' who threw dice with Death to enjoy the delights of fear, because when he escaped he tasted the intense joys of living."[5]

He continued: "It is the same in stock gambling—the delightful uncertainty; the grim 'now you see it and now you don't' of luck; the little chills of pleasure; the leaden sinking of disappointment; the magnified joys of anticipation; the exquisite expectancy—all this fires the blood of the young, as does love, and of the old, as love no longer can."[6]

The stories were later adapted into plays, movies, and television shows. In Lefevre's time, the sobriquet "Suicide Club" was also given to the Tank Corps commanded in France during World War I by Col. George Patton in 1918.

"Prentiss," I said to him, "it is a cardinal principle of stock manipulation to put up a stock in order to sell it. But you don't sell in bulk on the advance. You can't. The big selling is done on the way down from the top. I cannot put up your stock to 125 or 130. I'd like to, but it can't be done. So you will have to begin your selling from this level. In my opinion all stocks are going down, and Petroleum Products isn't going to be the one exception. It is better for it to go down now on the pool's selling than for it to break next month on selling by some one else. It will go down anyhow."

I can't see that I said anything harrowing, but you could have heard his howls in China. He simply wouldn't listen to such a thing. It would never do. It would play the dickens with the stock's record, to say nothing of inconvenient possibilities at the banks where the stock was held as collateral on loans, and so on.

I told him again that in my judgment nothing in the world could prevent Pete Products from breaking fifteen or twenty points, because the entire market was headed that way, and I once more said it was absurd to expect his stock to be a dazzling exception. But again my talk went for nothing. He insisted that I support the stock.

Here was a shrewd business man, one of the most successful promoters of the day, who had made millions in Wall Street deals and knew much more than the average man about the game of specula-tion, actually insisting on supporting a stock in an incipient bear market. It was his stock, to be sure, but it was nevertheless bad business. So much so that it went against the grain and I again began to argue with him. But it was no use. He insisted on putting in supporting orders.

Of course when the general market got weak and the decline began in earnest Pete Products went with the rest. Instead of selling I actually bought stock for the insiders' pool—by Prentiss' orders.

The only explanation is that Prentiss did not believe the bear market was right on top of us. I myself was confident that the bull market was over. I had verified my first surmise by tests not alone in Pete Products but in other stocks as well. I didn't wait for the bear market to announce its safe ar-rival before I started selling. Of course I didn't sell a share of Pete Products, though I was short of other stocks.

The Pete Products pool, as I expected, was hung up with all they held to begin with and with all they had to take in their futile effort to hold up the price. In the end they did liquidate; but at much lower figures than they would have got if Prentiss had let me sell when and as I wished. It could not be other-wise. But Prentiss still thinks he was right—or says he does. I understand he says the reason I gave him the advice I did was that I was short of other stocks and the general market was going up. It implies, of course, that the break in Pete Products that would have resulted from selling out the pool's holdings at any price would have helped my bear position in other stocks.

That is all tommyrot. I was not bearish because I was short of stocks. I was bearish because that was the way I sized up the situation, and I sold stocks short only after I turned bearish. There never is much money in doing things wrong end to; not in the stock market. My plan for selling the pool's stock was based on what the experience of twenty years told me alone was feasible and therefore wise. Prentiss ought to have been enough of a trader to see it as plainly as I did. It was too late to try to do anything else.

I suppose Prentiss shares the delusion of thousands of outsiders who think a manipulator can do anything. He can't. The biggest thing Keene did was his manipulation of U. S. Steel common and preferred in the spring of 1901. He succeeded not because he was clever and resourceful and not because he had a syndicate of the richest men in the country back of him. He succeeded partly because of those reasons but chiefly because the general market was right and the public's state of mind was right. ⟨21.8⟩

It isn't good business for a man to act against the teachings of experience and against common sense. But the suckers in Wall Street are not all outsiders. Prentiss' grievance against me is what I have just told you. He feels sore because I did my manipulation not as I wanted to but as he asked me to.

There isn't anything mysterious or underhanded or crooked about manipulation designed to sell a stock in bulk provided such operations are not accompanied by deliberate misrepresentations. Sound manipulation must be based on sound trading principles. People lay great stress on old-time practices, such as wash sales. But I can assure you that the mere mechanics of deception count for very little. The difference between stock-market manipulation

21.8 Here Livermore is referring to the boom times of 1901, a period marked by intense public participation in stock speculation as new industrial combinations were formed, new shares issued, and business prospered in the wake of President McKinley's reaffirmation of the gold standard.

He wants the reader to understand the stark difference between the enthusiasm seen in a real bull market and the torpor of the sideways market in which he found himself entombed with Prentiss.

It's impossible to overstate the craze for stocks that entranced the public in 1901, helping Keene unload his U.S. Steel shares. Henry Clews compared amateur stock bulls at the time to drunkards in an epitaph that could be applied again to every subsequent bull cycle:

> They have been engaged now for such a prolonged period in buying, buying, buying, making profits on all their ventures, as to make them like the inebriate, callous to all adverse factors whenever they come up. High prices don't frighten them; scarcity and high rates for money don't frighten them; strikes don't frighten them. Buying and holding on have simply become chronic with them.[7]

A history of the New York Stock Exchange added: "From Maine to Texas small-bore investors rushed to the savings bank or the woolen stocking and appears as buyers of the new securities. What prices they were paying they seemed not even to care to understand."[8]

Surveying the frenzy, historian Alexander Dana Noyes wrote that "old and experienced capitalists lost their heads, asserted publically that the old traditions of finance no longer held and that a new order of things must now be reckoned with, and joined the dance." As for everyone else, he said, "The 'outside public,' meantime, seemed to lose all restraint. A stream of excited customers, of every description, brought their money down to Wall Street, and spent their days in offices near the Stock Exchange."[9]

and the over-the-counter sale of stocks and bonds is in the character of the clientele rather than in the character of the appeal. J. P. Morgan & Co. sell an issue of bonds to the public—that is, to investors. A manipulator disposes of a block of stock to the public—that is, to speculators. An investor looks for safety, for permanence of the interest return on the capital he invests. The speculator looks for a quick profit.

The manipulator necessarily finds his primary market among speculators—who are willing to run a greater than normal business risk so long as they have a reasonable chance to get a big return on their capital. I myself never have believed in blind gambling. I may plunge or I may buy one hundred shares. But in either case I must have a reason for what I do.

I distinctly remember how I got into the game of manipulation—that is, in the marketing of stocks for others. It gives me pleasure to recall it because it shows so beautifully the professional Wall Street attitude toward stock-market operations. It happened after I had "come back"—that is, after my Bethlehem Steel trade in 1915 started me on the road to financial recovery.

I traded pretty steadily and had very good luck. I have never sought newspaper publicity, but neither have I gone out of my way to hide myself. At the same time, you know that professional Wall Street exaggerates both the successes and the failures of whichever operator happens to be active; and, of course, the newspapers hear about him and print rumors. I have been broke so many times, according to the gossips, or have made so many millions, according to the same authorities, that my only reaction to such reports is to wonder how and where they are born. And how they grow! I have had broker friend after broker friend bring the same story to me, a little changed each time, improved, more circumstantial.

All this preface is to tell you how I first came to undertake the manipulation of a stock for someone else. The stories the newspapers printed of how I had paid back in full the millions I owed did the trick. My plungings and my winnings were so magnified by the newspapers that I was talked about in Wall Street. The day was past when an operator swinging a line of two hundred thousand shares of stock could dominate the market. But, as you know, the public always desires to find successors to the old leaders. It was Mr. Keene's reputation as a skilful stock operator, a winner of millions on his own hook, that made promoters and banking houses apply to him for selling large blocks of securities. In short, his services as manipulator were in demand because of the stories the Street had heard about his previous successes as a trader.

But Keene was gone—passed on to that heaven where he once said he wouldn't stay a moment unless he found Sysonby ⟨**21.9**⟩ there waiting for him. Two or three other men who made stock-market history for a few months had relapsed into the obscurity of prolonged inactivity. I refer particularly to certain of those plunging Westerners who came to Wall Street in 1901 and after making many millions out of their Steel holdings remained in Wall Street. They were in reality superpromoters rather than operators of the Keene type. But they were extremely able, extremely rich and extremely successful in the securities of the companies which they and their friends controlled. They were not really great manipulators, like Keene or Governor Flower. ⟨**21.10**⟩ Still, the Street found in them plenty to gossip about and they certainly had a following among the professionals and the sportier commission houses. After they ceased to trade actively the Street found itself without manipulators; at least, it couldn't read about them in the newspapers.

21.9 Sysonby, a racehorse born in Kentucky in 1902, is ranked 30th in a list of the top 100 Thoroughbred champions of the twentieth century. Upon his death in June 1906, the *New York Times* ran a long obituary, calling Sysonby "possibly the greatest race horse of the American turf."[10]

Keene had bought Sysonby's mother at an auction, bred her in Kentucky, and then reaped the benefit of careful development by top trainer James G. Rowe.[11] Sysonby won all but one of the major stakes races in which he was entered—and that single loss stemmed from being drugged by a corrupt stable hand. Sysonby was inducted into the National Museum of Racing and Hall of Fame in Saratoga, New York, in 1956.[12] When the horse's life was cut short by blood poisoning, the *New York Times* reported that Keene was "greatly shocked by the news of his loss, as Sysonby was his favorite above all the great horses that he had ever owned."

21.10 ▶ **Roswell Pettibone Flower,** born in 1835, was the governor of New York from 1892 to 1894 and also served two terms in the U.S. Congress. He was best remembered by Livermore, however, as a legendary Wall Street financier and operator who owned the banking firm R. P. Flower & Co.

The sixth of nine boys born to a wool carder in upstate New York, Flower worked at a store for $5 a month to earn enough to attend high school, then launched his first career as teacher who boarded with his pupils.[13] He later became a deputy postmaster at $50 a month and loved to tell trader friends later that after buying a gold watch for $50 one day, he turned around and sold it to another man for $53. After six years, Roswell had saved enough money to buy a half interest in a jewelry store for $1,000 and soon managed to buy out his partner and expand the business. He made a strong impression on a wealthy railroad president, Henry Keep, who married his wife's sister, and when that man died, Flower found himself the trustee of the widow's $4 million estate.

Flower moved to Manhattan to manage the funds and accumulated his own fortune as a stock operator in the 1870s. He spent the next two and a half decades in politics and returned to Wall Street in the late 1880s. The *New York Times* reported that he made a fortune in 1898 by wading confidently into the panic that resulted from the sinking of the USS *Maine* in Havana Harbor—the incident that sparked the Spanish-American War. The report said: "He came into the market with a vigor and showed such confidence that he became apparently the master of the situation. Under his leadership the markets started upward, and gains in market value were tremendous."[14]

The *Times* reported that Flower declared himself bullish on U.S. stocks with this statement: "I am a believer in American stocks and a buyer of American stocks because I am a believer in our country." The newspaper said he faced "violent opposition" from the powerful speculators James Keene and Russell Sage, but his stocks rose by $100 million and "have since been continually strong and have been more popular than any other group in the Street." When his optimism won out, the *Times* crowed that the former governor had "whipped the enemy entire."[15]

Following his death in the evening of May 12, 1899, from heart disease, a mini panic ensued as the stocks he frequently bulled fell by as much as 30 points on the loss of such a strident supporter. The lows came in the opening minutes of trading, with New York Air Brake falling from $185 to $125 with declines of $5 to $10 between transactions before recovering to close at $164.[16] But the damage was done as the bull market of 1899 died along with Flower. Henry Clews writes that Flower had "a very plain exterior" and "used language that was noticeable more for its force and directness and emphasis, than it was for polish."[17]

You remember the big bull market that began when the Stock Exchange resumed business in 1915. As the market broadened and the Allies' purchases in this country mounted into billions we ran into a boom. As far as manipulation went, it wasn't necessary for anybody to lift a finger to create an unlimited market for a war bride. Scores of men made millions by capitalizing contracts or even promises of contracts. They became successful promoters, either with the aid of friendly bankers or by bringing out their companies on the Curb market. The public bought anything that was adequately touted.

When the bloom wore off the boom, some of these promoters found themselves in need of help from experts in stock salesmanship. When the public is hung up with all kinds of securities, some of them purchased at higher prices, it is not an easy task to dispose of untried stocks. After a boom the public is positive that nothing is going up. It isn't that buyers become more discriminating, but that the blind buying is over. It is the state of mind that has changed. Prices don't even have to go down to make people pessimistic. It is enough if the market gets dull and stays dull for a time.

In every boom companies are formed primarily if not exclusively to take advantage of the public's appetite for all kinds of stocks. Also there are belated promotions. The reason why promoters make that mistake is that being human they are unwilling to see the end of the boom. Moreover, it is good business to take chances when the possible profit is big enough. The top is never in sight when the vision is vitiated by hope. The average man sees a stock that nobody wanted at twelve dollars or fourteen dollars a share suddenly advance to thirty—which surely is the top—until it rises to fifty. That is absolutely the end of the rise. Then it goes to sixty; to seventy; to seventy-five. It then becomes a certainty that this stock, which a few weeks ago was selling for less than fifteen, can't go any higher. But it goes to eighty; and to eighty-five. Whereupon the average man, who never thinks of values but of prices, and is not governed in his actions by conditions but by fears, takes the easiest way—he stops thinking that there must be a limit to the advances. That is why those outsiders who are wise enough not to buy at the top make up for it by not taking profits. The big money in booms is always made first by the public—on paper. And it remains on paper.

ENDNOTES

1 Frederick Lewis Allen, *The Lords of Creation* (1935), 34.

2 "Prentiss' Rise Spectacular," *New York Times*, February 3, 1927, 2.

3 "Col. J.W. Prentiss, Broker, Dies at 62," *New York Times*, March 19, 1938, 15.

4 "Jesse Livermore Ends Life in Hotel." *New York Times*, November 29, 1940, 1.

5 Edwin Lefevre, "Boom Days in Wall Street." *Munsey's Magazine*, 1901, 39.

6 Ibid.

7 Henry Clews, *Fifty Years in Wall Street* (1907), 757.

8 Edmund Clarence Stedman, ed., *The New York Stock Exchange* (1905), 394.

9 Alexander Dana Noyes, *Forty Years of American Finance* (1909), 301.

10 "Famous Sysonby Dead of Blood Poisoning," *New York Times*, June 18, 1906, 1.

11 "Famous Race Horses: Sysonby," Horseracing.com.

12 National Museum of Racing and Hall of Fame, racingmuseum.org/hall.

13 "Roswell P. Flower Dies Suddenly," *New York Times*, May 13, 1899, 1.

14 Ibid.

15 Ibid.

16 Stedman, *The New York Stock Exchange,* 384.

17 Clews, *Fifty Years in Wall Street,* 703.

One day Jim Barnes,  who not only was one of my principal brokers but an intimate friend as well, called on me. He said he wanted me to do him a great favour. He never before had talked that way, and so I asked him to tell me what the favour was, hoping it was something I could do, for I certainly wished to oblige him. He then told me that his firm was interested in a certain stock; in fact, they had been the principal promoters of the company and had placed the greater part of the stock. Circumstances had arisen that made it imperative for them to market a rather large block. Jim wanted me to undertake to do the marketing for him. The stock was Consolidated Stove.

I did not wish to have anything to do with it for various reasons. But Barnes, to whom I was under some obligations, insisted on the personal-favour phase of the matter, which alone could overcome my objections. He was a good fellow, a friend, and his firm, I gathered, was pretty heavily involved, so in the end I consented to do what I could.

It has always seemed to me that the most picturesque point of difference between the war boom and other booms was the part that was played by a type new in stock-market affairs—the boy banker. **22.2**

The boom was stupendous and its origins and causes were plainly to be grasped by all. But at the same time the greatest banks and trust companies in the country certainly did all they could to help make millionaires overnight of all sorts and conditions of promoters and munition makers. It got so that all

22.1 James Barnes was a member of the New York Stock Exchange for almost 50 years, retiring from the firm Barnes Brothers at age 72 in 1927.[1] He was born in New York in 1855 and started work as a stockbroker in 1879.

Livermore says he was surprised that Barnes sought a favor because he had "never before talked that way." This may be because Barnes Brothers had developed a reputation as a brokerage that did not care much for shenanigans. In an August 22, 1908, NYSE session that the *New York Times* called "wildly manipulated," Barnes Brothers was among a group of brokerages that strongly denounced the "flagrant violation of recognized standards of trading," and refused to accept suspicious orders.[2]

22.2 Livermore expresses distaste for the trend toward the hiring of young men as bankers in the boom-time prelude to U.S. involvement in World War I. He sarcastically says that all that was required to borrow money from "trusting trust companies" for a new war supplies business was the moxie to bluff the "boy bankers" into thinking you had an inside relationship with an Allied commission.

He jokes that banks were looking for ways of "impounding" some of the flood of gold pouring into the United States from England and France for munitions and other military goods, and laments the lack of "gray-haired presidents of banks" who would have misgivings about the lending excesses that would later lead to a deep postwar recession and bear market. The Dow Jones Industrial Average soared 128% from 1914 to 1919, then crashed by almost 50% from 1919 to 1921.

Livermore's view was echoed nine decades later by investors who were aghast at the lending excesses by youthful MBAs at investment banks amid the technology boom in the late 1990s and the real estate boom of the early 2000s, both of which also led to painful recessions and bear markets.

22.3 ▶ Livermore delighted in observing other operators fail in their attempts to manipulate the public into purchasing an iffy stock. In this passage, he describes the bungled effort by a hapless pool, organized by his friend Barnes, to merge three small stove companies into a single firm and take it public with the backing of the young, ambitious president of a small bank. He notes that this occurred at the tail end of a time when the public had been "buying any old thing in the way of engraved stock certificates" and that by the time the crew he describes as "stupid" and "hoggish" had finagled $3.5 million in underwriting from the boy banker, the market was already saturated with new issues.

At the point when Livermore is tapped for assistance, he notes with an exasperation that would be familiar to modern investors that banks' excesses had finally made their directors think twice. Banks started calling in loans, he says, the "day of the boy banker was over," and it was time for an adult to come in and clean up the mess—which he does as a favor to Barnes even though it seemed like a hopeless task. He then launches into an amusing description of the way he managed to unload the syndicate's shares by taking advantage of news reports that he was about to launch an operation on behalf of the syndicate.

The tale ends with a twist when it turns out some members of the syndicate messed up by separately buying more shares on the advance; when they cannot sell those more inflated shares, they ungratefully blame Livermore and plead with him to manipulate it higher again. He turns them down, and they storm off. The three men mentioned—broker Clifton P. Kane, ex-senator Samuel Gordon, and veteran trader Joshua Wolff—do not appear in any contemporary newspaper articles or books, so they must be pseudonyms for people that Livermore thought better of defaming explicitly.

The long anecdote serves three purposes: Livermore shows how insiders often take advantage of positive publicity to sell shares, not buy them. He also gets even with some ill-mannered ex-partners who double-crossed and disrespected him in an operation. And Lefevre gets to provide one more cautionary tale about why the public should not seek or take advice from conflicted insiders because they will inevitably end up with tainted information, at best, as either "the third stratum of tip-takers" or the "fourth, fifth and possibly sixth strata of suckers."

a man had to do was to say that he had a friend who was a friend of a member of one of the Allied commissions and he would be offered all the capital needed to carry out the contracts he had not yet secured. I used to hear incredible stories of clerks becoming presidents of companies doing a business of millions of dollars on money borrowed from trusting trust companies, and of contracts that left a trail of profits as they passed from man to man. A flood of gold was pouring into this country from Europe and the banks had to find ways of impounding it.

The way business was done might have been regarded with misgivings by the old, but there didn't seem to be so many of them about. The fashion for gray-haired presidents of banks was all very well in tranquil times, but youth was the chief qualification in these strenuous times. The banks certainly did make enormous profits.

Jim Barnes and his associates, enjoying the friendship and confidence of the youthful president of the Marshall National Bank, decided to consolidate three well-known stove companies and sell the stock of the new company to the public that for months had been buying any old thing in the way of engraved stock certificates. ◀**22.3**

One trouble was that the stove business was so prosperous that all three companies were actually earning dividends on their common stock for the first time in their history. Their principal stockholders did not wish to part with the control. There was a good market for their stocks on the Curb; and they had sold as much as they cared to part with and they were content with things as they were. Their individual capitalisation was too small to justify big market movements, and that is where Jim Barnes' firm came in. It pointed out that the consolidated company must be big enough to list on the Stock Exchange, where the new shares could be made more valuable than the old ones. It is an old device in Wall Street— to change the colour of the certificates in order to make them more valuable. ⟨**22.4**⟩ Say a stock ceases to be easily vendible at par. Well, sometimes by quadrupling the stock you may make the new shares sell at 30 or 35. This is equivalent to 120 or 140 for the old stock—a figure it never could have reached.

It seems that Barnes and his associates succeeded in inducing some of their friends who held speculatively some blocks of Gray Stove Company—a large concern—to come into the consolidation on the basis of four shares of Consolidated for each share of Gray. Then the Midland and the Western followed their big sister and came in on the basis of share for share. Theirs had been quoted on the Curb at around 25 to 30, and the Gray, which was better known and paid dividends, hung around 125.

In order to raise the money to buy out those holders who insisted upon selling for cash, and also to provide additional working capital for improvements and promotion expenses, it became necessary to raise a few millions. So Barnes saw the president of his bank, who kindly lent his syndicate three million five hundred thousand dollars. The collateral was one hundred thousand shares of the newly organised corporation. The syndicate assured the president, or so I was told, that the price would not go below 50. It would be a very profitable deal as there was big value there.

The promoters' first mistake was in the matter of timeliness. The saturation point for new stock issues had been reached by the market, and they should have seen it. But even then they might have made a fair profit after all if they had not tried to duplicate the unreasonable killings which other promoters had made at the very height of the boom.

Now you must not run away with the notion that Jim Barnes and his associates were fools or inexperienced kids. They were shrewd men. All of them were familiar with Wall Street methods and some of them were exceptionally successful stock traders. But they did rather more than merely overestimate the public's

22.4 If a company was having a hard time selling its shares at par, or $100, it would sometimes declare a 2 to 1, 3 to 1, or 4 to 1 split. The price would be cut in half or some other fraction, and the number of shares would at least double. This had the effect of making each share seem cheaper even though it also represented a smaller slice of a company's earnings power.

Following a split, new certificates with a different tint or engraving would be issued. In this case, Livermore calls attention to the trick of changing the color of the certificates, observing that a pool operator might quadruple the number of shares of a stock that was hard to sell at $100 in order to try to find more buyers at $25. Then it was easier to manipulate the shares to $35, where they would be worth $140 of the old denomination. Stock splits are of course still common today, and for the same reason.

22.5 Livermore appears to be engaging in hyperbole because there was very little in the newspapers at this time about publicly traded stove companies. The only major mention of the industry came on May 11, 1916, when the National Association of Stove Manufacturers held its 45th annual convention at the Hotel Astor in New York with record attendance. The paper quoted the group's Illinois-based president as stating that business over the past 12 months had been good, but factory owners were hampered by a shortage of railroad cars, freight embargoes overseas, and the high cost of materials due to "phenomenal demand for metal abroad by the Allies for war munition manufactures."[3]

buying capacity. After all, that capacity was something that they could determine only by actual tests. Where they erred more expensively was in expecting the bull market to last longer than it did. I suppose the reason was that these same men had met with such great and particularly with such quick success that they didn't doubt they'd be all through with the deal before the bull market turned. They were all well known and had a considerable following among the professional traders and the wire houses.

The deal was extremely well advertised. The newspapers certainly were generous with their space. The older concerns were identified with the stove industry of America and their product was known the world over. **22.5** It was a patriotic amalgamation and there was a heap of literature in the daily papers about the world conquests. The markets of Asia, Africa and South America were as good as cinched.

The directors of the company were all men whose names were familiar to all readers of the financial pages. The publicity work was so well handled and the promises of unnamed insiders as to what the price was going to do were so definite and convincing that a great demand for the new stock was created. The result was that when the books were closed it was found that the stock which was offered to the public at fifty dollars a share had been oversubscribed by 25 per cent.

Think of it! The best the promoters should have expected was to succeed in selling the new stock at that price after weeks of work and after putting up the price to 75 or higher in order to average 50. At that, it meant an advance of about 100 per cent in the old prices of the stocks of the constituent companies. That was the crisis and they did not meet it as it should have been met. It shows you that every business has its own needs. General wisdom is less valuable than specific savvy. The promoters, delighted by the unexpected oversubscription, concluded that the public was ready to pay any price for any quantity of that stock. And they actually were stupid enough to underallot the stock. After the promoters made up their minds to be hoggish they should have tried to be intelligently hoggish.

What they should have done, of course, was to allot the stock in full. That would have made them short to the extent of 25 per cent of the total amount offered for subscription to the public, and that, of course, would have enabled them to support the stock when necessary and at no cost to themselves. Without any effort on their part they would have been in the strong strategic position that I always try to find myself in when I am manipulating a stock. They could have kept the price from sagging, thereby inspiring confidence in the new stock's price stability and in the underwriting syndicate back of it. They should have remembered that their work was not over when they sold the stock offered to the public. That was only a part of what they had to market. ⟨**22.6**⟩

They thought they had been very successful, but it was not long before the consequences of their two capital blunders became apparent. The public did not buy any more of the new stock, because the entire market developed reactionary tendencies. The insiders got cold feet and did not support Consolidated Stove; and if insiders don't buy their own stock on recessions, who should? The absence of inside support is generally accepted as a pretty good bear tip.

There is no need to go into statistical details. The price of Consolidated Stove fluctuated with the rest of the market, but it never went above the initial market quotations, which were only a fraction above 50. Barnes and his friends in the end had to come in as buyers in order to keep it above 40. Not to have supported that stock at the outset of its market career was regrettable. But not to have sold all the stock the public subscribed for was much worse.

At all events, the stock was duly listed on the New York Stock Exchange and the price of it duly kept sagging until it nominally stood at 37. And it stood there

22.6 A full-court press of publicity and price support for new mergers, initial public offerings, and secondary offerings was considered essential by pros like Livermore. So he despaired when seeing lesser operators bungle an operation by only doing half the job.

Livermore would have been impressed with the manipulations undertaken on behalf of new issues in the 1990s tech stock craze, when underwriters locked arms with investment banks, brokers, and the media to herald the prospects of untested young companies to the public with promotions disguised as research. Brokerages originally told clients that staff analysts issuing "strong buy" recommendations worked independently of their equity underwriting departments. But investigations after the collapse of dozens of stocks in the ensuing 2000–2002 bear market revealed that many of the blatantly manipulative tactics of turn-of-the-century operators had come eerily back to life. Once their scam was laid bare, brokerages were forced to accept new curbs on the marketing of securities. Yet as usual on Wall Street, insiders in the late 1990s got rich, the public lost a fortune, and very few frauds went to jail.

because Jim Barnes and his associates had to keep it there because their bank had loaned them thirty-five dollars a share on one hundred thousand shares. If the bank ever tried to liquidate that loan there was no telling what the price would break to. The public that had been eager to buy it at 50, now didn't care for it at 37, and probably wouldn't want it at 27.

As time went on the banks' excesses in the matter of extensions of credits made people think. The day of the boy banker was over. The banking business appeared to be on the ragged edge of suddenly relapsing into conservatism. Intimate friends were now asked to pay off loans, for all the world as though they had never played golf with the president.

There was no need to threaten on the lender's part or to plead for more time on the borrower's. The situation was highly uncomfortable for both. The bank, for example, with which my friend Jim Barnes did business, was still kindly disposed. But it was a case of "For heaven's sake take up that loan or we'll all be in a dickens of a mess!"

The character of the mess and its explosive possibilities were enough to make Jim Barnes come to me to ask me to sell the one hundred thousand shares for enough to pay off the bank's three-million-five-hundred-thousand-dollar loan. Jim did not now expect to make a profit on that stock. If the syndicate only made a small loss on it they would be more than grateful.

It seemed a hopeless task. The general market was neither active nor strong, though at times there were rallies, when everybody perked up and tried to believe the bull swing was about to resume.

The answer I gave Barnes was that I'd look into the matter and let him know under what conditions I'd undertake the work. Well, I did look into it. I didn't analyse the company's last annual report. My studies were confined to the stock-market phases of the problem. I was not going to tout the stock for a rise on its earnings or its prospects, but to dispose of that block in the open market. All I considered was what should, could or might help or hinder me in that task.

I discovered for one thing that there was too much stock held by too few people—that is, too much for safety and far too much for comfort. Clifton P. Kane & Co., bankers and brokers, members of the New York Stock Exchange, were carrying seventy thousand shares. They were intimate friends of Barnes and had been influential in effecting the consolidation, as they had made a specialty of stove stocks for years. Their customers had been let into the good thing. Ex-Senator Samuel Gordon, who was the special partner in his nephews' firm, Gordon Bros., was the owner of a second block of seventy thousand shares; and the famous Joshua Wolff had sixty thousand shares. This made a total of two hundred thousand shares of Consolidated Stove held by this handful of veteran Wall Street professionals. They did not need any kind person to tell them when to sell their stock. If I did anything in the manipulating line calculated to bring in public buying—that is to say, if I made the stock strong and active—I could see Kane and Gordon and Wolff unloading, and not in homeopathic doses either. The vision of their two hundred thousand shares Niagaraing into the market was not exactly entrancing. Don't forget that the cream was off the bull movement and that no overwhelming demand was going to be manufactured by my operations, however skilfully conducted they might be. Jim Barnes had no illusions about the job he was modestly sidestepping in my favour. He had given me a waterlogged stock to sell on a bull market that was about to breathe its last. Of course there was no talk in the newspapers about the ending of the bull market, but I knew it, and Jim Barnes knew it, and you bet the bank knew it.

Still, I had given Jim my word, so I sent for Kane, Gordon and Wolff. Their two hundred thousand shares was the sword of Damocles. I thought I'd like to substitute a steel chain for the hair. The easiest way, it seemed to me, was by some sort of reciprocity agreement. If they helped me passively by holding off while I sold the bank's one hundred

22.7 This passage again highlights Livermore's constant yearning to find a moral center on Wall Street, as he despairs of his co-conspirators' unprofessionalism. The manipulator expects some kind of honor among thieves, but fears Kane, Gordon, and Wolff will only think of themselves. He wishes that they would exercise an "intelligent unselfishness in order not to be unintelligently selfish."

By calling their 200,000 shares a "sword of Damocles," Livermore refers to a Greek legend in which a rich tyrant in Syracuse named Dionysius II decides to show a sycophantic member of his court that his life isn't as cushy as it appears. He lets the courtier, named Damocles, enjoy his food, wine, silver, and lovely servants for a day, but the man's pleasure evaporates when he discovers a sharp sword hanging over his head by a horsehair. Dionysius meant for Damocles to understand that the life of a powerful man is fraught with danger.[4] The Roman orator Cicero made the story famous by including it in one his speeches to explain further that happiness is fragile.[5]

A moment later, Livermore notes, again with a moralizing tone, "it never pays to be a dog in the manger in Wall Street or anywhere else." This is a reference to an Aesop fable in which a stray dog lay down to sleep in a section of a stable where an ox normally ate. When the ox returned from his work, he tries to eat the straw but the dog awakens in a rage, barking and snapping at the ox. The ox gives up hope of having lunch, and walks away muttering, "Ah, people often begrudge others what they cannot enjoy themselves." Livermore evidently means that he hopes the syndicate will recognize they'll ruin the deal for everyone if they don't cooperate with him.

thousand shares, I would help them actively by trying to make a market for all of us to unload on. As things were, they couldn't sell one-tenth of their holdings without having Consolidated Stove break wide open, and they knew it so well that they had never dreamed of trying. All I asked of them was judgment in timing the selling and an intelligent unselfishness in order not to be unintelligently selfish. It never pays to be a dog in the manger in Wall Street or anywhere else. **22.7** I desired to convince them that premature or ill-considered unloading would prevent complete unloading. Time urged.

I hoped my proposition would appeal to them because they were experienced Wall Street men and had no illusions about the actual demand for Consolidated Stove. Clifton P. Kane was the head of a prosperous commission house with branches in eleven cities and customers by the hundreds. His firm had acted as managers for more than one pool in the past.

Senator Gordon, who held seventy thousand shares, was an exceedingly wealthy man. His name was as familiar to the readers of the metropolitan press as though he had been sued for breach of promise by a sixteen-year-old manicurist possessing a five-thousand-dollar mink coat and one hundred and thirty-two letters from the defendant. He had started his nephews in business as brokers and he was a special partner in their firm. He had been in dozens of pools. He had inherited a large interest in the Midland Stove Company and he got one hundred thousand shares of Consolidated Stove for it. He had been carrying enough to disregard Jim Barnes' wild bull tips and had cashed in on thirty thousand shares before the market petered out on him. He told a friend later that he would have sold more only the other big holders, who were old and intimate friends, pleaded with him not to sell any more, and out of regard for them he stopped. Besides which, as I said, he had no market to unload on.

The third man was Joshua Wolff. He was probably the best known of all the traders. For twenty years everybody had known him as one of the plungers on the floor. In bidding up stocks or offering them down he had few equals, for ten or twenty thousand shares meant no more to him than two or three hundred. Before I came to New York I had heard of him as a plunger. He was then trailing with a sporting coterie that played a no limit game, whether on the race track or in the stock market.

They used to accuse him of being nothing but a gambler, but he had real ability and a strongly developed aptitude for the speculative game. At the same time his reputed indifference to highbrow pursuits made him the hero of numberless anecdotes. One of the most widely circulated of the yarns was that Joshua was a guest at what he called a swell dinner and by some oversight of the hostess several of the other guests began to discuss literature before they could be stopped.

A girl who sat next to Josh and had not heard him use his mouth except for masticating purposes, turned to him and looking anxious to hear the great financier's opinion asked him, "Oh, Mr. Wolff, what do you think of Balzac?"

Josh politely ceased to masticate, swallowed and answered, "I never trade in them Curb stocks!" **22.8**

Such were the three largest individual holders of Consolidated Stove. When they came over to see

22.9 Livermore typically asked to be paid for his operations not in cash but in call options on the stock he was asked to manipulate. Calls are leveraged derivatives that give the holder the right to buy a certain quantity of shares of a security at specified price up to certain date. By taking his payment in calls, Livermore was aligning his own interests with those of his client.

22.10 This was the steel goliath formed in the late 1890s by conglomerateur John W. Gates out of many smaller firms, including Consolidated Steel & Wire Co. and Salem Wire Co. In its heyday, the company controlled as much as 75% of the wire and steel rod production in the nation.[6] As Livermore implies, there was not much love between Gates and his contemporaries. One historian recounts a meeting between Gates and John Stevenson Jr., the head of New Castle Wire Nail Co., a firm he wished to bring into his fold. Said Stevenson: "Gates used to joke me, 'You had better surrender and come in with us.' That was all there was about it. I felt like a kind of Ishmaelite, with everybody's hand against everybody else, and there was no profit for any of us, or very little, and I know there was none for me, I will tell you that."[7]

me I told them that if they formed a syndicate to put up some cash and gave me a call on their stock at a little above the market I would do what I could to make a market. **22.9** They promptly asked me how much money would be required.

I answered, "You've had that stock a long time and you can't do a thing with it. Between the three of you you've got two hundred thousand shares, and you know very well that you haven't the slightest chance of getting rid of it unless you make a market for it. It's got to be some market to absorb what you've got to give it, and it will be wise to have enough cash to pay for whatever stock it may be necessary to buy at first. It's no use to begin and then have to stop because there isn't enough money. I suggest that you form a syndicate and raise six millions in cash. Then give the syndicate a call on your two hundred thousand shares at 40 and put all your stock in escrow. If everything goes well you chaps will get rid of your dead pet and the syndicate will make some money."

As I told you before, there had been all sorts of rumours about my stock-market winnings. I suppose that helped, for nothing succeeds like success. At all events, I didn't have to do much explaining to these chaps. They knew exactly how far they'd get if they tried to play a lone hand. They thought mine was a good plan. When they went away they said they would form the syndicate at once.

They didn't have much trouble in inducing a lot of their friends to join them. I suppose they spoke with more assurance than I had of the syndicate's profits. From all I heard they really believed it, so theirs were no conscienceless tips. At all events the syndicate was formed in a couple of days. Kane, Gordon and Wolff gave calls on the two hundred thousand shares at 40 and I saw to it that the stock itself was put in escrow, so that none of it would come out on the market if I should put up the price. I had to protect myself. More than one promising deal has failed to pan out as expected because the members

22.11 **The Seligmans** were the most prominent Jewish banking family in America in the 1800s and early 1900s. Family patriarch Joseph Seligman, born in Germany in 1819, immigrated to the United States at 18 and, after engaging in a variety of clothing and retail businesses in Pennsylvania and Alabama, started a bank, J. & W. Seligman & Co., with his brothers. Before long, it had branches in New York, San Francisco, New Orleans, London, Paris, and Frankfurt. The firm acted as broker for many of Jay Gould's transactions and itself became a prominent investor in railroads. It also served as underwriter for many stock and bond issuances in industries ranging from steel and railroads to mining, shipbuilding, and bicycles.[8]

Joseph Seligman was believed to have developed a close relationship with Abraham Lincoln, who appreciated his efforts to place bonds of the young, unstable country with investors in Europe to help finance the Civil War. Historian Isaac Markens says Seligman played a major role in recommending General Ulysses S. Grant, whom he knew as a lieutenant from previous dealings, to run the U.S. Army in the Civil War. Markens says Seligman was also instrumental in taking care of Lincoln's wife financially after the president's assassination.[9] The banker was later offered the post of Treasury secretary by President Grant, but he turned it down. A decade later, his firm helped President Rutherford Hayes refinance the lingering war debt.

Two decades later, family member Henry Seligman was one of Gates's top financiers and served on the board of American Wire.[10] J. & W. Seligman & Co. ultimately grew into a prominent money management firm specializing in technology stocks. It was purchased by Ameriprise Financial in 2008, and the name has survived as the firm's Seligman Funds division.

of the pool or clique failed to keep faith with one another. Dog has no foolish prejudices against eating dog in Wall Street. At the time the second American Steel and Wire Company **22.10** was brought out the insiders accused one another of breach of faith and trying to unload. There had been a gentlemen's agreement between John W. Gates and his pals and the Seligmans **22.11** and their banking associates. Well, I heard somebody in a broker's office reciting this quatrain, which was said to have been composed by John W. Gates:

> The tarantula jumped on the centipede's back
> And chortled with ghoulish glee:
> "I'll poison this murderous son of a gun.
> If I don't he'll poison me!"

Mind you, I do not mean for one moment to imply that any of my friends in Wall Street would even dream of double-crossing me in a stock deal. But on general principles it is just as well to provide for any and all contingencies. It's plain sense.

After Wolff and Kane and Gordon told me that they had formed their syndicate to put up six millions in cash there was nothing for me to do but wait for the money to come in. I had urged the vital need of haste. Nevertheless the money came in driblets. I think it took four or five installments. I don't know what the reason was, but I remember that I had to send out an S O S call to Wolff and Kane and Gordon.

That afternoon I got some big checks that brought the cash in my possession to about four million dollars and the promise of the rest in a day or two. It began at last to look as though the syndicate might do something before the bull market passed away. At best it would be no cinch, and the sooner I began work the better. The public had not been particularly keen about new market movements in inactive stocks. But a man could do a great deal to arouse interest in any stock with four millions in cash. It was enough to absorb all the probable offerings. If time urged, as I had said, there was no sense in waiting for the other two millions. The sooner the stock got up to 50 the better for the syndicate. That was obvious.

The next morning at the opening I was surprised to see that there were unusually heavy dealings in Consolidated Stove. As I told you before, the stock had been waterlogged for months. The price had been pegged at 37, Jim Barnes taking good care not to let it go any lower on account of the big bank loan at 35. But as for going any higher, he'd as soon expect to see the Rock of Gibraltar shimmying across the Strait as to see Consolidated Stove do any climbing on the tape.

Well, sir, this morning there was quite a demand for the stock, and the price went up to 39. In the first hour of the trading the transactions were heavier than for the whole previous half year. It was the sensation of the day and affected bullishly the entire market. I heard afterwards that nothing else was talked about in the customers' rooms of the commission houses.

I didn't know what it meant, but it didn't hurt my feelings any to see Consolidated Stove perk up. As a rule I do not have to ask about any unusual movement in any stock because my friends on the floor—brokers who do business for me, as well as personal friends among the room traders—keep me posted. They assume I'd like to know and they telephone me any news or gossip they pick up. On this day all I heard was that there was unmistakable inside buying in Consolidated Stove. There wasn't any washing. It was all genuine. The purchasers took all the offerings from 37 to 39 and when importuned for reasons or begged for a tip, flatly refused to give any. This made the wily and watchful traders conclude that there was something doing; something big. When a stock goes up on buying by insiders who refuse to encourage the world at large to follow suit the ticker hounds begin to wonder aloud when the official notice will be given out.

I didn't do anything myself. I watched and wondered and kept track of the transactions. **22.12** But on the next day the buying was not only greater in volume but more aggressive in character. The selling orders that had been on the specialists' books for months at above the pegged price of 37 were absorbed without any trouble, and not enough new selling orders came in to check the rise. Naturally, up went the price. It crossed 40. Presently it touched 42.

The moment it touched that figure I felt that I was justified in starting to sell the stock the bank held as collateral. Of course I figured that the price would go down on my selling, but if my average on the entire line was 37 I'd have no fault to find. I knew what the stock was worth and I had gathered some idea of the vendibility from the months of inactivity. Well, sir, I let them have stock carefully until I had got rid of thirty thousand shares. And the advance was not checked!

That afternoon I was told the reason for that opportune but mystifying rise. It seems that the floor traders had been tipped off after the close the night before and also the next morning before the opening, that I was bullish as blazes on Consolidated Stove

22.12 Unlike most traders, Livermore typically worked outside of the confines of Wall Street. For several years, starting in 1917, he worked out of a building at 11 Broadway, which was about four blocks away from the New York Stock Exchange. In the mid-1920s, he moved to the Squibb Building in midtown, overlooking Central Park. Time magazine described his operation:

The door, bearing no name, was guarded by a plug-ugly who kept its key locked inside a little green cabinet. No one could leave as long as the market was open; only outgoing telephone calls were allowed. Trader Livermore sat in a jungle of telephone wires, his sharp blue eyes glued to the private board which recorded the minute-to-minute gyrations of his vast paper empire. During trading hours he was nervous, excited, jubilant as a boy. At 3 o'clock, when the ticker went blank, he bit down hard on his cigar, retired in silence to an inner chamber to study his day's trades. Often he stayed until 8.[11]

22.13 The *New York Times* and other newspapers did in fact publish articles when reporters discovered what Livermore was trading. In August 1925, the *Times* reported he had taken a 50,000 share position in U.S. Steel and an "important position" in White Motors.[12]

The latter firm, by the way, built the first presidential limousine, in 1909, for President William Howard Taft—a steam-powered, seven-seat touring car. By the 1920s White became a specialist in tractors and trucks; in the 1930s it built the famed M3 White Scout patrol car seen frequently in World War II movies ferrying officers around; and its fleet of small, specialty buses with roll-up canvas convertible tops are still seen today in Glacier and Yellowstone national parks, where they're known as Red Jammers. Its U.S. assets were sold out of bankruptcy in 1981 to Volvo.

and was going to rush the price right up fifteen or twenty points without a reaction, as was my custom—that is, my custom according to people who never kept my books. The tipster in chief was no less a personage than Joshua Wolff. It was his own inside buying that started the rise of the day before. His cronies among the floor traders were only too willing to follow his tip, for he knew too much to give wrong steers to his fellows.

As a matter of fact, there was not so much stock pressing on the market as had been feared. Consider that I had tied up three hundred thousand shares and you will realise that the old fears had been well founded. It now proved less of a job than I had anticipated to put up the stock. After all, Governor Flower was right. Whenever he was accused of manipulating his firm's specialties, like Chicago Gas, Federal Steel or B. R. T., he used to say: "The only way I know of making a stock go up is to buy it." That also was the floor traders' only way, and the price responded.

On the next day, before breakfast, I read in the morning papers what was read by thousands and what undoubtedly was sent over the wires to hundreds of branches and out-of-town offices, and that was that Larry Livingston was about to begin active bull operations in Consolidated Stove. **22.13** The additional details differed. One version had it that I had formed an insiders' pool and was going to punish the overextended short interest. Another hinted at dividend announcements in the near future. Another reminded the world that what I usually did to a stock I was bullish on was something to remember. Still another accused the company of concealing its assets in order to permit accumulation by insiders. And all of them agreed that the rise hadn't fairly started.

By the time I reached my office and read my mail before the market opened I was made aware that the Street was flooded with red-hot tips to buy Consolidated Stove at once. My telephone bell kept ringing and the clerk who answered the calls heard the same question asked in one form or another a hundred times that morning: Was it true that Consolidated Stove was going up? I must say that Joshua Wolff and Kane and Gordon—and possibly Jim Barnes—handled that little tipping job mighty well.

I had no idea that I had such a following. Why, that morning the buying orders came in from all over the country—orders to buy thousands of shares of a stock that nobody wanted at any price three days before. And don't forget that, as a matter of fact, all that the public had to go by was my newspaper reputation as a successful plunger; something for which I had to thank an imaginative reporter or two.

Well, sir, on that, the third day of the rise, I sold Consolidated Stove; and on the fourth day and the fifth; and the first thing I knew I had sold for Jim Barnes the one hundred thousand shares of stock which the Marshall National Bank held as collateral on the three-million-five-hundred-thousand-dollar loan that needed paying off. If the most successful manipulation consists of that in which the desired end is gained at the least possible cost to the manipulator, the Consolidated Stove deal is by all means the most successful of my Wall Street career. Why, at no time did I have to take any stock. I didn't have to buy first in order to sell the more easily later on. I did not put up the price to the highest possible point and then begin my real selling. I didn't even do my principal selling on the way down, but on the way up. It was like a dream of Paradise to find an adequate buying power created for you without your stirring a finger to bring it about, particularly when you were in a hurry. I once heard a friend of Governor Flower's say that in one of the great bull-leader's operations for the account of a pool in B. R. T. the pool sold fifty thousand shares of the stock at a profit, but Flower & Co. got commissions on more than two hundred and fifty thousand shares and W. P. Hamilton says that to distribute two hundred and twenty thousand shares of Amalgamated Copper, James R. Keene must have traded in at least seven hundred thousand shares of the stock during the necessary manipulation. Some commission bill! Think of that and then consider that the only commissions that I had to pay were the commissions on the one hundred thousand shares I actually sold for Jim Barnes. I call that some saving.

Having sold what I had engaged to sell for my friend Jim, and all the money the syndicate had agreed to raise not having been sent in, and feeling no desire to buy back any of the stock I had sold, I rather think I went away somewhere for a short vacation. I do not remember exactly. But I do remember very well that I let the stock alone and that it was not long before the price began to sag. One day, when the entire market was weak, some disappointed bull wanted to get rid of his Consolidated Stove in a hurry, and on his offerings the stock broke below the call price, which was 40. Nobody seemed to want any of it. As I told you before, I wasn't bullish on the general situation and that made me more grateful than ever for the miracle that had enabled me to dispose of the one hundred thousand shares without having to put the price up twenty or thirty points in a week, as the kindly tipsters had prophesied.

Finding no support, the price developed a habit of declining regularly until one day it broke rather badly and touched 32. That was the lowest that had ever been recorded for it, for, as you will remember, Jim Barnes and the original syndicate had pegged it at 37 in order not to have their one hundred thousand shares dumped on the market by the bank.

I was in my office that day peacefully studying the tape when Joshua Wolff was announced. I said I would see him. He rushed in. He is not a very large man, but he certainly seemed all swelled up—with anger, as I instantly discovered.

He ran to where I stood by the ticker and yelled, "Hey? What the devil's the matter?"

"Have a chair, Mr. Wolff," I said politely and sat down myself to encourage him to talk calmly.

"I don't want any chair! I want to know what it means!" he cried at the top of his voice.

"What does what mean?"

"What in hell are you doing to it?"

"What am I doing to what?"

"That stock! That stock!"

"What stock?" I asked him.

But that only made him see red, for he shouted, "Consolidated Stove! What are you doing to it?"

"Nothing! Absolutely nothing. What's wrong?" I said.

He stared at me fully five seconds before he exploded: "Look at the price! Look at it!"

He certainly was angry. So I got up and looked at the tape.

I said, "The price of it is now 31¼."

"Yeh! Thirty-one and a quarter, and I've got a raft of it."

"I know you have sixty thousand shares. You have had it a long time, because when you originally bought your Gray Stove——"

But he didn't let me finish. He said, "But I bought a lot more. Some of it cost me as high as 40! And I've got it yet!"

He was glaring at me so hostilely that I said, "I didn't tell you to buy it."

"You didn't what?"

"I didn't tell you to load up with it."

"I didn't say you did. But you were going to put it up——"

"Why was I?" I interrupted.

He looked at me, unable to speak for anger. When he found his voice again, he said, "You were going to put it up. You had the money to buy it."

"Yes. But I didn't buy a share," I told him.

That was the last straw.

"You didn't buy a share, and you had over four millions in cash to buy with? You didn't buy any?"

"Not a share!" I repeated.

22.14 Livermore is not exaggerating when he complains that Wolff's tips to the media would have an impact on trading, as his name ultimately took on the status of legend.

On February 11, 1926, for instance, The Times reported in a gossipy column titled "Topics in Wall Street," that professional speculators "who believe that many stocks are too high are making no great secret of the fact that they are going around 'seeking whom they may devour.' "

It then went on to report that Livermore was reported to be one of those speculators, stating: "Wall Street had a story yesterday—which flashed from brokerage house to brokerage house and did not pass unnoticed in the banks—that Jesse L. Livermore was once more selling stocks and that some of the weakness in a few issues could be attributed to his liquidation. The story may or may not be true, because the subject of it is naturally not in the habit of saying what he is doing in the market. Nevertheless, 'Livermore selling' was a convenient excuse for Wall Street to use for some of the declines."[13]

Livermore Reported Selling.

Wall Street had a story yesterday—which flashed from brokerage house to brokerage house and did not pass unnoticed in the banks—that Jesse L. Livermore was once more selling stocks and that some of the weakness in a

He was so mad by now that he couldn't talk plainly. Finally he managed to say, "What kind of a game do you call that?"

He was inwardly accusing me of all sorts of unspeakable crimes. I sure could see a long list of them in his eyes. It made me say to him: "What you really mean to ask me, Wolff, is, why I didn't buy from you above 50 the stock you bought below 40. Isn't that it?"

"No, it isn't. You had a call at 40 and four millions in cash to put up the price with."

"Yes, but I didn't touch the money and the syndicate has not lost a cent by my operations."

"Look here, Livingston—" he began.

But I didn't let him say any more.

"You listen to me, Wolff. You knew that the two hundred thousand shares you and Gordon and Kane held were tied up, and that there wouldn't be an awful lot of floating stock to come on the market if I put up the price, as I'd have to do for two reasons: The first to make a market for the stock; and the second to make a profit out of the call at 40. But you weren't satisfied to get 40 for the sixty thousand shares you'd been lugging for months or with your share of the syndicate profits, if any; so you decided to take on a lot of stock under 40 to unload on me when I put the price up with the syndicate's money, as you were sure I meant to do. You'd buy before I did and you'd unload before I did; in all probability I'd be the one to unload on. I suspect you figured on my having to put the price up to 60. It was such a cinch that you probably bought ten thousand shares strictly for unloading purposes, and to make sure somebody held the bag if I didn't, you tipped off everybody in the United States, Canada and Mexico without thinking of my added difficulties. All your friends knew what I was supposed to do. **22.14** Between their buying and mine you were going to be all hunky. Well, your intimate friends to whom you gave the tip passed it on to their friends after they had bought their lines, and the third stratum of tip-takers planned to supply the fourth, fifth and possibly sixth strata of suckers, so that when I finally came to do some selling I'd find myself anticipated by a few thousands of wise speculators. It was a friendly thought, that notion of yours, Wolff. You can't imagine how surprised I was when Consolidated Stove began to go up before I even thought of buying a single share; or how grateful, either, when the underwriting syndicate sold one hundred thousand shares around 40 to the people who were going to sell those same shares to me at 50 or 60. I sure was a sucker not to use the four millions to make money for them, wasn't I? The cash was supplied to buy stock with, but only if I thought it necessary to do so. Well, I didn't."

Joshua had been in Wall Street long enough not to let anger interfere with business. He cooled off as he heard me, and when I was through talking he said in a friendly tone of voice, "Look here, Larry, old chap, what shall we do?"

"Do whatever you please."

"Aw, be a sport. What would you do if you were in our place?"

"If I were in your place," I said solemnly, "do you know what I'd do?"

"What?"

"I'd sell out!" I told him.

He looked at me a moment, and without another word turned on his heel and walked out of my office. He's never been in it since.

Not long after that, Senator Gordon also called. He, too, was quite peevish and blamed me for their troubles. Then Kane joined the anvil chorus. They forgot that their stock had been unsalable in bulk when they formed the syndicate. All they could remember was that I didn't sell their holdings when I had the syndicate's millions and the stock was active at 44, and that now it was 30 and dull as dishwater. To their way of thinking I should have sold out at a good fat profit.

Of course they also cooled down in due time. The syndicate wasn't out a cent and the main problem remained unchanged: to sell their stock. A day or two later they came back and asked me to help them out. Gordon was particularly insistent, and in the end I made them put in their pooled stock at 25½. My fee for my services was to be one-half of whatever I got above that figure. The last sale had been at about 30.

There I was with their stock to liquidate. Given general market conditions and specifically the behaviour of Consolidated Stove, there was only one way to do it, and that was, of course, to sell on the way down and without first trying to put up the price, and I certainly would have got stock by the ream on the way up. But on the way down I could reach those buyers who always argue that a stock is cheap when it sells fifteen or twenty points below the top of the movement, particularly when that top is a matter of recent history. A rally is due, in their opinion. After seeing Consolidated Stove sell up to close to 44 it sure looked like a good thing below 30.

It worked out as always. Bargain hunters bought it in sufficient volume to enable me to liquidate the pool's holdings. But do you think that Gordon or Wolff or Kane felt any gratitude? Not a bit of it. They are still sore at me, or so their friends tell me. They often tell people how I did them. They cannot forgive me for not putting up the price on myself, as they expected.

As a matter of fact I never would have been able to sell the bank's hundred thousand shares if Wolff and the rest had not passed around those red-hot bull tips of theirs. If I had worked as I usually do— that is, in a logical natural way—I would have had to take whatever price I could get. I told you we ran into a declining market. The only way to sell on such a market is to sell not necessarily recklessly but really regardless of price. No other way was possible, but I suppose they do not believe this. They are still angry. I am not. Getting angry doesn't get a man anywhere. More than once it has been borne in on me that a speculator who loses his temper is a goner. In this case there was no aftermath to the grouches. But I'll tell you something curious. One day Mrs. Livingston went to a dressmaker who had been warmly rec-

22.15 ▶ **Livermore** was notoriously secretive as he played his lone hand and regularly expresses surprise and indifference at the attention he stirs up among reporters seeking heroes and villains for every kink of market activity. While he did not give tips in the way that modern fund managers often do, he did agree to an interview with *New York Evening World* reporter Rose Tillotson at his office not long after he had made a killing in cotton in August 1908.

Calling him "the Napoleon of Cotton," the reporter reports that he turned a bankroll of $15 into a fortune of millions after arriving 15 years earlier from Boston. She says he was an unknown quantity until the spring, when he added $2.5 million to his savings by a single coup in cotton "and since then he has been recognized by grizzled bulls and bears as a mighty lively factor."[14]

Tillotson met him in the back room of the E. F. Hutton office at 35 New Street and describes her first impression of his "extreme youthfulness" with flaxen hair, blue eyes, and determined mouth and chin. He scarcely glances up from the ticker tape while he answers her questions about whether it was easier to make a million dollars now than 40 years ago, as E. H. Harriman had recently claimed.

Then he launches into some real advice. "Millions were made just as rapidly then as now. Look at the Rothschilds....Success is, of course, primarily a matter of opportunity, but the difficulty with a young man is that he has not had enough experience, as a general thing, to always recognize the opportunity."

Tillotson then asks Livermore to name the essentials for success on Wall Street, and the trader finally looks up from the tape. "Anticipation, intuition and experience," he answers. "A young man must school himself to look ahead, keeping himself informed as to the situation not only in this country but in foreign countries. I have always done that. Unless a man is born with strong powers of intuition he should keep out of speculation. It is a most important part of the Wall Street game."

Livermore adds: "Experience is of course the most important requisite of all, and here is the chief difficulty the young man encounters. He should seek it, and reason every situation out so that he will realize the benefit from it. Since I started in Boston 15 years ago, I have never valued money for itself but as a means of gaining wider experiences and increasing my opportunities."

Considering his belief that experience and intuition are hard-won, you can see why he takes such a dim view of people who want to shortcut the process by seeking and accepting a quick tip.

ommended to her. The woman was competent and obliging and had a very pleasing personality. At the third or fourth visit, when the dressmaker felt less like a stranger, she said to Mrs. Livingston: "I hope Mr. Livingston puts up Consolidated Stove soon. We have some that we bought because we were told he was going to put it up, and we'd always heard that he was very successful in all his deals."

I tell you it isn't pleasant to think that innocent people may have lost money following a tip of that sort. Perhaps you understand why I never give any myself. ◀**22.15** That dressmaker made me feel that in the matter of grievances I had a real one against Wolff.

ENDNOTES

1 "James Barnes Dies; a Retired Broker," *New York Times,* December 3, 1929, 29.

2 "Wild Day in Stocks Starts an Inquiry," *New York Times,* August 23, 1908, 1.

3 "Stove Makers in Session." *New York Times*, May 11, 1916, 18.

4 James Baldwin, *Favorite Tales of Long Ago* (New York: E.P. Dutton, 1955), 78.

5 Cicero, *On the Good Life* (New York: Penguin Classics, 1971), 84.

6 Naomi R. Lamoreaux, *The Great Merger Movement in American Business, 1895–1904* (Cambridge University Press, 2008), 74.

7 Ibid.

8 "Mr. Seligman's Career: Came to New York in Steerage—Died Worth Over $20,000,000," *New York Times,* April 24, 1894, 5.

9 Isaac Markens, *Abraham Lincoln and the Jews* (1909), 31.

10 "John W. Gates Has Left the Country," *New York Times,* May 11, 1900, 5.

11 "Business: Fourth Down," *Time*. March 19, 1934.

12 "Livermore Trading Again," *New York Times*, August 26, 1925.

13 "Livermore Reported Selling," *New York Times*, February 11, 1926.

14 Rose Tillotson, "Fortune No Kinder to Young Men Today Than 40 Years Ago, Livermore Says," *New York Evening World*, August 11, 1908, 3.

Speculation in stocks will never disappear. It isn't desirable that it should. It cannot be checked by warnings as to its dangers. You cannot prevent people from guessing wrong no matter how able or how experienced they may be. Carefully laid plans will miscarry because the unexpected and even the unexpectable will happen. Disaster may come from a convulsion of nature or from the weather, from your own greed or from some man's vanity; from fear or from uncontrolled hope. But apart from what one might call his natural foes, a speculator in stocks has to contend with certain practices or abuses that are indefensible morally as well as commercially.

As I look back and consider what were the common practices twenty-five years ago when I first came to Wall Street, I have to admit that there have been many changes for the better. The old-fashioned bucket shops are gone, though bucketeering "brokerage" houses still prosper at the expense of men and women who persist in playing the game of getting rich quick. The Stock Exchange is doing excellent work not only in getting after these out-and-out swindlers but in insisting upon strict adherence to its rules by its own members. Many wholesome regulations and restrictions are now strictly enforced but there is still room for improvement. The ingrained conservatism of Wall Street rather than ethical callousness is to blame for the persistence of certain abuses.

John Pierpont Morgan

Junius Spencer Morgan

23.1 So much can be said of **John Pierpont Morgan,** who is mentioned repeatedly in *Reminiscences* as a model of speculation, empire building and public service. He was Warren Buffett, George Soros, and Jamie Dimon rolled up into one larger-than-life figure. He was a banker, a railroad builder, and a manager of great enterprises. From his early days battling with Jay Gould to his skirmishes with E. H. Harriman, and of course to his crowning achievement of saving the American financial system from calamity in the Panic of 1907, J. P. Morgan dominated the Gilded Age period between the Civil War and World War I. The *Times* of London captured his role beautifully:

The life of Mr. Morgan furnished perhaps the most conspicuous example the modern world has seen of the power which the mere possession of wealth may place in the hands of an individual without assistance from official position, title, or the inherited prestige of an historic name. It may also fairly be said to have furnished a not unadmirable example of the intelligent use of that wealth and power.

Mr. Morgan had to bear his full share of abuse, often virulent and scurrilous, but it was the impersonal abuse of those who saw in him only the monstrous outgrowth of what they considered an iniquitous social system, and it is no small tribute to his character that with so great a willingness to discover a cause of grievance against him so little was found to be said in criticism of his integrity or of any individual act of his career. No one, indeed, who had an intimate knowledge of him would hesitate to say that the greatest factor of his success was the confidence which the financial world learned to have in his trustworthiness and singleness of purpose. The game which he played, for such large stakes, he played strictly according to the rules, and if the result was non-moral or injurious to the community, the fault lay not in the play but in the game.[1]

Morgan had distinguished lineage for his future role as an entrepreneur. His father's family descended from Captain Miles Morgan, who sailed from Bristol, England, in 1636 and was one of the founders of Springfield, Massachusetts. His grandfather, Joseph Morgan, began life as a farmer but leveraged a small inheritance into two taverns, a stagecoach line, a hotel in Hartford, Connecticut, a founding stake in the Aetna Fire Insurance Co., and investments in banks, canals, railroads and steamships. Joseph left his one son, Junius Spencer Morgan, a $3 million inheritance. Junius used it to start a bank, then left to become a partner in a large dry-goods business. He later headed to London to become a partner in a bank that would be renamed J. S. Morgan & Co. When he died, Junius in turn left his one son, John Pierpont Morgan, a $10 million inheritance.

Difficult as profitable stock speculation always has been it is becoming even more difficult every day. It was not so long ago when a real trader could have a good working knowledge of practically every stock on the list. In 1901, when

John Pierpont Morgan Jr.

J. P. was born in 1837 in Hartford. He attended a Boston high school before moving to Germany to study mathematics, history, and political economy at the University of Göttingen. In 1860, upon returning to the United States, he was made the American agent for his father's business. In 1871, Morgan joined with Anthony Drexel and formed the firm Drexel, Morgan & Co. Upon his father's death in 1890, Morgan inherited the London business and its global connections. And with Drexel's death in 1893, Morgan became the patriarch of a vast financial empire. In 1895, the firm was renamed J. P. Morgan & Co.

The firm was the first global American bank. In 1899, it extended a loan to the Mexican government to restructure its national debt. Later it helped the British fund the Boer War in South Africa, and helped Thomas Edison form General Electric. By 1901, J. P. Morgan & Co. was worth some $1.1 billion, or $28 billion in today's dollars.[2]

Morgan diversified. He won control of various railroads, including the New York Central and the New York, New Haven & Hartford. He was a director of Western Union, Aetna Insurance, and General Electric companies. Morgan would typically gain control of entities by reorganizing them once they fell into bankruptcy—a process that became known as re-Morganizing. Banker Henry Clews, who said Morgan had "the driving power of a locomotive," described the process: "They have been financial physicians, healing sick corporate bodies; monetary surgeons, amputating needless expenditures and reckless methods; or, in perhaps more happy figure, skilful pruners of the vine, that the ultimate vintage might be more abundant."[3]

Morgan also assumed the mantle of responsibility of ensuring the stability of the financial system that was later given to the Federal Reserve after its creation in 1913. Of course, there was also a profit to be had for Morgan's interests, for altruism was not one of his main personality traits. He took advantage of the Panic of 1907 to secure control of Tennessee Iron & Coal, a competitor to his U.S. Steel conglomerate, for instance, and also turned a buck in helping the U.S. Treasury rebuild its gold reserves in 1895–1896.

Good examples of his breathless confidence occurred during his formative years. In 1859 while in New Orleans, on a whim he bought an entire boatload of Brazilian coffee that had arrived in port without a buyer. He later resold it for a profit. Later, he helped finance a man's endeavor to buy old, surplus smoothbore rifles from the U.S. Army, have the barrels fixed for better range and accuracy, and sell them back to the government at six times the price.[4] And he was not above using extraordinary means to achieve his purposes. In his fight against the Gould forces over control of the Albany & Susquehanna railroad, Morgan allegedly "hurled chubby Jim Fisk down a flight of stairs," according to a biographer.

In his private life, Morgan enjoyed collecting rare books and works of art for his library. He died in 1913 while traveling in Rome. The New York Stock Exchange remained closed the morning of his funeral out of respect. When trading resumed, volume was very light.[6] Carrying on the family tradition, J. P. left his fortune and business to his only son, John Pierpont Morgan Jr.[5]

Morgan's name lives on. After the Glass-Steagall Act of 1933 forced banks to separate investment banking activities from commercial banking, some of the partners of J. P. Morgan & Co. left to form Morgan Stanley. The two banks maintained a close relationship with each other and with their London cousin, Morgan, Grenfell & Co. Regulatory changes and mergers pulled the old House of Morgan apart. Morgan, Grenfell was acquired by Deutsche Bank in 1990, and later J. P. Morgan & Co. merged with Chase Manhattan Bank to form one of the top three banks in the United States.

J. P. Morgan ⟨**23.1**⟩ brought out the United States Steel Corporation, which was merely a consolidation of lesser consolidations most of which were less than two years old, the Stock Exchange had 275 stocks on its list and about 100 in its "unlisted

23.2 Traditionally, securities that were unable to meet the listing requirements of the New York Stock Exchange were traded in alternative exchanges or "on the curb." In March 1885, the NYSE formed a special department to handle unlisted securities. This came just weeks after the Consolidated Exchange opened and presented a new competitive threat. One of the main distinctions was that the unlisted securities were not granted an official quotation from the exchange.[7]

Shares of industrial companies dominated the unlisted department in its early years (steelmakers and railroads dominated the main exchange). In 1895, some 435 industrial companies traded in the unlisted category, though just three of those—American Sugar Refining, National Lead, and U.S. Leather—comprised 94% of the group's $13.6 million trade volume.[8]

The unlisted department was not around for long. In 1910, the NYSE abolished it and adopted new rules requiring that stocks traded on the exchange meet strict listing requirements, including publication of financial reports.[9]

23.3 Guaranteed stocks were a class of equity similar to bonds that had higher standing than preferred shares. They had a set dividend that was guaranteed by a lease issued to a second company and would be paid regardless of the earnings of the issuing company. In the event of default, guaranteed stockholders were secondary to bondholders but ahead of the common stockholders.[10] Guaranteed stocks were not subject to state and local taxes.

Railroad companies were the primary issuers of guaranteed stocks, as larger lines would lease track rights from smaller lines. For example, the Albany & Susquehanna railroad would issue guaranteed stock backed by a lease paid by the larger Delaware & Hudson line.

There were considerable risks in the securities due to illiquidity, as Livermore mentions. According to a contemporary account: "There are…some serious disadvantages to even the best of such stocks, the foremost being the limited market and extreme inactivity of the stock, which makes it more or less difficult to dispose of immediately should such a contingency arise."[11]

department"; **23.2** and this included a lot that a chap didn't have to know anything about because they were small issues, or inactive by reason of being minority or guaranteed stocks **23.3** and therefore lacking in speculative attractions. In fact, an overwhelming majority were stocks in which there had not been a sale in years. Today there are about 900 stocks on the regular list and in our recent active markets about 600 separate issues were traded in. **23.4** Moreover, the old groups or classes of stocks were easier to keep track of. They not only were fewer but the capitalization was smaller and the news a trader had to be on the lookout for did not cover so wide a field. But today, a man is trading in everything; almost every industry in the world is represented. It requires more time and more work to keep posted and to that extent stock speculation has become much more difficult for those who operate intelligently.

There are many thousands of people who buy and sell stocks speculatively but the number of those who speculate profitably is small. As the public always is "in" the market to some extent, it follows that there are losses by the public all the time. The speculator's deadly enemies are: Ignorance, greed, fear and hope. All the statute books in the world and all the rules of all the Exchanges on earth cannot eliminate these from the human animal. Accidents which knock carefully conceived plans skyhigh also are beyond regulation by

Issuing Company	Guarantor	Guaranteed annual dividend
Albany & Susquehanna.............	Delaware & Hudson................	9%
Boston & Albany....................	New York Central..................	8½%
Connecticut River R. R...........	New York, New Haven & Hartford.	10%
Fitchburg (pfd.)...................	Boston & Maine....................	5%
Morris & Essex....................	Delaware, Lackawanna & Western..	7¼%
Pittsburgh, Ft. Wayne & Chicago..	Pennsylvania......................	7%
Rensselaer & Saratoga.............	Delaware & Hudson................	8%

bodies of cold-blooded economists or warm-hearted philanthropists. There remains another source of loss and that is, deliberate misinformation as distinguished from straight tips. And because it is apt to come to a stock trader variously disguised and camouflaged, it is the more insidious and dangerous.

The average outsider, of course, trades either on tips or on rumours, spoken or printed, direct or implied. Against ordinary tips you cannot guard. For instance, a lifelong friend sincerely desires to make you rich by telling you what he has done, that is, to buy or sell some stock. His intent is good. If the tip goes wrong what can you do? Also against the professional or crooked tipster the public is protected to about the same extent that he is against gold-bricks or wood-alcohol. **23.5** But against the typical Wall Street rumours, the speculating public has neither protection nor redress. Wholesale dealers in securities, manipulators, pools and individuals resort to various devices to aid them in disposing of their surplus holdings at the best possible prices. The circulation of bullish items by the newspapers and the tickers is the most pernicious of all.

Get the slips of the financial news-agencies any day and it will surprise you to see how many statements of an implied semi-official nature they print. The authority is some "leading insider" or "a prominent director" or "a high official" or someone "in authority" who presumably knows what he is talking about. Here are today's slips. I pick an item at random. Listen to this: "A leading banker says it is too early yet to expect a declining market."

Did a leading banker really say that and if he said it why did he say it? Why does he not allow his name to be printed? Is he afraid that people will believe him if he does?

Here is another one about a company the stock of which has been active this week. This

23.4 Livermore's lament about the complexity of tracking the industry trends and business developments between 1901 and the 1920s surely pales in comparison to how he would feel about today's marketplace: In mid-2009, the NYSE Euronext listed over 4,000 tradable issues. The NYSE Amex, the successor to the Curb Market of Livermore's time, listed another 676 equity securities, and the NASDAQ listed 2,820 issues.

23.5 The terms "gold-bricks" and "wood-alcohol" are more slang for a fraud or swindle. "Gold-brick" was a term used to describe con men who would sell bricks of "gold" that were in reality lead or some other weighty material coated with gold. John Hill wrote *Gold Bricks of Speculation*, a resource for the average investor, in the hope it would "make the difference between legitimate and illegitimate methods so clear that the reader will not be duped into buying any of the 'Gold Bricks of Speculation.'"[12]

Wood-alcohol, or methyl alcohol, was a cheap but poisonous substitute for ethyl or drinking alcohol used during Prohibition. Bootleggers would try to cook the methyl alcohol out of industrial alcohol through boiling, but their customers risked blindness or even death.[13] While methyl alcohol is a distillate of wood, ethyl alcohol comes from the fermentation of fruits or grains.

23.6 Livermore rails against the media's practice of allowing insiders to provide self-serving comments without furnishing their names. He would have been aghast at the current situation in which anyone with a computer connection can hold themselves out to be an expert in stocks on a blog, and create the mysterious aura required to influence public opinion.

He would also have been appalled at the ease by which canny short sellers could manipulate public opinion in minutes by spreading false rumors virally through social-media web sites. A famous *New Yorker* cartoon of the early online era showed a mutt typing into a computer while remarking to another mutt at his side, "On the Internet, no one knows you're a dog."[14] The anonymity that Livermore found so harmful in the 1920s has thus been magnified today, for on Twitter and in chat rooms, no one knows whether a bearish commenter on a stock is a short seller, a disgruntled employee with an ax to grind, or a rival company exec.

In August, 2000, the Securities and Exchange Commission tried to rein in some of the most abusive practices of insiders through a new rule, Regulation FD. It banned the selective disclosure of information by issuers to an inner circle of stock analysts or major shareholders, and instead demanded that any material new data be made available to both pros and the public at the same time. The unfortunate result was a dramatic decrease in the dissemination of any information.

time the man who makes the statement is a "prominent director." Now which—if any—of the company's dozen directors is doing the talking? It is plain that by remaining anonymous nobody can be blamed for any damage that may be done by the statement.

Quite apart from the intelligent study of speculation everywhere the trader in stocks must consider certain facts in connection with the game in Wall Street. In addition to trying to determine how to make money one must also try to keep from losing money. It is almost as important to know what not to do as to know what should be done. It is therefore well to remember that manipulation of some sort enters into practically all advances in individual stocks and that such advances are engineered by insiders with one object in view and one only and that is to sell at the best profit possible. However, the average broker's customer believes himself to be a business man from Missouri if he insists upon being told why a certain stock goes up. Naturally, the manipulators "explain" the advance in a way calculated to facilitate distribution. I am firmly convinced that the public's losses would be greatly reduced if no anonymous statements of a bullish nature were allowed to be printed. I mean statements calculated to make the public buy or hold stocks.

The overwhelming majority of the bullish articles printed on the authority of unnamed directors or insiders convey unreliable and misleading impressions to the public. The public loses many millions of dollars every year by accepting such statements as semi-official and therefore trustworthy. **23.6**

Say for example that a company has gone through a period of depression in its particular line of business. The stock is inactive. The quotation represents the general and presumably accurate belief of its actual value. If the stock were too cheap at that level somebody would know it and buy it and it would advance. If too dear somebody would know enough to sell it and the price would decline. As nothing happens one way or another nobody talks about it or does anything.

The turn comes in the line of business the company is engaged in. Who are the first to know it, the insiders or the public? You can bet it isn't the public. What happens next? Why, if the improvement continues the earnings will increase and the company will be in position to resume dividends on the stock; or, if dividends were not discontinued, to pay a higher rate. That is, the value of the stock will increase.

Say that the improvement keeps up. Does the management make public that glad fact? Does the president tell the stockholders? Does a philanthropic director come out with a signed statement for the benefit of that part of the public that reads the financial page in the newspapers and the slips of the news agencies? Does some modest insider pursuing his usual policy of anonymity come out with an unsigned statement to the effect that the company's future is most promising? Not this time. Not a word is said by anyone and no statement whatever is printed by newspapers or tickers.

The value-making information is carefully kept from the public while the now taciturn "prominent insiders" go into the market and buy all the cheap stock they can lay their hands on. As this well-informed but unostentatious buying keeps on, the stock rises. The financial reporters, knowing that the insiders ought to know the reason for the rise, ask questions. The unanimously anonymous insiders unanimously declare that they have no news to give out. They do not know that there is any warrant for the rise. Sometimes they even state that they are not particularly concerned with the vagaries of the stock market or the actions of stock speculators.

The rise continues and there comes a happy day when those who know have all the stock they want or can carry. The Street at once begins to hear all kinds of bullish rumours. The tickers tell the traders "on good authority" that the company has definitely turned the corner. The same modest director who did not wish his name used when he said he knew no warrant for the rise in the stock is now quoted— of course not by name—as saying that the stock-holders have every reason to feel greatly encouraged over the outlook.

Urged by the deluge of bullish news items the public begins to buy the stock. These purchases help to put the price still higher. In due course the predictions of the uniformly unnamed directors come true and the company resumes dividend payments; or increases the rate, as the case may be. With that the bullish items multiply. They not only are more numerous than ever but much more enthusiastic. A "leading director," asked point blank for a statement of conditions, informs the world that the improvement is more than keeping up. A "prominent insider," after much coaxing, is finally induced by a news-agency to confess that the earnings are nothing short of phenomenal. A "well-known banker," who is affiliated in a business way with the company, is made to say that the expansion in the volume of sales is simply unprecedented in the history of the trade. If not another order came in the company would run night and day for heaven knows how many months. A "member of the finance committee," in a double-leaded manifesto, expresses his astonishment at the public's astonishment over the stock's rise. The only astonishing thing is the stock's moderation in the climbing line. Anybody who will analyse the forthcoming annual report can easily figure how much more than the market-price the book-value of the stock is. But in no instance is the name of the communicative philanthropist given. ◁**23.7**▷

23.7 While Lefevre paints a portrait here of omnipotent directors who used their industry knowledge to cheat the public, the truth is that even in the 1920s being an insider was no instant path to riches. There were plenty of corporate titans who blew their fortunes in the market.

One of the most sensational rises and failures was experienced by William Crapo Durant, the eccentric founder of General Motors. The grandson of a Michigan governor who was born in Boston in 1861, Durant started his career as a cigar salesman but showed an early entrepreneurial streak by parlaying a $2,000 investment in a horse-drawn carriage business in Flint, Michigan, into a $2 million business with worldwide sales in the mid-1890s.

He was among the few in the buggy-whip set to transition to autos, and created General Motors in 1908 by consolidating 13 small car makers and 10 parts makers, including Cadillac, Buick, and Oldsmobile. Big investors in the new firm ousted him in 1911 over complaints about his risk taking, but he then started a new economy-car firm with famed racer Louis Chevrolet, and later managed to win back GM through a clever series of stock transactions: Leading the bull pool himself, he acquired shares in the company cheaply during a weak spot in the economy, and then manipulated the stock from $82 in January 1916 to $558 in December that year. "The visionary gambler was on the loose," said historian Kenneth Fisher.[15]

During his second term at the helm of GM, he brought in the managers who would ultimately create the midcentury glory of the firm—organizational genius Alfred Sloan and inventor Charles Kettering—but World War I was harsh on the company's sales, and ultimately Durant was wiped out of stock he had bought on 10% margin. Shares rose in the 1919 expansion, but then plunged again in the 1920 recession, wiping Durant out a third time. Chemicals tycoon Pierre DuPont, who was a major GM shareholder, brought in J. P. Morgan & Co. to reorganize GM and issue new stock, and although Durant worked tirelessly in bull syndicates to bolster the price, he ended up $90 million in debt and was booted again from his firm.[16]

In the mid-1920s bull market, the ultimate car salesman was back on his feet again and became a major player on the Street right alongside Livermore, launching a new firm, Durant Motors, and running bull pools in a variety of stocks in conjunction with other dilettantes from the fast-growing auto industry, including the Fisher brothers, who had made a fortune in carriage and auto frames.

But being an insider didn't help Durant avoid the devastating first leg of the 1929 crash, or the hubris of borrowing to buy more stocks in 1930 just ahead of the second leg of the crash. By 1932, he had lost his fortune once and for all. He declared bankruptcy in 1936, and ended his years living on a small GM pension and managing a bowling alley in Flint. He died in 1947 at age 86.

As long as the earnings continue good and the insiders do not discern any sign of a let up in the company's prosperity they sit on the stock they bought at the low prices. There is nothing to put the price down, so why should they sell? But the moment there is a turn for the worse in the company's business, what happens? Do they come out with statements or warnings or the faintest of hints? Not much. The trend is now downward. Just as they bought without any flourish of trumpets when the company's business turned for the better, they now silently sell. On this inside selling the stock naturally declines. Then the public begins to get the familiar "explanations." A "leading insider" asserts that everything is O.K. and the decline is merely the result of selling by bears who are trying to affect the general market. If on one fine day, after the stock has been declining for some time, there should be a sharp break, the demand for "reasons" or "explanations" becomes clamorous. Unless somebody says something the public will fear the worst. So the news-tickers now print something like this: "When we asked a prominent director of the company to explain the weakness in the stock, he replied that the only conclusion he could arrive at was that the decline today was caused by a bear drive. Underlying conditions are unchanged. The business of the company was never better than at present and the probabilities are that unless something entirely unforeseen happens in the meanwhile, there will be an increase in the rate at the next dividend meeting. The bear party in the market has become aggressive and the weakness in the stock was clearly a raid intended to dislodge weakly held stock." The news-tickers, wishing to give good measure, as likely as not will go on to state that they are "reliably informed" that most of the stock bought on the day's decline was taken by inside interests and that the bears will find that they have sold themselves into a trap. There will be a day of reckoning.

In addition to the losses sustained by the public through believing bullish statements and buying stocks, there are the losses that come through being dissuaded from selling out. The next best thing to having people buy the stock the "prominent insider" wishes to sell is to prevent people from selling the same stock when he does not wish to support or accumulate it. What is the public to believe after reading the statement of the "prominent director"? What can the average outsider think? Of course, that the stock should never have gone down; that it was forced down by bear-selling and that as soon as the bears stop the insiders will engineer a punitive advance during which the shorts will be driven to cover at high prices. The public properly believes this because it is exactly what would happen if the decline had in truth been caused by a bear raid.

The stock in question, notwithstanding all the threats or promises of a tremendous squeeze of the over-extended short interest, does not rally. It keeps on going down. It can't help it. There has been too much stock fed to the market from the inside to be digested.

And this inside stock that has been sold by the "prominent directors" and "leading insiders" becomes a football among the professional traders. It keeps on going down. There seems to be no bottom for it. The insiders knowing that trade conditions will adversely affect the company's future earnings do not dare to support that stock until the next turn for the better in the company's business. Then there will be inside buying and inside silence.

I have done my share of trading and have kept fairly well posted on the stock market for many years and I can say that I do not recall an instance when a bear raid caused a stock to decline extensively. What was called bear raiding was nothing but selling based on accurate knowledge of real conditions. But it would not do to say that the stock declined on inside selling or on inside non-buying. Everybody would hasten to sell and when everybody sells and nobody buys there is the dickens to pay.

The public ought to grasp firmly this one point: That the real reason for a protracted decline is never bear raiding. When a stock keeps on going down you can bet there is something wrong with it, either with the market for it or with the

23.8 ▶ In a typical corporate strategy at the time, even in the face of recent antitrust regulation, Charles Mellen set about reducing the competitive threat faced by the New Haven. Mellen was eager to make a name for himself in the Morgan empire after playing a small role at the Northern Pacific, boxed in by members of the James Hill family. Morgan, according to historian Ron Chernow, wanted "to take over every form of transportation in New England and wantonly usurped steamship lines, interurban electric trolleys, rapid transit systems—anything that threatened their monopoly."[17]

Burton Hendrick, writing in *McClure's Magazine*, expands on the events:

> Mellen first proceeded to put an end to the "intolerable" trolley situation. In seizing nearly all of the trolley lines in Connecticut, Rhode Island, and western Massachusetts, he paid little attention to expense. Wherever he saw a trolley line he proceeded to lay hand upon it. The prices demanded by the speculative adventurers who had "reorganized" to properties did not frighten Mellen for the movement....In Mellen's view-point, however, the proceeding justified itself; it took the whole trolley business of two states out of the hands of possible competitors, and anchored it, for all time, in the possession of the New Haven road.[18]

In the end, New Haven was not able to sustain the massive debt load it assumed during its acquisition frenzy. A scandal followed as it was revealed that Mellen handed out millions of dollars in bribes to keep politicians and regulators out of his way. He even paid a Harvard professor to deliver lectures favoring lenient regulation of railways.

It soon became apparent that something was wrong. New Haven, which had earned a reputation for thriftiness and conservatism in the years before Mellen and Morgan, was forced to cut expenses to stay solvent. Staff cuts and mechanical neglect resulted in 11 deadly train wrecks in 1911 and 1912. As the public grew outraged, and the government's Interstate Commerce Commission recommended that the New Haven be separated from its steamship and trolley holdings, J. P. Morgan's son, Jack Morgan, fired Mellen.[19]

company. If the decline were unjustified the stock would soon sell below its real value and that would bring in buying that would check the decline. As a matter of fact, the only time a bear can make big money selling a stock is when that stock is too high. And you can gamble your last cent on the certainty that insiders will not proclaim that fact to the world.

Of course, the classic example is the New Haven. Everybody knows today what only a few knew at the time. The stock sold at 255 in 1902 and was the premier railroad investment of New England. A man in that part of the country measured his respectability and standing in the community by his holdings of it. If somebody had said that the company was on the road to insolvency he would not have been sent to jail for saying it. They would have clapped him in an insane asylum with other lunatics. But when a new and aggressive president was placed in charge by Mr. Morgan and the débâcle began, it was not clear from the first that the new policies would land the road where it did. But as property after property began to be saddled in the Consolidated Road at inflated prices, a few clear sighted observers began to doubt the wisdom of the Mellen policies. A trolley system ◁**23.8** was bought for two million and sold to the New Haven ◁**23.9** for $10,000,000; whereupon a reckless man or two committed lèse majeste by saying that the management was acting recklessly. Hinting that not even the New Haven could stand such extravagance was like impugning the strength of Gibraltar.

Of course, the first to see breakers ahead were the insiders. They became aware of the real condition of the company and they reduced their holdings of the stock. On their selling as well as on their non-support, the price of New England's gilt-edged railroad stock began to yield. Questions were asked, and explanations were demanded as usual; and the usual explanations were promptly forthcoming. "Prominent insiders" declared that there was nothing wrong that they knew of and that the decline was due to reckless bear selling. So the "investors" of New England kept their holdings of New York, New Haven & Hartford stock. Why shouldn't they? Didn't insiders say there was nothing wrong and cry bear selling? Didn't dividends continue to be declared and paid?

In the meantime the promised squeeze of the bears did not come but new low records did. The insider selling became more urgent and less disguised. Nevertheless public spirited men in Boston were denounced as stock-jobbers and demagogues for demanding a genuine explanation for the stock's deplorable decline that meant appalling losses to everybody in New England who had wanted a safe investment and a steady dividend payer.

That historic break from $255 to $12 a share never was and never could have been a bear drive. It was not started and it was not kept up by bear operations. The insiders sold right along and always at higher prices than they could have done if they had told the truth or allowed the truth to be told. It did not matter whether the price was 250 or 200 or 150 or 100 or 50 or 25, it still was too high for that stock, and the insiders knew it and the public did not. The public might profitably consider the disadvantages under which it labours when it tries to make money buying and selling the stock of a company concerning whose affairs only a few men are in position to know the whole truth.

The stocks which have had the worst breaks in the past 20 years did not decline on bear raiding. But the easy acceptance of that form of explanation has been responsible for losses by the public amounting to millions upon millions of dollars. It has kept people from selling who did not like the way his stock was acting and would have liqui-

23.9 The New York & New Haven Railroad was incorporated in Connecticut in 1844, and the original 63-mile line was completed four years later. Passenger volumes grew rapidly as the road lay along the important overland route between New York and Boston. Tragedy struck in 1853 when an early-morning express steamed through an open drawbridge, killing 42 people and resulting in a $500 million lawsuit. The following year, company president Robert Schuyler, a nephew of the first secretary of the Treasury, Alexander Hamilton, fled to Italy after illegally issuing $2 million in stock. A magazine writer at the time noted:

The discovery of the…fraud created a universal panic that for a while threatened to break up the railroad system throughout the country. Stocks precipitately declined, and were unsalable even at a mere nominal price; while those who had borrowed money upon railroad stocks or bonds…were required to make immediate payment.[20]

A second road, the Hartford & New Haven, was chartered in 1833 and finished a few years later. The two roads were merged in 1872. By 1885, the New Haven, as the road was commonly called, was 265 miles long and had annual revenues of roughly $4 million. By 1900, the road stretched for 2,000 miles throughout Connecticut, Massachusetts, and Rhode Island and revenues totaled $40 million.[21]

J. P. Morgan took control of the New Haven shortly thereafter and selected Charles S. Mellen, the former president of the Northern Pacific, to take the reins. Mellen was later censured by the government for monopolistic practices and neglecting maintenance. He resigned in 1913, the same year J. P. Morgan died. The road struggled despite its favorable location before going bankrupt in 1935. Eventually, the New Haven's properties were absorbed into the Penn Central amalgamation of 1969 before becoming part of Amtrak in the 1970s. Amtrak's high-speed Acela Express runs on old New Haven track.

23.10 Charles F. Woerishoffer was one of the most famous bear operators of the mid-1800s. Born in Gelnhausen, Germany, in 1843, he came to the United States as a boy in search of his fortune. He appeared in Wall Street in 1865 first as a clerk and later as a cashier for Rutten & Bonn, a banking and brokerage operation.[22] By 1870, Woerishoffer had his own seat on the NYSE.

Woerishoffer & Co. soon followed, and it was prosperous from the start.[23] A colleague remarked on his daring: "He could have marched upon a cannon's mouth with a jest on his lips."[24] And he won notoriety in 1879 by taking on Jay Gould and Russell Sage in a fight over control of a majority of the bonds of the Kansas Pacific Railroad, which was eventually merged into the Union Pacific.

Later, German investors would help Woerishoffer build the Denver and Rio Grande Railroad. Other exploits included the pricking of the Northern Pacific bubble blown by Henry Villard in 1883. Woerishoffer had examined the line and found that the underlying earnings did not justify the road's fanciful stock price. He went against the established powers of the time, which included Drexel, Morgan & Co., and won millions "for his allegiance to the fact that stocks cannot be bulled with much satisfaction for any length of time with net earnings out of the question" according to the *Times*.[25]

He was not beholden to the bear side but, like Livermore, would seek out opportunities as they arose. The trader understood the importance of good sources of information: In one example, he went short after learning the railroads were not saving enough of their net earnings. Pneumonia killed him in 1886 at the age of 43 just as he was preparing for a trip back to Germany.

Henry Clews compared Woerishoffer favorably to Bismarck, Napoleon, and Ulysses S. Grant, saying, "The results of his life work show what can be accomplished by any man who sets himself at work upon an idea, and who devotes himself steadily and persistently to a course of action for the development and perfection of the principle which actuates his life."[26] His natural bearishness can be traced to a disappointment in the failures of men and a lack of confidence in their corporations. He believed history had shown that most companies were destined to failure as the ravages of capitalism wore down their competitive advantages. Said Clews: "It does not matter how successful the development of the business industries of this country may be hereafter, there will always be found men who will speculate upon their ruination."[27]

dated if they had not expected the price to go right back after the bears stopped their raiding. I used to hear Keene blamed in the old days. Before him they used to accuse Charley Woerishoffer **23.10** or Addison Cammack. Later on I became the stock excuse.

I recall the case of Intervale Oil. There was a pool in it that put the stock up and found some buyers on the advance. The manipulators ran the price to 50. There the pool sold and there was a quick break. The usual demand for explanations followed. Why was Intervale so weak? Enough people asked this question to make the answer important news. One of the financial news tickers called up the brokers who knew the most about Intervale Oil's advance and ought to be equally well posted as to the decline. What did these brokers, members of the bull pool, say when the news agency asked them for a reason that could be printed and sent broadcast over the country? Why, that Larry Livingston was raiding the market! And that wasn't enough. They added that they were going to "get" him. But of course, the Intervale pool continued to sell. The stock only stood then about $12 a share and they could sell it down to 10 or lower and their average selling price would still be above cost.

It was wise and proper for insiders to sell on the decline. But for outsiders who had paid 35 or 40, it was a different matter. Reading what the tickers printed there outsiders held on and waited for Larry Livingston to get what was coming to him at the hands of the indignant inside pool.

In a bull market and particularly in booms the public at first makes money which it later loses simply by overstaying the bull market. This talk of "bear raids" helps them to overstay. The public should beware of explanations that explain only what unnamed insiders wish the public to believe. **23.11**

23.11 After spending decades in the business as a bull, a bear, a trader, an investor, a syndicator, and a manipulator, Livermore knew every trick in the book and made up more as he went along. Yet despite many successes, massive losses haunted his career.

A decade after *Reminiscences* was published, he would declare bankruptcy for the fourth time in March, 1934.[28] He had made millions by being short stocks during the great crash of 1929, but suffered a series of setbacks following a very sharp, multimonth rally that began in mid-1932.

The *New York Times'* account of that bankruptcy shed light on all of Livermore's setbacks, since they were each variations of the same theme. The *Times* said the plunger's assets amounted to only $184,900, which included a life insurance policy worth $150,000; seats on the Chicago Board of Trade and Commodity Exchange valued at $10,500; and $20,000 worth of jewelry pledged as collateral for loans. His liabilities included $561,000 for unpaid federal and state income taxes; $9,000 promised to a dancer for keeping him "cheered and amused"[29] while getting his second divorce; $250,000 promised to a Russian woman in his office; $125,000 owed to his second wife; $100,000 to his current wife; and $142,525 to disgraced banker Joseph W. Harriman of the failed Harriman National Bank.

Here's how *Time* magazine described his fall from grace that week:

When the Coolidge market broke, there were angry stories that Jesse L. Livermore had smashed it. As the public began to get out of Wall Street, his fame receded. For the first time in 25 years he did not seem to prosper in a falling market. He gave up the big office overlooking the park. His second wife divorced him in 1932 and promptly married a onetime Federal Prohibition agent. For his third wife he took a brewer's daughter. The great Livermore estate at Great Neck, where the shrubbery alone was worth $150,000, netted $168,000 at auction. Last December Jesse Livermore was a 27-hour news headliner when he walked out of his Park Avenue apartment one afternoon, lost his bearings, spent the night at a hotel, and returned home the next day.

Perhaps Jesse L. Livermore will come back as he has done three times before. That was what his lawyers had in mind last week when they declared: 'Mr. Livermore has made three very large fortunes.... He has failed three times, on each occasion has paid 100 cents on the dollar with interest, and hopes to do so again.[30]

Yet his luck had run out. Livermore's name would surface again with reverence whenever the subject of great traders and manipulations arose, but new regulations in 1933 and 1934 essentially brought his era to an end.

Livermore, Plunger, Bankrupt Fourth Time; $2,259,212 Debts, $184,900 Assets Listed

ENDNOTES

1 "Mr. Pierpont Morgan," *New York Times*, April 1, 1913, 6.

2 "John Pierpont Morgan," *National Cyclopaedia of American Biography* (1910), 66.

3 Henry Clews, *Fifty Years in Wall Street* (New York: Irving Publishing Company, 1908), 681.

4 Ron Chernow, *The House of Morgan* (1990), 21–22.

5 Ibid., 31.

6 "Financial Markets," *New York Times*, April 15, 1913, 14.

7 Robert Sobel, *The Curbstone Brokers* (2000), 57.

8 Lance E. David and Robert J. Cull, *International Capital Markets and American Economic Growth, 1820–1914* (2002), 45.

9 S. N. D. North, ed., *The American Year Book* (1911), 387.

10 David Francis Jordan, *Jordan on Investments* (1920), 113.

11 Thomas Conway and Albert William Atwood. *Investment and Speculation* (1911), 132.

12 John Hill Jr., *Gold Bricks of Speculation* (1904), 19.

13 "The Trust about Poison Liquor," *Popular Science* (April 1927): 17.

14 *The New Yorker.* July 5, 1993, 61.

15 Kenneth L. Fisher. *100 Minds That Made the Market* (Hoboken, NJ: John Wiley & Sons, 2007).

16 Ibid.

17 Chernow, *The House of Morgan,* 175.

18 Burton J. Hendrick, "Bottling Up New England," *McClure's Magazine* (1912): 552.

19 Chernow, *The House of Morgan,* 177.

20 "Commercial Chronicle and Review," *Hunt's Merchants' Magazine and Commercial Review* (1854): 207.

21 John F. Stover, *Historical Atlas of the American Railroads* (1999), pp. 104–105

22 "August Rutten," *New York Times,* August 23, 1895, 2.

23 "C. F. Woerishoffer Dead," *New York Times,* May 11, 1886, 1.

24 Maury Klein, *The Life and Legend of Jay Gould* (1986), 320.

25 Ibid.

26 Clews, *Fifty Years in Wall Street,* 425.

27 Ibid., 427.

28 "Livermore, Plunger, Bankrupt Fourth Time," *New York Times,* March 6, 1934, 1.

29 "Fourth Down," *Time,* March 19, 1934.

30 Ibid.

XXIV

The public always wants to be told. That is what makes tip-giving and tip-taking universal practices. It is proper that brokers should give their customers trading advice through the medium of their market letters ◁**24.1**▷ as well as by word of mouth. But brokers should not dwell too strongly on actual conditions because the course of the market is always from six to nine months ahead of actual conditions. ◁**24.2**▷ Today's earnings do not justify brokers in advising their customers to buy stocks unless there is some assurance that six or nine months from today the business outlook will warrant the belief that the same rate of earnings will be maintained. If on looking that far ahead you can see, reasonably clearly, that conditions are developing which will change the present actual power, the argument about stocks being cheap today will disappear. The trader must look far ahead, but the broker is concerned with getting commissions now; hence the inescapable fallacy of the average market letter. Brokers make their living out of commissions from the public and yet they will try to induce the public through their market letters or by word of mouth to buy the same stocks in which they have received selling orders from insiders or manipulators.

It often happens that an insider goes to the head of a brokerage concern and says: "I wish you'd make a market in which to dispose of 50,000 shares of my stock."

24.1 ▶ Lefevre held brokerage-based advisors in low regard, but in all fairness, not all market letters during this period were merely advertisements for commission business. It is true that some were of dubious quality. *Benner's Prophecies of Future Ups and Downs in Prices,* in which Addison Cammack put great faith, was more about horoscopes than fundamental analysis. Its author based his predictions of the prices of hogs, corn, cotton, and pig iron on price cycles derived from the movements of the planets.

Many letters were impressive, however, and were written with an artistry that you will not see in any modern Wall Street research note. Banker Henry Clews prominently featured his market letters in his book *Fifty Years in Wall Street.* Here is an excerpt from one dated December 24, 1906, in which Clews laments the conditions created by a merger and acquisition spree among the railroads:

> Remember what I tell you: that the accumulation of stock as I have described has produced the present congested money market, and the unlocking of the former will, after a short time, unlock the other; then all will be well again. The present turbulent waves will pass over without many shipwrecks, and then will come calm weather and smooth sea. Patience is a great virtue; exercise it, and wait for bottom; then get in and get rich.[1]

24.2 ▶ This last chapter appears to have been added mostly to allow Lefevre some last licks on his favorite topics and insights. This was one of them. Writing in *Munsey's Magazine* in 1901, some 21 years before the original publication of *Reminiscences of a Stock Operator,* Edwin Lefevre said:

> Professional Wall Street invariably "discounts" events. It lives by foreseeing what is going to happen. It must take time by a long forelock. If it waited until the event actually occurred, everybody would prosper equally; and that would not be conducive to Wall Street wealth. Therefore, booms in stocks "discount" booms in trade.[2]

389

24.3 Lefevre loved to skewer get-rich-quick schemes like this one. He had observed them so often, and in such great variety, at the turn of the century that he used the theme for his novel *Samson Rock of Wall Street* in 1907. The story details the stock-market manipulations of a railroad magnate.

When the *New York Times* profiled Lefevre after the book's publication, he said: "There are two big motive powers in men, 'love and greed.' I made Wall Street the background to my story, because it is the meeting place of the 'greed stricken.'"

Speaking of the era *Samson Rock* evokes, a period of rapid-fire panics and booms from 1898 to 1906, he added: "This country exported so much more than we imported that we had a Johnstown flood of wealth—and you know what Americans do when they have money. They gambled in stocks and improved railroads and consolidated industries, but mostly they gambled in stocks."[3]

The broker asks for further details. Let us say that the quoted price of that stock is 50. The insider tells him: "I will give you calls on 5000 shares at 45 and 5000 shares every point up for the entire fifty thousand shares. I also will give you a put on 50,000 shares at the market."

Now, this is pretty easy money for the broker, if he has a large following and of course this is precisely the kind of broker the insider seeks. A house with direct wires to branches and connections in various parts of the country can usually get a large following in a deal of that kind. Remember that in any event the broker is playing absolutely safe by reason of the put. If he can get his public to follow he will be able to dispose of his entire line at a big profit in addition to his regular commissions.

I have in mind the exploits of an "insider" who is well-known in Wall Street.

He will call up the head customers' man of a large brokerage house. At times he goes even further and calls up one of the junior partners of the firm. He will say something like this:

"Say, old man, I want to show you that I appreciate what you have done for me at various times. I am going to give you a chance to make some real money. **24.3** We are forming a new company to absorb the assets of one of our companies and we'll take over that stock at a big advance over present quotations. I'm going to send in to you 500 shares of Bantam Shops at $65. The stock is now quoted at 72."

The grateful insider tells the thing to a dozen of the headmen in various big brokerage houses. Now since these recipients of the insider's bounty are in Wall Street what are they going to do when they get that stock that already shows them a profit? Of course, advise every man and woman they can reach to buy that stock. The kind donor knew this. They will help to create a market in which the kind insider can sell his good things at high prices to the poor public.

There are other devices of stock-selling promoters that should be barred. The Exchanges should not allow trading in listed stocks that are offered outside to the public on the partial payment plan. To have the price officially quoted gives a sort of sanction to any stock. Moreover, the official evidence of a free market, and at times the difference in prices, is all the inducement needed.

Another common selling device that costs the unthinking public many millions of dollars and sends nobody to jail because it is perfectly legal, is that of increasing the capital stock exclusively by reason of market exigencies. The process does not really amount to much more than changing the color of the stock certificates.

The juggling whereby 2 or 4 or even 10 shares of new stock are given in exchange for one of the old, is usually prompted by a desire to make the old merchandise more easily vendible. The old price was $1 per pound package and hard to move. At 25 cents for a quarter-pound box it might go better; and perhaps at 27 or 30 cents.

Why does not the public ask why the stock is made easy to buy? It is a case of the Wall Street philanthropist operating again, but the wise trader bewares of the Greeks bearing gifts. 〈**24.4**〉 It is all the warning needed. The public disregards it and loses millions of dollars annually.

The law punishes whoever originates or circulates rumors calculated to affect adversely the credit or business of individuals or corporations, that is, that tend to depress the values of securities by influencing the public to sell. Originally, the chief intention may have been to reduce the danger of panic by punishing anyone who doubted aloud the solvency of banks in times of stress. But of course, it serves also to protect the public against selling stocks below their real value. In other words the law of the land punishes the disseminator of bearish items of that nature.

24.4 ▶ This refers to a stratagem employed by Greek soldiers to sneak into Troy and sack the city, according to classical legend. The story of the Trojan horse is told the in *The Aeneid*, an epic poem written by Latin poet Virgil in around 20 BC.

Virgil said in verse that that the Greeks had lain siege to Troy for 10 years before they hit on a plan: Build a giant hollow horse—an animal that was sacred to Trojans—out of wood. Inscribe it as a gift to the goddess Athena, and leave it on the beach near the city gates. Secretly stuff the belly full of soldiers. Sail out of town, seemingly in defeat, but hide nearby. Wait for Trojans to roll the behemoth into town as a trophy. Then break out of the "gift horse," and attack in the night.

Trojan priest Laocoon was wary, and warned the city against accepting it. "Timeo Danaos et dona ferentes," he said, according to Virgil, which roughly means, "Do not trust Greeks bearing gifts." He and his two young sons were promptly devoured by sea serpents, which Trojans took as a sign that they would displease Athena if they did not accept the offering.

Bad move. Troy was slaughtered. Lefevre suggests the same lies in store for the public when they accept conflicted advice.

Four centuries earlier than Virgil, the Greek playwright Sophocles penned a similar line in his play *Ajax* that is just as applicable to traders: "Foes' gifts are no gifts—no, nor profitable."[4] Marble statue of Laocoon and his sons, below, is in the Vatican Museum.

24.5 This was one of Lefevre's favorite points. Indeed, his motivation for interviewing Livermore was to see if the great bear would confirm his theories on the "unbeatable" game of speculation. In the opening chapter of the *Reminiscences of a Stock Operator* series of articles in the *Saturday Evening Post*, which was cut out of the book version of the work, Lefevre elaborates on this in detail. He describes their chilly initial meeting and the conversation that followed:

> We shook hands, still neutral. I at once proceeded to tell him why I had sought him. As I talked I kept my eyes on his face to judge the effect of my words on him, but I could not tell what his thoughts were, nor, indeed, whether he was thinking at all. His eyes were full of that baffling intelligence that you see in the eyes of some babies. They were of a clean, clear, blue gray, and so steady that they impressed me as being more than merely organs of vision, as if they greatly helped him in his listening....
>
> I told him that I had certain theories about the game of speculation, as well as of the psychology of speculators, big or little. "I've read some of your articles." He spoke so noncommittally that I said, "Well?"
>
> "Well, you are one writer who is not afraid to tell the truth, even though it might hurt the brokers' business to tell it."
>
> "But the truth does not hurt the brokers' business," I said. He merely nodded. "I'd like to ask you some questions," I said.
>
> "I'll answer any question you ask me," he said confidently.[5]

It is for readers to decide whether Lefevre refuted or reinforced his preconceived notions with this work. If we are to believe Lefevre was pleading his case that Wall Street should not be considered a road to easy fortune but instead a den of thieves ready to prey on the uninitiated, then he succeeded. Time after time, in both Livermore's life as well as in the lives of the men he interacted with, we see that luck mixed with dedication, cunning, and detailed study were required for successful speculation. Quick tips, we are told, will inevitably lead to ruin.

Lefevre was born in 1870 in Panama before relocating as a boy to Colombia. He was the son of Henry Lefevre, a Civil War veteran working in Panama as an American agent for the Pacific Mail Steamship Co., and Emilia Lefevre, daughter of a former chief justice of the Panama Supreme Court. Lefevre's brother Ernest became president of Panama.[6]

How is the public protected against the danger of buying stocks above their real value? Who punishes the distributor of unjustified bullish news items? Nobody; and yet, the public loses more money buying stocks on anonymous inside advice when they are too high than it does selling out stocks below their value as a consequence of bearish advice during so-called "raids."

If a law were passed that would punish bull liars as the law now punishes bear liars, I believe the public would save millions.

Naturally, promoters, manipulators and other beneficiaries of anonymous optimism will tell you that anyone who trades on rumors and unsigned statements has only himself to blame for his losses. One might as well argue that any one who is silly enough to be a drug addict is not entitled to protection.

The Stock Exchange should help. It is vitally interested in protecting the public against unfair practices. If a man in position to know wishes to make the public accept his statements of fact or even his opinions, let him sign his name. Signing bullish items would not necessarily make them true. But it would make the "insiders" and "directors" more careful.

The public ought always to keep in mind the elementals of stock trading. When a stock is going up no elaborate explanation is needed as to why it is going up. It takes continuous buying to make a stock keep on going up. As long as it does so, with only small and natural reactions from time to time, it is a pretty safe proposition to trail along with it. But if after a long steady rise a stock turns and gradually begins to go down, with only occasional small rallies, it is obvious that the line of least resistance has changed from upward to downward. Such being the case why should any one ask for explanations? There are probably very good reasons why it should go down, but these reasons are known only to a few people who either keep those reasons to themselves, or else actually tell the public that the stock is cheap. The nature of the game as it is played is such that the public should realise that the truth cannot be told by the few who know.

Many of the so-called statements attributed to "insiders" or officials have no basis in fact. Sometimes the insiders are not even asked to make a statement, anonymous or signed. These stories are invented by somebody or other who has a large interest in the market. At a certain stage of an advance in the market-price of a security the big insiders are not averse to getting the help of the professional element to trade in that stock. But while the insider might tell the big plunger the right time to buy, you can bet he will never tell when is the time to sell. That puts the big professional in the same position as the public, only he has to have a market big enough for him to get out on. Then is when you get the most misleading "information." Of course, there are certain insiders who cannot be trusted at any stage of the game. As a rule the men who are at the head of big corporations may act in the market upon their inside knowledge, but they don't actually tell lies. They merely say nothing, for they have discovered that there are times when silence is golden.

I have said many times and cannot say it too often that the experience of years as a stock operator has convinced me that no man can consistently and continuously beat the stock market ⟨**24.5**⟩ though he may make money in individual stocks on certain occasions. No matter how experienced a trader is the possibility of his making losing plays is always present because speculation cannot be made 100 per cent safe. Wall Street professionals know that acting on "inside" tips will break a man more quickly than famine, pestilence, crop failures, political readjustments or what might be called normal accidents. There is no asphalt boulevard to success in Wall Street or anywhere else. Why additionally block traffic?

THE END

Lefevre had a cosmopolitan upbringing. At age 10, his father sent him on a solitary voyage to China to help him recover from a bout of typhoid fever. Although enchanted by the strange land, Lefevre was slightly confused by the similar styles of traditional dress for Chinese men and women. He returned to Panama and learned deep-sea diving from pearl fishers.[7]

Young Lefevre eventually found his way to San Francisco, where he attended public school before going on to study geology at Lehigh University from 1887 to 1890. He went on to work as a reporter for the *New York Sun* and later became assistant financial editor at the *New York Commercial Advertiser* and the *New York Commercial*. Lefevre was also a successful novelist, penning *Samson Rock of Wall Street*, *The Golden Flood*, and *Wall Street Stories*.

In 1909, the government of Panama appointed him ambassador to Spain, Portugal, and Italy. Upon his return to the United States, he returned to writing about Wall Street, gathering the contacts and anecdotes that would later figure in *Reminiscences*.

Lefevre died in 1943, leaving a widow and two sons. One of those sons, Reid, became well known throughout the eastern seaboard both as owner of the King Reid Show, a large traveling carnival, and as a long-serving Vermont legislator with a gift for gab who became a confidant of *Saturday Evening Post* artist Norman Rockwell.

In short, Lefevre led a quintessentially sprawling American life in which *Reminiscences*—his classic tale of speculation, psychology, biography, and history—was the cornerstone.

ENDNOTES

1 Henry Clews, *Fifty Years in Wall Street* (New York: Irving Publishing Company, 1907), 724–725.

2 Edwin Lefevre, "Boom Days in Wall Street," *Munsey's Magazine* (April 1901): 32.

3 Otis Notman, "Men of Affairs Who Write Novels" *New York Times*, March 9, 1907, BR142.

4 Robert Whitelaw, *Sophocles Translated into English Verse.* (Longman, Greens & Co., 1904), 336.

5 Edwin Lefevre, *Reminiscences of a Stock Operator: Illustrated Edition* (2005), 10.

6 "Edwin Lefevre, 73, Financial Writer," *New York Times,* February 24, 1943, 21.

7 "Sketches of Writers: Edwin Lefevre," *The Writer* (1907): 87.

Dow Jones
Industrial Average
(1895–1929)

Dow Jones Industrial Average (1895–1929)

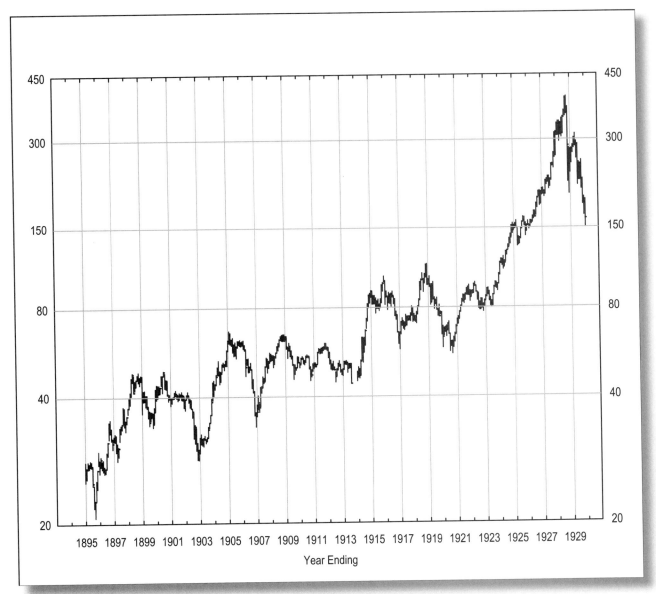

Year Ending

Source: Thechartstore.com

PAUL TUDOR JONES ON
REMINISCENCES

One of Edwin Lefevre's key messages in *Reminiscences* was that the stock market is an unbeatable game that chews up players without remorse. And judging from the trader profiles written as annotations for this edition, it's easy to agree with that conclusion. Most could be shortened to read: "Born in poverty. Made a fortune. Lost it all. Died in poverty."

It was a rare player who could out-think and out-work his competitors, win big on a titanic scale, and exercise enough risk control to secure a generational fortune. Harriman, Rockefeller, Morgan and Baruch were able. Livermore, tragic hero of the saga, was not—though paradoxically his insightful ruminations on his flaws have proven to be a rich legacy.

Paul Tudor Jones II, chairman and chief executive of the Tudor Investment Corporation, is a full-blooded example of a modern player along the lines of Morgan: Not a permanent bull nor bear, but a consistent winner. And it turns out he has been a longtime admirer of *Reminiscences* due to its timeless message of persistence under pressure.

To add fresh perspective to this edition for a new generation of traders, I asked Jones to answer a few questions about his relationship with the book and its themes.

Before we get to his answers, let me tell you a little more about him. Yes, one more annotation.

After growing up in Memphis, Tennessee, and graduating from the University of Virginia in 1976, Jones began his career as a commodities broker in New York, specializing in cotton futures. At age 25, he became a highly successful "local" on the New York Cotton Exchange, trading just for himself. In 1982, on the cusp of a two-decade bull market, he left the floor of the exchange to branch out into equities and bonds. His Tudor Futures Fund has not recorded a single losing year in its 25 years of operation.

Jones built an asset management business from scratch that now invests $11 billion on behalf of institutions, pension funds, and individuals worldwide. He has held seats on the major exchanges, chaired the New York Cotton Exchange, innovated investment products, and led efforts to educate newcomers on strategies and ethics.

He has also become a leading philanthropist on Wall Street, founding an elementary school and after-school programs for under-served children in New York and leading efforts to preserve wildlife in East Africa and Florida. His Robin Hood Foundation, founded in 1988, has partnered with hundreds of grass-roots organizations to invest more than $1 billion in long-term solutions for New Yorkers in need.

Throughout this remarkable journey, the stirring narration of *Reminiscences* has served as a touchstone for Jones—a reminder to anticipate changes in basic conditions by leveraging experience and intuition, and to listen to the message of the tape as trends develop. He gives the book to new employees to make sure they're on the same page.

Much like Livermore might have responded in the 1920s while sailing off the coast of Miami, Jones answered my queries in June 2009 while flying to meetings in Tanzania, India, and the United Kingdom before returning to the United States. He typed out his answers on a laptop computer, and emailed them from his ports of call.

Q: Out of the hundreds of books written about trading since the early 1900s, why do you think this one has become a classic?

Jones: Let's call the book what it really is, and that is a historical novel. Because the book is written by a journalist who is interviewing one of the greatest speculators of all time, it combines the best of two worlds. As you noted in the annotations, the journalist borrowed many of the great trading tenets of the time in composing the mythical Livingston character in the book. This character was partly modeled after the very colorful lifestyle of Jesse Livermore, who had a penchant for high living and fast times to create a larger-than-life, full-blooded character who happened to embody every great trading maxim of the time. As the book states very early on, there is nothing new under the sun in the art of speculation, and everything that was said then completely applies to the markets of today. My guess is that the same will hold true for time eternal as long as man's basic emotions remain intact—fear, greed, happiness, sorrow, elation, dejection, excitement, and apathy.

Q: **Part of the appeal of the book is Livermore's journey of self-discovery as a person and as a trader. Have you had the same experience as a trader and portfolio manager, or was your path easier or harder?**

Jones: Probably the best lessons to be learned from this book come from his repeated failures and how he dealt with them. In the book I think he lost his entire fortune four or five times. I did the same thing but was fortunate enough to do it all in my early twenties on very small stakes of capital. I think I lost $10,000 when I was 22, and when I was 25 I lost about $50,000, which was all I had to my name. It felt like a fortune at the time. It was then that my father flew up from Memphis and sat me down in my tiny New York City apartment and began lecturing me as lawyers do. He commanded, "Leave the gambling den behind. Come home and get a real job in a safe profession like real estate." Of course, I did not, and the rest is history. And real estate these past few years has been about as safe as shooting craps to pay the rent, so I was twice blessed. If I'd have taken my father's advice, I might have lost all of my money again these past few years in my fifties.

Anyway, I think it's no coincidence that our greatest champions, our greatest artists, our greatest leaders, our greatest everything all seem to have experienced some kind of gut-wrenching loss. I think their greatness, in part, was fashioned on the crucible of that defeat. Two years before Lincoln was elected as maybe our finest president, he lost that monumental Senate race to Stephen Douglas. To a certain extent, I think that holds true in my field as well, and I am leery of traders who have never lost it all. I think that intense feeling of desperation that accompanies such a horrifically deflating experience indelibly cauterizes great risk management reflexes into a trader's very being.

There are two unpleasant experiences that every trader will face in his lifetime at least once and most likely multiple times. First, there will come a day after a devastatingly brutal and agonizing stretch of losing trades that you'll wonder if you will ever make a winning trade again. And second, there will come a point when you begin to ask yourself why it is you make money and if this is truly sustainable. That first experience tests an individual's grit; does he have the stamina, courage, guts, and smarts to get up and engage the battle again? That second moment of enlightenment is the one that is actually scarier because it acknowledges a certain lack of control over anything. I think I was almost 38 years old when one day, in a moment of frightening enlightenment, I knew that I really did not know exactly how and why I had made all the money that I had over the prior 17 years. This threw my confidence for a jolt. It sent me down a path of self-discovery that today is still a work in progress.

Q: Sections of the book that deal with trading psychology sound as if they could have been written this year, the issues and insights are so fresh. Do you have a sense that this was the result of Livermore's insightful explanation of his craft to his biographer, or Lefevre's strength as an observer and writer?

Jones: I put this down to Lefevre the biographer. There were any number of people he could have chosen to be the centerpiece of his book, but he brilliantly picked Jesse Livermore. It was not random chance. He did that because of his training. While attending the University of Virginia, I took some summer courses at Memphis State in journalism and at the same time worked editing my father's small business paper. Looking back on my education, I would say that journalism was the single most important element of my development as a trader and as a businessman, more so than any of the economics and business classes I took at the University of Virginia. Newspaper journalism teaches you how to fact find, analyze, and condense a story down to its most essential points and then to communicate those in a series of paragraphs that read from the most important to the least important. A copy editor has to be able to cut a story from the bottom up so that all the important stories can fit onto one page. Knowing this, a writer immediately focuses on those essential points that need to be communicated in any story and how to deliver those points in a way that answers the who, what, where, when, how, and why in short order. Learning to report and communicate in this fashion is far and away the best training any businessman, investor, or trader can have. It's a vital yet surprisingly underestimated skill that really enhances one's ability to be able to frame, analyze, and solve problems in the most expeditious fashion. Lefevre had this skill, and it was his journalistic training that made this book the all-encompassing, spectacular compendium of knowledge on the profession of trading that it is. An untrained writer, even with all the skills and personality Jesse Livermore brought to bear as a subject, could never have written such a classic piece of prose.

Incidentally, this gets to why so many other books on business and trading are so bad; the person writing them, oftentimes the businessman himself, can't write in an interesting manner that clearly and concisely communicates what he's trying to say. Also, you asked about the sections that deal with trading psychology. Many of us are blind to key psychological elements of ourselves; that's why people go to therapists or get outside help for any number of problems. This very thing happened to me in 1993, 17 years into my career, when a combination of people helped me discover, completely unbeknownst to me, that my trading style had incorporated some inimical traits. These bad habits were responsible for the worst year of my career and the only one that came close to being negative for my trading accounts. It's easier for someone on the outside to understand why people do what they do than it is for people to figure it out themselves. Individually, each of us probably thinks we are just about perfect, which of course is why marriage was invented to kill that delusion. In many ways, it was easier for Lefevre, on the outside, to figure out the psychology of Jesse Livermore's trading than it was for Jesse. It's not so easy to see yourself, and it's even harder to clearly describe what you might see in yourself. Lefevre could see what was unique about Livermore more easily than Livermore could ever have seen it himself, and he had the writing skills to clearly describe what he saw.

Q: **Technology has sped up trading immeasurably since the early 1900s and yet the fundamentals of trading remain the same. Can you reflect on how trading is much the same now as it was in the 1880s and 1900s despite technological advances?**

Jones: The book says it the best on the second page: "There is nothing new in Wall Street." And even that sentiment is hardly new. King Solomon beat Lefevre to the punch by about 5,000 years when, in the Book of Ecclesiastes, he wrote, "There is nothing new beneath the sun." But back to Wall Street: The game is the same though the actors have changed. And the content is essentially the same although it's taken on some new forms. Specialists and floor traders who used to be well-paid gatekeepers of short-term liquidity for customer orders have been supplanted by high-frequency trading programs that provide moment-to-moment liquidity and harvest billions annually from the markets. Instead of working 40-hour weeks as most of our trading forebearers did, we work 80-hour weeks now because the information available has probably multiplied by 1,000 times in what oftentimes is an information race.

But at the end of the day, markets will always be driven by greed and fear, valuations will always swing from too cheap to too dear, and there will always be a new generation to rationalize why this time it is different. But I guarantee that for as long as I live I will always be able to find a chart that will look like another chart from another era, showing once again how Mr. Market ran the full gamut of emotions from bottom to top, and top to bottom all over again. Remember, he was known as King Solomon the Wise, not King Solomon the Clueless. As it is written, there is nothing new beneath the sun or on Wall Street.

Q: Most investors today seem to believe that the banking and credit problems witnessed in the past two years are unique, yet a study of Livermore's era seem to show that investors 100 years ago faced many of the same concerns. Why do you think that every generation seems to confront the same problems of credit excesses, and it is possible for the cycle to ever be truly smoothed out by better understanding of economics and business processes?

Jones: That is a very interesting question, and I would be reluctant to think that men will ever be smart and farsighted enough to avoid the next bubble unless man's basic greed can be excised. We know wars are not good, but they seem to be a permanent staple of humanity. Why not bubbles? It seems pretty clear that excess leverage ultimately leads to a very painful unwind. But is this new news? The extreme type of leverage we saw in the 1920s certainly contributed to the stock market crash, and partly in response, Congress over the next decade passed the Securities Act of 1933, the Securities Exchange Act of 1934, and the Glass-Steagall Act in 1933. These laws were designed to prevent the extreme types of leverage that we had in the 1920s, and for over 60 years they worked beautifully until 2000, when Congress, at the behest of the brokerage and banking lobby, decided to repeal aforementioned critical elements of this historical and well-functioning regulatory infrastructure. This legislation never would have made it to the Senate floor had it been opposed by our leading financial regulators or officials. But they, like their counterparts in the Hoover administration of the late 1920s, generally believed in the perfection of the free market system and the inviolate sanctity of noninterference. And that's in large part why we are where we are today. Because there will always be a powerful contingent of very well connected and very wealthy power brokers who, probably innocently, believe it will be different this time. It will take a fundamental change in human nature to ever truly control this.

Q: Livermore/Livingston lays down numerous rules during the book. Do you ever think about these particular insights as you manage your own trades today, or are there any phrases or anecdotes that linger with you more than the others?

Jones: There are two rules from this book by which I now live during these later stages of my constitution. First is the tenet "The trend is your friend," which is repeated often—but not often enough. You will simply never make any money unless you begin and end every trading thought with that in mind. Second is the old adage actually popularized in the 1880s, as I learned in your annotations: "Sell down to the sleeping point." I remember in 1994, during the great bond bear market of that year, I had bought way too many British gilts for just a quick flip one afternoon. Gilts closed three hours before U.S. Treasuries did back then, and Treasuries proceeded to get hammered that afternoon. I knew gilts were going to open substantially lower the next day, and I dreaded the proverbial wake-up call I was going to get from my London desk. Around 2:00 A.M., my wife, Sonia, woke me up and said, "What the hell did you do to our bed?" It was soaking wet; sure enough, the bed was totally drenched. I was also drenched from head to toe as in my sleep I had literally sweated out probably a pound of fluid from the dread of the beating I was about to take. It was the last time I ever went home with an overly large countertrend position.

Q: **If you were born in Livermore's era, what role do you think you'd have liked to play: speculator, railroad baron, deal maker, government financier, or observer, and why?**

Jones: How about (F) All of the above? But if I had to say, I would have been the speculator. I simply love the markets too much, and those were some great markets, by the way. Ever since I was a kid, I liked playing games whether it is chess, bridge, backgammon, poker, or sports. I don't know a single great trader who doesn't share the same trait. If doing this was about the money, I would have quit a long time ago. Being a deal maker or working in government at that time would have conceivably provided a great social value, and that is very important for me. But I think my highest and best purpose in my professional life is to make as much money as I possibly can and give it away in a very targeted fashion to have a lasting and important social and environmental impact. That is why I still work today.

Q: **To what extent do you think that private and/or private/government cliques still attempt to manipulate equity and commodity markets? Crude oil in the first half of 2008 might be an example, or the run on banks' credit default swaps and equity in the winter of 2008. If so, how are current methods of manipulation different from the 1890s to 1920s?**

Jones: Generally speaking, the markets at a micro level are much freer and less subject to manipulation than in the days of Livermore. There is a veritable alphabet soup of global regulatory agencies providing a significant deterrent against the type of pump-and-dump schemes that were so rampant in the 1920s. Limits on controlling interest, disclosure requirements, and prohibitions against insider trading have all but eradicated market manipulation as described in that book—certainly by private interests.

But "manipulation" of a sort certainly still occurs. Today it is practiced on a much larger, policy-driven scale by sovereign governments and central banks. From agricultural subsidies to currency management, governments practice it daily and with abandon. Certainly, the most glaring example in the past two decades would be the dollar peg enforced by the People's Republic of China. History will probably remember it as the greatest single misallocation of economic resources in the history of modern civilization. It was not just what they did but the countries that imitated them also. The peg was a significant contributing factor to the Great Credit Bubble as their purchases of public and private debt in the United States sparked a massively unsustainable boom in consumption. That was Act 1. And now that the Chinese own $2 trillion of U.S. debt, my guess is that equally large market moves will be forthcoming in a variety of asset classes as the Chinese one day will try to reduce this unnatural position.

You mention the rise in crude oil in 2008 as a possible example of manipulation. I would characterize that as more of a bubble. Institutional investment in commodity indexes simply swamped what is in reality a very small market. And the price action became self-reinforcing as is always the case in any great bull market, until it reached bubble-like proportions. The exact same thing happened in 1999 with the tech bubble, as evidenced by the fourfold rise in the Nasdaq 100. But there was no manipulation. And certainly, there existed significant regulatory apparatus in both instances to have at least partially prevented them. But the Federal Reserve Board, in the case of the Nasdaq bubble, and the CFTC [Commodity Futures Trading Commission], in the case of the crude oil bubble, chose to let the market take its course. This was very reminiscent of the late 1920s and early '30s and had as much to do with the prevailing financial wisdom of the times as anything.

One last postscript. We have spent a lot of time in the last two questions discussing the rationale behind recent events in modern financial history and how it compared to that era. It is not fitting to end on this note. The whole point of *Reminiscences* was that all of those very serious economic issues should be largely irrelevant to a great operator. Yes, they are interesting to debate, important to know, but always secondary to the tale the tape tells us on a continual basis.

SELECTED QUOTES

Reminiscences of a Stock Operator has endured as a classic as much because of the richness of its narrative as for the truth of its insights. But if you just want to get a quick read on its big ideas without the framework of the storytelling, here are most of the key passages.

There is nothing new in Wall Street. There can't be because speculation is as old as the hills. Whatever happens in the stock market to-day has happened before and will happen again.

■■■

The tape does not concern itself with the why and wherefore. It doesn't go into explanations. I didn't ask the tape why when I was fourteen, and I don't ask it to-day, at forty. The reason for what a certain stock does today may not be known for two or three days, or weeks, or months. But what the dickens does that matter? Your business with the tape is now—not to-morrow. The reason can wait.

I always made money when I was sure I was right before I began. What beat me was not having brains enough to stick to my own game—that is, to play the market only when I was satisfied that precedents favored my play. There is a time for all things, but I didn't know it. And that is precisely what beats so many men in Wall Street who are very far from being in the main sucker class. There is the plain fool, who does the wrong thing at all times everywhere, but there is the Wall Street fool, who thinks he must trade all the time. No man can always have adequate reasons for buying or selling stocks daily—or sufficient knowledge to make his play an intelligent play.

■■■

The desire for constant action irrespective of underlying conditions is responsible for many losses in Wall Street even among the professionals.

■■■

A stock operator has to fight a lot of expensive enemies within himself.

■■■

I don't know whether I make myself plain, but I never lose my temper over the stock market. I never argue with the tape. Getting sore at the market doesn't get you anywhere.

It takes a man a long time to learn all the lessons of all his mistakes. They say there are two sides to everything. But there is only one side to the stock market; and it is not the bull side or the bear side, but the right side.

■ ■ ■

I have been flat broke several times, but my loss has never been a total loss. Otherwise, I wouldn't be here now. I always knew I would have another chance and that I would not make the same mistake a second time. I believed in myself.

■ ■ ■

Speculation is a hard and trying business, and a speculator must be on the job all the time or he'll soon have no job to be on.

■ ■ ■

I owe my early success as a trader…not to brains or knowledge, because my mind was untrained and my ignorance was colossal. The game taught me the game. And it didn't spare the rod while teaching.

■ ■ ■

If somebody had told me my method would not work I nevertheless would have tried it out to make sure for myself, for when I am wrong only one thing convinces me of it, and that is, to lose money. And I am only right when I make money. That is speculating.

■ ■ ■

Ignorance at twenty-two isn't a structural defect.

■ ■ ■

If the unusual never happened there would be no difference in people and then there wouldn't be any fun in life. The game would become merely a matter of addition and subtraction. It would make of us a race of bookkeepers with plodding minds. It's the guessing that develops a man's brain power.

When a man is right he wants to get all that is coming to him for being right.

■ ■ ■

[Brokers] always had the hope of getting away from me what I had taken from them. They regarded my winnings as temporary loans.

The first change I made in my play was in the matter of time. I couldn't wait for the sure thing to come along and then take a point or two out of it.…I had to start much earlier.…In other words, I had to study what was going to happen; to anticipate stock movements…the essential difference between betting on fluctuation and anticipating inevitable advances and declines, between gambling and speculating.

■ ■ ■

I discovered that although I often was 100 percent right on the market—that is, in my diagnosis of conditions and general trend—I was not making as much money as my market "rightness" entitled me to.

■ ■ ■

They say you never grow poor taking profits. No, you don't. But neither do you grow rich taking a four-point profit in a bull market. Where I should have made twenty thousand dollars I made two thousand. That was what my conservatism did for me.

■ ■ ■

Suckers differ among themselves according to the degree of experience. The tyro knows nothing, and everybody, including himself, knows it. . . . The second-grade sucker knows how to keep from losing his money in some of the ways that get the raw beginner. It is this semisucker rather than the 100 per cent article who is the real all-the-year-round support of the commission houses. He lasts about three and a half years on an average, as compared with a single season of from three to thirty weeks, which is the usual Wall Street life of a first offender. It is naturally the semisucker who is always quoting the famous trading aphorisms and the various rules of the game. He knows all the don'ts that ever fell from the oracular lips of the old stagers—excepting the principal one, which is: Don't be a sucker!

■ ■ ■

The customer would finish the tale of his perplexity and then ask: "What do you think I ought to do?" Old Turkey would cock his head to one side, contemplate his fellow customer with a fatherly smile, and finally he would say very impressively, "You know, it's a bull market!" Time and again I heard him say, "Well, this is a bull market, you know!" as though he were giving to you a priceless talisman wrapped up in a million-dollar accident insurance policy. And of course I did not get his meaning. . . .

■ ■ ■

What old Mr. Partridge said did not mean much to me until I began to think about my own numerous failures to make as much money as I ought to when I was so right on the general market. The more I studied the more I realized how wise that old chap was. He had evidently suffered from the same defect in his young days and knew his own human weaknesses. He would not lay himself open to a temptation that experience had taught him was hard to resist and had always proved expensive to him, as it was to me. I think it was a long step forward in my trading education when I realized at last that when old Mr. Partridge kept on telling the other customers, "Well, you know this is a bull market!" he really meant to tell them that the big money was not in the individual fluctuations but in the main movements—that is, not in reading the tape but in sizing up the entire market and its trend.

■ ■ ■

After spending many years in Wall Street and after making and losing millions of dollars I want to tell you this: It never was my thinking that made the big money for me. It always was my sitting. Got that? My sitting tight! It is no trick at all to be right on the market. You always find lots of early bulls in bull markets and early bears in bear markets. I've known many men who were right at exactly the right time, and began buying or selling stocks when prices were at the very level which should show the greatest profit. And their experience invariably matched mine—that is, they made no real money out of it. Men who can both be right and sit tight are uncommon. I found it one of the hardest things to learn. But it is only after a stock operator has firmly grasped this that he can make big money. It is literally true that millions come easier to a trader after he knows how to trade than hundreds did in the days of his ignorance.

■■■

A man may see straight and clearly and yet become impatient or doubtful when the market takes its time about doing as he figured it must do. That is why so many men in Wall Street, who are not at all in the sucker class, not even in the third grade, nevertheless lose money. The market does not beat them. They beat themselves, because though they have brains they cannot sit tight.

■■■

Disregarding the big swing and trying to jump in and out was fatal to me. Nobody can catch all the fluctuations. In a bull market your game is to buy and hold until you believe that the bull market is near its end. To do this you must study general conditions and not tips or special factors affecting individual stocks.

■■■

One of the most helpful things that anybody can learn is to give up trying to catch the last eighth—or the first. These two are the most expensive eighths in the world. They have cost stock traders, in the aggregate, enough millions of dollars to build a concrete highway across the continent.

■■■

Without faith in his own judgment no man can go very far in this game. That is about all I have learned—to study general conditions, to take a position and stick to it. I can wait without a twinge of impatience. I can see a setback without being shaken, knowing that it is only temporary.

■■■

If I learned all this so slowly it was because I learned by my mistakes, and some time always elapses between making a mistake and realizing it, and more time between realizing it and exactly determining it.

VI

It isn't a hunch but the subconscious mind, which is the creative mind, at work. That is the mind which makes artists do things without their knowing how they came to do them. Perhaps with me it was the cumulative effect of a lot of little things individually insignificant but collectively powerful.

■■■

I began to think of basic conditions instead of individual stocks. I promoted myself to a higher grade in the hard school of speculation. It was a long and difficult step to take.

VII

People don't seem to grasp easily the fundamentals of stock trading....When I am bearish and I sell a stock, each sale must be at a lower level than the previous sale. When I am buying, the reverse is true. I must buy on a rising scale. I don't buy long stock on a scale down, I buy on a scale up.

■■■

Remember that stocks are never too high for you to begin buying or too low to begin selling. But after the initial transaction, don't make a second unless the first shows you a profit. Wait and watch.

VIII

I was utterly free of speculative prejudices. The bear side doesn't appeal to me any more than the bull side, or vice versa. My one steadfast prejudice is against being wrong.

■ ■ ■

I never argue with the tape. To be angry at the market because it unexpectedly or even illogically goes against you is like getting mad at your lungs because you have pneumonia.

■ ■ ■

I have always played a lone hand. . . . It is the way my mind works. I have to do my own seeing and my own thinking. But I can tell you after the market began to go my way I felt for the first time in my life that I had allies—the strongest and truest in the world: underlying conditions. They were helping me with all their might.

IX

It was an old trading theory of mine that when a stock crosses 100 or 200 or 300 for the first time the price does not stop at the even figure but goes a good deal higher, so that if you buy it as soon as it crosses the line it is almost certain to show you a profit. Timid people don't like to buy a stock at a new high record. But I had the history of such movements to guide me.

■ ■ ■

The only thing to do when a man is wrong is to be right by ceasing to be wrong.

■ ■ ■

My greatest discovery was that a man must study general conditions, to size them so as to be able to anticipate probabilities. In short I had learned that I had to work for my money. I was no longer betting blindly or concerned with mastering the technique of the game, but with earning my successes by hard study and clear thinking.

■ ■ ■

My biggest winnings were not in dollars but in the intangibles: I had learned what a man must do in order to make big money; I was permanently out of the gambler class; I had at last learned to trade intelligently in a big way. It as a day of days for me.

X

If a man is both wise and lucky, he will not make the same mistake twice. But he will make any one of the ten thousand brothers or cousins of the original. The Mistake family is so large that there is always one of them around when you want to see what you can do in the fool-play line.

■ ■ ■

Losing money is the least of my troubles. A loss never bothers me after I take it. I forget it overnight. But being wrong—not taking the loss—that is what does the damage to the pocketbook and to the soul.

■ ■ ■

Money creates needs or encourages their multiplication. I mean that after a man makes money in the stock market he very quickly loses the habit of not spending. But after he loses his money it takes him a long time to lose the habit of spending.

■ ■ ■

I would rather play commodities than stocks. There is no question about their greater legitimacy. . . . It partakes more of the nature of a commercial venture than trading in stocks does. A man can approach it as he might any mercantile problem. It may be possible to use fictitious arguments for or against a certain trend in a commodity market; but success will be only temporary, for in the end the facts are bound to prevail, so that a trader gets dividends on study and observation, as he does in a regular business.

■ ■ ■

In the long run commodity prices are governed but by one law—the economic law of demand and supply. The business of the trader in commodities is simply to get facts about the demand and the supply, present and prospective. He does not indulge in guesses about a dozen things as he does in stocks.

■ ■ ■

Prices, like everything else, move along the line of least resistance. They will do whatever comes easiest.

■ ■ ■

The trend has been established before the news is published, and in bull markets bear items are ignored and bull news exaggerated, and vice versa.

■ ■ ■

A man has to guard against many things, and most of all against himself—that is, against human nature. That is the reason why I say that the man who is right always has two forces working in his favor—basic conditions and the men who are wrong.

■ ■ ■

In a narrow market, when prices are not getting anywhere to speak of but move within a narrow range, there is no sense in trying to anticipate what the next big movement is going to be—up or down. The thing to do is to watch the market, read the tape to determine the limits of the get-nowhere prices, and make up your mind that you will not take an interest until the price breaks through the limit in either direction. A speculator must concern himself with making money out of the market and not with insisting that the tape must agree with him. Never argue with it or ask it for reasons or explanations. Stock-market post-mortems don't pay dividends.

■ ■ ■

It is surprising how many experienced traders there are who look incredulous when I tell them that when I buy stocks for a rise I like to pay top prices and when I sell I must sell low or not at all. . . . [A trader] should accumulate his line on the way up. Let him buy one-fifth of his full line. If that does not show him a profit he must not increase his holdings because he has obviously begun wrong; he is wrong temporarily and there is no profit in being wrong at any time.

■■■

It is simple arithmetic to prove that it is a wise thing to have the big bet down only when you win, and when you lose to lose only a small exploratory bet....If a man trades in the way I have described, he will always be in the profitable position of being able to cash in on the big bet.

■■■

The average speculator has arrayed against him his own nature. The weaknesses that all men are prone to are fatal to success in speculation—usually those very weaknesses that make him likable to his fellows or that he himself particularly guards against in those other ventures of his where they are not nearly so dangerous as when he is trading.

■■■

The speculator's chief enemies are always boring from within. It is inseparable from human nature to hope and to fear. In speculation when the market goes against you hope that every day will be the last day—and you lose more than you should had you not listened to hope—the same ally that is so potent a success-bringer to empire builders and pioneers, big and little. And when the market goes your way you become fearful that the next day will take away your profit, and you get out—too soon. Fear keeps you from making as much money as you ought to. The successful trader has to fight these two deep-seated instincts. He has to reverse what you might call his natural impulses. Instead of hoping he must fear; instead of fearing he must hope. He must fear that his loss may develop into a much bigger loss, and hope that his profit may become a big profit. It is absolutely wrong to gamble in stocks the way the average man does.

■■■

I have been in the speculative game ever since I was fourteen. It is all I have ever done. I think I know what I am talking about. And the conclusion that I have reached after nearly thirty years of constant trading, both on a shoestring and with millions of dollars back of me, is this: A man may beat a stock or a group at a certain time, but no man living can beat the stock market!

A trader gets to play the game as the professional billiard player does—that is, he looks far ahead instead of considering the particular shot before him. It gets to be an instinct to play for position.

■■■

That is one trouble about trading on a large scale. You cannot sneak out as you can when you pike along. You cannot always sell out when you wish or when you think it wise. You have to get out when you can; when you have a market that will absorb your entire line. Failure to grasp the opportunity to get out may cost you millions. You cannot hesitate. If you do you are lost.

⌐XII⌐

A man cannot be convinced against his own convictions, but he can be talked into a state of uncertainty and indecision, which is even worse, for that means that he cannot trade with confidence and comfort.

■ ■ ■

I have done nothing in my life but trade in stocks and commodities. I naturally think that if it is wrong to be bearish it must be right to be a bull. And if it is right to be a bull it is imperative to buy. As my old Palm Beach friend said Pat Hearne used to say, "You can't tell till you bet!"

■ ■ ■

I did precisely the wrong thing. The cotton showed me a loss and I kept it. The wheat showed me a profit and I sold it out. It was an utterly foolish play….Of all speculative blunders there are few greater than trying to average a losing game….Always sell what shows you a loss and keep what shows you a profit.

■ ■ ■

It cost me millions to learn that another dangerous enemy to a trader is his susceptibility to the urgings of a magnetic personality when plausibly expressed by a brilliant mind. It has always seemed to me, however, that I might have learned my lesson quite as well if the cost had been only one million. But Fate does not always let you fix the tuition fee. She delivers the educational wallop and presents her own bill, knowing you have to pay it, no matter what the amount might be.

■ ■ ■

The hope of making the stock market pay your bill is one of the most prolific sources of loss in Wall Street….There isn't a man in Wall Street who has not lost money trying to make the market pay for an automobile or a bracelet or a motor boat or a painting. I could build a huge hospital with the birthday presents that the tight-fisted stock market has refused to pay for. In fact, of all hoodoos in Wall Street I think the resolve to induce the stock market to act as a fairy godmother is the busiest and the most persistent.

⌐XIII⌐

It was improper and unwise for me as a speculator to allow myself to be influenced by any consideration to act against my own judgment. *Noblesse oblige*—but not in the stock market, because the tape is not chivalrous and moreover does not reward loyalty.

■ ■ ■

I was very lucky. I was rampantly bullish in a wild bull market [in 1916]. Things were certainly coming my way so that there wasn't anything to do but to make money. It made me remember a saying of the late H. H. Rogers of the Standard Oil Company, to the effect that there were times when a man could no more help making money than he could help getting wet if he went out in a rainstorm without an umbrella.

∎∎∎

Nowhere does history indulge in repetitions so often or so uniformly as in Wall Street. When you read contemporary accounts of booms or panics the one thing that strikes you most forcibly is how little either stock speculation or stock speculators to-day differ from yesterday. The game does not change and neither does human nature.

∎∎∎

A market does not culminate in one grand blaze of glory. Neither does it end with a sudden reversal of form. A market can and does often cease to be a bull market long before prices generally begin to break. My long expected warning came to me when I noticed that, one after another, those stocks which had been the leaders of the market reacted several points from the top and—for the first time in many months—did not come back. Their race evidently was run.

∎∎∎

It is enough for the experienced trader to perceive that something is wrong. He must not expect the tape to become a lecturer. His job is to listen for it to say "Get out!" and not wait for it to submit a legal brief for approval.

One day the entire market became quite weak and prices of all stocks began to fall. When I had a profit of at least four points in each and every one of the twelve stocks that I was short of, I knew that I was right. The tape told me it was now safe to be bearish, so I promptly doubled up.... After I doubled up, I didn't make another trade for a long time.

∎∎∎

Never try to sell at the top. It isn't wise. Sell after a reaction if there is no rally.

∎∎∎

In a bear market it is always wise to cover if complete demoralization suddenly develops. That is the only way, if you swing a good-sized line, of turning a big paper profit into real money.

XIV

We ran smack into a long moneyless period; four mighty lean years....As Billy Henriquez once said, "It was the kind of market in which not even a skunk could make a scent."

∎∎∎

I have come to feel that it is as necessary to know how to read myself as to know how to read the tape.

XVI

It has always seemed to me the height of damfoolishness to trade on tips....I sometimes think that tip-takers are like drunkards. There are some who can't resist the craving and always look forward to those jags which they consider indispensable to their happiness. It is so easy to open your ears and let the tip in. To be told precisely what to do to be happy and in such a manner that you can easily obey is the next nicest thing to being happy....It is not so much greed made blind by eagerness as it is hope bandaged by the unwillingness to do any thinking.

■ ■ ■

Old Baron Rothschild's recipe for wealth winning applies with greater force than ever to speculation. Somebody asked him if making money in the Bourse was not a very difficult matter and he replied that, on the contrary, he thought it was very easy. . . . "I will tell you my secret if you wish. It is this: I never buy at the bottom and I always sell too soon."

⌐XVII⌐

The training of a stock trader is like a medical education. The physician has to spend long years learning anatomy, physiology, materia medica and collateral subjects by the dozen. He learns the theory and then proceeds to devote his life to the practice. He observes and classifies all sorts of pathological phenomena. He learns to diagnose. If his diagnosis is correct—and that depends upon the accuracy of his observation—he ought to do pretty well in his prognosis, always keeping in mind, of course, that human fallibility and the utterly unforeseen will keep him from scoring one-hundred per cent of bull's-eyes. And then, as he gains in experience he learns not only to do the right thing but to do it instantly, so that many people will think he does it instinctively. It really isn't automatism. It is that he has diagnosed the case according to his observations of such cases during a period of many years; and, naturally, after he has diagnosed it, he can only treat it in the way that experience has taught him is the proper treatment. You can transmit knowledge—that is, your particular collection of card-indexed facts—but not your experience. A man may know what to do and lose money—if he doesn't do it quickly enough.

■ ■ ■

Observation, experience, memory and mathematics—these are what the successful trader must depend on. . . . He must bet always on probabilities—that is, try to anticipate them.

■ ■ ■

I have found that experience is apt to be a steady dividend payer in this game and that observation gives you the best tips of all. The behavior of a certain stock is all you need at times.

■ ■ ■

I never buy a stock even in a bull market, if it doesn't act as it ought to act in that kind of market.

■ ■ ■

An old broker once said to me: "If I am walking along a railroad track and I see a train coming toward me at sixty miles an hour, do I keep walking on the ties? Friend, I side-step. And I do not even pat myself on the back for being so wise and prudent."

■ ■ ■

Experiences had taught me to beware of buying a stock that refuses to follow the group-leader.

XVIII

It was not difficult to be both fearless and patient. A speculator must have faith in himself and in his judgment. The late Dickson G. Watts…says that courage in a speculator is merely confidence to act on the decision of his mind. With me, I cannot fear to be wrong because I never think I'm wrong until I am proven wrong. In fact, I am uncomfortable unless I am capitalizing my experience.

XIX

The study of the psychology of speculators is as valuable as it ever was. I think the clearest summing up of the whole thing was expressed by Thomas F. Woodlock when he declared: "The principles of successful stock speculation are based on the supposition that people will continue in the future to make the mistakes that they have made in the past."

■■■

In booms, which is when the public is in the market in the greatest numbers, there is never any need of subtlety, so there is no sense of wasting time discussing either manipulation or speculation during such times; it would be like trying to find the differences in raindrops that are falling synchronously on the same roof across the street.

■■■

People who look for easy money invariably pay for the privilege of proving conclusively that it cannot be found on this sordid earth. At first, when I listened to the accounts of old-time deals and devices I used to think that people were more gullible in the 1860s and 70's than in the 1900's. But I was sure to read in the newspapers that very day or the next something about the latest Ponzi or the bust-up of some bucketing broker and about the millions of sucker money gone to join the silent majority of vanished savings.

XX

A brilliant operator, James R. Keene!…That he did not argue with the tape is plain. He was utterly fearless but never reckless. He could and did turn in a twinkling, if he found he was wrong.

■■■

There is no question that advertising is an art, and manipulation is the art of advertising through the medium of the tape. The tape should tell the story the manipulator wishes its readers to see.

■■■

It is well to remember a rule of manipulation, a rule that Keene and his able predecessors well knew. It is this: Stocks are manipulated to the highest point possible and then sold to the public on the way down.

■■■

The first step in a bull movement in a stock is to advertise the fact that there is a bull movement on…to make the stock active and strong. After all is said and done, the greatest publicity agent in the wide world is the ticker, and by far the best advertising medium is the tape.

∎∎∎

It is always well to make it plain to the traders—and to the public also—that there is a demand for the stock on the way down. That tends to check both reckless short selling by the professionals and liquidation by frightened holders—which is the selling you usually see when a stock gets weaker and weaker.

XXI

The big money in booms is always made first by the public—on paper. And it remains on paper.

XXII

[In the boom of 1915] it got so that all a man had to do was to say that he had a friend who was a friend of a member of one of the Allied commissions and he would be offered all the capital needed to carry out the contracts he had not yet secured. I used to hear incredible stories of clerks becoming presidents of companies doing a business of millions of dollars on money borrowed from trusting trust companies, and of contracts that left a trail of profits as they passed from man to man. A flood of gold was pouring into this country from Europe and the banks had to find ways of impounding it.

∎∎∎

The way business was done might have been regarded with misgivings by the old, but there didn't seem to be so many of them about. The fashion for gray-haired presidents of banks was all very well in tranquil times, but youth was the chief qualification in these strenuous times. The banks certainly did make enormous profits.

XXIII

Manipulation of some sort enters into practically all advances in individual stocks and … such advances are engineered by insiders with one object in view and one only and that is to sell at the best profit possible.

XXIV

The public ought always to keep in mind the elementals of stock trading. When a stock is going up no elaborate explanation is needed as to why it is going up. It takes continuous buying to make a stock keep on going up. As long as it does so, with only small and natural reactions from time to time, it is a pretty safe proposition to trail along with it. But if after a long steady rise a stock turns and gradually begins to go down, with only occasional small rallies, it is obvious that the line of least resistance has changed from upward to downward. Such being the case why should any one ask for explanations? There are probably very good reasons why it should go down, but these reasons are known only to a few people who either keep those reasons to themselves, or else actually tell the public that the stock is cheap. The nature of the game as it is played is such that the public should realize that the truth cannot be told by the few who know.

CREDITS

I

1.2   *Haight & Freese's Guide to Investor.* New York: Haight & Freese, 1899)

1.3   Richard Wheatley, "The New York Stock Exchange," *Harper's Magazine* (November 1885): 849.

1.7   *Haight & Freese's Guide to Investors* (New York: Haight & Freese, 1899).

1.8   "Gates, John Warne." *The Cyclopædia of American Biography*, vol. 8 New York: The Press Association Compilers, 1915), 61.

1.13   Public domain.

1.14   Barron, Clarence Walker, Vincent Carosso, and Joseph Gregory Martin. "The Boston Stock Exchange." 1975

II

2.1   Samuel Armstrong Nelson, *The ABC of Wall Street* (New York: S.A. Nelson, 1900), Frontispiece.

2.3   Edwin Lefevre, "Boom Days in Wall Street," *Munsey's Magazine* (April 1901): 35.

2.4   Merrill Teague. "Bucket-Shop Sharks." *Everybody's Magazine*. (June, 1906), 723.

2.6   Edward F. Hutton, public domain.

2.10   Larry Bohn.

2.11   Public domain.

2.16   Edwin Griswold Nourse, *Brokerage*. (New York: Universal Business Institute, 1918), 228.

2.17   Postcard collection of Maggie Land Blanck

2.18   Public domain.

2.19   David Hochfelder, "'Where the Common People Could Speculate': The Ticker, Bucket Shops, and the Origins of Popular Participation in Financial Markets, 1880–1920," *Journal of American History* (September 2006): 354.

III

3.1   Henry Hall, How *Money Is Made in Security Investments* (1907). Page 116–117. New York: The De Vinne Press.

3.6a   Edwin Lefevre, "Harriman," American Magazine (June 1907), 114.

3.6b   Samuel Armstrong Nelson, "The Jews of Wall Street," *American Magazine* 60 (May 1905–October 1905): 147.

3.6c   *The Economist*, May 4, 1901.

3.7a   George H. Cushing, "Hill Against Harriman," *American Magazine* (September 1909): 427.

3.7b   Edwin Lefevre, "Harriman," *American Magazine* (June 1907, 117.

3.7c   "Disaster and Ruin in Falling Market," New York Times, May 10, 1901, 1.

IV

4.1a   Harrison Hardy Brace, *The Value of Organized Speculation* (Boston: Houghton Mifflin Company, 1913), 57.

4.1b   Samuel Armstrong Nelson, *The ABC of Wall Street* (New York: S. A. Nelson, 1900), 66.

4.2a   Richard Wheatly, "The New York Produce Exchange," *Harper's Magazine* (June–September 1886): 197.

4.2b   Richard Wheatly, "The New York Produce Exchange," *Harper's Magazine* (June–September 1886): 205.

4.3   Finance Publishing Syndicate, *How to Avoid Losses in Your Investing* (New York: Finance Publishing Syndicate, 1920), 21.

4.10   Advertisement from the *Wall Street Journal*, June 22, 1905, 1.

V

5.1a   Edwin Lefevre, "James R. Keene, Manipulator," *World's Work* 2 (May 1900–October 1901): 995.

5.1b   Edwin Lefevre, "Stock Manipulation," *Saturday Evening Post*, March 27, 1909, 12.

5.3   Rollo Tape, "Studies in Stock Speculation," *Ticker and Investment* Digest (1910): 10.

5.4   *Ticker and Investment Digest* (October 1910): 284.

5.5   Stockcharts.com.

5.7   Stockcharts.com.

5.8   *New York Times.*

XVI

16.2   *Time*, May 7, 1934.

16.3   Public domain.

16.4   Public domain.

16.10 Public domain.

XVII

17.2   Edwin Lefevre, "James Robert Keene," *Cosmopolitan* (November 1902–April 1903): 93.

17.3   Library of Congress.

17.4   Library of Congress.

17.14 Library of Congress.

17.15 *From the Collection of The Public Library of Cincinnati and Hamilton County.*

XVIII

18.1   Meade Minnigerode, *Certain Rich Men* (1927), 88.

18.2   Meade Minnigerode, *Certain Rich Men* (1927), 98.

18.5   Library of Congress.

18.6   Dickinson Watts, Public domain.

18.7   *How To Trade in Stocks.*

XIX

19.2   Henry Clews, *Fifty Years in Wall Street* (1908), 12.

19.6   Advertisement, *Popular Science* (November 1953): 267.

19.7   William Worthington Fowler, *Ten Years in Wall Street* (1870), Frontispiece.

19.12 William Worthington Fowler, *Ten Years in Wall Street* (1870), 183.

19.15 "Mr. Jay Gould's New Yacht, the Atalanta," *Harper's Weekly* (June 1883).

19.16 Henry Clews, *Fifty Years in Wall Street* (1908), 451.

19.17 Library of Congress.

19.18 William Worthington Fowler, *Ten Years in Wall Street* (1870), 369.

XX

20.1   "'Jim' Keene, *The Avatar of Wall Street*," Current Literature (1910), 499.

20.3a Library of Congress.

20.3b Charles Edward Russell, "Where Did You Get It, Gentlemen?" *Everybody's Magazine* 17 (July–December 1907): 202.

20.6a Library of Congress.

20.6b Henry Clews, *Fifty Years in Wall Street* (1908), 869.

20.6c Library of Congress.

20.8a Henry Clews, *Fifty Years in Wall Street* (1908), 728.

20.8b Henry Clews, *Fifty Years in Wall Street* (1908), 712.

20.11 Library of Congress.

20.12 "Wall Street," *Munsey's Magazine* 10 (October 1893–March 1894): 371.

20.13 Public domain.

20.14a Public domain.

20.14b Public domain.

XXI

21.4   Other Oil Stocks, *The Financial Review*. 1921. 312

21.5   *New York Times*, http://bit.ly/13bIW7.

21.7   Public domain.

21.10a www.gegoux.com/gov_flow.htm.

21.10b "Mammoth Stock Sold." *New York Times*. October 10, 1922. 33.

XXII

22.8   Honore de Balzac, Public domain.

22.11 www.unc.edu/~ageller/hist22web/assets/seligman.jpg.

22.14 "Topics in Wall Street," *Times*.

22.15 New York Public Library, Astor, Lenox and Tilden Foundation, http://chroniclingamerica.loc.gov/lccn/sn83030193/1908-08-11/ed-1/seq-3/.

XXIII

23.1a Library of Congress.

23.1b Carl Hovery, *The Life Story of J. Pierpont Morgan* (1911), 14.

23.1c John Pierpont Morgan Jr. Public domain

23.3   David Francis Jordan, *Jordan on Investments* (1920), 114.

23.7   William C. Durant, early 1890s. Public domain.

23.11 *New York Times*.

XXIV

24.4   Public Domain.

24.5   "Sketches of Writers: Edwin Lefevre," *The Writer* (1907): 87.

ABOUT THE AUTHOR

Jon D. Markman is an award-winning journalist, investment adviser and portfolio manager. He won a Gerald Loeb Award for Distinguished Financial Journalism for his columns exposing flaws in the S&P 500 Index in 2002; a Society of Professional Journalists award for his 2001 reporting on Enron and the post–September 11 investment environment; and a Society of American Business Editors and Writers award for columns in 2007 that forcast and explained the credit crisis and bear market of 2008. Markman was a pioneer in the development of stock-rating system and screening software; a portfolio manager at a hedge fund; managing editor at CNBC on *MSN Money*; and investment columnist and investigative reporter at the *Los Angeles Times*. He now provides long-term investment management for individuals and institutions through his firm Markman Portfolios, and tactical investment guidance daily to subscribers of his *Strategic Advantage* and *Trader's Advantage* research services.